# Volvo S40 & V40
## Service and Repair Manual

## Mark Coombs & Spencer Drayton

**Models covered**

(3569 - 320 - 7AH2)

Volvo S40 Saloon & V40 Estate models with petrol engines, including turbo and GDI versions, T4 and special/limited editions
1.6 litre (1588cc), 1.8 litre (1731, 1783 & 1834cc), 1.9 litre (1855cc) & 2.0 litre (1948cc)

*Does NOT cover Diesel or bi-fuel models, or new S40/V50 range introduced March 2004*

© Haynes Publishing 2004

ABCD

A book in the **Haynes Service and Repair Manual Series**

ISBN 978 1 78521 044 0

**British Library Cataloguing in Publication Data**
A catalogue record for this book is available from the British Library.

Printed in Malaysia

**Haynes Publishing**
Sparkford, Yeovil, Somerset BA22 7JJ, England

**Haynes North America, Inc**
859 Lawrence Drive, Newbury Park, California 91320, USA

*Printed using NORBRITE BOOK 48.8gsm (CODE: 40N6533) from NORPAC; procurement system certified under Sustainable Forestry Initiative standard. Paper produced is certified to the SFI Certified Fiber Sourcing Standard (CERT - 0094271)*

# Contents

## LIVING WITH YOUR VOLVO S40 & V40

## Roadside repairs

## Weekly checks

## Lubricants and fluids

## Tyre pressures

## MAINTENANCE

## Routine maintenance and servicing

# Contents

Many people see the words 'advanced driving' and believe that it won't interest them or that it is a style of driving beyond their own abilities. Nothing could be further from the truth. Advanced driving is straightforward safe, sensible driving - the sort of driving we should all do every time we get behind the wheel.

An average of 10 people are killed every day on UK roads and 870 more are injured, some seriously. Lives are ruined daily, usually because somebody did something stupid. Something like 95% of all accidents are due to human error, mostly driver failure. Sometimes we make genuine mistakes - everyone does. Sometimes we have lapses of concentration. Sometimes we deliberately take risks.

For many people, the process of 'learning to drive' doesn't go much further than learning how to pass the driving test because of a common belief that good drivers are made by 'experience'.

Learning to drive by 'experience' teaches three driving skills:

☐ Quick reactions. (Whoops, that was close!)
☐ Good handling skills. (Horn, swerve, brake, horn).
☐ Reliance on vehicle technology. (Great stuff this ABS, stop in no distance even in the wet...)

Drivers whose skills are 'experience based' generally have a lot of near misses and the odd accident. The results can be seen every day in our courts and our hospital casualty departments.

Advanced drivers have learnt to control the risks by controlling the position and speed of their vehicle. They avoid accidents and near misses, even if the drivers around them make mistakes.

The key skills of advanced driving are **concentration,** effective all-round **observation, anticipation** and **planning.** When **good vehicle handling** is added to these skills, all driving situations can be approached and negotiated in a safe, methodical way, leaving nothing to chance.

**Concentration** means applying your mind to safe driving, completely excluding anything that's not relevant. Driving is usually the most dangerous activity that most of us undertake in our daily routines. It deserves our full attention.

**Observation** means not just looking, but seeing and seeking out the information found in the driving environment.

**Anticipation** means asking yourself what is happening, what you can reasonably expect to happen and what could happen unexpectedly. (One of the commonest words used in compiling accident reports is 'suddenly'.)

**Planning** is the link between seeing something and taking the appropriate action. For many drivers, planning is the missing link.

If you want to become a safer and more skilful driver and you want to enjoy your driving more, contact the Institute of Advanced Motorists at www.iam.org.uk, phone 0208 996 9600, or write to IAM House, 510 Chiswick High Road, London W4 5RG for an information pack.

Working on your car can be dangerous. This page shows just some of the potential risks and hazards, with the aim of creating a safety-conscious attitude.

# General hazards

### Scalding

• Don't remove the radiator or expansion tank cap while the engine is hot.
• Engine oil, automatic transmission fluid or power steering fluid may also be dangerously hot if the engine has recently been running.

### Burning

• Beware of burns from the exhaust system and from any part of the engine. Brake discs and drums can also be extremely hot immediately after use.

### Crushing

• When working under or near a raised vehicle, always supplement the jack with axle stands, or use drive-on ramps. *Never venture under a car which is only supported by a jack.*

• Take care if loosening or tightening high-torque nuts when the vehicle is on stands. Initial loosening and final tightening should be done with the wheels on the ground.

### Fire

• Fuel is highly flammable; fuel vapour is explosive.
• Don't let fuel spill onto a hot engine.
• Do not smoke or allow naked lights (including pilot lights) anywhere near a vehicle being worked on. Also beware of creating sparks (electrically or by use of tools).
• Fuel vapour is heavier than air, so don't work on the fuel system with the vehicle over an inspection pit.
• Another cause of fire is an electrical overload or short-circuit. Take care when repairing or modifying the vehicle wiring.
• Keep a fire extinguisher handy, of a type suitable for use on fuel and electrical fires.

### Electric shock

• Ignition HT voltage can be dangerous, especially to people with heart problems or a pacemaker. Don't work on or near the ignition system with the engine running or the ignition switched on.

• Mains voltage is also dangerous. Make sure that any mains-operated equipment is correctly earthed. Mains power points should be protected by a residual current device (RCD) circuit breaker.

### Fume or gas intoxication

• Exhaust fumes are poisonous; they often contain carbon monoxide, which is rapidly fatal if inhaled. Never run the engine in a confined space such as a garage with the doors shut.
• Fuel vapour is also poisonous, as are the vapours from some cleaning solvents and paint thinners.

### Poisonous or irritant substances

• Avoid skin contact with battery acid and with any fuel, fluid or lubricant, especially antifreeze, brake hydraulic fluid and Diesel fuel. Don't syphon them by mouth. If such a substance is swallowed or gets into the eyes, seek medical advice.
• Prolonged contact with used engine oil can cause skin cancer. Wear gloves or use a barrier cream if necessary. Change out of oil-soaked clothes and do not keep oily rags in your pocket.
• Air conditioning refrigerant forms a poisonous gas if exposed to a naked flame (including a cigarette). It can also cause skin burns on contact.

### Asbestos

• Asbestos dust can cause cancer if inhaled or swallowed. Asbestos may be found in gaskets and in brake and clutch linings. When dealing with such components it is safest to assume that they contain asbestos.

# Special hazards

### Hydrofluoric acid

• This extremely corrosive acid is formed when certain types of synthetic rubber, found in some O-rings, oil seals, fuel hoses etc, are exposed to temperatures above 400°C. The rubber changes into a charred or sticky substance containing the acid. *Once formed, the acid remains dangerous for years. If it gets onto the skin, it may be necessary to amputate the limb concerned.*
• When dealing with a vehicle which has suffered a fire, or with components salvaged from such a vehicle, wear protective gloves and discard them after use.

### The battery

• Batteries contain sulphuric acid, which attacks clothing, eyes and skin. Take care when topping-up or carrying the battery.
• The hydrogen gas given off by the battery is highly explosive. Never cause a spark or allow a naked light nearby. Be careful when connecting and disconnecting battery chargers or jump leads.

### Air bags

• Air bags can cause injury if they go off accidentally. Take care when removing the steering wheel and/or facia. Special storage instructions may apply.

### Diesel injection equipment

• Diesel injection pumps supply fuel at very high pressure. Take care when working on the fuel injectors and fuel pipes.

⚠️ *Warning: Never expose the hands, face or any other part of the body to injector spray; the fuel can penetrate the skin with potentially fatal results.*

# Remember...

## DO

• Do use eye protection when using power tools, and when working under the vehicle.

• Do wear gloves or use barrier cream to protect your hands when necessary.

• Do get someone to check periodically that all is well when working alone on the vehicle.

• Do keep loose clothing and long hair well out of the way of moving mechanical parts.

• Do remove rings, wristwatch etc, before working on the vehicle – especially the electrical system.

• Do ensure that any lifting or jacking equipment has a safe working load rating adequate for the job.

## DON'T

• Don't attempt to lift a heavy component which may be beyond your capability – get assistance.

• Don't rush to finish a job, or take unverified short cuts.

• Don't use ill-fitting tools which may slip and cause injury.

• Don't leave tools or parts lying around where someone can trip over them. Mop up oil and fuel spills at once.

• Don't allow children or pets to play in or near a vehicle being worked on.

The range received a major facelift in May 2000, with new lights and bumpers, suspension revisions, 2.0 litre variable valve timing engines, and a new 5-speed automatic transmission. A further facelift in April 2002 resulted in a new-look Volvo radiator grille and other minor changes.

Provided that regular servicing is carried out in accordance with the manufacturer's recommendations, the S40/V40 should prove reliable and economical. The engine compartment is well-designed, and most of the items requiring frequent attention are easily accessible.

# Your Volvo S40 & V40 manual

The aim of this manual is to help you get the best value from your vehicle. It can do so in several ways. It can help you decide what work must be done (even should you choose to get it done by a garage). It will also provide information on routine maintenance and servicing, and give a logical course of action and diagnosis when random faults occur. However, it is hoped that you will use the manual by tackling the work yourself. On simpler jobs it may even be quicker than booking the car into a garage and going there twice, to leave and collect it. Perhaps most important, a lot of money can be saved by avoiding the costs a garage must charge to cover its labour and overheads.

The manual has drawings and descriptions to show the function of the various components so that their layout can be understood. Tasks are described and photographed in a clear step-by-step sequence.

References to the 'left' and 'right' of the vehicle are in the sense of a person in the driver's seat facing forwards.

The Volvo S40/V40 was introduced into the UK in May of 1996 as a replacement for the 400 series. The S40/V40 range was developed jointly with Mitsubishi, and is built along with its sister car, the Mitsubishi Carisma, at the NedCar plant in Holland. At its launch, the S40 Saloon and V40 Estate models were available with a choice of either 1.8 litre (1731 cc) or 2.0 litre (1948 cc) petrol engines, with either a 5-speed manual transmission or a 4-speed automatic. Both engines were newly-designed 16-valve double overhead camshaft (DOHC) units.

All models have fully-independent front and rear suspension, and are equipped with anti-lock disc brakes all round.

In early 1997, a 1.6 litre (1588 cc) version of the petrol engine was introduced, initially in Saloon models only. Towards the end of 1997, two turbocharged petrol engines were also introduced; the high-powered 1855 cc engine (fitted to the T4 model) and a low-pressure turbo version of the 1948 cc engine.

In March 1998, the first models with the Mitsubishi-designed 1.8 litre (1834 cc) GDI engine were introduced, while in early 1999, the first diesel models (not covered in this manual) were added to the range. Also in 1999, the 1.6 and 1.8 litre engines (except the GDI engine) gained variable valve timing, and a consequent boost in power – the 1.8 litre unit also grew slightly in capacity at this time, from 1731 cc to 1783 cc.

## Acknowledgements

Certain illustrations are the copyright of Volvo Car Corporation, and are used with their permission. Thanks are also due to Draper Tools Limited, who provided some of the workshop tools, and to all those people at Sparkford who helped in the production of this manual.

**We take great pride in the accuracy of information given in this manual, but vehicle manufacturers make alterations and design changes during the production run of a particular vehicle of which they do not inform us. No liability can be accepted by the authors or publishers for loss, damage or injury caused by any errors in, or omissions from, the information given.**

The following pages are intended to help in dealing with common roadside emergencies and breakdowns. You will find more detailed fault finding information at the back of the manual, and repair information in the main chapters.

## If your car won't start and the starter motor doesn't turn

- ☐ If it's a model with automatic transmission, make sure the selector is in the P or N position.
- ☐ Open the bonnet and make sure that the battery terminals are clean and tight (unclip the battery cover for access).
- ☐ Switch on the headlights and try to start the engine. If the headlights go very dim when you're trying to start, the battery is probably flat. Get out of trouble by jump starting (see next page) using another car.

## If your car won't start even though the starter motor turns as normal

- ☐ Is there fuel in the tank?
- ☐ Has the engine immobiliser been deactivated? This should happen automatically, on inserting the ignition key. However, if a replacement key has been obtained (other than from a Volvo dealer), it may not contain the transponder chip necessary to deactivate the system.
- ☐ Is there moisture on electrical components under the bonnet? Switch off the ignition, then wipe off any obvious dampness with a dry cloth. Spray a water-repellent aerosol product (WD-40 or equivalent) on ignition and fuel system electrical connectors like those shown in the photos. Pay special attention to the ignition coils wiring connector.

**A** Check the condition and security of the battery connections

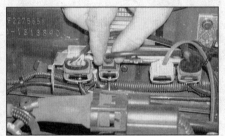

**B** Unclip the plastic cover from the centre of the bulkhead and check that the engine management system wiring connectors are all securely joined

**C1** If possible, remove the engine cover to . . .

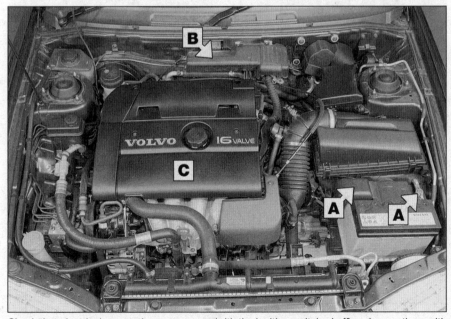

Check that electrical connections are secure (with the ignition switched off) and spray them with a water dispersant spray like WD-40 if you suspect a problem due to damp.

**C2** . . . check that the ignition coil wiring connectors are securely connected . . .

**C3** . . . and the HT leads (non-GDI engines) are securely connected to both the coils and spark plugs

# Jump starting

When jump-starting a car using a booster battery, observe the following precautions:

✔ Before connecting the booster battery, make sure that the ignition is switched off.

✔ Ensure that all electrical equipment (lights, heater, wipers, etc) is switched off.

✔ Take note of any special precautions printed on the battery case.

✔ Make sure that the booster battery is the same voltage as the discharged one in the vehicle.

✔ If the battery is being jump-started from the battery in another vehicle, the two vehicles MUST NOT TOUCH each other.

✔ Make sure that the transmission is in neutral (or PARK, in the case of automatic transmission).

**1** Connect one end of the red jump lead to the positive (+) terminal of the flat battery

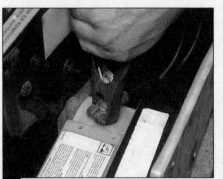

**2** Connect the other end of the red lead to the positive (+) terminal of the booster battery.

**3** Connect one end of the black jump lead to the negative (-) terminal of the booster battery

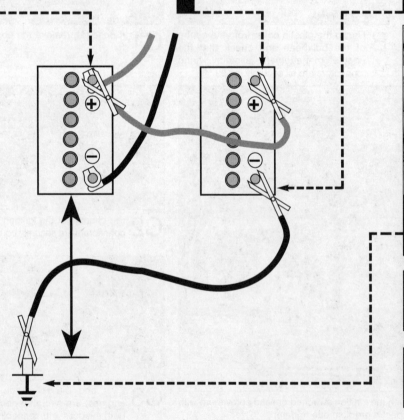

**4** Connect the other end of the black jump lead to a bolt or bracket on the engine block, well away from the battery, on the vehicle to be started.

**5** Make sure that the jump leads will not come into contact with the fan, drive-belts or other moving parts of the engine.

**6** Start the engine using the booster battery and run it at idle speed. Switch on the lights, rear window demister and heater blower motor, then disconnect the jump leads in the reverse order of connection. Turn off the lights etc.

# Identifying leaks

Puddles on the garage floor or drive, or obvious wetness under the bonnet or underneath the car, suggest a leak that needs investigating. It can sometimes be difficult to decide where the leak is coming from, especially if the engine bay is very dirty already. Leaking oil or fluid can also be blown rearwards by the passage of air under the car, giving a false impression of where the problem lies.

 *Warning: Most automotive oils and fluids are poisonous. Wash them off skin, and change out of contaminated clothing, without delay.*

 **HAYNES HiNT** *The smell of a fluid leaking from the car may provide a clue to what's leaking. Some fluids are distinctively coloured. It may help to clean the car carefully and to park it over some clean paper overnight as an aid to locating the source of the leak.*
*Remember that some leaks may only occur while the engine is running.*

## Sump oil

Engine oil may leak from the drain plug...

## Oil from filter

...or from the base of the oil filter.

## Gearbox oil

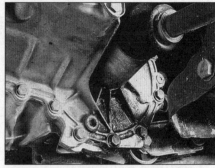

Gearbox oil can leak from the seals at the inboard ends of the driveshafts.

## Antifreeze

Leaking antifreeze often leaves a crystalline deposit like this.

## Brake fluid

A leak occurring at a wheel is almost certainly brake fluid.

## Power steering fluid

Power steering fluid may leak from the pipe connectors on the steering rack.

# Towing

When all else fails, you may find yourself having to get a tow home – or of course you may be helping somebody else. Long-distance recovery should only be done by a garage or breakdown service. For shorter distances, DIY towing using another car is easy enough, but observe the following points:
☐ Use a proper tow-rope – they are not expensive. The vehicle being towed must display an ON TOW sign in its rear window.
☐ Always turn the ignition key to the 'on' position when the vehicle is being towed, so

that the steering lock is released, and that the direction indicator and brake lights will work.
☐ Both front and rear towing eyes are provided. They are located centrally, below the front and rear bumpers.
☐ Before being towed, release the handbrake and select neutral on the transmission. On models with automatic transmission, special precautions apply. If in doubt, do not tow, or transmission damage may result.
☐ Note that greater-than-usual pedal pressure will be required to operate the brakes, since the vacuum servo unit is only

operational with the engine running.
☐ On models with power steering, greater-than-usual steering effort will also be required.
☐ The driver of the car being towed must keep the tow-rope taut to avoid snatching.
☐ Make sure that both drivers know the route before setting off.
☐ Only drive at moderate speeds and keep the distance towed to a minimum. Drive smoothly and allow plenty of time for slowing down at junctions.

# Wheel changing

Some of the details shown here will vary according to model.

**Warning: Do not change a wheel in a situation where you risk being hit by another vehicle. On busy roads, try to stop in a lay-by or a gateway. Be wary of passing traffic while changing the wheel - it is easy to become distracted by the job in hand.**

## Preparation

☐ When a puncture occurs, stop as soon as it is safe to do so.
☐ Park on firm level ground, if possible, and well out of the way of other traffic.
☐ Use hazard warning lights if necessary.

☐ If you have one, use a warning triangle to alert other drivers of your presence.
☐ Apply the handbrake and engage first or reverse gear (or Park on models with automatic transmission).

☐ Chock the wheel diagonally opposite the one being removed – a couple of large stones will do for this.
☐ If the ground is soft, use a flat piece of wood to spread the load under the jack.

## Changing the wheel

**1** Lift up the luggage compartment floor and remove the toolkit then unscrew the retainer and lift out the spare wheel . . .

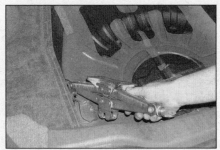

**2** . . . and the jack from the luggage compartment (Saloon model shown).

**3** Slacken each wheel nut by half a turn. On some wheels it will be necessary to remove the centre cap/wheel trim (as applicable) to gain access to the nuts.

**4** Where Volvo anti-theft wheel nuts are fitted, use the adaptor supplied (try looking in the glovebox) to enable the special wheel nut to be slackened.

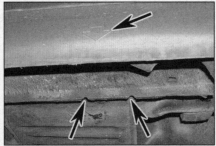

**5** Make sure the jack is located on firm ground and engage the jack head with the lifting point on the sill. The lifting point is in between the two notches on the sill seam; on models with plastic sill trim panels an arrow on the trim panel indicates its location.

**6** Ensure that the jack head is correctly located in the sill seam cutout and the base of the jack is directly underneath the sill seam. Using the wheelbrace and hooked rod in the tool kit, raise the jack until the wheel is clear of the ground.

**7** Unscrew the wheel nuts and remove the wheel. Fit the spare wheel and screw on the nuts. Lightly tighten the nuts with the wheelbrace then lower the vehicle to the ground.

**8** Securely tighten the wheel nuts in a diagonal sequence then refit the centre cap/wheel trim (where removed).

## Finally...

☐ Remove the wheel chocks.
☐ Stow the punctured wheel, jack and tools in the correct locations in the car.
☐ Check the tyre pressure on the wheel just fitted. If it is low, or if you don't have a pressure gauge with you, drive slowly to the next garage and inflate the tyre to the correct pressure.
☐ Have the damaged tyre or wheel repaired as soon as possible.
☐ Note that the wheel nuts should be slackened and retightened to the specified torque at the earliest possible opportunity.

## Introduction

There are some very simple checks which need only take a few minutes to carry out, but which could save you a lot of inconvenience and expense.

These *Weekly checks* require no great skill or special tools, and the small amount of time they take to perform could prove to be very well spent, for example;

☐ Keeping an eye on tyre condition and pressures, will not only help to stop them wearing out prematurely, but could also save your life.

☐ Many breakdowns are caused by electrical problems. Battery-related faults are particularly common, and a quick check on a regular basis will often prevent the majority of these.

☐ If your car develops a brake fluid leak, the first time you might know about it is when your brakes don't work properly. Checking the level regularly will give advance warning of this kind of problem.

☐ If the oil or coolant levels run low, the cost of repairing any engine damage will be far greater than fixing the leak, for example.

## Underbonnet check points

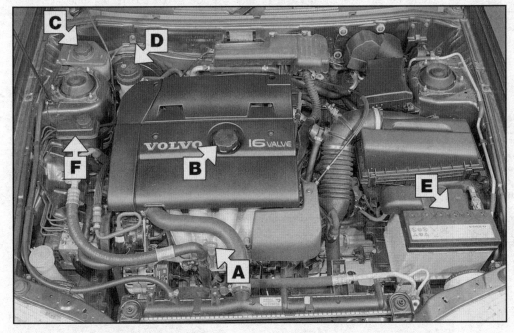

**◄ 2.0 litre engine (others similar)**

**A** *Engine oil level dipstick*

**B** *Engine oil filler cap*

**C** *Coolant expansion tank*

**D** *Brake (and clutch) fluid reservoir*

**E** *Battery*

**F** *Power steering fluid reservoir*

# Engine oil level

## Before you start
✔ Make sure that your car is on level ground.
✔ Check the oil level before the car is driven, or at least 5 minutes after the engine has been switched off.

 **HAYNES HINT** *If the oil is checked immediately after driving the vehicle, some of the oil will remain in the upper engine components, resulting in an inaccurate reading on the dipstick.*

## The correct oil
Modern engines place great demands on their oil. It is very important that the correct oil for your car is used (See *Lubricants and fluids* on page 0•17).

## Car Care
● If you have to add oil frequently, you should check whether you have any oil leaks. Place some clean paper under the car overnight, and check for stains in the morning. If there are no leaks, the engine may be burning oil.

● Always maintain the level between the upper and lower dipstick marks (see photo 3). If the level is too low severe engine damage may occur. Oil seal failure may result if the engine is overfilled by adding too much oil.

**1** The dipstick is located at the front of the engine (see *Underbonnet check points* on page 0•11 for exact location). Withdraw the dipstick.

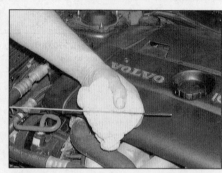

**2** Using a clean rag or paper towel remove all oil from the dipstick. Insert the clean dipstick into the tube as far as it will go, then withdraw it again.

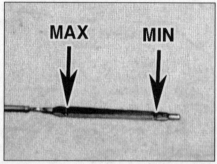

**3** Note the oil level on the end of the dipstick which should be between the upper (MAX) mark and lower (MIN) mark. Approximately 1.9 litres of oil (1.0 litre on GDI engines) will raise the level from the lower mark to the upper mark.

**4** Oil is added through the filler cap. Unscrew the cap and top-up the level, a funnel will help to prevent spillage. Add the oil slowly, checking the level on the dipstick often. Do not overfill.

---

# Coolant level

⚠ **Warning: DO NOT attempt to remove the expansion tank pressure cap when the engine is hot, as there is a very great risk of scalding. Do not leave open containers of coolant about, as it is poisonous.**

## Car Care
● With a sealed-type cooling system, adding coolant should not be necessary on a regular basis. If frequent topping-up is required, it is likely there is a leak. Check the radiator, all hoses and joint faces for signs of staining or wetness, and rectify as necessary.

● It is important that antifreeze is used in the cooling system all year round, not just during the winter months. Don't top-up with water alone, as the antifreeze will become too diluted.

**1** The coolant level varies with engine temperature. When the engine is cold, the coolant level should be between the MAX and MIN level marks on the side of the expansion tank. When the engine is hot, the level will rise.

**2** If topping-up is necessary, **wait until the engine is cold**. Slowly unscrew the expansion tank cap, to release any pressure present in the cooling system, and remove it.

**3** Add a mixture of water and antifreeze to the expansion tank until the coolant level is in between the level marks then securely refit the expansion cap tank.

# Brake and clutch* fluid level

*On manual transmission models, the brake fluid reservoir also supplies fluid to the clutch master cylinder.*

 **Warning:**
● **Brake fluid can harm your eyes and damage painted surfaces, so use extreme caution when handling and pouring it.**
● **Do not use fluid that has been standing open for some time, as it absorbs moisture from the air, which can cause a dangerous loss of braking effectiveness.**

 ● *Make sure that your car is on level ground.*
● *The fluid level in the reservoir will drop slightly as the brake pads wear down, but the fluid level must never be allowed to drop below the MIN mark.*

## Safety First!
● If the reservoir requires repeated topping-up this is an indication of a fluid leak somewhere in the system, which should be investigated immediately.
● If a leak is suspected, the car should not be driven until the braking system has been checked. Never take any risks where brakes are concerned.

**1** The upper (MAX) and lower (MIN) fluid level markings are on the side of the reservoir, which is located in the right-hand rear corner of the engine compartment. The fluid level must always be kept in between these two marks.

**2** If topping-up is necessary, first wipe clean the area around the filler cap to prevent dirt entering the hydraulic system.

**3** Carefully add fluid, taking care not to spill it onto the surrounding components. Use only the specified fluid; mixing different types can cause damage to the system. After topping-up to the correct level, securely refit the cap and wipe off any spilt fluid

# Power steering fluid level

## Before you start
✔ Park the vehicle on level ground.
✔ Set the steering wheel straight-ahead.
✔ The engine should be turned off.

 *For the check to be accurate, the steering must not be turned once the engine has been stopped.*

## Safety first!
● The need for frequent topping-up indicates a leak, which should be investigated immediately.

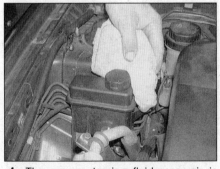

**1** The power steering fluid reservoir is located on the right-hand side of the engine compartment, and the fluid should be cold when checking the level. Wipe clean the reservoir before unscrewing and removing the cap.

**2** Wipe clean the filler cap dipstick then refit the filler cap and remove it again. Note the fluid level on the dipstick.

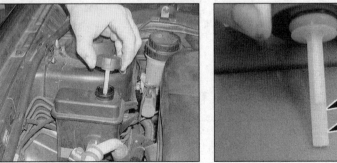

**3** When the fluid is cold the fluid level should be between upper (MAX) and lower (MIN) level marks on the dipstick. Top-up the fluid level using the specified type of fluid (do not overfill) then securely refit the filler cap

# Battery

*Caution: Before carrying out any work on the vehicle battery, read the precautions given in 'Safety first!' at the start of this manual.*

✔ Make sure that the battery tray is in good condition, and that the clamp is tight. Corrosion on the tray, retaining clamp and the battery itself can be removed with a solution of water and baking soda. Thoroughly rinse all cleaned areas with water. Any metal parts damaged by corrosion should be covered with a zinc-based primer, then painted.

✔ Periodically (approximately every three months), check the charge condition of the battery, as described in Chapter 5A.

✔ If the battery is flat, and you need to jump start your vehicle, see *Roadside repairs*.

**1** The battery is located at the front left-hand corner of the engine compartment. The exterior of the battery should be inspected periodically for damage, such as a cracked case or cover, and leads should be checked for signs of damage.

**2** Check that both battery lead clamps are securely fitted to ensure good electrical connections.

*Battery corrosion can be kept to a minimum by applying a layer of petroleum jelly to the clamps and terminals after they are reconnected.*

**3** If corrosion (white, fluffy deposits) is evident, remove the cables from the battery terminals, clean them with a small wire brush, then refit them. Automotive stores sell a tool for cleaning the battery post . . .

**4** . . . as well as the battery cable clamps.

# Electrical systems

✔ Check all external lights and the horn. Refer to the appropriate Sections of Chapter 12 for details if any of the circuits are found to be inoperative, and replace the fuse if necessary.

✔ Visually check all accessible wiring connectors, harnesses and retaining clips for security, and for signs of chafing or damage.

*If you need to check your brake lights and indicators unaided, back up to a wall or garage door and operate the lights. The reflected light should show if they are working properly.*

**1** If a single indicator light, brake light or headlight has failed, it is likely that a bulb has blown and will need to be renewed. Refer to Chapter 12 for details. If both stop-lights have failed, it is possible that the switch is faulty (see Chapter 9).

**2** If more than one indicator light or tail light has failed it is likely that either a fuse has blown or that there is a fault in the circuit (see Chapter 12). Most fuses are located in the fusebox, behind the driver's side lower facia panel; remove the cover to gain access. Additional fuses can be found in the engine compartment fuse/relay box.

**3** To replace a blown fuse, remove it using the fuse removal tool (which is clipped to the cover) and renew it with a fuse of the correct rating (shown with lower facia panel removed). If the new fuse blows as well, it is important that you find the reason why (see *Electrical fault finding* in Chapter 12).

# Tyre condition and pressure

It is very important that tyres are in good condition, and at the correct pressure - having a tyre failure at any speed is highly dangerous. Tyre wear is influenced by driving style - harsh braking and acceleration, or fast cornering, will all produce more rapid tyre wear. As a general rule, the front tyres wear out faster than the rears. Interchanging the tyres from front to rear ("rotating" the tyres) may result in more even wear. However, if this is completely effective, you may have the expense of replacing all four tyres at once! Remove any nails or stones embedded in the tread before they penetrate the tyre to cause deflation. If removal of a nail does reveal that

the tyre has been punctured, refit the nail so that its point of penetration is marked. Then immediately change the wheel, and have the tyre repaired by a tyre dealer.

Regularly check the tyres for damage in the form of cuts or bulges, especially in the sidewalls. Periodically remove the wheels, and clean any dirt or mud from the inside and outside surfaces. Examine the wheel rims for signs of rusting, corrosion or other damage. Light alloy wheels are easily damaged by "kerbing" whilst parking; steel wheels may also become dented or buckled. A new wheel is very often the only way to overcome severe damage.

New tyres should be balanced when they are fitted, but it may become necessary to re-balance them as they wear, or if the balance weights fitted to the wheel rim should fall off. Unbalanced tyres will wear more quickly, as will the steering and suspension components. Wheel imbalance is normally signified by vibration, particularly at a certain speed (typically around 50 mph). If this vibration is felt only through the steering, then it is likely that just the front wheels need balancing. If, however, the vibration is felt through the whole car, the rear wheels could be out of balance. Wheel balancing should be carried out by a tyre dealer or garage.

**1 Tread Depth - visual check**
The original tyres have tread wear safety bands (B), which will appear when the tread depth reaches approximately 1.6 mm. The band positions are indicated by a triangular mark on the tyre sidewall (A).

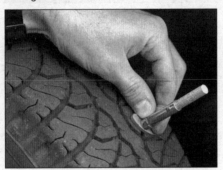

**2 Tread Depth - manual check**
Alternatively, tread wear can be monitored with a simple, inexpensive device known as a tread depth indicator gauge.

**3 Tyre Pressure Check**
Check the tyre pressures regularly with the tyres cold. Do not adjust the tyre pressures immediately after the vehicle has been used, or an inaccurate setting will result. Tyre pressures are shown on page 0•17.

# Tyre tread wear patterns

### Shoulder Wear

**Underinflation (wear on both sides)**
Under-inflation will cause overheating of the tyre, because the tyre will flex too much, and the tread will not sit correctly on the road surface. This will cause a loss of grip and excessive wear, not to mention the danger of sudden tyre failure due to heat build-up.
*Check and adjust pressures*
**Incorrect wheel camber (wear on one side)**
*Repair or renew suspension parts*
**Hard cornering**
*Reduce speed!*

### Centre Wear

**Overinflation**
Over-inflation will cause rapid wear of the centre part of the tyre tread, coupled with reduced grip, harsher ride, and the danger of shock damage occurring in the tyre casing.
*Check and adjust pressures*

*If you sometimes have to inflate your car's tyres to the higher pressures specified for maximum load or sustained high speed, don't forget to reduce the pressures to normal afterwards.*

### Uneven Wear

Front tyres may wear unevenly as a result of wheel misalignment. Most tyre dealers and garages can check and adjust the wheel alignment (or "tracking") for a modest charge.
**Incorrect camber or castor**
*Repair or renew suspension parts*
**Malfunctioning suspension**
*Repair or renew suspension parts*
**Unbalanced wheel**
*Balance tyres*
**Incorrect toe setting**
*Adjust front wheel alignment*
**Note:** The feathered edge of the tread which typifies toe wear is best checked by feel.

## Screen washer fluid level

● Screenwash additives not only keep the windscreen clean during bad weather, they also prevent the washer system freezing in cold weather – which is when you are likely to need it most. Don't top up using plain water, as the screenwash will become diluted and will freeze in cold weather.
*On no account use coolant antifreeze in the washer system - this could discolour or damage paintwork.*

**1** The filler neck for the washer reservoir is located in the front, right-hand corner of the engine compartment. One reservoir supplies all the car's washer systems.

**2** When topping-up the reservoir, a screen-wash additive should be added in the quantities recommended on the bottle.

## Wiper blades

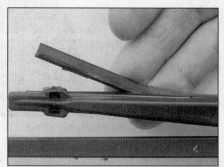

**1** Check the condition of the wiper blades; if they are cracked or show any signs of deterioration, or if the glass swept area is smeared, renew them. Wiper blades should be renewed annually.

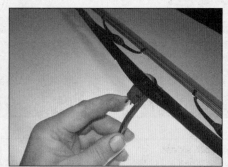

**2** To remove a windscreen wiper blade, pull the arm fully away from the screen until it locks. Swivel the blade through 90°, press the locking tab with your fingers and slide the blade out of the arm's hooked end.

## Lubricants and fluids

| | |
|---|---|
| Engine . . . . . . . . . . . . . . . . . . . . . . . . . . . . . . . . . . . . . . . . . . | Multigrade engine oil, viscosity SAE 10W/30, 10W/40, or 15W/40, to ACEA A1 or A3, API SH or SJ |
| Cooling system . . . . . . . . . . . . . . . . . . . . . . . . . . . . . . . . . . | Ethylene glycol-based antifreeze |
| **Manual transmission** | |
| M3P, M5P, M5D . . . . . . . . . . . . . . . . . . . . . . . . . . . . . . . . . | Volvo synthetic gearbox oil 3345534-6 |
| M5M42/F5M45 . . . . . . . . . . . . . . . . . . . . . . . . . . . . . . . . . | Volvo synthetic gearbox oil 1161520-7 |
| M56 . . . . . . . . . . . . . . . . . . . . . . . . . . . . . . . . . . . . . . . . . . . . | Volvo synthetic gearbox oil 1161423-7 |
| **Automatic transmission** | |
| AW50-42 (4-speed, up to 2001) . . . . . . . . . . . . . . . . . . | Volvo synthetic gearbox oil (Dexron III type) |
| AW55-50 (5-speed, 2001-on) . . . . . . . . . . . . . . . . . . . . | Volvo synthetic gearbox oil 1161540-8 (to JWS 3309) |
| Braking system . . . . . . . . . . . . . . . . . . . . . . . . . . . . . . . . . . | Brake and clutch fluid to DOT 4+ |
| Power steering . . . . . . . . . . . . . . . . . . . . . . . . . . . . . . . . . . | Dexron type ATF |

## Choosing your engine oil

Engines need oil, not only to lubricate moving parts and minimise wear, but also to maximise power output and to improve fuel economy.

### HOW ENGINE OIL WORKS

#### • Beating friction

Without oil, the moving surfaces inside your engine will rub together, heat up and melt, quickly causing the engine to seize. Engine oil creates a film which separates these moving parts, preventing wear and heat build-up.

#### • Cooling hot-spots

Temperatures inside the engine can exceed 1000° C. The engine oil circulates and acts as a coolant, transferring heat from the hot-spots to the sump.

#### • Cleaning the engine internally

Good quality engine oils clean the inside of your engine, collecting and dispersing combustion deposits and controlling them until they are trapped by the oil filter or flushed out at oil change.

### OIL CARE - FOLLOW THE CODE

To handle and dispose of used engine oil safely, always:

0800 66 33 66
www.oilbankline.org.uk

• **Avoid skin contact with used engine oil. Repeated or prolonged contact can be harmful.**
• **Dispose of used oil and empty packs in a responsible manner in an authorised disposal site. Call 0800 663366 to find the one nearest to you. Never tip oil down drains or onto the ground.**

## Tyre pressures (cold)

**Note:** *Pressures apply to original-equipment tyres only, and may vary if any other make or type of tyre is fitted; check with the tyre manufacturer or supplier for correct pressures if necessary.*
**Note:** *Tyre pressures must always be checked with the tyres cold to ensure accuracy. The following are typical pressures, for the exact recommendations for your vehicle are given on a sticker attached to the driver's door, directly below the lock.*

| | Front | Rear |
|---|---|---|
| Up to 3 passengers . . . . . . . . . . . . . . . . . . . . . . . . . . . . . | 32 psi (2.2 bar) | 29 psi (2.0 bar) |
| Fully loaded . . . . . . . . . . . . . . . . . . . . . . . . . . . . . . . . . . . . | 34 psi (2.3 bar) | 34 psi (2.3 bar) |
| Space-saver spare . . . . . . . . . . . . . . . . . . . . . . . . . . . . . | 60 psi (4.1 bar) | 60 psi (4.1 bar) |

# Chapter 1
# Routine maintenance and servicing

## Contents

## Degrees of difficulty

 **Easy,** suitable for novice with little experience

 **Fairly easy,** suitable for beginner with some experience

 **Fairly difficult,** suitable for competent DIY mechanic

 **Difficult,** suitable for experienced DIY mechanic

**Very difficult,** suitable for expert DIY or professional

**Lubricants and fluids** . . . . . . . . . . . . . . . . . . . . . . . . . . . . . . . . . . .   Refer to end of *Weekly checks* on page 0•17

## Capacities

**Engine oil (including filter)**
Models up to 1997 . . . . . . . . . . . . . . . . . . . . . . . . . . . . . . . . . . . . . . .   5.3 litres
Models from 1998, except GDI engine . . . . . . . . . . . . . . . . . . . . . . . .   5.4 litres
GDI engine models . . . . . . . . . . . . . . . . . . . . . . . . . . . . . . . . . . . . . . .   3.8 litres

**Cooling system**
From dry:
   Non-turbo models, except GDI engine . . . . . . . . . . . . . . . . . . . . . .   6.3 litres
   GDI engine models . . . . . . . . . . . . . . . . . . . . . . . . . . . . . . . . . . . .   6.0 litres
   Turbo models . . . . . . . . . . . . . . . . . . . . . . . . . . . . . . . . . . . . . . . .   5.7 litres
Drain and refill (approximate) . . . . . . . . . . . . . . . . . . . . . . . . . . . . . . .   5.0 litres

**Manual transmission**
Non-turbo models, except GDI engine . . . . . . . . . . . . . . . . . . . . . . . .   3.4 litres
GDI engine models . . . . . . . . . . . . . . . . . . . . . . . . . . . . . . . . . . . . . . .   2.2 litres
Turbo models . . . . . . . . . . . . . . . . . . . . . . . . . . . . . . . . . . . . . . . . . . .   2.1 litres

**Automatic transmission**
4-speed:
   Total (including fluid cooler and hoses) . . . . . . . . . . . . . . . . . . . . . .   7.7 litres
   Torque converter only . . . . . . . . . . . . . . . . . . . . . . . . . . . . . . . . . . .   2.5 litres
   Difference between MAX and MIN levels on dipstick . . . . . . . . . . . .   0.5 litres
5-speed:
   Total (including fluid cooler and hoses) . . . . . . . . . . . . . . . . . . . . . .   7.5 litres
   Difference between MAX and MIN levels on dipstick . . . . . . . . . . . .   0.2 litres

**Washer fluid reservoir**
Without headlight washers . . . . . . . . . . . . . . . . . . . . . . . . . . . . . . . . . .   3.5 litres
With headlight washers . . . . . . . . . . . . . . . . . . . . . . . . . . . . . . . . . . . .   4.5 litres

**Fuel tank** . . . . . . . . . . . . . . . . . . . . . . . . . . . . . . . . . . . . . . . . . . . . . .   60 litres

## Cooling system

Antifreeze mixture:
   50% antifreeze . . . . . . . . . . . . . . . . . . . . . . . . . . . . . . . . . . . . . . . .   Protection down to -37°C (5°F)
   55% antifreeze . . . . . . . . . . . . . . . . . . . . . . . . . . . . . . . . . . . . . . . .   Protection down to -45°C (-22°F)
**Note:** *Refer to antifreeze manufacturer for latest recommendations.*

## Ignition system

| | Spark plug type | Gap |
| --- | --- | --- |
| 1.6 litre models . . . . . . . . . . . . . . . . . . . . . . . . . . . . . . . . . . . . . . . | Bosch FGR 7 DQE 0 | 1.4 mm |
| 1.8 litre models: | | |
|    Except GDI . . . . . . . . . . . . . . . . . . . . . . . . . . . . . . . . . . . . . . . | Bosch FGR 7 DQE 0 | 1.4 mm |
|    GDI . . . . . . . . . . . . . . . . . . . . . . . . . . . . . . . . . . . . . . . . . . . . | Bosch FR 7 DTC | 0.8 mm |
| 1.9 litre models . . . . . . . . . . . . . . . . . . . . . . . . . . . . . . . . . . . . . . . | Bosch FR 7 DPP 10 | 0.7 mm |
| 2.0 litre: | | |
|    Non-turbo models . . . . . . . . . . . . . . . . . . . . . . . . . . . . . . . . . . | Bosch FGR 7 DQE 0 | 1.4 mm |
|    Turbo models . . . . . . . . . . . . . . . . . . . . . . . . . . . . . . . . . . . . . | Bosch FR 7 DPP 10 | 0.7 mm |

## Brakes

Brake pad material minimum thickness (front/rear) . . . . . . . . . . . . . . .   2.0 mm

## Torque wrench settings

| | Nm | lbf ft |
| --- | --- | --- |
| Alternator pivot nut . . . . . . . . . . . . . . . . . . . . . . . . . . . . . . . . . . . . . | 44 | 32 |
| Engine sump drain plug: | | |
|    Except GDI engine . . . . . . . . . . . . . . . . . . . . . . . . . . . . . . . . . . | 35 | 26 |
|    GDI engine . . . . . . . . . . . . . . . . . . . . . . . . . . . . . . . . . . . . . . . | 39 | 29 |
| Ignition coil mounting bolts . . . . . . . . . . . . . . . . . . . . . . . . . . . . . . . | 10 | 7 |
| Oil filter (models with renewable filter cartridge): | | |
|    Except GDI engine . . . . . . . . . . . . . . . . . . . . . . . . . . . . . . . . . . | 25 | 18 |
|    GDI engine . . . . . . . . . . . . . . . . . . . . . . . . . . . . . . . . . . . . . . . | 14 | 10 |
| Manual transmission drain plug: | | |
|    Non-turbo models, except GDI . . . . . . . . . . . . . . . . . . . . . . . . . | 22 | 16 |
|    GDI models . . . . . . . . . . . . . . . . . . . . . . . . . . . . . . . . . . . . . . | 32 | 24 |
|    Turbo models . . . . . . . . . . . . . . . . . . . . . . . . . . . . . . . . . . . . . | 35 | 26 |
| Manual transmission filler/level plug: | | |
|    Non-turbo models except GDI (plastic plug) . . . . . . . . . . . . . . . | Finger-tight | Finger-tight |
|    GDI models . . . . . . . . . . . . . . . . . . . . . . . . . . . . . . . . . . . . . . | 32 | 24 |
|    Turbo models . . . . . . . . . . . . . . . . . . . . . . . . . . . . . . . . . . . . . | 35 | 26 |
| Roadwheel nuts . . . . . . . . . . . . . . . . . . . . . . . . . . . . . . . . . . . . . . . | 110 | 81 |
| Spark plugs . . . . . . . . . . . . . . . . . . . . . . . . . . . . . . . . . . . . . . . . . . | 25 | 18 |

The maintenance intervals in this manual are provided with the assumption that you, not the dealer, will be carrying out the work. These are the minimum maintenance intervals recommended by us for cars driven daily. If you wish to keep your car in peak condition at all times, you may wish to perform some of these procedures more often. We encourage frequent maintenance, because it enhances the efficiency, performance and resale value of your car.

If the car is driven in dusty areas, used to tow a trailer, or driven frequently at slow speeds (idling in traffic) or on short journeys, more frequent maintenance intervals are recommended.

When the car is new, it should be serviced by a factory-authorised dealer service department, in order to preserve the factory warranty.

## Every 5000 miles (7500 km) or 6 months

☐ Renew the engine oil and filter (Section 3)
☐ Reset the service reminder indicator (Section 4)

**Note:** *Frequent oil and filter changes are good for the engine. We recommend changing the oil at the mileage specified here, or at least twice a year if the mileage covered is less.*

## Every 10 000 miles (15 000 km) or 12 months, whichever comes first

☐ Renew the pollen filter (Section 5)
☐ Check the operation of the starter inhibitor – models with automatic transmission (Section 6)
☐ Check all components, pipes and hoses for fluid leaks (Section 7)
☐ Check the condition of the auxiliary drivebelt (Section 8)
☐ Check the condition of the coolant (Section 9)
☐ Check the manual transmission oil level (Section 10)
☐ Check the automatic transmission fluid level (Section 11)
☐ Check the operation of the handbrake (Section 12)
☐ Check the brake pads and discs for wear (Section 13)
☐ Check the condition of the exhaust system (Section 14)
☐ Check the condition of the driveshaft gaiters (Section 15)
☐ Check the steering and suspension components for condition and security (Section 16)
☐ Lubricate all door locks and hinges, door stops, bonnet lock and release, and tailgate lock and hinges (Section 17)
☐ Check and if necessary adjust the headlight beam alignment (Section 18)
☐ Check the operation of the wiper/washer systems (Section 19)
☐ Clean the electric aerial (Section 20)
☐ Carry out a road test (Section 21)

## Every 20 000 miles (30 000 km) or 2 years, whichever comes first

☐ Renew the brake/clutch fluid (Section 22)
☐ Check the underbody sealant for signs of damage (Section 23)

## Every 30 000 miles (45 000 km) or 3 years, whichever comes first

☐ Renew the spark plugs (Section 24)
☐ Renew the air filter element (Section 25)

## Every 40 000 miles (60 000 km) or 4 years, whichever comes first

☐ Renew the automatic transmission fluid – only on cars used for towing or stop-start driving (Section 26)
☐ Clean the brake servo vacuum pipes and ports – GDI engine only (Section 27)
☐ Clean the throttle housing – GDI engine only (Section 28)
☐ Check the engine crankcase ventilation system and renew the flame trap (Section 29)

## Every 80 000 miles (120 000 km) or 8 years, whichever comes first

☐ Renew the fuel filter (Section 30)
☐ Renew the timing belt (Section 31)*
☐ Renew the auxiliary drivebelt (Section 32)

***Note:** *Although this is the normal interval for timing belt renewal, it is strongly recommended that the interval is reduced to 40 000 miles/ 4 years on cars which are subjected to intensive use, ie, mainly short journeys or a lot of stop-start driving. The actual belt renewal interval is therefore very much up to the individual owner, but bear in mind that severe engine damage will result if the belt breaks.*

## Every 2 years, regardless of mileage

☐ Renew the coolant (Section 33)

## Underbonnet view of a 1.8 litre GDI model (engine cover removed)

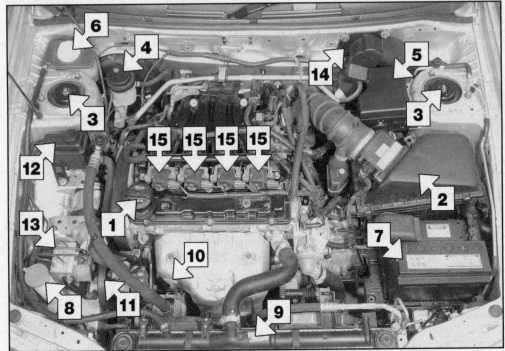

1 Engine oil filler cap
2 Air cleaner
3 Front suspension strut upper mounting
4 Brake (and clutch) fluid reservoir
5 Auxiliary fuse and relay box
6 Cooling system expansion tank
7 Battery
8 Washer fluid reservoir
9 Radiator
10 Engine oil level dipstick
11 Power steering pump
12 Power steering fluid reservoir
13 Anti-lock braking system (ABS) unit
14 Windscreen wiper motor
15 Ignition coils

## Underbonnet view of a 2.0 litre non-turbo model (others similar)

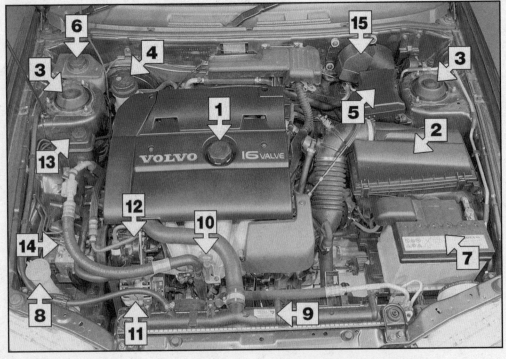

1 Engine oil filler cap
2 Air cleaner
3 Front suspension strut upper mounting
4 Brake (and clutch) fluid reservoir
5 Auxiliary fuse and relay box
6 Cooling system expansion tank
7 Battery
8 Washer fluid reservoir
9 Radiator
10 Engine oil level dipstick
11 Alternator
12 Power steering pump
13 Power steering fluid reservoir
14 Anti-lock braking system (ABS) unit
15 Windscreen wiper motor

## Front underbody view of a 2.0 litre non-turbo model (others similar)

1. Exhaust front downpipe
2. Oil filter
3. Engine oil drain plug
4. Air conditioning system compressor
5. Front suspension lower arm
6. Steering track rod
7. Driveshaft
8. Engine/transmission crossmember
9. Gearchange linkage
10. Charcoal canister

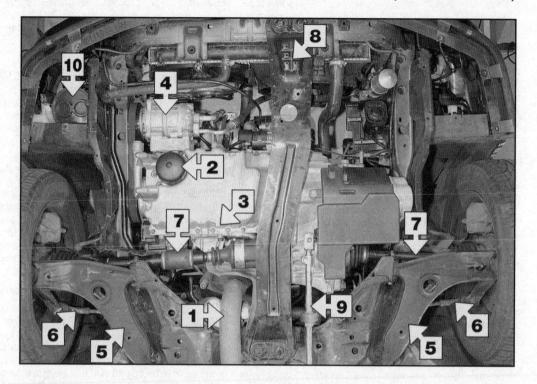

## Rear underbody view of a 2.0 litre non-turbo model (others similar)

1. Exhaust rear silencer
2. Fuel tank
3. Rear suspension anti-roll bar
4. Rear suspension lower arm
5. Rear suspension control link
6. Rear suspension upper link
7. Rear suspension trailing arm

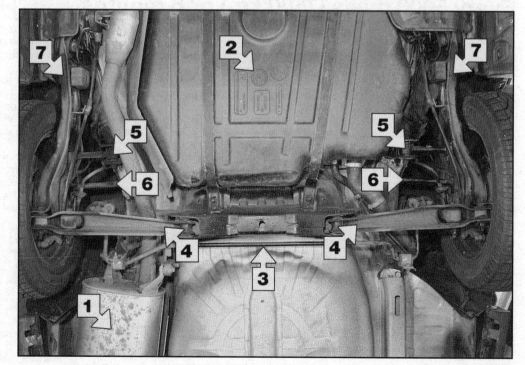

## 1 General information

This Chapter is designed to help the home mechanic maintain his/her car for safety, economy, long life and peak performance.

The Chapter contains a master maintenance schedule, followed by Sections dealing specifically with each task in the schedule. Visual checks, adjustments, component renewal and other helpful items are included. Refer to the accompanying illustrations of the engine compartment and the underside of the car for the locations of the various components.

Servicing your car in accordance with the mileage/time maintenance schedule and the following Sections will provide a planned maintenance programme, which should result in a long and reliable service life. This is a comprehensive plan, so maintaining some items but not others at the specified service intervals, will not produce the same results.

As you service your car, you will discover that many of the procedures can – and should – be grouped together, because of the particular procedure being performed, or because of the proximity of two otherwise-unrelated components to one another. For example, if the car is raised for any reason, the exhaust can be inspected at the same time as the suspension and steering components.

The first step in this maintenance programme is to prepare yourself before the actual work begins. Read through all the Sections relevant to the work to be carried out, then make a list and gather all the parts and tools required. If a problem is encountered, seek advice from a parts specialist, or a dealer service department.

## 2 Routine maintenance

If, from the time the car is new, the routine maintenance schedule is followed closely, and frequent checks are made of fluid levels and high-wear items, as suggested throughout this manual, the engine will be kept in relatively good running condition, and the need for additional work will be minimised.

It is possible that there will be times when the engine is running poorly due to the lack of regular maintenance. This is even more likely if a used car, which has not received regular and frequent maintenance checks, is purchased. In such cases, additional work may need to be carried out, outside of the regular maintenance intervals.

If engine wear is suspected, a compression test (refer to Chapter 2A or 2B) will provide valuable information regarding the overall performance of the main internal components. Such a test can be used as a basis to decide on the extent of the work to be carried out. If, for example, a compression test indicates serious internal engine wear, conventional maintenance as described in this Chapter will not greatly improve the performance of the engine, and may prove a waste of time and money, unless extensive overhaul work is carried out first.

The following series of operations are those most often required to improve the performance of a generally poor-running engine:

### Primary operations

a) Clean, inspect and test the battery (refer to 'Weekly checks').
b) Check all the engine-related fluids (refer to 'Weekly checks').
c) Check the condition of the auxiliary drivebelt (Section 8).
d) Renew the spark plugs (Section 24).
e) Check the condition of the air filter, and renew if necessary (Section 25).
f) Renew the fuel filter (Section 30).
g) Check the condition of all hoses, and check for fluid leaks (Section 7).

If the above operations do not prove effective, carry out the following secondary operations:

### Secondary operations

All items listed under *Primary operations*, plus the following:
a) Check the charging system (refer to Chapter 5A).
b) Check the ignition system (refer to Chapter 5B).
c) Check the fuel system (refer to Chapter 4A or 4B).

# Every 5000 miles (7500 km) or 6 months

## 3 Engine oil and filter renewal

1 Frequent oil changes are the best preventive maintenance the home mechanic can give the engine, because ageing oil becomes diluted and contaminated, which leads to premature engine wear.
2 Make sure that you have all the necessary tools before you begin this procedure. You should also have plenty of rags or newspapers handy, for mopping-up any spills. The oil should preferably be changed when the engine is still fully warmed-up to normal operating temperature, just after a run; warm oil and sludge will flow out more easily. Take care, however, not to touch the exhaust or any other hot parts of the engine when working under the car. To avoid any possibility of scalding, and to protect yourself from possible skin irritants and other harmful contaminants in used engine oils, it is advisable to wear gloves when carrying out this work.

3 Access to the underside of the car is greatly improved if the car can be lifted on a hoist, driven onto ramps, or supported by axle stands (see *Jacking and vehicle support*). Whichever method is chosen, make sure that the car remains level, or if it is at an angle, that the sump drain plug is at the lowest point. On some models, it will be necessary to remove the engine undershield for access to the sump and filter.
4 Position the draining container under the drain plug, and unscrew the plug **(see illustration)**. If possible, try to keep the plug pressed into the sump while unscrewing it by hand the last couple of turns.

> **HAYNES HINT** *As the drain plug releases from the threads, move it away sharply, so the stream of oil issuing from the sump runs into the container, not up your sleeve.*

5 Wait until all the old oil has drained into the container, noting that it may be necessary to reposition the container as the oil flow slows to a trickle **(see illustration)**.
6 When the oil has completely drained, wipe

**3.4 Unscrew the sump drain plug . . .**

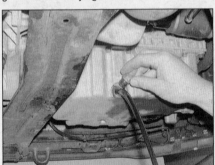

**3.5 . . . and allow the oil to drain into the container**

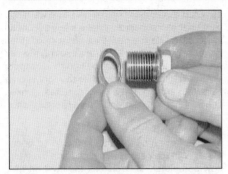

3.6a Fit a new sealing washer to the plug . . .

3.6b . . . then refit the plug to the sump, tightening it to the specified torque

3.7 Some models have a plastic or metal guard plate fitted round the oil filter

3.8 Unscrew the filter body using a close-fitting filter removal tool (later model with plastic filter body shown)

3.10a Remove the old filter element . . .

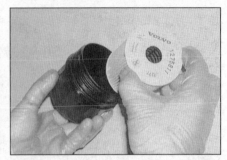

3.10b . . . then fit the new one, pushing it into place until the centre is felt to engage with the lug on the inside of the casing

clean the drain plug and its threads in the sump. Fit a new sealing washer to the plug, then refit the plug to the sump, tightening it to the specified torque (see illustrations).

7 The oil filter is located at the base of the sump on the right-hand side. On some models, a plastic or metal cover may be fitted over the filter, secured by two bolts – remove the cover for access to the filter (see illustration).

8 Reposition the draining container under the oil filter then, using a suitable filter removal tool if necessary, slacken the filter initially, then unscrew it by hand the rest of the way; be prepared for some oil spillage. Empty the oil in the old filter into the container. Note that on some later models, a plastic oil filter body containing a renewable filter element is fitted. To avoid damaging the plastic casing when removing this kind of filter, use a strap wrench, or a close-fitting filter removal tool that engages with the hexagon-shaped casing (see illustration).

9 Using a clean, lint-free rag, wipe clean the cylinder block around the filter mounting. Check the old filter to make sure that the rubber sealing ring hasn't stuck to the engine; if it has, carefully remove it.

10 On models with a renewable filter element, withdraw the old filter element from the plastic filter casing, or the engine if it has stuck there. Clean out the filter casing using a clean cloth, then fit the new filter element, pushing it firmly into place until the centre is felt to engage with the lug on the inside of the casing. Fit the new sealing ring supplied with the filter element over the threads of the filter

casing and coat it with clean engine oil (see illustrations).

11 Screw the filter into position on the engine until it seats, then tighten it firmly by hand only – do not use any tools.

3.10c Fit the new sealing ring supplied with the filter element over the threads of the filter casing . . .

3.12a Screw the plastic filter casing into position on the engine . . .

12 On models with a renewable filter element, screw the plastic filter casing into position on the engine until it seats, then tighten it firmly by hand. Finally tighten the casing to the specified torque, using the same

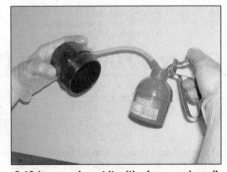

3.10d . . . and coat it with clean engine oil

3.12b . . . then tighten the casing to the specified torque, using the same tool employed during removal (later model with plastic filter body shown)

3.14a Remove the dipstick . . .

3.14b . . . and the oil filler cap from the engine

3.14c Fill the engine with oil, using the correct grade and type of oil . . .

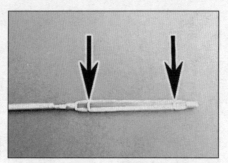

3.14d . . . adding oil a small quantity at a time, until the level is midway between the lower and upper marks on the dipstick

strap wrench or tool employed during removal **(see illustrations)**. Where applicable, refit the oil filter cover.

13 Remove the oil drain container and all tools from under the car, then lower the car to the ground.

14 Remove the dipstick and the oil filler cap from the engine. Fill the engine with oil, using the correct grade and type of oil (see *Lubricants and fluids*). Pour in half the specified quantity of oil first, then wait a few minutes for the oil to fall to the sump. Continue adding oil a small quantity at a time, until the level is midway between the lower and upper marks on the dipstick **(see illustrations)**.

15 Start the engine. The oil pressure warning light on the dashboard will take a few seconds to go out while the new filter fills with oil; the pressure should then build-up, causing the oil pressure warning light to extinguish – do not rev the engine above idle while the light is on. Run the engine for a few minutes, while checking for leaks around the oil filter seal and the drain plug.

16 Switch off the engine, and wait a few minutes for the oil to settle in the sump once more. With the new oil circulated and the filter now completely full, recheck the level on the dipstick. Add more oil, as necessary, to bring the level up to the MAX marking on the dipstick.

17 Dispose of the used engine oil safely and in accordance with environmental regulations (see *General repair procedures*).

## 4 Service reminder indicator – resetting

1 Start with the ignition switched off. Press and hold the reset button for the trip meter, then switch on the ignition, keeping the trip meter button pressed.

2 If the trip meter button is released within 4 seconds of switching the ignition on, there will be an audible signal to confirm that the light has been reset, and the light will go out.

3 If the button is held in for longer than 10 seconds with the ignition on, the light will start to flash, but this does not mean the light has been reset. If the 4 second period is missed, switch off the ignition and repeat the procedure.

# Every 10 000 miles (15 000 km) or 12 months

## 5 Pollen filter renewal

1 Slacken and remove the retaining screws and remove the passenger side lower panel from the facia. The pollen filter is fitted to the underside of the duct/evaporator housing (as

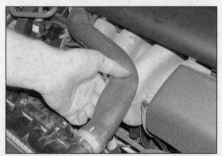

7.1 Carefully check the radiator and heater hoses along their entire length – cracks show up better if the hose is squeezed

applicable) linking the blower motor housing to the heating/ventilation housing.

2 Release the retaining clip and slide the pollen filter assembly out of position, noting which way around it is fitted.

3 Slide the new filter assembly into the duct/housing, making sure it is fitted the correct way around. Ensure the filter is clipped securely in position then refit the lower panel to the facia.

## 6 Automatic transmission starter inhibitor check

**Note:** *This procedure applies to models with automatic transmission only.*

1 Park the car on a level surface and switch off the ignition.

2 Check that the engine can only be started with the selector lever in either the P or N positions.

3 If the engine can be started with any other gear selected, there is a fault with the

gearshift position sensor, which must be rectified as soon as possible (see Chapter 7B, Section 5).

## 7 Hose and fluid leak check

### Cooling system

 *Warning: Refer to the safety information given in 'Safety first!' and Chapter 3 before disturbing any of the cooling system components.*

1 Carefully check the radiator and heater coolant hoses along their entire length. Renew any hose which is cracked, swollen or which shows signs of deterioration. Cracks will show up better if the hose is squeezed **(see illustration)**. Pay close attention to the clips that secure the hoses to the cooling system components. Hose clips that have been over-tightened can pinch and puncture hoses, resulting in cooling system leaks.

*A leak in the cooling system will usually manifest itself as white or rust-coloured, crusty deposits on the area adjacent to the leak.*

2 Inspect all the cooling system components (hoses, joint faces, etc) for leaks. Where any problems of this nature are found on system components, renew the component or gasket with reference to Chapter 3 **(see Haynes Hint)**.

## Fuel system

 *Warning: Refer to the safety information given in 'Safety first!' and Chapter 4A or 4B before disturbing any of the fuel system components.*

3 Petrol leaks are difficult to pinpoint, unless the leakage is significant and hence easily visible. Fuel tends to evaporate quickly once it comes into contact with air, especially in a hot engine bay. Small drips can disappear before you get a chance to identify the point of leakage. If you suspect that there is a fuel leak from the area of the engine bay, leave the car overnight then start the engine from cold, with the bonnet open. Metal components tend to shrink when they are cold, and rubber seals and hoses tend to harden, so any leaks will be more apparent whilst the engine is warming-up from a cold start.

4 Check all fuel lines at their connections to the fuel rail, fuel pressure regulator and fuel filter, and examine each rubber fuel hose along its length for splits or cracks. Check for leakage from the crimped joints between rubber and metal fuel lines. Examine the unions between the metal fuel lines and the fuel filter housing. Also check the area around the fuel injectors for signs of O-ring leakage **(see illustration)**.

5 To identify fuel leaks between the fuel tank and the engine bay, the car should raised and securely supported on axle stands. Inspect the petrol tank and filler neck for punctures, cracks and other damage. The connection between the filler neck and tank is especially critical. Sometimes a rubber filler neck or connecting hose will leak due to loose retaining clamps or deteriorated rubber.

6 Carefully check all rubber hoses and metal fuel lines leading away from the petrol tank. Check for loose connections, deteriorated hoses, kinked lines, and other damage. Pay particular attention to the vent pipes and hoses, which often loop up around the filler

**7.4 Check the fuel lines at their quick-release connections to the fuel rail**

neck and can become blocked or kinked, making tank filling difficult. Follow the fuel supply and return lines to the front of the car, carefully inspecting them all the way for signs of damage or corrosion. Renew damaged sections as necessary.

## Engine oil

7 Inspect the area around the camshaft cover, cylinder head, oil filter and sump joint faces. Bear in mind that, over a period of time, some very slight seepage from these areas is to be expected – what you are really looking for is any indication of a serious leak caused by gasket failure. Engine oil seeping from the base of the timing belt cover or the transmission bellhousing may be an indication of crankshaft or transmission input shaft oil seal failure. Should a leak be found, renew the failed gasket or oil seal by referring to the appropriate Chapters in this manual.

## Automatic transmission fluid

8 Where applicable, check the hoses leading to the transmission fluid cooler at the front of the engine bay for leakage. Look for deterioration caused by corrosion and damage from grounding, or debris thrown up from the road surface. Automatic transmission fluid is a thin oil, and is usually red in colour.

## Power steering fluid

9 Examine the hose running between the fluid reservoir and the power steering pump, and the return hose running from the steering rack to the fluid reservoir. Also examine the high-pressure supply hose between the pump and the steering rack.

10 Check the condition of each hose carefully. Look for deterioration caused by corrosion and damage from grounding, or debris thrown up from the road surface.

11 Pay particular attention to crimped unions, and the area surrounding the hoses that are secured with adjustable worm drive clips **(see illustration)**. Like automatic transmission fluid, PAS fluid is a thin oil, and is frequently red in colour.

## Air conditioning refrigerant

 *Warning: Refer to the safety information given in 'Safety first!' and Chapter 3, regarding the*

**7.11 Check the condition of the power steering pump fluid hoses, paying particular attention to crimped unions**

*dangers of disturbing any of the air conditioning system components.*

12 The air conditioning system is filled with a liquid refrigerant, which is retained under high pressure. If the air conditioning system is opened and depressurised without the aid of specialised equipment, the refrigerant will immediately turn into gas and escape into the atmosphere. If the liquid comes into contact with your skin, it can cause severe frostbite. In addition, the refrigerant contains substances which are environmentally damaging; for this reason, it should not be allowed to escape into the atmosphere.

13 Any suspected air conditioning system leaks should be immediately referred to a Volvo dealer or air conditioning specialist. Leakage will be shown up as a steady drop in the level of refrigerant in the system.

14 Note that water may drip from the condenser drain pipe, underneath the car, immediately after the air conditioning system has been in use. This is normal, and should not be cause for concern.

## Brake fluid

 *Warning: Refer to the safety information given in 'Safety first!' and Chapter 9, regarding the dangers of handling brake fluid.*

15 With reference to Chapter 9, examine the area surrounding the brake pipe unions at the master cylinder for signs of leakage. Check the area around the base of fluid reservoir for signs of leakage caused by seal failure **(see illustration)**. Also examine the brake pipe unions at the ABS hydraulic unit.

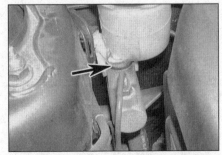

**7.15 Check the area around the base of brake fluid reservoir for signs of leakage caused by seal failure**

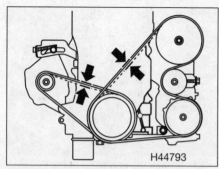

**8.6 Checking drivebelt deflections on GDI engine (model with air conditioning shown)**

16 If fluid loss is evident, but the leak cannot be pinpointed in the engine bay, the brake calipers and underbody brake lines should be carefully checked with the car raised and supported on axle stands. Leakage of fluid from the braking system is a serious fault that must be rectified immediately.

17 Brake/clutch hydraulic fluid is a toxic substance with a watery consistency. New fluid is almost colourless, but it becomes darker with age and use.

### Unidentified fluid leaks

18 If there are signs that a fluid of some description is leaking from the car, but you cannot identify the type of fluid or its exact origin, park the car overnight and slide a large piece of card underneath it. Providing that the card is positioned in roughly the right location, even the smallest leak will show up on the card. Not only will this help you to pinpoint the exact location of the leak, it should be easier to identify the fluid from its colour. Bear in mind, though, that the leak may only be occurring when the engine is running!

### Vacuum hoses

19 Although the braking system is hydraulically-operated, the brake servo unit amplifies the effort applied at the brake pedal, by making use of the vacuum in the inlet manifold generated by the engine. Vacuum is ported to the servo by means of a large-bore hose. Any leaks that develop in this hose will reduce the effectiveness of the braking system, and may affect the running of the engine.

**10.1a Undo the securing screws and remove the splash guard from the underside of the transmission**

20 In addition, a number of the underbonnet components, particularly the emission control components, are driven by vacuum supplied from the inlet manifold via narrow-bore hoses. A leak in a vacuum hose means that air is being drawn into the hose (rather than escaping from it) and this makes leakage very difficult to detect. One method is to use an old length of vacuum hose as a form of stethoscope – hold one end close to (but not in!) your ear and use the other end to probe the area around the suspected leak. When the end of the hose is directly over a vacuum leak, a hissing sound will be heard clearly through the hose. Care must be taken to avoid contacting hot or moving components, as the engine must be running when testing in this manner. Renew any vacuum hoses that are found to be defective.

## 8 Auxiliary drivebelt check

1 The auxiliary drivebelt transmits power from the crankshaft pulley to the alternator, power steering pump and air conditioning compressor (as applicable). Models with the GDI engine have two separate belts.

### Check

2 With the engine and ignition switched off, open and support the bonnet, then locate the auxiliary drivebelt at the crankshaft pulley end (right-hand side) of the engine. On turbo models, remove the engine right-hand cover, and the cover fitted over the right-hand headlight (right as seen from the driver's seat).

3 Using an inspection light or a small electric torch, and rotating the engine when necessary with a spanner applied to the crankshaft pulley nut, check the whole length of the drivebelt for cracks, separation of the rubber, and torn or worn ribs. Also check for fraying and glazing, which gives the drivebelt a shiny appearance.

4 Both sides of the drivebelt should be inspected, which means you will have to twist the drivebelt to check the underside. Use your fingers to feel the drivebelt where you can't see it. If you are in any doubt as to the condition of the drivebelt, renew it (see Section 32). As there is minimal working clearance, it may be beneficial to jack up and support the front of the car on axle stands. Then, with the roadwheel removed, the inner wheel arch panel can be folded back to give access to the crankshaft pulley.

5 On all except models with the GDI engine, depress the belt with your thumb at a point midway along its longest run, between the crankshaft and power steering pump pulleys. Check that the automatic belt tensioner moves freely as you exert pressure on the belt. Check also that the tensioner retracts, taking up all freeplay in the belt when the pressure is removed. Renew the tensioner if its condition is in doubt.

6 On models with the GDI engine, both drivebelts have manual tensioners. In normal service, the drivebelt tension should not normally need adjusting. Check the tension by pressing down on the top run of each belt, midway between the two pulleys. The total belt deflection (up-and-down) should be between 10 and 12 mm – any more than this, and the belts need adjusting as described in Section 32 (see illustration).

## 9 Antifreeze concentration check

⚠ **Warning: Wait until the engine is cold before starting this procedure. Do not allow coolant to come in contact with your skin, or with the painted surfaces. Rinse off spills immediately with plenty of water.**

1 Note that a tester will be required to check the antifreeze concentration (specific gravity); these can be obtained relatively cheaply from most motor accessory shops.

2 With the engine completely cold, unscrew and remove the filler cap from the coolant expansion tank. Following the instructions supplied with the tester, check the antifreeze mixture is sufficient to give protection down to temperatures well below freezing. If the coolant has been renewed at the specified intervals this shouldn't be a problem. However, if the coolant mixture is not strong enough to provide sufficient protection, it will be necessary to drain the cooling system and renew the coolant (see Section 33).

3 Once the test is complete, check the coolant level is correct (see Weekly checks) then securely refit the expansion tank cap.

## 10 Manual transmission oil level check

1 The manual transmission does not have a dipstick. To check the oil level, raise the car and support it securely on axle stands, making sure that the car is level (see Jacking and vehicle support). Undo the securing screws and remove the splash guard. On the forward-facing surface of the transmission casing you will see the filler/level plug (may be marked OIL), and on the underside of the transmission casing, a drain plug. On turbo models, the filler/level and drain plugs are located on the rear of the differential casing, facing the left-hand side of the car. The filler/level plug is the upper of the two (see illustrations).

2 Wipe all around the filler/level plug with a clean rag then unscrew and remove it. If the lubricant level is correct, the oil should be up to the lower edge of the hole. Note that a small quantity of oil may have collected behind the filler/level plug and then escaped

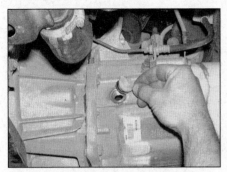

**10.1b Removing the filler/level plug (non-turbo models)**

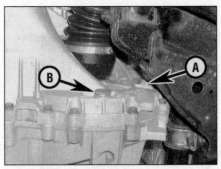

**10.1c Filler/level plug (A) and drain plug (B) locations (turbo models)**

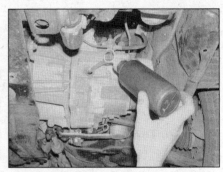

**10.3 Topping-up the transmission oil**

as you removed the plug; this does not necessarily mean that the oil level is correct.

**3** If the transmission needs more lubricant (if the oil level is not up to the hole), use a syringe, or a plastic bottle and tube, to add more. Stop filling the transmission when the lubricant begins to run out of the hole in a steady stream. Make sure that you use the correct type of lubricant **(see illustration)**.

**4** Ensure that the filler/level plug sealing ring is in good condition, then refit the plug to the transmission, and tighten it. On models with a metal plug, observe the correct tightening torque. On later non-turbo models with a plastic plug, hand-tighten only. Drive the car a short distance, then check for leaks.

**5** A need for regular topping-up can only be due to a leak, which should be found and rectified without delay.

**6** Although not part of the manufacturer's routine maintenance schedule, it is a good idea to change the transmission oil after a high mileage has been completed, or perhaps periodically on a car which does a lot of towing. A drain plug is provided – see Chapter 7A for details.

## 11 Automatic transmission fluid level check

**1** The level of the automatic transmission fluid should be carefully maintained. Low fluid level can lead to slipping or loss of drive, while overfilling can cause foaming, loss of fluid and transmission damage.

**2** The transmission fluid level should be checked when the transmission is hot (at its normal operating temperature of around 80°C), ie, when the car has just been driven for about 30 minutes.

**3** Park the car on level ground, apply the handbrake, and start the engine. With the engine idling and the brake pedal depressed, move the selector lever through all gear positions, holding the lever in each gear for about 3 seconds before moving to the next. On completion, return the lever to the P position.

**4** Wait two minutes then, with the engine still idling, remove the dipstick from its tube which is located at the front of the engine. Note the

condition and colour of the fluid on the dipstick.

**5** Wipe the fluid from the dipstick with a clean rag, and re-insert it into the filler tube until the cap seats.

**6** Pull the dipstick out again, and note the fluid level. The level should be between the MIN and MAX marks, on the upper section of the dipstick (marked HOT) **(see illustration)**. If the level is on the MIN mark, stop the engine, and add the specified automatic transmission fluid through the dipstick tube, using a clean funnel if necessary. Cleanliness is of great importance; it is vitally important not to introduce dirt into the transmission when topping-up.

**7** Add the fluid a little at a time, and keep checking the level as previously described until it is correct. The difference between the MIN and MAX marks on the dipstick is approximately 0.5 litre (4-speed transmission, fitted up to 2000) or 0.2 litre (5-speed transmission, year 2001-on). The transmission must not be overfilled – this will result in increased operating temperatures and fluid leaks. If overfilling occurs, the excess should be drained off (refer to Chapter 7B).

**8** If the car has not been driven and the engine and transmission are cold, carry out the procedures in paragraphs 3 to 7, but use the lower section of the dipstick marked COLD. Bear in mind that, when the transmission is cold, the fluid level will only be a few millimetres up from the bottom of the dipstick.

**9** The need for regular topping-up of the transmission fluid indicates a leak, which should be found and rectified without delay.

**11.6 Automatic transmission fluid dipstick markings**

**10** The condition of the fluid should also be checked along with the level. If the fluid at the end of the dipstick is black or a dark reddish-brown colour, or if it has a burned smell, the fluid should be changed. If you are in doubt about the condition of the fluid, purchase some new fluid, and compare the two for colour and smell. Refer to Chapter 7B for further information.

## 12 Handbrake check

**1** Handbrake adjustment is checked by counting the number of clicks emitted from the lever ratchet mechanism whilst apply the handbrake. Fully release the handbrake lever and apply as normal; the handbrake should be fully applied between the 5th and 7th notch of the ratchet mechanism. If necessary, adjust the handbrake as described in Chapter 9.

**2** Also check that the handbrake warning light and the handbrake lever ratchet mechanism both function correctly. Investigate any problems using the information in Chapters 9 and 12.

## 13 Brake pad and disc check

**1** Firmly apply the handbrake, loosen the front wheel nuts, then jack up the front of the car and support it securely on axle stands. Remove the front roadwheels.

**2** For a comprehensive check, the brake pads should be removed and cleaned. The operation of the caliper can then also be checked, and the condition of the brake disc itself can be fully examined on both sides. Refer to Chapter 9.

**3** If any pad's friction material is worn to the specified thickness or less, *all four pads must be renewed as a set* **(see Haynes Hint overleaf)**.

**4** Once the front brakes have been checked, refit the front roadwheels then lower the car to the ground and tighten the roadwheel nuts to the specified torque.

**5** Chock the front wheels, loosen the rear wheel nuts, then jack up the rear of the car and support it on axle stands. Remove the rear roadwheels and repeat the check on the rear brakes.

**6** On completion, refit the roadwheels then lower the car to the floor and tighten the rear roadwheel nuts to the specified torque.

## 14 Exhaust system check

**1** With the engine cold (at least three hours after the car has been driven), check the complete exhaust system, from its starting point at the engine to the end of the tailpipe. Ideally, this should be done on a hoist, where unrestricted access is available; if a hoist is not available, raise and support the car on axle stands (see *Jacking and vehicle support*).

**2** Check the pipes and connections for evidence of leaks, severe corrosion, or damage. Make sure that all brackets and rubber mountings are in good condition, and tight; if any of the mountings are to be renewed, ensure that the new ones are of the correct type. Leakage at any of the joints or in other parts of the system will usually show up as a black sooty stain in the vicinity of the leak.

**3** At the same time, inspect the underside of the body for holes, corrosion, open seams, etc, which may allow exhaust gases to enter the passenger compartment. Seal all body openings with silicone or body putty.

**4** Rattles and other noises can often be traced to the exhaust system, especially the rubber mountings. Try to move the system, silencer(s) and catalytic converter. If any components can touch the body or suspension parts, secure the exhaust system with new mountings.

## 15 Driveshaft gaiter check

**1** With the car raised and securely supported on stands, turn the steering onto full lock,

**15.1 Check the condition of the driveshaft gaiters**

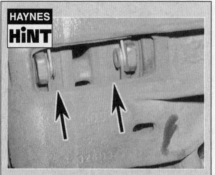

*Brake pad wear can be assessed by observing the thickness of the pad material, visible through the aperture at the front of the brake caliper.*

then slowly rotate the roadwheel. Inspect the condition of the outer constant velocity (CV) joint rubber gaiters, squeezing the gaiters to open out the folds **(see illustration)**. Check for signs of cracking, splits or deterioration of the rubber, which may allow the grease to escape, and lead to water and grit entry into the joint. Also check the security and condition of the retaining clips. Repeat these checks on the inner CV joints. If any damage or deterioration is found, the gaiters should be renewed as described in Chapter 8.

**2** At the same time, check the general condition of the CV joints themselves by first holding the driveshaft and attempting to rotate the wheel. Repeat this check by holding the inner joint and attempting to rotate the driveshaft. Any appreciable movement indicates wear in the joints, wear in the driveshaft splines, or possibly a loose hub nut.

## 16 Suspension and steering check

### Front suspension and steering

**1** Raise the front of the car, and securely support it on axle stands (see *Jacking and vehicle support*).

**2** Visually inspect the balljoint dust covers and the steering rack-and-pinion gaiters for splits, chafing or deterioration. Any wear of these components will cause loss of lubricant, together with dirt and water entry, resulting in rapid deterioration of the balljoints or steering gear.

**3** On cars with power steering, check the fluid hoses for chafing or deterioration, and the pipe and hose unions for fluid leaks. Also check for signs of fluid leakage under pressure from the steering gear rubber gaiters, which would indicate failed fluid seals within the steering gear.

**4** Grasp the roadwheel at the 12 o'clock and 6 o'clock positions, and try to rock it **(see illustration)**. Very slight free play may be felt, but if the movement is appreciable, further

investigation is necessary to determine the source. Continue rocking the wheel while an assistant depresses the footbrake. If the movement is now eliminated or significantly reduced, it is likely that the hub bearings are at fault. If the free play is still evident with the footbrake depressed, then there is wear in the suspension joints or mountings.

**5** Now grasp the wheel at the 9 o'clock and 3 o'clock positions, and try to rock it as before. Any movement felt now may again be caused by wear in the hub bearings or the steering track rod balljoints. If the outer balljoint is worn, the visual movement will be obvious. If the inner joint is suspect, it can be felt by placing a hand over the rack-and-pinion rubber gaiter and gripping the track rod. If the wheel is now rocked, movement will be felt at the inner joint if wear has taken place.

**6** Using a large screwdriver or flat bar, check for wear in the suspension mounting bushes by levering between the relevant suspension component and its attachment point. Some movement is to be expected, as the mountings are made of rubber, but excessive wear should be obvious. Also check the condition of any visible rubber bushes, looking for splits, cracks or contamination of the rubber.

**7** With the car standing on its wheels, have an assistant turn the steering wheel back-and-forth, about an eighth of a turn each way. There should be very little, if any, lost movement between the steering wheel and roadwheels. If this is not the case, closely observe the joints and mountings previously described. In addition, check the steering column universal joints for wear, and also check the rack-and-pinion steering gear itself.

### Rear suspension

**8** Chock the front wheels, then jack up the rear of the car and support securely on axle stands (see *Jacking and vehicle support*).

**9** Working as described previously for the front suspension, check the rear hub bearings, the suspension bushes and the strut or shock absorber mountings (as applicable) for wear.

### Shock absorber

**10** Check for any signs of fluid leakage around the shock absorber body, or from the

**16.4 Check for wear in the hub bearings by grasping the wheel and trying to rock it**

rubber gaiter around the piston rod. Should any fluid be noticed, the shock absorber is defective internally, and should be renewed. **Note:** *Shock absorbers should always be renewed in pairs on the same axle.*

**11** The efficiency of the shock absorber may be checked by bouncing the car at each corner. Generally speaking, the body will return to its normal position and stop after being depressed. If it rises and returns on a rebound, the shock absorber is probably suspect. Also examine the shock absorber upper and lower mountings for any signs of wear.

## 17 Hinge and lock lubrication

**1** Work around the car and lubricate the hinges of the bonnet, doors and tailgate with light oil.

**2** Lightly lubricate the bonnet release mechanism and exposed section of inner cable with a smear of grease.

**3** Check carefully the security and operation of all hinges, latches and locks, adjusting them where required. Check the operation of the central locking system.

**4** Check the condition and operation of the boot lid/tailgate struts, renewing them if either is leaking or no longer able to support the boot lid/tailgate securely when raised.

## 18 Headlight beam alignment check

Refer to Chapter 12 for details.

## 19 Wiper/washer system check

**1** Check that each of the washer jet nozzles are clear and that each nozzle provides a strong jet of washer fluid. The jets should be aimed to spray at a point slightly above the centre of the screen/headlight. On the windscreen washer nozzles where there are two jets, aim one of the jets slightly above then centre of the screen and aim the other just below to ensure complete coverage of the screen. If necessary, adjust the jets using a pin, noting that only vertical adjustment is possible.

## 20 Electric aerial cleaning

**1** If an electric aerial is fitted, extend the aerial and remove all traces of dirt from its mast.

**2** Lubricate the aerial mast with a silicone-spray type lubricant (Volvo recommend the use of spray P/N 1161398 – available from your Volvo dealer) then retract and extend the aerial several times. Wipe off all excess lubricant and retract the aerial.

## 21 Road test

### Braking system

**1** Make sure that the car does not pull to one side when braking, and that the wheels do not lock when braking hard.

**2** Check that there is no vibration through the steering when braking. On models equipped with ABS brakes, if vibration is felt through the pedal under heavy braking, this is a normal characteristic of the system operation, and is not a cause for concern.

**3** Check that the handbrake operates correctly, without excessive movement of the lever, and that it holds the car stationary on a slope.

**4** With the engine switched off, test the operation of the brake servo unit as follows. Depress the footbrake four or five times to exhaust the vacuum, then start the engine. As the engine starts, there should be a noticeable give in the brake pedal as vacuum builds-up. Allow the engine to run for at least two minutes, and then switch it off. If the brake pedal is now depressed again, it should be possible to detect a hiss from the servo as the pedal is depressed. After about four or five applications, no further hissing should be heard, and the pedal should feel considerably harder.

### Steering and suspension

**5** Check for any abnormalities in the steering, suspension, handling or road feel.

**6** Drive the car, and check that there are no unusual vibrations or noises.

**7** Check that the steering feels positive, with no excessive sloppiness or roughness, and check for any suspension noises when cornering and driving over bumps.

### Drivetrain

**8** Check the performance of the engine, transmission and driveline.

**9** Check that the engine starts correctly, both when cold and hot.

**10** Listen for any unusual noises from the engine and transmission.

**11** Make sure that the engine runs smoothly when idling, and that there is no hesitation when accelerating.

**12** On manual transmission models, check that all gears can be engaged smoothly without noise, and that the gear lever action is smooth and not abnormally vague or notchy.

**13** On automatic transmission models, make sure that the drive seems smooth without jerks or engine speed flare-ups. Check that all the gear positions can be selected with the car at rest.

### Clutch

**14** Check that the clutch pedal moves smoothly and easily through its full travel, and that the clutch itself functions correctly, with no trace of slip or drag. If the movement is uneven or stiff in places, check the system components with reference to Chapter 6.

### Instruments and electrical equipment

**15** Check the operation of all instruments and electrical equipment.

**16** Make sure that all instruments read correctly, and switch on all electrical equipment in turn, to check that it functions properly.

# Every 20 000 miles (30 000 km) or 2 years

## 22 Brake fluid renewal

⚠ *Warning: Brake hydraulic fluid can harm your eyes and damage painted surfaces, so use extreme caution when handling and pouring it. Do not use fluid that has been standing open for some time, as it absorbs moisture from the air. Excess moisture can cause a dangerous loss of braking effectiveness.*

**1** The procedure is similar to that for the bleeding of the hydraulic system as described in Chapter 9, except that the brake fluid reservoir should be emptied by syphoning, using a clean poultry baster or similar before starting, and allowance should be made for the old fluid to be expelled when bleeding a section of the circuit.

**2** Working as described in Chapter 9, open the first bleed screw in the sequence, and pump the brake pedal gently until nearly all the old fluid has been emptied from the master cylinder reservoir.

| HAYNES HiNT | *Old hydraulic fluid is invariably much darker in colour than the new, making it easy to distinguish the two.* |

**3** Top-up to the upper (MAX) level mark with new fluid, and continue pumping until only the new fluid remains in the reservoir, and new fluid can be seen emerging from the bleed screw. Tighten the screw, and top the reservoir level up to the upper (MAX) level line.

**4** Work through all the remaining bleed screws in the sequence until new fluid can be seen at all of them. Be careful to keep the master cylinder reservoir topped-up to above the lower (MIN) level at all times, or air may enter the system and greatly increase the length of the task.

**5** When the operation is complete, check that all bleed screws are securely tightened, and that their dust caps are refitted. Wash off all traces of spilt fluid, and recheck the master cylinder reservoir fluid level.

**6** Check the operation of the brakes before taking the car on the road.

### 23 Body corrosion check

**1** Check the paintwork for signs of scratches or blemishes. If any damage is found to have penetrated the undercoat, it should be touched in to prevent corrosion occurring.

**2** With the car raised and securely supported, carry out a thorough check of the underbody sealant for signs of damage. If any area of the underbody sealant shows visible damage, the affected area should be repaired to prevent possible problems with corrosion occurring at a later date.

# Every 30 000 miles (45 000 km) or 3 years

### 24 Spark plug renewal

**1** It is vital for the correct running, full performance and proper economy of the engine that the spark plugs perform with maximum efficiency. The most important factor in ensuring this is that the plugs fitted are appropriate for the engine (a suitable type is specified at the beginning of this Chapter). If this type is used and the engine is in good condition, the spark plugs should not need attention between scheduled renewal intervals. Spark plug cleaning is rarely necessary, and should not be attempted unless specialised equipment is available, as damage can easily be caused to the firing ends.

**24.3 Undo the screws and remove the plastic engine cover from the top of the cylinder head**

**24.6 Disconnect the HT leads from the spark plugs**

**2** Spark plug removal and refitting requires a spark plug socket, with an extension which can be turned by a ratchet handle or similar. This socket is lined with a rubber sleeve, to protect the porcelain insulator of the spark plug, and to hold the plug while you insert it into the spark plug hole. You will also need a set of feeler blades, to check and adjust the spark plug electrode gap, and a torque wrench to tighten the new plugs to the specified torque.

**3** To remove the spark plugs, open the bonnet, undo the screws, unscrew the engine oil filler cap (where necessary) and remove the plastic engine cover from the top of the cylinder head **(see illustration)**.

#### Early non-GDI engines

**4** Note how the HT leads are routed and secured by clips along the top of the cylinder head. To prevent the possibility of mixing up HT leads, it is a good idea to try to work on one spark plug at a time.

**5** If the marks on the original-equipment HT leads cannot be seen, mark the leads 1 to 4, to correspond to the cylinder the lead serves.

**6** Disconnect the leads by gripping the rubber boot, not the lead, otherwise the lead connection may be fractured **(see illustration)**. Each lead has a rigid extension pillar attached to its end, which connects to top of the spark plug. Note that on turbo

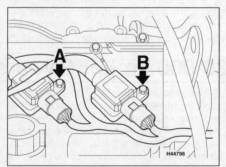

**24.9 Ignition coil mounting bolts (arrowed) – later non-GDI engines**

A No 3 spark plug ignition coil (grey wiring plug)

B No 4 spark plug ignition coil (blue wiring plug)

models, the spark plugs for cylinders Nos 3 and 4 have ignition coil units built into their HT leads. These can be removed by removing the securing bolts and then pulling the coil units carefully from the tops of the spark plugs, after disconnecting the LT wiring from each unit.

#### Later non-GDI engines

**7** Disconnect the wiring plugs from the two ignition coils fitted over Nos 3 and 4 spark plugs. The grey wiring plug is fitted to the coil on No 3 plug (which serves plugs 2 and 3), and the blue plug is fitted to the coil on No 4 plug (which serves plugs 1 and 4).

**8** Carefully pull upwards on the HT lead connectors (not the leads themselves) on Nos 1 and 2 plugs, and disconnect them from the spark plugs below.

**9** Remove the bolt securing each coil, and pull them carefully upwards off their respective spark plugs **(see illustration)**.

#### GDI engine

**10** Disconnect the wiring plug from each of the four ignition coils which are fitted over the spark plugs **(see illustration)**.

**11** Remove the two mounting bolts from each coil, noting the earth wire fitted to one of the bolts, and carefully pull the coils upwards off the spark plugs **(see illustrations)**. Although it appears there would be no serious consequences if the coils were mixed up, it makes sense to mark them for position as they are removed (No 1 at the timing belt end of the engine).

**24.10 Disconnect the wiring plug from each coil . . .**

24.11a . . . then remove the two mounting bolts, noting the earth wires . . .

24.11b . . . and pull the coil upwards to remove it

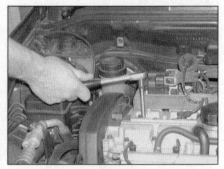

24.12 Unscrew the spark plugs from the cylinder head

24.13 Examine each spark plug as it is removed

24.18 Refit the spark plugs and tighten them to specified torque

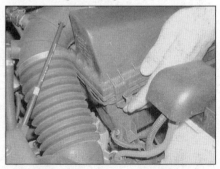

**TOOL TiP**

*Especially on engines where the plugs are deeply recessed, there is a danger of cross-threading the plugs as they are screwed in. To avoid this possibility, fit a short length of rubber hose over the end of the spark plug. The flexible hose acts as a universal joint to help align the plug with the plug hole. Should the plug begin to cross-thread, the hose will slip on the spark plug, preventing thread damage to the aluminium cylinder head.*

### All engines

**12** Unscrew the spark plugs, ensuring that the socket is kept in alignment with each plug – if the socket is forcibly moved to either side, the porcelain top of the plug may be broken off **(see illustration)**. On GDI engines in particular, a very slim-walled socket will be needed. If any undue difficulty is encountered when unscrewing any of the spark plugs, carefully check the cylinder head threads and sealing surfaces for signs of wear, excessive corrosion or damage; if any of these conditions is found, seek the advice of a dealer as to the best method of repair.

**13** As each plug is removed, examine it as follows – this will give a good indication of the condition of the engine **(see illustration)**:

a) *If the insulator nose of the spark plug is clean and white, with no deposits, this is indicative of a weak mixture.*

b) *If the tip and insulator nose are covered with hard black-looking deposits, then this is indicative that the mixture is too rich.*

c) *Should the plug be black and oily, then it is likely that the engine is fairly worn, as well as the mixture being too rich.*

d) *If the insulator nose is covered with light tan to greyish-brown deposits, then the mixture is correct, and it is likely that the engine is in good condition.*

**14** The spark plug electrode gap is of considerable importance as, if it is too large or too small, the size of the spark and its efficiency will be seriously impaired. The gap should be set to the value given in the Specifications. Note that on certain types of spark plug with

specially-shaped or multiple electrodes it is not necessary or possible to adjust the electrode gap; check with the manufacturer's instructions.

**15** To set the electrode gap, where possible, measure the gap with a feeler blade or adjusting tool, and then bend open, or closed, the outer plug electrode until the correct gap is achieved. The centre electrode should never be bent, as this may crack the insulation and cause plug failure, if nothing worse. If the outer electrode is not exactly over the centre electrode, bend it gently to align them.

**16** Before fitting the spark plugs, check that the threaded connector sleeves at the top of the plugs are tight, and that the plug exterior surfaces and threads are clean.

**17** On installing the spark plugs, first check that the cylinder head thread and sealing surface are as clean as possible; use a clean rag wrapped around a paintbrush to wipe clean the sealing surface. Ensure that the spark plug threads are clean and dry then screw them in by hand where possible. Take extra care to enter the plug threads correctly.

**18** When each spark plug is started correctly on its threads, screw it down until it just seats lightly, then tighten it to the specified torque wrench setting **(see illustration and Tool tip)**.

**19** Reconnect the HT leads/ignition coils in their correct order, pressing each one firmly into position.

**20** On models with coils fitted over the plugs, make sure the wiring clips and earth wires are refitted as noted before removal, and tighten the coil mounting bolts to the specified torque.

**21** Finally, refit the engine cover.

### 25 Air cleaner element renewal

**1** Release the spring clips which secure the air cleaner lid to the housing **(see illustration)**. Where necessary, also disconnect the wiring connector from the mass airflow sensor, to avoid straining the wiring.

25.1 Release the spring clips which secure the air cleaner lid to the housing

25.2 Lift off the lid, and remove the air cleaner element

25.3 Wipe clean inside the housing and lid with a cloth

**2** Lift off the lid, and remove the air cleaner element **(see illustration)**.

**3** Wipe clean inside the housing and lid with a cloth **(see illustration)**. Be careful not to sweep debris into the air inlet on the lid of the air cleaner housing – this is particularly important on turbo models.

**4** Fit the new element, making sure it is the right way up. Press the seal on the rim of the element into the groove on the housing.

**5** Refit the lid and secure it with the spring clips.

# Every 40 000 miles (60 000 km) or 4 years

## 26 Automatic transmission fluid renewal

See Chapter 7B.

## 27 Brake servo vacuum hose check (GDI engine)

**1** Trace the brake servo vacuum hose from the servo unit on the driver's side of the engine compartment to the inlet manifold main connection (remove the engine top cover for access). Typically, there will also be a rigid pipe section on top of the manifold – the hose connections here should be checked as well **(see illustration)**.

**2** Before removing the hose, check it externally for signs of damage, typically in the form of splits (at ends or bends), chafing or melting/burning (through close contact with moving or hot components).

**3** Disconnect the vacuum hose from the inlet manifold by pressing down the retaining clip – those at the rigid pipe section on top of the manifold have spring-type clips, which may not survive being disconnected (obtain Jubilee clip substitutes) **(see illustration)**. Check inside the end of the hoses, and inside the pipe stubs, for any sign of blockage, and clean as necessary.

**4** On completion, securely refit the hose to the manifold. If desired, the operation of the servo can be checked as described in Section 21.

## 28 Throttle housing cleaning (GDI engine)

**1** For a thorough job of cleaning, the throttle housing should really be removed as described in Chapter 4B, Section 10.

**2** However, an adequate job may be done with the throttle housing in place. Remove the engine top cover, then loosen the hose clips securing the air inlet duct to the airflow meter and throttle housing. Disconnect the breather hose from the rear of the cylinder head, and carefully remove the inlet duct.

**3** Where applicable, prise out the tamperproof plug on the throttle housing which covers the idle adjusting screw.

**4** Slowly turn the idle screw into the throttle housing until it just seats, noting the number of turns required to do so – this will give you a reference setting to reset the screw on completion. Now remove the screw completely, together with its sealing O-ring.

**5** The throttle housing must now be cleaned internally. Volvo recommend using a nylon brush of some kind (an old toothbrush?) for this, to avoid damaging the internal surfaces. If the deposits are found to be heavy, carburettor cleaner may be used – as this is available in aerosol form, it's particularly useful for cleaning where access is limited, especially if the extension tube is fitted to the aerosol nozzle **(see illustration)**.

**6** Pay close attention to the throttle plate inside the throttle housing – deposits often accumulate at the lower edge of the plate, and these must be removed **(see illustration)**. Open the throttle by manually operating the throttle linkage to ensure complete cleaning is achieved.

**7** Make sure that the throttle housing air passages are clear, including the port containing the idle screw. Do not allow carbon debris to enter the engine, nor to block the air passages, during cleaning.

27.1 Brake servo hose connections over the inlet manifold

27.3 Disconnecting a servo hose from the top of the manifold

28.5 Spraying carburettor cleaner around the throttle plate

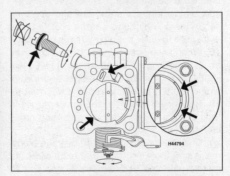

28.6 Details of throttle body cleaning – GDI engine

**8** On completion, refit the idle screw using a new O-ring, and reset its position by bottoming it, then unscrewing it the number of turns noted.

## 29 Crankcase ventilation system check

### Checking

**1** The components of this system require no attention other than to check that all ventilation hoses, and the ports they are connected to, are clear and undamaged. An ineffective crankcase ventilation system can cause high exhaust emissions readings, exhaust smoke and poor running. In extreme cases, the catalytic converter can also be damaged.

### Flame trap renewal

**2** Earlier models were fitted with a flame trap, and the manufacturer initially specified that this component should be renewed at the interval specified here. However, the flame trap was deleted on later models and, at the time of writing, it was unclear whether routine renewal of this component was still a requirement. We suggest that you seek up-to-date information relevant to your particular model from a Volvo dealer before proceeding. The renewal procedure is given here for reference.

**3** Undo the screw and remove the cover over the accelerator cable drum and linkage.

**4** Locate the flame trap housing which is situated in the duct elbow, in front of the throttle housing.

**5** Turn the flame trap housing to the left to release the bayonet fastening. Withdraw the housing but do not disconnect the ventilation hose.

**6** Remove the flame trap from the housing and clean the housing thoroughly. It is advisable to blow through all the hoses with compressed air and to change the engine oil whenever the flame trap is renewed.

**7** Fit the new flame trap using a reversal of the removal procedure.

# Every 80 000 miles (120 000 km) or 8 years

## 30 Fuel filter renewal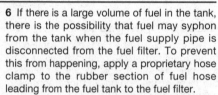

⚠️ **Warning: Before carrying out the following operation, refer to the precautions given in 'Safety first!' at the beginning of this manual, and follow them implicitly. Petrol is a highly-dangerous and volatile liquid, and the precautions necessary when handling it cannot be overstressed.**

**1** The fuel filter is located under the rear of the car, just forward and to the left of the fuel tank. Ensure that the engine has cooled completely before starting work.

**2** Depressurise the fuel system with reference to Chapter 4A or 4B.

**3** Disconnect the battery negative lead. Refer to *Disconnecting the battery* in the Reference section of this manual.

**4** Raise the rear of the car and support it securely on axle stands (see *Jacking and vehicle support*).

**5** Undo the securing screws and release the press-stud fixings, then remove the plastic cover panel(s) to expose the fuel filter **(see illustration)**.

**6** If there is a large volume of fuel in the tank, there is the possibility that fuel may syphon from the tank when the fuel supply pipe is disconnected from the fuel filter. To prevent this from happening, apply a proprietary hose clamp to the rubber section of fuel hose leading from the fuel tank to the fuel filter.

**7** Thoroughly clean the area around the fuel pipe couplings at each end of the filter, then cover both with absorbent cloths. Place a container underneath the fuel couplings to catch the spilt fuel.

**8** Disconnect the quick-release couplings using an open-ended spanner to push back the coupling sleeves. Be prepared for an initial release of fuel as the couplings are released, particularly from the fuel delivery line that leads to the engine compartment. Plug the coupling or clamp the flexible section of the fuel delivery line, to prevent further loss of fuel **(see illustration)**.

**9** Undo the filter mounting strap retaining bolt and remove the filter **(see illustrations)**.

**10** Fit the new filter, making sure it is the same way round as the old one. Observe the arrow on the new filter showing the direction of fuel flow **(see illustration)**.

**11** Secure the filter with the mounting strap then push the fuel pipe couplings firmly back on the filter outlets **(see illustration)**. Give each pipe coupling a tug to confirm that it has

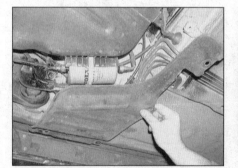

**30.5 Remove the plastic cover panel under the car to expose the fuel filter**

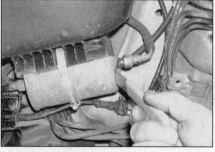

**30.8 Disconnect the quick-release couplings using an open-ended spanner or a forked tool to push back the coupling sleeves**

**30.9a Undo the filter mounting strap retaining bolt . . .**

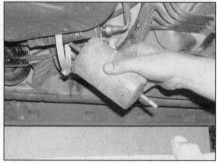

**30.9b . . . and remove the filter**

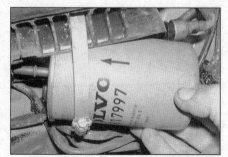

**30.10 Fit the new filter, observing the arrow on the new filter showing the direction of fuel flow**

reconnected correctly. On completion, refit the plastic cover panel securely.

**12** Reconnect the battery. Run the engine and check that there are no fuel leaks.

 *Warning: Dispose of the old filter safely; it will be highly flammable, and may explode if thrown on a fire.*

## 31 Timing belt renewal

Refer to the information given in Chapter 2A or 2B.

## 32 Auxiliary drivebelt renewal

### Except GDI engine

**1** The correct drivebelt tension is continually maintained by an automatic adjuster and tensioner assembly. This device is bolted to the front of the engine and incorporates a spring-loaded idler pulley.

**2** Unbolt and remove the metal guard from the power steering pump casing, to expose the top of the power steering pump pulley **(see illustration)**.

**3** The tensioner idler pulley must be released to allow removal of the drivebelt. To do this, fit a ring spanner to the idler pulley centre bolt

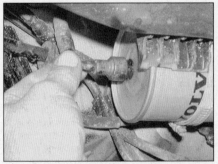

**30.11  Push the fuel pipe couplings firmly back on the filter outlets**

and pivot it clockwise until the locking holes on the tensioner body line up **(see illustrations)**. **Note:** *Access is very limited; if you find it difficult to reach the tensioner, try supporting the front of the car on axle stands and removing the left-hand front roadwheel. If the wheel arch liner is then removed, access to the side of the engine can be gained via the wheel arch.*

**4** Hold the pulley in the released position using the spanner, then pass a metal rod through the locking holes to hold the tensioner pulley in the released position – a twist drill bit is ideal for this purpose **(see illustration)**. The spanner can be removed once the tensioner has been locked in position.

**5** The drivebelt can now be slipped the belt off all the pulleys and removed from the engine compartment **(see illustration)**.

**6** Fit the new belt over each pulley in turn, ensuring that it is properly seated. Fit the ring spanner to the pulley centre bolt and apply pressure in a clockwise direction, then carefully remove the drill bit/locking tool and release the tensioner gradually. Do not allow the tensioner to fly back unchecked, as damage to spring mechanism may result.

**7** The tensioner mechanism should automatically take up the free play in the drivebelt; rotate the engine using a socket and wrench on the crankshaft sprocket to ensure that the belt is correctly located on all the pulleys.

**8** On completion, refit the metal guard over the power steering pump pulley, and tighten the bolts securely.

### GDI engine

### Power steering pump/air conditioning compressor drivebelt

**9** Loosen the right-hand front roadwheel nuts, then jack up the front of the car, and support on axle stands (see *Jacking and vehicle support*). Remove the wheel. For better access to the drivebelts from below, remove the wheel arch access panel, which is secured by three bolts (one in front of the washer reservoir, which will require the front undershield to be partially removed also) **(see illustrations)**.

**32.2  Unbolt and remove the metal guard from the power steering pump casing, to expose the top of the pump pulley**

**32.3a  Fit a ring spanner to the idler pulley centre bolt and pivot it clockwise until the locking holes on the tensioner body line up**

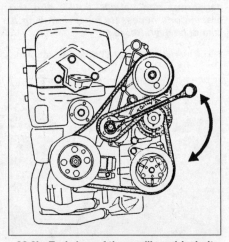

**32.3b  End view of the auxiliary drivebelt and pulleys – except GDI engine**

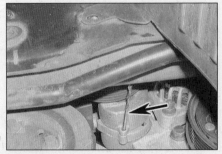

**32.4  Pass a metal rod (arrowed) through the locking holes to hold the tensioner pulley in the released position – a drill bit is ideal**

**32.5 The drivebelt can now be slipped off all its pulleys**

**32.9a  Remove a total of three bolts . . .**

**32.9b** . . . and take out the wheel arch access panel

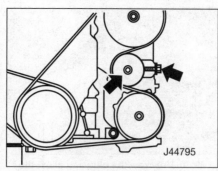

**32.10a** Tensioner pulley centre nut and adjuster bolt (arrowed)

**32.10b** Removing the drivebelt

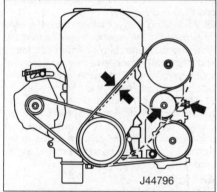

**32.12 Setting the drivebelt tension – note the drivebelt routing for models without air conditioning, shown by the dotted line**

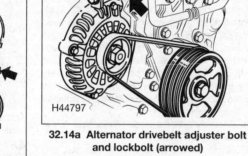

**32.14a** Alternator drivebelt adjuster bolt and lockbolt (arrowed)

**32.14b** Alternator pivot bolt nut (arrowed)

**10** Loosen the nut at the centre of the drivebelt tensioner pulley, then turn the adjuster bolt at the front of the engine to release the drivebelt tension until the belt can be slipped from the pulleys **(see illustrations)**. If both drivebelts are being removed or renewed, this belt comes off first, and goes back on last (it 'traps' the alternator belt when in place).

**11** Fit the new drivebelt around the pulleys. On models without air conditioning, note that the belt fits round the outside of the tensioner pulley, rather than the inside. Make sure the drivebelt is located properly in the pulley grooves, and is not displaced to one side by being one groove out.

**12** Turn the tensioner adjuster bolt to tension the belt. The tension is checked on the top run of the belt, midway between the two pulleys – a total deflection (up-and-down) of around 10 to 12 mm is the target **(see illustration)**. When the tension is correct, tighten the tensioner pulley centre nut. A new drivebelt will tend to stretch slightly after first use, but do not overtension the belt in anticipation, as expensive damage may be done to the driven components. Instead, recheck a new belt's tension after a few hundred miles.

### Alternator drivebelt

**13** Remove the power steering pump/air conditioning compressor drivebelt as described previously in this Section.

**14** Loosen the adjuster bolt and lockbolt located above the alternator at the rear of the engine, then, working from below, loosen the

pivot bolt nut at the base of the alternator **(see illustrations)**. Turn the adjuster bolt to release the drivebelt tension, until the alternator drivebelt can be removed.

**15** Fit the new drivebelt around the pulleys, making sure the drivebelt is located properly in the pulley grooves.

**16** Turn the adjuster bolt to tension the belt, then lock it in place with the lockbolt. The tension is checked on the top run of the belt, midway between the two pulleys – a total deflection (up-and-down) of around 10 to 12 mm is the target. As with the other belt, do not overtension it (or the alternator bearings will suffer), and recheck a new belt's tension after a few hundred miles.

**17** On completion, tighten the alternator pivot bolt nut, refit the other drivebelt, refit the engine undershields and lower the car to the ground.

# Every 2 years, regardless of mileage

## 33 Coolant renewal

### Cooling system draining

⚠ *Warning: Wait until the engine is cold before starting this procedure. Do not allow antifreeze to come in contact with your skin, or with the painted surfaces. Rinse off spills immediately with plenty of water. Never*

*leave antifreeze lying around in an open container, or in a puddle in the driveway or on the garage floor. Children and pets are attracted by its sweet smell, but antifreeze can be fatal if ingested.*

**1** With the engine completely cold, firmly apply the handbrake then jack up the front of the car and support it on axle stands. Remove the retaining screws/fasteners and remove the front section of the undershield to gain access to the base of the radiator.

**2** Unscrew and remove the expansion tank filler cap, then position a suitable container

beneath the coolant drain outlet at the base of the radiator.

**3** Loosen the drain plug (there is no need to remove it completely) and allow the coolant to drain into the container. If desired, a length of tubing can be fitted to the drain outlet to direct the flow of coolant during draining **(see illustrations)**.

**4** When the flow of coolant stops, reposition the container underneath the drain plug on the rear of the cylinder block (not fitted to all engines). Unscrew the drain plug and allow the remainder of the coolant to drain into the container.

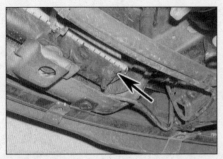

**33.3a Remove the front section of the engine undershield to gain access to the radiator drain plug (arrowed)**

**33.3b Unscrew the plug and allow the coolant to drain into a suitable container (note the tubing fitted to the drain outlet)**

**33.19 GDI engine bleed screw (arrowed) on thermostat housing**

**5** If the coolant has been drained for a reason other than renewal, then provided it is clean and less than two years old, it can be re-used, though this is not recommended.

**6** Securely tighten the radiator and cylinder block drain plugs on completion of draining.

### Cooling system flushing

**7** If coolant renewal has been neglected, or if the antifreeze mixture has become diluted, then in time, the cooling system may gradually lose efficiency, as the coolant passages become restricted due to rust, scale deposits, and other sediment. The cooling system efficiency can be restored by flushing the system clean.

**8** The radiator should be flushed independently of the engine, to avoid unnecessary contamination.

### Radiator flushing

**9** To flush the radiator, first tighten the radiator drain plug securely.

**10** Disconnect the top and bottom hoses and any other relevant hoses from the radiator, with reference to Chapter 3.

**11** Insert a garden hose into the radiator top inlet. Direct a flow of clean water through the radiator, and continue flushing until clean water emerges from the radiator bottom outlet.

**12** If after a reasonable period, the water still does not run clear, the radiator can be flushed with a good proprietary cleaning agent. It is important that their manufacturer's instructions are followed carefully. If the contamination is particularly bad, insert the hose in the radiator bottom outlet, and reverse-flush the radiator.

### Engine flushing

**13** To flush the engine, remove the thermostat as described in Chapter 3, then temporarily refit the thermostat cover.

**14** With the top and bottom hoses disconnected from the radiator, insert a garden hose into the radiator top hose. Direct a clean flow of water through the engine, and continue flushing until clean water emerges from the radiator bottom hose.

**15** On completion of flushing, refit the thermostat and reconnect the hoses with reference to Chapter 3.

### Cooling system filling

**16** Before attempting to fill the cooling system, make sure that all hoses and clips are in good condition, and that the clips are tight. Note that an antifreeze mixture must be used all year round, to prevent corrosion of the engine components (see following sub-Section). Also check that the radiator and cylinder block drain plugs are securely tightened, and all hoses disturbed on draining are reconnected and securely held in position by their retaining clips.

**17** Securely refit the undershield, then lower the car to the ground.

**18** Remove the expansion tank filler cap, and slowly fill the system until the coolant level reaches the MAX mark on the side of the expansion tank.

**19** On GDI and turbo engine models, loosen the bleed screw to remove any trapped air from the system; on GDI engines, the screw is located on top of the thermostat housing **(see illustration)**, while turbo models have a bleed screw in the bottom hose. As soon as coolant free of air bubbles flows from the hose, tighten the bleed screw securely. Check the coolant level in the expansion tank and top-up if necessary.

**20** On all models, refit and tighten the expansion tank filler cap.

**21** Start the engine, and allow it to run until it reaches normal operating temperature.

**22** Stop the engine, and allow it to cool, then recheck the coolant level with reference to *Weekly checks*. Top-up the level if necessary and refit the expansion tank filler cap.

### Antifreeze mixture

**23** The antifreeze should always be renewed at the specified intervals. This is necessary not only to maintain the antifreeze properties, but also to prevent corrosion which would otherwise occur as the corrosion inhibitors become progressively less effective.

**24** Always use an ethylene-glycol based antifreeze which is suitable for use in mixed-metal cooling systems. The quantity of antifreeze and levels of protection are given in the Specifications.

**25** Before adding antifreeze, the cooling system should be completely drained,

preferably flushed, and all hoses checked for condition and security.

**26** After filling with antifreeze, a label should be attached to the expansion tank, stating the type and concentration of antifreeze used, and the date installed. Any subsequent topping-up should be made with the same type and concentration of antifreeze.

**27** Do not use engine antifreeze in the windscreen/tailgate washer system, as it will cause damage to the paintwork. A screenwash additive should be added to the washer system in the quantities stated on the bottle.

### Airlocks

**28** If, after draining and refilling the system, symptoms of overheating are found which did not occur previously, then the fault is almost certainly due to trapped air at some point in the system, causing an airlock and restricting the flow of coolant; usually, the air is trapped because the system was refilled too quickly.

**29** If an airlock is suspected, first try gently squeezing all visible coolant hoses. A coolant hose which is full of air feels quite different to one full of coolant, when squeezed. After refilling the system, most airlocks will clear once the system has cooled, and been topped-up.

**30** While the engine is running at operating temperature, switch on the heater and heater fan, and check for heat output. Provided there is sufficient coolant in the system, any lack of heat output could be due to an airlock in the system.

**31** Airlocks can have more serious effects than simply reducing heater output – a severe airlock could reduce coolant flow around the engine. Check that the radiator top hose is hot when the engine is at operating temperature – a top hose which stays cold could be the result of an airlock (or a non-opening thermostat).

**32** If the problem persists, stop the engine and allow it to cool down **completely**, before unscrewing the expansion tank filler cap or loosening the hose clips and squeezing the hoses to bleed out the trapped air. In the worst case, the system will have to be at least partially drained (this time, the coolant can be saved for re-use) and flushed to clear the problem.

# Chapter 2 Part A:
# Engine (except GDI) in-car repair procedures

## Contents

## Degrees of difficulty

| Easy, suitable for novice with little experience  | Fairly easy, suitable for beginner with some experience  | Fairly difficult, suitable for competent DIY mechanic | Difficult, suitable for experienced DIY mechanic | Very difficult, suitable for expert DIY or professional  |
|---|---|---|---|---|

## Specifications

### General

| | |
|---|---|
| Type . . . . . . . . . . . . . . . . . . . . | Four-cylinder, twin overhead camshaft, 16-valve |

Engine codes:
| | |
|---|---|
| B4164S (1.6 litre) . . . . . . . . . . . . . . . . . . . . . . . . . . . . . . . . . . . . . . . | 1587 cc, non-turbo |
| B4164S2 (1.6 litre) . . . . . . . . . . . . . . . . . . . . . . . . . . . . . . . . . . . . . . | 1587 cc, non-turbo, variable valve timing (VVT) |
| B4184S (1.8 litre) . . . . . . . . . . . . . . . . . . . . . . . . . . . . . . . . . . . . . . | 1731 cc, non-turbo |
| B4184S2/3 (1.8 litre) . . . . . . . . . . . . . . . . . . . . . . . . . . . . . . . . . . . | 1783 cc, non-turbo, variable valve timing (VVT) |
| B4194T (1.9 litre) . . . . . . . . . . . . . . . . . . . . . . . . . . . . . . . . . . . . . . | 1855 cc, 16-valve, turbocharged (147 kW) |
| B4194T2 (1.9 litre) . . . . . . . . . . . . . . . . . . . . . . . . . . . . . . . . . . . . . | 1855 cc, 16-valve, turbocharged (147 kW), variable valve timing (VVT) |
| B4204S (2.0 litre) . . . . . . . . . . . . . . . . . . . . . . . . . . . . . . . . . . . . . . | 1948 cc, 16-valve, non-turbo |
| B4204S2 (2.0 litre) . . . . . . . . . . . . . . . . . . . . . . . . . . . . . . . . . . . . . | 1948 cc, 16-valve, non-turbo, variable valve timing (VVT) |
| B4204T (2.0 litre) . . . . . . . . . . . . . . . . . . . . . . . . . . . . . . . . . . . . . . | 1948 cc, 16-valve, turbocharged (118 kW) |
| B4204T2/3 (2.0 litre) . . . . . . . . . . . . . . . . . . . . . . . . . . . . . . . . . . . | 1948 cc, 16-valve, turbocharged (118 kW), variable valve timing (VVT) |
| B4204T5 (2.0 litre) . . . . . . . . . . . . . . . . . . . . . . . . . . . . . . . . . . . . . | 1948 cc, 16-valve, turbocharged (147 kW), variable valve timing (VVT) |

Bore/stroke:
| | |
|---|---|
| 1.6 litre . . . . . . . . . . . . . . . . . . . . . . . . . . . . . . . . . . . . . . . . . . . . . . | 81.0 mm/77.0 mm |
| 1.8 litre: | |
|   B4184S . . . . . . . . . . . . . . . . . . . . . . . . . . . . . . . . . . . . . . . . . . . | 83.0 mm/80.0 mm |
|   B4184S2/3 . . . . . . . . . . . . . . . . . . . . . . . . . . . . . . . . . . . . . . . . | 83.0 mm/82.4 mm |
| 1.9 litre . . . . . . . . . . . . . . . . . . . . . . . . . . . . . . . . . . . . . . . . . . . . . . | 81.0 mm/90.0 mm |
| 2.0 litre . . . . . . . . . . . . . . . . . . . . . . . . . . . . . . . . . . . . . . . . . . . . . . | 83.0 mm/90.0 mm |

Compression pressure:
| | |
|---|---|
| Non-turbo engines . . . . . . . . . . . . . . . . . . . . . . . . . . . . . . . . . . . . . | 13 to 15 bar (189 to 218 psi) |
| Turbo engines . . . . . . . . . . . . . . . . . . . . . . . . . . . . . . . . . . . . . . . . | 11 to 13 bar (160 to 189 psi) |
| Variation between cylinders . . . . . . . . . . . . . . . . . . . . . . . . . . . . . . | 2 bar (29 psi) maximum |
| Firing order . . . . . . . . . . . . . . . . . . . . . . . . . . . . . . . . . . . . . . . . . . . | 1 – 3 – 4 – 2 (No 1 at timing belt end of engine) |

### Lubrication system

Oil pressure (hot engine with new oil filter):
| | |
|---|---|
| At 750 rpm . . . . . . . . . . . . . . . . . . . . . . . . . . . . . . . . . . . . . . . . . . . | 1 bar (14.5 psi) minimum |
| At 4000 rpm . . . . . . . . . . . . . . . . . . . . . . . . . . . . . . . . . . . . . . . . . . | 3.5 bar (51 psi) minimum |
| Oil pump type . . . . . . . . . . . . . . . . . . . . . . . . . . . . . . . . . . . . . . . . . | Gear, driven from crankshaft |
| Maximum oil pressure . . . . . . . . . . . . . . . . . . . . . . . . . . . . . . . . . . . | 7 bar (102 psi) |
| Relief valve opening pressure . . . . . . . . . . . . . . . . . . . . . . . . . . . . . | 5 bar (73 psi) |
| Pressure relief valve spring free height . . . . . . . . . . . . . . . . . . . . . . | 82.13 mm |
| Outer rotor-to-housing clearance . . . . . . . . . . . . . . . . . . . . . . . . . . | 0.35 mm |

## Torque wrench settings*

| | Nm | lbf ft |
|---|---|---|
| Auxiliary drivebelt tensioner pulley | 25 | 18 |
| Camshaft position sensor trigger wheel bolt | 17 | 13 |
| Camshaft sprocket bolts: | | |
|   Conventional sprocket (three bolts) | 20 | 15 |
|   VVT sprocket centre bolt | 90 | 66 |
|   VVT sprocket centre plug | 35 | 26 |
| Crankshaft pulley-to-sprocket bolts: | | |
|   Stage 1 | 25 | 18 |
|   Stage 2 | Angle-tighten a further 30° | |
| Crankshaft sprocket centre nut | 180 | 133 |
| Cylinder head lower section to block**: | | |
|   Stage 1 | 20 | 15 |
|   Stage 2 | 60 | 44 |
|   Stage 3 | Angle-tighten a further 130° | |
| Cylinder head upper section to lower section | 17 | 13 |
| Engine mountings: | | |
|   Engine/transmission crossmember to bodywork | 69 | 51 |
|   Front mounting to engine bracket | 55 | 41 |
|   Front mounting to engine/transmission crossmember | 35 | 26 |
|   Left-hand mounting: | | |
|     Engine mounting to bodywork bracket | 98 | 72 |
|     Engine mounting-to-transmission bracket nuts | 45 | 33 |
|     Rear mounting to engine/transmission bracket | 55 | 41 |
|     Rear mounting to engine/transmission crossmember | 35 | 26 |
|   Right-hand mounting: | | |
|     Engine mounting to bodywork bracket: | | |
|       Stage 1 | 50 | 37 |
|       Stage 2 | Angle-tighten a further 60° | |
|     Engine mounting to engine: | | |
|       Stage 1 | 67 | 49 |
|       Stage 2 | Angle-tighten a further 60° | |
| Flywheel/driveplate**: | | |
|   Stage 1 | 45 | 33 |
|   Stage 2 | Angle-tighten a further 65° | |
| Knock sensor | 20 | 15 |
| Manifold nuts/bolts | 25 | 18 |
| Oil pickup | 18 | 13 |
| Oil pressure switch | 25 | 18 |
| Oil pump to cylinder block | 10 | 7 |
| Pipe unions | 26 | 19 |
| Roadwheel nuts | 110 | 81 |
| Sump drain plug | 35 | 26 |
| Timing belt idler pulley | 25 | 18 |
| Timing belt automatic tensioner bolts | 25 | 18 |
| Timing belt automatic tensioner pulley | 40 | 30 |
| Timing belt manual tensioner centre bolt | 20 | 15 |
| VVT control valve mounting bolts | 10 | 7 |

*Oiled threads unless otherwise stated*
** *New nuts/bolts must **always** be used*

## 1 General information

### How to use this Chapter

This Part of Chapter 2 describes those repair procedures that can reasonably be carried out on the non-GDI engine while it remains in the car (owners of the GDI engine should refer to Part B of this Chapter). If the engine has been removed from the car and is being dismantled as described in Part C, any preliminary dismantling procedures can be ignored.

Note that, while it may be possible physically to overhaul items such as the piston/connecting rod assemblies while the engine is in the car, such tasks are not normally carried out as separate operations. Usually, several additional procedures (not to mention the cleaning of components and oilways) have to be carried out. For this reason, all such tasks are classed as major overhaul procedures, and are described in Part C of this Chapter.

Part C describes the removal of the engine/transmission from the vehicle, and the full overhaul procedures that can then be carried out.

### Engine description

All engines in the S40 & V40 range are 4-cylinder, in-line units, of the double overhead camshaft type incorporating two inlet valves and two exhaust valves per cylinder. The engine is mounted transversely on a subframe in the engine bay.

The entire engine is constructed of aluminium, and consists of five sections. The cylinder head comprises an upper and lower section, with the cylinder block, intermediate section and sump forming the other three. The upper and lower sections of the cylinder head are mated along the centre line of the camshafts, while the cylinder block and intermediate section are mated along the crankshaft centre line. A conventional cylinder head gasket is used between the cylinder head and block, with liquid gaskets being used in the joints between the other main sections.

The cylinder block incorporates four cast-iron dry cylinder liners, which are cast into the block and cannot be renewed. Cast-iron reinforcements are also used in the intermediate section as strengthening agents in the main bearing areas.

Drive to the camshaft is by a toothed timing belt and sprockets, incorporating an automatic or manual tensioning mechanism (depending on model). The timing belt also drives the coolant pump. All accessories are driven from the crankshaft pulley by a single multi-ribbed auxiliary drivebelt.

The cylinder head is of the crossflow type, the inlet ports being at the front of the engine and the exhaust ports at the rear. The upper section of the cylinder head functions as a combined valve cover and camshaft cover, the camshafts run in plain bearings integral to the two cylinder head sections. Valve actuation is by maintenance-free hydraulic tappets, acted upon directly by the camshaft lobes. Models from approximately 1999 onwards feature variable valve timing (VVT), where the exhaust camshaft timing is varied under the control of the engine management system to boost both low-speed torque and top-end power.

The crankshaft runs in five shell-type main bearings; the connecting rod big-end bearings are also of the shell type. Crankshaft endfloat is taken by thrustwashers which are an integral part of the No 3 main bearing shells.

The lubrication system is of the full-flow, pressure-feed type. Oil is drawn from the sump by a gear-type pump, driven from the right-hand end of the crankshaft. Oil under pressure passes through a filter before being fed to the various shaft bearings and to the valve gear. An external oil cooler, incorporated in the oil filter housing, is fitted to turbocharged models. Turbo models are also equipped with separate oil feed and return lines for the turbocharger bearings.

### Operations with engine in car

The following work can be carried out with the engine in the car:
a) Compression pressure – testing.
b) Timing belt – removal and refitting.
c) Camshaft oil seals – renewal.
d) Camshafts and tappets – removal and refitting.
e) Cylinder head – removal and refitting.
f) Cylinder head and pistons – decarbonising.
g) Crankshaft oil seals – renewal.
h) Oil pump – removal and refitting.
i) Flywheel/driveplate – removal and refitting.
j) Engine mountings – removal and refitting.

## 2  Compression test – description and interpretation

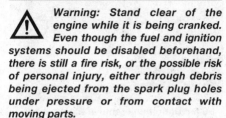

> **Warning: Stand clear of the engine while it is being cranked. Even though the fuel and ignition systems should be disabled beforehand, there is still a fire risk, or the possible risk of personal injury, either through debris being ejected from the spark plug holes under pressure or from contact with moving parts.**

1 When engine performance is down, or if misfiring occurs which cannot be attributed to the ignition or fuel systems, a compression test can provide diagnostic clues as to the engine's condition. If the test is performed regularly, it can give warning of trouble before any other symptoms become apparent.

2 The engine must be fully warmed-up to normal operating temperature, the battery must be fully-charged, and all the spark plugs must be removed (see Chapter 1). The aid of an assistant will also be required.

3 Disable the ignition system by disconnecting the crankshaft sensor wiring at the connector located just above the inlet manifold. Also disconnect the wiring connectors to each fuel injector to prevent unburned fuel from damaging the catalytic converter (alternatively, locate and temporarily remove fuse number 17 from the engine compartment fusebox).

4 Fit a compression tester to the No 1 cylinder spark plug hole – the type of tester which screws into the plug thread is to be preferred.

5 Have the assistant hold the throttle wide open, and crank the engine on the starter motor; after one or two revolutions, the compression pressure should build-up to a maximum figure, and then stabilise. Record the highest reading obtained.

6 Repeat the test on the remaining cylinders, recording the pressure in each.

7 All cylinders should produce very similar pressures; a difference of more than 2 bars between any two cylinders indicates a fault. Note that the compression should build-up quickly in a healthy engine; low compression on the first stroke, followed by gradually-increasing pressure on successive strokes, indicates worn piston rings. A low compression reading on the first stroke, which does not build-up during successive strokes, indicates leaking valves or a blown head gasket (a cracked cylinder head could also be the cause). Deposits on the undersides of the valve heads can also cause low compression.

8 If the pressure in any cylinder is low, carry out the following test to isolate the cause. Introduce a teaspoonful of clean oil into that cylinder through its spark plug hole, and repeat the test.

9 If the addition of oil temporarily improves the compression pressure, this indicates that bore or piston wear is responsible for the pressure loss. No improvement suggests that leaking or burnt valves, or a blown head gasket, may be to blame.

10 A low reading from two adjacent cylinders is almost certainly due to the head gasket having blown between them; the presence of coolant in the engine oil will confirm this.

11 If one cylinder is about 20 percent lower than the others and the engine has a slightly rough idle, a worn camshaft lobe could be the cause.

12 If the compression reading is unusually high, the combustion chambers are probably coated with carbon deposits. If this is the case, the cylinder head should be removed and decarbonised.

13 On completion of the test, refit the spark plugs and reconnect the ignition system and fuel injectors.

## 3  Timing belt – removal and refitting

### Automatic belt tensioner

#### Removal

1 Disconnect the battery negative lead (see *Disconnecting the battery*), and remove the engine top cover panel.

2 Remove the auxiliary drivebelt as described in Chapter 1.

3 Undo the bolts and remove the timing belt upper covers **(see illustration)**. The outer cover is secured by one bolt down the side of the engine, and a spring clip front and rear. The inner cover is held on by two bolts on top of the engine.

4 Position an engine hoist, or an engine lifting beam across the engine compartment and attach the jib to the right-hand engine lifting eyelet **(see illustration)**. Raise the lifting gear to take up the slack, so that it is just supporting the combined weight of the engine and transmission.

5 Unbolt both parts of the engine right-hand mounting bracket from the bodywork and engine, as described in Section 11. On models with air conditioning, it will necessary to release the refrigerant hoses that pass over the engine mounting by unbolting their support brackets.

**3.3  Undo the bolts and remove the timing belt front cover**

3.4 Support the engine using a hoist or lifting beam attached to the engine right-hand lifting eyelet

3.6a Unbolt and remove the auxiliary drivebelt idler pulley . . .

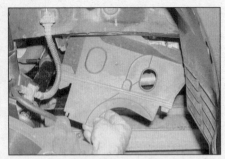

3.6b . . . then undo the securing screws and remove the lower timing belt lower cover

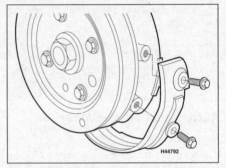

3.8 Timing belt lower guard removal details

3.9a Counterhold the crankshaft pulley . . .

3.9b . . . and remove the pulley centre nut

**6** Unbolt and remove the auxiliary drivebelt idler pulley from the side of the engine, then undo the securing screws and remove the timing belt lower cover **(see illustrations)**.
**7** Jack up the front of the car and support it on axle stands (see *Jacking and vehicle support*). Remove the right-hand front roadwheel.
**8** Release the fasteners securing the inner wheel arch liner, and fold back the liner for access to the crankshaft pulley. Where applicable, unbolt and remove the belt lower guard, mounted underneath the crankshaft sprocket **(see illustration)**.
**9** The crankshaft pulley must now be held stationary while its centre retaining nut is slackened. If the Volvo holding tool 999 5433 cannot be obtained, it will be necessary to fabricate a home-made alternative. This will be essentially the same as the camshaft sprocket holding tool described in Section 4, but instead of bending the prongs of the forks through 90°, leave them straight, and drill a suitable hole in each. The four bolts securing the crankshaft pulley to the sprocket are then removed, allowing the tool to be bolted to the pulley using two of the bolts. Hold the tool securely and undo the pulley centre retaining nut using a socket and bar. Remove the tool and lift the pulley off the sprocket **(see illustrations)**. **Note**: *It may be necessary to lower the engine slightly, using the lifting beam, to gain clear access to the crankshaft pulley centre nut.*
**10** Using a large spanner on the temporarily-refitted crankshaft sprocket centre nut, rotate the crankshaft clockwise (viewed from the right-hand side of the car) until the timing marks on the camshaft sprocket rims align with the notches on the timing belt inner cover (temporarily refit the inner cover to check). In this position, the timing mark on the crankshaft sprocket should also be aligned with the projection cast into the outer surface of the oil pump housing. Note that these markings are very faint and hence difficult to see **(see illustrations)**.

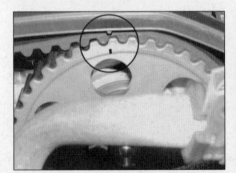

3.9c Slacken and withdraw the four securing bolts

3.9d . . . and remove the pulley from the sprocket

3.10a Camshaft timing marks

3.10b Crankshaft timing marks

**11** Undo the timing belt tensioner upper retaining bolt, and slacken the lower one. Move the tensioner assembly anti-clockwise to free it from the tensioner pulley **(see illustration)**.

**12** Remove the previously-slackened tensioner lower bolt and remove the tensioner. Collect the plastic horseshoe-shaped spacer collar fitted to the top of the tensioner **(see illustration)**.

**13** Mark the running direction of the belt if it is to be re-used, then slip it off the sprockets, tensioner and idler pulleys, and remove it. Clearance is very limited at the crankshaft sprocket, and a certain amount of manipulation is necessary. Do not rotate the crankshaft or camshafts with the belt removed, as there is the risk of piston-to-valve contact.

**14** Spin the tensioner and idler pulleys, and check for roughness or shake; renew if necessary. Check that the tensioner pulley arm is free to move up-and-down under the action of the tensioner. If the arm is at all stiff, remove the unit, clean it thoroughly, then lubricate sparingly and refit. It is considered good practice to renew the belt pulleys along with the timing belt – to this end, Volvo dealers (and some motor factors) now sell timing belt 'kits', containing all the relevant parts.

**15** Check the timing belt carefully for any signs of uneven wear, splitting, or oil contamination. Pay particular attention to the roots of the teeth. Renew the belt if there is the slightest doubt about its condition. If the engine is undergoing an overhaul, and has covered more than 36 000 miles (60 000 km) with the existing belt fitted, renew the belt as a matter of course, regardless of its apparent condition. The cost of a new belt is negligible when compared to the cost of engine repairs, should the belt break in service. If signs of oil contamination are found, trace the source of the oil leak, and rectify it. Wash down the engine timing belt area and all related components, to remove all traces of oil.

**16** Renew the tensioner assembly if there are signs of oil leaks, if there is no resistance to compression of the plunger, or if the plunger cannot be compressed.

### Refitting and tensioning

**17** Prior to refitting the timing belt, it will be necessary to compress and lock the tensioner plunger, before the tensioner assembly is refitted to the engine. To do this, mount the assembly in a vice with protected jaws; the jaws in contact with the tensioner body and the plunger.

**18** Tighten the vice until resistance is felt, then tighten it very slowly a little further. Pause for a few seconds and tighten slowly a little further again. Continue this procedure until the hole in the tensioner body and corresponding hole in the plunger are aligned. It will probably take about five minutes to do this; don't rush it, or the internal seals will be

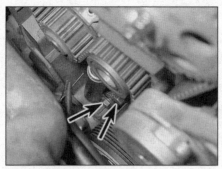

**3.11 Timing belt tensioner retaining bolts (arrowed)**

damaged by trying to force oil between the internal chambers too quickly. When the two holes are finally aligned, insert length of metal rod (a drill bit is ideal) through all the holes to lock the assembly **(see illustration)**.

**19** Refit the locked tensioner to the engine, and secure with the two bolts tightened to the specified torque.

**20** Before refitting the timing belt, make sure that the sprockets are aligned in their correct positions (see paragraph 10). Slip the belt over the crankshaft sprocket, keep it taut and feed it over the idler pulley, front camshaft sprocket, rear camshaft sprocket, coolant pump sprocket, and finally over the tensioner pulley. Observe the correct running direction if the old belt is being re-used.

**21** Recheck the alignment of the sprocket marks, then release the belt tensioner by pulling out the locking pin with pliers. Check that the tensioner plunger moves out to tension the belt.

**22** Refit the horseshoe-shaped spacer collar (where fitted) to the top of the tensioner.

**23** Refit the timing belt inner cover, and secure with the two bolts.

**24** Turn the crankshaft clockwise through two complete revolutions, then check that all the timing marks can be realigned.

**25** With reference to Section 11, refit the right-hand mounting to the engine and tighten the securing bolts to the specified torque. Insert the engine mounting-to-bodywork bolt loosely – do not tighten it at this stage.

**26** Lower the engine lifting equipment slowly until the weight of the engine and trans-

**3.18 Lock the compressed tensioner using a 2.0 mm drill bit**

**3.12 Collect the plastic horseshoe-shaped spacer collar fitted to the top of the tensioner**

mission rests on the engine right-hand mounting. Remove the lifting gear from the engine compartment, then tighten the engine mounting-to-bodywork bolt to the specified torque.

**27** Refit the upper and lower timing belt covers, then tighten the retaining screws securely.

**28** Refit the crankshaft pulley, and tighten the securing bolts and centre nut to the specified torque.

**29** Refit the auxiliary drivebelt idler pulley assembly, and tighten the securing bolt.

**30** Refit the auxiliary drivebelt as described in Chapter 1.

**31** On models with air conditioning, refit the refrigerant hose support brackets and tighten the securing bolts securely.

**32** Fold back the wheel arch liner, refit the engine splash guard and secure with the fasteners.

**33** Refit the roadwheel and lower the car to the ground. Tighten the wheel nuts in a diagonal sequence to the specified torque.

**34** On completion, reconnect the battery negative lead, and refit the engine top cover panel.

### Manually-adjusted belt tensioner

*Note: The manufacturer recommends that the tensioner assembly is renewed at the same service interval as the timing belt.*

### Removal

**35** Carry out the operations described in paragraphs 1 to 10 inclusive in the previous sub-Section.

**36** Unscrew the securing bolts and release the power steering fluid reservoir from the bodywork. Move the reservoir to one side, noting that it will not be necessary to disconnect the fluid hoses from the reservoir.

**37** Gradually slacken the belt tensioner centre bolt, whilst rotating the tensioner pulley with an Allen key, until all tension is removed from the timing belt **(see illustration)**.

**38** Mark the running direction of the belt if it is to be re-used, then slip it off the sprockets tensioner and idler pulleys and remove it **(see illustrations)**. Clearance is very limited at the crankshaft sprocket and a certain amount of

**3.37 Slacken the belt tensioner centre bolt and turn the tensioner pulley with an Allen key to release the timing belt**

**3.38a Remove the timing belt from the crankshaft sprocket . . .**

**3.38b . . . and camshaft sprockets**

**3.41 Fit the tensioner to the engine, then insert the centre bolt and tighten lightly**

**3.42 Ensure the locating tab (arrowed) on the tensioner indicator is to the left of the cast web**

**3.43 Fit the timing belt over the sprockets, finishing at the tensioner pulley**

manipulation is necessary. The upper timing belt cover may be temporarily removed if necessary to allow greater clearance. Do not rotate the crankshaft or camshafts with the belt removed, as there the risk of piston-to-valve contact.

**39** Spin the tensioner and idler pulleys and check for roughness or shake; renew if necessary. It is considered good practice to renew the belt pulleys along with the timing belt – to this end, Volvo dealers (and some motor factors) now sell timing belt 'kits', containing all the relevant parts.

**40** Check the timing belt carefully for any signs of uneven wear, splitting, or oil contamination. Pay particular attention to the roots of the teeth. Renew the belt if there is the slightest doubt about its condition. If the engine is undergoing an overhaul, and has covered more than 36 000 miles (60 000 km) with the existing belt fitted, renew the belt as a

matter of course, regardless of its apparent condition. The cost of a new belt is negligible when compared to the cost of engine repairs, should the belt break in service. If signs of oil contamination are found, trace the source of the oil leak, and rectify it. Wash down the engine timing belt area and all related components, to remove all traces of oil.

### Refitting and tensioning

**41** If a new tensioner assembly is to be fitted (as per the manufacturer's recommendation), fit the tensioner to the side of the engine, then insert the centre bolt **(see illustration)**.

**42** Tighten the tensioner centre bolt hand-tight initially, to hold in place. Ensure that the locating tab on the rear of the tensioner pointer is to the left of the web cast into the side of the cylinder block **(see illustration)**.

**43** Before refitting the timing belt, make sure that the camshaft and crankshaft sprockets

are in the correct positions (see paragraph 10). Slip the belt over the crankshaft sprocket, keeping it taut and feed it in anti-clockwise direction over the idler pulley, inlet camshaft sprocket, exhaust camshaft sprocket, coolant pump sprocket and finally over the tensioner pulley **(see illustration)**. Observe the correct running direction if the old belt is being re-used.

**44** Refit the upper timing belt inner cover, then check the alignment of the camshaft and crankshaft sprocket markings.

**45** Fit a 6 mm Allen key into the adjustment hole in the plate on the side of the tensioner pulley. Rotate the tensioner pulley anti-clockwise using the Allen key, until the pointer is aligned centrally between the two indicators. Keep the tensioner in this position and then tighten the tensioner centre bolt to its specified torque **(see illustrations)**.

**46** Using thumb pressure only, press on the

**3.45a Using a 6mm Allen key, rotate the tensioner pulley anti-clockwise . . .**

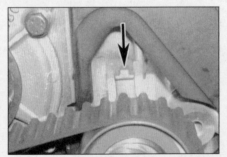

**3.45b . . . until the pointer (arrowed) is aligned centrally between the two indicators . . .**

**3.45c . . . keep the tensioner in this position and then tighten the tensioner centre bolt to the specified torque**

**4.5 Prise the sealing cap from the left-hand end of the cylinder head, to expose the end of the inlet camshaft**

outer surface of the timing at a point midway between the exhaust camshaft sprocket and the coolant pump sprocket. Check that the tensioner pointer moves backwards and forwards freely as you press on the belt.

**47** Using a large spanner on the temporarily-refitted crankshaft sprocket centre nut, turn the crankshaft in its normal direction of rotation (ie, clockwise as viewed from the right-hand side of the car) through two complete revolutions. Bring all three camshaft and crankshaft sprocket markings back into alignment.

**48** Check that the tensioner pointer is still aligned centrally between the two indicators. If this is not the case, slacken the tensioner centre bolt and then repeat the steps detailed in paragraphs 43 to 45 inclusive.

**49** Carry out the steps described in paragraphs 25 to 34 inclusive.

## 4  Camshaft right-hand oil seals – renewal

**Note:** *For this procedure, the Volvo camshaft locking tool 999 5452 will be required to set the positions of the camshafts and crankshaft while the sprockets are timing belt are*

removed. Details for fabricating home-made alternatives are given in the text. Do not attempt to carry out the work without locking the camshafts, or the valve timing may be irretrievably lost.

**1** Remove the cover panel from the top of the engine, then remove the timing belt as described in Section 3.

**2** Refer to Chapter 4A and remove the complete air cleaner assembly and inlet ducts as necessary for clear access to the end of both camshafts on the left-hand side of the cylinder head.

**3** Disconnect the brake servo vacuum hose from the throttle housing by pressing the locking collar down with the tip of a screwdriver, and at the same time pulling up on the hose.

**4** Unscrew the bolt and release the fuel pipe support bracket from the end of the cylinder head.

**5** Prise the sealing cap from the left-hand end of the cylinder head, to expose the end of the inlet camshaft **(see illustration)**. The cap cannot be re-used, so the easiest way to remove it is to punch a small hole in the centre of the cap and lever it out with a stout screwdriver. Take care to ensure that no debris falls into the camshaft oil return hole.

**6** Disconnect the camshaft position sensor wiring, at the connector located on top of the sensor housing at the end of the exhaust camshaft.

**7** Remove the screws and release the wiring harness guide from the end of the cylinder head. Unclip the wiring from the cylinder head as necessary.

**8** Undo the two screws and remove the camshaft position sensor housing from the left-hand end of the cylinder head (left as seen from the driver's seat). Undo the bolt and remove the sensor trigger wheel from the end of the exhaust camshaft (see Chapter 4A, Section 10, for details).

**9** Observe the position of the slots in the rear of the camshafts. The camshafts must be positioned so that these slots are parallel to the join between the upper and lower cylinder

*Tool Tip 1:  To make a camshaft locking tool, obtain a length of angle-iron and cut it to length so that it will fit across the rear of the cylinder head. Mark and drill two holes so that it can be bolted to a distributor cap and camshaft position sensor bolt hole. Obtain a length of steel strip of suitable thickness to fit snugly in the slots in the camshafts. Cut the strip into two lengths and drill accordingly so that both strips can be bolted to the angle-iron. Using spacer washers, nuts and bolts, position and secure the strips to the angle-iron so that the camshafts can be locked with their slots horizontal. Pack out the strips with spacers to cater for the offset of the slots.*

head sections, and then locked in that position. Note also that the slots are very slightly offset from the centreline; one slightly above and one slightly below.

**10** To lock the camshafts in the correct position for refitting, obtain Volvo tool 999 5452 or fabricate a home-made alternative **(see Tool Tip 1)**.

**11** Check that the crankshaft sprocket timing marks are still aligned, then attach the Volvo tool or the home-made alternative to the cylinder head. It may be necessary to rotate the camshafts very slightly to bring their slots exactly to the horizontal position to allow the tool to fit **(see illustrations)**.

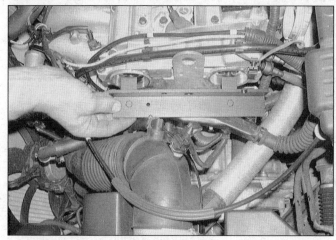

**4.11a Attach the home-made camshaft locking tool to the cylinder head**

**4.11b It may be necessary to rotate the camshafts slightly so their slots are exactly horizontal to fit the tool**

*Tool Tip 2: To make a camshaft sprocket holding tool, obtain two lengths of steel strip about 6 mm thick by 30 mm wide or similar, one 600 mm long, the other 200 mm long (all dimensions approximate). Bolt the two strips together to form a forked end, leaving the bolt slack so that the shorter strip can pivot freely. At the end of each 'prong' of the fork, bend the strips through 90° about 50 mm from their ends to act as the fulcrums; these will engage with the holes in the sprockets. It may be necessary to grind or cut off their sides slightly to allow them to fit the sprocket holes.*

**12** If both camshaft sprockets are to be removed, suitably mark them inlet and exhaust for identification when refitting. On all engines, the inlet sprocket is nearest the front of the car.

**4.15a Withdraw the securing bolts . . .**

**4.15b . . . and remove the inlet camshaft sprocket**

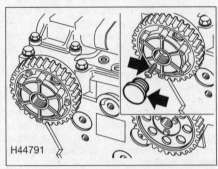

**4.14 VVT camshaft sprocket removal details**

**13** Undo the three bolts and remove the appropriate camshaft sprocket for access to the failed seal. Restrain the sprockets with a suitable tool through the holes in their faces **(see Tool Tip 2)**.

**14** On models with variable valve timing (VVT), the exhaust camshaft sprocket is removed differently. First, a centre cap is unscrewed, using a Torx (T55) bit, to give access to the single sprocket bolt (also a T55) **(see illustration)**. The sprocket will not turn, provided the special tool remains in place in the ends of the camshafts.

**15** Withdraw the appropriate sprocket from the camshaft **(see illustrations)**. As the VVT sprocket is removed, be prepared for a small amount of oil spillage.

**16** Carefully extract the seal by prising it out with a small screwdriver or hooked tool. Take great care to avoid damaging the shaft sealing face.

> **HAYNES HiNT** *Sometimes, a seal can be loosened by pushing it in on one side – this tilts the seal outwards on the opposite side, and it can then be gripped with pliers and removed.*

**17** Clean the seal seat. Examine the shaft sealing face for wear or damage which could cause premature failure of the new seal.

**18** Lubricate the new oil seal. Fit the seal over the shaft, lips inwards, and tap it home with a large socket or piece of tube until its outer face is flush with the housing **(see illustration)**. On models with VVT, note that the two oil seals

**4.18 Fit the new oil seal over the camshaft**

are different – compare old and new parts to be sure of fitting the right one.

**19** Refit the conventional (three-bolt) camshaft sprocket(s), with the timing marks aligned, and secure with only two of the retaining bolts for each sprocket. If only one sprocket has been removed, slacken the three bolts on the other sprocket and remove one of them. Tighten the bolts so that they just touch the sprockets, but allow the sprockets to turn within the limits of their elongated bolt holes. Position the sprockets so that the bolts are at the centre of their elongated holes **(see illustration)**.

**20** Where applicable refit the VVT sprocket, again only tightening the single bolt so that the sprocket can still turn.

**21** On models with automatic timing belt tensioners, carry out the operations described in Section 3, paragraphs 17 to 21. Release the timing belt tensioner by pulling out the locking pin with pliers. Check that the tensioner plunger moves out to tension the belt. Depress the belt hard by hand, then tap it with a plastic mallet in two locations; between the camshaft sprockets and between the camshaft sprocket and the coolant pump sprocket.

**22** On models with manually-adjusted timing belt tensioners, carry out the operations described in Section 3, paragraphs 42 to 46.

**23** Refit the remaining bolt to each conventional camshaft sprocket, and tighten all three bolts to the specified torque.

**24** Similarly, on models with VVT, tighten the single sprocket bolt to the specified torque, then fit and tighten the centre cap.

**25** Remove the locking tool from the camshafts.

**26** Turn the crankshaft clockwise through two complete revolutions, then check that all the timing marks can be realigned.

**27** Continue with the timing belt refitting procedure as described in the relevant part of Section 3. Do not reconnect the battery at this stage.

**28** Refit the camshaft position sensor trigger wheel and housing, then reconnect the sensor wiring.

**29** Press a new inlet camshaft cover cap into position at the left end of the cylinder head, then refit the wiring harness guide.

**4.19 Position the sprockets so that the bolts are at the centre of their elongated holes (arrowed) – bolt slackened to show elongated hole**

30 Reconnect the brake servo vacuum hose to the throttle housing, ensuring that it is securely held by the locking collar.
31 Refit the air cleaner assembly and air ducts.
32 Refit the cover panel to the top of the engine.
33 Reconnect the battery negative lead.

## 5 Camshaft left-hand oil seals – renewal

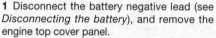

1 Disconnect the battery negative lead (see *Disconnecting the battery*), and remove the engine top cover panel.
2 Refer to Chapter 4A and remove the complete air cleaner assembly and inlet ducts as necessary for clear access to the end of both camshafts on the left-hand side of the cylinder head, as seen from the driver's seat.
3 Unscrew the bolt and release the fuel pipe support bracket from the end of the cylinder head.
4 Carefully prise the sealing cap from the left-hand end of the cylinder head, to expose the end of the inlet camshaft. The cap cannot be re-used, so the easiest way to remove it is to punch a small hole in the centre of the cap and lever it out with a stout screwdriver. Take care to ensure that no debris falls into the camshaft oil return hole.
5 Disconnect the camshaft position sensor wiring at the connector located at the rear of the engine compartment.
6 Remove the screws and release the wiring harness guide from the end of the cylinder head.
7 Undo the two screws and remove the camshaft position sensor housing from the left-hand end of the cylinder head. Undo the bolt and remove the sensor trigger wheel from the end of the exhaust camshaft.
8 Carefully extract the seal by prising it out with a small screwdriver or hooked tool. Do not damage the shaft sealing face.

> **HAYNES HINT** *Sometimes, a seal can be loosened by pushing it in on one side – this tilts the seal outwards on the opposite side, and it can then be gripped with pliers and removed.*

9 Clean the seal seat. Examine the shaft sealing face for wear or damage which could cause premature failure of the new seal.
10 Lubricate the new oil seal. Fit the seal over the shaft, lips inwards, and tap it home with a large socket or piece of tube until its outer face is flush with the housing. Note that if the end of the camshaft shows signs of wear caused by the old seal, the new seal may be driven into its housing by a further 2 mm.
11 Refit the camshaft position sensor, wiring harness guide, camshaft sealing cap and fuel

pipe support bracket using a reversal of removal procedure, then reconnect the camshaft position sensor wiring.
12 Refit the air cleaner and ducts, then reconnect the battery. Refit the engine top cover.

## 6 Camshafts and tappets – removal, inspection and refitting

**Note:** *For this procedure, Volvo special tools 999 5451, 999 5452, 999 5453 and 999 5454 will be required to lock the camshafts in position in the cylinder head upper section during refitting, and to pull the upper section into place. Details for fabricating home-made alternatives are given in the text. Do not attempt to carry out the work without these tools. A tube of liquid gasket and a short-haired application roller (available from Volvo dealers) will also be required.*

### Removal

1 Disconnect the battery negative lead (see *Disconnecting the battery*).
2 With reference to Chapter 1, drain the cooling system and remove the spark plugs.
3 Remove the timing belt as described in Section 3. On models with variable valve timing (VVT), remove the VVT control valve as described in Section 12.
4 Disconnect the brake servo vacuum hose from the throttle housing by pressing the locking collar down with the tip of a screwdriver, and at the same time pulling up on the hose.
5 Unscrew the bolt and release the fuel pipe support bracket from the end of the cylinder head.
6 Prise the sealing cap from the left-hand end of the cylinder head, to expose the end of the inlet camshaft **(see illustration 4.5)**. The cap cannot be re-used, so the easiest way to remove it is to punch a small hole in the centre of the cap and lever it out with a stout screwdriver. Take care to ensure that no debris falls into the camshaft oil return hole.
7 Disconnect the camshaft position sensor wiring, at the connector located on top of the sensor housing at the end of the exhaust camshaft.
8 Remove the screws and release the wiring harness guide from the end of the cylinder head. Unclip the wiring from the cylinder head as necessary.
9 Undo the two screws and remove the camshaft position sensor housing from the left-hand end of the cylinder head (left as seen from the driver's seat). Undo the bolt and remove the sensor trigger wheel from the end of the exhaust camshaft (see Chapter 4A, Section 10, for details).
10 Observe the position of the slots in the rear of the camshafts. The camshafts must be positioned so that these slots are parallel to the join between the upper and lower cylinder

**6.14 On non-turbo models, unbolt and remove the ignition coil support bracket**

head sections, and then locked in that position. Note also that the slots are very slightly offset from the centreline; one slightly above and one slightly below.
11 To lock the camshafts in the correct position for refitting, obtain Volvo tool 999 5452 or fabricate a home-made alternative (see **Tool Tip 1** in Section 4).
12 Check that the crankshaft sprocket timing marks are still aligned, then attach the Volvo tool or the home-made alternative to the rear of the cylinder head. It may be necessary to rotate the camshafts very slightly to bring their slots exactly to the horizontal position to allow the tool to fit **(see illustrations 4.11a and 4.11b)**.
13 Remove the camshaft sprockets as described in Section 4.
14 Release the wiring harness guide from the end of the cylinder head, then remove the ignition coils as described in Chapter 5B. On non-turbo models, unbolt and remove the ignition coil support bracket **(see illustration)**.
15 In a progressive diagonal sequence, working inwards, slacken then remove all the bolts securing the cylinder head upper section.
16 Using a soft-faced mallet, gently tap, or alternatively prise, the cylinder head upper section upwards off the lower section. Note that parting lugs are provided to allow the upper section to be struck or prised against without damage **(see illustration)**. Do not insert a screwdriver or similar tool into the joint between the two sections as a means of separation. The upper section will be quite tight, as it is located on several dowels.

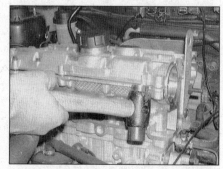

**6.16 Gently tap the upper section upwards off the lower section, using the parting lugs**

6.17 Lift the upper section squarely from the cylinder head

6.18 Withdraw the sealing O-rings from the top of the spark plug recesses in the lower section

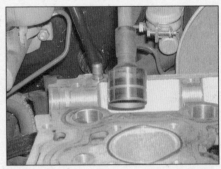

6.22 Lift out the tappets, using a suction cup if necessary

**17** Once the upper section is free, lift it squarely from the cylinder head **(see illustration)**. The camshafts will rise up under the pressure of the valve springs – be careful they don't tilt and jam in either section.

**18** Withdraw the sealing O-rings from the top of the spark plug recesses in the lower section. Obtain new O-rings for reassembly **(see illustration)**.

**19** Suitably mark the camshafts – inlet and exhaust – and lift them out complete with left- and right-hand oil seals. Be careful of the lobes, as they may have sharp edges.

**20** Remove the oil seals from the camshafts, noting their fitted positions. Obtain new seals for reassembly.

**21** Have ready a suitable box divided into sixteen segments, or some containers or other means of storing and identifying the hydraulic tappets after removal. The box or containers must be oil-tight, and deep enough to allow the tappets to be almost totally submerged in oil. Mark the segments in the box or the containers with the cylinder number for each tappet, together with identification for its position in the cylinder head (ie, inlet front/inlet rear, exhaust front/exhaust rear).

**22** Lift out the tappets, using a suction cup if necessary (Volvo state that a magnet should

not be used). Keep them identified for position, and place them upright in their respective positions in the box or containers **(see illustration)**. Once all the tappets have been removed, add clean engine oil to the box or container so that the oil hole in the side of the tappet is submerged.

### Inspection

**23** Inspect the cam lobes and the camshaft bearing journals for scoring or other visible evidence of wear. Once the surface hardening of the cam lobes has been eroded, wear will occur at an accelerated rate. **Note:** *If these symptoms are visible on the tips of the camshaft lobes, check the corresponding tappet, as it will probably be worn as well.*

**24** No specific bearing journal diameters or running clearances are specified by Volvo for the camshafts or journals. However, if there is a visual deterioration, then component renewal will be necessary.

**25** Inspect the tappets for scuffing, cracking or other damage; measure their diameter in several places with a micrometer. Renew the tappets if they are damaged or worn.

### Preparation for refitting

**26** Thoroughly clean the sealant from the mating surfaces of the upper and lower cylinder head sections. Use a suitable liquid gasket dissolving agent together with a soft putty knife; do not use a metal scraper, or the faces will be damaged. As there is no conventional gasket used, the cleanliness of the mating faces is of the utmost importance.

**27** Clean off any oil, dirt or grease from both components, and dry with a clean, lint-free cloth. Ensure that all the oilways are completely clean.

**28** For reassembly, the camshafts are installed in the upper section, and retained in place in the correct position using special tools. This assembly is then fitted to the lower section, clamped in place against the pressure of the valve springs with more special tools, and finally bolted down. If possible, obtain the Volvo special tools mentioned in the note at the beginning of this section, and use them in accordance with the instructions provided. Alternatively, fabricate a set of home-made tools as follows.

**29** To position and secure the camshafts at the left-hand end, the angle-iron tool described in Section 4 is required.

**30** To secure the camshafts at the right-hand end, make up a strap as shown **(see Tool Tip 1)**.

**31** Finally, it will be necessary to make up a tool which will allow the upper section to be clamped down against the pressure of the valve springs **(see Tool Tip 2)**.

### Refitting

**32** Commence refitting by liberally oiling the tappet bores and the camshaft bearings in the cylinder head lower section with clean engine oil.

**33** Insert the tappets into their original bores (unless new ones are being fitted). Fill new tappets with oil through the oil hole in their side before fitting.

**Tip 1:** *To retain the camshafts in the cylinder head upper section at the front when refitting, make a retaining strap out of welding rod, bent to shape, which will locate under the camshaft projections at the front and can be secured to the upper section with two bolts.*

**Tip 2:** *To pull the cylinder head upper section down against valve spring pressure, obtain two old spark plugs and carefully break away all the porcelain so that only the lower threaded portion remains. Drill out the centre of the spark plugs as necessary, then fit a long bolt or threaded rod to each, and secure tightly with nuts. The bolts or rods must be long enough to project up from the spark plug wells to above the level of the assembled cylinder head. Drill a hole in the centre of two 6 mm thick strips of steel which are long enough to fit across the cylinder head upper section. Fit the strips, then fit a nut and locknut to each bolt or rod.*

6.36  Apply an even coat of Volvo liquid gasket to the mating face of the cylinder head upper section only

6.40a  With the camshafts correctly positioned, lock them by fitting the left-hand locking and holding tool

6.40b  Now secure the camshafts at the right using the second home-made holding tool

6.41  Place new sealing O-rings into the recesses around each spark plug well in the lower section

6.44  Insert the pull-down tools into Nos 1 and 4 spark plug holes and tighten securely

6.45  Refit the cylinder head upper section bolts

**34** Ensure that the mating faces of both cylinder head sections are clean, and free of any oil or grease.

**35** Check that the crankshaft timing marks are still aligned.

**36** Using the short-haired roller, apply an even coating of Volvo liquid gasket solution to the mating face of the cylinder head upper section only **(see illustration)**. Ensure that the whole surface is covered, but take care to keep the solution out of the oilways; a thin coating is sufficient for a good seal.

**37** Lubricate the camshaft journals in the upper section sparingly with oil, taking care not to allow the oil to spill over onto the liquid gasket.

**38** Lay the camshafts in their correct locations in the upper section, remembering that the inlet camshaft is at the front.

**39** Turn the camshafts so that their slots are parallel to the upper section joint, noting that the slots in each camshaft are offset with regards to the centreline. When viewing the upper section the right way up, ie, as it would be when fitted, the slot on the inlet camshaft is offset above the centreline, and the exhaust camshaft slot is offset below the centreline. Verify this by looking at the other end of the camshafts. Again, with the upper section the right way up, there should be two sprocket bolt holes above the centreline on the inlet camshaft, and two bolt holes below the centreline on the exhaust camshaft.

**40** With the camshafts correctly positioned,

lock them at the left-hand end by fitting the locking and holding tool. It should not be possible to rotate the camshafts at all with the tool in place. Now secure the camshafts at the right-hand end using the holding tool or the home-made alternative **(see illustrations)**.

**41** Place new sealing O-rings into the recesses around each spark plug well in the lower section **(see illustration)**.

**42** Lift up the assembled upper section, with camshafts, and lay it in place on the lower section.

**43** Insert the pull-down tools into Nos 1 and 4 spark plug holes and tighten securely. If using the home-made tool, make sure that the bolt or threaded rod is a secure fit in the spark plug, or you will not be able to remove the tool later.

**44** Lay the pull-down tool top plates, or the home-made steel strips, over the bolts or threaded rods and secure with the nuts **(see illustration)**. Slowly and carefully tighten the nuts, a little at a time, so that the tools pull the upper section down onto the lower section. Remember there will be considerable resistance from the valve springs. Make sure that the upper section stays level, or the locating dowels will jam.

**45** Refit the upper section retaining bolts and tighten them in a progressive diagonal sequence, working outwards, to the specified torque **(see illustration)**.

**46** With the upper section secure, remove the pull-down tool and the camshaft right-

hand end holding tool. Leave the left-hand locking tool in place.

**47** Lubricate the lips of four new oil seals. Fit each seal the correct way round over the camshaft, and tap it home with a large socket or piece of tube until its outer face is flush with the housing; refer to the information in Sections 4 and 5 for guidance.

**48** For the remainder of refitting, refer to Section 4 and carry out the operations from paragraph 19 onwards.

**49** On completion, refill the cooling system as described in Chapter 1.

## 7  Cylinder head – removal and refitting

### Removal

**1** Disconnect the battery negative lead (see *Disconnecting the battery*), then drain the cooling system as described in Chapter 1.

**2** With reference to Chapter 4A, remove the complete air cleaner assembly and inlet ducts, followed by the inlet manifold and fuel rail.  Remove the exhaust manifold as described in Chapter 4C.

**3** Remove timing belt, followed by the upper section of the cylinder head together with the camshafts, followed by the tappets, as described in Sections 3 and 6.

**4** Unbolt the engine right-hand mounting

**7.4a Unbolt the engine right-hand mounting bracket from the engine**

**7.4b Engine right-hand mounting bracket locating dowel (arrowed)**

**7.8 Undo the two bolts securing the coolant pipe flange to the rear of the cylinder head**

**7.9a Slackening the cylinder head bolts**

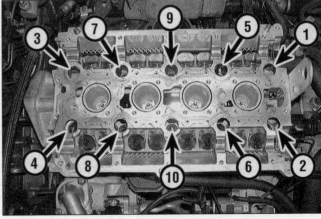
**7.9b Cylinder head bolt *slackening* sequence (tightening sequence is the reverse)**

bracket from the engine (right as seen from the driver's seat). The bracket can be difficult to remove, as it located by a tight-fitting dowel **(see illustrations)**.

**5** Undo the bolt and remove the earth lead at the rear of the cylinder head.

**6** Slacken the clips and remove the radiator top hose from the thermostat housing and radiator.

**7** Remove the expansion tank hose from the thermostat housing.

**8** Undo the two bolts securing the coolant pipe flange to the rear of the cylinder head **(see illustration)**.

**9** Slacken the cylinder head bolts, half a turn at a time to begin with, in the order shown.

Remove the bolts. Note that new bolts will be required for refitting **(see illustrations)**.

**10** Lift off the cylinder head, and set it down on wooden blocks to avoid damage to protruding valves. Recover the old head gasket.

**11** If the cylinder head is to be dismantled for overhaul, refer to Part C of this Chapter.

### Preparation for refitting

**12** The mating faces of the cylinder head and cylinder block must be perfectly clean before refitting the head. Use a soft putty knife to remove all traces of gasket and carbon; also clean the piston crowns. Take particular care during the cleaning operations, as aluminium alloy is easily damaged.

**13** Make sure that the carbon is not allowed to enter the oil and water passages – this is particularly important for the lubrication system, as carbon could block the oil supply to the engine's components. Using adhesive tape and paper, seal the water, oil and bolt holes in the cylinder block.

**14** To prevent carbon entering the gap between the pistons and bores, smear a little grease in the gap. After cleaning each piston, use a small brush to remove all traces of grease and carbon from the gap, then wipe away the remainder with a clean rag. Clean all the pistons in the same way.

**15** Check the mating surfaces of the cylinder block and the cylinder head for nicks, deep scratches and other damage. If slight, they may be removed carefully with a file, but if excessive, machining may be the only alternative to renewal.

**16** If warpage of the cylinder head gasket surface is suspected, use a straight-edge to check it for distortion. Refer to the overhaul information given in Part C of this Chapter if necessary.

### Refitting

**17** Commence refitting by placing a new head gasket on the cylinder block. Make sure it is the right way up; the surface marked with the word TOP should face upwards **(see illustration)**.

**7.9c Removing a cylinder head bolt**

**7.17 Make sure the cylinder head gasket is the right way up; surface marked TOP should face upwards**

**18** Remove the starter motor as described in Chapter 5A, to gain access to the crankshaft locking aperture. Prise the plug from the crankshaft access hole in the front of the engine block. Insert the Volvo special tool 999 5451 (or an equivalent, such as twist drill bit of suitable diameter) into the aperture, then using a socket and wrench on the crankshaft sprocket, slowly turn the crankshaft anti-clockwise, until it can be felt to touch the locking tool. No further anti-clockwise rotation of the crankshaft should now be possible.

**19** Lower the cylinder head into position, then oil the threads of the new cylinder head bolts. Fit the bolts and tighten them to the specified Stage 1 torque, in the *reverse* of the slackening sequence **(see illustration 7.9b)**.

**20** In the same sequence, tighten the bolts to the Stage 2 torque, then, again in the reverse of the slackening sequence, tighten the bolts through the angle specified for Stage 3 using an angle-tightening gauge.

**21** Using a new gasket, refit the coolant pipe flange to the rear of the cylinder head and secure with the two bolts.

**22** Refit the radiator top hose to the thermostat housing, and tighten the hose clip securely.

**23** Refit the earth lead to the rear of the cylinder head.

**24** Remove the locking tool from the crankshaft and refit the plug. Refit the starter motor as described in Chapter 5A.

**25** Refit the camshaft and tappets as described in Section 6, paragraphs 32 to 48. Do not reconnect the battery at this stage.

**26** Refit the inlet manifold, fuel rail and exhaust manifold as described in Chapters 4A and 4C.

**27** On completion, refill cooling system as described in Chapter 1, and reconnect the battery negative lead.

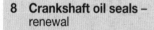

**8 Crankshaft oil seals – renewal**

### Right-hand seal

**1** Remove the timing belt as described in Section 3. Lower the engine slightly, by adjusting the engine lifting equipment, until clear access to the crankshaft pulley can be gained.

**2** The crankshaft pulley must be held stationary while its centre retaining nut is slackened. If the Volvo holding tool 999 5433 cannot be obtained, it will be necessary to fabricate a home-made alternative. This will be essentially the same as the camshaft sprocket holding tool described in Section 4, but instead of bending the prongs of the forks through 90°, leave them straight and drill a suitable hole in each. The four bolts securing the crankshaft pulley to the sprocket are then removed, allowing the tool to be bolted to the pulley using two of the bolts.

**8.4 Draw the crankshaft sprocket off using a universal puller**

**8.7a Fit the new seal over the crankshaft . . .**

**3** Hold the tool securely and undo the pulley centre retaining nut using a socket and bar. Remove the tool and lift the pulley off the sprocket (refer to the illustrations in Section 3, paragraphs 6 to 9 for greater detail).

**4** With the pulley removed, insert two of the retaining bolts and draw the sprocket off the crankshaft using a universal puller. Engage the puller legs with the protruding bolts at the rear **(see illustration)**. Avoid damaging the sprocket teeth.

**5** With the sprocket removed, carefully prise out the old oil seal **(see illustration)**. Do not damage the oil pump housing or the surface of the crankshaft. Alternatively, punch or drill two small holes opposite each other in the oil seal. Screw a self-tapping screw into each, and pull on the screws with pliers to extract the seal.

**HAYNES HINT** *Sometimes, a seal can be loosened by pushing it in on one side – this tilts the seal outwards on the opposite side, and it can then be gripped with pliers and removed.*

**6** Clean the oil seal location and the crankshaft. Inspect the crankshaft for a wear groove or ridge left by the old seal.

**7** Lubricate the housing, the crankshaft and the new seal. Fit the seal, lips inwards, and use a piece of tube (or the old seal, inverted) to tap it into place until flush **(see illustrations)**.

**8** Refit the crankshaft sprocket and pulley using a reverse of the removal procedure.

**8.5 Carefully prise out the old oil seal**

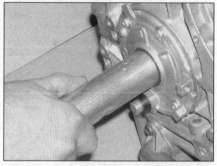

**8.7b . . . and use a piece of tube to tap it into place until it is flush with its housing**

Note that the crankshaft nose has a master spline to ensure that the sprocket is correctly refitted **(see illustration)**.

**9** Refit the timing belt as described in Section 3.

### Left-hand seal

**10** Remove the flywheel or driveplate as described in Section 10.

**11** Carefully prise out the old oil seal. Do not damage the block mating surfaces or the crankshaft flange. Alternatively, punch or drill two small holes opposite each other in the oil seal. Screw a self-tapping screw into each, and pull on the screws with pliers to extract the seal.

**12** Inspect the crankshaft for a wear groove or ridge left by the old seal. If necessary, use emery cloth to clean up the crankshaft flange, wrapped round the flange (not in-and-out).

**8.8 Note that the crankshaft nose has a master spline (arrowed) to ensure that the sprocket is correctly refitted**

**8.14a Fit the new oil seal over the crankshaft . . .**

**8.14b . . . and use a length of wood to tap it into place until it is flush with its housing**

## Removal

**1** Carry out the operations described in Section 8, paragraphs 1 to 4.
**2** Undo the four bolts securing the oil pump to the cylinder block.
**3** Carefully withdraw the pump assembly by levering behind the upper and lower parting lugs using a screwdriver. Remove the pump and recover the gasket.
**4** Thoroughly clean the pump and cylinder block mating faces and remove all traces of old gasket.

## Inspection

**5** Remove the two screws which hold the two halves of the pump together **(see illustration)**.
**6** Remove the gear cover from the pump body. Be prepared to catch the pressure relief valve spring **(see illustration)**.
**7** Remove the relief valve spring and plunger and the pump gears **(see illustrations)**.
**8** Remove the crankshaft oil seal by carefully levering it out of the cover **(see illustration)**. Obtain a new seal for refitting.
**9** Clean all components thoroughly, then inspect the gears, body and gear cover for signs of wear or damage.
**10** Measure the free height of the pressure relief valve spring, and compare the dimension with that given in the Specifications. Renew it if it is weak or distorted. Also inspect the plunger for scoring or other damage **(see illustration)**.
**11** Refit the gears to the pump body, with the markings on the large gear uppermost. Using feeler blades, check the clearance between

**13** Clean the oil seal location and the crankshaft – it's vital that there is no thread-lock debris (from the flywheel/driveplate bolts) or other dirt present, as this will result in leaks.
**14** Lubricate the housing, the crankshaft and

the new seal – use clean engine oil, not grease. Fit the seal, lips inwards, and use a piece of tube (or the old seal, inverted) to tap it into place until flush **(see illustrations)**. Make sure the seal is pressed in to a uniform depth all round, as this further reduces the chances of the new seal leaking.
**15** Refit the flywheel or driveplate as described in Section 10.

**9.5 Remove the two screws which hold the two halves of the pump together**

| 9 | Oil pump – removal, inspection and refitting |

**Note:** *Four new copper washers should be obtained, to be fitted to the pump mounting bolts when refitting the pump. The washers are a revised fitment – early models may be found not to have any washers on dismantling.*

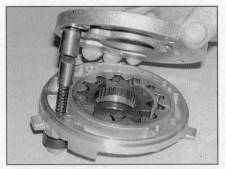

**9.6 Remove the gear cover from the pump body**

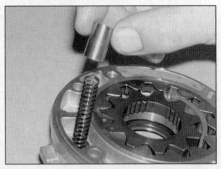

**9.7a Remove the relief valve spring and plunger . . .**

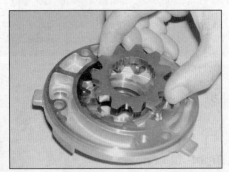

**9.7b . . . and inner . . .**

**9.7c . . . and outer pump gears**

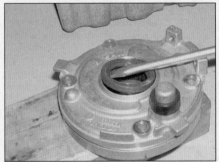

**9.8 Remove the crankshaft oil seal by carefully levering it out of the cover**

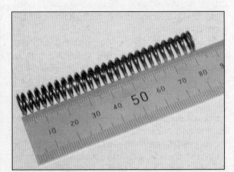

**9.10 Measure the free height of the pressure relief valve spring**

the large gear and the pump body. If the clearance is outside the specified limit, renew the pump **(see illustration)**.

**12** If the clearance is satisfactory, liberally lubricate the gears. Lubricate and fit the relief valve plunger and spring.

**13** Fit a new O-ring seal to the pump body then fit the cover and secure with the two screws **(see illustration)**.

### Refitting

**14** Using a new gasket, fit the pump to the block. Fit new copper washers to the pump retaining bolts, then use the bolts as guides and draw the pump into place with the crankshaft pulley nut and spacers. Take care not to damage the seal in the oil pump as it is fitted; also note that the crankshaft must not turn as the pump is being fitted. With the pump seated, tighten the retaining bolts diagonally to the specified torque **(see illustrations)**.

**15** Lubricate the cover, crankshaft and the new oil seal. Fit the seal, lips inwards, and use a piece of tube (or the old seal, inverted) to tap it into place until flush.

**16** Refit the crankshaft sprocket and pulley using a reverse of the removal procedure.

**17** Refit the timing belt as described in Section 3.

**10 Flywheel/driveplate –**
removal, inspection
and refitting

**Note**: *New flywheel/driveplate retaining bolts will be required for refitting.*

### Removal

#### Flywheel

**1** Remove the transmission as described in Chapter 7A.

**2** Remove the clutch assembly as described in Chapter 6.

**3** Make alignment marks so that the flywheel can be refitted in the same position relative to the crankshaft.

**4** Unbolt the flywheel and remove it – the bolts will be tight, as thread-locking compound is used. Prevent crankshaft rotation by inserting a large screwdriver in the ring gear teeth and in contact with an adjacent dowel in the engine/transmission mating face.

**5** Discard the old flywheel bolts once they have been removed. The bolts are subject to very high loads in service, and are tightened to a high torque – re-using them may be dangerous.

#### Driveplate

**6** Remove the automatic transmission as described in Chapter 7B.

**7** Make alignment marks so that the driveplate can be refitted in the same position relative to the crankshaft.

**8** Unbolt the driveplate and remove it, preventing crankshaft rotation as described

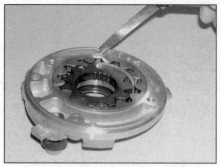

**9.11  Check the clearance between the outer gear and its housing**

previously. As with the flywheel bolts on manual transmission models, the old driveplate bolts must not be re-used.

### Inspection

**9** On manual transmission models, if the flywheel's clutch mating surface is deeply scored, cracked or otherwise damaged, the flywheel must be renewed. However, it may be possible to have it surface-ground; seek the advice of a Volvo dealer or engine reconditioning specialist. If the ring gear is badly worn or has missing teeth, flywheel renewal will also be necessary.

**10** On models equipped with automatic transmission, check the torque converter driveplate carefully for signs of distortion. Look for any hairline cracks around the bolt holes or radiating outwards from the centre, and inspect the ring gear teeth for signs of wear or chipping. If any signs of wear or

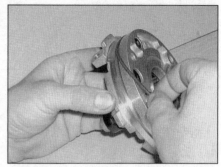

**9.13  Fit a new O-ring seal to the pump body**

damage are found, the driveplate must be renewed.

### Refitting

#### Flywheel

**11** Clean the mating surfaces of the flywheel and crankshaft. Remove any remaining locking compound from the threads of the crankshaft holes, using the correct-size tap, if available.

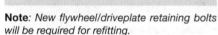
*If a suitable tap is not available, cut two slots into the threads of one of the old flywheel bolts and use the bolt to remove the locking compound from the threads.*

**12** Continue refitting by reversing the removal operations. Note that the flywheel is

**9.14a  Using a new gasket . . .**

**9.14b  . . . fit the pump to the block**

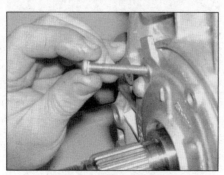

**9.14c  Insert the retaining bolts with new washers (not shown here) . . .**

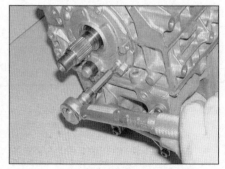

**9.14d  . . . and tighten them diagonally to the specified torque**

**10.12a The flywheel is located by a roll-pin pressed into the crankshaft mating surface**

**10.12b Insert the new flywheel retaining bolts . . .**

**10.12c . . . and tighten them to the specified torque . . .**

**10.12d . . . and through the specified angle**

located by a roll-pin pressed into the crankshaft mating surface. Apply thread-locking fluid to the threads of the new flywheel retaining bolts, and then tighten them to the specified torque and angle **(see illustrations)**.

**13** Refit the clutch as described in Chapter 6, and the transmission as described in Chapter 7A.

### Driveplate

**14** Proceed as described above for manual transmission models but ignoring any references to clutch. Refit the transmission as described in Chapter 7B.

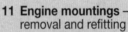

## 11 Engine mountings – removal and refitting

### Inspection

**1** If improved access is required, raise the front of the car and support it securely on axle stands.

**2** Check the rubber section of the relevant mounting to see if it is cracked, hardened or separated from the metal at any point; renew the mounting if any such damage or deterioration is evident.

**3** Check that all the mounting's fasteners are securely tightened; use a torque wrench to check if possible.

**4** Using a large screwdriver or a crowbar, check for wear in the mounting by carefully levering against it to check for free play. Where this is not possible, enlist the aid of an

assistant to move the engine/transmission unit back-and-forth, or from side-to-side, while you watch the mounting. While some free play is to be expected even from new components, excessive wear should be obvious. If excessive free play is found, check first that the fasteners are correctly secured, then renew any worn components as described below.

### *Renewal*

#### Right-hand mounting

**5** Disconnect the battery negative lead (see *Disconnecting the battery*).

**6** Place a jack beneath the engine (but not under the sump), with a block of wood on the jack head. Raise the jack until it is supporting the weight of the engine. Alternatively, position a lifting beam across the engine

**11.7 Slacken and remove the through-bolt securing the rubber mounting to the vehicle body bracket**

compartment and attach the jib to the right-hand engine lifting eyelet, located on the side of the cylinder head.

**7** Slacken and remove the through-bolt securing the rubber mounting to the vehicle body bracket **(see illustration)**. Note that on models with air conditioning, it will be necessary to unbolt the refrigerant pipe support bracket from the bodywork to gain access to the engine mounting. Access can be further improved by unbolting the power steering fluid reservoir and moving it one side.

**8** Slacken and remove the three bolts securing the right-hand mounting to the engine bracket and then remove the mounting from the vehicle **(see illustration)**. If required, the bracket fitted to the engine can also be removed (after removing the timing belt upper cover as described in Section 3) by removing the four mounting bolts; the bracket is located on a dowel, which can make removal difficult.

**9** Check carefully for signs of wear or damage on all components, and renew them where necessary.

**10** On reassembly, offer the mounting up to the engine bracket, then insert the three bolts and tighten them to the specified torque.

**11** Fit the through-bolt to secure the engine mounting to the bodywork bracket, fit the nut, but do not tighten it yet.

**12** Lower the engine lifting equipment or jack as applicable, until the weight of the engine is resting on the engine mounting. Rock the engine back-and-forth to settle the mounting, then tighten the through-bolt nut to the specified torque. Remove the lifting equipment or jack as applicable, then reconnect the battery negative lead.

#### Left-hand mounting

**13** Refer to Chapter 4A and remove the complete air cleaner assembly and inlet ducts as necessary for clear access to the left-hand engine mounting, at the top of the transmission casing.

**14** Place a jack beneath the transmission, with a block of wood on the jack head. Raise the jack until it is supporting the weight of the transmission. Take care to avoid damaging the gearshift mechanism. On some models it may be necessary to first remove the plastic cover panel from the underside of the transmission.

**11.8 Slacken and remove the three bolts securing the right-hand mounting to the engine bracket**

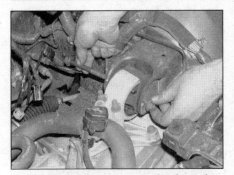

**11.15 Slacken and remove the through-bolt securing the rubber mounting to the vehicle body bracket**

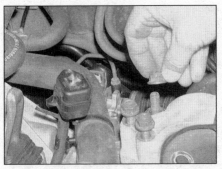

**11.16a Slacken and remove the three nuts securing the left-hand mounting to the transmission bracket . . .**

**11.16b . . . and then remove the mounting from the vehicle**

15 Slacken and remove the through-bolt securing the rubber mounting to the vehicle body bracket **(see illustration)**.
16 Slacken and remove the three nuts securing the left-hand engine mounting to the transmission bracket and then remove the mounting from the vehicle **(see illustrations)**.
17 Check carefully for signs of wear or damage on all components, and renew them where necessary.
18 Refit the engine mounting to the transmission bracket, tightening its mounting nuts to the specified torque.
19 Position the mounting in the bodywork bracket, ensuring that the protective rubber flaps are correctly located between the sides of the mounting and the bodywork bracket, then insert the through-bolt and fit the retaining nut. Do not tighten it at this stage.
20 Lower the jack until the weight of the engine is resting on the engine mounting. Rock the engine back-and-forth to settle the mounting, then tighten the through-bolt nut to the specified torque.
21 Remove the jack from underneath the transmission, then refit the air cleaner and air ducting as described in Chapter 4A.

**Front and rear mountings**

22 Position a lifting beam across the engine compartment and attach the jib to the engine lifting eyelets, located at either end of the cylinder head. Adjust the beam so that it just takes the combined weight of the engine and transmission.
23 If not already done, firmly apply the handbrake, then jack up the front of the vehicle and support it securely on axle stands.
24 Working at the underside of the engine compartment, slacken and remove the through-bolt securing the front and rear engine mountings to their respective engine brackets **(see illustration)**.
25 Unbolt and remove the engine/transmission crossmember from the underside of the engine compartment.
26 Slacken and remove the two bolts securing the relevant engine mounting to the engine/transmission crossmember, then remove the mounting from the beam.
27 Check carefully for signs of wear or

**11.24 Slacken and remove the through-bolt securing the front mounting to its engine bracket**

damage on all components, and renew them where necessary.
28 Refitting is a reversal of removal, noting the following points **(see illustration)**:
a) *Front mounting: position the engine mounting such that the square orientation hole in the left-hand side of the engine mounting bracket faces the front of the vehicle (front mounting) or the rear of the vehicle (rear mounting).*
b) *Ensure that the engine/transmission crossmember securing bolts and associated components are refitted as shown.*
c) *Tighten all nuts and bolts to the specified torque, but rock the engine back-and-forth to settle the engine mounting, before tightening the through-bolt last of all.*

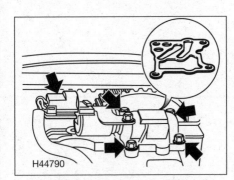

**12.3 Removing the VVT control valve – wiring plug and mounting bolts arrowed**

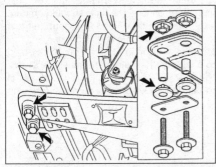

**11.28 Ensure that the engine/transmission crossmember securing bolts and associated components are refitted as shown**

## 12 Variable valve timing control valve – removal and refitting

### Removal

1 Remove the timing belt upper covers (inner and outer) as described in Section 3.
2 Clean the area around the base of the control valve, prior to removing it – no dirt or debris must be allowed to enter the valve ports.
3 Disconnect the control valve wiring connector, then undo the four mounting bolts and take off the valve – be prepared for a small amount of oil spillage as the valve is removed. Recover the gasket from the cylinder head surface – a new one must be used when refitting **(see illustration)**. Again, take care once the valve is removed that no contaminated oil or dirt enters the valve block, nor the ports on the engine.

### Refitting

4 Clean the gasket surfaces on the engine and the valve, and fit a new gasket.
5 Refit the valve, and tighten the four mounting bolts evenly to the specified torque.
6 Reconnect the wiring plug to the valve.
7 Check and if necessary top-up the engine oil level as described in *Weekly checks*. If desired, before refitting the timing belt covers,

the engine may be run to check for any sign of oil leaks (taking care to keep any loose clothing, etc, clear of the timing belt and sprockets).

**8** On completion, refit the timing belt covers, using the information in Section 3 if necessary.

### 13 Oil pressure switch – removal and refitting

**1** The oil pressure switch is a vital early warning of low oil pressure. The switch operates the oil warning light on the instrument panel – the light should come on with the ignition, and go out almost immediately when the engine starts.

**2** If the light does not come on, there could be a fault on the instrument panel, the switch wiring, or the switch itself. If the light does not go out, low oil level, worn oil pump (or sump pick-up blocked), blocked oil filter, or worn main bearings could be to blame – or again, the switch may be faulty.

**3** If the light comes on while driving, the best advice is to turn the engine off immediately, and not to drive the car until the problem has been investigated – ignoring the light could mean expensive engine damage.

### Removal

**4** The engine oil pressure switch is located on the front of the engine block, adjacent to the dipstick tube. Access is possible from above, but is easier from below – jack up the front of the car, support on axle stands (see *Jacking and vehicle support*), and remove the engine undershield.

**5** Disconnect the switch wiring connector, then unscrew the switch from the engine and recover the sealing washer. There may be a very slight weep of oil as the switch is removed, but only if the engine has very recently been running.

### Inspection

**6** Examine the switch for signs of cracking or splits. If the top part of the switch is loose, this is an early indication of impending failure.

**7** Check that the wiring terminals at the switch are not loose, then trace the wire from the switch connector until it enters the main loom – any wiring defects will give rise to apparent oil pressure problems.

### Refitting

**8** Refitting is the reverse of the removal procedure, noting the following points:

a) *Fit a new sealing washer, and tighten the switch to the specified torque wrench setting.*

b) *Reconnect the switch connector securely, and ensure that the wiring is routed away from any hot or moving parts.*

c) *Check the engine oil level and top-up if necessary (see 'Weekly checks').*

d) *Check for signs of oil leaks once the engine has been restarted and warmed-up to normal operating temperature.*

# Chapter 2 Part B:
## Engine (GDI) in-car repair procedures

## Contents

## Degrees of difficulty

| **Easy,** suitable for novice with little experience |  | **Fairly easy,** suitable for beginner with some experience |  | **Fairly difficult,** suitable for competent DIY mechanic |  | **Difficult,** suitable for experienced DIY mechanic | | **Very difficult,** suitable for expert DIY or professional | |

## Specifications

### General

| | |
|---|---|
| Type . . . . . . . . . . . . . . . . . . . . . . . . . . . . . . . . . . . . . . . . . . . . . . . . | Four-cylinder, 1.8 litre twin overhead camshaft, 16-valve, direct petrol injection |
| Engine codes: | |
|   B4184SM . . . . . . . . . . . . . . . . . . . . . . . . . . . . . . . . . . . . . . . . . . | 1834 cc, non-turbo, 92kW |
|   B4184SJ . . . . . . . . . . . . . . . . . . . . . . . . . . . . . . . . . . . . . . . . . . | 1834 cc, non-turbo, 90kW |
| Bore/stroke . . . . . . . . . . . . . . . . . . . . . . . . . . . . . . . . . . . . . . . . . . | 81.0 mm/89.0 mm |
| Compression ratio . . . . . . . . . . . . . . . . . . . . . . . . . . . . . . . . . . . . . | 12.5:1 |
| Compression pressure: | |
|   Nominal . . . . . . . . . . . . . . . . . . . . . . . . . . . . . . . . . . . . . . . . . . | 15.8 bar (229 psi) |
|   Minimum . . . . . . . . . . . . . . . . . . . . . . . . . . . . . . . . . . . . . . . . . . | 12.8 bar (186 psi) |
| Variation between cylinders . . . . . . . . . . . . . . . . . . . . . . . . . . . . . | 1 bar (14.5 psi) maximum |
| Firing order . . . . . . . . . . . . . . . . . . . . . . . . . . . . . . . . . . . . . . . . . . | 1 – 3 – 4 – 2 (No 1 at timing belt end of engine) |

### Lubrication system

| | |
|---|---|
| Oil pressure (hot engine with new oil filter): | |
|   Below 1500 rpm . . . . . . . . . . . . . . . . . . . . . . . . . . . . . . . . . . . . . | 1.0 to 3.0 bar (14.5 to 43.5 psi) |
|   Above 1500 rpm . . . . . . . . . . . . . . . . . . . . . . . . . . . . . . . . . . . . . | 3.0 to 4.9 bar (43.5 to 71.1 psi) |
| Oil pressure switch operating value . . . . . . . . . . . . . . . . . . . . . . . | Less than 0.3 bar (4.4 psi) |
| Oil pump type . . . . . . . . . . . . . . . . . . . . . . . . . . . . . . . . . . . . . . . . | Gear, driven from crankshaft |
| Outer rotor-to-housing clearance (maximum) . . . . . . . . . . . . . . . . | 0.35 mm |

### Cylinder head

| | |
|---|---|
| Warp limit (measured diagonally – refer to Chapter 2C) . . . . . . . . . . | 0.05 mm |
| Head bolt maximum length . . . . . . . . . . . . . . . . . . . . . . . . . . . . . . | 96.4 mm |

## Torque wrench settings

| | Nm | lbf ft |
|---|---|---|
| Alternator drivebelt adjuster bracket bolts . . . . . . . . . . . . . . . . . . . . . . | 23 | 17 |
| Camshaft sprocket bolt . . . . . . . . . . . . . . . . . . . . . . . . | 88 | 65 |
| Crankshaft pulley bolt (oiled threads) . . . . . . . . . . . . . . . . . . . . . . . . | 180 | 133 |
| Cylinder head to block (oiled threads): | | |
|    Stage 1 . . . . . . . . . . . . . . . . . . . . . . . . . . . . . . . . | 74 | 55 |
|    Stage 2 . . . . . . . . . . . . . . . . . . . . . . . . . . . . . . . . | Slacken completely | |
|    Stage 3 . . . . . . . . . . . . . . . . . . . . . . . . . . . . . . . . | 20 | 15 |
|    Stage 4 . . . . . . . . . . . . . . . . . . . . . . . . . . . . . . . . | Angle-tighten a further 90° | |
|    Stage 5 . . . . . . . . . . . . . . . . . . . . . . . . . . . . . . . . | Angle-tighten a further 90° | |
| Cylinder head upper section bolts: | | |
|    M6 bolts . . . . . . . . . . . . . . . . . . . . . . . . . . . . . . . . | 11 | 8 |
|    M8 bolts . . . . . . . . . . . . . . . . . . . . . . . . . . . . . . . . | 21 | 15 |
|    Retaining plate bolts (for timing belt upper cover) . . . . . . . . . | 10 | 7 |
| Engine mountings: | | |
|    Front mounting bolts . . . . . . . . . . . . . . . . . . . . . . . . . . | 35 | 26 |
|    Front mounting through-bolt nut . . . . . . . . . . . . . . . . . . | 59 | 44 |
|    Left-hand mounting-to-body nuts . . . . . . . . . . . . . . . . . . | 45 | 33 |
|    Left-hand mounting through-bolt nut . . . . . . . . . . . . . . . . | 98 | 72 |
|    Rear mounting bolts . . . . . . . . . . . . . . . . . . . . . . . . . . | 35 | 26 |
|    Rear mounting through-bolt nut . . . . . . . . . . . . . . . . . . . . | 59 | 44 |
|    Right-hand mounting engine bracket (lower section) . . . . . . . . . . . | 50 | 37 |
|    Right-hand mounting through-bolt nut . . . . . . . . . . . . . . . . . . | 98 | 72 |
|    Right-hand mounting upper section nuts/bolt . . . . . . . . . . . | 76 | 56 |
|    Support member bolts . . . . . . . . . . . . . . . . . . . . . . . . | 69 | 51 |
| Exhaust manifold-to-downpipe nuts . . . . . . . . . . . . . . . . . . . . . . | 44 | 32 |
| Flywheel bolts (with locking fluid/oiled heads) . . . . . . . . . . . . . . . . | 98 | 72 |
| Oil pressure switch (with locking fluid) . . . . . . . . . . . . . . . . . . . . | 10 | 7 |
| Oil pump cover screws . . . . . . . . . . . . . . . . . . . . . . . . . . . . . . | 10 | 7 |
| Oil pump mounting bolts . . . . . . . . . . . . . . . . . . . . . . . . . . . . . . | 14 | 10 |
| Oil pump pick-up bolts . . . . . . . . . . . . . . . . . . . . . . . . . . . . . . | 19 | 14 |
| Oil pump pressure relief valve spring retaining plug . . . . . . . . . . . . . | 44 | 32 |
| Roadwheel nuts . . . . . . . . . . . . . . . . . . . . . . . . . . . . . . . . . . | 110 | 81 |
| Sump: | | |
|    Lower pan bolts . . . . . . . . . . . . . . . . . . . . . . . . . . . . . | 7 | 5 |
|    Main sump bolts: | | |
|       M6 bolts . . . . . . . . . . . . . . . . . . . . . . . . . . . . . . . | 9 | 7 |
|       M8 bolts (x4) . . . . . . . . . . . . . . . . . . . . . . . . . . . . . | 24 | 18 |
|       Sump-to-transmission bolts (x2) . . . . . . . . . . . . . . . . . . | 50 | 37 |
| Thermostat housing bolts . . . . . . . . . . . . . . . . . . . . . . . . . . . . | 23 | 17 |
| Timing belt automatic tensioner bolts . . . . . . . . . . . . . . . . . . . . . | 13 | 10 |
| Timing belt tensioner pulley centre bolt . . . . . . . . . . . . . . . . . . . . | 48 | 35 |
| Timing belt cover bolts . . . . . . . . . . . . . . . . . . . . . . . . . . . . . . | 9 | 7 |

## 1  General information

### How to use this Chapter

This Part of Chapter 2 describes those repair procedures that can reasonably be carried out on the GDI engine while it remains in the car. If the engine has been removed from the car and is being dismantled as described in Part C, any preliminary dismantling procedures can be ignored.

Note that, while it may be possible physically to overhaul items such as the piston/connecting rod assemblies while the engine is in the car, such tasks are not normally carried out as separate operations. Usually, several additional procedures (not to mention the cleaning of components and oilways) have to be carried out. For this reason, all such tasks are classed as major

overhaul procedures, and are described in Part C of this Chapter.

Part C describes the removal of the engine/transmission from the car, and the full overhaul procedures that can then be carried out.

### Engine description

The GDI engine is a Mitsubishi design, also used in the S40/V40's sister car, the Carisma. In many ways, the GDI unit is similar to the other engines covered by this manual – it is a 4-cylinder in-line unit, with twin overhead camshafts and four valves per cylinder, mounted transversely on a subframe in the engine bay. The main distinction of the GDI unit is the direct fuel injection system fitted, which means several of the air/fuel and ignition system components are unique to this engine (more details on the GDI fuel and ignition systems in Chapters 4B and 5B respectively). The design of the cylinder head is very unusual for a petrol engine, with air

entering the cylinders via a manifold on top, fuel injectors screwed directly into the head at the rear, and a conventional exhaust manifold on the front.

The bulk of the engine is constructed of aluminium, and consists of five sections. The cylinder head comprises an upper and lower section, with the cylinder block, main bearing ladder and sump forming the other three. The upper and lower sections of the cylinder head are mated along the centre line of the camshafts, while the cylinder block and intermediate section are mated along the crankshaft centre line. A conventional cylinder head gasket is used between the cylinder head and block, with liquid gaskets being used in the joints between the other main sections.

The cylinder block incorporates four cast-iron dry cylinder liners, which are cast into the block and cannot be renewed. Cast-iron is also used for the main bearing ladder, while the sump is pressed-steel.

Drive to the camshaft is by a toothed timing belt and sprockets, incorporating an automatic tensioning mechanism. The timing belt also drives the coolant pump. All accessories are driven from the crankshaft pulley by two multi-ribbed auxiliary drivebelts.

The cylinder head features inlet ports on top of the engine, and the exhaust ports at the front. The upper section of the cylinder head has a separate pressed-steel camshaft cover (some engines have a cover for each camshaft); the camshafts run in plain bearings integral to the two cylinder head sections. Valve actuation is by maintenance-free hydraulic tappets, acted upon indirectly by rockers from the camshaft lobes.

The crankshaft runs in five shell-type main bearings; the connecting rod big-end bearings are also of the shell type. The main bearing caps are 'joined together' in a one-piece ladder which bolts to the bottom of the crankcase. Crankshaft endfloat is taken by thrustwashers either side of the No 3 main bearing.

The lubrication system is of the full-flow, pressure-feed type. Oil is drawn from the sump by a gear-type pump, driven from the right-hand end of the crankshaft. Oil under pressure passes through a filter before being fed to the various shaft bearings and to the valve gear.

### Operations with engine in car

The following work can be carried out with the engine in the car:
a) Compression pressure – testing.
b) Timing belt – removal and refitting.
c) Camshaft oil seals – renewal.
d) Camshafts and tappets – removal and refitting.
e) Cylinder head – removal and refitting.
f) Cylinder head and pistons – decarbonising.
g) Crankshaft oil seals – renewal.
h) Oil pump – removal and refitting.
i) Flywheel – removal and refitting.
j) Engine mountings – removal and refitting.

## 2 Compression test –
description and interpretation

**Warning: Stand clear of the engine while it is being cranked. Even though the fuel and ignition systems should be disabled beforehand, there is still a fire risk, or the possible risk of personal injury, either through debris being ejected from the spark plug holes under pressure or from contact with moving parts.**

1 When engine performance is down, or if misfiring occurs which cannot be attributed to the ignition or fuel systems, a compression test can provide diagnostic clues as to the engine's condition. If the test is performed regularly, it can give warning of trouble before any other symptoms become apparent.

2 The engine must be fully warmed-up to normal operating temperature, the battery must be fully-charged, and all the spark plugs must be removed (see Chapter 1). The aid of an assistant will also be required.

3 Disable the ignition system by disconnecting the engine speed sensor wiring at the connector located to the rear of the timing belt top cover. Also disconnect the wiring connectors to each fuel injector, to prevent unburned fuel from damaging the catalytic converter (alternatively, locate and temporarily remove fuse number 17 from the engine compartment fusebox).

4 Fit a compression tester to the No 1 cylinder spark plug hole – the type of tester which screws into the plug thread is to be preferred.

5 Have the assistant hold the throttle wide open, and crank the engine on the starter motor; after one or two revolutions, the compression pressure should build-up to a maximum figure, and then stabilise. Record the highest reading obtained.

6 Repeat the test on the remaining cylinders, recording the pressure in each.

7 All cylinders should produce very similar pressures; a difference of more than 2 bars between any two cylinders indicates a fault. Note that the compression should build-up quickly in a healthy engine; low compression on the first stroke, followed by gradually-increasing pressure on successive strokes, indicates worn piston rings. A low compression reading on the first stroke, which does not build-up during successive strokes, indicates leaking valves or a blown head gasket (a cracked cylinder head could also be the cause). Deposits on the undersides of the valve heads can also cause low compression.

8 If the pressure in any cylinder is low, carry out the following test to isolate the cause. Introduce a teaspoonful of clean oil into that cylinder through its spark plug hole, and repeat the test.

9 If the addition of oil temporarily improves the compression pressure, this indicates that bore or piston wear is responsible for the pressure loss. No improvement suggests that leaking or burnt valves, or a blown head gasket, may be to blame.

10 A low reading from two adjacent cylinders is almost certainly due to the head gasket having blown between them; the presence of coolant in the engine oil will confirm this.

11 If one cylinder is about 20 percent lower than the others and the engine has a slightly rough idle, a worn camshaft lobe could be the cause.

12 If the compression reading is unusually high, the combustion chambers are probably coated with carbon deposits. If this is the case, the cylinder head should be removed and decarbonised.

13 On completion of the test, refit the spark plugs and reconnect the ignition system and fuel injectors.

## 3 Timing belt –
removal and refitting

**Note:** *Before starting this procedure, it is recommended that a sprocket locking tool is obtained (the Volvo tool is 999 5714, but aftermarket alternatives are available), to hold the camshaft sprockets against the tension of the valve springs when the timing belt is removed. However, provided that a simpler sprocket-holding tool (described in Section 4) can be made up, and an assistant is available to hold it, the special sprocket locking tool should not be necessary. An assistant will also be required to help move the engine on its mountings, as there is insufficient clearance to remove several of the bolts (especially those for the engine right-hand mounting). An engine support bar or hoist is recommended also, as the engine must be raised/lowered on its remaining mountings at various points in this procedure.*

### Removal

1 Disconnect the battery negative lead (see *Disconnecting the battery*), and remove the engine top cover panel, which is secured by a total of six bolts, with a rubber washer fitted beneath each one **(see illustration)**.

2 Disconnect the engine speed sensor wiring plug clipped to the timing belt upper cover, towards the rear **(see illustration)**. Release the wiring harness from the inlet manifold bracket, and move it to one side.

**3.1 Removing the engine top cover**

**3.2 Disconnecting the engine speed sensor wiring plug**

3.4a Undo the four bolts (this one hidden behind the power steering pump pulley) . . .

3.4b . . . and remove the timing belt upper cover

3 Remove the auxiliary drivebelts as described in Chapter 1.

4 Undo the four bolts and remove the timing belt upper cover **(see illustrations)**.

5 The alternator drivebelt tensioner and its

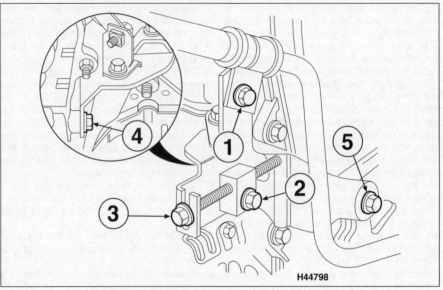

3.5a Removing the alternator drivebelt adjuster bracket – suggested order of dismantling

mounting bracket must now be unbolted from the engine. First, remove the bolt securing the power steering fluid hose at the top of the bracket, then loosen the adjuster locking bolt and unhook the adjuster bolt itself. The bracket is now held by two further bolts at the rear and side of the engine – the rear one comes out easily, but the side one is hard to reach (access from below only), very tight, and will not come right out even when loose, as there's insufficient clearance. Leave the

side bolt loosely in place, then it, and the bracket, can be removed later when the engine mounting has been taken off **(see illustrations)**.

6 If not already done, release the fasteners securing the wheel arch liner, and fold back the liner for access to the crankshaft pulley. It's preferable to remove the liner completely, which also means removing the front section of the engine undershield **(see illustration)**.

7 The crankshaft pulley must now be held stationary while its centre retaining nut is slackened. If the Volvo holding tool 999 5705 cannot be obtained, it will be necessary to fabricate a home-made alternative. This will be essentially the same as the camshaft sprocket holding tool described in Section 4, securely engaged in the pulley spokes. Alternatively, remove the starter motor as described in Chapter 5A, and jam the flywheel ring gear to prevent the engine turning. Undo the pulley centre retaining bolt using a socket and bar – make sure the car is securely supported, and that good-quality, close-fitting tools are used, as considerable force will be required. Lift the pulley off, together with the belt guard plate behind **(see illustrations)**.

3.5b Unbolt the power steering hose bracket . . .

3.5c . . . then unhook the adjuster bolt

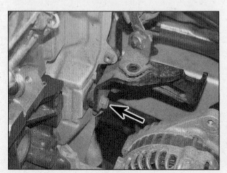

3.5d Alternator adjuster bracket rear bolt (arrowed)

3.6 Removing the wheel arch liner

3.7a Loosen the bolt using a home-made sprocket-holding tool . . .

3.7b . . . then remove the bolt, noting the washer fitted behind . . .

3.7c . . . take off the crankshaft pulley, noting how it fits on the Woodruff key . . .

3.7d . . . then slip off the belt guard plate

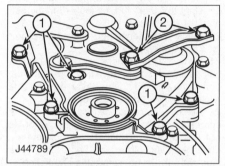

3.9a  Timing belt lower cover bolts (1) and power steering pump brace bolts (2)

3.9b  Loosening the power steering pump brace lower bolt

3.11a  Remove the five (or six) bolts . . .

*Later models have an additional lower cover bolt in the centre*

**8** Position an engine hoist (or an engine support bar across the engine compartment) and attach the jib to the engine right-hand lifting eyelet. Raise the lifting gear to take up the slack, so that it is just supporting the combined weight of the engine and transmission.

**9** Unbolt the brace between the power steering pump and the engine mounting bracket. Note that the bolt at the lower end of the brace is one of the engine mounting bracket bolts, and again, it cannot be removed at this stage, due to lack of clearance between the engine and inner wing **(see illustrations)**.

**10** Unbolt the coolant pipe support bracket from the underside of the inner wing – once the pipe is free to move, this allows extra clearance for removing several of the components.

**11** Undo the five bolts securing the timing belt lower cover (later models have six bolts in total). Pull the timing belt lower cover downwards, unclip the wiring harness, and remove the cover **(see illustrations)**.

**12** Both parts of the engine right-hand mounting must now be removed from the inner wing and engine. Before starting, make sure that the weight of the engine is fully and safely supported. First, remove the two bolts securing the power steering fluid reservoir to the inner wing, and move it to one side without disconnecting the hoses **(see illustration)**.

**13** Remove the nut from the (horizontal) through-bolt on the upper section of the engine mounting, then raise the engine slightly. Remove the two nuts, and the bolt in between, from the inner side of the upper

3.11b . . . and pull down the timing belt lower cover

3.13a  Undo the nut on the engine mounting through-bolt . . .

section of mounting, then tap out the through-bolt and lift off the mounting **(see illustrations)**.

**14** The remaining two bolts securing the lower section of the engine mounting can now

3.12  Unbolt the power steering fluid reservoir, and move it clear

3.13b . . . then remove the remaining nuts and bolts, and lift off the upper section

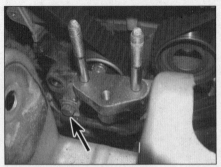

**3.14 This small bolt (arrowed) secures a power steering pipe bracket to the engine mounting lower section**

**3.15 Lift out the lower section of the engine right-hand mounting**

be loosened. Note that there is a further small bolt used for a power steering pipe bracket – this must also be removed **(see illustration)**.

**15** At this stage, the various bolts which could not previously be removed have to come out. It will be necessary to experiment with raising and lowering the engine on its remaining mountings until sufficient clearance can be gained. The following advice is based on our experience in the workshop:

a) To remove the side bolt for the alternator adjuster bracket, raise the engine, then have an assistant push the engine rearwards.

b) To remove the two most-difficult engine mounting bracket bolts, lower the engine, then have an assistant pull (or push) the engine sideways to increase the clearance between the engine and inner wing. With the two bolts removed, the lower section

of the engine mounting can be removed **(see illustration)**.

**16** Before removing the timing belt, if the same belt is going to be refitted (only advisable if the belt is known to be nearly new), Volvo recommend marking the belt's fitted position on the camshaft sprockets, and refitting it in the same place. Also mark the belt's running direction.

**17** To turn the engine so the timing marks can be aligned, temporarily refit the crankshaft pulley bolt, and use a spanner on the bolt to turn the engine in its normal direction (clockwise, seen from the timing belt end of the engine).

**18** There are alignment marks on both the camshaft sprockets, which correspond with marks on the cylinder head. On the crankshaft toothed sprocket, there are two markings – a dot punched in the front face, and an

arrowhead on a plate behind the sprocket – which should both align at the 12 o'clock position with a raised mark on the oil pump **(see illustrations)**.

**19** Before removing the timing belt from the sprockets, Volvo dealers use a small special tool (999 5714) with side ribs which locate into the camshaft sprockets, locking them together in the TDC position **(see illustration)**. If this tool is not used, when the belt is removed, the camshaft sprockets will spring towards each other, under pressure from the valve springs. The sprocket alignment can be reset to the marks as the new belt is fitted, but a spanner and sprocket-holding tool will be needed, with help from an assistant to either hold the tools or fit the belt onto the sprockets.

**20** Slacken the tensioner pulley centre bolt **(see illustration)**.

**21** Remove the two bolts securing the timing belt tensioner, and remove it from the engine, noting how it fits to the lever arm for the tensioner pulley **(see illustration)**.

**22** Remove the timing belt carefully from the sprockets, so that (if the Volvo special tool is not used) the camshaft sprockets are disturbed as little as possible **(see illustration)**. Do not rotate the crankshaft or camshafts more than a few degrees with the belt removed, as there is the risk of piston-to-valve contact.

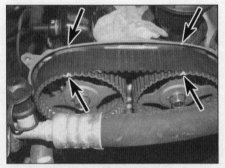

**3.18a Align the camshaft sprocket markings (arrowed) . . .**

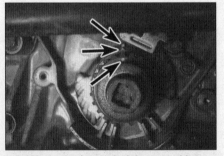

**3.18b . . . and a total of three markings (arrowed) on the crankshaft sprocket and oil pump housing**

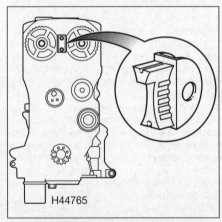

H44765

**3.19 Volvo tool 999 5714 used to lock together the camshaft sprockets**

**3.20 Slacken the tensioner pulley centre bolt**

**3.21 Removing the timing belt tensioner**

**3.22 Removing the timing belt**

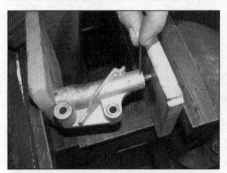

**3.27a Mount the tensioner in a vice, and slowly compress the plunger . . .**

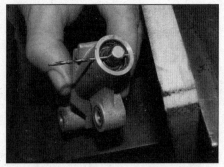

**3.27b . . . until a 2 mm twist drill fits through the outer body and plunger**

**23** Spin the tensioner and idler pulleys, and check for roughness or shake; renew if necessary. Check that the tensioner pulley arm is free to move up-and-down under the action of the tensioner. If the arm is at all stiff, remove the unit, clean it thoroughly, then lubricate sparingly and refit. It is considered good practice to renew the belt pulleys along with the timing belt – to this end, Volvo dealers (and some motor factors) now sell timing belt 'kits', containing all the relevant parts.

**24** Check the timing belt carefully for any signs of uneven wear, splitting, or oil contamination. Pay particular attention to the roots of the teeth. Renew the belt if there is the slightest doubt about its condition. If the engine is undergoing an overhaul, and has covered more than 36 000 miles (60 000 km) with the existing belt fitted, renew the belt as a matter of course, regardless of its apparent condition. The cost of a new belt is negligible when compared to the cost of engine repairs, should the belt break in service. If signs of oil contamination are found, trace the source of the oil leak, and rectify it. Wash down the engine timing belt area and all related components, to remove all traces of oil.

**25** Renew the tensioner assembly if there are signs of oil leaks, if there is no resistance to compression of the plunger, or if the plunger cannot be compressed. With no pressure applied, the plunger should protrude from the tensioner body by approximately 11 mm.

### Refitting and tensioning

**26** Prior to refitting the timing belt, it will be necessary to compress and lock the tensioner plunger, before the tensioner assembly is refitted to the engine. To do this, mount the assembly in a vice with protected jaws; the jaws in contact with the tensioner body and the plunger.

**27** Tighten the vice until resistance is felt, then tighten it very slowly a little further. Pause for a few seconds and tighten slowly a little further again. Continue this procedure until the hole in the tensioner body and corresponding hole in the plunger are aligned. It will probably take about five minutes to do this; don't rush it, or the internal seals will be damaged by trying to force oil between the internal chambers too quickly. When the two holes are finally aligned, insert length of metal rod (a 2 mm drill bit is ideal) through all the holes to lock the assembly **(see illustrations)**.

**28** Clean the mating surfaces, then refit the locked tensioner to the engine, and secure with the two bolts tightened to the specified torque.

**29** Before refitting the timing belt, make sure that the camshaft sprockets are aligned in their correct positions (see paragraph 17) – if the Volvo special locking tool is available, fit it now. The crankshaft sprocket should still be aligned with the 12 o'clock mark on the oil pump. However, before the belt is fitted, turn the crankshaft sprocket anti-clockwise (backwards) by half a tooth – this seems an unusual instruction, but is precisely what's advised by Volvo, and we followed their method without encountering any problems.

**30** Slip the belt over the crankshaft sprocket, keep it taut, and feed it over the coolant pump sprocket, idler pulley, front camshaft sprocket, rear camshaft sprocket, and finally over the tensioner pulley **(see illustration)**. Observe the correct running direction if the old belt is being re-used. If the sprocket-locking tool is not used, the front camshaft sprocket must first be held with a spanner (turning the sprocket clockwise against the spring tension) so its timing marks align as the belt is fitted. A sprocket-holding tool will then be needed to push the rear sprocket backwards (anti-clockwise) to align its markings for the belt to be fitted.

**31** Before proceeding with setting the belt tension, check that all the alignment markings appear to be in line, then (if used) remove the locking tool from the camshaft sprockets. As a further (rough) guide, if the belt appears to be 'bulging' upwards significantly between the two camshaft sprockets, something may be wrong.

**32** Press down on the tensioner pulley's lever arm (turn anti-clockwise) so that it just contacts the end of the (still locked) tensioner. Hold the arm in this position, and tighten the tensioner pulley centre bolt to the specified torque.

**33** Recheck the alignment of the sprocket marks, then turn the engine approximately a quarter-turn (90°) anti-clockwise.

**34** Slacken the tensioner pulley centre bolt, then using a suitable pair of circlip pliers in the holes in the front of the pulley, turn the pulley anti-clockwise to take up the slack in the belt (make sure the belt is fully seated on all the sprockets) **(see illustration)**. This is an operation which requires a certain amount of 'feel' – the belt shouldn't be ridiculously-tight

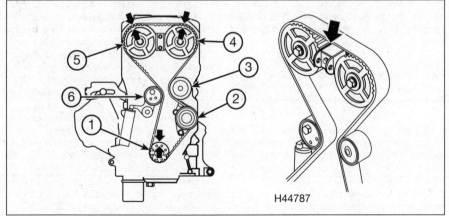

**3.30 Timing belt fitting details – timing marks, order of fitting, and Volvo special tool (arrowed)**

1  Crankshaft sprocket
2  Coolant pump
3  Idler pulley
4  Exhaust camshaft sprocket
5  Inlet camshaft sprocket
6  Tensioner pulley

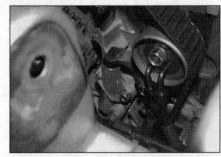

**3.34 Use a pair of circlip pliers to turn the pulley, then hold in position and tighten the centre bolt**

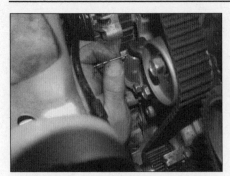

**3.36 Remove the locking pin from the tensioner**

at this point, just not loose. When the tensioner is released, the belt tension is self-setting to a large extent – the trick here is to give the tensioner less work to do, by removing the excess slack. Retighten the pulley centre bolt to the specified torque on completion, ensuring that the pulley does not turn as this is done.

**35** Turn the engine clockwise through two complete turns, and check that the alignment markings come back into line.

**36** Remove the locking pin from the tensioner – this should slide out quite easily **(see illustration)**.

**37** Turn the engine clockwise a further two turns clockwise, then leave in this position for approximately two minutes.

**38** Try and refit the locking pin to the tensioner. Ideally, it should slip into position quite easily. If not, there is no problem, providing the tensioner pushrod is only

**TOOL TiP**

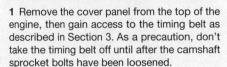

*To make a camshaft sprocket holding tool, obtain two lengths of steel strip about 6 mm thick by 30 mm wide or similar, one 600 mm long, the other 200 mm long (all dimensions approximate). Bolt the two strips together to form a forked end, leaving the bolt slack so that the shorter strip can pivot freely. At the end of each 'prong' of the fork, bend the strips through 90° about 50 mm from their ends to act as the fulcrums; these will engage with the holes in the sprockets. It may be necessary to grind or cut off their sides slightly to allow them to fit the sprocket holes.*

protruding from the tensioner body by approximately 4 mm. If this is not the case, the locking pin should be refitted (have an assistant press down on the tensioner pulley's lever arm), and the procedure in paragraphs 33 and 34 repeated.

**39** Refit the engine mounting bracket to the engine, referring to Section 11 if necessary. Bear in mind that, as noted during removal, two of the bracket bolts will not fit easily, and some manipulation of the engine will be needed. Tighten the bolts to the specified torque – if possible – space limitations may prohibit the use of a torque wrench.

**40** Loosely fit the upper section of the engine mounting into place, then adjust the height of the engine until the mounting is sufficiently lined up to refit all the nuts/bolts, and the through-bolt. Refit the upper section of the mounting with reference to Section 11, and tighten all the fasteners to the specified torque.

**41** Refit the timing belt lower cover, and refit the coolant pipe bracket to the inner wing, where applicable.

**42** Fit the timing belt guard plate before refitting the crankshaft pulley. Lightly oil the bolt threads and under the bolt head, and stop the engine turning as per removal, while the pulley bolt is tightened. Volvo do not state that a new bolt is required, but obviously, if the old bolt's condition is in any way suspect, using a new one is advisable. Tighten the bolt to the specified torque, again ensuring that the car is securely supported, and that only good-quality tools are used.

**43** Refit the alternator drivebelt adjuster bracket using a reversal of the removal procedure, then refit the timing belt upper cover. Fit and tension the alternator and power steering drivebelts as described in Chapter 1.

**44** Refit the roadwheel and lower the car to the ground. Tighten the wheel nuts in a diagonal sequence to the specified torque.

**45** Refit the power steering fluid reservoir, and reconnect the engine speed sensor, ensuring that the wiring is correctly routed.

**46** On completion, reconnect the battery negative lead, and refit the engine top cover panel.

### 4 Camshaft right-hand oil seals – renewal

**1** Remove the cover panel from the top of the engine, then gain access to the timing belt as described in Section 3. As a precaution, don't take the timing belt off until after the camshaft sprocket bolts have been loosened.

**2** To hold the camshaft sprockets and stop them turning while their bolts are being loosened, obtain Volvo tool 999 5199, or fabricate a home-made alternative **(see Tool Tip)**.

**3** Loosen and remove the camshaft sprocket bolts, then remove the sprockets. The

sprockets are pegged in position on their respective camshafts, and it should not be possible to mix them up – mark them if necessary. The inlet camshaft is the rear one.

**4** Carefully extract the seal by prising it out with a small screwdriver or hooked tool. Take great care to avoid damaging the shaft sealing face.

**HAYNES HiNT** *Sometimes, a seal can be loosened by pushing it in on one side – this tilts the seal outwards on the opposite side, and it can then be gripped with pliers and removed.*

**5** Clean the seal seat. Examine the shaft sealing face for wear or damage which could cause premature failure of the new seal.

**6** Lubricate the new oil seal with clean engine oil. Fit the seal over the shaft, lips inwards, and tap it home with a large socket or piece of tube until its outer face is flush with the housing.

**7** Refit the camshaft sprockets, locating them over the pegs on the ends of the camshafts and aligning the timing marks. Secure each sprocket with its bolt, done up hand-tight so that the sprocket is firmly in position, to take the timing belt.

**8** Refit the timing belt over the sprockets as described in Section 3. Before tensioning the belt, tighten the camshaft sprocket bolts to the specified torque, preventing the camshafts from turning as per removal.

**9** Complete the timing belt refitting and tensioning procedure described in Section 3.

### 5 Camshafts and tappets – removal, inspection and refitting

#### Removal

**1** With reference to Chapter 1, drain the cooling system and remove the spark plugs.

**2** Depressurise the fuel system as described in Chapter 4B, then disconnect the battery negative lead (see *Disconnecting the battery*).

**3** Remove the inlet manifold, fuel pump and camshaft position sensor housing from the cylinder head, as described in Chapter 4B.

**4** Remove the camshaft sprockets as described in Section 4, paragraphs 1 to 3.

**5** Disconnect the crankcase breather hose from the rear of the camshaft cover.

**6** The camshaft cover (or two separate covers, on some models) must now be removed. Work around the cover(s) removing the bolts, noting that at least one is also used to secure a wiring plug bracket. Lift off the cover(s), and recover the gasket(s).

**7** Remove the two retaining plates fitted at the timing belt end of the head, which are used to secure the timing belt upper cover, and act as additional braces for the cylinder head upper section.

**8** The upper section of the cylinder head is secured by a total of thirty-two bolts. It is essential that these are unscrewed progressively, as the upper section is effectively the camshaft bearing cap, and it must not be allowed to distort. Although not stipulated by Volvo, it might be wise to refer to the refitting part of this section, and work in the reverse order of the bolt tightening sequence, loosening each bolt by no more than a quarter-turn at a time until they are all fully loose.

**9** Remove the bolts, noting their locations as they are of different size and design. On some models, a stud is fitted, which can be unscrewed once the upper section has been removed, by fitting two nuts, tightening them against each other, and using a spanner on the lower one.

**10** Lift off the cylinder head upper section carefully, and recover the rubber gasket fitted down the centre of the head. A new gasket should be fitted when reassembling. If the upper section is stuck (unlikely, as pressure from the valve springs will tend to lift it), avoid prising it up if at all possible – to loosen it, first try tapping it from the sides, using a wooden or rubber mallet.

**11** Note the fitted positions of the locating pegs for the camshaft sprockets – this is essential to locating the camshafts in the correct position when refitting. Suitably mark the camshafts – inlet and exhaust – and lift them out complete with the oil seals. Be careful of the lobes, as they may have sharp edges.

**12** Remove the oil seals from the camshafts. Obtain new seals for reassembly.

**13** Have ready a suitable box divided into sixteen segments, or some containers or other means of storing and identifying the hydraulic tappets and rockers after removal. The box or containers must be oil-tight, and deep enough to allow the tappets to be almost totally submerged in oil. Mark the segments in the box or the containers with the cylinder number for each tappet, together with identification for its position in the cylinder head (ie, inlet front/inlet rear, exhaust front/exhaust rear).

**14** Working on each valve in turn, lift off the rocker, then lift out the tappet, using a suction cup if necessary (Volvo state that a magnet should **not** be used). Keep them identified for position, and place them upright in their respective positions in the box or containers. Once all the tappets have been removed, add clean engine oil to the box or container so that the oil hole in the side of the tappet is submerged.

**15** If required, the cylinder head can now be completely stripped, and the valve components removed (refer to Chapter 2C).

## Inspection

**16** Inspect the cam lobes and the camshaft bearing journals for scoring or other visible evidence of wear. Once the surface hardening of the cam lobes has been eroded, wear will occur at an accelerated rate. **Note:** *If these symptoms are visible on the tips of the camshaft lobes, check the corresponding rocker, as it will probably be worn as well.*

**17** No specific bearing journal diameters or running clearances are specified by Volvo for the camshafts or journals. However, if there is a visual deterioration, then component renewal will be necessary.

**18** Inspect the rockers and tappets for scuffing, cracking or other damage; measure the tappet diameter in several places with a micrometer. Renew the rockers and tappets as a set if they are damaged or worn – if new camshafts are being fitted, it makes sense to fit a full set of new components anyway. Note that new tappets come prefilled with special fluid, so immersion in an oil bath prior to fitting is not necessary.

## Preparation for refitting

**19** Thoroughly clean the sealant from the mating surfaces of the upper and lower cylinder head sections. Use a suitable liquid gasket dissolving agent, together with a soft putty knife; do not use a metal scraper, or the faces will be damaged. As there is no conventional gasket used, the cleanliness of the mating faces is of the utmost importance.

**20** Clean off any oil, dirt or grease from both cylinder head sections, and dry with a clean, lint-free cloth. Ensure that all the oilways are completely clean. Similarly, clean off both camshafts, and the rockers – it is vital that no dirt is introduced as the cylinder head is being reassembled.

**21** To avoid any possibility of piston-to-valve contact as the upper section is bolted down, turn the crankshaft sprocket approximately one quarter-turn anti-clockwise, to move the pistons down the bores.

## Refitting

**22** Commence refitting by oiling the tappet bores and the camshaft bearings in the cylinder head lower section with clean engine oil. Do not apply too much, or it will have to be cleaned off before the sealant is applied to the grooves in the lower section.

**23** Insert the tappets into their original bores, then place the rockers onto their original valves and tappets (unless new parts are being fitted).

**24** Lubricate the camshafts, then place them in position. Set the camshaft sprocket locating pegs as noted prior to removal **(see illustration)**. As further identification, the exhaust camshaft (fitted at the front of the engine) has a threaded hole facing the flywheel end of the engine, to take the camshaft position sensor.

**25** Ensure that the mating faces of both cylinder head sections are clean, and free of any oil or grease.

**26** Referring to the accompanying

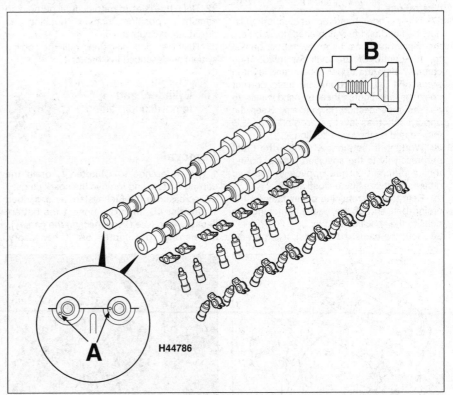

**5.24 Camshaft and tappet refitting details**

A  *Camshaft sprocket locating pegs in correct position*

B  *Threaded hole in exhaust camshaft*

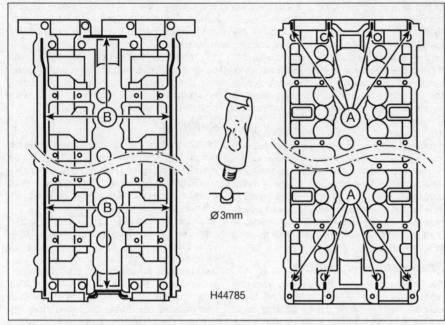

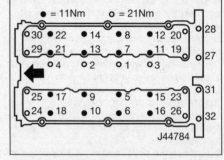

**5.28 Cylinder head upper section bolt tightening sequence (timing belt end arrowed)**

**5.26 Application points for Volvo sealant on cylinder head upper (A) and lower (B) sections**

illustration, apply a continuous 3 mm bead of Volvo sealant (part number 1161231) to the grooves in the lower section of the cylinder head. Also apply a small amount of sealant to the positions shown on the upper section **(see illustration)**.

**27** The cylinder head upper section must now be fitted and fully tightened down before the sealant hardens. Fit a new rubber gasket to the centre of the cylinder head, then carefully align the upper section and lay it in place. Fit all the bolts in their correct positions, and tighten them by hand initially to pull the upper section down evenly. Keep the upper section as level as possible until it is fully seated on the lower section.

**28** Working in sequence, tighten the bolts progressively to the specified torque, noting that a different torque applies to the two different bolt sizes **(see illustration)**.

**29** Refit the two retaining plates fitted at the timing belt end of the head, tightening the bolts to the specified torque.

**30** Refit the camshaft cover(s), using a new

gasket (or gaskets), and tighten the bolts from the middle outwards. Refit the crankcase breather hose and the wiring plug bracket.

**31** Fit new camshaft oil seals as described in Section 4.

**32** Refit the inlet manifold, fuel pump and camshaft position sensor housing as described in Chapter 4B.

**33** Refit the spark plugs and refill the cooling system as described in Chapter 1.

## 6 Cylinder head – removal and refitting

### Removal

**1** With reference to Chapter 1, drain the cooling system and remove the spark plugs.

**2** Depressurise the fuel system as described in Chapter 4B, then disconnect the battery negative lead (see *Disconnecting the battery*).

**3** Referring to Chapter 5A if necessary,

remove the battery and battery tray (this isn't absolutely essential, but it does provide greater working room).

**4** Referring to Chapter 4B if necessary, remove the air cleaner and air inlet duct.

**5** Noting carefully how it is clipped in place and routed, work around the top of the engine and disconnect all the relevant wiring from it. In particular, there are several earth points to disconnect **(see illustrations)**. Move the wiring harness to one side.

**6** Place some absorbent rags or paper towel around and under the fuel supply and return connections to the fuel pump (at the transmission end of the head). Carefully remove the fuel pipes, including the small hose to the charcoal canister.

**7** Loosen the hose clamps for the radiator top and bottom hoses on the front of the engine, and for the heater hoses at the rear of the engine compartment. Anticipating some spillage of residual coolant, carefully disconnect the hoses, noting that some manipulation might be needed to break the seal at each connection.

**8** Remove the inlet manifold as described in Chapter 4B.

**9** Using the information in Chapter 10, unbolt the power steering pump from the engine, and move it to one side without disconnecting the hoses.

**10** Remove the timing belt as described in Section 3.

**11** Remove the three bolts securing the thermostat housing to the cylinder head, and tap the housing to release it **(see illustration)**.

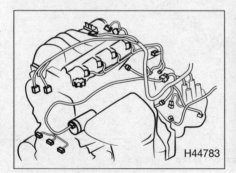

**6.5a Wiring harness layout around the cylinder head**

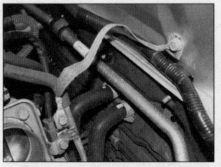

**6.5b Earth strap attached to throttle housing**

**6.11 Thermostat housing bolts (arrowed)**

Using a twisting motion, detach the housing from the engine coolant pipe, and recover the sealing O-ring (a new one will be needed when refitting). Remove the engine coolant pipe retaining bolt at the rear of the cylinder head.

**12** Under the front of the car, unscrew and remove the three nuts securing the exhaust downpipe to the manifold. If the nuts are in poor condition, obtain some new ones for reassembly.

**13** Disconnect the crankcase breather hose from the rear of the camshaft cover, and unbolt the wiring plug support bracket. Unbolt and remove the cover(s), and recover the gasket(s).

**14** If the cylinder head is to be completely stripped (such as to service the valve components), it would be preferable to first remove the cylinder head upper section, camshafts, rockers and tappets, as described in Section 5. To remove the cylinder head complete (such as to renew the head gasket), proceed as follows.

**15** Using the reverse sequence to that shown later in the refitting part of this section, gradually loosen the ten cylinder head bolts. Do not confuse the head bolts with the smaller ones used to secure the upper section to the lower section. Loosen the head bolts by no more than a quarter-turn each at a time, in sequence, until they are all loose.

**16** Remove the head bolts and washers, using a magnet if necessary (the bolts are quite recessed).

**17** Release the head by tapping it lightly on the sides with a wooden or rubber mallet. The head is located on two dowels, so it will not move much as this is done.

**18** Lift off the cylinder head, and set it down on wooden blocks to avoid damage to protruding valves. Recover the old head gasket and the two locating dowels. If the cylinder head is to be dismantled for overhaul, refer to Section 5 (if not already done) and to Part C of this Chapter.

### Preparation for refitting

**19** The mating faces of the cylinder head and cylinder block must be perfectly clean before refitting the head. Use a soft putty knife to remove all traces of gasket and carbon; also clean the piston crowns. Take particular care during the cleaning operations, as aluminium alloy is easily damaged.

**20** Make sure that the carbon is not allowed to enter the oil and water passages – this is particularly important for the lubrication system, as carbon could block the oil supply to the engine's components. Using adhesive tape and paper, seal the water, oil and bolt holes in the cylinder block.

**21** To prevent carbon entering the gap between the pistons and bores, smear a little grease in the gap. After cleaning each piston, use a small brush to remove all traces of grease and carbon from the gap, then wipe away the remainder with a clean rag. Clean all the pistons in the same way.

**22** Check the mating surfaces of the cylinder block and the cylinder head for nicks, deep scratches and other damage. If slight, they may be removed carefully with a file, but if excessive, machining may be the only alternative to renewal.

**23** If warpage of the cylinder head gasket surface is suspected, use a straight-edge to check it for distortion. Refer to the overhaul information given in Part C of this Chapter if necessary.

**24** Check the condition of the cylinder head bolts, if they are to be re-used. Ideally, a new set of bolts should be obtained, but the old ones can be refitted, provided there's no damage to the threads, and that the bolt length (measured from the underside of the bolt head, without washer) is not longer than specified. If there is any doubt about any one bolt, or if the bolts are known to have been re-used more than once, buying a new set is advisable.

**25** If possible, run the correct-size tap down the bolt holes, to make sure they're clean. This is particularly important if the threads of any of the old bolts appear damaged.

### Refitting

**26** To avoid any possibility of piston-to-valve contact as the cylinder head is bolted down, turn the crankshaft sprocket approximately one quarter-turn anti-clockwise, to move the pistons down the bores.

**27** Commence refitting by inserting the two dowels into the block top surface, in the locations at opposite corners.

**28** Place a new head gasket on the cylinder block, locating it over the two dowels. Make sure it is the right way up; the surface marked with the word TOP should face upwards.

**29** Check that the mating faces of the exhaust manifold and downpipe are clean. Place a new gasket on the exhaust downpipe flange.

**30** Place the cylinder head into position, locating it over the two dowels. Keep the head square to the block surface at this point, or it may jam on the dowels (they are a precision fit). Also check that the exhaust manifold-to-downpipe studs fit through the holes in the downpipe gasket.

**31** Lightly oil the bolts and washers, and fit the washer so that the bevelled edge on the washer faces upwards. Insert the bolts and washers as carefully into their locations as possible, and tighten them lightly by hand initially.

**32** Working in sequence, tighten all the head bolts to the Stage 1 torque, then use the reverse of the sequence to completely slacken all the bolts (Stage 2) **(see illustration)**. This process serves to initially compress the new gasket.

**33** Working again in the tightening sequence, tighten the bolts to the Stage 3 torque setting.

**34** Tighten the bolts further, working in the sequence, by turning each bolt through the number of degrees specified for Stage 4 – a process known as angle-tightening. Angle gauges are available from tool suppliers, which can be fitted between a socket/ extension and socket handle, to make the process more accurate. In practice, 90 degrees is a right-angle, and can be approximated by looking at the initial and final position of the socket handle, relative to the engine. Each turn should be completed in one smooth movement, if possible.

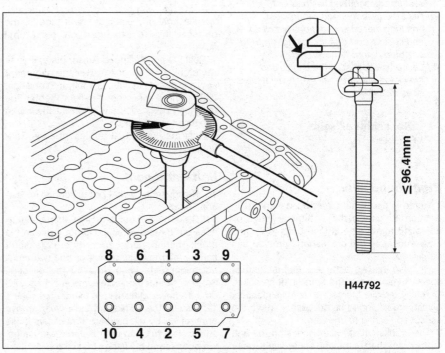

**6.32 Cylinder head refitting details – tightening sequence, head bolt length and washer fitment**

**35** Once all ten bolts have been tightened to Stage 4, the final stage is to go round once more in the tightening sequence, and tighten all ten bolts a further 90 degrees.

**36** If the cylinder head has been stripped, the upper section should now be refitted as described in Section 5.

**37** Refit the camshaft cover(s), using a new gasket (or gaskets), and tighten the bolts from the middle outwards. Refit the crankcase breather hose and the wiring plug bracket.

**38** Clean and dry the mating surfaces for the thermostat housing, then refit it as follows. Lubricate a new O-ring with neat antifreeze, and slide it onto the engine coolant pipe. Apply a 3 mm bead of sealant around the inside of the bolt holes on the housing mating surface, then fit the housing onto the coolant pipe and finally onto the cylinder head **(see illustration)**. Tighten the three mounting bolts to the specified torque.

**39** Using new nuts if necessary, refit the exhaust downpipe to the manifold, tightening the nuts to the specified torque.

**40** Further refitting is a reversal of removal, noting the following points:

a) *Refit the timing belt as described in Section 3.*
b) *Refit the power steering pump as described in Chapter 10.*
c) *Refit the inlet manifold and air cleaner/air inlet duct as described in Chapter 4B.*
d) *Securely refit the coolant hoses to the heater/engine, and the fuel hoses to the fuel pump.*
e) *If removed, refit the battery, with reference to Chapter 5A.*
f) *Refit the spark plugs and refill the cooling system as described in Chapter 1.*
g) *Refit the cylinder head wiring loom, ensuring that all connections are clean and secure, and that the wiring is routed as noted before removal.*
h) *On completion, start the engine and check for leaks from all joints which have been disturbed.*

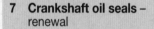

**7  Crankshaft oil seals –**
renewal

### *Right-hand seal*

**1** Remove the timing belt as described in Section 3. Lower the engine slightly, by adjusting the engine lifting equipment, until clear access to the crankshaft sprocket can be gained.

**2** Remove the two bolts securing the engine speed sensor above the crankshaft sprocket. Carefully remove the sensor from its location, unclipping its wiring as necessary. Move the sensor and wiring to one side.

**3** The crankshaft sprocket slides off the end of the crankshaft (it may be necessary to lever it off, working round it using a suitable screwdriver). As the sprocket is removed,

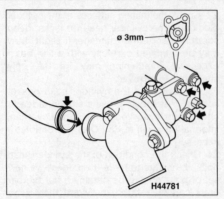

**6.38  Refitting the thermostat housing**

recover the alignment key if it is loose; also slide off the engine speed sensor plate.

**4** With the sprocket removed, carefully prise out the old oil seal. Do not damage the oil pump housing or the surface of the crankshaft. Alternatively, punch or drill two small holes opposite each other in the oil seal. Screw a self-tapping screw into each, and pull on the screws with pliers to extract the seal.

 *Sometimes, a seal can be loosened by pushing it in on one side – this tilts the seal outwards on the opposite side, and it can then be gripped with pliers and removed.*

**5** Clean the oil seal location and the crankshaft. Inspect the crankshaft for a wear groove or ridge left by the old seal.

**6** Lubricate the housing, the crankshaft and the new seal with oil (not grease). Fit the seal, lips inwards, and use a piece of tube (or the old seal, inverted) to tap it into place until flush.

**7** Refit the engine speed sensor plate, then fit the crankshaft sprocket over the alignment key, and ensure that it seats fully into position.

**8** Refit the engine speed sensor, tighten the mounting bolts securely, and refit the wiring into its retaining clips.

**9** Refit the timing belt as described in Section 3.

### *Left-hand seal*

**10** Remove the flywheel as described in Section 10.

**11** Clean the surrounding area, then carefully prise out the old oil seal. Do not damage the block mating surfaces or the crankshaft flange. Alternatively, punch or drill two small holes opposite each other in the oil seal. Screw a self-tapping screw into each, and pull on the screws with pliers to extract the seal.

**12** Inspect the crankshaft for a wear groove or ridge left by the old seal. If necessary, use emery cloth to clean up the crankshaft flange, wrapped round the flange (not in-and-out).

**13** Clean the oil seal location and the crankshaft – it's vital that there is no thread-

lock debris (from the flywheel bolts) or other dirt present, as this will result in leaks.

**14** Lubricate the housing, the crankshaft and the new seal – use clean engine oil, not grease. Fit the seal, lips inwards, and use a piece of tube (or the old seal, inverted) to tap it into place until flush. Make sure the seal is pressed in to a uniform depth all round, as this further reduces the chances of the new seal leaking.

**15** Refit the flywheel as described in Section 10.

**8  Oil pump –**
removal, inspection
and refitting

**Note:** *New copper washers should be obtained, to be fitted to the pump mounting bolts when refitting the pump. The washers are a revised fitment – early models may be found not to have any washers on dismantling.*

### *Removal*

**1** Remove the timing belt as described in Section 3. Lower the engine slightly, by adjusting the engine lifting equipment, until clear access to the crankshaft sprocket can be gained.

**2** Remove the two bolts securing the engine speed sensor above the crankshaft sprocket. Carefully remove the sensor and its backplate.

**3** The crankshaft sprocket slides off the end of the crankshaft (it may be necessary to lever it off, working round it using a suitable screwdriver). As the sprocket is removed, recover the alignment key if it is loose.

**4** Remove the screw securing the cover plate located at the rear of the engine, behind the timing belt tensioner assembly. Remove the cover plate.

**5** Remove the alternator as described in Chapter 5A.

**6** Disconnect the wiring for the oil pressure switch, which is located at the rear of the engine, next to the oil filter.

**7** Remove the sump as described in Section 9.

**8** Undo the five bolts securing the oil pump to the cylinder block – note the fitted position of each bolt, as only two are identical. Where applicable, recover the copper washers fitted to the bolts – new washers must be fitted on reassembly (regardless of whether washers were present on removal).

**9** Carefully withdraw the pump assembly by prising it free. Remove the pump.

**10** Thoroughly clean the pump and cylinder block mating faces, and remove all traces of old sealant.

### *Inspection*

**11** Remove the six screws which hold the gear cover to the pump body – an impact driver may well be required for this. Recover the gasket from the cover.

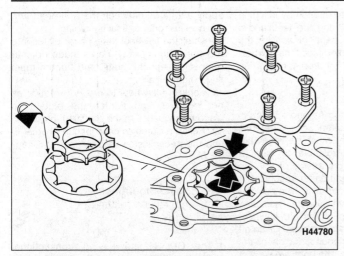

**8.19 Reassembling the oil pump – lubricate and align marks on gears**

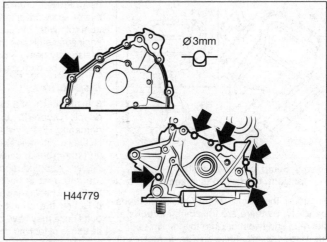

**8.21 Refitting the oil pump – apply sealant as shown, tighten bolts (arrowed)**

**12** Mark the oil pump gears in relation to each other, then remove them from the oil pump housing.

**13** Unscrew the plug which retains the pressure relief valve spring, taking care that the spring does not fly out as the plug is removed. Recover the piston from inside the valve bore.

**14** Prise out the crankshaft right-hand oil seal from the pump housing.

**15** Clean all components thoroughly, then inspect the gears, body and gear cover for signs of wear or damage.

**16** Renew the relief valve spring if it is weak or distorted. Also inspect the piston for scoring or other damage.

**17** Refit the gears to the pump body, aligning the markings made prior to removal. Using feeler blades, check the clearance between the large gear and the pump body. If the clearance is outside the specified limit, renew the pump.

**18** If the clearance is satisfactory, liberally lubricate the gears. Lubricate and fit the relief valve piston and spring, tightening the retaining plug to the specified torque.

**19** Fit a new gasket to the pump body, then fit the cover and secure with the six screws **(see illustration)**.

**20** Fit a new crankshaft right-hand oil seal to the oil pump – the seal lips should face inwards when the pump is fitted to the engine.

### Refitting

**21** Check once more that the mating surfaces of the oil pump and block and clean and dry. Referring to the accompanying illustration, apply a 3 mm diameter bead of sealant to the oil pump **(see illustration)**. The pump must then be fitted before the sealant has a chance to set.

**22** Lightly oil the nose of the crankshaft, to allow the pump and its oil seal to pass over it without damage.

**23** Refit the pump to the block, offering it squarely into place. Fit new copper washers

to the pump retaining bolts, then use the bolts as guides, and draw the pump into place with the crankshaft pulley bolt and sprocket. Take care not to damage the seal in the oil pump as it is fitted; also note that the crankshaft must not turn as the pump is being fitted. With the pump seated, tighten the retaining bolts diagonally to the specified torque.

**24** Refit the sump as described in Section 9, and reconnect the oil pressure switch wiring.

**25** Refit the alternator as described in Chapter 5A.

**26** Refit the cover plate located behind the timing belt tensioner assembly.

**27** Refit the engine speed sensor plate, then fit the crankshaft sprocket over the alignment key, and ensure that it seats fully into position.

**28** Refit the engine speed sensor, tighten the mounting bolts securely, and refit the wiring into its retaining clips.

**29** Refit the timing belt as described in Section 3.

### 9  Sump – removal and refitting

**1** The sump is in two parts – the main sump and a smaller lower pan **(see illustration)**. The

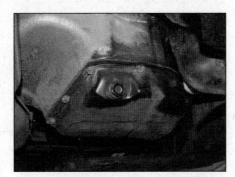

**9.1 View of engine from underneath, showing lower sump pan**

lower pan is removable separately, but this only necessary if a leak has been noted from that area of the sump – otherwise, the two sections can be removed in one piece.

**2** Drain the engine oil and remove the oil filter, using the information in Chapter 1 if necessary.

**3** Remove the exhaust downpipe as described in Chapter 4C. If only the lower pan is being removed, this may not be essential, though access will be easier with the downpipe removed.

### Lower pan

#### Removal

**4** Unscrew and remove the bolts securing the sump lower pan to the main sump.

**5** Use a sharp knife in the joint to cut through the bead of sealant which now holds the lower pan in place. Using a wide-bladed tool, carefully prise off the lower pan (if a screwdriver is used, take care not to deform the sealing edges of the pan).

**6** Clean the mating surfaces of the lower pan and main sump, removing all traces of oil and old sealant.

#### Refitting

**7** Apply a 4 mm bead of sealant to the lower pan, running it to the inside of the bolt holes. Do not apply too much, as excess sealant may end up in the engine oil, and partially block the oil pick-up in the sump.

**8** Offer the lower pan into position, then fit and tighten the bolts in a diagonal sequence to the specified torque **(see illustration)**. Clean away any excess sealant.

**9** Refit the exhaust downpipe (if removed) using the information in Chapter 4C.

**10** Fit a new oil filter, then refill the engine with oil as described in Chapter 1.

### Main sump

#### Removal

**11** Unscrew and remove all the bolts

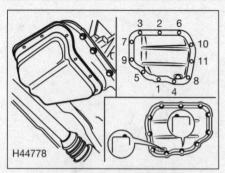

**9.8 Sump lower pan refitting – apply sealant, tighten bolts in sequence**

securing the sump, noting their positions carefully, as there are four long M8 bolts at the rear, and two more into the transmission.

**12** Use a sharp knife in the joint to cut through the bead of sealant which now holds the lower pan in place. Using a wide-bladed tool, carefully prise off the lower pan (if a screwdriver is used, take care not to deform the sealing edges). Note that the sump is located on two dowels.

**13** Recover the two dowels from the engine. Clean the mating surfaces of the sump and engine, removing all traces of oil and old sealant.

### Refitting

**14** Apply a 4 mm bead of sealant to the sump, running it to the inside of the bolt holes. Do not apply too much, as excess sealant may end up in the engine oil, and partially block the oil pick-up in the sump.

**15** Refit the two dowels to the engine.

**16** Offer the lower pan into position over the dowels. Starting at the transmission end, fit and tighten the bolts to the specified torque, noting the different torques applied to the different-size bolts. Clean away any excess sealant.

**17** Refit the exhaust downpipe using the information in Chapter 4C.

**18** Fit a new oil filter, then refill the engine with oil as described in Chapter 1.

### 10 Flywheel –
removal, inspection and refitting

### Removal

**1** Remove the transmission as described in Chapter 7A.

**2** Remove the clutch assembly as described in Chapter 6.

**3** The flywheel will only fit one way, but making alignment marks will allow the flywheel to be offered up in exactly the right position, making refitting quicker and easier. Various spacer plates are fitted either side of the flywheel, and it's important to note their order of fitting as the flywheel is removed.

**4** Unbolt the flywheel and remove it – the bolts will be tight, as thread-locking compound is

used. Prevent crankshaft rotation by inserting a large screwdriver in the ring gear teeth and in contact with an adjacent dowel in the engine/transmission mating face. The flywheel is also very heavy – do not drop it, or the ring gear may be damaged.

### Inspection

**5** If the flywheel's clutch mating surface is deeply scored, cracked or otherwise damaged, the flywheel must be renewed. However, it may be possible to have it surface-ground; seek the advice of a Volvo dealer or engine reconditioning specialist. If the ring gear is badly worn or has missing teeth, flywheel renewal will also be necessary.

**6** Check the condition of the old flywheel bolts once they have been removed. Clean off all traces of locking compound, and check the condition of the threads. The bolts are subject to very high loads in service, and are tightened to a high torque – re-using them may be dangerous, and it is recommended that new bolts are obtained.

**7** Do not remove the six bolts fitted around the outer edge of the flywheel – these are fitted at the factory, and act to balance the flywheel.

### Refitting

**8** Clean the mating surfaces of the flywheel and crankshaft. Remove any remaining locking compound from the threads of the crankshaft holes, using the correct-size tap, if available.

> **HAYNES HINT** *If a suitable tap is not available, cut two slots into the threads of one of the old flywheel bolts (assuming new bolts have been obtained) and use the bolt to remove the locking compound from the threads.*

**9** Volvo state that the flywheel bolts should be refitted with the underside of the bolt heads oiled, and the threads coated in locking fluid. Since it is obviously important not to mix oil and locking compound, this could prove difficult in practice. One solution might be to coat the bolt threads with locking compound as advised, fit the bolts finger-tight, then

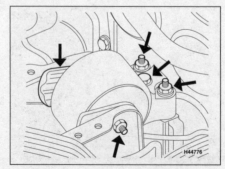

**11.9 Engine right-hand mounting removal details**

apply a little oil between the bolt head and flywheel just prior to final tightening.

**10** Offer the flywheel and spacer plates into position, aligning any marks made prior to removal. Insert the bolts, and tighten them finger-tight initially.

**11** Lock the flywheel to prevent rotation as per removal, and tighten the bolts in a diagonal sequence to the specified torque.

**12** Refit the clutch as described in Chapter 6, and the transmission as described in Chapter 7A.

### 11 Engine mountings –
removal and refitting

**1** The GDI engine has a conventional mounting either side, and a support member running centrally from front to rear under the engine, with a front and rear mounting attached. References to 'left' and 'right' are as seen from the driver's seat.

### Inspection

**2** If improved access is required, raise the front of the car and support it securely on axle stands.

**3** Check the rubber section of the relevant mounting to see if it is cracked, hardened or separated from the metal at any point; renew the mounting if any such damage or deterioration is evident.

**4** Check that all the mounting's fasteners are securely tightened; use a torque wrench to check if possible.

**5** Using a large screwdriver or a crowbar, check for wear in the mounting by carefully levering against it to check for free play. Where this is not possible, enlist the aid of an assistant to move the engine/transmission unit back-and-forth, or from side-to-side, while you watch the mounting. While some free play is to be expected even from new components, excessive wear should be obvious. If excessive free play is found, check first that the fasteners are correctly secured, then renew any worn components as described below.

### Renewal

#### Right-hand mounting

**6** Disconnect the battery negative lead (see *Disconnecting the battery*).

**7** Place a jack beneath the engine (but not under the sump), with a block of wood on the jack head. Raise the jack until it is supporting the weight of the engine. Alternatively, position a lifting beam across the engine compartment and attach the jib to the right-hand engine lifting eyelet, located on the side of the cylinder head.

**8** Slacken and remove the nut from the (horizontal) through-bolt securing the rubber mounting to the inner wing, then remove the through-bolt.

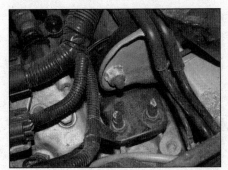

**11.14 Engine left-hand mounting with air cleaner removed**

**9** Raise the engine slightly, then slacken and remove the two nuts and single bolt securing the mounting to the engine bracket. Lift away the mounting, and remove it **(see illustration)**. If required, the engine bracket can also be removed – this is described in Section 3, as part of the timing belt removal procedure.

**10** Check carefully for signs of wear or damage on all components, and renew them where necessary.

**11** On reassembly, offer the mounting onto the engine bracket studs, and secure with the two nuts, followed by the single bolt, tightened to the specified torque.

**12** Adjust the height of the engine as necessary, then fit the through-bolt to secure the engine mounting to the inner wing bracket, fit the nut, but do not tighten it yet.

**13** Lower the engine lifting equipment or jack as applicable, until the weight of the engine is resting on the engine mounting. Rock the engine back-and-forth to settle the mounting, then tighten the through-bolt nut to the specified torque. Remove the lifting equipment or jack as applicable, then reconnect the battery negative lead.

### Left-hand mounting

**14** Referring to Chapter 4B, remove the complete air cleaner assembly and inlet ducts as necessary for clear access to the left-hand engine mounting, at the top of the transmission casing **(see illustration)**.

**15** Place a jack beneath the transmission, with a block of wood on the jack head. Raise

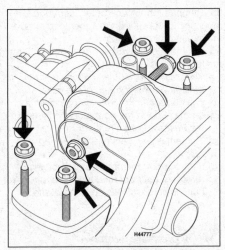

**11.17 Removing the engine left-hand mounting**

the jack until it is supporting the weight of the transmission. Take care to avoid damaging the gearshift mechanism. On some models it may be necessary to first remove the plastic cover panel from the underside of the transmission.

**16** Slacken and remove the through-bolt securing the rubber mounting to the vehicle body bracket.

**17** Slacken and remove the four nuts securing the left-hand mounting to the transmission bracket, then remove the mounting from the car **(see illustration)**.

**18** Check carefully for signs of wear or damage on all components, and renew them where necessary.

**19** Refit the engine mounting to the transmission bracket, tightening its mounting nuts to the specified torque.

**20** Position the mounting in the bodywork bracket, ensuring that the protective rubber flaps are correctly located between the sides of the mounting and the bodywork bracket, then insert the through-bolt and fit the retaining nut. Do not tighten it at this stage.

**21** Lower the jack, until the weight of the engine is resting on the engine mounting. Rock the engine back-and-forth to settle the mounting, then tighten the through-bolt nut to the specified torque.

**11.26 Engine front mounting through-bolt (arrowed)**

**22** Remove the jack from underneath the transmission, then refit the air cleaner and air ducting as described in Chapter 4B.

### Front mounting

**23** Providing the engine left- and right-hand mountings have not been removed (and are in good condition), the engine front and rear mountings can be removed without arranging additional engine support. Be prepared, however, for the engine to tilt slightly as the mountings are released – it may be necessary to have a jack ready under the car, to re-align the mountings when refitting.

**24** If not already done, firmly apply the handbrake, then jack up the front of the car and support it securely on axle stands.

**25** Remove the engine undershield for access to the support member.

**26** Slacken the nut and remove the through-bolt securing the front mounting to the support member **(see illustration)**.

**27** Remove the two bolts securing the support member to the car body, noting the fitted order of the spacers, plate, and rubbers **(see illustration)**.

**28** Remove the two bolts securing the mounting to the support member, and remove the mounting from the car.

**29** Refitting is a reversal of removal, noting the following points:

a) *The small square hole at the side of the mounting faces the front of the car (see illustration).*

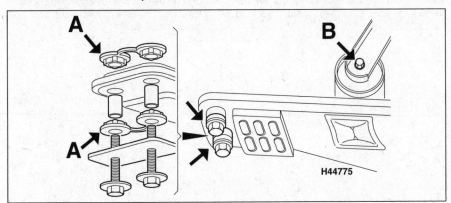

**11.27 Support member front bolts (A) and front mounting through-bolt (B)**

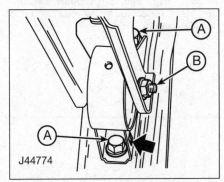

**11.29 Engine front mounting bolts (A) and through-bolt nut (B) – hole (arrowed) faces front**

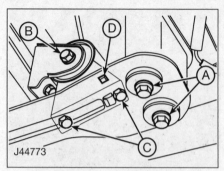

11.34 Engine rear mounting details

A *Support member rear bolts*
B *Mounting through-bolt*
C *Mounting bolts*
D *Square hole (faces rear)*

b) *The correct fitted order of components for the support member mountings must be preserved when refitting.*
c) *Tighten all fasteners to the specified torque.*
d) *If the support member was completely removed, the front mounting through-bolt nut should be fully tightened last when refitting.*

## Rear mounting

**30** Providing the engine left- and right-hand mountings have not been removed (and are in good condition), the engine front and rear mountings can be removed without arranging additional engine support. Be prepared, however, for the engine to tilt slightly as the mountings are released – it may be necessary to have a jack ready under the car, to re-align the mountings when refitting.
**31** If not already done, firmly apply the handbrake, then jack up the front of the car and support it securely on axle stands.
**32** Remove the engine undershield for access to the support member.
**33** Remove the two bolts securing the support member to the car body, noting the fitted order of the spacers, plate, and rubbers **(see illustration 11.27)**.
**34** Slacken the nut and remove the through-bolt securing the mounting to the support member, then pull the support member downwards for access to the mounting bolts **(see illustration)**.

**35** Remove the two bolts securing the mounting to the support member, and remove the mounting from the car.
**36** Refitting is a reversal of removal, noting the following points:
a) *The small square hole at the side of the mounting faces the rear of the car.*
b) *The correct fitted order of components for the support member mountings must be preserved when refitting.*
c) *Tighten all fasteners to the specified torque.*
d) *If the support member was completely removed, the front mounting through-bolt nut should be fully tightened last when refitting.*

## 12 Oil pressure switch – removal and refitting

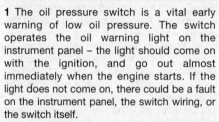

**1** The oil pressure switch is a vital early warning of low oil pressure. The switch operates the oil warning light on the instrument panel – the light should come on with the ignition, and go out almost immediately when the engine starts. If the light does not come on, there could be a fault on the instrument panel, the switch wiring, or the switch itself.
**2** If the light does not go out, low oil level, worn oil pump (or sump pick-up blocked), blocked oil filter, or worn main bearings could be to blame – or again, the switch may be faulty.
**3** If the light comes on while driving, the best advice is to turn the engine off immediately, and not to drive the car until the problem has been investigated – ignoring the light could mean expensive engine damage.

### Removal

**4** The oil pressure switch is located at the rear of the engine – access to it is easiest from below **(see illustration)**. Jack up the front of the car, and support it securely on axle stands (see *Jacking and vehicle support*).
**5** Remove the rear section of the undershield for access to the rear of the engine.
**6** Reach up behind the sump to the oil pressure switch, then disconnect the wiring from it.

12.4 Oil pressure switch (arrowed) at rear of engine – seen with inlet manifold removed

**7** Unscrew the switch using an open-ended spanner, and remove it. The switch may be quite tight, as thread-locking fluid is used to secure it. There should be no more than a few drops of oil lost as the switch is removed (provided the engine has been switched off for some time), since the switch is above the oil in the sump.

### Inspection

**8** Examine the switch for signs of cracking or splits. If the top part of the switch is loose, this is an early indication of impending failure.
**9** Check that the wiring terminals at the switch are not loose, then trace the wire from the switch connector until it enters the main loom – any wiring defects will give rise to apparent oil pressure problems.

### Refitting

**10** Refitting is a reversal of removal, noting the following points:
a) *If the original switch is being refitted, clean the switch threads thoroughly. Also check that the inner end of the switch is clean.*
b) *Apply a drop of thread-locking fluid to the switch threads, ensuring that the fluid does not block the inner end of the switch.*
c) *Tighten the switch to the specified torque.*
d) *Reconnect the wiring securely, ensuring that the wire is routed clear of any hot or moving components.*
e) *On completion, run the engine to check for correct switch operation, and also check for oil leaks.*

# Chapter 2 Part C:
# Engine removal and overhaul procedures

## Contents

## Degrees of difficulty

| Easy, suitable for novice with little experience |  | Fairly easy, suitable for beginner with some experience |  | Fairly difficult, suitable for competent DIY mechanic | | Difficult, suitable for experienced DIY mechanic | | Very difficult, suitable for expert DIY or professional | 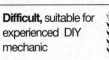 |
|---|---|---|---|---|---|---|---|---|---|

## Specifications

### Non-GDI engines

**Cylinder head**

Warp limit – maximum acceptable for use:
| | |
|---|---|
| Lengthways | 0.5 mm |
| Across | 0.2 mm |

Height:
| | |
|---|---|
| New | 128.95 to 129.05 mm |
| Maximum height reduction after machining | 0.3 mm |
| Cylinder head bolts maximum length | Less than 158.0 mm |

**Inlet valves**

| | |
|---|---|
| Head diameter | 30.85 to 31.15 mm |
| Stem diameter | 6.955 to 6.970 mm |
| Length | 104.05 to 104.45 mm |
| Valve seat angle | 44° 30' |

**Exhaust valves**

| | |
|---|---|
| Head diameter | 26.85 to 27.15 mm |

Stem diameter:
| | |
|---|---|
| Non-turbo engines | 6.955 to 6.97 mm |
| Turbo engines | 6.945 to 6.96 mm |

Length:
| | |
|---|---|
| Non-turbo engines | 103.10 to 103.50 mm |
| Turbo engines | 103.00 to 103.60 mm |
| Valve seat angle | 44° 30' |

**Valve seat inserts**

Diameter (standard):
| | |
|---|---|
| Inlet | 32.61 mm |
| Exhaust | 28.61 mm |
| Oversizes available | + 0.50 mm |
| Valve seat angle | 45° 00' |

**Valve guides**

| | |
|---|---|
| Valve stem-to-guide clearance | 0.03 to 0.05 mm |
| Fitted height above cylinder head | 12.8 to 13.2 mm |
| External oversizes available | 2 (marked by grooves) |

## Non-GDI engines (continued)

### Valve springs
External diameter ............................................... 27.70 to 28.10 mm
Length (unloaded) .............................................. 42.4 mm

### Cylinder bores
Diameter:
  B4184S, B4204S, B4204T engines:
    Nominal ................................................... 83.00 to 83.05 mm
    Wear limit ................................................ 0.10 mm
  B4164S, B4194T engines:
    Nominal ................................................... 81.00 to 81.05 mm
    Wear limit ................................................ 0.10 mm

### Pistons
Diameter (nominal):
  B4164S, B4194T ............................................ 80.98 to 81.01 mm
  B4184S, B4204S, B4204T .................................. 82.98 to 83.01 mm
Piston-to-bore clearance ...................................... 0.01 to 0.03 mm
Weight variation in same engine ............................. 10 g max
Gudgeon pin diameter, standard ............................ 22.996 to 23.000 mm

### Piston rings
Clearance in groove:
  Top compression ......................................... 0.050 to 0.085 mm
  Second compression ..................................... 0.030 to 0.065 mm
  Oil control ................................................ 0.020 to 0.055 mm
End gap (measured in cylinder):
  Top compression ......................................... 0.20 to 0.40 mm
  Second compression ..................................... 0.20 to 0.40 mm
  Oil control ................................................ 0.25 to 0.50 mm

### Crankshaft
Endfloat ......................................................... 0.19 mm max
Main bearing journal diameter:
  Standard .................................................. 64.984 to 65.003 mm
  Undersize ................................................. 64.750 mm
Main bearing running clearance .............................. 0.025 to 0.045 mm
Main bearing journal out-of-round ........................... 0.004 mm max
Main bearing journal taper ................................... 0.004 mm max
Big-end bearing journal diameter:
  Standard .................................................. 49.984 to 50.000 mm
  Undersize ................................................. 49.750 mm
Big-end bearing running clearance .......................... n/a
Big-end bearing out-of-round ................................ 0.004 mm max
Big-end rod bearing taper ................................... 0.004 mm max
Intermediate section M10 bolts maximum length ............ 118 mm

### Torque wrench settings

**Note**: *Refer to Chapter 2A for additional engine torque wrench settings.*

| | Nm | lbf ft |
|---|---|---|
| Big-end bearing cap bolts*: | | |
| Stage 1 ............................................... | 20 | 15 |
| Stage 2 ............................................... | Tighten through a further 90° | |
| Driveplate bolts: | | |
| Stage 1 ............................................... | 45 | 33 |
| Stage 2 ............................................... | Tighten through a further 65° | |
| Flywheel bolts: | | |
| Stage 1 ............................................... | 45 | 33 |
| Stage 2 ............................................... | Tighten through a further 65° | |
| Intermediate section to cylinder block**: | | |
| Stage 1 (M10 bolts only) ............................. | 20 | 15 |
| Stage 2 (M10 bolts only) ............................. | 45 | 33 |
| Stage 3 (M8 bolts only) .............................. | 24 | 18 |
| Stage 4 (M7 bolts only) .............................. | 17 | 13 |
| Stage 5 (M10 bolts only) ............................. | Tighten through a further 90° | |
| Oil pick-up pipe bolt ................................. | 17 | 13 |
| Sump bolts ........................................... | 17 | 13 |
| Transmission-to-engine bolts ......................... | 50 | 37 |

*  New bolts must always be used.
** M10 bolts should be renewed if their length exceeds 118 mm.

## GDI engine

### Cylinder head

| | |
|---|---|
| Warp limit (measured diagonally) | 0.05 mm |
| Cylinder head bolt maximum length | 96.4 mm |
| Valve spring minimum free length | 43.8 mm |

### Cylinder bores

| | |
|---|---|
| Diameter (nominal) | 81.00 to 81.03 mm |

### Pistons

| | |
|---|---|
| Diameter | n/a |
| Piston-to-bore clearance | 0.02 to 0.04 mm |
| Gudgeon pin diameter | 19.00 mm |

### Piston rings

| | |
|---|---|
| Clearance in groove: | |
| Top compression | 0.03 to 0.07 mm |
| Second compression | 0.02 to 0.06 mm |
| End gap (measured in cylinder): | |
| Top compression | 0.25 to 0.40 mm |
| Second compression | 0.40 to 0.55 mm |
| Oil control | 0.10 to 0.35 mm |

### Crankshaft

| | |
|---|---|
| Endfloat: | |
| Nominal | 0.05 to 0.25 mm |
| Maximum | 0.40 mm |
| Main bearing journal diameter | n/a |
| Main bearing running clearance: | |
| Nominal | 0.02 to 0.04 mm |
| Maximum | 0.1 mm |
| Main bearing bolts maximum length | 71.1 mm |
| Big-end bearing journal diameter | 45.000 to 44.980 mm |
| Big-end bearing running clearance: | |
| Nominal | 0.02 to 0.05 mm |
| Maximum | 0.1 mm |
| Big-end bearing out-of-round | 0.0025 mm max |
| Big-end bearing taper | 0.0050 mm max |
| Runout | 0.01 mm max |

## Torque wrench settings

**Note**: *Refer to Chapter 2B for additional engine torque wrench settings.*

| | Nm | lbf ft |
|---|---|---|
| Big-end bearing cap nuts: | | |
| Stage 1 | 20 | 15 |
| Stage 2 | Angle-tighten a further 95° | |
| Crankshaft oil seal carrier bolts | 11 | 8 |
| Engine oil dipstick tube mounting bolt | 13 | 10 |
| Main bearing ladder bolts (oiled)*: | | |
| Stage 1 | 25 | 18 |
| Stage 2 | Angle-tighten a further 90° | |
| Transmission-to-engine bolts | 48 | 35 |

* New bolts to be fitted if their length exceeds 71.1 mm.

### 1  General information

Included in this part of Chapter 2 are details of removing the engine/transmission from the car, and general overhaul procedures for the cylinder head, cylinder block and all other engine internal components.

The information ranges from advice concerning preparation for an overhaul and the purchase of new parts, to detailed step-by-step procedures covering removal, inspection, renovation and refitting of engine internal components.

After Section 7, all instructions are based on the assumption that the engine has been removed from the car. For information concerning engine in-car repair, as well as removal and installation of those external components necessary for full overhaul, refer to Part A or B of this Chapter, and to Section 5. Ignore any preliminary dismantling operations described in Part A or B that are no longer relevant once the engine has been removed from the car.

### 2  Engine/transmission removal – preparation and precautions

If you have decided that an engine must be removed for overhaul or major repair work, several preliminary steps should be taken.

Locating a suitable place to work is extremely important. Adequate work space, along with storage space for the car, will be needed. If a workshop or garage is not available, at the very least, a flat, level, clean work surface is required.

If possible, clear some shelving close to the work area and use it to store the engine components and ancillaries as they are removed and dismantled. In this manner the components stand a better chance of staying clean and undamaged during the overhaul. Laying out components in groups together with their fixing bolts, screws, etc, will save time and avoid confusion when the engine is refitted.

Clean the engine compartment and engine/transmission before beginning the removal procedure; this will help visibility and help to keep tools clean.

The help of an assistant should be available; there are certain instances when one person cannot safely perform all of the operations required to remove the engine from the car. Safety is of primary importance, considering the potential hazards involved in this kind of operation. A second person should always be in attendance to offer help in an emergency. If this is the first time you have removed an engine, advice and aid from someone more experienced would also be beneficial.

Plan the operation ahead of time. Before starting work, obtain (or arrange for the hire of) all of the tools and equipment you will need. Access to the following items will allow the task of removing and refitting the engine/transmission to be completed safely and with relative ease: an engine hoist – rated in excess of the combined weight of the engine/transmission, a heavy-duty trolley jack, complete sets of spanners and sockets as described at the rear this manual, wooden blocks, and plenty of rags and cleaning solvent for mopping-up spilled oil, coolant and fuel. A selection of different-sized plastic storage bins will also prove useful for keeping dismantled components grouped together. If any of the equipment must be hired, make sure that you arrange for it in advance, and perform all of the operations possible without it beforehand; this may save you time and money.

Plan on the car being out of use for quite a while, especially if you intend to carry out an engine overhaul. Read through the whole of this Section and work out a strategy based on your own experience and the tools, time and workspace available to you. Some of the overhaul processes may have to be carried out by a Volvo dealer or an engineering works – these establishments often have busy schedules, so it would be prudent to consult them before removing or dismantling the engine, to get an idea of the amount of time required to carry out the work.

When removing the engine from the car, be methodical about the disconnection of external components. Labelling cables and hoses as they removed will greatly assist the refitting process.

Always be extremely careful when lifting the engine/transmission assembly from the engine bay. Serious injury can result from careless actions. If help is required, it is better to wait until it is available rather than risk personal injury and/or damage to components by continuing alone. By planning ahead and taking your time, a job of this nature, although major, can be accomplished successfully and without incident.

On all models covered by this manual, the engine and transmission are removed as a complete assembly, upwards and out of the engine bay. The engine and transmission are then separated with the assembly on the bench.

**3 Engine and transmission (except GDI)** – removal, separation and refitting

### Removal

**1** Open the bonnet, then remove the stop bolts from both bonnet hinges to allow the bonnet to be raised to its fully extended (vertical) position. Alternatively, unbolt the bonnet from its hinges and remove it, as described in Chapter 11.

**2** Refer to Chapter 5A and remove the battery and its tray.

**3** Undo the securing screws and remove the cover panel from the top of the engine, then unclip the cover panel from the relay box.

**4** With reference to Chapter 4A, remove the air cleaner assembly and all air ducting, including the turbocharger/intercooler ducts (where applicable).

**5** With reference to Chapter 4C, Section 9, disconnect the oxygen sensor wiring at the connector at the rear of the engine compartment.

**6** Refer to Chapter 1 and carry out the following:
a) Drain the cooling system.
b) If the engine is going to be dismantled, drain the engine oil.
c) Remove the auxiliary drivebelt.

**7** If the car is fitted with cruise control, disconnect the wiring and vacuum hose to the vacuum pump.

**8** On models with air conditioning, unbolt the refrigerant pipe support bracket from above the right-hand engine mounting.

**9** Chock the rear wheels and apply the handbrake, then jack up the front of the car and rest it securely on axle stands. Remove both front roadwheels.

**10** Working in either wheel arch, remove the ABS wheel sensors from the steering knuckles and release the sensor wiring from the suspension strut brackets.

**11** Extract the spring clips and release the brake hose from the bracket on the steering knuckle.

**12** Remove the securing screws then lower the front and rear splash guards away from the underside of the engine compartment.

**13** Position an engine hoist over the engine compartment. Attach the jib to the lifting eyelets at either end of the cylinder head. Raise the hoist so that it supports the engine securely; the engine will tend to pivot towards the rear of the engine compartment as the front and rear engine mountings are removed (see next paragraph) so adjust the lifting hoist to compensate for this.

**14** Working underneath the engine compartment, unbolt the front and rear engine/transmission mountings from the engine/transmission crossmember beam, with reference to Chapter 2A.

**15** Refer to Chapter 4C and unbolt and remove the exhaust system front pipe. Take care to avoid straining the oxygen sensor wiring as you do this.

**16** With reference to Chapter 10, Section 4, remove the securing bolts and withdraw the lower end of each suspension strut from the tops of the steering knuckles.

**17** On models with automatic transmission, release the track rod control arms from the steering knuckles as described in Chapter 10, Section 28.

**18** On models with manual transmission, drain the oil from the transmission with reference to Chapter 7A. On models with automatic transmission, drain the fluid with reference to Chapter 7B.

**19** Unbolt and remove the driveshaft heat shield(s).

**20** On the left-hand side of the transmission, release the driveshaft inner CV joint from the transmission as described in Chapter 8, noting that on non-turbo models, the driveshaft need not be separated from the steering knuckle. Take care not to damage the transmission oil seal or the inner CV joint gaiter. Tie the driveshaft to the anti-roll bar to keep it away from the work area.

**21** At the right-hand wheelarch, swivel the suspension strut and steering knuckle assembly outwards and pull the right-hand driveshaft out of the transmission, as described in Chapter 8, again noting that the driveshaft need not be separated from the steering knuckle. On turbo models, it will be necessary to undo the two bolts and remove the cap from the support bearing on the rear of the engine, to allow the intermediate shaft to be withdrawn from the transmission. Tie the driveshaft back away from the engine.

**22** On models with manual transmission, disconnect the selector cables/rod (as applicable) from the transmission as described in Chapter 7A. Disconnect the wiring connector from the reversing light switch.

**23** On models with automatic transmission, refer to Chapter 7B and disconnect the selector cable from the transmission. Unplug the wiring from the shift solenoids and the vehicle speed, fluid temperature, shift position and engine speed sensors at the connectors located on the top of the transmission casing.

**24** Remove the securing screws and detach the wiring harness clip(s) from the top of the transmission casing.

**25** Unbolt the earth lead from the transmission and position it to one side.

**26** On models with air conditioning, unbolt the refrigerant compressor, with reference to Chapter 3. Tie the compressor to the front of the engine compartment away from the engine; note that there is no need to disconnect the refrigerant pipes from the compressor.

**27** On models with automatic transmission, undo the union bolts and disconnect the transmission fluid cooler pipes from the transmission – be prepared for some fluid loss. Plug the open ports and pipes to minimise fluid loss and to prevent the ingress of dirt. Unbolt the fluid pipe support bracket from the transmission casing.

**28** With reference to Chapter 4A, carry out the following:

a) *Disconnect the accelerator cable from the throttle housing and mounting bracket.*
b) *Depressurise the fuel system (Section 2).*
c) *Disconnect the fuel supply and return hoses at the quick-release connectors to the right of the cylinder head.*

**29** Disconnect the evaporative loss system vacuum hose from the port on the inlet manifold.

**30** On non-turbo models with manual transmission, remove the clutch slave cylinder from the top of the transmission casing with reference to Chapter 6. Wrap a cable-tie around the slave cylinder to prevent the piston from being pushed out.

**31** On turbo models with manual transmission, undo the union and disconnect the slave cylinder hydraulic pipe at the coupling at the top of the transmission casing; be prepared for some hydraulic fluid spillage.

**32** Extract the spring clip and release the clutch hydraulic pipe from the support bracket on the front of the transmission casing.

**33** Refer to Chapter 3 and carry out the following:

a) *Remove the electric cooling fan(s) from the radiator.*
b) *Slacken the hose clips and disconnect the heater supply and return hoses from the connections at the engine compartment bulkhead.*
c) *Slacken the hose clips and remove the radiator top and bottom hoses.*
d) *Slacken the hose clips and disconnect the coolant hose from the expansion tank.*
e) *Remove the radiator.*

**34** With reference to Chapter 10, unbolt the power steering pump from its mounting bracket, and tie it to the front of the engine compartment. Note that there is no need to disconnect the hydraulic fluid pipes from the pump.

**35** Disconnect the brake servo vacuum hose from the inlet manifold, with reference to Chapter 9.

**36** Locate the main engine wiring harness, at the front right-hand corner of the engine compartment. Trace each branch of the wiring to all sensors, actuators and ancillaries on the engine and unplug the wiring at the connector. Label each connector to ensure correct refitting.

**37** Disconnect the vacuum hoses from the manifold pressure sensor (where applicable).

**38** Disconnect the vacuum hoses from the EGR and evaporative loss system solenoid valves (where applicable).

**39** Check that the hoist is supporting the weight of the engine and transmission, then remove the right- and left-hand engine mountings as described Chapter 2A.

**40** Check that no wires, hoses, etc, have been overlooked. Raise the engine and transmission as a unit, and manipulate it to clear all adjacent components with the aid of an assistant **(see illustration)**. In particular, take great care to avoid damaging the ABS hydraulic modulator on the right-hand side of the engine compartment as the engine is being manoeuvred. If not already done, removing the engine mounting brackets will provide more clearance. The engine will need to be angled upwards slightly at the timing belt end to clear the engine bay.

**41** When sufficient height exists, lift it over the front panel, clear of the engine bay, and lower it to the ground or onto a workbench.

### Separation

**42** With the engine/transmission removed, support the assembly on suitable blocks of wood, on a workbench (or failing that, on a clean area of the workshop floor).

**43** Remove the starter motor.

### Manual transmission models

**44** Remove the bolts securing the transmission to the engine.

**45** With the aid of an assistant, draw the transmission off the engine **(see illustration)**. Once it is clear of the dowels, do not allow the input shaft to hang on the clutch driven plate.

### Automatic transmission models

**46** Rotate the crankshaft, using a socket on the pulley nut, until one of the torque converter-to-driveplate retaining bolts becomes accessible through the opening on the rear facing side of the engine. Working through the opening, undo the bolt. Rotate the crankshaft as necessary and remove the remaining bolts in the same way. Note that new bolts will be required for refitting.

**47** Remove the bolts securing the transmission to the engine.

**48** With the aid of an assistant, draw the transmission squarely off the engine dowels making sure that the torque converter remains in position on the transmission. Use the access hole in the transmission housing to hold the converter in place.

### Refitting

### Manual transmission models

**49** Where removed, refit the clutch to the engine using the information given in Chapter 6. Make sure that the clutch is correctly centred

**3.40 Raise the engine and transmission as a unit**

and that the clutch release components are fitted to the transmission bellhousing. Do not apply any grease to the transmission input shaft, the guide sleeve, or the release bearing itself as these components have a friction-reducing coating which does not require lubrication.

**50** Manoeuvre the transmission squarely into position and engage it with the engine dowels. Refit the bolts securing the transmission to the engine, and tighten them to the specified torque. Refit the starter motor.

### Automatic transmission models

**51** Before refitting the transmission, flush out the oil cooler with fresh transmission fluid. To do this, attach a hose to the upper union, pour ATF through the hose, and collect it in a container positioned beneath the return hose.

**52** Clean the contact surfaces on the torque converter and driveplate, and the transmission and engine mating faces. Lightly lubricate the torque converter guide projection and the engine/transmission locating dowels with grease.

**53** Check that the torque converter is fully seated by measuring the distance from the edge of the transmission housing face to the retaining bolt tabs on the converter. The dimension should be approximately 14 mm.

**54** Manoeuvre the transmission squarely into position and engage it with the engine dowels. Refit the bolts securing the transmission to the engine and tighten lightly first in a diagonal sequence, then again to the specified torque.

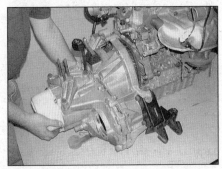

**3.45 Withdrawing the transmission from the engine**

**55** Attach the torque converter to the driveplate using new bolts. Rotate the crankshaft for access to the bolts as was done for removal, then rotate the torque converter by means of the access hole in the transmission housing. Fit and tighten all the bolts hand tight first then tighten again to the specified torque.

### All models

**56** The remainder of refitting is essentially a reversal of removal, noting the following points:

a) *Tighten all fastenings to the specified torque and, where applicable, torque angle. Refer to the relevant Chapters of this manual for torque wrench settings not directly related to the engine.*

b) *When refitting the fuel rail and injectors, check that the injector O-rings and manifold seals are in good condition and renew them if necessary; smear them with petroleum jelly or silicone grease as an assembly lubricant.*

c) *When refitting the left-hand driveshaft, ensure that the inner CV joint is pushed fully into the transmission so that the retaining circlip locks into place in the differential gear.*

d) *Ensure that the ABS sensor, and sensor location in the steering knuckle, are perfectly clean before refitting.*

e) *When reconnecting the manual transmission selector cables, note that the outermost cable attaches to the vertical selector lever on the end of the transmission.*

f) *On automatic transmission models, reconnect and adjust the selector cable as described in Chapter 7B.*

g) *Refit the air cleaner assembly and reconnect the accelerator cable as described in Chapter 4A.*

h) *Refit the auxiliary drivebelt, then refill the engine with coolant and oil as described in Chapter 1.*

i) *Refill the transmission with lubricant if necessary as described in Chapter 1, 7A or 7B as applicable.*

j) *Refer to Section 18 before starting the engine.*

### 4  Engine and transmission (GDI) – removal, separation and refitting

**1** Open the bonnet, then remove the stop-bolts from both bonnet hinges to allow the bonnet to be raised to its fully extended (vertical) position. Alternatively, unbolt the bonnet from its hinges and remove it, as described in Chapter 11.

**2** Depressurise the fuel system, and remove the air cleaner and inlet duct, as described in Chapter 4B.

**3** Remove the battery and its tray as described in Chapter 5A.

**4** Drain the cooling system as described in Chapter 1.

**5** At the rear of the engine compartment, remove the two bolts securing the fuse/relay box, and release the box from its bracket – move it aside as far as possible without disconnecting the wiring.

**6** Unscrew the three nuts securing the fuel injector output stage (large heat sink) to its mounting bracket on the left-hand inner wing (left as seen from the driver's seat). Lift out the unit, then clean round the connector plug before releasing the locking catch and disconnecting the plug. The output stage will be hot if the car has recently been driven.

**7** Noting carefully how it is clipped in place and routed, work around the top of the engine and disconnect all the relevant wiring from it (see illustration 6.5a in Chapter 2B). In particular, there are several earth points to disconnect. Move the wiring harness to one side.

**8** Place some absorbent rags or paper towel around and under the fuel supply and return connections to the fuel pump (at the transmission end of the head). Carefully remove the fuel pipes, including the small hose to the charcoal canister.

**9** On early models, open the throttle quadrant fully by hand, and unhook the throttle cable end fitting from it. Remove the two bolts securing the throttle cable bracket to the inlet manifold, and move the cable back from the engine.

**10** Mark the gear selector cables for position, then pull out the wire clips and recover the washers from the end fittings. To remove the cables from the mounting brackets, carefully prise out the pushed-in tags on the retaining clips, then slide the clips off to release the cables.

**11** Loosen the hose clamps for the radiator top and bottom hoses on the front of the engine, and for the heater hoses at the rear of the engine compartment. Anticipating some spillage of residual coolant, carefully disconnect the hoses, noting that some manipulation might be needed to break the seal at each connection.

**12** Remove the clutch slave cylinder with reference to Chapter 6. Wrap a cable-tie around the slave cylinder to prevent the piston from being pushed out.

**13** Release the hose clip, and disconnect the brake servo flexible hose from the rigid hose attached to the inlet manifold.

**14** Loosen the front wheel nuts, then jack up the front of the car, and support it on axle stands (see *Jacking and vehicle support*). Remove the front wheels and the engine undershields.

**15** Referring to Chapter 4C if necessary, remove the exhaust downpipe and (front) oxygen sensor from the car. Recover the manifold-to-downpipe gasket – a new gasket (and possibly, some new mounting nuts) should be obtained for refitting.

**16** Remove the auxiliary drivebelts as described in Chapter 1.

**17** On models so equipped, unscrew the four mounting bolts and separate the air conditioning compressor from the engine. Without disconnecting or bending the pipework, tie the compressor up out of the way.

**18** Similarly, unbolt the power steering pump from the engine (refer to Chapter 10 if necessary). Hang the pump up out of the way, without disconnecting any of the fluid hoses.

**19** Drain the transmission oil, referring to Chapter 7A if necessary. Refit the drain plug with a new washer, and tighten to the specified torque (Chapter 7A Specifications).

**20** Using the information in Chapter 8, disconnect the driveshafts from the transmission. The shafts don't have to be removed completely – instead, release them at the inner ends only, and tie them up to prevent damage to the CV joints.

**21** Referring to Chapter 2B if necessary, unbolt and remove the engine front and rear mountings, and the support member from under the car. This will leave the engine suspended only by the left- and right-hand mountings.

**22** Position a suitable engine crane/hoist over the engine, and attach its lifting chain/rope to the lifting eyes provided at the front and rear of the cylinder head. Raise the crane/hoist so that it is taking the weight of the engine/transmission, then remove the engine left- and right-hand engine mountings as described Chapter 2B.

**23** Check that no wires, hoses, etc, have been overlooked. Raise the engine and transmission as a unit, and manipulate it to clear all adjacent components with the aid of an assistant. In particular, take great care to avoid damaging the ABS hydraulic modulator on the right-hand side of the engine compartment as the engine is being manoeuvred. If not already done, removing the engine mounting brackets will provide more clearance. The engine will need to be angled upwards slightly at the timing belt end to clear the engine bay.

**24** When sufficient height exists lift it over the front panel, clear of the engine bay, and lower it to the ground or onto a workbench.

### Separation

**25** With the engine/transmission removed, support the assembly on suitable blocks of wood, on a workbench (or failing that, on a clean area of the workshop floor).

**26** Remove the starter motor.

**27** Remove the bolts securing the transmission to the engine.

**28** With the aid of an assistant, draw the transmission off the engine. Once it is clear of the dowels, do not allow the input shaft to hang on the clutch driven plate.

## 5 Engine overhaul – preliminary information

It is much easier to dismantle and work on the engine if it is mounted on a portable engine stand. These stands can often be hired from a tool hire shop. Before the engine is mounted on a stand, the flywheel/driveplate should be removed so that the stand bolts can be tightened into the end of the cylinder block/crankcase.

If a stand is not available, it is possible to dismantle the engine with it suitably supported on a sturdy, workbench or on the floor. Be careful not to tip or drop the engine when working without a stand.

If you intend to obtain a reconditioned engine, all ancillaries must be removed first, to be transferred to the new engine (just as they will if you are doing a complete engine overhaul yourself). These components include the following.

a) Engine mountings and brackets (Chapter 2A or 2B).
b) Alternator including accessories mounting bracket (Chapter 5A).
c) Starter motor (Chapter 5A).
d) The ignition system and HT components including all sensors, coil modules and spark plugs (Chapters 1 and 5B).
e) Exhaust manifold, with turbocharger if fitted (Chapter 4C).
f) Inlet manifold with fuel injection components (Chapter 4A or 4B).
g) All electrical switches, actuators and sensors and the engine wiring harness (Chapters 4A, 4B and 5B).
h) Coolant pump, thermostat, hoses, and distribution pipe (Chapter 3).
i) Clutch components – manual transmission models (Chapter 6).
j) Flywheel/driveplate (Chapter 2A or 2B).
k) Oil filter (Chapter 1).
l) Dipstick, tube and bracket.

**Note:** When removing the external components from the engine, pay close attention to details that may be helpful or important during refitting. Note the fitting positions of gaskets, seals, washers, bolts and other small items.

If you are obtaining a short engine (cylinder block/crankcase, crankshaft, pistons and connecting rods all assembled), then the cylinder head, timing belt (together with tensioner, tensioner and idler pulleys and covers) and auxiliary drivebelt tensioner will have to be removed also.

If a complete overhaul is planned, the engine can be dismantled in the order given below:

a) Inlet and exhaust manifolds, EGR housing and turbocharger (where applicable).
b) Timing belt, sprockets, tensioner, pulleys and covers.
c) Cylinder head.
d) Oil pump.
e) Flywheel/driveplate.
f) Sump.
g) Oil pick-up pipe.
h) Intermediate section/main bearing ladder.
i) Pistons/connecting rods.
j) Crankshaft.

## 6 Cylinder head – dismantling, cleaning, inspection and reassembly

**Note:** New and reconditioned cylinder heads are available from the manufacturer, and from engine overhaul specialists. Specialist tools are required for the dismantling and inspection procedures, and new components may not be readily available. It may, therefore, be more practical and economical for the home mechanic to purchase a reconditioned head rather than dismantle, inspect and recondition the original head.

### Dismantling

**1** Remove the cylinder head as described in Part A or B of this Chapter.
**2** If still in place, remove the camshafts and tappets as described in Part A or B of this Chapter.
**3** According to components still fitted, remove the thermostat housing (Chapter 3), the spark plugs (Chapter 1) and any other unions, pipes, sensors or brackets as necessary.
**4** Tap each valve stem smartly, using a light hammer and drift, to free the spring and associated items.
**5** Fit a deep-reach type valve spring compressor to each valve in turn, and compress each spring until the collets are exposed. Lift out the collets; a small screwdriver, a magnet or a pair of tweezers may be useful. Carefully release the spring compressor and remove it.
**6** Remove the valve spring upper seat and the valve spring. Pull the valve out of its guide.
**7** Pull off the valve stem oil seal with a pair of long-nosed pliers. It may be necessary to use a tool such as a pair of electrician's wire strippers, the legs of which will engage under the seal, if the seal is tight.
**8** Recover the valve spring lower seat. If there is much carbon build-up round the outside of the valve guide, this will have to be scraped off before the seat can be removed.
**9** It is essential that each valve is stored together with its collets, spring and seats. The valves should also be kept in their correct sequence, unless they are so badly worn or burnt that they are to be renewed. If they are going to be kept and used again, place each valve assembly in a labelled polythene bag or similar container.
**10** Continue removing all the remaining valves in the same way.

### Cleaning

**11** Thoroughly clean all traces of old gasket material and sealing compound from the cylinder head upper and lower mating surfaces. Use a suitable liquid gasket dissolving agent together with a soft putty knife; do not use a metal scraper or the faces will be damaged.
**12** Remove the carbon from the combustion chambers and ports, then clean all traces of oil and other deposits from the cylinder head, paying particular attention to the bearing journals, tappet bores, valve guides and oilways.
**13** Wash the head thoroughly with paraffin or a suitable solvent. Take plenty of time and do a thorough job. Be sure to clean all oil holes and galleries very thoroughly and then dry the head completely.
**14** Scrape off any heavy carbon deposits that may have formed on the valves, then use a power-operated wire brush to remove deposits from the valve heads and stems.

### Inspection

**Note:** Be sure to perform all the following inspection procedures before concluding that the services of an engineering works are required. Make a list of all items that require attention.

#### Cylinder head

**15** Inspect the head very carefully for cracks, evidence of coolant leakage, and other damage. If cracks are found, a new cylinder head should be obtained.
**16** Use a straight-edge and feeler blade to check that the cylinder head gasket surface is not distorted. If it is, it may be possible to resurface it; consult your dealer or engine overhaul specialist **(see illustration)**.
**17** Examine the valve seats in each of the combustion chambers. If they are severely pitted, cracked or burned, then they will need to be renewed or re-cut by an engine overhaul specialist. If they are only slightly pitted, this can be removed by grinding-in the valve heads and seats with fine valve-grinding compound, as described below.
**18** If the valve guides appear worn, indicated by a side-to-side motion of the valve, new guides must be fitted. The renewal of valve guides should be carried out by an engine overhaul specialist.
**19** If the valve seats are to be recut, this must be done *only after* the guides have been renewed.

**6.16 Use a straight-edge and feeler blade to check for distortion of the cylinder head gasket surface**

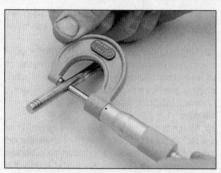

**6.23 Measure the valve stem diameter using a micrometer**

**20** The threaded holes in the cylinder head must be clean to ensure accurate torque readings when tightening fixings during reassembly. Carefully run the correct-size tap (which can be determined from the size of the relevant bolt which fits in the hole) into each of the holes to remove rust, corrosion, thread sealant or other contamination, and to restore damaged threads. If possible, use compressed air to clear the holes of debris produced by this operation. Do not forget to clean the threads of all bolts and nuts as well.

**21** Any threads which cannot be restored in this way can often be reclaimed by the use of thread inserts. If any threaded holes are damaged, consult your dealer or engine overhaul specialist and have them install any thread inserts where necessary.

### Valves

**22** Examine the head of each valve for pitting, burning, cracks and general wear, and check the valve stem for scoring and wear ridges. Rotate the valve, and check for any obvious indication that it is bent. Look for pits and excessive wear on the tip of each valve stem. Renew any valve that shows any such signs of wear or damage.

**23** If the valve appears satisfactory at this stage, measure the valve stem diameter at several points, using a micrometer **(see illustration)**. Any significant difference in the readings obtained indicates wear of the valve stem. Should any of these conditions be apparent, the valve(s) must be renewed.

**24** If the valves are in satisfactory condition, they should be ground (lapped) into their respective seats, to ensure a smooth gas-tight seal. If the seat is only lightly pitted, or if it has been recut, fine grinding compound *only* should be used to produce the required finish. Coarse valve-grinding compound should *not* be used unless a seat is badly burned or deeply pitted; if this is the case, the cylinder head and valves should be inspected by an expert, to decide whether seat recutting, or even the renewal of the valve or seat insert, is required.

**25** Valve grinding is carried out as follows. Place the cylinder head upside-down on a bench, with a block of wood at each end to give clearance for the valve stems.

**26** Smear a trace of (the appropriate grade) valve-grinding compound on the seat face, and press a suction grinding tool onto the valve head. With a semi-rotary action, grind the valve head to its seat, lifting the valve occasionally to redistribute the grinding compound. A light spring placed under the valve head will greatly ease this operation.

**27** If coarse grinding compound is being used, work only until a dull, matt even surface is produced on both the valve seat and the valve, then wipe off the used compound, and repeat the process with fine compound. When a smooth unbroken ring of light grey matt finish is produced on both the valve and seat, the grinding operation is complete. *Do not* grind in the valves any further than absolutely necessary, or the seat will be prematurely sunk into the cylinder head.

**28** When all the valves have been ground-in, carefully wash off *all* traces of grinding compound, using paraffin or a suitable solvent, before reassembly of the cylinder head.

### Valve components

**29** Examine the valve springs for signs of damage and discoloration, and also measure their free length by comparing each of the existing springs with a new component.

**30** Stand each spring on a flat surface, and check it for squareness. If any of the springs are damaged, distorted, or have lost their tension, obtain a complete set of new springs. It is normal to fit new springs as a matter of course if a major overhaul is being carried out.

**31** Renew the valve stem oil seals regardless of their apparent condition.

### *Reassembly*

**32** Fit the first lower spring seat in position over the valve guide, then oil the stem of the corresponding valve and insert it into the guide **(see illustrations)**.

**33** The new valve stem oil seals should be supplied with a plastic fitting sleeve to protect the seal when it is fitted over the valve. If not, wrap a thin piece of polythene around the valve stem allowing it to extend about 10 mm above the end of the valve stem.

**34** With the fitting sleeve, or polythene in place around the valve, fit the valve stem oil seal, pushing it onto the valve guide as far as it will go with a suitable socket or piece of tube **(see illustration)**. Once the seal is seated, remove the protective sleeve or polythene.

**35** Fit the valve spring and upper seat.

**6.32a Fit the first lower spring seat in position . . .**

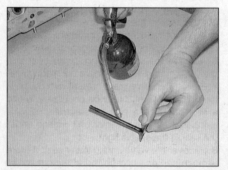

**6.32b . . . then oil the stem of the corresponding valve . . .**

**6.32c . . . and insert it into the guide**

**6.34 Fit the new valve stem oil seal over the valve guide**

**6.35a Fit the valve spring . . .**

6.35b . . . followed by the upper spring seat

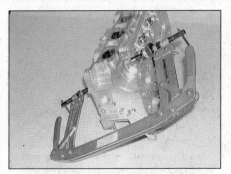

6.35c  Compress the spring using the spring compressors . . .

6.35d . . . and fit the two collets in the recesses in the valve stem, using a small screwdriver or similar

Compress the spring and fit the two collets in the recesses in the valve stem. Carefully release the compressor **(see illustrations)**.

> **HAYNES HiNT**
>
> *Use a little dab of grease to hold the collets in position on the valve stem while the spring compressor is released.*

**36** Cover the valve stem with a cloth and tap it smartly with a light hammer to verify that the collets are properly seated.

**37** Repeat these procedures on all the other valves.

**38** Refit the remainder of the disturbed components then refit the cylinder head as described in Part A of this Chapter.

### 7  Sump and intermediate section (except GDI engine) – removal

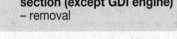

**1** If not already done, drain the engine oil then remove the oil filter, referring to Chapter 1 if necessary.

**2** Remove the oil pump as described in Part A of this Chapter.

**3** If the pistons and connecting rods are to be removed later, rotate the crankshaft to position all the pistons approximately half-way down their bores.

**4** Undo the bolts securing the sump to the intermediate section, noting the different bolt lengths and their locations.

**5** Carefully tap the sump free using a rubber or hide mallet. Recover the O-ring seals.

**6** Undo the mounting bracket bolt and remove the oil pick-up pipe. Recover the O-ring seal on the end of the pipe **(see illustrations)**.

**7** Undo all the M7 bolts securing the intermediate section to the cylinder block in the **reverse** order to that shown. With all the M7 bolts removed, undo the M10 bolts in the same order **(see illustrations)**.

**8** Carefully tap the intermediate section free using a rubber or hide mallet. Lift off the intermediate section complete with crankshaft lower main bearing shells. If any of the shells have stayed on the crankshaft, transfer them to their correct locations in the intermediate section.

**9** Remove the crankshaft oil seal.

7.6a  Undo the mounting bracket bolt . . .

7.6b  . . . and remove the oil pick-up pipe

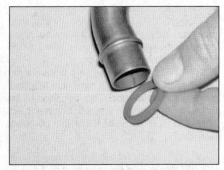

7.6c  Recover the O-ring seal from the end of the pipe

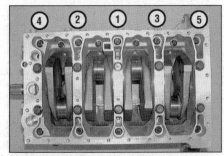

7.7a  Intermediate section tightening sequence; slacken the bolts in the REVERSE order

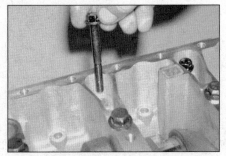

7.7b  Undo all the M7 bolts securing the intermediate section to the cylinder block in the REVERSE order to that shown

7.7c  With all the M7 bolts removed, undo the M10 bolts in the same order

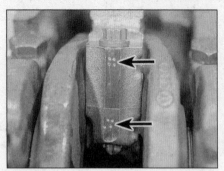

**9.3 Mark the big-end caps and connecting rods with their cylinder numbers**

## 8 Main bearing ladder (GDI engine) – removal

**1** If not already done, drain the engine oil then remove the oil filter, referring to Chapter 1 if necessary.

**2** Remove the oil pump as described in Part B of this Chapter.

**3** If the pistons and connecting rods are to be removed later, rotate the crankshaft to position all the pistons approximately half-way down their bores.

**4** Progressively unscrew the bolts securing the main bearing ladder to the base of the engine, loosening each bolt by no more than a quarter-turn at a time until all the bolts are loose.

**5** Remove the bolts, then prise up the bearing ladder and remove it together with the bearing shells. Tape the shells to the relevant position on the ladder, if they are to be re-used.

**6** Recover the thrustwashers from their locations either side of No 3 main bearing – note which way round they are fitted. Store them with the bearing ladder.

**7** Check that the main bearing bolts are not longer than the specified maximum length. If there is any doubt about the condition of the bolts, or if they are known to have been tightened more than once, obtain a complete new set.

## 9 Pistons and connecting rods – removal and inspection

### Removal

**1** Remove the cylinder head, oil pump and flywheel/driveplate as described in Part A or B of this Chapter. On the GDI engine, remove the main sump as described in Chapter 2B; on all other engines, remove the sump and intermediate section as described in Section 7.

**2** Feel inside the tops of the bores for a pronounced wear ridge. It is recommended that you remove such a ridge (with a scraper or ridge reamer) before attempting to remove the pistons, as the pistons rings may jam beneath the ridge making removal difficult.

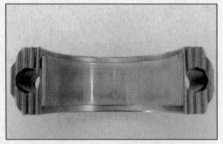

**9.4 On non-GDI engines, the big-end bearing shells do not have locating tabs – make a careful note of the position of the shell in the bearing cap**

Note that a ridge large enough to cause complications such as this will almost certainly mean that a rebore and new pistons/rings are needed.

**3** Check that there are identification numbers or marks on each connecting rod and cap; paint or punch suitable marks if necessary, so that each rod can be refitted in the same position and the same way round **(see illustration)**.

**4** On non-GDI engines, remove the two connecting rod bolts. Tap the cap with a soft-faced hammer to free it. Remove the bearing cap, and note that the lower bearing shell does not have locating tabs **(see illustration)**. Make a careful note of the position of the shell in the bearing cap – during refitting the shell must be refitted to the cap in exactly the same position; no alignment markings or locating tabs are provided. **Note:** *New big-end bearing cap bolts will be needed for reassembly.*

**5** On the GDI engine, the connecting rod bearing caps are secured by two nuts. The cap may need a light tap to free it from the rod. The bearing cap shell has a locating tab which corresponds to a cut-out in the cap itself – tape the shell to the cap if new ones are not being fitted.

**6** Push the connecting rod and piston up and out of the bore, and recover the upper bearing shell. The upper shell has no locating tabs or alignment markings. Make a careful note of the position of the shell in the connecting rod – during refitting the shell must be refitted to the rod in exactly the same position.

**7** Refit the cap to the connecting rod, the correct way round, so that they do not get mixed up. On non-GDI engines, note that the

**9.7 On non-GDI engines, the serrations on the bearing cap and connecting rod mating surfaces ensure correct refitting**

serrations on the bearing cap and connecting rod mating surfaces ensure that the cap can only be fitted the correct way round **(see illustration)**. On the GDI engine, the connecting rod studs are slightly offset, to ensure correct refitting.

**8** Check to see if there is an arrow on the top of the piston which should be pointing toward the timing belt end of the engine **(see illustration)**. If no arrow can be seen, make a suitable direction mark yourself. On the GDI engine, this is less important, as the hollow combustion chamber in the top of the piston faces the inlet (rear) side of the engine.

**9** Without rotating the crankshaft, repeat the operations on the remaining connecting rods and pistons.

### Inspection

**10** Before the inspection process can be carried out, the piston/connecting rod assemblies must be cleaned, and the original piston rings removed from the pistons.

**11** Carefully expand the old rings and remove them from the top of the pistons. The use of two or three old feeler blades will be helpful in preventing the rings dropping into empty grooves **(see illustration)**. Be careful not to scratch the pistons with the ends of the ring. The rings are brittle, and will snap if they are spread too far. They are also very sharp – protect your hands and fingers.

**12** Scrape all traces of carbon from the top of the piston. A hand-held wire brush (or a piece of fine emery cloth) can be used, once the majority of the deposits have been scraped away.

**9.8 The arrow on the piston crown points towards the timing belt end of the engine**

**9.11 Removing the piston rings using a feeler blade**

**9.21 Push the gudgeon pin out of the piston and connecting rod**

**9.22a Measure the diameter of each piston using a micrometer (see text)**

**9.22b Piston/cylinder grade stamped on the edge of the cylinder block**

**13** Remove the carbon from the ring grooves in the piston, using an old ring. Break the ring in half to do this (be careful not to cut your fingers – piston rings are sharp). Be careful to remove only the carbon deposits – do not remove any metal, and do not nick or scratch the sides of the ring grooves.

**14** Once the deposits have been removed, clean the piston/rod assemblies with paraffin or a suitable solvent, and dry thoroughly. Make sure the oil return holes in the ring grooves, where applicable, are clear.

**15** If the pistons and cylinder bores are not damaged or worn excessively, and if the cylinder block does not need to be rebored, the original pistons can be refitted. Normal piston wear appears as even vertical wear on the piston thrust surfaces, and slight looseness of the top ring in its groove. New piston rings should always be used when the engine is reassembled.

**16** Carefully inspect each piston for cracks around the skirt, around the gudgeon pin holes, and at the ring lands (between the ring grooves).

**17** Look for scoring and scuffing on the piston skirt, holes in the piston crown, and burned areas at the edge of the crown. If the skirt is scored or scuffed, the engine may have been suffering from overheating and/or abnormal combustion, which caused excessively-high operating temperatures. The cooling and lubrication systems should be checked thoroughly. Scorch marks on the sides of the piston show that blow-by has occurred. A hole in the piston crown or burned areas at the edge of the piston crown, indicates that abnormal combustion (pre-ignition, knocking, or detonation) has been occurring. If any of the above problems exist, the causes must be investigated and corrected, or the damage will occur again. The causes may include inlet air leaks, incorrect fuel/air mixture or an emission control system fault.

**18** Corrosion of the piston, in the form of pitting, indicates that coolant has been leaking into the combustion chamber and/or the crankcase. Again, the cause must be corrected, or the problem may persist in the rebuilt engine.

**19** Examine each connecting rod carefully for signs of damage, such as cracks around the

big-end and small end bearings. Check that the rod is not bent or distorted. Damage is highly unlikely, unless the engine has been seized or badly overheated. Detailed checking of the connecting rod assembly can only be carried out by an engine overhaul specialist with the necessary equipment.

**20** The gudgeon pins are of the floating type, secured in position by two circlips. Where necessary, the pistons and connecting rods can be separated as follows.

**21** Remove one of the circlips which secure the gudgeon pin. Push the gudgeon pin out of the piston and connecting rod **(see illustration)**.

**22** Using a micrometer, measure the diameter of all four pistons at a point 10 mm from the bottom of the skirt, at right-angles to the gudgeon pin axis. Compare the measurements obtained with those listed in the Specifications. Note that four standard size grades are available – the grade letter is stamped on the piston crown and on the cylinder block **(see illustrations)**. If new pistons are to be obtained, they must be of the same grade marking as the cylinder bore to which they will be fitted.

**23** If the diameter of any of the pistons is out of the tolerance band listed for its particular grade, then all four pistons must be renewed. Note that if the cylinder block was rebored during a previous overhaul, oversize pistons may have been fitted. Record the measurements and use them to check the piston-to-bore clearance when the cylinder bores are measured later in this Chapter.

**24** Hold a new piston ring in the appropriate groove and measure the ring-to-groove clearance using a feeler blade **(see illustration)**. Note that the rings are of different sizes, so use the correct ring for the groove. Compare the measurements with those listed in the Specifications; if the clearances are outside the tolerance range, then the pistons must be renewed.

**25** Check the fit of the gudgeon pin in the connecting rod bush and in the piston. If there is perceptible play, a new bush or an oversize gudgeon pin must be fitted. Consult a Volvo dealer or engine reconditioning specialist.

**26** Examine all components and obtain any new parts required. If new pistons are

purchased, they will be supplied complete with gudgeon pins and circlips. Circlips can also be purchased separately.

**27** Oil the gudgeon pin. Reassemble the connecting rod and piston, making sure the rod is the right way round, and secure the gudgeon pin with the circlip. Position the circlip so that its opening is facing downward.

**28** Repeat these operations for the remaining pistons.

## 10 Crankshaft – removal and inspection

**Note:** *If no work is to be done on the pistons and connecting rods, then removal of the cylinder head and pistons will not be necessary. Instead, the pistons need only be pushed far enough up the bores so that they are positioned clear of the crankpins.*

### Removal

**1** With reference to Part A or B of this Chapter, and earlier Sections of this part as applicable, carry out the following:
a) *Remove the oil pump.*
b) *Remove the sump and intermediate section.*
c) *Remove the clutch components and flywheel/driveplate.*
d) *Remove the pistons and connecting rods (refer to the Note above).*

**2** Before the crankshaft is removed, it is advisable to check the endfloat. To do this, temporarily refit the intermediate section or main bearing ladder, then mount a dial gauge

**9.24 Measure the ring-to-groove clearance using a feeler blade**

with the stem in line with the crankshaft and just touching the crankshaft nose.

3 Push the crankshaft fully away from the gauge, and zero it. Next, lever the crankshaft towards the gauge as far as possible, and check the reading obtained. The distance that the crankshaft moved is its endfloat; if it is greater than specified, check the crankshaft thrust surfaces for wear. If no wear is evident, new thrustwashers should correct the endfloat. The thrustwashers are integral with the main bearing shells on non-GDI engines, while the GDI engine has separate washers fitted either side of No 3 bearing.

4 Remove the intermediate section or main bearing ladder again, then lift out the crankshaft. On the GDI engine, it will first be necessary to unbolt and remove the crankshaft oil seal carrier, which is secured by four bolts, and located on two dowels – undo the bolts, then prise off the carrier (it may be stuck on, due to the sealant used as a gasket).

5 Remove the upper half main bearing shells from their seats in the crankcase by pressing the end of the shell furthest from the locating tab. Keep all the shells in order.

### Inspection

6 Clean the crankshaft using paraffin or a suitable solvent, and dry it, preferably with compressed air if available. Be sure to clean the oil holes with a pipe cleaner or similar probe to ensure that they are not obstructed.

 **Warning: Wear eye protection when using compressed air.**

7 Check the main and big-end bearing journals for uneven wear, scoring, pitting and cracking.

8 Big-end bearing wear is accompanied by distinct metallic knocking when the engine is running (particularly noticeable when the engine is pulling from low speed) and some loss of oil pressure.

9 Main bearing wear is accompanied by severe engine vibration and rumble – getting progressively worse as engine speed increases – and again by loss of oil pressure.

10 Check the bearing journal for roughness by running a finger lightly over the bearing surface. Any roughness (which will be accompanied by obvious bearing wear) indicates that the crankshaft requires regrinding (where possible) or renewal.

11 Using a micrometer, measure the diameter of the main and big-end journals, and compare the results with the Specifications **(see illustration)**. By measuring the diameter at a number of points around each journal's circumference, you will be able to determine whether or not the journal is out-of-round. Take the measurement at each end of the journal, near the webs, to determine if the journal is tapered.

12 If the crankshaft journals are outside the tolerance range specified, a new crankshaft will be needed as only graded, standard-size bearing shells are available from the

manufacturer. However, seek the advice of an engine overhaul specialist first, as to whether regrinding may be possible and graded bearing shells can be supplied to match.

13 Check the oil seal contact surfaces at each end of the crankshaft for wear and damage. If either seal has worn a deep groove in the surface of the crankshaft, consult an engine overhaul specialist; repair may be possible, otherwise a new crankshaft will be required.

14 Refer to Section 12 for details of main and big-end bearing selection.

### 11 Cylinder block/crankcase – cleaning and inspection

#### Cleaning

1 Prior to cleaning, remove all external components and senders, and any gallery plugs or caps that may be fitted.

2 If any of the castings are extremely dirty, all should be steam-cleaned.

3 After the castings are returned from steam-cleaning, clean all oil holes and oil galleries one more time. Flush all internal passages with warm water until the water runs clear. If you have access to compressed air, use it to speed the drying process, and to blow out all the oil holes and galleries.

 **Warning: Wear eye protection when using compressed air.**

4 If the castings are not very dirty, you can do an adequate cleaning job with hot soapy water (as hot as you can stand!) and a stiff brush. Take plenty of time, and do a thorough job. Regardless of the cleaning method used, be sure to clean all oil holes and galleries very thoroughly, and to dry all components completely. Apply clean engine oil to the cylinder bores to prevent rusting.

5 The threaded holes in the cylinder block must be clean, to ensure accurate torque readings when tightening fixings during reassembly. Carefully run the correct-size tap (which can be determined from the size of the relevant bolt which fits in the hole) into each of the holes to remove rust, corrosion, thread sealant or other contamination, and to restore

**10.11 Use a micrometer to measure the crankshaft journal diameters**

damaged threads. If possible, use compressed air to clear the holes of debris produced by this operation. Do not forget to clean the threads of all bolts and nuts as well.

6 Any threads which cannot be restored in this way can often be reclaimed by the use of thread inserts. If any threaded holes are damaged, consult your dealer or engine overhaul specialist and have them install any thread inserts where necessary.

7 If the engine is not going to be reassembled right away, cover it with a large plastic bag to keep it clean; protect the machined surfaces as described above, to prevent rusting.

### Inspection

8 Visually check the castings for cracks and corrosion. Look for stripped threads in the threaded holes. If there has been any history of internal coolant leakage, it may be worthwhile having an engine overhaul specialist check the cylinder block/crankcase for cracks with special equipment. If defects are found, have them repaired, if possible, or renew the assembly.

9 Check the condition of the cylinder head mating face and the intermediate section mating surfaces. Check the surfaces for any possible distortion using the straight-edge and feeler blade method described earlier for cylinder head inspection. If distortion is slight, consult an engine overhaul specialist as to the best course of action.

10 Check each cylinder bore for scuffing and scoring. Check for signs of a wear ridge at the top of the cylinder, indicating that the bore is excessively worn.

11 If the necessary measuring equipment is available, measure the diameter of each cylinder at the top (just under the ridge area), centre and bottom of the cylinder bore, parallel to the crankshaft axis using a cylinder bore gauge. Next, measure the bore diameter at the same three locations across the crankshaft axis. Note the measurements obtained. Have this work carried out by an engine overhaul specialist if you do not have access to the measuring equipment needed.

12 To obtain the piston-to-bore clearance, measure the piston diameter as described earlier in this Chapter, and subtract the piston diameter from the largest bore measurement.

13 Repeat these procedures for the remaining pistons and cylinder bores.

14 If any bore measurement is significantly different from the others (indicating that the bore is tapered or oval), the piston or bore is excessively-worn.

15 On non-GDI engines, note that each cylinder is identified by a classification letter marking stamped into the rear of the cylinder block. The GDI engine has a similar system of grading, etched into the top of the block at the timing belt end. There are several classifications (or grades) for standard diameter cylinder bores, and oversize classifications for some engines. In all cases, consult a Volvo dealer or engine reconditioning specialist before selecting any new components.

**16** If any of the cylinder bores are badly scuffed or scored, or if they are excessively-worn, out-of-round or tapered, the usual course of action would be to have the cylinder block/crankcase rebored, and to fit new, oversized, pistons on reassembly. Consult a dealer or engine reconditioning specialist for advice.

**17** If the bores are in reasonably good condition and not excessively-worn, then it may only be necessary to renew the piston rings.

**18** If this is the case, the bores should be honed, to allow the new rings to bed-in correctly and provide the best possible seal. Honing is an operation that will be carried out for you by an engine reconditioning specialist – on the GDI engine, Volvo state that honing be carried out in cylinder order 2-4-1-3, to avoid possible heat distortion of the block.

**19** After all machining operations are completed, the entire block/crankcase must be washed very thoroughly with warm soapy water to remove all traces of abrasive grit produced during the machining operations. When the cylinder block/crankcase is completely clean, rinse it thoroughly and dry it, then lightly oil all exposed machined surfaces, to prevent rusting.

**20** The final step is to measure the length of the M10 bolts used to secure the intermediate section to the cylinder block (or the main bearing ladder bolts, on the GDI engine). If the length of any is greater than that given in the Specifications, they should be renewed. As with all bolts that are tightened through a torque angle, they are prone to stretch, often up to the extent of their elastic limit (shearing). It is virtually impossible to judge the strain that this imposes on a particular bolt, and if any are in any way flawed, breakage when retightening, or failure in service, could be the result.

## 12 Main and big-end bearings – inspection and selection

### Inspection

**1** Even though the main and big-end bearing shells should be renewed during the engine overhaul, the old shells should be retained for close examination, as they may reveal valuable information about the condition of the engine.

**2** Bearing failure occurs because of lack of lubrication, the presence of dirt or other foreign particles, overloading the engine, and corrosion. Regardless of the cause of bearing failure, the cause must be corrected (where applicable) before the engine is reassembled, to prevent it from happening again.

**3** When examining the bearing shells, remove them from the cylinder block/crankcase and main bearing caps, and from the connecting rods and the big-end bearing caps, then lay

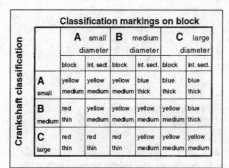

**12.11a Main bearing selection table (non-GDI engines)**

| Crankshaft classification | | A small diameter | | B medium diameter | | C large diameter | |
|---|---|---|---|---|---|---|---|
| | | block | int. sect. | block | int. sect. | block | int. sect. |
| **A** small | | yellow medium | yellow medium | yellow medium | blue thick | blue thick | blue thick |
| **B** medium | | red thin | yellow medium | yellow medium | yellow medium | yellow medium | blue thick |
| **C** large | | red thin | red thin | red thin | yellow medium | yellow medium | yellow medium |

them out on a clean surface in the same general position as their location in the engine. This will enable you to match any bearing problems with the corresponding crankshaft journal. *Do not* touch any of the shell's bearing surface with your fingers while checking it, or the delicate surface may be scratched.

**4** Dirt or other foreign matter gets into the engine in a variety of ways. It may be left in the engine during assembly, or it may pass through filters or the crankcase ventilation system. It may get into the oil, and from there into the bearings. Metal chips from machining operations and normal engine wear are often present. Abrasives are sometimes left in engine components after reconditioning, especially when parts are not thoroughly cleaned using the proper cleaning methods. Whatever the source, these foreign objects often end up embedded in the soft bearing material, and are easily recognised. Large particles will not embed in the material, and will score or gouge the shell and journal. The best prevention for this cause of bearing failure is to clean all parts thoroughly, and to keep everything spotlessly-clean during engine assembly. Frequent and regular engine oil and filter changes are also recommended.

**5** Lack of lubrication (or lubrication breakdown) has a number of inter-related causes. Excessive heat (which thins the oil),

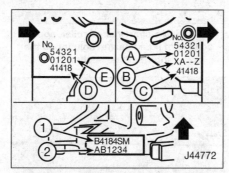

**12.11c ... and on the top surface of the block, at the timing belt end, on GDI engines**

*A/E* Main bearing internal diameter code
*B* Cylinder bore letter code
*C/D* Date of manufacture
*1* Engine type code (at transmission end)
*2* Serial number

**12.11b Main bearing classifications stamped onto the edge of the cylinder block on non-GDI engines ...**

overloading (which squeezes the oil from the bearing face) and oil leakage (from excessive bearing clearances, worn oil pump or high engine speeds) all contribute to lubrication breakdown. Blocked oil passages, which usually are the result of misaligned oil holes in a bearing shell, will also starve a bearing of oil, and destroy it. When lack of lubrication is the cause of bearing failure, the bearing material is wiped or extruded from the shell's steel backing. Temperatures may increase to the point where the steel backing turns blue from overheating.

**6** Driving habits can have a definite effect on bearing life. Full-throttle, low-speed operation (labouring the engine) puts very high loads on bearings, which tends to squeeze out the oil film. These loads cause the shells to flex, which produces fine cracks in the bearing face (fatigue failure). Eventually, the bearing material will loosen in pieces, and tear away from the steel backing.

**7** Short-distance driving leads to corrosion of bearings, because insufficient engine heat is produced to drive off condensed water and corrosive gases. These products collect in the engine oil, forming acid and sludge. As the oil is carried to the engine bearings, the acid attacks and corrodes the bearing material.

**8** Incorrect shell refitting during engine assembly will lead to bearing failure as well. Tight-fitting shells leave insufficient bearing running clearance, and will result in oil starvation. Dirt or foreign particles trapped behind a bearing shell result in high spots on the bearing, which lead to failure.

**9** *Do not* touch any shell's bearing surface with your fingers during reassembly; there is a risk of scratching the delicate surface, or of depositing particles of dirt on it.

### Selection

**10** To ensure that the main bearing running clearance will be correct, there are several different grades of bearing shell. The grades are indicated by a colour-coding marked on each bearing shell, which denotes the shell's thickness.

**11** New main bearing shells for each journal can be selected using the reference letters/numbers which are stamped on the cylinder block and on the crankshaft **(see illustrations)**.

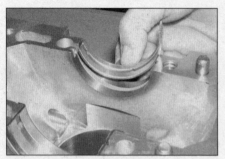

**14.3a Insert the previously-selected upper shells into their correct position in the crankcase**

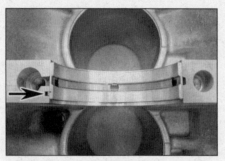

**14.3b Press the shells home so that the tangs (arrowed) engage in the recesses provided**

**14.4 Liberally lubricate the bearing shells in the crankcase with clean engine oil**

**12** Big-end bearing shells are also graded on the GDI engine (though not for the others in the S40/V40 range).

**13** It is recommended that the advice of a Volvo dealer or engine reconditioning specialist is sought before selecting new components. Assessing engine wear and obtaining the correct running clearances is a job for an expert.

## 13 Engine overhaul – reassembly sequence

**1** Before reassembly begins, ensure that all new parts have been obtained and that all necessary tools are available. Read through the entire procedure to familiarise yourself with the work involved, and to ensure that all items necessary for reassembly of the engine

are at hand. In addition to all normal tools and materials, thread locking compound will be needed in most areas during engine reassembly. A tube of Volvo liquid gasket solution together with a short-haired application roller will also be needed to assemble the main engine sections.

**2** In order to save time and avoid problems, engine reassembly can be carried out in the following order:
- a) Crankshaft.
- b) Pistons/connecting rods.
- c) Sump.
- d) Oil pump.
- e) Flywheel/driveplate.
- f) Cylinder head.
- g) Camshaft and tappets.
- h) Timing belt, tensioner, sprockets and idler pulleys.
- i) Engine external components.

**3** At this stage, all engine components should

be absolutely clean and dry, with all faults repaired. The components should be laid out (or in individual containers) on a completely clean work surface.

## 14 Crankshaft – refitting

**1** Crankshaft refitting is the first stage of engine reassembly following overhaul. It is assumed at this point that the cylinder block/crankcase and crankshaft have been cleaned, inspected and repaired or reconditioned as necessary. Position the cylinder block on a clean level work surface, with the crankcase facing upwards.

### Non-GDI engines

**2** If they're still in place, remove the old bearing shells from the block and the intermediate section.

**3** Wipe clean the main bearing shell seats in the crankcase and clean the backs of the bearing shells. Insert the previously-selected upper shells into their correct position in the crankcase. Press the shells home so that the tangs engage in the recesses provided **(see illustrations)**.

**4** Liberally lubricate the bearing shells in the crankcase with clean engine oil **(see illustration)**.

**5** Wipe clean the crankshaft journals, then lower the crankshaft into position **(see illustration)**. Make sure that the shells are not displaced.

**6** Inject oil into the crankshaft oilways, then wipe any traces of excess oil from the crankshaft and intermediate section mating faces.

**7** Using the short-haired application roller, apply an even coating of Volvo liquid gasket to the cylinder block mating face of the intermediate section **(see illustration)**. Ensure that the whole surface is covered – a thin coating is sufficient for a good seal.

**8** Wipe clean the main bearing shell seats in the intermediate section and clean the backs of the bearing shells. Insert the previously-selected lower shells into their correct position in the intermediate section. Press the shells home so that the tangs engage in the recesses provided **(see illustrations)**.

**14.5 Lower the crankshaft into position, making sure that the bearing shells are not displaced**

**14.7 Using a short-haired roller, apply a coating of liquid gasket solution to the intermediate section**

**14.8a Insert the previously-selected lower shells into their correct position in the intermediate section**

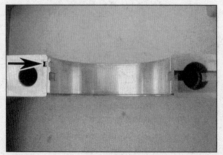

**14.8b Press the shells home so that the tangs (arrowed) engage in the recesses provided**

**9** Lightly lubricate the bearing shells in the intermediate section, but take care to keep the oil away from the liquid gasket **(see illustration)**.

**10** Lay the intermediate section on the crankshaft and cylinder block **(see illustration)**.

**11** Oil the threads of the intermediate section retaining bolts, then insert and tighten them in the stages listed in the Specifications, to the specified torque and torque angle, in the sequence shown in illustration 7.7a **(see illustrations)**.

**12** Rotate the crankshaft. Slight resistance is to be expected with new components, but there must be no tight spots or binding.

**13** It is a good idea at this stage to once again check the crankshaft endfloat as described in Section 10. If the thrust surfaces of the crankshaft have been checked and new bearing shells have been fitted, then the endfloat should be within specification.

**14** Lubricate the oil seal location, the crankshaft, and a new oil seal. Fit the seal, lips inwards, and use a piece of tube (or the old seal, inverted) to tap it into place until flush.

### GDI engine

**15** Ensure that the main bearing ladder, bearing shells, thrustwashers and crankshaft are completely clean and dry.

**16** Fit the upper bearing shells (with the central oil grooves) into their locations in the crankcase, locating them in place with the tabs.

**17** Similarly, position the lower (plain) bearing shells into the main bearing ladder, using the tabs provided to locate them.

**18** Place the two thrustwashers into the crankcase, one either side of the centre (No 3) main bearing location, with the oil grooves facing outwards. If necessary, the thrustwashers may be held in place using a little grease to 'stick' them to the bearing.

**19** Lubricate all the bearing shells and the thrustwashers with clean engine oil, then lay the crankshaft into place.

**20** It is a good idea at this stage to once again check the crankshaft endfloat as described in Section 10.

**21** Carefully lay the main bearing ladder, complete with shells, into position on the crankshaft and crankcase. The arrow marking on the ladder should point towards the timing belt end of the engine. Take care that the dipstick lower tube is not damaged as the ladder is fitted.

**22** Lightly oil the main bearing bolt threads and heads before fitting them to the ladder. The bolts may be re-used, providing their length (measured from below the bolt heads) does not exceed that specified.

**23** Working in sequence, tighten all the bolts to the specified Stage 1 torque setting **(see illustration)**.

**24** Tighten the bolts further, working in the sequence, by turning each bolt through the number of degrees specified for Stage 2 – a process known as angle-tightening. Angle gauges are available from tool suppliers, which can be fitted between a socket/extension and socket handle, to make the process more accurate. In practice, 90 degrees is a right-angle, and can be approximated by looking at

the initial and final position of the socket handle, relative to the engine. Each turn should be completed in one smooth movement, if possible.

**25** Once all the bolts have been tightened, check that it is still possible to turn the crankshaft. If new parts have been fitted, the crankshaft may be slightly stiff to turn, but it should not be binding.

**26** Check that the mating faces of the crankshaft oil seal carrier and block are completely clean, with all traces of sealant removed.

**27** Apply a 3 mm diameter bead of sealant to the carrier **(see illustration)**, then offer the carrier into position, locating it over the two dowels fitted to the block.

**28** Press the carrier firmly home, then fit and tighten the four bolts to the specified torque. Clean off any excess sealant.

**29** Fit a new oil seal using the information in Chapter 2B.

## 15 Pistons and piston rings – assembly

**1** At this stage it is assumed that the pistons have been correctly assembled to their respective connecting rods, and that the piston ring-to-groove clearances have been checked. If not, refer to the end of Section 9.

**2** Before the rings can be fitted to the pistons, the end gaps must be checked with the rings inserted into the cylinder bores.

**14.9 Lightly lubricate the bearing shells in the intermediate section**

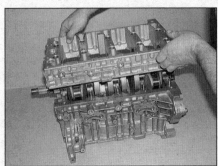
**14.10 Lay the intermediate section on the crankshaft and cylinder block**

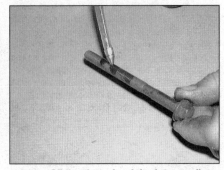
**14.11a Oil the threads of the intermediate section retaining bolts**

**14.11b Tighten the intermediate section bolts to the correct torque and the specified sequence**

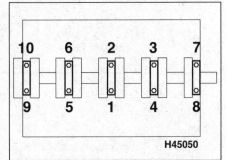
**14.23 Main bearing ladder bolt tightening sequence (GDI engine)**

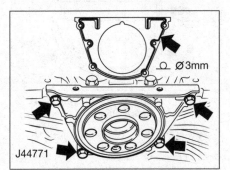
**14.27 Refitting the GDI engine crankshaft oil seal carrier (bolts arrowed)**

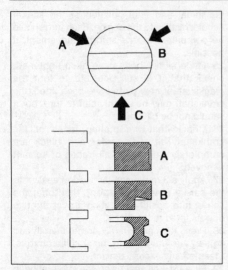

**15.12 Piston ring identification and end gap positioning (non-GDI engines)**

**3** Lay out the piston assemblies and the new ring sets so the components are kept together in their groups, during and after end gap checking. Position the cylinder block on the work surface, on its side, allowing access to the top and bottom of the bores.

**4** Take the No 1 piston top ring, and insert it into the top of the first cylinder. Push it down the bore using the top of the piston – this will ensure that the ring remains square with the cylinder walls. Position the ring near the bottom of the cylinder bore, at the lower limit of ring travel. Note that the top and second compression rings are different. The second ring is easily identified by the step on its lower surface (the GDI engine has T or T1 on the top ring, T2 on the second).

**5** Measure the ring gap using feeler blades.

**6** Repeat the procedure with the ring at the top of the cylinder bore, at the upper limit of its travel and compare the measurements with the figures given in the Specifications.

**7** If new rings are being fitted, it is unlikely that the end gaps will be too small. If a measurement is found to be undersize, it must be corrected or there is the risk that the ring ends may contact each other during engine operation, possibly resulting in engine damage. Ideally, new piston rings providing the correct end gap should be fitted, however, as a last resort the end gaps can be increased by filing the ring ends very carefully with a fine file. Mount the file in a vice equipped with soft jaws, slip the ring over the file with the ends contacting the file face, and slowly move the ring to remove material from the ends. Take care, as piston rings are sharp and are easily broken.

**8** It is equally unlikely that the end gap will be too large. If the gaps are too large, check that you have the correct rings for your engine and for the cylinder bore size.

**9** Repeat the checking procedure for each ring in the first cylinder, and then for the rings in the remaining cylinders. Remember to keep rings, pistons and cylinders matched up.

**10** Once the ring end gaps have been checked and if necessary corrected, the rings can be fitted to the pistons.

**11** Fit the piston rings using the same technique as for removal. Fit the bottom scraper ring first, and work up.

**12** On non-GDI engines, observe the text markings on one side of the top and bottom rings; this must face upwards when the rings are fitted **(see illustration)**. The middle ring is bevelled, and the bevel must face downwards when installed.

**13** On the GDI engine, first fit the oil scraper to the bottom groove – this ring is in three parts. First, fit the spacer ring (the ring ends should touch), then add the upper and lower rings above and below it – the upper and lower oil scraper rings are identical.

**14** Do not expand the compression rings (first and second rings) too far, or they will break. **Note:** *Always follow any instructions supplied with the new piston ring sets – different manufacturers may specify different procedures. Do not mix up the top and second compression rings, as they have different cross-sections.*

**15** When all the rings are in position, arrange the ring gaps 120° apart (non-GDI engines) or as shown (GDI engine) **(see illustration)**.

## 16 Pistons and connecting rod assemblies – refitting

**1** Before refitting the piston/connecting rod assemblies, the cylinder bores must be perfectly clean, the top edge of each cylinder must be chamfered, and the crankshaft and intermediate section must be in place.

**2** Remove the big-end bearing cap from No 1 cylinder connecting rod.

**3** Remove the original bearing shells (observing the notes in Section 9, relating to the position of the shells in the bearing cap and connecting rod) and wipe the bearing recesses of the connecting rod and cap with a clean, lint-free cloth. They must be kept spotlessly-clean. Ensure that new big-end bearing cap retaining bolts are available.

**4** Clean the back of the new upper bearing shell, fit it to No 1 connecting rod, then fit the other shell of the bearing to the big-end bearing cap. Fit the new shells in exactly the same positions as the old shells.

**5** Position the piston ring gaps in their correct positions around the piston, lubricate the piston and rings with clean engine oil, and attach a piston ring compressor to the piston **(see illustration)**. Leave the piston crown protruding slightly, to guide the piston into the cylinder bore. The rings must be compressed until they're flush with the piston.

**6** Rotate the crankshaft until No 1 big-end journal is at BDC (Bottom Dead Centre), and apply a coat of engine oil to the cylinder walls.

**7** Arrange the No 1 piston/connecting rod assembly so that the arrow on the piston crown points to the timing belt end of the engine. Gently insert the assembly into the No 1 cylinder bore, and rest the bottom edge of the ring compressor on the engine block.

**8** Tap the top edge of the ring compressor to make sure it's contacting the block around its entire circumference.

**9** Gently tap on the top of the piston with the end of a wooden hammer handle, whilst guiding the connecting rod big-end onto the crankpin with the aid of a long screwdriver (non-GDI engines) or a pair of long-nosed pliers (GDI engine) **(see illustrations)**. The

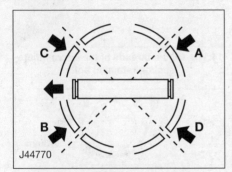

**15.15 Piston ring end gap positions (GDI engine)**

A  Top compression ring
B  Second compression ring
C  Upper ring, oil scraper
D  Lower ring, oil scraper
   Arrow from gudgeon pin indicates timing belt end

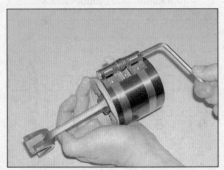

**16.5 Attach a ring compressor to the piston**

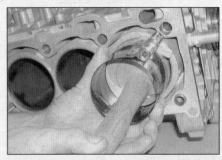

**16.9a Insert the piston assembly into the No 1 cylinder bore, and gently tap on the top of the piston with the end of a wooden hammer handle**

**16.9b Guide the connecting rod onto the crankpin using a long screwdriver (non-GDI engines)**

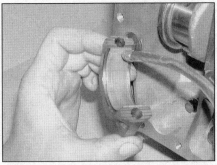

**16.10 Apply clean engine oil to the bearing cap surfaces**

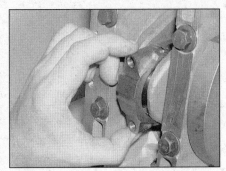

**16.11a Refit the big-end bearing cap . . .**

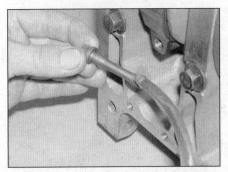

**16.11b . . . lubricate the threads of the bearing cap bolts (nuts on the GDI engine) . . .**

**16.11c . . . tighten them to the Stage 1 torque . . .**

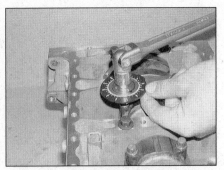

**16.11d . . . then angle-tighten them to the Stage 2 torque**

piston rings may try to pop out of the ring compressor just before entering the cylinder bore, so keep some pressure on the ring compressor. Work slowly, and if any resistance is felt as the piston enters the cylinder, stop immediately. Find out what is binding, and fix it before proceeding. *Do not, for any reason, force the piston into the cylinder – you might break a ring and/or the piston.*

**10** Make sure the bearing surfaces are perfectly clean, then apply a uniform layer of clean engine oil to both of them **(see illustration)**. You may have to push the piston back up the cylinder bore slightly to expose the bearing surface of the shell in the connecting rod.

**11** Slide the connecting rod back into place on the big-end journal, refit the big-end bearing cap. Lubricate the bolt threads, fit the bolts/nuts and tighten them in stages to the correct torque, as detailed in the Specifications **(see illustrations)**.

**12** Repeat the entire procedure for the remaining piston/connecting rod assemblies.

*Caution: Do not rotate the crankshaft until the first pair of big-end bearing caps have been tightened to their final torque settings, or the bearing shells may be dislodged.*

**13** The important points to remember are:
a) *Keep the backs of the bearing shells and the recesses of the connecting rods and*

caps perfectly clean when assembling them.
b) *Make sure you have the correct piston/rod assembly for each cylinder.*
c) *On non-GDI engines, the arrow on the piston crown must face the timing belt end of the engine (see Section 9).*
d) *On the GDI engine, the hollow in the piston crown should face the inlet (rear) side of the engine.*
e) *Lubricate the cylinder bores with clean engine oil.*
f) *Lubricate the bearing surfaces before fitting the big-end bearing caps.*

**14** After all the piston/connecting rod assemblies have been properly installed, rotate the crankshaft a number of times by hand, to check for any obvious binding.

**17.2 Locate new O-rings in the recesses in the intermediate section**

## 17 Sump (except GDI engine) – refitting

**1** Place a new O-ring on the oil pick-up pipe and insert the pipe into its location. Secure with the bracket retaining bolt tightened to the specified torque.

**2** Wipe off any oil smears from the sump and intermediate section joint faces, then locate new O-rings in the recesses in the intermediate section **(see illustration)**.

**3** Using the short-haired application roller, apply an even coating of Volvo liquid gasket to the sump mating face **(see illustration)**. Ensure that the whole surface is covered – a thin coating is sufficient for a good seal.

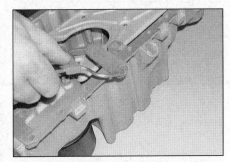

**17.3 Using a short-haired roller, apply an even coating liquid gasket solution to the sump mating face**

**17.4 Place the sump in position on the intermediate section**

**17.5 Using a straight-edge, ensure that the rear edges of the sump and cylinder block are flush**

**17.6 Refit the remaining bolts and tighten all progressively, working towards the centre, to the specified torque**

**17.7a Fit new O-rings to the oil cooler thermostat housing mating surface . . .**

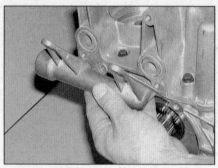

**17.7b . . . then refit the housing . . .**

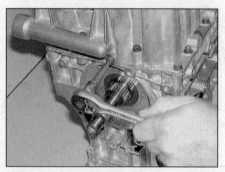

**17.7c . . . and tighten the retaining bolts securely**

**4** Place the sump in position and insert four of the retaining bolts, tightened finger-tight only **(see illustration)**.

**5** Using a straight-edge, ensure that the rear edges of the sump and cylinder block are flush, then tighten the four bolts to just hold the sump in position **(see illustration)**.

**6** Refit the remaining bolts and tighten all progressively, working towards the centre, to the specified torque **(see illustration)**.

**7** Where applicable, fit new O-rings to the oil cooler thermostat housing mating surface, then refit the housing and tighten the retaining bolts securely **(see illustrations)**.

## 18 Engine – initial start-up after overhaul and reassembly

**1** Refit the remainder of the engine components in the order listed in Section 13, with reference to the relevant Sections of this part of Chapter 2, and Part A or B. Refit the engine and transmission to the car as described in Section 3 or 4 of this Part. Double-check the engine oil and coolant levels, and make a final check that everything has been reconnected. Make sure that there are no tools or rags left in the engine compartment.

**2** Remove the spark plugs and disable the ignition system by disconnecting the camshaft position sensor wiring at the connector (non-GDI engines) or by disconnecting the engine speed sensor wiring at the connector located just in front of the timing belt top cover. Disconnect the fuel injector wiring connectors to prevent fuel being injected into the cylinders (alternatively, locate and temporarily remove fuse number 17 from the engine compartment fusebox).

**3** Turn the engine over on the starter motor until the oil pressure warning light goes out. If the light fails to extinguish after several seconds of cranking, check the engine oil level and oil filter tightness. Assuming these are correct, check the security of the oil pressure sensor wiring – do not progress any further until you are sure that oil is being pumped around the engine at sufficient pressure.

**4** Refit the spark plugs, and reconnect the camshaft position/engine speed sensor and fuel injector wiring connectors (or refit fuse 17).

**5** Start the engine, noting that this also may take a little longer than usual, due to the fuel system components being empty.

**6** While the engine is idling, check for fuel, coolant and oil leaks. Don't be alarmed if there are some odd smells and smoke from parts getting hot and burning off oil deposits. Note also that it may initially be a little noisy until the hydraulic tappets fill with oil.

**7** Keep the engine idling until hot water is felt circulating through the top hose, check that it idles reasonably smoothly and at the usual speed, then switch it off.

**8** After a few minutes, recheck the oil and coolant levels, and top-up as necessary (see Chapter 1).

**9** If new components such as pistons, rings or crankshaft bearings have been fitted, the engine must be run-in for the first 500 miles (800 km). Do not operate the engine at full-throttle, or allow it to labour in any gear during this time. It is recommended that the oil and filter be changed at the end of this period.

# Chapter 3
# Cooling, heating and ventilation systems

## Contents

## Degrees of difficulty

| Easy, suitable for novice with little experience |  | Fairly easy, suitable for beginner with some experience | | Fairly difficult, suitable for competent DIY mechanic |  | Difficult, suitable for experienced DIY mechanic | | Very difficult, suitable for expert DIY or professional | |
|---|---|---|---|---|---|---|---|---|---|

## Specifications

### General

Maximum system pressure:
| | |
|---|---|
| Up to 1997 model year ........................................ | 1.1 to 1.3 bar (16 to 19 psi) |
| 1997 model year onwards .................................... | 1.4 to 1.6 bar (20 to 23 psi) |

### Thermostat

Opening temperature (approximate):
| | |
|---|---|
| Starts opening ............................................... | 90°C |
| Fully open ................................................... | 105°C |

### Torque wrench settings

| | Nm | lbf ft |
|---|---|---|
| Blower motor housing nuts ............................... | 25 | 18 |
| Coolant pump bolts: | | |
|   Non-GDI engines ..................................... | 20 | 15 |
|   GDI engine ........................................... | 24 | 18 |
| Cooling fan/shroud nuts and bolts ....................... | 10 | 7 |
| Evaporator housing nut and bolts ........................ | 25 | 18 |
| Facia support bracket bolts .............................. | 10 | 7 |
| Heating/ventilation housing mounting nuts ............... | 25 | 18 |
| Radiator mounting bracket bolts – normally-aspirated engine ....... | 25 | 18 |
| Thermostat housing bolts: | | |
|   Non-GDI engines ..................................... | 17 | 13 |
|   GDI engine ........................................... | 23 | 17 |

## 1 General information and precautions

The cooling system is of pressurised type, comprising a coolant pump (driven by the engine timing belt), an aluminium crossflow radiator, an electric cooling fan, a thermostat, heater matrix, and all associated hoses and switches.

The system functions as follows. Cold coolant in the bottom of the radiator passes through the bottom hose to the coolant pump, where it is pumped around the cylinder block and head passages, and through the oil cooler (where fitted). After cooling the cylinder bores, combustion surfaces and valve seats, the coolant reaches the underside of the thermostat, which is initially closed. The coolant passes through the heater, and is returned via the cylinder block to the coolant pump.

When the engine is cold, the coolant circulates only through the cylinder block, cylinder head, and heater. When the coolant reaches a predetermined temperature, the thermostat opens, and the coolant passes through the top hose to the radiator. As the coolant circulates through the radiator, it is cooled by the inrush of air when the car is in forward motion. The airflow is supplemented by the action of the electric cooling fan when necessary. Upon reaching the bottom of the radiator, the coolant has now cooled, and the cycle is repeated.

The cooling fan(s) is/are controlled by the engine management ECU, via the cooling fan relay(s), using the information supplied by the coolant temperature sensor and (where fitted) air conditioning system pressure switch.

**2.3 Disconnecting the radiator top hose**

## Precautions

 **Warning: Do not attempt to remove the expansion tank filler cap, or to disturb any part of the cooling system, while the engine is hot, as there is a high risk of scalding. If the expansion tank filler cap must be removed before the engine and radiator have fully cooled (even though this is not recommended), the pressure in the cooling system must first be relieved. Cover the cap with a thick layer of cloth to avoid scalding, and slowly unscrew the filler cap until a hissing sound is heard. When the hissing has stopped, indicating that the pressure has reduced, slowly unscrew the filler cap until it can be removed; if more hissing sounds are heard, wait until they have stopped before unscrewing the cap completely. At all times, keep well away from the filler cap opening, and protect your hands.**

**Warning: Do not allow antifreeze to come into contact with your skin, or with the painted surfaces of the car. Rinse off spills immediately, with plenty of water. Never leave antifreeze lying around in an open container, or in a puddle in the driveway or on the garage floor. Children and pets are attracted by its sweet smell, but antifreeze can be fatal if ingested.**

**Warning: If the engine is hot, the electric cooling fan may start rotating even if the engine is not running. Be careful to keep your hands, hair, and any loose clothing well clear when working in the engine compartment.**

 **Warning: Refer to Section 10 for precautions to be observed when working on models equipped with air conditioning.**

## 2 Cooling system hoses – disconnection and renewal

**Note:** *Refer to the warnings given in Section 1 of this Chapter before proceeding. Hoses should only be disconnected once the engine has cooled sufficiently to avoid scalding.*

**1** If the checks described in Chapter 1, Section 7, reveal a faulty hose, it must be renewed as follows.

**2** First drain the cooling system (see Chapter 1). If the coolant is not due for renewal, it may be re-used, providing it is collected in a clean container.

**3** To disconnect a hose, release the retaining clips and move them along the hose, clear of the relevant inlet/outlet. There are two different types of clip, the original crimp-type clip fitted by Volvo, and conventional Jubilee clips; where the crimped type clips are fitted, cut them to release them and use Jubilee hose clips **(see illustration)**. Carefully work the hose free; hoses can be removed with relative ease when new – on an older car, they may have stuck.

**4** If a hose proves to be difficult to remove, try to release it by rotating its ends before attempting to free it. Gently prise the end of the hose with a blunt instrument (such as a flat-bladed screwdriver), but do not apply too much force, and take care not to damage the pipe stubs or hoses. Note in particular that the radiator stubs are fragile; do not use excessive force when attempting to remove the hose.

**5** When fitting a hose, first slide the clips onto the hose, then work the hose into position. On some hose connections, alignment marks are provided on the hose and union; if marks are present, ensure they are correctly aligned.

**HAYNES HiNT** *If the hose is stiff, use a little soapy water as a lubricant, or soften the hose by soaking it in hot water. Do not use oil or grease, which may attack the rubber.*

**6** Ensure the hose is correctly routed, then secure it in position with the retaining clips.

**7** Refill the cooling system with reference to Chapter 1.

**8** Check thoroughly for leaks as soon as possible after disturbing any part of the cooling system.

## 3 Radiator – removal, inspection and refitting

**Note:** *If leakage is the reason for removing the radiator, bear in mind that minor leaks can often be cured using a radiator sealant with the radiator in situ.*

### Removal

**1** Disconnect the battery negative lead (see *Disconnecting the battery*), then drain the cooling system as described in Chapter 1. Proceed as described under the relevant sub-heading.

### Non-turbo models

**2** Remove the cooling fan(s) as described in Section 5. On models with air conditioning, it will not be possible to remove the cooling fan due to lack of clearance; unbolt and position the fan assembly clear of the radiator.

**3** Release the retaining clips and disconnect the top and bottom hoses and the coolant expansion tank hoses from the radiator **(see illustrations)**.

**4** On automatic transmission models, remove all traces of dirt from the fluid cooler unions on the radiator. Unscrew the union nuts and disconnect both pipes from the radiator. Plug the pipe ends and radiator unions to minimise fluid loss and prevent the entry of dirt into the hydraulic system.

**5** Slacken and remove the mounting bolts securing the radiator mounting brackets to the bonnet lock crossmember and remove both brackets **(see illustration)**.

**6** Lift the radiator to disengage it from its lower mountings, and remove it from the engine compartment. Recover the rubbers from the lower mountings and examine them for damage or deterioration **(see illustrations)**.

**3.3a Release the retaining clips and disconnect the top hose . . .**

**3.3b . . . expansion tank hose . . .**

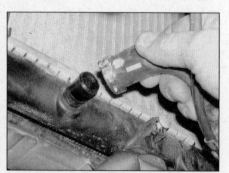

**3.3c . . . and bottom hoses from the radiator**

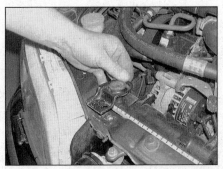

**3.5 Slacken and remove the mounting bolts and lift off the radiator upper mountings**

**3.6a Lift the radiator carefully out of position . . .**

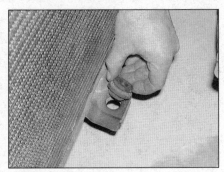

**3.6b . . . and recover the lower mounting rubbers**

## Turbo models

**Note:** *The following procedure describes radiator removal, leaving the intercooler assembly in situ on the car, and requires the use of an engine support bar or hoist to support the engine/transmission whilst the crossmember is removed. Another option is to remove the intercooler assembly and then separate the cooling fans and radiator from the intercooler with the assembly on the bench (refer to Chapter 4A for intercooler removal and refitting details).*

**7** Remove the cooling fan assembly as described in Section 5.

**8** Release the retaining clips and disconnect the top and bottom hoses from the radiator.

**9** Free the radiator from the rear of the intercooler and remove it from the car. The mounting brackets can then be unclipped and remove from the radiator, if necessary.

## Inspection

**10** If the radiator has been removed due to suspected blockage, reverse-flush it as described in Chapter 1. Clean dirt and debris from the radiator fins, using an air line (in which case, wear eye protection) or a soft brush. Be careful, as the fins are sharp, and easily damaged.

**11** If necessary, a radiator specialist can perform a flow test on the radiator, to establish whether an internal blockage exists.

**12** A leaking radiator must be referred to a specialist for permanent repair. Do not attempt to weld or solder a leaking radiator,

as damage to the plastic components may result.

**13** In an emergency, minor leaks from the radiator can be cured by using a suitable radiator sealant, in accordance with its manufacturer's instructions, with the radiator *in situ.*

**14** If the radiator is to be sent for repair or renewed, remove the cooling fan switch.

**15** Inspect the condition of the radiator lower mounting rubbers, and renew them if necessary.

## Refitting

### Non-turbo models

**16** Refitting is a reversal of removal, bearing in mind the following points:
   *a) Ensure that the radiator is correctly engaged with its lower mounting rubbers, then refit the upper mounting brackets and tighten the retaining bolts to the specified torque.*
   *b) Make sure all coolant hoses are correctly reconnected and securely retained by their clips.*
   *c) On completion, refill the cooling system as described in Chapter 1.*

### Turbo models

**17** Ensure that the mounting brackets are correctly fitted to the radiator, then manoeuvre the radiator into position and engage it with the intercooler.

**18** Reconnect the coolant hoses to the radiator and secure them in position with the retaining clips.

**19** Refit the cooling fans as described in Section 5.

**20** On completion, refill the cooling system as described in Chapter 1.

## 4 Thermostat – removal, testing and refitting

### Removal

**1** Disconnect the battery negative lead (see *Disconnecting the battery*), then drain the cooling system as described in Chapter 1.

**2** Slacken and remove the retaining screws and remove the cover from the top of the engine (front of the engine, on GDI models).

**3** Slacken the hose clip and disconnect the coolant hose from the thermostat cover **(see illustrations)**.

**4** Unscrew the retaining bolts and remove the thermostat housing cover.

**5** Lift out the thermostat and sealing ring. Discard the sealing ring, a new one should be used on refitting.

### Testing

**6** A rough test of the thermostat may be made by suspending it with a piece of string in a container full of water. Heat the water to bring it to the boil – the thermostat must open by the time the water boils. If not, renew it.

**7** If a thermometer is available, the precise opening temperature of the thermostat may be determined; compare with the figures given in the Specifications. The opening temperature should also be marked on the thermostat.

**8** A thermostat which fails to close as the water cools must also be renewed.

### Refitting

**9** Fit the sealing ring to the thermostat then seat the thermostat correctly in its housing.

**10** Refit the thermostat housing cover and tighten its retaining bolts to the specified torque.

**11** Securely reconnect the coolant hose then refit the engine cover.

**12** Refill the cooling system as described in Chapter 1 and reconnect the battery.

**4.3a Coolant hose connection to the thermostat cover on non-GDI engines . . .**

**4.3b . . . and on the GDI engine**

**5.5 Disconnect the cooling fan wiring connector . . .**

**5.6 . . . then slacken and remove the retaining bolts (arrowed) and lift the cooling fan out of position**

**5.7 Unscrew the retaining bolts and separate the motor from its shroud**

## 5 Cooling fan(s) – testing, removal and refitting

### Testing

**1** The cooling fan(s) is/are (as applicable) controlled by the engine management ECU, via the cooling fan relay(s), using the information supplied by the coolant temperature sensor and (where fitted) air conditioning system pressure switch.

**2** If a fan does not appear to work but the engine is running correctly, the fault is likely to be in either the cooling fan relay(s) or the motor(s). If either the ECU or temperature sensor are faulty it is likely that the engine will be running roughly and/or the engine management warning light in the instrument panel will be illuminated.

**3** The motor can be checked by disconnecting the wiring connector and connecting a 12 volt supply directly to it. The best way to check a cooling fan relay is by substitution with a new relay which is known to function correctly.

### Removal and refitting – non-turbo models

**4** Disconnect the battery negative terminal (see *Disconnecting the battery*) and proceed as described under the relevant sub-heading.

#### Cooling fan – without air conditioning

**5** Disconnect the wiring connector from the fan motor, then unclip the wiring/hoses from the fan shroud **(see illustration)**. If necessary, to gain access from underneath, firmly apply the handbrake then jack up the front of the car and support it on axle stands. Remove the retaining screws/fasteners and remove the

front section of the engine/transmission undershield.

**6** Slacken and remove the retaining bolts securing the fan shroud to the top of the radiator, then manoeuvre the fan assembly out of position **(see illustration)**.

**7** If necessary, unclip the wiring, then slacken and remove the retaining bolts and separate the motor and shroud **(see illustration)**.

**8** Refitting is the reverse of removal. Make sure the shroud is correctly located in its lower mounting, then tighten its retaining bolts to the specified torque. Ensure the fan wiring is securely clipped to the shroud and in no danger of contacting the fan blade.

#### Cooling fan – with air conditioning

**9** Carry out the operations described in paragraphs 5 and 6, and unbolt the fan assembly from the radiator.

**10** Position the fan clear of the radiator then remove the radiator as described in Section 3.

**11** Manoeuvre the cooling fan out of position and, if necessary, slacken and remove the retaining bolts and separate the motor and shroud **(see illustration)**.

**12** Refitting is the reverse of removal.

#### Auxiliary cooling fan

**13** Disconnect the wiring connector from the fan motor, then unclip the wiring/hoses from the fan shroud **(see illustration)**.

**14** Slacken and remove the upper retaining bolts securing the fan shroud to the top of the radiator. Loosen the lower mounting bolt and manoeuvre the fan assembly out of position **(see illustrations)**.

**5.11 On models with air conditioning it will be necessary to remove the radiator to enable the cooling fan to be removed**

**5.13 Disconnect the wiring connector from the auxiliary cooling fan**

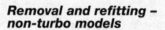

**5.14a Remove the upper mounting bolts (arrowed) . . .**

**5.14b . . . then slacken the lower bolt (arrowed) . . .**

**5.14c . . . and lift the auxiliary cooling fan out of position**

**5.17a  On turbo models, remove both headlight access covers . . .**

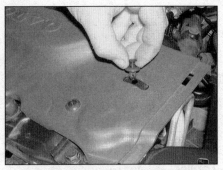

**5.17b  . . . then remove the retaining fasteners . . .**

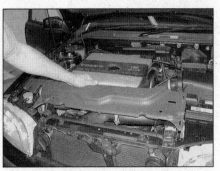

**5.17c  . . . and lift off the cover from the top of the radiator**

15 If necessary, remove the retaining nut/clip (as applicable) and remove the fan blade from the motor shaft. Release the wiring then undo the retaining nuts and separate the motor and shroud.
16 Refitting is the reverse of removal, tightening the bolts to the specified torque. Ensure the fan wiring is securely clipped to the shroud and in no danger of contacting the fan blade.

### Removal and refitting – turbo models

**Note:** *An engine support bar or hoist will be required to support the engine/transmission whilst the crossmember is removed.*

17 Release the securing clips and remove both headlight access covers. Undo the retaining fasteners (slacken the centre screws a few turns then pull out the complete fastener) and remove the cover from the top of the radiator **(see illustrations)**.
18 Disconnect the canister hose from the evaporative emission system purge valve and free the hose from the fan shroud. Release the purge valve from its mounting and position it clear of the shroud.
19 Disconnect the wiring connector from the intake air temperature sensor (screwed into the top of the intercooler) and right-hand cooling fan unclip the wiring harness from the shroud.
20 Slacken and remove the upper retaining screws securing the fan shroud to the radiator.
21 Chock the rear wheels, firmly apply the handbrake, then jack up the front of the car and support on axle stands.
22 Remove the retaining screws/fasteners and remove the undershield from beneath the engine.
23 Attach a support bar or engine hoist to the lifting hook on the cylinder head and use it to support the weight of the engine/transmission. Alternatively, support the engine/transmission with a jack and block of wood.
24 Slacken and remove the through-bolts from the front and rear mountings, then undo the mounting bolts and remove the crossmember from beneath the engine/transmission. Recover the upper and lower mounting rubbers and spacers from the crossmember mountings, noting their correct

fitted locations. Renew the mounting rubbers if they show signs of damage or deterioration.
25 Slacken the retaining clip and disconnect the lower air hose from the intercooler.
26 Disconnect the left-hand cooling fan wiring connector, and free the wiring from the fan shroud.
27 Ensure all wiring/hoses have been unclipped from the fan shroud then undo the two lower retaining screws and manoeuvre the fan assembly out from underneath the car, taking care not to displace the radiator.
28 If necessary, remove the retaining nut/clip (as applicable) and remove the fan blade from the motor shaft. Release the wiring then undo the retaining nuts/bolts and separate the motor and shroud.
29 Refitting is the reverse of removal, noting the following:
a) Tighten the fan nuts/bolts to the specified torque.
b) Ensure the wiring/hoses are all correctly clipped to the shroud and in no danger of contacting the fan blades.
c) Ensure the upper and lower mounting rubbers and the spacers are correctly fitted to the engine/transmission crossmember. Tighten the crossmember mounting bolts to the specified torque, then refit the through-bolts to the engine/transmission mountings. Remove the support bar/hoist/jack (as applicable) and rock the engine to settle it in position, then tighten the engine/transmission rear mounting through-bolt to the specified torque, followed by the front mounting through-bolt.

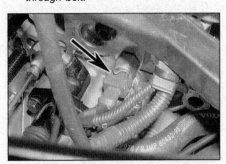

**6.1  On non-GDI engines, the coolant temperature gauge sensor (arrowed) screws into the cylinder head**

### 6  Cooling system electrical switches and sensors – testing, removal and refitting

### *Coolant temperature sensor*

**Note:** *On turbo and later GDI engines, the temperature gauge is operated by the engine temperature sensor.*

#### Testing

1 On non-GDI engines, the coolant temperature sensor is fitted to the left-hand end of the cylinder head **(see illustration)**. On the GDI engine, the sensor is screwed into the side of the thermostat housing – only the early GDIs have a separate sensor for the gauge (see Chapter 4B, Section 10, for more details).
2 The temperature gauge is fed with a stabilised voltage from the instrument panel feed (via the ignition switch and a fuse). The gauge earth is controlled by the sensor. The sensor contains a thermistor – an electronic component whose electrical resistance decreases at a predetermined rate as its temperature rises. When the coolant is cold, the sensor resistance is high, current flow through the gauge is reduced, and the gauge needle points towards the cold end of the scale. As the coolant temperature rises and the sensor resistance falls, current flow increases, and the gauge needle moves towards the upper end of the scale. If the sensor is faulty, it must be renewed.
3 If the gauge develops a fault, first check the other instruments; if they do not work at all, check the instrument panel electrical feed. If the readings are erratic, there may be a fault in the instrument panel printed circuit board (see Chapter 12). If the fault lies in the temperature gauge alone, check it as follows.
4 If the gauge needle remains at the cold end of the scale when the engine is hot, disconnect the sensor wiring plug, and earth the relevant wire to the cylinder head. If the needle then deflects when the ignition is switched on, the sensor unit is proved faulty, and should be renewed. If the needle still does not move, remove the instrument panel (Chapter 12) and check the continuity of the wire between the sensor unit and the gauge,

**6.11 The engine management system temperature sensor (arrowed) is screwed into the thermostat housing**

and the feed to the gauge unit. If continuity is shown, and the fault still exists, then the gauge is faulty, and the gauge should be renewed.

5 If the gauge needle remains at the hot end of the scale when the engine is cold, disconnect the sensor wire. If the needle then returns to the cold end of the scale when the ignition is switched on, the sensor unit is proved faulty, and should be renewed. If the needle still does not move, check the remainder of the circuit as described previously.

### Removal

**Note:** *The engine should be cold before removing the switch.*

6 Either partially drain the cooling system to just below the level of the sensor (as described in Chapter 1), or have ready a suitable plug which can be used to plug the sensor aperture whilst it is removed. If a plug is used, take great care not to damage the sensor unit aperture, and do not use anything which will allow foreign matter to enter the cooling system.

7 Ensure the ignition is switched off, then disconnect the sensor wiring connector. Unscrew the sensor from the engine and recover its sealing washer (where fitted).

### Refitting

8 Where a sealing washer was fitted, fit a new washer then fit the sensor and tighten securely.

9 Where no sealing washer is used, ensure

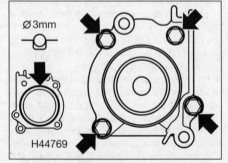

**7.5 Coolant pump refitting on the GDI engine – apply sealant and tighten bolts (arrowed)**

the sensor threads are clean and dry, then apply a smear of suitable sealant to them. Fit the sensor to the engine and tighten it securely.

10 Reconnect the wiring connector, then refill the cooling system as described in Chapter 1 or top-up as described in *Weekly checks*.

## Engine temperature sensor

**Note:** *On turbo and later GDI engines, the sensor also operates the coolant temperature gauge.*

### Testing

11 The engine temperature sensor is screwed into the thermostat housing, or into the cylinder head on GDI engines **(see illustration)**.

12 The sensor is a thermistor (see paragraph 2). The engine management electronic control unit (ECU) supplies the sensor with a set voltage and then, by measuring the current flowing in the sensor circuit, it determines the engine's temperature. This information is then used, in conjunction with other inputs, to control the injector timing, the idle speed, etc.

13 If the sensor circuit should fail to provide adequate information, the ECU's back-up facility will override the sensor signal. In this event, the ECU assumes a predetermined setting which will allow the engine management system to run, albeit at reduced efficiency. When this occurs, the warning light on the instrument panel will come on, and the advice of a Volvo dealer should be sought. The sensor itself can only be tested using special Volvo diagnostic equipment (see Chapter 4A or 4B). *Do not* attempt to test the circuit using any other equipment, as there is a high risk of damaging the ECU.

### Removal and refitting

14 Refer to Chapter 4A or 4B.

## 7 Coolant pump – removal and refitting

### Removal

1 Remove the timing belt as described in Chapter 2A or 2B.

2 Drain the cooling system as described in Chapter 1.

3 Slacken and remove the pump retaining bolts and remove the pump from the cylinder block. Recover the gasket and discard it; a new one must be used on refitting. On the GDI engine, sealant is used in place of a regular gasket.

### Refitting

4 Ensure the pump and cylinder block mating surfaces are clean and dry. On the GDI engine, ensure that all traces of old sealant have been removed.

5 Fit the new gasket (on the GDI engine, apply a 3 mm bead of sealant to the pump's

inner surface as shown) and locate the pump in the cylinder block. Refit the pump retaining bolts and tighten them to the specified torque **(see illustration)**.

6 Refit the timing belt as described in Chapter 2A or 2B.

7 On completion, refill the cooling system as described in Chapter 1.

## 8 Heating and ventilation system – general information

**Note:** *Refer to Section 10 for information on the air conditioning side of the system.*

### Manual heating/ ventilation system

1 The heating/ventilation system consists of a fully-adjustable blower motor, face-level vents in the centre and at each end of the facia, and air ducts to the front and rear footwells. The main assemblies of the system are the blower motor housing, located behind the passenger's end of the facia, and the heating/ ventilation housing which is located centrally behind the facia. On models not fitted with air conditioning, the two housings are linked with a large air duct; on models with air conditioning, they are joined by the evaporator housing.

2 Cold air enters the system through the grille at the rear of the bonnet. The air flows through the blower motor housing to the heating/ ventilation housing, where it is distributed through the relevant ducts and outlets. Stale air is expelled through ducts at the rear of the car. If warm air is required, the cold air is passed over the heater matrix (contained in the heating/ventilation housing), which is heated by the engine coolant. The rate of airflow can be increased by operating the blower motor.

3 The facia-mounted control panel is connected to the heating/ventilation housing by two cables; one operates the temperature control flap, and the other the air distribution flap. The flap valves deflect and mix the air flowing through the heating/ventilation housing, which acts as a central distribution unit, passing air to the various ducts and vents, according to the control panel settings.

4 An air recirculation switch is provided to close off the outside air supply to the car. The switch operates a flap on the blower motor housing, via an electrical motor, which closes off the heating/ventilation air intake. This prevents unpleasant odours entering from outside the car but should only be used briefly, as the recirculated air inside the car will soon become stale.

### Electronic climate control system

5 A fully-automatic electronic climate control air conditioning system was offered as an option on some models. The main components of the system are exactly the same as those described above – the only

major difference being that the temperature and distribution flaps in the heating/ventilation housing are operated by electric motors rather than by cables.

**6** The operation of the system is controlled by the ECC control module, which is housed inside the facia control panel, along with the following sensors.

   a) *Interior temperature sensor – informs the control module of the temperature inside the passenger compartment of the car.*

   b) *Outside air temperature sensor – informs the control module of the air temperature entering the heating/ventilation system.*

   c) *Evaporator temperature sensor – informs the control module of the evaporator temperature to prevent over-cooling of the system.*

   d) *Coolant temperature sensor – informs the control module of the temperature of the coolant in the heater matrix.*

   e) *Sun sensor – informs the control module when the sun is shining.*

**7** All the above information is analysed by the control module and, based on this, the module determines the appropriate settings for the heating/ventilation system to maintain the passenger compartment temperature at the desired setting on the control panel.

**8** If the ECC system develops a fault, the car should be taken to a Volvo dealer at the earliest opportunity. A complete test of the ECC system can then be carried out, using a special electronic diagnostic test unit (Volvo Scan Tool) which is plugged into the diagnostic (Data link) connector. The connector is located at the front of the centre console on the driver's side.

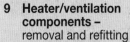

### 9  Heater/ventilation components – removal and refitting

#### Manual heating/ventilation system

##### Control panel

**1** Disconnect the battery negative terminal (see *Disconnecting the battery*).

**2** Undo the retaining screws securing the left- and right-hand side panels in position, then carefully unclip the panels and remove them

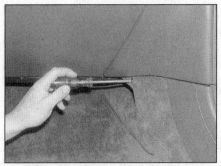

**9.2a  Undo the retaining screw . . .**

**9.2b  . . . and remove each side panel from the front of the centre console**

**9.5a  Pull off all the control knobs . . .**

**9.5b  . . . then pull the faceplate off the heating/ventilation control panel (panel retaining screws arrowed)**

from the front of the centre console **(see illustrations)**.

**3** Remove the radio/cassette player as described in Chapter 12.

**4** Where necessary, unclip and remove the storage compartment from the centre of the facia.

**5** Pull off all the control knobs from the heating/ventilation control panel. Reach in through the control knob apertures and carefully ease the faceplate off from the front of the control panel **(see illustrations)**.

**6** Slacken and remove the heater control panel retaining screws, and free the panel from the facia.

**7** Slacken and remove the screw securing the base of the facia centre panel to the centre console. Carefully ease the centre panel out of position and remove it from the facia – disconnect its wiring connectors as they become accessible **(see illustrations)**.

**8** Free the control panel from the facia, then disconnect the control cables and wiring connector(s) and remove the panel from the car. The control cable end fittings are clipped into position.

**9** Refitting is the reverse of removal. Prior to refitting the radio/cassette player, check the operation of the control panel knobs and make any necessary adjustments at the heater/ventilation housing end of the cable. Remove the facia lower panel to gain access to the cable end, then make adjustments by repositioning the outer cable in its retaining clip.

##### Blower motor

**10** Slacken and remove the retaining screws and remove the passenger's side lower panel from the facia **(see illustration)**. Fold back the carpet to gain access to the blower motor, which is fitted to the underside of the housing.

**9.7a  Undo the retaining screw . . .**

**9.7b  . . . then remove the facia centre panel, disconnecting the wiring from the panel switches**

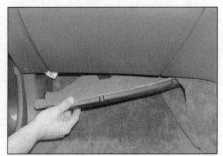

**9.10  Remove the lower panel from the passenger side of the facia to gain access to the blower motor**

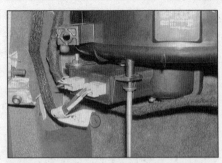

9.11 Undo the retaining screws and position the relay unit clear of the blower motor housing

9.12a Disconnect the blower motor wiring . . .

9.12b . . . then undo the retaining screws (arrowed) . . .

11 Where necessary, slacken and remove the retaining screws and free the relay from the underside of the blower motor housing (see illustration).

12 Disconnect the wiring connector, then undo three retaining screws and manoeuvre the motor assembly out of position (see illustrations).

13 Refitting is the reverse of removal ensuring the blower motor seal is in good condition.

### Blower motor resistor

14 Slacken and remove the retaining screws and remove the passenger's side lower panel from the facia. Fold back the carpet to gain access to the blower resistor which is fitted to the underside of the duct/evaporator housing (as applicable).

15 Disconnect the wiring connector, then undo the retaining screws and remove the resistor from the car (see illustrations).

16 Refitting is the reverse of removal.

### Heater matrix

17 Working in the engine compartment, locate the heater matrix unions on the engine compartment bulkhead. Clamp both coolant hoses to minimise coolant loss, and position a wad of rag beneath the matrix unions, to catch any spilt coolant. Release the retaining clips and disconnect both hoses. Mop up any spilt coolant and rinse off with water.

18 Remove the facia panel assembly as described in Chapter 11.

19 Disconnect the wiring connector(s)/hose/control cables (as applicable) and remove the heating/ventilation control panel.

20 Disconnect all the wiring connectors from

the heating/ventilation housing then unclip the wiring from the housing and facia support bracket and position it clear.

21 Undo the retaining bolts and remove both the facia support brackets (see illustrations).

22 On models with air conditioning, slacken and remove the evaporator housing mounting nut and bolts (see illustrations). Free the evaporator housing from the heating/ventilation housing assembly, taking care not to place any strain on the refrigerant pipes. If necessary, free the pipes from their retaining clips/brackets in the engine compartment. Also slacken and remove the three retaining nuts securing the blower motor housing to the bulkhead.

> ⚠ **Warning: Do not disconnect the refrigerant pipes. Refer to the precautions given in Section 10.**

9.12c . . . and lower the motor assembly out of position

9.15a Disconnect the wiring connector . . .

9.15b . . . then undo the retaining screws . . .

9.15c . . . and remove the blower motor resistor

9.21a Unscrew the retaining bolts . . .

9.21b . . . and remove both the facia support brackets

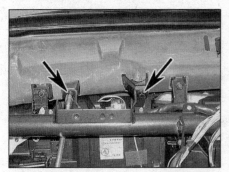

**9.22a  On models with air conditioning, unscrew the evaporator housing upper . . .**

**9.22b  . . . and lower retaining nuts (arrowed)**

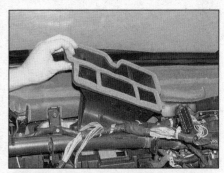

**9.24  Unclip the upper outlet from the heating/ventilation housing**

23  On models not fitted with air conditioning, disconnect the wiring connector from the blower motor resistor. Remove the fasteners (press out the centre pins then remove the fastener clip) securing the duct to the blower motor and heater/ventilation housing and ease the duct out of position.

24  Unclip the upper outlet and remove it from the top of the heating/ventilation housing **(see illustration)**.

25  Slacken and remove the retaining screw, then detach the footwell vent outlet from the base of the heating/ventilation housing. Push down on the footwell vents and manoeuvre the outlet out of position **(see illustrations)**.

26  Slacken and remove the housing retaining nuts, then free the assembly from the bulkhead and remove it from the car **(see illustrations)**. As the unit is removed, make sure all the necessary clips and ties have been released, and try and keep the heater matrix unions uppermost to prevent coolant spillage. Mop up any spilt coolant immediately.

*Caution: On models with air conditioning, take great care not to place any strain on the evaporator housing refrigerant pipes as the housing is removed.*

27  Slacken and remove the screws securing the matrix coolant pipe retaining bracket to the heating/ventilation housing. Free the pipe bracket from the housing, and slide the pipe and matrix assembly carefully out of the housing **(see illustrations)**.

28  Slacken the clamps and separate the pipe assembly from matrix unions **(see**

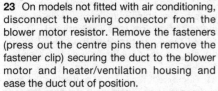

**9.25a  Remove the retaining screw . . .**

**9.25b  . . . then unclip the footwell vent outlet from the base of the housing**

**illustration)**. Recover the sealing ring from each union and discard them – new ones must be used on refitting. Inspect the matrix seal for signs of damage, and renew if necessary.

29  Prior to refitting, inspect all seals for signs of damage and renew/repair as necessary.

30  Fit new sealing rings and reassemble the coolant pipe and matrix, tightening the clamps lightly only. Slide the assembly into

**9.26a  Unscrew the heating/ventilation housing upper . . .**

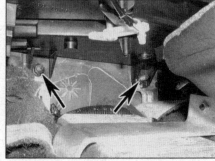

**9.26b  . . . and lower retaining nuts (arrowed) . . .**

**9.26c  . . . then manoeuvre the housing out of position**

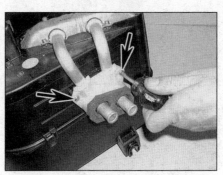

**9.27a  Slacken and remove the pipe bracket retaining screws (arrowed) . . .**

**9.27b  . . . then slide the matrix assembly out of position**

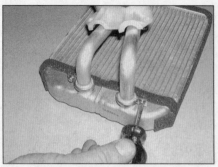

**9.28 Slacken the clamps and separate the pipe assembly from the matrix**

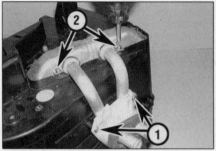

**9.30 Tighten the pipe bracket screws (1) first then securely tighten the pipe/matrix clamps (2)**

**9.38 Release the retaining clip and detach the servo motor link rod from the linkage**

the housing, and locate the pipe bracket in position. Securely tighten the bracket screws, then tighten the pipe/matrix union clamps securely **(see illustration)**.

31 Locate the heating/ventilation housing on its mounting, and lightly tighten its retaining nuts. On models with air conditioning, lightly tighten the evaporator unit nut and bolts and the blower motor housing nuts.

32 Refit the lower outlet securely to the housing then reconnect the footwell ducts, tightening the retaining screw securely.

33 On models not fitted with air conditioning, refit the duct linking the blower motor and heating ventilation housings, and reconnect the wiring connector to the resistor. Ensure the duct is correctly seated, and secure it in position with the retaining clips.

34 On models with air conditioning, ensure the evaporator housing is correctly seated in both the blower motor and heating/ventilation

housing, then tighten its mounting nut and bolts to the specified torque. Also tighten the blower motor housing nuts to the specified torque.

35 On all models, ensure the housing/duct joins are correctly sealed, then tighten the heating/ventilation housing nuts to the specified torque. Refit the facia support brackets, and tighten their retaining bolts to the specified torque.

36 The remainder of refitting is the reverse of removal. On completion, top-up the cooling system as described in *Weekly checks*.

### Air recirculation flap servo motor

37 Remove the facia panel as described in Chapter 11. The servo motor is mounted onto the blower motor housing.

38 Rotate the locking clip away from the link rod, and detach the rod from flap linkage **(see illustration)**.

39 Disconnect the wiring connector, then undo the retaining screws and remove servo motor from the car **(see illustrations)**.

40 Fit the servo motor to the blower motor housing, and securely tighten its retaining screws.

41 Reconnect the link rod to the flap linkage, and securely clip the locking clip onto the rod.

42 Reconnect the servo unit wiring connector, then refit the facia panel as described in Chapter 11.

### *Electronic climate control system*

#### Control panel

43 Carry out the operations described in paragraphs 1 to 4.

44 Remove the faceplate from the heater control panel. To do this, release the faceplate retaining clips by inserting a small, flat-bladed screwdriver in through the top vent on either side, then carefully ease the faceplate out of position **(see illustrations)**.

45 Slacken and remove the heater control panel retaining screws, and free the panel from the facia.

46 Slacken and remove the screw securing the base of the facia centre panel to the centre console. Carefully ease the centre panel out of position and remove it from the facia – disconnect its wiring connectors as they become accessible.

47 Free the control panel from the facia, then disconnect the hose and wiring connector, and remove the panel from the car **(see illustrations)**.

**9.39a Disconnect the wiring connector then undo the retaining screws (arrowed) . . .**

**9.39b . . . and remove the recirculation flap motor from the housing**

**9.44a Release the retaining clips, accessible through the upper vent slots (arrowed) . . .**

**9.44b . . . then carefully unclip the faceplate from the control panel**

**9.47a Free the control panel from the facia . . .**

**48** Refitting is the reverse of removal, ensuring the hose and wiring connectors are securely refitted.

**Blower motor**

**49** Refer to paragraphs 10 to 13.

**Blower motor control module**

**50** Slacken and remove the retaining screws, and remove the passenger's side lower panel from the facia. The control module is fitted to the side of the evaporator housing.
**51** Disconnect the wiring connector then undo the retaining screws and remove the module from the car. Note that access to the upper retaining screw is very limited but can only be improved by removing the complete facia panel (see Chapter 11).
**52** Refitting is the reverse of removal.

**Heater matrix**

**53** Refer to paragraphs 17 to 36.

**Air recirculation flap servo motor**

**54** Refer to paragraphs 37 to 42.

**Air temperature flap and distribution flap servo motors**

**55** Removal and refitting of these servo motors should be entrusted to a Volvo dealer. Once the new motor has been installed it will be necessary to have the control module reprogrammed to ensure the ECC system functions correctly. This can only be done using the special Volvo Scan Tool which is plugged into the diagnostic socket (see Section 8).

**System control module**

**56** The control module is an integral part of the control panel assembly and cannot be renewed separately.

**Interior temperature sensor**

**57** The interior temperature sensor is an integral part of the control panel assembly and cannot be renewed separately.

**Outside air temperature sensor**

**58** Remove the facia panel assembly as described in Chapter 11.
**59** Disconnect the wiring connectors from the blower motor and the air recirculation flap servo motor.
**60** Slacken and remove the evaporator housing mounting nut and bolts.
**61** Slacken and remove the mounting nuts then free the blower motor housing assembly from the evaporator housing and manoeuvre it out of position.
**62** The outside air temperature sensor is clipped to the blower motor side of the evaporator. Disconnect the wiring connector then carefully unclip the sensor and ease it out from the evaporator housing.
**63** Refitting is the reverse of removal making sure the sensor is securely clipped in position. Ensure the evaporator housing and blower motor housing seals are all securely joined before tightening the mounting nuts and bolts to the specified torque.

**9.47b . . . then disconnect its wiring connector . . .**

**Evaporator temperature sensor**

**64** Remove the heating/ventilation housing as described in paragraphs 17 to 26.
**65** The outside air temperature sensor is clipped to the heating/ventilation housing side of the evaporator. Disconnect the wiring connector then carefully unclip the sensor and ease it out from the evaporator housing.
**66** Refitting is the reverse of removal making sure the sensor is securely clipped in position. Refit the heating/ventilation housing as described in paragraphs 31 to 36.

**Coolant temperature sensor**

**67** Undo the retaining screw and remove the passenger's side trim panel from the front of the centre console.
**68** Undo the retaining screws and remove the passenger's side lower panel from the facia.
**69** Locate the coolant temperature sensor, which is fitted to the base of the heating/ventilation housing, directly beneath the heater matrix.
**70** Disconnect the wiring connector, then pull the sensor out from the housing.
**71** Refitting is the reverse of removal, making sure the sensor is correctly located in the housing and making good contact with the heater matrix.

**Sun sensor**

**72** Carefully ease the loudspeaker grille out from the top of the passenger's end of the facia panel to gain access to the sun sensor.
**73** Unclip the sensor from the facia and disconnect it from the wiring connector.
**74** Refitting is the reverse of removal.

**10  Air conditioning system –**
general information and precautions

**1** An air conditioning system is available on certain models. It enables the temperature of incoming air to be lowered, and also dehumidifies the air, which makes for rapid demisting and increased comfort.
**2** The cooling side of the system works in the same way as a domestic refrigerator.

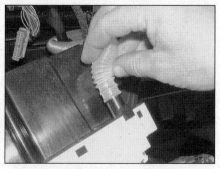

**9.47c . . . and hose**

Refrigerant gas is drawn into a belt-driven compressor (the compressor is fitted with an electrically-operated clutch to enable it be switched on and off as required), and passes into a condenser mounted on the front of the radiator, where it loses heat and becomes liquid. The liquid passes through an expansion valve to an evaporator, where it changes from liquid under high pressure to gas under low pressure. This change is accompanied by a drop in temperature, which cools the evaporator. The refrigerant returns to the compressor, and the cycle begins again.
**3** Air blown through the evaporator passes to the heating/ventilation housing, where it is mixed with hot air blown through the heater matrix to achieve the desired temperature in the passenger compartment.
**4** The heating side of the system works in the same way as on models without air conditioning (see Section 8).
**5** Any problems with the air conditioning system should be referred to a Volvo dealer.

**Precautions**

**6** When an air conditioning system is fitted, it is necessary to observe special precautions when dealing with any part of the system, or its associated components.
• Never attempt to open any air conditioning system pipe/hose union – the system is under constant pressure. If for any reason the system must be disconnected, the car should be taken to a Volvo dealer or air conditioning system specialist with the necessary equipment to safely discharge the refrigerant before opening the circuit. Once the work is complete, they can then safely recharge the circuit with the correct type and amount of fresh refrigerant.
• The refrigerant is potentially dangerous, and should only be handled by qualified persons. Uncontrolled discharging of the refrigerant is dangerous for the following reasons:
a) *If it is splashed onto the skin, it can cause frostbite.*
b) *The refrigerant is heavier than air and so displaces oxygen. In a confined space which is not adequately ventilated, this could lead to a risk of suffocation. The*

gas is odourless and colourless, so there is no warning of its presence in the atmosphere.
c) *Although not poisonous, in the presence of a naked flame (including a cigarette) it forms a noxious gas which causes nausea, headaches, etc.*

• Do not operate the air conditioning system if it is known to be short of refrigerant, as this could damage the compressor.

## 11 Air conditioning system components – removal and refitting

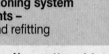

**⚠ Warning: Never attempt to open the refrigerant circuit before the circuit has been professionally discharged. Refer to the precautions given in Section 10.**

The only operation which can be carried out easily without discharging the refrigerant is the renewal of the auxiliary drivebelt for the compressor – this is described in Chapter 1. If necessary, the compressor can be unbolted and moved aside, without disconnecting the refrigerant pipes, after removing the drivebelt. All other operations should be entrusted to a Volvo dealer or an air conditioning specialist.

# Chapter 4 Part A:
# Fuel system (except GDI engine)

## Contents

## Degrees of difficulty

| **Easy,** suitable for novice with little experience |  | **Fairly easy,** suitable for beginner with some experience |  | **Fairly difficult,** suitable for competent DIY mechanic | | **Difficult,** suitable for experienced DIY mechanic | | **Very difficult,** suitable for expert DIY or professional | 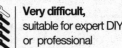 |
|---|---|---|---|---|---|---|---|---|---|

## Specifications

### System type
Non-turbo engines . . . . . . . . . . . . . . . . . . . . . . . . . . . . . . . . . . . . Fenix 5.1 or EMS 2000 engine management system
Turbocharged engines . . . . . . . . . . . . . . . . . . . . . . . . . . . . . . . . . EMS 2000 engine management system

### Fuel delivery system data
Fuel tank capacity . . . . . . . . . . . . . . . . . . . . . . . . . . . . . . . . . . . . . 60 litres
Idle speed (all models)* . . . . . . . . . . . . . . . . . . . . . . . . . . . . . . . . . 750 rpm
Idle mixture CO content* . . . . . . . . . . . . . . . . . . . . . . . . . . . . . . . . < 0.2%
Fuel pump unregulated delivery pressure . . . . . . . . . . . . . . . . . . . . 4.8 to 8.0 bar (70 to 116 psi)
Regulated fuel pressure . . . . . . . . . . . . . . . . . . . . . . . . . . . . . . . . . 3.0 bar (44 psi)
Fuel delivery rate:
   Non-turbo engines . . . . . . . . . . . . . . . . . . . . . . . . . . . . . . . . . . 120 litres/hour @ 3.0 bar and 12.5V
   Turbocharged engines . . . . . . . . . . . . . . . . . . . . . . . . . . . . . . . . 150 litres/hour @ 3.0 bar and 12.5V
Fuel injectors:

| Colour code: | **Up to 1999** | **2000 onwards** |
|---|---|---|
|   Non-turbo engines | Lilac/black | Green/black |
|   Turbocharged engines | Grey/black | Dark green/green |
|   Electrical resistance (all models) | 14.0 to 15.0 ohms | |

*Non-adjustable – controlled by ECU*

### Engine management system data (typical)
Sensor/actuator electrical resistance (at 20°C):
   Inlet air temperature sensor . . . . . . . . . . . . . . . . . . . . . . . . . . . . 3500 ohms @ 20°C
   Crankshaft sensor . . . . . . . . . . . . . . . . . . . . . . . . . . . . . . . . . . . 260 to 340 ohms @ 20°C
   Coolant temperature sensor:
      Non-turbo engines (to 1999) . . . . . . . . . . . . . . . . . . . . . . . . . 2800 ohms @ 20°C
      Non-turbo engines (from 2000) . . . . . . . . . . . . . . . . . . . . . . . 2450 ohms @ 20°C
      Turbocharged engines . . . . . . . . . . . . . . . . . . . . . . . . . . . . . . 2450 ohms @ 20°C
   Throttle position sensor (at idle) . . . . . . . . . . . . . . . . . . . . . . . . . 960 to 1440 ohms @ 20°C
   Idle air control valve . . . . . . . . . . . . . . . . . . . . . . . . . . . . . . . . . 8.6 to 10.6 ohms @ 20°C

### Recommended fuel
Octane rating:
   Recommended . . . . . . . . . . . . . . . . . . . . . . . . . . . . . . . . . . . . . . 95 RON unleaded
   Minimum . . . . . . . . . . . . . . . . . . . . . . . . . . . . . . . . . . . . . . . . . . 91 RON unleaded

## Torque wrench settings

| | Nm | lbf ft |
|---|---|---|
| Coolant temperature sensor | 10 | 7 |
| Crankshaft sensor | 20 | 15 |
| Fuel pump plastic retaining nut | 40 | 30 |
| Fuel rail to inlet manifold | 10 | 7 |
| Inlet manifold bolts | 20 | 15 |
| Inlet manifold support bracket bolts | 20 | 15 |
| Oxygen sensor | 55 | 41 |
| Throttle housing | 10 | 7 |

## 1 General information and precautions

### General information

All models covered in this manual are equipped with an electronic engine management system which controls the fuelling and ignition. Details of the type of system fitted to each model in the range are given in the Specifications. This Chapter deals with the those parts of the engine management system which are concerned with fuel injection – refer to Chapter 5B for details of the ignition system components.

The fuel injection system comprises a fuel tank, an electric fuel pump, a fuel filter, fuel supply and return lines, a throttle housing, four fuel injectors, and an Electronic Control Unit (ECU) together with its associated sensors, actuators and wiring.

The fuel pump delivers a constant supply of fuel through a cartridge filter to the throttle housing, and the fuel pressure regulator (integral with the throttle housing) maintains a constant fuel pressure at the fuel injector, and returns excess fuel to the tank via the return line. This constant-flow system also helps to reduce fuel temperature, and prevents vapourisation.

The fuel injectors are opened and closed by an Electronic Control Unit (ECU), which calculates the injection timing and duration according to engine speed, throttle position and rate of opening, inlet air temperature, coolant temperature and exhaust gas oxygen content information, received from sensors mounted on and around the engine.

Inlet air is drawn into the engine through the air cleaner, which contains a renewable paper filter element. On non-turbo engines, the inlet air temperature is regulated by a thermostatically-controlled valve mounted in the air cleaner, which blends air at ambient temperature with hot air, drawn from over the exhaust manifold.

Idle speed is controlled by an Idle Air Control Valve (IAC), located on the side of the throttle housing. Cold starting enrichment is controlled by the ECU, using the coolant temperature and inlet air temperature parameters, to increase the injector opening duration.

The exhaust gas oxygen content is constantly monitored by the ECU via the lambda sensor, which is mounted in the exhaust downpipe. On later engines, two oxygen sensors are fitted, one before the catalytic converter, and one after – this improves sensor response time and accuracy, and the ECU compares the signals from each sensor to confirm that the converter is working correctly. The ECU then uses this information to modify the injection timing and duration to maintain the optimum air/fuel ratio. An exhaust catalyst is fitted to all models.

Depending on engine type, models for some market territories are also equipped with an exhaust gas recirculation (EGR) system, a secondary air injection system, and an activated charcoal filter evaporative loss system as part of an emissions control package. Further details of these systems will be found in Part C of this Chapter.

It should be noted that engine management system fault diagnosis is only possible with dedicated electronic test equipment. Problems with the system should therefore be referred to a fuel injection specialist or a Volvo dealer for assessment. Once the fault has been identified, the removal/refitting procedures detailed in the following Sections can then be followed.

### Precautions

⚠️ **Warning: Petrol is extremely flammable – great care must be taken when working on any part of the fuel system. Do not smoke or allow any naked flames or uncovered light bulbs near the work area. Note that gas powered domestic appliances with pilot flames, such as heaters, boilers and tumble dryers, also present a fire hazard – bear this in mind if you are working in an area where such appliances are present.**

**2.4 Unscrew the dust cap from the service valve at the right-hand end of the fuel rail**

*Always keep a suitable fire extinguisher close to the work area and familiarise yourself with its operation before starting work. Wear eye protection when working on fuel systems and wash off any fuel spilt on bare skin immediately with soap and water. Note that fuel vapour is just as dangerous as liquid fuel; a vessel that has just been emptied of liquid fuel will still contain vapour and can be potentially explosive. Petrol is a highly dangerous and volatile liquid, and the precautions necessary when handling it cannot be overstressed.*

- *Many of the operations described in this Chapter involve the disconnection of fuel lines, which may cause an amount of fuel spillage. Before commencing work, refer to the above Warning and the information in 'Safety first!' at the beginning of this manual.*
- *When working with fuel system components, pay particular attention to cleanliness – dirt entering the fuel system may cause blockages which will lead to poor running.*

## 2 Depressurising the fuel system

1 This procedure should be carried out before attempting any work on the fuel system. The injection system operates at such a high pressure, residual pressure will remain in the system for several hours after the engine is switched off. Opening any of the fuel lines in this condition will result in an uncontrolled spray of fuel, which is at best unpleasant, and at worst highly-dangerous.

2 Although relieving the system pressure will prevent fuel being sprayed out, note that it will not empty the fuel lines, and appropriate precautions against fuel spillage (such as wrapping the connection with clean cloth before opening it) should still be observed.

### Method 1

3 Undo the securing screws and remove the plastic cover from the top of the engine. Disconnect the battery negative lead (see *Disconnecting the battery*).

4 Unscrew the dust cap from the service valve at the right-hand end of the fuel rail **(see illustration)**.

5 Place wads of absorbent cloth underneath

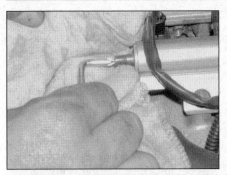

**2.5  Depress the fuel rail service valve pin with a pointed instrument**

and around the service valve, then depress the pin at the centre of the valve with a pointed instrument. Be prepared for the release of fuel which may be ejected under pressure. When the pressure has been relieved, refit the dust cap to the service valve **(see illustration)**.

### Method 2

**6** Locate and remove fuse number 17 from the engine compartment fusebox.
**7** Start the engine, and let it run until it cuts out. If the engine will not start with the fuel pump fuse removed, turn it over on the starter for approximately 10 seconds. The fuel system will now be depressurised.
**8** On completion, switch off the ignition, disconnect the battery negative lead (see *Disconnecting the battery*), and refit the fuel pump fuse.

### 3  Air cleaner assembly and air ducts – removal and refitting

#### Removal

**Air cleaner assembly**

**1** Remove the battery from its mounting tray, with reference to Chapter 5A.
**2** On turbo models, release the fixings and remove the cover panel from the front left-hand side of the engine compartment, above the throttle housing.
**3** Where applicable, disconnect the

crankcase ventilation hose from the air cleaner ducting **(see illustration)**.
**4** On turbo models, unplug the wiring connector from the mass airflow sensor, then remove the two securing screws and disconnect the air mass meter from the air cleaner. Slacken the hose clip and detach the air mass meter from the air inlet hose, then remove the meter from the engine compartment. Recover the gasket.
**5** On turbo models, release the turbocharger boost control valve from the side of the air cleaner; there is no need to disconnect the vacuum hoses from it.
**6** On non-turbo models, disconnect the vacuum hose from the warm air control valve, at the side of the air cleaner.
**7** Detach the warm-air inlet duct or turbocharger inlet duct, as applicable, from the base of the air cleaner housing **(see illustration)**.
**8** Slacken and withdraw the air cleaner housing securing screws. Lift the housing upwards at the engine side to release it from the lower locating lugs, then move it sideways to disengage the side locating peg **(see illustration)**.
**9** Withdraw the cold air intake duct from the bodywork, then detach it from the side of the air cleaner housing **(see illustration)**.
**10** Remove the housing from the car.

**Air ducts**

**11** All ducting is retained either by simple snap-fit connectors or by hose clips. The routing of the ducts varies between models, but in all cases removal is straightforward and

self-explanatory **(see illustration)**. To gain access to the lower ducts, it will be necessary to remove the air cleaner assembly as previously described.

#### Refitting

**12** In all cases, refit by reversing the removal operations.

### 4  Intake air preheating system – testing

**1** An inlet air preheating system is incorporated in the air cleaner housing on non-turbo models for certain markets. The system utilises a flap valve arrangement controlled by a wax thermostat capsule to blend cold air from the inlet adjacent to the radiator, with warm air from the exhaust manifold heat shield. The capsule responds to ambient temperature to move the flap valve accordingly.
**2** To gain access to the unit, remove the air cleaner assembly as described in Section 3.
**3** Detach the inlet body from the air cleaner housing by removing the securing screws and pulling the body free.
**4** Check the condition of the spindle bearings, capsule and spring, then test the operation of the capsule as follows.
**5** Cool the unit by placing it in a refrigerator for a few minutes. Check that at a temperature of approximately 5°C or less, the flap valve has moved to shut off the cold air inlet.

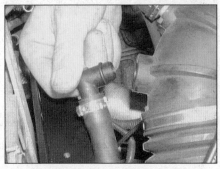

**3.3  Disconnect the crankcase ventilation hose from the air cleaner ducting**

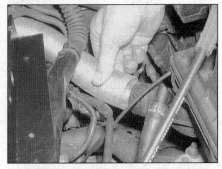

**3.7  Detach the warm-air inlet duct from the base of the air cleaner housing**

**3.8  Slacken and withdraw the air cleaner housing securing screws**

**3.9  Lift the air cleaner housing and withdraw the cold air intake duct from the bodywork**

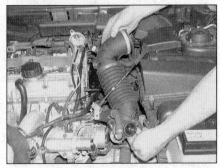

**3.11  Removing the air cleaner-to-throttle housing ducting**

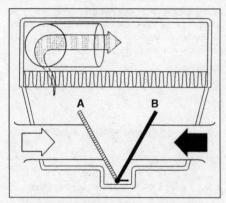

**4.6 Inlet air preheating system flap positions**

A  Cold position          B  Hot position

**5.2a Unhook the inner cable from the throttle spindle quadrant . . .**

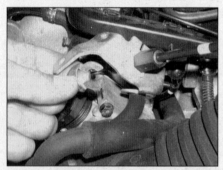

**5.2b . . . release the retaining clip from the accelerator cable adjuster . . .**

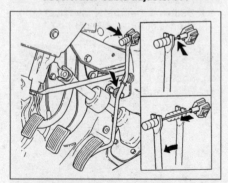

**5.4 Release the cable nipple from the top of the accelerator pedal, then pass the cable inner through the slotted hole to release it from the pedal**

6 As the unit warms in response to room temperature, check that at approximately 10°C the flap valve is in the mid-position, and that at 15°C or higher, the flap has moved to shut off the warm air inlet **(see illustration)**.
7 If the unit does not function as described, it should be renewed.
8 On completion, reassemble the inlet body, then refit the air cleaner assembly as described in Section 3.

## 5  Accelerator cable – removal, refitting and adjustment

### Removal

1 Undo the screws and remove the engine cover to gain access to the throttle housing.
2 Unhook the inner cable from the throttle spindle quadrant, release the retaining clip from the accelerator cable adjuster and extract the outer cable from the support bracket **(see illustrations)**.
3 Undo the screws, release the clips and remove the trim/sound proofing panel from under the facia on the driver's side. Where applicable, remove the cruise control vacuum unit.
4 Release the cable nipple from the top of the accelerator pedal, then pass the cable inner through the slotted hole to release it from the pedal **(see illustration)**.

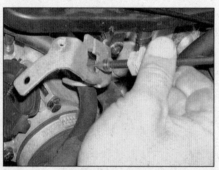

**5.2c . . . and extract the outer cable from the support bracket**

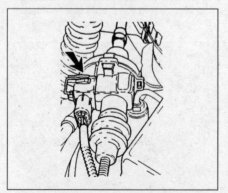

**5.6 On automatic transmission models from 1998 onwards, disconnect the kickdown switch wiring connector**

5 On manual transmission models, depress the locking tabs and release the cable grommet from the bulkhead and pull the cable into the engine compartment. Note the routing of the cable, release it from any clips or ties, and remove it.
6 On automatic transmission models from 1998 onwards, disconnect the wiring connector from the kickdown switch attached to the cable at the bulkhead entry. Release the kickdown switch from the bulkhead by depressing the switch lugs with a screwdriver, whilst at the same time pushing the cable through **(see illustration)**. Note the routing of the cable, release it from any clips or ties, and remove it.

### Refitting

7 Refit by reversing the removal operations, ensuring that, on automatic transmission models, the kickdown switch lugs fully engage in the bulkhead (where applicable), and that the switch wiring connector is upright. Check along the entire length of the cable to ensure that there are no kinks, bends or restrictions that might cause it to stick in operation. Adjust the cable as follows.

### Adjustment

8 Reconnect the inner cable to the throttle spindle quadrant. With the accelerator pedal in the rest position, check that the throttle spindle quadrant is seated against the idle stop on the throttle mounting bracket.
9 Secure the accelerator outer cable in its mounting bracket with the retaining clip. Depress the accelerator pedal to the floor, and check that the quadrant reaches the wide-open throttle stop. Release the pedal and check that the quadrant returns to the idle stop; there should be no freeplay in the cable inner.

## 6  Fuel pump/gauge sender unit – removal and refitting

**Note:** *Observe the precautions in Section 1 before working on any component in the fuel system.*

### Removal

1 Disconnect the battery negative lead (see *Disconnecting the battery*).
2 Fold down the rear seat backrest and release the front edge of the load space carpet. Remove the support panel under the carpet.
3 Undo the screws, then remove the access cover and the protective cage from the top of the fuel pump/sender unit **(see illustrations)**.
4 Unplug the wiring from the top of the fuel pump/gauge sender unit at the connector **(see illustration)**.
5 Identify the fuel hose connections on top of the pump, to aid refitting. The delivery hose should be marked with a yellow band with a corresponding yellow mark on top of the

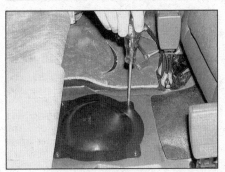

**6.3a  Undo the screws . . .**

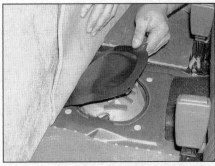

**6.3b  . . . then remove the access cover . . .**

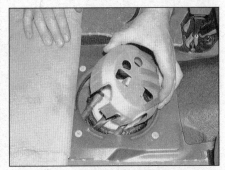

**6.3c  . . . and the protective cage**

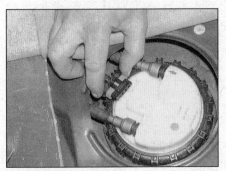

**6.4  Unplug the wiring from the top of the fuel pump/gauge sender unit at the connector**

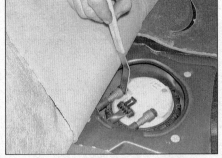

**6.6  Disconnect the quick-release couplings using a forked tool**

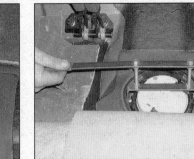

**6.7  Using a home-made tool to unscrew the large diameter fuel pump retaining nut**

pump flange. Make your own marks if none are visible. Arrows on the top of the fuel pump unit indicate fuel flow direction.

**6** Place absorbent rags around the fuel hose connections then disconnect the quick-release couplings using a forked tool. Insert the tool under the edge of the outer sleeve of each coupling, and lever upwards without squeezing the sleeve **(see illustration)**. Be prepared for an initial release of fuel under pressure as the couplings are released.

**7** Unscrew the large-diameter plastic retaining nut using a wide-opening pair of grips, or water pump pliers. Certain types of oil filter removal tools are an ideal alternative. A removal tool can be fabricated from lengths of steel and threaded rod **(see illustration)**.

**8** Withdraw the fuel pump/gauge sender unit from the tank slightly, and allow it to drain for a few seconds **(see illustration)**. Recover the seal, then temporarily refit the plastic nut to

the tank while the pump is removed, to prevent the pipe stub swelling.

## Refitting

**9** Lubricate a new seal sparingly with petroleum jelly and fit to the fuel tank stub, ensuring that it is correctly seated.

**10** Refit the fuel pump/gauge sender unit to the tank, so that the assembly markings on the unit and tank are aligned. Refit the plastic nut and tighten securely.

**11** Lubricate the fuel hose coupling O-rings with petroleum jelly, position them squarely over the pump outlets, and push down on the outer sleeves to lock. Ensure that the hoses are fitted to their correct outlets as noted during removal.

**12** Restore the wiring harness connection at the top of the fuel pump/gauge sender unit.

**13** The remainder of refitting is a reversal of removal.

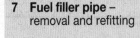

**7  Fuel filler pipe –**
  removal and refitting

## Removal

**1** Drain all fuel from the fuel tank, as described in Section 8.

**2** Open the flap and remove the fuel filler cap.

**3** Disconnect the earth connection's spade terminal above the filler neck **(see illustration)**.

**4** Release the rubber seal and drip tray around the filler neck, then pull out the drain hose below it.

**5** Unscrew the three bolts that secure the filler neck to the bodywork.

**6** Select first gear or Park as applicable, and then chock the front wheels. Raise the rear of the car and rest it securely on axle stands.

**6.8  Withdraw the fuel pump/gauge sender unit from the tank**

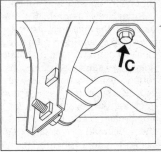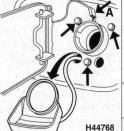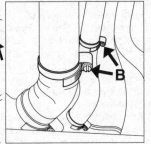

H44768

**7.3  Fuel filler neck removal details**

*A  Earth connection*          *B  Filler and breather hose clips*          *C  Filler pipe-to-floorpan bolt*

**7** Remove the bolt that secures the filler pipe bracket to the floorpan.

**8** Slacken the hose clips, then disconnect the fuel filler and breather hoses from fuel tank.

### Refitting

**9** Refitting is a reversal of removal. Fit a new sealing rubber between the filler pipe and the bodywork.

## 8  Fuel tank – removal and refitting

**Note:** *Observe the precautions in Section 1 before working on any component in the fuel system.*

### Removal

**1** Before the tank can be removed, it must be drained of as much fuel as possible. To avoid the dangers and complications of fuel handling and storage, it is advisable to carry out this operation with the tank almost empty. Any fuel remaining can be drained as follows.

**2** Disconnect the battery negative lead (see *Disconnecting the battery*).

**3** Using a hand-pump or syphon inserted through the filler neck, remove any remaining fuel from the bottom of the tank. Alternatively, chock the front wheels then jack up the rear of the car and support it on axle stands (see *Jacking and vehicle support*). Place a suitable large-capacity container under the fuel filter. Clean the fuel inlet quick-release coupling on the filter, place rags around the coupling, then disconnect it. Be prepared for an initial release of fuel under pressure as the coupling is released. Hold the disconnected fuel line over the container and allow the fuel to drain; remove the fuel filler cap to improve the flow. Store the collected fuel in a suitable sealed container.

**4** Carry out the operations described in paragraphs 1 to 6 of Section 6.

**5** Disconnect the filler pipe and breather hose from the side of the fuel tank with reference to Section 7.

**6** Refer to Chapter 1 and disconnect the fuel supply pipe from the fuel filter cartridge at the quick-release connector. Disconnect the fuel return pipe (and, where applicable, the evaporative emissions pipe) from the tank at the quick-release connector.

**7** Remove the securing screws and detach the heat shields from the front of the fuel tank.

**8** Position a trolley jack under the centre of the tank. Insert a protective wooden pad between the jack head and the underside of the tank, then raise the jack to just take the weight of the tank.

**9** Undo the nuts and release the front edges of the tank retaining straps. Carefully lower the jack and tank slightly. When sufficient clearance exists, disconnect the vent hoses leading to the front of the car. The hoses between the tank and filler tube can be left in place. Also detach the wiring harness and its support from the top of the tank.

**10** Lower the jack and tank, and remove the tank from under the car.

**11** If the tank is contaminated with sediment or water, remove the gauge sender unit and the fuel pump as described previously, and disconnect the ventilation hoses and filler tube. Swill the tank out with clean fuel. The tank is moulded from a synthetic material and if damaged, it should be renewed. However, in certain cases it may be possible to have small leaks or minor damage repaired. Seek the advice of a dealer or suitable specialist concerning tank repair.

**12** If a new tank is to be fitted, transfer all the components from the old tank to the new. Always renew the filler tube seal and the seals and the large plastic nut securing the fuel pump. Once used, they may not seat and seal properly on a new tank.

### Refitting

**13** Refitting is a reversal of removal, bearing in mind the following points:

a) *Locate the tank in position and tighten the rear strap mountings. Push the tank forward and centre the fuel pump plastic nut with respect to its access hole in the floorpan. Now tighten the front strap mountings.*

b) *Lubricate the filler neck seals and ensure that they are properly located. Make sure that the drain tube is on the inside of the inner seal.*

c) *On completion, refill the tank with fuel and check exhaustively for signs of leakage before driving the car on the road.*

## 9  Fuel injection systems – general information

The Fenix 5.1 and EMS 2000 systems covered in this Chapter are both full engine management systems, controlling both the fuel injection and ignition functions; refer to the Specifications for system application data. As the layout and overall operation of each of the systems is very similar, a general description is given in the following paragraphs. Section 10 contains fault finding information, and Section 11 details fuel injection component removal and refitting information. Refer to Chapter 5B for information relating to the ignition system.

All systems employ closed-loop fuelling by means of a catalytic converter and a lambda sensor, to minimise exhaust gas emissions. On some models, exhaust emissions are further reduced by a secondary air injection system. A fuel vapour evaporative loss emission control system is also integrated, to minimise the escape of unburned hydrocarbons into the atmosphere from the fuel tank. Chapter 4C contains information relating to the removal and refitting of these emission control system components.

The main components of the fuel side of the system and their individual operation are as follows.

### Electronic control unit

The ECU is microprocessor-based, and controls the entire operation of the fuel system. Contained in the unit memory is software which controls the timing and opening duration of the fuel injectors. The program enters sub-routines to alter these parameters, according to inputs from the other components of the system. In addition to this, the engine idle speed is also controlled by the ECU, which uses an idle air control valve to open or close an air passage as required. The ECU also incorporates a self-diagnostic facility in which the entire fuel system is continuously monitored for correct operation. Any detected faults are logged as fault codes which can be displayed by activating the on-board diagnostic unit. In the event of a fault in the system due to loss of a signal from one of the sensors, the ECU reverts to an emergency (limp-home) program. This will allow the car to be driven, although engine operation and performance will be limited.

### Fuel injectors

Each fuel injector consists of a solenoid-operated needle valve, which opens under commands from the ECU. Fuel from the fuel rail is then delivered through the injector nozzle into the inlet manifold.

### Coolant temperature sensor

This resistive device is screwed into the thermostat housing; the sensor probe is immersed the engine coolant. Changes in coolant temperature are detected by the ECU as a change in voltage measured across the sensor, caused by a change in its electrical resistance. Signals from the coolant temperature sensor are also used by the ignition system ECU and by the temperature gauge in the instrument panel.

### Mass airflow sensor

The mass airflow sensor measures the mass flow rate of the air entering the engine on models fitted with EMS 2000 engine management system. The sensor is of the hot-film type, containing four different resistive elements and related circuitry. The unit is located in the air cleaner inlet; intake air passing over the heated resistive elements causes a temperature drop proportional to the speed and density of the air passing over it and this is in turn alters the electrical resistance of the elements and hence the voltage across it. By comparing this change in voltage with a reference voltage, the ECU can establish the inlet air temperature and the inlet air mass flow rate.

### Throttle position sensor

The throttle position sensor is a

potentiometer attached to the throttle shaft in the throttle housing. The unit sends a linear signal to both the fuel and ignition system ECUs proportional to throttle opening.

### Idle air control (IAC) valve

The idle air control valve contains a small electric motor that open or shuts a bypass air passage inside the valve. The valve only operates when the throttle is closed, and in response to signals from the ECU, maintains the engine idle speed at a constant value irrespective of any additional load from the various accessories.

### Fuel pump

The electric fuel pump is located in the fuel tank, and is totally submerged in fuel. Fuel flows through the pump housing, and acts as a coolant to control the temperature of the pump motor during operation. The unit is a two-stage device, consisting of an electric motor which drives an impeller pump to draw in fuel, and a gear pump to discharge it under pressure. The fuel is then supplied to the fuel rail on the inlet manifold via an in-line fuel filter.

### Fuel pressure regulator

The regulator is a vacuum-operated mechanical device, which ensures that the pressure differential between fuel in the fuel rail and fuel in the inlet manifold is maintained at a constant value. As manifold depression increases, the regulated fuel pressure is reduced in direct proportion. When fuel pressure in the fuel rail exceeds the regulator setting, the regulator opens to allow fuel to return via the return line to the tank.

### System relay

The main system relay is energised by the fuel system ECU, and provides power for the fuel pump.

### Manifold absolute pressure sensor

Instead of the mass airflow sensor used in the EMS 2000 systems, the Fenix system utilises a MAP sensor and a separate inlet air temperature sensor (see following sub-section) to calculate the volume of air being drawn into the engine. The MAP sensor is connected to the inlet manifold via a hose, and uses a piezo-electrical crystal to convert manifold depression to an electrical signal to be transmitted to the ECU.

### Ambient pressure sensor

This sensor is fitted to the EMS 2000 system only, and provides the ECU with a signal proportional to the ambient atmospheric pressure. Changes in ambient air pressure and density (encountered for example when driving on mountainous roads at high altitudes) have an effect on the amount of oxygen being drawn into the engine, and so affect combustion. The ambient pressure

sensor allows the ECU to provide the correct fuelling (and turbocharger boost pressure, where applicable) to suit all conditions.

### Intake air temperature sensor

This resistive device is located in the air inlet ducting, where its element is in direct contact with the air entering the engine. Changes in intake air temperature are detected by the ECU as a change in voltage measured across the sensor, caused by a change in its electrical resistance. From the signals received from the inlet air temperature sensor and manifold absolute pressure sensor, the ECU can calculate the volume of air inducted into the engine.

### Camshaft position (CMP) sensor

The camshaft position sensor is mounted on the left-hand side of the cylinder head, and is driven by the exhaust camshaft. It informs the ECU when cylinder No 1 is on its combustion stroke, allowing sequential fuel injection and ignition timing (for combustion knock control) to be employed.

### Crankshaft position sensor

The crankshaft position sensor provides a datum for the ECU to calculate the rotational speed and position of the crankshaft in relation to TDC. The sensor is triggered by a series of teeth machined into the flywheel/driveplate.

### Heated oxygen sensor (HO$_2$S)

The oxygen sensor provides the ECU with constant feedback on the oxygen content of the exhaust gases, allowing closed-loop fuelling to be employed. The sensor has an integral heating element to bring it up to operating temperature quickly after the engine has been started. Several models are fitted with two oxygen sensors, one upstream of the catalytic converter and one downstream of it.

### Turbocharger Control Valve (TCV)

Boost pressure (the pressure of the intake air in the inlet manifold) is limited by a wastegate valve, mounted on the turbocharger and operated by a vacuum actuator, which diverts the exhaust gas away from the turbine wheel. The wastegate valve is controlled by the engine management system ECU, via the turbocharger control valve (TCV). The ECU opens and closes (modulates) the turbocharger control valve several times a second; this results in manifold vacuum being applied to the wastegate valve actuator in a series of rapid pulses – the duty ratio of the pulses depends primarily on engine speed and load. The overall function is to manage the supply of boost pressure to engine, giving optimum driveability by increasing boost pressure smoothly under acceleration, and by venting excess boost pressure under deceleration, preventing turbocharger compressor stall and reducing turbo lag.

## 10 Fuel injection system – fault finding

1 If a fault appears in the fuel injection system, first ensure that all the system wiring connectors are securely connected and free of corrosion – also refer to paragraphs 6 to 9 below. Then ensure that the fault is not due to poor maintenance; ie, check that the air cleaner filter element is clean, the spark plugs are in good condition and correctly gapped, the cylinder compression pressures are correct, the ignition system wiring is in good condition and securely connected, and the engine breather hoses are clear and undamaged, referring to Chapter 1, Chapter 2A and Chapter 5B.

2 If these checks fail to reveal the cause of the problem, the car should be taken to a suitably-equipped Volvo dealer for testing. A diagnostic connector is incorporated in the engine management system wiring harness, into which dedicated electronic test equipment can be plugged (the connector is located behind the facia, at the right-hand side of the centre console. The test equipment is capable of 'interrogating' the engine management system ECU electronically and accessing its internal fault log (reading fault codes).

3 Fault codes can only be extracted from the ECU using a dedicated fault code reader. A Volvo dealer will obviously have such a reader, but they are also available from other suppliers. It is unlikely to be cost-effective for the private owner to purchase a fault code reader, but a well-equipped local garage or auto-electrical specialist will have one.

4 Using this equipment, faults can be pinpointed quickly and simply, even if their occurrence is intermittent. Testing all the system components individually in an attempt to locate the fault by elimination is a time-consuming operation that is unlikely to be fruitful (particularly if the fault occurs dynamically), and carries a high risk of damage to the ECU's internal components.

5 Experienced home mechanics equipped with an accurate tachometer and a carefully-calibrated exhaust gas analyser may be able to check the exhaust gas CO content and the engine idle speed; if these are found to be out of specification, then the car must be taken to a suitably-equipped Volvo dealer for assessment. Neither the air/fuel mixture (exhaust gas CO content) nor the engine idle speed are manually adjustable; incorrect test results indicate the need for maintenance (possibly, injector cleaning) or a fault within the fuel injection system.

6 Certain faults, such as failure of one of the engine management system sensors, will cause the system will revert to a backup (or 'limp-home') mode. This is intended to be a 'get-you-home' facility only – the engine management warning light will come on when this mode is in operation.

**11.1a Intake air temperature sensor location**

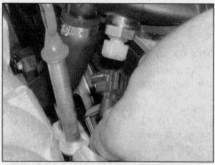

**11.1b Intake air temperature sensor location (turbo models, and later non-turbo models)**

**11.6 Disconnect the manifold vacuum pipe from the port at the base of the sensor**

**11.11 Use a forked tool to separate the fuel pipe unions**

7 In this mode, the signal from the defective sensor is substituted with a fixed value (it would normally vary), which may lead to loss of power, poor idling, and generally-poor running, especially when the engine is cold.

8 However, the engine may in fact run quite well in this situation, and the only clue (other than the warning light) would be that the exhaust CO emissions (for example) will be higher than they should be.

9 Bear in mind that, even if the defective sensor is correctly identified and renewed, the engine will not return to normal running until the fault code is erased. This also applies even if the cause of the fault was a loose connection or damaged piece of wire – until the fault code is erased, the system will continue in 'limp-home' mode.

**11.12 Undo the securing screw and release the fuel pipe support bracket**

---

## 11 Fuel injection system components – removal and refitting

**Note:** *Ensure that the engine has cooled completely before working on any of the fuel*

**11.13 Release the hose clip and disconnect the fuel return rubber hose from the rigid pipe**

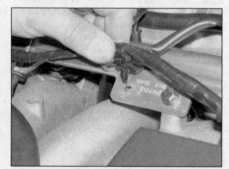

**11.14 Release the wiring harness clips from the fuel rail**

system components, and refer to the precautions given in Section 1.
**Caution: Ensure that the ignition is switched off before working on any of the engine management system components.**

### *Intake air temperature sensor*

#### Removal

1 On most models, the sensor is mounted in the flexible intake air ducting elbow that runs between the air cleaner and the throttle body. Turbo models, and later non-turbo models, have the sensor mounted in the rigid intake air ducting elbow, directly above the radiator **(see illustrations)**.

2 Disconnect the wiring plug, then carefully unscrew, or prise, the sensor out of the air ducting.

#### Refitting

3 Refit by reversing the removal operations.

### *Manifold absolute pressure sensor*

#### Removal

4 The MAP sensor is mounted on a bracket at the rear of the engine compartment.

5 Detach the plastic cover panel to expose the sensor.

6 Disconnect the manifold vacuum pipe from the port at the base of the sensor **(see illustration)**.

7 Unplug the wiring from the sensor at the connector.

8 Undo the securing screws, detach the sensor from its mounting bracket and remove the sensor from the engine compartment.

#### Refitting

9 Refit by reversing the removal operations.

### *Fuel rail and injectors*

#### Removal

10 Depressurise the fuel system as described in Section 2.

11 Locate the fuel feed and return pipes unions, at the left-hand side of the cylinder head. Use a forked tool to retract the union collars, the separate the pipes by gently puling them apart **(see illustration)**. Place absorbent rags around the unions and be prepared for an initial release of fuel as the unions are slackened.

12 Undo the securing screw and release the fuel pipe support bracket from the side of the cylinder head **(see illustration)**.

13 Release the hose clip and disconnect the fuel return rubber hose from the rigid pipe – this will allow the fuel hose to pass in front of the cylinder head cover breather hose **(see illustration)**.

14 Release the wiring harness clips from the fuel rail **(see illustration)**.

15 Unplug the wiring harness from each of the fuel injectors at the connectors **(see illustration)**.

**11.15 Unplug the wiring harness from each of the fuel injectors at the connectors**

**11.16 Undo the two bolts securing the fuel rail to the inlet manifold**

**19** Individual injectors may now be removed from the rail by removing the screws, withdrawing the retaining plate and pulling the injectors from the rail **(see illustrations)**.

### Refitting

**20** Refit by reversing the removal operations. Check that the injector O-rings and manifold seals are in good condition and renew them if necessary; smear them with petroleum jelly as an assembly lubricant **(see illustration)**. Apply thread-locking fluid to the fuel rail retaining bolts, then insert and tighten them to the specified torque setting.

## Fuel pressure regulator

### Removal

**21** Disconnect the battery negative lead (see *Disconnecting the battery*).
**22** Remove the fuel rail and injectors as described previously, but leave the injectors in place in the fuel rail.
**23** Undo the two screws and remove the fuel pressure regulator from the fuel rail **(see illustrations)**.

**11.17 Disconnect the vacuum hose from the fuel pressure regulator**

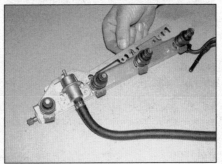

**11.18 Remove the fuel rail complete with injectors and fuel pressure regulator**

### Refitting

**24** Refit the regulator to the fuel rail, then refit the fuel rail and injectors as described previously.

## Idle air control valve

### Removal

**25** Remove the plastic cover panel from the front left-hand corner of the engine compartment, to expose the throttle body.

**16** Undo the two bolts securing the fuel rail to the inlet manifold. Pull the rail upwards to release the injectors from the manifold **(see illustration)**.

**17** Disconnect the vacuum hose from the fuel pressure regulator **(see illustration)**.
**18** Remove the fuel rail complete with injectors and fuel pressure regulator **(see illustration)**.

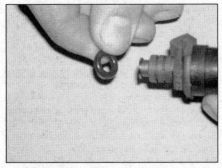

**11.19a Individual injectors may now be removed from the rail by removing the screws . . .**

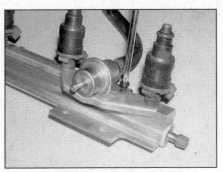

**11.19b . . . withdrawing the retaining plate . . .**

**11.19c . . . and pulling the injectors from the rail**

**11.20 Renew the injector O-ring seals if necessary**

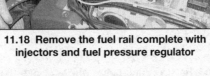

**11.23a Undo the two screws . . .**

**11.23b . . . and remove the fuel pressure regulator from the fuel rail**

**11.26 Disconnect the wiring connector from the end of the idle air control valve**

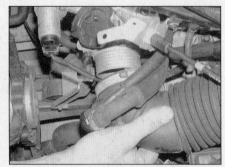

**11.31 Disconnect the air inlet duct from the throttle housing**

**11.33a Remove the bolts . . .**

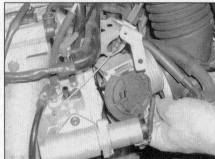

**11.33b . . . and withdraw the throttle housing from the manifold**

**26** Disconnect the wiring connector from the end of the valve **(see illustration)**.
**27** Undo the retaining bolts and withdraw the valve from the inlet manifold.

### Refitting

**28** Refit by reversing the removal operations.

## Throttle housing

### Removal

**29** Remove the plastic cover panel from the front left-hand corner of the engine compartment, to expose the throttle housing.
**30** Disconnect the throttle position sensor wiring connector.
**31** Slacken the large-diameter hose clip and disconnect the air inlet duct from the throttle housing **(see illustration)**.
**32** Disconnect the accelerator cable from the throttle valve operating lever, with reference to Section 5.

**33** Remove the bolts which secure the housing and withdraw it from the manifold **(see illustrations)**. Recover the gasket.

### Refitting

**34** Refit by reversing the removal operations, using a new gasket, and hose clips if necessary.

## Throttle position sensor

### Removal

**35** Remove the throttle housing with reference to the previous sub-section.
**36** Remove the two bolts which secure the sensor and withdraw it from the throttle housing.

### Refitting

**37** Refit by reversing the removal operations. If a new sensor has been fitted, have the car checked by a Volvo dealer using the correct

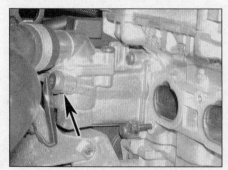

**11.38 The coolant temperature sensor is mounted on the thermostat housing**

**11.51a Undo the screws . . .**

diagnostic equipment, to ensure that the new sensor is correctly adapted to the engine management system.

## Coolant temperature sensor

### Removal

**38** The coolant temperature sensor is mounted on, or next to, the thermostat housing, at the front right-hand side of the engine (refer to Chapter 3 for details) **(see illustration)**.
**39** Partially drain the cooling system with reference to Chapter 1, then disconnect the radiator top hose from the thermostat housing, with reference to the radiator removal and refitting procedures given in Chapter 3.
**40** Unplug the wiring from the connector and the end of the sensor flying lead.
**41** Unscrew the sensor from its location. Recover the sealing ring, where fitted.

### Refitting

**42** Refit the sensor using a reversal of the removal procedure.

## Electronic control unit (ECU)

### Removal

**43** The ECU is located inside the passenger compartment, behind the centre console.
**44** Working in the driver's footwell, remove the screw and detach the carpet trim panel from the lower right-hand side of the centre console.
**45** Release the locking strap from the ECU, then remove the case securing screws.
**46** Ensure that the ignition is switched off, then unplug the wiring harness from the ECU at the multi-plug connector and remove the ECU from the car. Release the two catches on the side of the module box lid. Lift off the lid and place it to one side.

### Refitting

**47** Refit the ECU by reversing the removal procedure. Ensure that the wiring connector is securely reconnected.

## Camshaft position sensor

### Removal

**48** The camshaft position sensor is mounted at the left-hand side of the cylinder head, at the end of the exhaust camshaft.
**49** Remove the fuel rail and injectors as described earlier in this section.
**50** Unplug the wiring from the sensor at the connector, which is located on the connector mounting bracket at the rear of the engine compartment, under a plastic cowl.
**51** Undo the screws and remove the sensor body from the cylinder head **(see illustrations)**.
**52** Remove the timing belt upper cover, then brace the exhaust camshaft sprocket with a suitable tool **(see illustration)**.
**53** Unscrew the centre bolt and remove the sensor trigger wheel, together with its washer, from the end of the camshaft **(see illustrations)**.

**11.51b . . . and remove the sensor body from the cylinder head**

**11.52 Brace the exhaust camshaft sprocket with a suitable tool . . .**

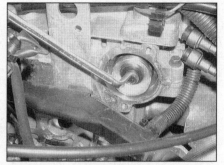

**11.53a . . . then unscrew the centre bolt . . .**

**11.53b . . . and remove the sensor rotor, together with its washer, from the end of the camshaft**

**11.58 Undo the securing screws and withdraw the crankshaft sensor**

**11.61 Slide the turbocharger control valve from its mountings, behind the air cleaner housing**

## Refitting

**54** Refitting is a reversal of removal. The sensor rotor is keyed to ensure correct alignment on refitting.

### Crankshaft position sensor

#### Removal

**55** The crankshaft position sensor is located on the left-hand side of the engine, at the top of the transmission bellhousing.

**56** Remove the air cleaner and intake ducting to gain access to the top of the transmission casing.

**57** Unplug the wiring from the sensor at the connector, which is located on the connector mounting bracket at the rear of the engine compartment, under a plastic cowl.

**58** Undo the securing screws and withdraw the sensor, together with its mounting bracket from the bellhousing **(see illustration)**.

#### Refitting

**59** Refit the sensor by reversing the removal procedure.

### Turbocharger control valve (TCV)

#### Removal

**60** The turbocharger control valve is located behind the air cleaner housing.

**61** Slide the control valve from its mountings and unplug the wiring from the valve at the connector **(see illustration)**.

**62** Make a careful note of the fitted position

of each vacuum hose; label them if necessary to aid correct refitting later.

**63** Release the hose clips and disconnect the vacuum hoses from the control valve ports.

**64** Remove it the valve from the engine compartment.

#### Refitting

**65** Refitting is a reversal of removal, but ensure that the vacuum hoses are reconnected to the correct ports on the turbocharger control valve.

### Ambient pressure sensor

#### Removal

**66** The ambient pressure sensor is mounted on a bracket at the rear of the engine compartment, beneath a plastic cowl.

**67** Remove the plastic cowl, then unplug the wiring from the sensor at the connector.

**68** Undo the securing screw and remove the sensor from its mounting bracket.

#### Refitting

**69** Refit the sensor by reversing the removal procedure.

### Mass airflow sensor

#### Removal

**70** Disconnect the battery negative lead (see *Disconnecting the battery*).

**71** Slacken the hose clip and detach the air outlet duct and, where applicable the crankcase ventilation hose at the air cleaner cover.

**72** Spring back the retaining clips and lift off the air cleaner cover.

**73** Undo the two screws and remove the sensor from the air cleaner cover. Recover the large O-ring seal.

#### Refitting

**74** Refit by reversing the removal operations. Check the condition of the O-ring seal, and fit a new one if necessary.

## 12 Cruise control –
component removal and refitting

### General information

**1** The cruise control system allows the car to maintain a steady speed selected by the driver, regardless of gradients or prevailing winds.

**2** The main components of the system are a control unit, a control switch, a vacuum servo and a vacuum pump. Brake and (when applicable) clutch pedal switches protect the engine against excessive speeds or loads should a pedal be depressed whilst the system is in use.

**3** In operation, the driver accelerates to the desired speed and then brings the system into use by means of the switch. The control unit then monitors vehicle speed (from the speedometer pulses) and opens or closes the throttle by means of the servo to maintain the set speed. If the switch is moved to OFF, or the brake or clutch pedal is depressed, the servo immediately closes the throttle. The set speed is stored in the control unit memory and the system can be reactivated by moving the switch to RESUME, provided that vehicle speed has not dropped below 25 mph.

**4** The driver can override the cruise control for overtaking simply by depressing the throttle pedal. When the pedal is released, the set speed will be resumed.

**5** The cruise control cannot be engaged at speeds below 25 mph, and should not be used in slippery or congested conditions.

### Control module

#### Removal

**6** The control unit is located under the right-hand side of the facia. Working in the driver's footwell, first remove the screws and detach the carpet trim panel from the base of the right-hand side of the centre console.

**7** Detach the connector locking strap from the unit by drilling out the rivet, then unplug the connector from the unit.

**8** Undo the two securing screws and lift the control unit from its mountings.

#### Refitting

**9** Refitting is a reversal of removal.

### Vacuum servo

#### Removal

**10** The servo unit is mounted above the accelerator pedal mounting bracket. Working in the driver's footwell, first remove the screws and detach the carpet trim panel from the base of the right-hand side of the centre console.

**11** Unplug the vacuum hose from the top of the servo unit.

**12** Undo the retaining nut to release the servo from the mounting bracket.

**13** Prise the pushrod balljoint off the accelerator pedal pivot arm, and remove the unit from the car.

#### Refitting

**14** Fit the servo unit to the mounting bracket, passing the stud through lower hole and vacuum port through the upper hole. Fit the retaining nut and tighten it securely.

**15** With the accelerator pedal in the rest position, check that the pushrod balljoint socket lines up with the corresponding ball on the pedal pivot arm, without extending or retracting it against the pressure of the internal membrane. If necessary, adjust the length of the servo unit pushrod as follows. Loosen the adjusting bush by turning it anti-clockwise, then slide the bush in or out to achieve the correct length. When the length is correct, turn the locking bush clockwise to tighten it.

**16** Press the balljoint socket onto the pivot arm so that it clicks home.

**17** Reconnect the vacuum hose to the servo unit.

**18** Refit the facia side panel.

**19** Before bringing the car back into service, check that the vacuum servo unit does not preload the accelerator pedal when the cruise control system is switched off.

### Vacuum pump and regulator

#### Removal

**20** The vacuum pump and regulator are located on the bulkhead, at the rear left-hand side of the engine compartment.

**21** Unplug the wiring connector from the side of the vacuum pump.

**22** Disconnect the vacuum hose from the base of the pump/regulator unit.

**23** Undo the securing bolts and remove the unit from the bulkhead. Recover the rubber mountings.

#### Refitting

**24** Refitting is a reversal of removal.

### Brake pedal vacuum valve

#### Removal

**25** The brake pedal vacuum valve is mounted above the brake pedal mounting bracket. To gain access, first remove trim the panel beneath the right-hand side of the facia.

**26** Disconnect the vacuum hose from the top of the valve.

**27** Unplug the wiring connector from the top of the valve.

**28** Depress the locking catches and remove the vale from the mounting bracket.

#### Refitting

**29** Refitting is a reversal of removal.

### Clutch pedal vacuum valve

#### Removal

**30** The clutch pedal vacuum valve is mounted above the clutch pedal mounting bracket. To gain access, first remove trim the panel beneath the right-hand side of the facia.

**31** Disconnect the vacuum hose from the top of the valve.

**32** Unplug the wiring connector from the top of the valve.

**33** Depress the locking catches and remove the valve from the mounting bracket.

#### Refitting

**34** Refitting is a reversal of removal.

### Stop-light switch

**35** Refer to the information given in Chapter 9.

### Steering column switch

**36** Refer to the information in Chapter 12, Section 4.

### Transmission gearshift position sensor

**37** Refer to the information in Chapter 7B, Section 5.

### 13 Dynamic Stability Assistance (DSA) system – information and component renewal

#### Information

**1** The traction control system fitted to the S40 and V40 models covered in this manual is referred to as Dynamic Stability Assistance (DSA) by Volvo and is different to the TRACS traction control system fitted to other Volvo models. Its purpose is to prevent wheel spin under acceleration.

**2** The DSA system components consist of a single electronic control unit and its associated wiring harness. The system has no sensors or actuators of its own; all input signals are provided by the engine management system ECU (engine speed, injector pulse width, accelerator pedal position) and the anti-lock braking (ABS) system ECU (front and rear roadwheel speed).

**3** Wheel spin is detected by comparing front and rear roadwheel speeds. When one or both of the driving wheels loses grip, the DSA system sends a request to the engine management system ECU to reduce the torque of the engine. This is achieved by decreasing the fuel injector pulse width, with the decrease being carried out gradually in a series of small steps. The amount of engine torque reduction is dependent on a number of factors including road speed, the gear currently selected and the accelerator pedal position.

**4** A DSA indicator light on the instrument panel illuminates when the ignition is switched on, to indicate the state of the system. Under normal circumstances, the light will extinguish after a short period if the system is operating correctly. If the light remains lit, a fault exists. If wheel spin occurs during driving and the DSA system becomes active as a result, the indicator light flashes to indicate operation.

**5** The DSA system may be disabled by pressing the control button on the centre console, in front of the gear lever. The system is then automatically enabled again, the next time the ignition is switched on.

#### DSA electronic control unit

#### Removal

**6** With reference to Chapter 11, Section 29, remove the trim panel from the base of the right-hand A-pillar, at the underside of the facia.

**7** Remove the securing screw, then slide the DSA control unit down from its mounting bracket.

**8** Unplug the wiring connector and remove the unit from the car.

#### Refitting

**9** Refitting is a reversal of removal.

#### DSA switch

#### Removal

**10** Ensure the ignition is switched off, then

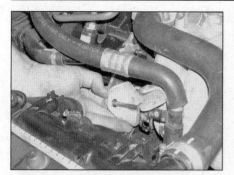

**14.10 Unscrew the three bolts and remove the bracket between the alternator upper mounting and the inlet manifold**

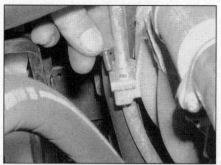

**14.11a Undo the bolt securing the dipstick tube to the manifold . . .**

**14.11b . . . then twist the tube away from the manifold and pull it upwards to extract it from the engine block**

carefully prise the switch body from the centre console, using a thin plastic blade. Pad the surface of the centre console with card to prevent damage.

**11** Unplug the wiring from the base of the switch and remove it.

### Refitting

**12** Refitting is a reversal of removal.

**14.13a Unscrew the securing bolts . . .**

**14.13b . . . and remove the inlet manifold support bracket**

---

## 14 Inlet manifold –
removal and refitting

**Note:** *Observe the precautions in Section 1 before working on any component in the fuel system.*

### Removal

**1** Disconnect the battery negative lead (see *Disconnecting the battery*).

**2** Slacken and withdraw the securing screws, then lift the cover panel from the top of the engine.

**3** Remove the securing screw and detach the hose support bracket from the inlet manifold.

**4** Disconnect the air inlet duct from the throttle housing.

**5** Disconnect the wiring plug from each fuel injector. If difficulty is experienced, pull off the fuel rail cover over the injectors for greater access.

**6** Disconnect the vacuum hose from the pressure regulator on the underside of the fuel rail.

**7** Undo the two bolts securing the fuel rail to the inlet manifold. Pull the rail upwards to release the injectors from the manifold and lay the fuel rail with injectors on the top of the engine. Take care not to damage the injector tips.

**8** On turbo models, unbolt and remove the engine bay front cover panel, then release the turbocharger inlet ducting.

**9** Remove the throttle housing as described in Section 10.

**10** Unclip the wiring harness from the bracket between the alternator upper mounting and the inlet manifold, then unscrew the three bolts and remove the bracket **(see illustration)**.

**11** Undo the bolt securing the dipstick tube to the manifold, then twist the tube away from the manifold and pull it upwards to extract it from the engine block **(see illustrations)**.

Recover the O-ring seal at the base of the tube.

**12** Apply the handbrake firmly and chock the rear wheels, then raise the front of the car and rest it securely on axle stands.

**13** Working underneath the engine compartment, unscrew the securing bolts and remove the inlet manifold support bracket **(see illustrations)**.

**14** Slacken the lower manifold retaining bolts by about two or three turns, and remove all the upper manifold bolts **(see illustration)**.

**15** Lift the manifold upwards, feeding the crankcase ventilation hose through the ducts (where applicable), then remove the manifold from the cylinder head **(see illustrations)**. Note that the lower bolt holes are slotted allowing the manifold to slide up and off, leaving them in position. If the manifold will not lift up, make sure that the gasket has not

**14.14 Slacken the lower manifold retaining bolts, and remove all the upper manifold bolts**

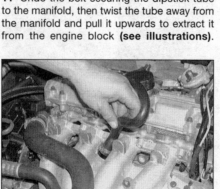

**14.15a Feed the crankcase ventilation hose through the ducts . . .**

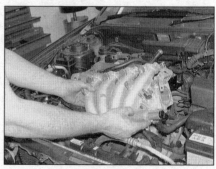

**14.15b . . . then remove the manifold from the cylinder head**

**15.2  Detach the EVAP purge valve from the radiator and position it to one side**

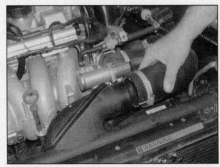

**15.5  Detach the intake air ducts from the ports at the top of the intercooler**

**15.7  Disconnect the air ducting from the base of the intercooler**

stuck to the manifold face; the gasket lower holes are not slotted, and it must remain on the engine to allow manifold removal.

**16** With the manifold removed, take out the lower bolts and remove the gasket.

**17** If required, the components remaining on the manifold can be removed with reference to earlier Sections of this Chapter.

### Refitting

**18** Refit by reversing the removal operations, noting the following points:

a) *Use a new inlet manifold gasket.*
b) *Fit new and new seals and O-rings to the fuel injectors.*
c) *Fit a new O-ring seal to the base of the dipstick tube.*
d) *Coat the threads of the fuel rail securing screws with thread-locking fluid.*
e) *Locate the manifold gasket on the cylinder head and fit the lower manifold bolts a few turns, prior to placing the manifold in position.*
f) *Remember to pass the crankcase*

*ventilation hose up between the second and third manifold ducts.*
g) *Tighten the inlet manifold bolts to the specified torque.*
h) *Refit and adjust the accelerator cable as described in Section 5.*

### 15  Intercooler – removal and refitting

### Removal

**1** Release the retaining clips and screws, and remove the engine compartment front cover panels.

**2** Detach the EVAP purge valve (located at the top left-hand side of the radiator) from its mountings, and position it to one side **(see illustration)**.

**3** Drain the cooling system as described in Chapter 1.

**4** Slacken the hose clip and disconnect the

top hose from the radiator.

**5** Slacken the hose clips and detach the intake air ducts from the ports at the top of the intercooler **(see illustration)**.

**6** Unplug the wiring from the inlet air temperature sensor and the cooling fan motors. Release the wiring from the clips on the rear of the radiator assembly.

**7** Working underneath the engine compartment, undo the hose clip and disconnect the air ducting from the base of the intercooler **(see illustration)**.

**8** Disconnect the bottom hose from the radiator **(see illustration)**.

**9** Unbolt the radiator upper mounting brackets from the bodywork, then lift the radiator, intercooler and cooling fans from the engine compartment **(see illustration)**.

**10** Undo the securing bolts and detach the intercooler and cooling fans from the radiator.

### Refitting

**11** Refit the intercooler by reversing the removal procedure.

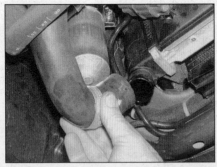

**15.8  Disconnect the bottom hose from the radiator**

**15.9  Lift the radiator, intercooler and cooling fans from the engine compartment**

# Chapter 4 Part B:
# Fuel system (GDI engine)

## Contents

## Degrees of difficulty

| Easy, suitable for novice with little experience |  | Fairly easy, suitable for beginner with some experience |  | Fairly difficult, suitable for competent DIY mechanic | | Difficult, suitable for experienced DIY mechanic | | Very difficult, suitable for expert DIY or professional |  |
|---|---|---|---|---|---|---|---|---|---|

## Specifications

### System type

| | |
|---|---|
| General . . . . . . . . . . . . . . . . . . . . . . . . . . . . . . . . . . . . . . . . . . . . . | Mitsubishi GDI (Gasoline Direct Injection) |
| Engine code B4184SM (up to 2001 model year) . . . . . . . . . . . . . . . . | Melco 1 engine management system |
| Engine code B4184SJ (2001 model year onwards) . . . . . . . . . . . . . | Melco 2 engine management system |

### Fuel delivery system data

| | |
|---|---|
| Fuel tank capacity . . . . . . . . . . . . . . . . . . . . . . . . . . . . . . . . . . . . . . | 60 litres |
| Idle speed* . . . . . . . . . . . . . . . . . . . . . . . . . . . . . . . . . . . . . . . . . . . . | 620 rpm |
| Idle mixture CO content* . . . . . . . . . . . . . . . . . . . . . . . . . . . . . . . . . | < 0.2% |
| Fuel tank pump: | |
|    Unregulated delivery pressure . . . . . . . . . . . . . . . . . . . . . . . . . . . . | 4.8 to 8.0 bar (70 to 116 psi) |
|    Regulated fuel pressure . . . . . . . . . . . . . . . . . . . . . . . . . . . . . . . . | 3.2 bar (46.4 psi) minimum |
|    Fuel delivery rate . . . . . . . . . . . . . . . . . . . . . . . . . . . . . . . . . . . . . | 120 litres/hour @ 3.0 bar and 12.5V |
| Injector pump system pressure . . . . . . . . . . . . . . . . . . . . . . . . . . . . | 50 bar (725 psi) approx |
| Fuel injector electrical resistance . . . . . . . . . . . . . . . . . . . . . . . . . . . | 13.0 to 16.0 ohms |

*Non-adjustable – controlled by ECU*

### Engine management system data (typical)

Sensor/actuator electrical resistance (@ 20°C):

| | |
|---|---|
|    Inlet air temperature sensor . . . . . . . . . . . . . . . . . . . . . . . . . . . . . | 2300 to 3000 ohms |
|    Crankshaft sensor . . . . . . . . . . . . . . . . . . . . . . . . . . . . . . . . . . . . | 260 to 340 ohms |
|    Coolant temperature sensor . . . . . . . . . . . . . . . . . . . . . . . . . . . . . | 2400 to 2500 ohms |
|    Oil temperature sensor . . . . . . . . . . . . . . . . . . . . . . . . . . . . . . . . | 950 to 2050 ohms |
|    Throttle position sensor . . . . . . . . . . . . . . . . . . . . . . . . . . . . . . . | 3500 to 6000 ohms |
|    Idle air control valve . . . . . . . . . . . . . . . . . . . . . . . . . . . . . . . . . . | 28 to 32 ohms |

### Recommended fuel

Octane rating:

| | |
|---|---|
|    Recommended . . . . . . . . . . . . . . . . . . . . . . . . . . . . . . . . . . . . . . | 95 RON unleaded |
|    Minimum . . . . . . . . . . . . . . . . . . . . . . . . . . . . . . . . . . . . . . . . . . . | 91 RON unleaded |

## Torque wrench settings

| | Nm | lbf ft |
|---|---|---|
| Camshaft position sensor | 13 | 10 |
| Coolant temperature sensor (thermostat housing) | 29 | 21 |
| Crankshaft sensor | 8 | 6 |
| EGR valve housing | 21 | 15 |
| Engine temperature sensor (cylinder head) | 30 | 22 |
| Fuel delivery pipe flange bolts | 12 | 9 |
| Fuel injector retaining plate bolt | 22 | 16 |
| Fuel rail mounting bolts | 12 | 9 |
| Fuel unions | 13 | 10 |
| Injector pump bolts: | | |
| Stage 1 | 5 | 4 |
| Stage 2 | 17 | 13 |
| Inlet manifold | 20 | 15 |
| Knock sensor | 22 | 16 |
| Lambda sensor | 55 | 41 |
| Oil temperature sensor | 32 | 24 |
| Throttle housing | 20 | 15 |

## 1  General information and precautions

### General information

All models covered in this manual are equipped with an electronic engine management system which controls the fuelling and ignition. Details of the type of system fitted to each model in the range are given in the Specifications. This Chapter deals with the those parts of the engine management system which are concerned with fuel injection – refer to Chapter 5B for details of the ignition system components.

The Mitsubishi-designed GDI engine used in the S40/V40 uses a unique direct fuel injection system, similar in some ways to a modern diesel fuel system setup. The intention is to offer significant improvements in fuel efficiency over similar-sized conventional petrol engines, without compromise. The system comprises a fuel tank, an electric fuel lift pump, a fuel filter, fuel supply and return lines, a mechanically-driven high-pressure injector fuel pump, a throttle housing, four fuel injectors, and an Electronic Control Unit (ECU) together with its associated sensors, actuators and wiring.

The tank-mounted fuel pump (which has a built-in fuel pressure regulator) delivers a constant supply of fuel through a cartridge filter to the high-pressure fuel injector pump. The injector pump has its own high-pressure regulator which maintains a constant fuel pressure at the fuel rail, and returns excess fuel to the tank via the return line. This constant-flow system also helps to reduce fuel temperature, and prevents vapourisation. The injector pump, driven from the inlet camshaft, increases the fuel pressure from around 3 bar to nearly 50 bar, and delivers the fuel to the fuel rail serving the four fuel injectors which are fitted directly into the rear of the cylinder head.

The fuel injectors are opened and closed by an Electronic Control Unit (ECU), which calculates the injection timing and duration according to engine speed, throttle position and rate of opening, inlet air temperature, coolant temperature, exhaust gas oxygen content information, and even gearbox oil temperature, received from sensors mounted on and around the engine. The injection timing varies more widely than on a conventional engine, with two distinct 'modes' of operation possible – 'performance', in which injection takes place during the inlet stroke (as normal), and 'lean-burn' operation, when injection occurs during the compression stroke (similar to a diesel). The appropriate mode of operation is selected by the ECU, and is largely dependent on throttle position – reducing the throttle opening will result in a change back to lean-burn operation, and greater fuel economy.

Inlet air is drawn into the engine through the air cleaner, which contains a renewable paper filter element. The airflow sensor fitted downstream of the air cleaner measures the volume of air entering the engine, and also contains sensors to give the ECU air temperature and pressure information. The air passes through the throttle housing, and enters the engine through the inlet manifold, via ports in the top of the cylinder head. The air mixes with the injected fuel in a combustion chamber formed in the specially-shaped piston crown.

Idle speed is controlled on early models by the idle air control valve, located on the throttle housing – later models have a stepper motor on the throttle housing which provides idle speed control. Cold starting enrichment is controlled by the ECU, using the engine temperature and inlet air temperature parameters, to increase the injector opening duration.

The exhaust gas oxygen content is constantly monitored by the ECU via the oxygen (or lambda) sensor, which is mounted in the exhaust downpipe. On later engines, two oxygen sensors are fitted, one before the catalytic converter, and one after – this improves sensor response time and accuracy, and the ECU compares the signals from each sensor to confirm that the converter is working correctly. The ECU then uses this information to modify the injection timing and duration to maintain the optimum air/fuel ratio. An exhaust catalyst is fitted to all models.

All GDI engines are also equipped with an exhaust gas recirculation (EGR) system and an activated charcoal filter evaporative loss system as part of an emissions control package. Further details of these systems will be found in Part C of this Chapter.

It should be noted that engine management system fault diagnosis is only possible with dedicated electronic test equipment. Problems with the system should therefore be referred to a fuel injection specialist or a Volvo dealer for assessment. Once the fault has been identified, the removal/refitting procedures detailed in the following Sections can then be followed.

### Precautions

⚠ **Warning: Petrol is extremely flammable – great care must be taken when working on any part of the fuel system. Do not smoke or allow any naked flames or uncovered light bulbs near the work area. Note that gas powered domestic appliances with pilot flames, such as heaters, boilers and tumble dryers, also present a fire hazard – bear this in mind if you are working in an area where such appliances are present. Always keep a suitable fire extinguisher close to the work area and familiarise yourself with its operation before starting work. Wear eye protection when working on fuel systems and wash off any fuel spilt on bare skin immediately with soap and water. Note that fuel vapour is just as dangerous as liquid fuel; a vessel that has just been emptied of liquid fuel will still contain vapour and can be potentially explosive. Petrol is a highly dangerous and volatile liquid, and the precautions necessary when handling it cannot be overstressed.**

• *Many of the operations described in this Chapter involve the disconnection of fuel lines, which may cause an amount of fuel spillage. Before commencing work, refer to the above Warning and the information in 'Safety first!' at the beginning of this manual.*
• *When working with fuel system components, pay particular attention to cleanliness – dirt entering the fuel system may cause blockages which will lead to poor running.*

## 2  Depressurising the fuel system

**1** This procedure should be carried out before attempting any work on the fuel system. The injection system operates at such a high pressure, residual pressure will remain in the system for several hours after the engine is switched off. Opening any of the fuel lines in this condition will result in an uncontrolled spray of fuel, which is at best unpleasant, and at worst highly-dangerous.
**2** Although relieving the system pressure will prevent fuel spraying out, it will not empty the fuel lines, and appropriate precautions against fuel spillage (such as wrapping the connection with clean cloth before opening it) should still be observed.
**3** With the ignition switched off, locate and remove fuse number 17 from the engine compartment fusebox. Alternatively, (also with

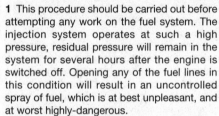

**3.2  Disconnect the airflow sensor wiring plug**

**3.4a  Remove the air cleaner mounting bolt in front . . .**

**2.3a  Removing the fuel pump fuse**

the ignition off) locate and pull out the fuel pump relay from the fuse board **(see illustrations)**.
**4** Start the engine, and let it run until it cuts out. If the engine will not start with the fuel pump fuse/relay removed, turn it over on the starter for approximately 10 seconds. The fuel system will now be depressurised.
**5** On completion, switch off the ignition, disconnect the battery negative lead (see *Disconnecting the battery*), and refit the fuel pump fuse or relay.

## 3  Air cleaner assembly and inlet air duct – removal and refitting

### Removal

**1** Referring to Chapter 5A if necessary,

**3.3  Remove the air inlet duct, complete with resonance chamber**

**3.4b  . . . and the one behind (arrows) . . .**

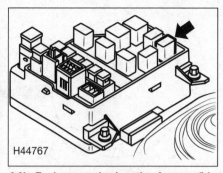
H44767

**2.3b  Fuel pump relay location (arrowed) in engine compartment fusebox**

remove the battery holding clamp, and slide the battery forwards in its mounting tray.
**2** Disconnect the wiring plug from the airflow sensor **(see illustration)**.
**3** Slacken the large hose clips at either end of the air inlet duct. Disconnect the breather hose which runs from the rear of the cylinder head to the air inlet duct, and remove the duct from the engine compartment **(see illustration)**.
**4** Remove the two air cleaner mounting bolts (one close to the battery on the inner wing, the other at the side of the air cleaner) and manoeuvre the air cleaner out of its location, lifting and turning it to free the locating peg at the base **(see illustrations)**.

### Refitting

**5** Refitting is a reversal of removal. Locate the peg on the base of the air cleaner in position first during refitting, and ensure that all hose connections are securely remade, to prevent air leaks.

## 4  Accelerator cable – removal, refitting and adjustment

**Note:** *Later models with the Melco 2 engine management system have a 'fly-by-wire' throttle, and a conventional cable is not fitted. Instead, a throttle position sensor on the pedal sends a signal, via the ECU, to the stepper motor fitted on the throttle housing.*

**3.4c  . . . then pull and twist to free the air cleaner from the lower locating peg, and remove it**

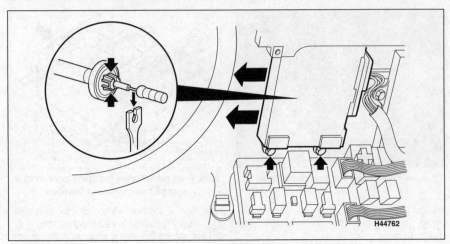

**4.6 Removing the accelerator cable inside the car**

## Removal

**1** Undo the screws and remove the engine cover to gain access to the throttle housing.

**2** Unhook the inner cable from the throttle spindle quadrant, and remove the two bolts securing the cable support bracket from the inlet manifold.

**3** On right-hand-drive models, pull up on the washer reservoir, and remove it to one side of the engine bay, to gain access to the cable where it passes through the bulkhead.

**4** On left-hand-drive models, trace the cable round the front of the inlet manifold, and release it from the two clips.

**5** Undo the screws, release the clips and remove the trim/soundproofing panel from under the facia on the driver's side. Where applicable, remove the cruise control vacuum unit.

**6** On right-hand-drive models, remove the two nuts at the base of the throttle control ECU, and slide it to the left. Release the locking washer securing the pedal return spring, and slide the pedal off its pivot – if necessary, also disconnect the pedal position sensor wiring **(see illustration)**.

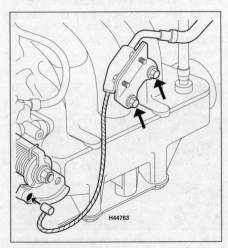

**4.10 Fitting and adjusting the accelerator cable**

**7** Release the cable nipple from the top of the accelerator pedal, then pass the cable inner through the slotted hole to release it from the pedal.

**8** Depress the locking tabs and release the cable grommet from the bulkhead and pull the cable into the engine compartment. Note the routing of the cable, release it from any clips or ties, and remove it.

### Refitting

**9** Refit by reversing the removal operations. Check along the entire length of the cable to ensure that there are no kinks, bends or restrictions that might cause it to stick in operation. On right-hand-drive models, grease the pedal pivot before refitting the pedal. Adjust the cable as follows.

### Adjustment

**10** The cable is adjusted using the two bolts which secure the cable bracket to the inlet manifold. Grasp the inner cable, then pull the outer upwards until all slack is removed. Tighten the cable bracket-to-inlet manifold bolts securely **(see illustration)**.

## 5 Fuel pump/gauge sender unit – removal and refitting

**Note:** *This section deals with the electric pump mounted in the fuel tank. For details of the engine-driven injector pump, refer to Section 10. Observe the precautions in Section 1 before working on any component in the fuel system.*

Refer to Chapter 4A, Section 6.

## 6 Fuel filler pipe – removal and refitting

Refer to Chapter 4A, Section 7.

## 7 Fuel tank – removal and refitting

Refer to Chapter 4A, Section 8.

## 8 Fuel injection systems – general information

The Melco system covered in this Chapter is a full engine management system, controlling both the fuel injection and ignition functions (refer to Chapter 5B for information relating to the ignition system). The Melco 2 system fitted to later models differs only in detail to the original system, and was introduced in response to tighter emissions regulations.

All systems employ closed-loop fuelling by means of a catalytic converter and a lambda sensor, to minimise exhaust gas emissions. Exhaust emissions are further reduced by an exhaust gas recirculation (EGR) system. A fuel vapour evaporative loss emission control system is also integrated, to minimise the escape of unburned hydrocarbons into the atmosphere from the fuel tank. Chapter 4C contains information relating to the removal and refitting of these emission control system components.

The main components of the fuel side of the system and their individual operation are as follows.

### Electronic control unit

The ECU is microprocessor-based, and controls the entire operation of the fuel system. Contained in the unit memory is software which controls the timing and opening duration of the fuel injectors. The program enters sub-routines to alter these parameters, according to inputs from the other components of the system. In addition to this, the engine idle speed is also controlled by the ECU, which uses an idle air control valve to open or close an air passage as required. The ECU also incorporates a self-diagnostic facility in which the entire fuel system is continuously monitored for correct operation. Any detected faults are logged as fault codes which can be displayed by activating the on-board diagnostic unit. In the event of a fault in the system due to loss of a signal from one of the sensors, the ECU reverts to an emergency (limp-home) program. This will allow the car to be driven, although engine operation and performance will be limited.

### Fuel injectors

Each fuel injector consists of a solenoid-operated needle valve, which opens under commands from the ECU. Fuel from the fuel rail is then delivered through the injector nozzle into the inlet manifold. The injectors on this system operate at fifteen times the pressure of a conventional injection system, and run at 100 volts. An output stage is fitted to the inner wing as part of the injector switching circuit – this steps up the injector voltage to the required level (and generates significant heat doing so, which explains its heat sink-like appearance).

### Coolant temperature sensor

This resistive device is screwed into the thermostat housing; the sensor probe is immersed the engine coolant. This sensor is used only by the temperature gauge on the facia panel, and is only fitted to early models with the Melco 1 engine management system.

### Engine temperature sensor

Similar to the coolant temperature sensor, the engine temperature sensor is screwed into the water passage at the transmission end of the cylinder head. It provides the ECU with a constantly-varying (analogue) voltage signal, corresponding to the temperature of the engine. This is used to refine the calculations made by the module, when determining the correct amount of fuel required to achieve the ideal air/fuel mixture ratio.

Early models with the Melco 1 system have both coolant and engine temperature sensors, while later models have just the engine temperature sensor, which also provides the gauge feed.

### Airflow sensor

The airflow sensor measures the flow rate of the air entering the engine. The unit is located on the engine side of the air cleaner, and contains sensors which also measure air temperature and atmospheric pressure, allowing the ECU to make fuelling adjustments for cold or altitude conditions.

### Accelerator pedal position sensor

Attached to the pedal itself, this sensor sends the ECU information on accelerator position and rate of change. In the at-rest (idle) position, the sensor signals the ECU to enter idle control mode; at full-throttle, the ECU is signalled to provide maximum fuelling.

### Throttle position sensor

The throttle position sensor is a potentiometer attached to the throttle shaft in the throttle housing. The unit sends a linear signal to both the fuel and ignition system ECUs proportional to throttle opening.

### Idle air control valve

Under the influence of the ECU, the valve allows a controlled air bleed into the throttle housing, to regulate idle speed as required by the varying loads placed on the engine. This valve is only fitted to Melco 1 system models – on the Melco 2 system, the idle speed is regulated by the stepper motor fitted to the throttle housing.

### Stepper motor

On the later Melco 2 system, the conventional throttle cable is replaced by the accelerator pedal position sensor and a stepper motor. A fully-electronic control system for the throttle allows faster response and offers greater control. When the pedal position sensor signals the ECU that the engine is in idle condition, the stepper motor is used by the ECU to provide the required idle speed, based on engine temperature and load information.

### Fuel pump

The electric fuel pump is located in the fuel tank, and is totally submerged in fuel. Fuel flows through the pump housing, and acts as a coolant to control the temperature of the pump motor during operation. The unit is a two-stage device, consisting of an electric motor which drives an impeller pump to draw in fuel, and a gear pump to discharge it under pressure. The fuel is then supplied to the high-pressure injector pump via an in-line fuel filter.

### Fuel pressure regulators

Both the tank pump and the injector pump have a built-in pressure regulator, to ensure that both the low and high fuel pressures are maintained around the nominal values. When fuel pressure in the fuel rail exceeds the injector pump regulator setting, the regulator opens to allow fuel to return via the return line to the tank.

### Injector pump

The GDI engine features direct injection of fuel into the combustion chamber, and this requires fuel delivery at a much higher pressure than normal (indirect) injection. A high-pressure injector pump is fitted, driven off the inlet camshaft, to supply the fuel rail.

### Fuel pressure sensor

Fitted directly into the fuel rail, the pressure sensor monitors the fuel pressure in the rail.

### System relay

The main system relay is energised by the fuel system ECU, and provides power for the fuel pump.

### Ambient pressure sensor

This sensor, built into the airflow sensor, provides the ECU with a signal proportional to the ambient atmospheric pressure. Changes in ambient air pressure and density (encountered for example when driving on mountainous roads at high altitudes) have an effect on the amount of oxygen being drawn into the engine, and so affect combustion. The ambient pressure sensor allows the ECU to provide the correct fuelling to suit all conditions.

### Intake air temperature sensor

This resistive device is located in the airflow sensor, where its element is in direct contact with the air entering the engine. Changes in

intake air temperature are detected by the ECU as a change in voltage measured across the sensor, caused by a change in its electrical resistance. From the signals received from the inlet air temperature sensor and ambient pressure sensor, the ECU can calculate the volume of air inducted into the engine.

### Camshaft position sensor

The camshaft position sensor is mounted on the left-hand side of the cylinder head, and monitors the exhaust camshaft. It informs the ECU when cylinder No 1 is on its combustion stroke, allowing sequential fuel injection and ignition timing (for combustion knock control) to be employed.

### Engine speed/crankshaft position sensor

This sensor provides a datum for the ECU to calculate the rotational speed and position of the crankshaft in relation to TDC. The sensor is triggered directly from the crankshaft sprocket.

### Oil temperature sensor

An oil temperature sensor is fitted to the transmission, to allow the ECU to finely adjust the idle speed, based on the transmission oil temperature.

### Power steering pressure switch

A pressure switch, fitted to the power steering fluid supply line, allows the ECU to raise the idle speed slightly, in response to the engine loads which may occur if the steering is turned to full-lock with the engine idling (such as during parking manoeuvres).

### Heated oxygen sensor

The oxygen sensor provides the ECU with constant feedback on the oxygen content of the exhaust gases, allowing closed-loop fuelling to be employed. The sensor has an integral heating element to bring it up to operating temperature quickly after the engine has been started. Several models are fitted with two oxygen sensors, one upstream of the catalytic converter and one downstream of it.

## 9  Fuel injection system – fault finding

1 If a fault appears in the fuel injection system, first ensure that all the system wiring connectors are securely connected and free of corrosion – also refer to paragraphs 6 to 9 below. Then ensure that the fault is not due to poor maintenance; ie, check that the air cleaner filter element is clean, the spark plugs are in good condition and correctly gapped, the cylinder compression pressures are correct, the ignition system wiring is in good condition and securely connected, and the engine breather hoses are clear and undamaged, referring to Chapter 1, Chapter 2B and Chapter 5B.

**2** If these checks fail to reveal the cause of the problem, the car should be taken to a suitably-equipped Volvo dealer for testing. A diagnostic connector is incorporated in the engine management system wiring harness, into which dedicated electronic test equipment can be plugged (the connector is located behind the facia, at the right-hand side of the centre console. The test equipment is capable of 'interrogating' the engine management system ECU electronically and accessing its internal fault log (reading fault codes).

**3** Fault codes can only be extracted from the ECU using a dedicated fault code reader. A Volvo dealer will obviously have such a reader, but they are also available from other suppliers. It is unlikely to be cost-effective for the private owner to purchase a fault code reader, but a well-equipped local garage or auto-electrical specialist will have one.

**4** Using this equipment, faults can be pinpointed quickly and simply, even if their occurrence is intermittent. Testing all the system components individually in an attempt to locate the fault by elimination is a time-consuming operation that is unlikely to be fruitful (particularly if the fault occurs dynamically), and carries a high risk of damage to the ECU's internal components.

**5** Experienced home mechanics equipped with an accurate tachometer and a carefully-calibrated exhaust gas analyser may be able to check the exhaust gas CO content and the engine idle speed; if these are found to be out of specification, then the car must be taken to a suitably-equipped Volvo dealer for assessment. Neither the air/fuel mixture (exhaust gas CO content) nor the engine idle speed are manually adjustable; incorrect test results indicate the need for maintenance (possibly, injector cleaning) or a fault within the fuel injection system.

**6** Certain faults, such as failure of one of the engine management system sensors, will cause the system will revert to a backup (or 'limp-home') mode. This is intended to be a 'get-you-home' facility only – the engine management warning light will come on when this mode is in operation.

**7** In this mode, the signal from the defective sensor is substituted with a fixed value (it would normally vary), which may lead to loss of power, poor idling, and generally-poor running, especially when the engine is cold.

**8** However, the engine may in fact run quite well in this situation, and the only clue (other than the warning light) would be that the exhaust CO emissions (for example) will be higher than they should be.

**9** Bear in mind that, even if the defective sensor is correctly identified and renewed, the engine will not return to normal running until the fault code is erased. This also applies even if the cause of the fault was a loose connection or damaged piece of wire – until the fault code is erased, the system will continue in 'limp-home' mode.

**10.15 Disconnecting the engine temperature sensor wiring plug**

## 10 Fuel injection system components – removal and refitting

**Note:** *Ensure that the engine has cooled completely before working on any of the fuel system components, and refer to the precautions given in Section 1.*
**Caution: Ensure that the ignition is switched off (take out the key) before working on any of the engine management system components. If a wiring plug is disconnected (or reconnected) while 'live', the component may be damaged.**

### Airflow sensor

#### Removal

**1** Disconnect the battery negative lead (see *Disconnecting the battery*).
**2** Slacken the hose clip and detach the air inlet duct.
**3** Disconnect the airflow sensor wiring plug, then release the wiring from the wire clip fitted to one of the airflow sensor mounting nuts.

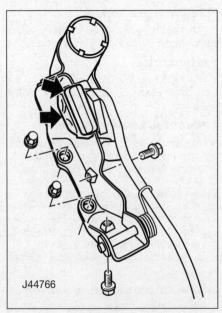

**10.18 Accelerator pedal position sensor removal details**

**4** Remove the four nuts securing the airflow sensor, noting that one of them secures the wire clip used for retaining the airflow sensor wiring. Remove the sensor from the air cleaner housing.

#### Refitting

**5** Refit by reversing the removal operations. Ensure that the mating surfaces of the sensor and air cleaner are clean, and tighten the nuts securely, to ensure there are no air leaks.

### Intake air temperature sensor

**6** The air temperature sensor is an integral part of the airflow sensor, and cannot be removed.

### Ambient pressure sensor

**7** The ambient pressure sensor is an integral part of the airflow sensor, and cannot be removed.

### Coolant temperature sensor

#### Removal

**8** The coolant temperature sensor is mounted on the thermostat housing, at the front left-hand side of the engine (left as seen from the driver's seat – refer to Chapter 3 for details).
**9** Partially drain the cooling system with reference to Chapter 1, then disconnect the radiator top hose from the thermostat housing, with reference to the radiator removal and refitting procedures given in Chapter 3.
**10** Unplug the wiring from the connector and the end of the sensor flying lead.
**11** Unscrew the sensor from the thermostat housing. Recover the sealing ring, where fitted.

#### Refitting

**12** Refit the sensor using a reversal of the removal procedure.

### Engine temperature sensor

#### Removal

**13** The sensor is screwed into the left-hand end of the cylinder head, at the front (left as seen from the driver's seat). Remove the engine top cover as necessary for access. The sensor is situated behind the thermostat housing – a deep 19 mm socket will be needed to remove it.
**14** Partially drain the cooling system with reference to Chapter 1, or else be prepared to fit the new sensor as soon as the old one is removed.
**15** Pull the large wiring harness from the bracket next to the sensor to further improve access. Disconnect the wiring plug, then unscrew and remove the sensor from the head **(see illustration)**.

#### Refitting

**16** Refitting is a reversal of removal.

### Accelerator pedal position sensor

#### Removal

**17** Make sure the ignition is switched off

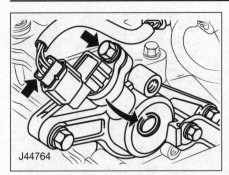

**10.21 Removing the camshaft position sensor**

**10.25 Crankshaft position sensor mounting bolts (arrowed)**

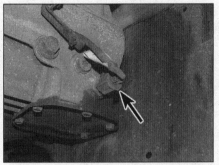

**10.28 Oil temperature sensor wiring plug (arrowed) at the front of the transmission**

(take out the key). Remove the driver's side lower facia panel for access to the pedal, disconnecting the courtesy light wiring in the process.

**18** The sensor is secured using two screws and two nuts **(see illustration)**. Disconnect the wiring plug, unscrew the fasteners, and remove the sensor from the pedal area.

### Refitting

**19** Refitting is a reversal of removal.

## Camshaft position sensor

### Removal

**20** The camshaft position sensor is fitted at the transmission end of the engine, on the exhaust (front) camshaft. Remove the engine top cover for access to the sensor.

**21** Disconnect the sensor wiring plug, then remove the single bolt and withdraw the sensor from its housing **(see illustration)**. Recover the O-ring seal from the base of the sensor – a new one should be used when refitting.

### Refitting

**22** Refitting is a reversal of removal. Lubricate the new O-ring with a little clean engine oil.

## Engine speed/crankshaft position sensor

### Removal

**23** The sensor is fitted directly above the crankshaft toothed sprocket (from which the timing belt is driven). To remove the sensor, refer to Chapter 2B and remove the timing belt covers – the timing belt itself does not have to be removed, though significant dismantling is required. The sensor wiring plug is attached to the timing belt lower cover, so removing the cover effectively disconnects the sensor.

**24** Clean the area around the sensor as far as possible.

**25** Remove the two mounting bolts, and lift out the sensor and its backplate **(see illustration)**.

### Refitting

**26** Refitting is a reversal of removal, referring to Chapter 2B as necessary.

## Oil temperature sensor

### Removal

**27** Ideally, this procedure should only be carried out when the transmission (and its oil) are completely cold. Volvo recommend that the transmission oil be drained before starting, if the work is to be carried out with the transmission at or near operating temperature (possibly due to the risk of scalding).

**28** The sensor is located on the front face of the transmission, next to the oil filler/level plug **(see illustration)**. The sensor's probe will be in constant contact with the oil – hence the risk of oil spillage when the sensor is removed. To improve access to the sensor, and possibly to reduce the risk of oil spillage if the transmission is not drained, jack up the left-hand side of the car, and support it on axle stands (see *Jacking and vehicle support*). If the car is at an angle, the amount of oil lost should be less.

**29** Working under the car, remove the left-hand section of the engine undershield.

**30** Ensure that the ignition is switched off (take out the key), then disconnect the sensor wiring plug.

**31** To reduce any possible oil spillage to a minimum, have the new sensor ready to fit immediately. Unscrew the sensor, fit the new one, and tighten (if possible) to the specified torque. Wipe up any oil spillage.

### Refitting

**32** Refitting is a reversal of removal. If a significant amount of oil was lost during the

**10.35 Pull off the evaporative emissions hose from the throttle body**

procedure, get the car level, then top-up the transmission oil as described in Chapter 1.

## Throttle housing

### Removal

**33** Depressurise the fuel system as described in Section 2. Remove the engine top cover to expose the throttle housing.

**34** Slacken the large-diameter hose clips at either end, then disconnect the breather hose from the cylinder head, and remove the air inlet duct from the air cleaner and throttle housing.

**35** Pull off the evaporative emissions hose(s) on top of the throttle housing **(see illustration)**.

**36** Unclip the wiring harness from the two mounting clips on the throttle housing bracket.

**37** Unbolt the earth strap from the side of the throttle housing **(see illustration)**.

**38** Disconnect the wiring plugs from the throttle position sensor on top of the housing, and from the throttle control motor (at the side) or from the idle air control valve (at the base), as applicable **(see illustrations)**.

**39** The coolant hose(s) must now be disconnected from the housing **(see illustration)**. Either partially drain the cooling system (see Chapter 1), use hose clamps, or be prepared for some loss of coolant. If the spring-type hose clips are used, obtain some new Jubilee hose clips for use when refitting.

**40** A total of seven bolts now secure the throttle housing and its mounting bracket – three securing the bracket to the cylinder

**10.37 Unbolt the throttle body earth strap**

10.38a Disconnect the throttle position sensor on top . . .

10.38b . . . and the throttle control motor at the side

10.39 Coolant hose connection to the throttle housing

head, and four around the 'mouth' of the housing (which secure the housing to the bracket). Strictly speaking, only the four housing-to-bracket bolts need be removed, but taking out the remaining three bolts will allow movement in the bracket itself, and this improves working room, especially if the throttle housing is being removed as part of another procedure. Remove the bolts, then lift away the housing and its gasket – a new

gasket must be used when refitting **(see illustrations)**.

### Refitting

**41** Refit by reversing the removal operations, using a new gasket. Tighten the throttle housing bolts to the specified torque. On completion, check and if necessary top-up the coolant.

## *Injector pump*

### Removal

**42** Depressurise the fuel system as described in Section 2.
**43** Remove the engine top cover to expose the injector pump.
**44** Release the spring-type hose clips, and pull off the two fuel return hoses from the injector pump, noting their respective positions for refitting **(see illustration)**. Carefully move the two hoses to one side. If

the spring-type hose clips are in poor condition, obtain some new Jubilee hose clips for use when refitting.
**45** Wrap some absorbent towel around the base of the fuel supply line flange, then undo the two bolts securing the flange and separate the joint **(see illustration)**. Recover the O-ring seal from the flange joint – a new one should be used when refitting. Move the fuel line away without bending it excessively.
**46** Remove the throttle housing as described previously in this Section, and the inlet manifold as described in Section 11.
**47** Remove the rigid fuel delivery pipe fitted between the injector pump and the fuel rail. The pipe is secured by a two-bolt flange at either end – remove the bolts and take off the pipe (careful prising will be needed to free the flanges) **(see illustrations)**. Recover the O-ring and washer from each flange, noting that the split washer is fitted at the bottom.

10.40a Throttle housing removal details

10.40b Throttle housing-to-bracket bolts (arrowed)

10.40c Separate the housing from its mounting bracket, and recover the gasket

10.44 Release the spring clips (arrowed) and disconnect the fuel return hoses

10.45 Undo the two flange bolts (arrowed) and disconnect the fuel supply pipe

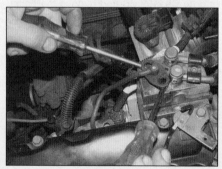

10.47a Prise the flange carefully to release the O-rings . . .

**10.47b ... then remove the fuel delivery pipe**

New O-rings should be used when refitting – remember, this system operates at a far higher pressure even than conventional fuel injection, and every precaution should be taken to prevent fuel leaks.

**48** The injector pump is secured by four bolts – remove the bolts, then carefully pull out the pump.

### Refitting

**49** Refitting is a reversal of removal, noting the following points:

a) *Tighten the four injector pump mounting bolts to the specified Stage 1 torque, in the sequence shown* **(see illustration)**. *Next, go round again in the same sequence, and tighten the bolts to the Stage 2 setting.*

b) *Use new O-rings on the fuel supply and delivery pipes, and lubricate them with clean engine oil before fitting. Fit the*

**10.53a Disconnecting the EGR valve wiring plug improved access to the fuel rail ...**

**10.54 Removing a fuel rail mounting bolt**

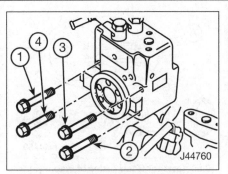

**10.49 Tightening sequence for injector pump mounting bolts**

*washer, then the O-ring to each flange, then fit the pipe and tighten the bolts to the specified torque.*

### Fuel rail and injectors

#### Removal

**50** Depressurise the fuel system as described in Section 2. Remove the engine top cover.

**51** Remove the inlet manifold as described in Section 11, and remove the fuel delivery pipe as described in paragraph 47.

**52** Disconnect the wiring plugs from each of the four injectors, noting that each plug contains a rubber seal (orange in colour) which should not be lost **(see illustration)**. Also disconnect the wiring plug from the fuel pressure sensor.

**53** To improve access to the left-hand end of the fuel rail, disconnect the wiring plug from

**10.53b ... unbolting it completely meant a new gasket was needed**

**10.55a The injectors each have a retaining plate ...**

**10.52 Disconnect the injector wiring plugs, and recover the rubber seals inside**

the EGR valve. To improve access still further, we unbolted the valve completely from the back of the head (without disconnecting the coolant pipe), but this meant a new gasket had to be fitted on reassembly **(see illustrations)**.

**54** Remove the four bolts securing the fuel rail **(see illustration)**. Each bolt has a spacer washer fitted between the fuel rail and cylinder head – if possible, ease the rail away from the head and recover these washers now, before they drop out as the rail is removed.

**55** Remove the bolt from each injector retaining plate, and recover the dished washer used, noting its fitted position. Remove the plate from each injector **(see illustrations)**.

**56** Carefully pull the fuel rail, complete with all four injectors, from the cylinder head. Try to keep the injectors in place as the fuel rail is removed, to preserve the fitted order of all washers and O-rings. It is possible that the injectors may be left behind in the head as the rail is removed – if so, take care to grip them only by their metal bases when extracting them **(see illustration)**. Recover the copper washers fitted at the base of each injector – new copper washers will be needed when refitting.

**57** Once the fuel rail and injectors are removed, the injectors can be pulled out. It is advisable (though not essential) to mark the injectors for position in the rail as they are removed, so they can be refitted in the same place. Note the fitted order of the washers and O-ring at the top of each injector – new O-rings should be obtained for refitting.

**10.55b ... and all four have to be unbolted to remove the fuel rail**

10.56 If any injectors get left behind, pull them out using pliers on the metal base only

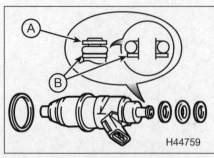

10.59 Correct fitted order of washers and O-ring seal – inset shows different profiles of upper washers (A and B)

10.60 Lubricate the O-rings and twist the injectors into position

10.61a Secure the copper washers in place using a little grease . . .

10.61b . . . this method is also useful on the injector lower washers

10.62 Fit the spacer washers to the fuel rail mounting bolt holes

## Refitting

**58** Lubricate the new O-ring on each injector with a little clean engine oil before fitting.

**59** Ensure that the two small washers fitted at the top of each injector are fitted as noted on removal – the thicker washer is fitted first **(see illustration)**.

**60** Fit the injectors into the fuel rail using a twisting motion **(see illustration)**, and turn them so the connector plugs are facing the right way. The injectors should be easy to turn in the rail, once fitted – if not, something has gone wrong, and the injector should be removed once more for checking. A defective, used, or poorly-seated O-ring is the most likely cause.

**61** Fit new copper washers to the cylinder head recesses, or alternatively, slip one over each injector, and secure it with a small dab of

grease. We found that the injector lower washers have a habit of falling off too, so these were also held on with a very small amount of grease **(see illustrations)**.

**62** Place the spacer washers in position on the rear of the engine – take care, as they are easily dislodged as the fuel rail is fitted (perhaps put a spot of grease on these too) **(see illustration)**.

**63** Press the fuel rail into position, ensuring everything remains in place, and tighten the four mounting bolts by hand to retain it **(see illustration)**.

**64** Fit the four injector retaining plates, then insert the bolt and dished washer for each **(see illustration)**, and tighten to the specified torque.

**65** Tighten the fuel rail mounting bolts to the specified torque.

**66** Connect the four fuel injector wiring plugs,

taking care not to displace the rubber seal fitted inside each plug.

**67** The remainder of refitting is a reversal of removal. On completion, start the engine and check for any sign of fuel leakage.

### Injector output stage

**68** The output stage (which looks like a large heat sink) is fitted at the rear of the engine compartment, sited in a bracket attached to the left-hand inner wing (left as seen from the driver's seat) **(see illustration)**. The output stage will be hot if the car has recently been driven.

**69** Disconnect the battery negative lead (see *Disconnecting the battery*).

**70** At the rear of the engine compartment, remove the two bolts securing the fuse/relay box, and release the box from its bracket – move it aside as far as possible without

10.63 Align the fuel rail carefully, and ensure nothing falls off as it is pressed into place

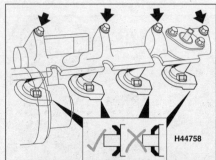

10.64 Fuel rail mounting bolts (arrowed) – inset shows correct fitment of injector retaining plate dished washers

10.68 Injector output stage – seen with air cleaner removed

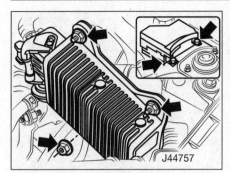

**10.71 Injector output stage mounting nuts (arrowed) – inset shows relay box bolts**

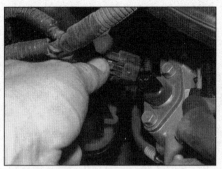

**10.78a Disconnect the wiring plug . . .**

**10.78b . . . then undo the two bolts and withdraw the fuel pressure sensor from the fuel rail**

disconnecting the wiring. Access to the output stage can be greatly improved by removing the air cleaner as described in Section 3.

**71** Unscrew the three nuts securing the output stage to its mounting bracket **(see illustration).**

**72** Lift out the unit, then clean round the connector plug before releasing the locking catch and disconnecting the plug.

### *Fuel (high) pressure regulator*

**Note:** *The low-pressure regulator is an integral part of the tank-mounted fuel pump, and cannot be renewed separately.*

#### Removal

**73** Remove the injector pump as described previously in this Section.

**74** The pressure regulator is secured by four Allen screws to the base of the injector pump. Undo the screws and take off the regulator.

#### Refitting

**75** Refitting is a reversal of removal.

### *Fuel pressure sensor*

#### Removal

**76** The fuel pressure sensor is fitted to the fuel rail. It should not be necessary to remove the fuel rail (described earlier in this Section) to remove the pressure sensor, but some dismantling will be required to gain access to it.

**77** Depressurise the fuel system as described in Section 2.

**78** Unplug the wiring connector from the sensor, then remove the two bolts and withdraw the sensor from the fuel rail **(see illustrations).** Recover the gasket/O-ring – a new one must be used when refitting.

#### Refitting

**79** Refitting is a reversal of removal.

### *Throttle position sensor*

#### Removal

**80** Depressurise the fuel system as described in Section 2. Remove the engine top cover to expose the throttle housing.

**81** Disconnect the sensor wiring plug, then remove the two bolts which secure the sensor and withdraw it from the throttle housing.

#### Refitting

**82** Refit by reversing the removal operations. If a new sensor has been fitted, have the car checked by a Volvo dealer using the correct diagnostic equipment, to ensure that the new sensor is correctly adapted to the engine management system.

### *Electronic control unit (ECU)*

#### Removal

**83** The ECU is located inside the passenger compartment, behind the centre console.

**84** Working in the driver's footwell, remove the screw and detach the carpet trim panel from the lower right-hand side of the centre console.

**85** On the right-hand side of the ECU is a tamperproof shear-bolt, which must be drilled out before the ECU can be removed. The shear-bolt is only fitted to discourage 'chipping' the ECU – an ordinary bolt could be used when refitting if preferred.

**86** On some models, a locking cap is fitted to the ECU bracket, which is released by turning it to the left.

**87** Ensure that the ignition is switched off, then release the locking catch on the ECU wiring plug by pressing upwards. Unplug the multi-plug connector and remove the ECU from the car.

#### Refitting

**88** Refit the ECU by reversing the removal procedure. Ensure that the wiring connector is securely reconnected. The ECU should in theory be resecured using a new shear-bolt, tightened until its head shears off. A new ECU

**11.4 Disconnect the evaporative emissions hose from the throttle housing**

will need to be programmed-in using the Volvo VADIS diagnostic equipment on completion.

### 11 Inlet manifold –
removal and refitting

**Note:** *Observe the precautions in Section 1 before working on any component in the fuel system.*

### *Removal*

**1** The inlet manifold on the GDI engine has its ports in the top of the cylinder head, which means there's a greater risk of dirt and debris being introduced directly into the engine when the manifold is removed. For this reason, it is advisable to clean around the top of the engine, preferably using compressed air, before starting. The inlet ports will also need to be plugged with suitable material once the manifold is off.

**2** Drain the cooling system as described in Chapter 1. Alternatively, provided that the coolant hoses to the throttle housing and EGR valve housing are not disconnected, the cooling system may be left undisturbed.

**3** Remove the air cleaner and inlet duct as described in Section 3.

**4** Disconnect the hose(s) for the evaporative emissions system from the top of the throttle housing **(see illustration).**

**5** At the rear of the manifold, disconnect the brake servo vacuum hose from the rigid pipe, after releasing the spring-type hose clip **(see illustration).**

**11.5 Disconnect the servo hose from the top of the manifold**

11.7 Disconnecting the engine speed sensor wiring plug

11.8a Disconnect the wiring plug for the oxygen sensor . . .

11.8b . . . and unclip the wiring from the back of the manifold

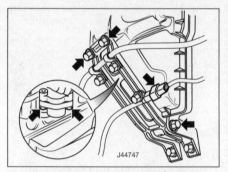

11.8c Inlet manifold support bracket removal details – early models

11.8d On later models, undo four bolts (two lower bolts arrowed) . . .

11.8e . . . and withdraw the manifold support bracket

6 Unbolt or unclip the mounting brackets securing the wiring harness to the manifold, and release the wiring from the twisted wire clips, where used.

7 At the timing belt cover, disconnect the wiring plug for the engine speed sensor, and move the wiring harness away from the manifold as far as possible (see illustration).

8 Working from underneath the car, remove the following from the rear of the manifold:

a) Two bolts securing the EGR elbow to the base of the manifold.

b) Wiring plug for the oxygen sensor. Detach the sensor wiring from the clips on the rear of the manifold (see illustrations).

c) On early models, two bolts from the top of the manifold support bracket, and a single bolt from the plastic resonance chamber, at the base of the manifold support bracket (see illustration).

d) On later models, the manifold support bracket is smaller, and secured by four bolts in total (see illustrations).

9 On early models, disconnect the accelerator cable from the inlet manifold, using the information in Section 4.

10 On later models, disconnect the wiring plugs on top of the manifold, for the EVAP system control valve and the EGR valve. Unclip the wiring from the locations on the manifold (see illustrations).

11 Remove the two bolts securing each of the four ignition coils which are fitted over the spark plugs, noting the earth wires which are also secured using the coil mounting bolts.

12 Disconnect the wiring plug from each coil, then carefully pull the coils upwards off the spark plugs. Although it appears there would be no serious consequences if the coils were mixed up, it makes sense to mark them for position as they are removed (No 1 at the timing belt end of the engine).

13 If not already done, disconnect the crankcase breather hose from either the throttle housing or the top of the manifold (see illustration).

11.10a Disconnect the EGR valve wiring plug . . .

11.10b . . . and unclip the wiring plug from the manifold

11.10c Similarly, disconnect the EVAP system wiring plug . . .

11.10d . . . and unclip the valve (with hoses) from the manifold

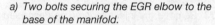

**11.13  Disconnecting the breather hose from the manifold at the timing belt end**

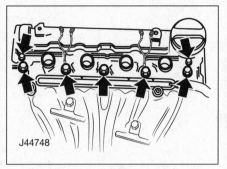

**11.15a  Inlet manifold nuts and bolts (arrowed)**

**11.15b  Two of the manifold bolts are also used to secure the ignition coil earth wiring**

**14** Remove the four bolts securing the throttle housing, and the further three bolts securing the throttle housing mounting bracket to the cylinder head.

**15** Remove the two outer nuts, then the row of five bolts, securing the inlet manifold – note that two of the bolts secure the ignition coil earth wiring. Check round the manifold to ensure that no wiring is still attached, then lift the manifold carefully over the outer studs, and remove it from the engine bay, together with the plastic resonance chamber. Recover the gaskets – new ones must be obtained for reassembly **(see illustrations)**. Cover or plug the manifold ports on the engine, to prevent any dirt entering the engine.

**16** If required, on early models, the resonance chamber fitted underneath the manifold can be removed by undoing two bolts and pulling it free.

### Refitting

**17** Refit by reversing the removal operations, noting the following points:

a) Clean the mating surfaces (making sure no dirt enters the engine), and use new inlet manifold gaskets **(see illustration)**.
b) Tighten the manifold nuts and bolts to the specified torque, starting with the centre bolt.

**12  Cruise control** – component removal and refitting

Refer to Chapter 4A.

**13  Dynamic Stability Assistance (DSA) system** – information and component renewal

Refer to Chapter 4A.

**11.15c  Lift off the inlet manifold, making sure the gaskets don't fall out**

**11.17  Use new gaskets when refitting the inlet manifold**

# Chapter 4 Part C:
# Exhaust & emission control systems

## Contents

## Degrees of difficulty

| Easy, suitable for novice with little experience  | Fairly easy, suitable for beginner with some experience  | Fairly difficult, suitable for competent DIY mechanic  | Difficult, suitable for experienced DIY mechanic | Very difficult, suitable for expert DIY or professional |
|---|---|---|---|---|

## Specifications

### Torque wrench settings

| | Nm | lbf ft |
|---|---|---|
| EGR system components (GDI engine) . . . . . . . . . . . . . . . . . . . . . . . . . | 19 | 14 |
| Exhaust front pipe: | | |
|   Non-GDI engines: | | |
|     Front pipe to catalytic converter (non-turbo models) . . . . . . . . . . | 30 | 22 |
|     Front pipe-to-intermediate pipe nuts/bolts . . . . . . . . . . . . . . . . . . | 60 | 44 |
|     Front pipe to turbocharger . . . . . . . . . . . . . . . . . . . . . . . . . . . . . | 30 | 22 |
|     Spring-loaded flange joint nuts . . . . . . . . . . . . . . . . . . . . . . . . . . . | 9 | 7 |
|   GDI engines: | | |
|     Front pipe-to-catalytic converter bolts . . . . . . . . . . . . . . . . . . . | 80 | 59 |
|     Front pipe-to-manifold nuts . . . . . . . . . . . . . . . . . . . . . . . . . . . | 44 | 32 |
|     Front pipe-to-block bracket nuts . . . . . . . . . . . . . . . . . . . . . . . . | 50 | 37 |
| Exhaust manifold heat shield bolts: | | |
|   M6 bolts . . . . . . . . . . . . . . . . . . . . . . . . . . . . . . . . . . . . . . . . . . . . | 10 | 7 |
|   M8 bolts . . . . . . . . . . . . . . . . . . . . . . . . . . . . . . . . . . . . . . . . . . . . | 16 | 12 |
| Exhaust manifold to cylinder head: | | |
|   Non-GDI engines . . . . . . . . . . . . . . . . . . . . . . . . . . . . . . . . . . . . . | 25 | 18 |
|   GDI engines . . . . . . . . . . . . . . . . . . . . . . . . . . . . . . . . . . . . . . . . | 29 | 21 |
| Exhaust tail pipe to intermediate pipe . . . . . . . . . . . . . . . . . . . . . . . | 55 | 41 |
| Heated oxygen sensor . . . . . . . . . . . . . . . . . . . . . . . . . . . . . . . . . . . | 55 | 41 |
| Oil separator bolts . . . . . . . . . . . . . . . . . . . . . . . . . . . . . . . . . . . . . . | 20 | 15 |
| Turbocharger coolant pipe unions . . . . . . . . . . . . . . . . . . . . . . . . . . | 25 | 18 |
| Turbocharger to manifold . . . . . . . . . . . . . . . . . . . . . . . . . . . . . . . . . | 25 | 18 |

## 1 General information

### Exhaust system

The exhaust system comprises the exhaust manifold, a front section incorporating the catalytic converter and front pipe, and a rear section incorporating the intermediate pipe, silencer and tail pipe. The system is supported under the car on rubber mountings.

On B4204T and B4194T engines, a water-cooled turbocharger is fitted to the exhaust manifold. Further information on the turbocharger unit is contained in Section 5.

### Emission control systems

All models covered by this manual have various features built into the fuel and exhaust systems to help minimise harmful emissions. These features fall broadly into three categories; crankcase emission control, evaporative emission control, and exhaust emission control. The main features of these systems are as follows.

### Crankcase emission control

To reduce the emissions of unburned hydrocarbons from the crankcase into the atmosphere, a Positive Crankcase Ventilation (PCV) system is used whereby the engine is sealed and the blow-by combustion gases and oil vapour are drawn from inside the crankcase, through an oil separator, into the inlet tract to be burned by the engine during normal combustion.

Under conditions of high manifold depression (idling, deceleration) the gases will be sucked positively out of the crankcase. Under conditions of low manifold depression (acceleration, full-throttle running) the gases are forced out of the crankcase by the (relatively) higher crankcase pressure; if the engine is worn, the raised crankcase pressure (due to increased blow-by) will cause some of the flow to return under all manifold conditions.

### Evaporative emission control

The evaporative emission control (EVAP) system is used to minimise the escape of unburned hydrocarbons (evaporated fuel) into the atmosphere. To do this, the fuel tank filler cap is sealed, and a carbon-filled canister is used to collect and store petrol vapours generated in the tank. When the engine is running, the vapours are purged from the canister by means of a vacuum-driven, ECU-controlled solenoid purge valve. The vapours are then passed into the inlet tract to be burned by the engine during normal combustion. To protect the catalyst and to ensure that the engine runs correctly when idling, the purge valve only operates when the engine is running under load. As a safety measure, a roll-over valve is incorporated into the system which closes when the car tilts sideways by more than 45°. This prevents fuel leakage in the event of an accident.

### Exhaust emission control

To minimise the amount of pollutants which escape into the atmosphere, all models are fitted with a catalytic converter in the exhaust system. The system is of the closed-loop type, in which a heated oxygen sensor in the exhaust system provides the fuel injection system ECU with constant feedback on the oxygen content of the exhaust gases. This enables the ECU to adjust the mixture by altering injector opening time, thus providing the best possible conditions for the converter to operate. The system functions in the following manner. The oxygen sensor has a built-in heating element, activated by the ECU to quickly bring the sensor's tip to an efficient operating temperature. The sensor's tip is sensitive to oxygen, and sends the control module a varying voltage depending on the amount of oxygen in the exhaust gases; if the inlet air/fuel mixture is too rich, the exhaust gas is low in oxygen, so the sensor sends a voltage signal that reflects the level of oxygen detected, the voltage altering as the mixture weakens and the amount of oxygen in the exhaust gas rises. Peak conversion efficiency of all major pollutants occurs if the inlet air/fuel mixture is maintained at the chemically-correct ratio for complete combustion of petrol – 14.7 parts (by weight) of air to 1 part of fuel (the stoichiometric ratio). The sensor output voltage alters in a large step at this point, the ECU using the signal change as a reference point, and correcting

the inlet air/fuel mixture accordingly, by altering the fuel injector opening time. On later engines, two oxygen sensors are fitted, one before the catalytic converter and one after – this improves sensor response time and accuracy, and the ECU compares the signals from each sensor to confirm that the converter is working correctly.

In addition to the catalytic converter, certain models are fitted with an exhaust gas recirculation (EGR) system. This system is designed to recirculate small quantities of exhaust gas into the inlet tract, and therefore into the combustion process. This reduces the level of oxides of nitrogen present in the final exhaust gas which is released into the atmosphere. The volume of exhaust gas recirculated is controlled by vacuum (supplied from the inlet manifold) via an EGR valve mounted on the inlet manifold. Before reaching the EGR valve, the vacuum from the manifold passes to an EGR controller. The purpose of which is to modify the vacuum supplied to the EGR valve according to engine operating conditions. The EGR system is controlled by the fuel/ignition ECU, which receives information on engine operating parameters from its various sensors.

A secondary air injection system is fitted to certain models intended for markets with stringent emission control regulations. The system is designed to inject fresh air into the exhaust passages in the cylinder head during the engine warm-up phase. This allows further fuel oxidation to take place in the exhaust to reduce HC and CO emissions upstream of the catalytic converter. The system comprises an electrically-driven air pump, solenoid, non-return valve, shut-off valve and interconnecting pipework. Under the control of the fuel/ignition ECU, the system operates for under two minutes, and starts approximately twenty seconds after the car has started to move.

> ⚠️ **Warning: Only work on the exhaust system components once the system has cooled sufficiently to avoid the risk of burns. The manifold, downpipe and catalytic converter run especially hot, and should not be touched until several hours after the engine was last run.**

## 2 Exhaust system – general information and component renewal

**Note:** *Refer to the warning at the end of Section 1 before proceeding.*

### General information

**1** The exhaust system consists of an exhaust manifold bolted to the cylinder head, a front section which comprises a front pipe and catalytic converter, and a rear section comprising an intermediate pipe and tailpipe. On turbocharged models, the turbocharger is mounted between the exhaust manifold and the exhaust system front pipe. The system is suspended from the underbody on rubber mountings, and a self-aligning ball-and-socket joint is used to connect the front and rear sections together. The front pipe-to-manifold connection is by either a spring-loaded flange joint, or a flange joint incorporating a flexible lattice-type coupling.

**2** The exhaust system should be examined for leaks, damage and security at regular intervals (see Chapter 1). To do this, apply the handbrake, and allow the engine to idle in a well-ventilated area. Lie down on each side of the car in turn, and check the full length of the system for leaks, while an assistant temporarily places a wad of cloth over the end of the tailpipe. If a leak is evident, stop the engine and use a proprietary repair kit to seal it. If the leak is excessive, or damage is evident, renew the section. Check the rubber mountings for deterioration, and renew them if necessary.

### Removal

#### Front section – non-GDI engines

**3** Jack up the front, and preferably the rear, of the car and support it on axle stands (see *Jacking and vehicle support*).
**4** Disconnect the heated oxygen sensor wiring connector(s) and release the wiring from any cable-ties.
**5** Undo the nuts securing the front pipe flange to the exhaust manifold. Recover the tension springs where fitted. Access may be improved removing the driveshaft heat shield to the left of the front section (**see illustrations**).

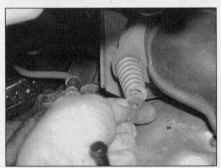

2.5a **Undo the nuts securing the front pipe flange to the exhaust manifold**

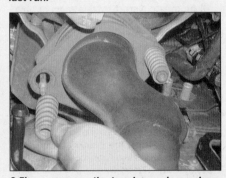

2.5b **. . . recover the tension springs where fitted**

2.5c **Access may be improved removing the driveshaft heat shield to the left of the front section**

**6** Undo the nuts and bolts at the ball-and-socket joint connecting the front and rear sections, and remove the clamps.

**7** Separate the front pipe-to-manifold joint, and remove the front section from under the car. Recover the gasket from the manifold flange joint **(see illustration)**.

### Front section – GDI engines

**8** Jack up the front, and preferably the rear, of the car and support it on axle stands (see *Jacking and vehicle support*).

**9** Disconnect the heated oxygen sensor wiring connector(s) and release the wiring from any cable-ties.

**10** Remove the clamp securing the downpipe to the bracket on the front of the block.

**11** Loosen the three nuts on the manifold-to-downpipe joint, and the three bolts at the joint to the catalytic converter.

**12** Unhook the downpipe from the two rubber mountings, then remove the nuts and bolts at the two joints, and remove it from under the car. Recover the gaskets.

### Rear section

**13** Jack up the rear, and preferably the front, of the car and support it on axle stands (see *Jacking and vehicle support*). The original rear section may be in one piece, which obviously makes removing it far more difficult than if a separate back box is fitted.

**14** Early models have a ball-and-socket joint connecting the front and rear sections, released by removing the nuts and bolts, and taking off the clamps. On later models, the rear section joints are conventional bolted flanges.

**15** Unhook the tailpipe and silencer from their rubber mountings, and slide the rear section forward until the tailpipe is clear of the rear suspension – on models with a separate back box, unbolt that first. Remove the system from under the car.

### *Refitting*

**16** Refitting is a reversal of removal, bearing in mind the following points:

a) *Use a new sealing ring or flange gasket, as applicable, on the front pipe-to-manifold joint.*

b) *When refitting the front section, loosely attach the front pipe to the manifold and the catalytic converter to the intermediate pipe. Align the system, then tighten the front pipe-to-manifold nuts first, followed by the intermediate pipe clamp nuts (or catalytic converter bolts), to the specified torque.*

c) *Where a gasket was used on any flanged joint, a new gasket should be used when refitting. Otherwise, use exhaust jointing compound, having first cleaned the joint faces of any old compound.*

d) *Ensure that there is adequate clearance between the exhaust system and underbody/suspension components (at least 20 mm).*

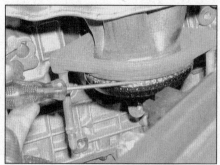

**2.7  Recover the gasket from the manifold flange joint**

---

3  **Catalytic converter –**
general information
and precautions

The catalytic converter is a reliable and simple device, which needs no maintenance in itself, but there are some facts of which an owner should be aware if the converter is to function properly for its full service life.

a) *DO NOT use leaded petrol/LRP in a vehicle equipped with a catalytic converter – the lead will coat the precious metals, reducing their converting efficiency, and will eventually destroy the converter.*

b) *Always keep the ignition and fuel systems well-maintained in accordance with the manufacturer's schedule (see Chapter 1).*

c) *If the engine develops a misfire, do not drive the vehicle at all (or at least as little as possible) until the fault is cured. The unburned fuel from the misfiring cylinder will enter the catalytic converter, where it can burn causing the converter to overheat.*

d) *DO NOT push – or tow-start the vehicle – this will soak the catalytic converter in unburned fuel, causing it to overheat when the engine does start.*

e) *DO NOT switch off the ignition at high engine speeds, ie, do not blip the throttle immediately before switching off.*

f) *DO NOT use fuel or engine oil additives – these may contain substances harmful to the catalytic converter.*

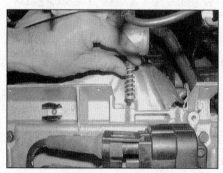

**4.5a  Undo the bolts . . .**

g) *DO NOT continue to use the vehicle if the engine burns oil to the extent of leaving a visible trail of blue smoke.*

h) *Remember that the catalytic converter operates at very high temperatures. DO NOT, therefore, park the vehicle in dry undergrowth, over long grass or piles of dead leaves, after a long run.*

i) *Remember that the catalytic converter is FRAGILE. Do not strike it with tools during servicing work.*

j) *In some cases, a sulphurous smell (like that of rotten eggs) may be noticed from the exhaust. This is common to many catalytic converter-equipped vehicles, particularly where fuel with a relatively high sulphur content is used. Once the vehicle has covered a few thousand miles, the problem should reduce – in the meantime, try changing the brand of petrol used.*

k) *The catalytic converter used on a well-maintained and well-driven vehicle should last up 100 000 miles. If the converter is no longer effective, it must be renewed.*

---

4  **Exhaust manifold –**
removal and refitting

**Note:** *Refer to the warning at the end of Section 1 before proceeding.*

### *Removal*

#### Non-GDI engines

**1** Disconnect the battery negative lead (see *Disconnecting the battery*).

**2** Undo the securing screws and remove the cover panel from the top of the engine.

**3** On turbo models, remove the turbocharger as described in Section 6.

**4** Refer to Part A of this Chapter and remove the air cleaner assembly and the hot air inlet duct from the manifold heat shield.

**5** Undo the bolts securing the heat shields to the exhaust manifold and the engine compartment bulkhead. Manoeuvre the heat shields out from behind the engine. Note that clearance is limited **(see illustrations)**.

**6** Jack up the front of the car and support it on axle stands (see *Jacking and vehicle support*).

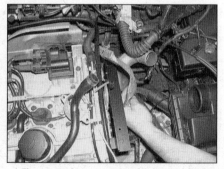

**4.5b  . . . and manoeuvre the heat shields out from behind the engine**

4.10 Manipulate the exhaust manifold out from the rear of the engine – clearance is very limited

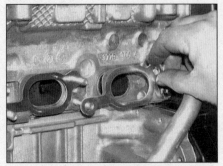

4.19a Use new individual gaskets when refitting the exhaust manifold (shown with engine removed for clarity)

4.19b Refit the manifold . . .

4.19c . . . and tighten all manifold nuts to the specified torque (shown with engine removed for clarity)

4.19d Refit the heat shield . . .

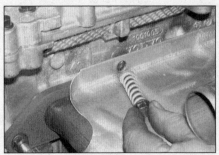

4.19e . . . and secure with the spring-loaded bolts (shown with engine removed for clarity)

**7** On non-turbo models, undo the nuts securing the exhaust front pipe flange to the manifold, with reference to Section 2. Recover the tension springs where fitted.

**8** Lower the car to the ground.

**9** Undo the nuts and spring-loaded bolts securing the manifold to the cylinder head, starting at the innermost nuts first of all.

**10** Move the manifold rearwards off the cylinder head studs, then separate the front pipe flange joint. Twist the manifold through 90° to the right and manipulate it out from the rear of the engine (see illustration). Again, clearance is very limited and considerable manoeuvring will be necessary.

**11** Recover the front pipe flange joint gasket or sealing ring and the individual manifold-to-cylinder head gaskets.

### GDI engines

**12** Disconnect the battery negative lead (see *Disconnecting the battery*).

**13** Undo the securing screws and remove the cover panel from the top of the engine.

**14** Separate the downpipe from the manifold, with reference to Section 2.

**15** Remove the bolts securing the heat shield over the manifold, and take off the heat shield. It's likely that these bolts may be in very poor condition, having suffered corrosion damage – make sure the spanner or socket used to remove them is a good fit, and spray the bolts with penetrating lubricant before trying to remove them. If the bolts are found to be in poor condition, it is advisable to obtain new bolts for reassembly.

**16** Remove the two bolts from underneath which secure the manifold to the cylinder block mounting bracket.

**17** Remove the nuts and washers used to secure the manifold to the cylinder head, then slide the manifold off the studs and remove it. Recover the gasket – a new one should be used when refitting. Again, if the manifold nuts are in poor condition, new ones should be obtained for reassembly.

**18** If any studs were removed with the nuts, these can be refitted to the head using two nuts tightened against each other. Volvo recommend that any studs which have to be refitted (or renewed, if their threads are in poor condition) are refitted using thread-locking fluid.

### Refitting

**19** Refitting is a reversal of removal bearing in mind the following points (see illustrations):

a) *Return any studs that were removed with their nuts back to the cylinder head, using thread-locking fluid.*

b) *Thoroughly clean the manifold and cylinder head mating faces prior to refitting.*

c) *Use new manifold gaskets and a new sealing ring or flange gasket as applicable on the front pipe-to-manifold joint.*

d) *Refit the turbocharger with reference to Section 6.*

e) *Tighten all nuts and bolts to the specified torque.*

### 5 Turbocharger – general information and precautions

#### General information

**1** A water-cooled turbocharger is used on all turbo models covered by this manual. The turbocharger increases the efficiency of the engine by raising the pressure in the inlet manifold above atmospheric pressure. Instead of the air/fuel mixture being simply sucked into the cylinders, it is forced in.

**2** Energy for the operation of the turbocharger comes from the exhaust gas. The gas flows through a specially-shaped housing (the turbine housing), and in so doing, spins the turbine wheel. The turbine wheel is attached to a shaft, at the other end of which is another vaned wheel known as the compressor wheel. The compressor wheel spins in its own separate housing and compresses the intake air on the way to the inlet manifold.

**3** After leaving the turbocharger, the compressed air passes through an intercooler, which is an air-to-air heat exchanger mounted next to the coolant radiator. Here, the air which was heated as a result of being compressed in the turbocharger, is now cooled and so reduces in volume. This volume reduction allows a greater mass of air to be forced into the combustion chambers, leading to a large improvement in engine efficiency. The temperature reduction also reduces the risk of detonation, or pinking.

**4** Turbocharger boost pressure (the pressure in the inlet manifold) is limited by a wastegate, which diverts the exhaust gas away from the turbine wheel in response to a pressure-sensitive actuator. The actuator is controlled by the turbocharger control valve, under signals from the fuel system electronic control unit – see Chapter 4A for more information.

**5** The turbo shaft is pressure-lubricated by means of a feed pipe from the engine's main oil gallery. The shaft floats on a cushion of oil. A drain pipe returns the oil to the sump.

**6** Water cooling reduces the operating temperature of the turbo bearings. Water supplied from the engine's coolant circuit continues to circulate by convection after the engine has stopped, so cooling the turbocharger if it is hot after a long run.

## Precautions

**7** The turbocharger operates at extremely high speeds and temperatures. Certain precautions must be observed to avoid premature failure of the turbo or injury to the operator.

 a) *Do not operate the turbo if the ports are exposed (open to air). Foreign objects falling onto the rotating vanes could cause extensive damage and (if ejected) personal injury.*

 b) *Do not race the engine immediately after start-up, especially if it is cold. Give the oil a few seconds to circulate.*

 c) *Always allow the engine to return to idle speed before switching it off – do not blip the throttle and switch off, as this will leave the turbo spinning without lubrication.*

 d) *Allow the engine to idle for several minutes before switching off after a high-speed run, to allow the heat in the turbocharger to dissipate.*

 e) *Observe the recommended intervals for oil and filter changing, and use a reputable oil of the specified quality. Neglect of oil changing, or use of inferior oil, can cause carbon formation on the turbo shaft and subsequent failure.*

**6.4  Unbolt the heat shield from the top of the turbocharger unit**

## 6  Turbocharger – removal and refitting

**Note:** *Refer to the warning at the end of Section 1 before proceeding.*

### Removal

**1** Disconnect the battery negative lead (see *Disconnecting the battery*).

**2** Drain the cooling system as described in Chapter 1.

**3** Undo the securing screws and remove the engine cover panel.

**4** Unbolt the heat shield from the top of the turbocharger unit **(see illustration)**.

**5** With reference to Chapter 4A, disconnect the vacuum hoses from the turbocharger control valve; make a careful note of their order of connection to aid correct refitting. Detach the valve from the side of the air cleaner, then remove the entire air cleaner assembly from the engine compartment (see Chapter 4A for more information).

**6** Slacken the hose clips and disconnect the inlet and outlet air ducts from the turbocharger.

**7** Slacken and remove the securing nuts and bolts then detach the heat shield from the engine compartment bulkhead.

**8** Undo the coolant supply and return pipe unions and the oil supply pipe union from the turbocharger housing. Recover the sealing washers as each union is released **(see illustrations)**.

**9** Jack up the front of the car and support it on axle stands (see *Jacking and vehicle support*).

**10** Undo the securing screws and remove the splash shield from the underside of the engine compartment.

**11** Undo the bolt and remove the clamp bracket securing the oil return pipe.

**12** Undo the oil supply pipe union at the engine block; be prepared for some oil spillage. Recover the union sealing washers. Delay extracting the oil return pipe from the engine block until the turbocharger is removed.

**13** Undo the four nuts securing the exhaust front pipe to the turbocharger. Pull the front pipe down to separate the joint, and recover the gasket.

**14** Disconnect the turbocharger control valve vacuum hoses from the turbocharger; make a careful note of the order of connection of the hoses to aid correct refitting **(see illustration)**.

**15** Undo the nuts securing the turbocharger to the exhaust manifold, then withdraw the turbocharger from the exhaust manifold. Carefully withdraw the oil return pipe from the engine block.

**16** Remove the turbocharger from the car and recover the gaskets.

### Refitting

**17** Refitting is a reversal of removal bearing in mind the following points:

 a) *Return any studs that were removed with their nuts back to their original locations; apply thread-locking fluid to their (cleaned) threads.*

 b) *Thoroughly clean the turbocharger and manifold mating faces prior to refitting.*

 c) *Use a new manifold gasket and new seals on all disturbed unions.*

 d) *Before refitting the oil supply pipe to the engine, first undo the adjacent water pipe union and move the pipe to side, to give greater access. On completion, reconnect the water pipe and tighten the union to the specified torque.*

 e) *Tighten all nuts and bolts to the correct torque, where specified.*

 f) *On completion, refill the cooling system as described in Chapter 1, then check and if necessary top-up the engine oil level as described in 'Weekly checks'.*

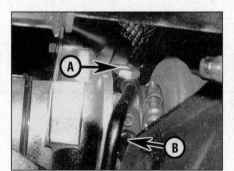

**6.8a  Coolant supply and return unions (A), oil return union (B) . . .**

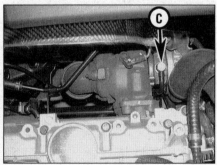

**6.8b  . . . and oil supply union (C) locations**

**6.14  Turbocharger control valve (air cleaner removed for clarity)**

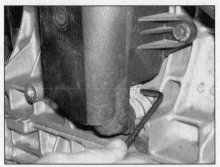

**7.3 Disconnect the hoses leading to the oil separator – non-GDI engine**

**7.4a Undo the two bolts . . .**

**7.4b . . . and remove the unit from the engine**

## 7 Crankcase emission control system – checking and component renewal

### Checking

**1** The components of this system require no attention other than to check that the hoses are clear and undamaged, and to renew the flame trap in the air cleaner at regular intervals. An ineffective crankcase ventilation system can cause high exhaust emissions readings, exhaust smoke and poor running. In extreme cases, the catalytic converter can also be damaged.

### Oil separator – non-GDI engines

**2** The oil separator is located on the front-facing side of the cylinder block, below the inlet manifold. Remove the inlet manifold as described in Part A of this Chapter.

**3** Disconnect the upper hose at the oil separator, and remove the inlet manifold support bracket. Where applicable, remove the clips securing the connecting hoses to the cylinder block connecting sleeves **(see illustration)**.

**4** Undo the two bolts and remove the unit from the engine **(see illustrations)**.

**5** Clean the oil separator seal surfaces in the cylinder block, and fit new seals to the oil separator stubs. Obtain a new separator top hose and securing clip.

**6** Refit the oil separator using a reversal of removal. Refit the inlet manifold as described in Part A of this Chapter.

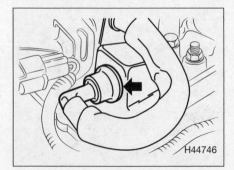

**7.7 Crankcase ventilation valve (arrowed) – GDI engine**

### PCV valve – GDI engine

**7** The crankcase ventilation valve is located on top of the engine, at the timing belt end **(see illustration)**.

**8** Carefully prise the valve to release it from the cylinder head, then pull it out of its location and disconnect its hose.

**9** Check that the valve and its hose are clear. It should be possible to blow through the valve, but in one direction only. If cleaning does not cure any blockage, a new valve should be fitted.

**10** When refitting the valve, check the condition of the rubber seal – fit a new one if its condition is in doubt.

## 8 Evaporative emission control system – checking and component renewal

### Checking

**1** Poor idle, stalling and poor driveability can be caused by an inoperative canister vacuum valve, a damaged canister, split or cracked hoses, or hoses connected to the wrong fittings. Check the fuel filler cap for a damaged or deformed gasket.

**2** Fuel loss or fuel odour can be caused by liquid fuel leaking from fuel lines, a cracked or damaged canister, an inoperative canister vacuum valve, and disconnected, misrouted, kinked or damaged vapour or control hoses.

**3** Inspect each hose attached to the canister for kinks, leaks and cracks along its entire length. Repair or renew as necessary.

**4** Inspect the canister. If it is cracked or damaged, renew it. Look for fuel leaking from the bottom of the canister. If fuel is leaking, renew the canister, and check the hoses and hose routing.

### Component renewal

#### Carbon canister

**5** The canister is located under the left-hand wheel arch at the front. Remove the left-hand foglight (where fitted) to gain access (see Chapter 12, Section 7), then remove the engine compartment splash guard.

**6** Note the location of the vacuum and fuel vent hose connections at the canister, and carefully disconnect them.

**7** Remove the screw securing the rear of the canister to the bodywork, then remove the two screws securing the front of the canister to the windscreen washer fluid reservoir. Lift the canister from the wheel arch.

**8** Refitting is a reversal of removal.

#### Purge valve

**9** The purge valve is mounted in the engine compartment, in front of the inlet manifold. The valve can be renewed by tracing back the vapour line from the canister to the valve, disconnecting the hoses and wiring connector and removing the valve from its location.

**10** Refitting is a reversal of removal.

## 9 Exhaust emission control systems – checking and component renewal

### Checking

**1** Checking of the system as a whole entails a close visual inspection of all hoses, pipes and connections for condition and security. Apart from this, any known or suspected faults should be referred to a Volvo dealer.

### Component renewal

#### Heated oxygen sensor

**Note:** *The sensor is delicate, and will not work if it is dropped or knocked, if its power supply is disrupted, or if any cleaning materials are used on it.*

**2** Jack up the front of the car and support it on axle stands (see *Jacking and vehicle support*).

**3** Disconnect the heated oxygen sensor wiring connector(s) and release the wiring from any cable-ties.

**4** Unscrew the sensor from the exhaust system front pipe and collect the sealing washer (where fitted).

**5** On refitting, clean the sealing washer (where fitted) and renew it if it is damaged or worn. Apply a smear of anti-seize compound to the sensor's threads, then refit the sensor, tightening it to the specified torque. Reconnect the wiring and secure with cable-ties where applicable.

### Catalytic converter

**6** The catalytic converter is part of the exhaust system front section. Refer to Sections 2 and 3 for renewal procedures and additional information.

### Air injection pump

**7** Remove the air cleaner assembly and intake ducting, as described in Chapter 4A. The air injection pump is located behind the air cleaner.

**8** Unplug the pump wiring at the base of the relay

**9** Unscrew the bolt and disconnect the bodywork earth cable.

**10** Disconnect the air hoses from the air injection pump, making a careful note of their order of connection.

**11** Unscrew and remove the mounting bolts, then remove the pump from the engine compartment.

**12** Refitting is a reversal of removal. Ensure that the earth cable is securely reconnected.

### EGR valve

**13** The EGR valve is located on the rear of the EGR housing, on top of the engine at the transmission end.

**14** To gain access to the valve to remove it, take off the starter motor as described in Chapter 5A.

**15** Disconnect the gear selector cables as described in Chapter 7A, and move them to one side.

**16** Disconnect the wiring plug on the top of the EGR valve.

**17** Remove the two valve mounting bolts, and remove the valve from the EGR housing.

**18** Refitting is a reversal of removal.

### EGR housing

**19** Unscrew the bolts from the EGR connecting pipe flanges, and separate the pipes from the housing. Recover the gaskets, and obtain new ones for reassembly.

**20** Anticipating some loss of coolant, release the spring-type hose clip and disconnect the coolant hose from the base of the housing.

**21** Remove the bolt at the top of the housing, noting that it is also used to secure the engine lifting eye.

**22** Remove the two nuts securing the EGR

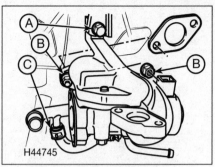

**9.22  Removing the EGR housing –
GDI engine**

*A  Upper mounting bolt*
*B  Mounting nuts*
*C  Coolant hose*

housing to the cylinder head, and remove it together with its gasket **(see illustration)**.

**23** Refitting is a reversal of removal, using new gaskets and tightening all fixings to the specified torque.

# Notes

# Chapter 5 Part A:
# Starting and charging systems

## Contents

## Degrees of difficulty

| | | | | | | | | | |
|---|---|---|---|---|---|---|---|---|---|
| **Easy,** suitable for novice with little experience |  | **Fairly easy,** suitable for beginner with some experience |  | **Fairly difficult,** suitable for competent DIY mechanic | | **Difficult,** suitable for experienced DIY mechanic |  | **Very difficult,** suitable for expert DIY or professional | 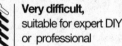 |

## Specifications

**System type** ........................................ 12 volt, negative earth

**Battery**
Type ............................................. Low-maintenance or maintenance-free sealed for life
Capacity .......................................... 50, 55, 62 or 72Ah (depending on model)

**Alternator**
Type ............................................. Bosch, Nippon-Denso, Valeo or Delco (depending on model)
Nominal output voltage ............................. 14V
Max current output ................................. 80 to 120A max

**Starter motor**
Type ............................................. Valeo or Delco (depending on model)
Minimum brush length .............................. 6.1 mm

| **Torque wrench settings** | **Nm** | **lbf ft** |
|---|---|---|
| Alternator drivebelt adjuster bracket bolts ..................... | 23 | 17 |
| Alternator pivot bolt nut ................................... | 44 | 32 |
| Starter motor mounting bolts ............................... | 50 | 37 |

## 1 General information and precautions

### General information

The engine electrical system consists mainly of the charging and starting systems. Because of their engine-related functions, these components are covered separately from the body electrical devices such as the lights, instruments, etc (which are covered in Chapter 12). Information on the ignition system is covered in Part B of this Chapter.

The electrical system is of the 12 volt negative-earth type.

The battery is of the low-maintenance or maintenance-free (sealed for life) type and is charged by the alternator, which is belt-driven from the crankshaft pulley.

The starter motor is of the pre-engaged type, incorporating an integral solenoid. On starting, the solenoid moves the drive pinion into engagement with the flywheel ring gear before the starter motor is energised. Once the engine has started, a one-way clutch prevents the motor armature being driven by the engine until the pinion disengages from the flywheel.

### Precautions

**Warning: It is necessary to take extra care when working on the electrical system to avoid damage to semi-conductor devices (diodes and transistors), and to avoid the risk of personal injury. In addition to the precautions given in 'Safety first!', observe the following when working on the system:**
• **Always remove rings, watches, etc, before working on the electrical system.**
Even with the battery disconnected, capacitive discharge could occur if a component's live terminal is earthed through a metal object. This could cause a shock or nasty burn.
• **Do not reverse the battery connections.** Components such as the alternator, electronic control units, or any other components having semi-conductor circuitry could be irreparably damaged.
• **Never disconnect the battery terminals, the alternator, any electrical wiring or any test instruments when the engine is running.**
• **Do not allow the engine to turn the alternator when the alternator is not connected.**
• **Never 'test' for alternator output by 'flashing' the output lead to earth.**
• **Always ensure that the battery negative lead is disconnected when working on the electrical system.**

• If the engine is being started using jump leads and a slave battery, connect the batteries **positive-to-positive** and **negative-to-negative** (see *Jump starting*). This also applies when connecting a battery charger.

• **Never** use an ohmmeter of the type incorporating a hand-cranked generator for circuit or continuity testing.

• Before using electric-arc welding equipment on the car, **disconnect the battery, alternator and components such as the electronic control units** (where applicable) to protect them from the risk of damage.

---

### 2 Battery – removal, refitting, testing and charging

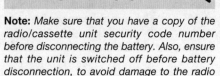

**Note:** *Make sure that you have a copy of the radio/cassette unit security code number before disconnecting the battery. Also, ensure that the unit is switched off before battery disconnection, to avoid damage to the radio microprocessor circuitry.*

### Removal

1 The battery is located at the front left-hand side of the engine compartment.

2 Slacken the clamp bolt and disconnect the clamp from the battery negative (earth) terminal (see *Disconnecting the battery*).

3 Remove the insulation cover (where fitted) and disconnect the positive terminal lead(s) in the same way.

4 Depress the locking plate and rotate to detach it from the battery tray. Slide the battery to the right to disengage it from the locating rails on the battery tray, then lift the battery out of the engine compartment **(see illustrations)**.

5 If required, the battery tray can now be removed, after unscrewing the four bolts.

### Refitting

6 Refitting is a reversal of removal, but smear petroleum jelly on the terminals after reconnecting the leads, to prevent corrosion. Always reconnect the positive lead first, and the negative lead last.

**2.4a Depress the locking plate and rotate to detach it from the battery tray**

### Testing

### Standard and low-maintenance battery

7 If the car covers a small annual mileage, it is worthwhile checking the specific gravity of the electrolyte every three months to determine the state of charge of the battery. Use a hydrometer to make the check and compare the results with the following:

| | |
|---|---|
| *Fully-charged:* | 1.280 (at 20°C) |
| *Recharge at:* | 1.210 (at 20°C) |

Note that the specific gravity readings assume an electrolyte temperature of 15°C (60°F); for every 10°C (18°F) below 15°C (60°F) subtract 0.007. For every 10°C (18°F) above 15°C (60°F) add 0.007.

8 If the battery condition is suspect, first check the specific gravity of electrolyte in each cell. A variation of 0.040 or more between any cells indicates loss of electrolyte or deterioration of the internal plates.

9 If the specific gravity variation is 0.040 or more, the battery should be renewed. If the cell variation is satisfactory but the battery is discharged, it should be charged as described later in this Section.

### Maintenance-free battery

10 In cases where a sealed for life maintenance-free battery is fitted, topping-up and testing of the electrolyte in each cell is not possible. The condition of the battery can therefore only be tested using a battery condition indicator or a voltmeter.

11 If testing the battery using a voltmeter, connect the voltmeter across the battery, and note the result. The test is only accurate if the battery has not been subjected to any kind of charge for the previous six hours. If this is not the case, switch on the headlights for 30 seconds, then wait four to five minutes before testing the battery after switching off the headlights. All other electrical circuits must be switched off, so check that the doors and tailgate are fully shut when making the test.

12 If the voltage reading is less than 11.0 volts, then the battery is discharged, whilst a reading of 11.1 to 11.9 volts indicates a partially-discharged condition.

13 If the battery is to be charged, remove it from the car and charge it as described later in this Section.

**2.4b Disengage the battery from the locating rails on the battery tray, then lift it from the engine compartment**

### Charging

**Note:** *The following is intended as a guide only. Always refer to the manufacturer's recommendations (often printed on a label attached to the battery) before charging a battery.*

### Standard and low-maintenance battery

14 Charge the battery at a rate of 3.5 to 4 amps and continue to charge the battery at this rate until no further rise in specific gravity is noted over a four hour period.

15 Alternatively, a trickle charger charging at the rate of 1.5 amps can safely be used overnight.

16 Boost chargers which are claimed to restore the power of the battery in 1 to 2 hours are not recommended, as they can cause irreparable damage to the battery plates through overheating.

17 While charging the battery, note that the temperature of the electrolyte should never exceed 37.8°C (100°F).

### Maintenance-free battery

18 This battery type takes considerably longer to fully recharge than the standard type, the time taken being dependent on the extent of discharge, but it can take anything up to three days.

19 A constant voltage type charger is required, to be set, when connected, to 13.9 to 14.9 volts with a charger current below 25 amps. Using this method, the battery should be usable within three hours, giving a voltage reading of 12.0 volts, but this is for a partially-discharged battery and, as mentioned, full charging can take considerably longer.

20 If the battery is to be charged from a fully-discharged state (condition reading less than 11.0 volts), have it recharged by your Volvo dealer or local automotive electrician, as the charge rate is higher and constant supervision during charging is necessary.

---

### 3 Charging system – general information and precautions

### General information

The charging system includes the alternator, an internal voltage regulator, a no-charge (or 'ignition') warning light, the battery, and the wiring between all the components. The charging system supplies electrical power for the ignition system, the lights, the radio, etc. The alternator is driven by the auxiliary drivebelt at the timing belt end of the engine.

The purpose of the voltage regulator is to limit the alternator's voltage to a preset value. This prevents power surges, circuit overloads, etc, during peak voltage output.

The charging system doesn't ordinarily require periodic maintenance. However, the drivebelt, battery and wires and connections should be inspected at the intervals outlined in Chapter 1.

The dashboard warning light should come on when the ignition key is turned to positions II or III, then should go off immediately the engine starts. If it remains on, or if it comes on while the engine is running, there is a malfunction in the charging system. If the light does not come on when the ignition key is turned, and the bulb is in working condition (see Chapter 12 for warning light bulbs), there is a fault in the alternator.

## Precautions

Be very careful when making electrical circuit connections to a car equipped with an alternator, and note the following:

a) *When reconnecting wires to the alternator from the battery, be sure to note the polarity.*

b) *Before using arc-welding equipment to repair any part of the car, disconnect the wires from the alternator and the battery terminals.*

c) *Never start the engine with a battery charger connected.*

d) *Always disconnect both battery leads before using a battery charger.*

e) *The alternator is driven by an engine drivebelt which could cause serious injury if your hand, hair or clothes become entangled in it with the engine running.*

f) *Because the alternator is connected directly to the battery, it could arc or cause a fire if overloaded or shorted-out.*

g) *If steam-cleaning or pressure-washing the engine, wrap a plastic bag over the alternator or any other electrical component and secure them with rubber bands **(do not forget to remove, before re-starting the engine).***

h) *Never disconnect the alternator terminals while the engine is running.*

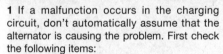

### 4 Charging system – testing

1 If a malfunction occurs in the charging circuit, don't automatically assume that the alternator is causing the problem. First check the following items:

a) *Check the tension and condition of the auxiliary drivebelt – renew it if it is worn or deteriorated (see Chapter 1).*

b) *Ensure the alternator mounting bolts and nuts are tight.*

c) *Inspect the alternator wiring harness and the electrical connections at the alternator; they must be in good condition, and tight.*

d) *Check the large main fuses in the engine compartment (see Chapter 12). If any are blown, determine the cause, repair the circuit and renew the fuse (the car won't start and/or the accessories won't work if the fuse is blown).*

e) *Start the engine and check the alternator for abnormal noises – for example, a*

**5.3 Unbolt the power steering pump from its mounting bracket, and tie it to the front if the engine compartment**

shrieking or squealing sound may indicate a badly-worn bearing or brush.

f) *Make sure that the battery is fully-charged – one bad cell in a battery can cause overcharging by the alternator.*

g) *Disconnect the battery leads (negative first, then positive). Inspect the battery posts and the lead clamps for corrosion. Clean them thoroughly if necessary (see 'Weekly checks'). Reconnect the leads.*

 **Warning: Never disconnect the alternator output wiring with the engine running.**

2 Using a voltmeter, check the battery voltage with the engine off. It should be approximately 12 volts.

3 Start the engine and check the battery voltage again. Increase engine speed until the voltmeter reading remains steady; it should now be approximately 13.5 to 14.6 volts.

4 Switch on as many electrical accessories (eg, the headlights, heated rear window and heater blower) as possible, and check that the alternator maintains the regulated voltage at around 13 to 14 volts. The voltage may drop and then come back up; it may also be necessary to increase engine speed slightly, even if the charging system is working properly.

5 If the voltage reading is greater than the specified charging voltage, renew the voltage regulator.

6 If the voltmeter reading is less than that specified, the fault may be due to worn brushes, weak brush springs, a faulty voltage regulator, a faulty diode, a severed phase

**5.5 Disconnect the wiring from the rear of the alternator**

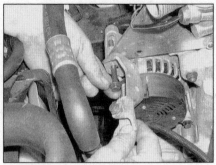

**5.4 Slacken and withdraw the bolt that secures the top of the alternator to the triangular bracket at the rear of the power steering pump**

winding, or worn or damaged slip-rings. The brushes and slip-rings may be checked, but if the fault persists, the alternator should be renewed or taken to an auto-electrician for testing and repair.

### 5 Alternator – removal and refitting

## Removal

### Non-GDI engines

1 Disconnect the battery negative lead (see *Disconnecting the battery*).

2 Remove the auxiliary drivebelt as described in Chapter 1.

3 With reference to Chapter 10, unbolt the power steering pump from its mounting bracket, and tie it to the front if the engine compartment; there is no need to disconnect the hydraulic fluid pipes **(see illustration)**.

4 Slacken and withdraw the bolt that secures the top of the alternator to the triangular bracket at the rear of the power steering pump **(see illustration)**.

5 Disconnect the wiring multi-plugs and the leads from the terminal studs at the rear of the alternator **(see illustration)**.

6 Slacken and withdraw the remaining alternator-to-inlet manifold bracket bolts, and remove the bracket from the engine compartment **(see illustration)**.

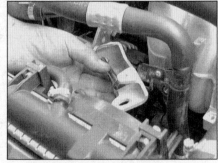

**5.6 Remove the alternator-to-inlet manifold bracket**

**5.7a Remove the upper and lower alternator mounting nuts and bolts (arrowed)**

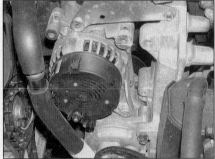

**5.7b ... and lift the alternator from the engine compartment (inlet manifold and radiator top hose removed for clarity)**

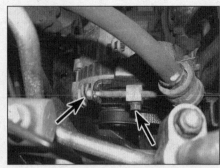

**5.9 Alternator drivebelt adjuster bolt and lockbolt (arrowed)**

**7** Remove the upper and lower alternator mounting nuts and bolts at the front and rear, and lift the alternator from the engine compartment **(see illustrations)**.

### GDI engine

**8** Remove the engine top cover, and disconnect the battery negative lead (see *Disconnecting the battery*).

**9** Unscrew the alternator drivebelt adjuster bolt and its lockbolt **(see illustration)**.

**10** With the front of the car raised and supported on axle stands (see *Jacking and vehicle support*), disconnect the alternator wiring from below. The positive supply cable is covered by a plastic cap, and secured by a nut, while the grey wiring connector just pulls off.

**11** Remove the auxiliary drivebelt from the alternator, as described in Chapter 1.

**12** On models with air conditioning, remove the bolts securing the alternator adjuster bracket to the engine, and the bolt from the power steering hose bracket **(see illustration)**.

**13** Remove the pivot bolt nut, then manoeuvre the alternator out from its location **(see illustration)**. On some models, it may be necessary to unclip the wiring for the oxygen

sensor, to make room to remove the alternator.

### Refitting

**14** Refitting is a reversal of removal. Refit the auxiliary drivebelt as described in Chapter 1.

---

### 6 Alternator – testing and overhaul

If the alternator is thought to be suspect, it should be removed from the car and taken to an auto-electrician for testing. Most auto-electricians will be able to supply and fit brushes at a reasonable cost. However, check on the cost of repairs before proceeding, as it may prove more economical to obtain a new or exchange alternator.

---

### 7 Starting system – testing

**Note:** *Refer to the precautions given in 'Safety first!' and in Section 1 of this Chapter before starting work.*

**1** If the starter motor fails to operate when the ignition key is turned to the appropriate position, the following possible causes may be to blame.
 a) *The battery is faulty.*
 b) *The electrical connections between the switch, solenoid, battery and starter motor are somewhere failing to pass the necessary current from the battery through the starter to earth.*
 c) *The solenoid is faulty.*
 d) *The starter motor is mechanically or electrically defective.*

**2** To check the battery, switch on the headlights. If they dim after a few seconds, this indicates that the battery is discharged – recharge (see Section 2) or renew the battery. If the headlights glow brightly, operate the ignition switch and observe the lights. If they dim, then this indicates that current is reaching the starter motor, therefore the fault must lie in the starter motor. If the lights continue to glow brightly (and no clicking sound can be heard from the starter motor solenoid), this indicates that there is a fault in the circuit or solenoid – see following paragraphs. If the starter motor turns slowly when operated, but the battery is in good condition, then this indicates that either the

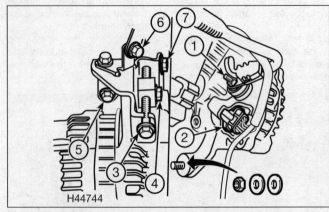

**5.12 Alternator removal details – GDI engine**

 1  *Positive cable nut*
 2  *Wiring plug*
 3  *Adjuster bolt*
 4  *Lockbolt*

 5  *Adjuster bracket bolt*
 6  *Power steering hose bracket*
 7  *Adjuster bracket bolt*

**5.13 Alternator pivot bolt nut (arrowed) – seen from below**

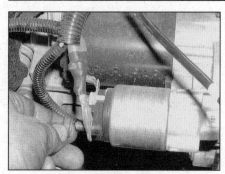

**8.4a Undo the nut . . .**

starter motor is faulty, or there is considerable resistance somewhere in the circuit.

**3** If a fault in the circuit is suspected, disconnect the battery leads (including the earth connection to the body), the starter/solenoid wiring and the engine/transmission earth strap. Thoroughly clean the connections, and reconnect the leads and wiring, then use a voltmeter or test lamp to check that full battery voltage is available at the battery positive lead connection to the solenoid, and that the earth is sound. Smear petroleum jelly around the battery terminals to prevent corrosion – corroded connections are amongst the most frequent causes of electrical system faults.

**4** If the battery and all connections are in good condition, check the circuit by disconnecting the wire from the solenoid blade terminal. Connect a voltmeter or test lamp between the wire end and a good earth (such as the battery negative terminal), and check that the wire is live when the ignition switch is turned to the start position. If it is, then the circuit is sound – if not the circuit wiring can be checked as described in Chapter 12, Section 2.

**5** The solenoid contacts can be checked by connecting a voltmeter or test lamp between the battery positive feed connection on the starter side of the solenoid and earth. When the ignition switch is turned to the start position, there should be a reading or lighted

bulb, as applicable. If there is no reading or lighted bulb, the solenoid is faulty and should be renewed.

**6** If the circuit and solenoid are proved sound, the fault must lie in the starter motor. In this event, it may be possible to have the starter motor overhauled by a specialist, but check on the cost of spares before proceeding, as it may prove more economical to obtain a new or exchange motor.

### 8 Starter motor – removal and refitting

## *Removal*

### Non-GDI engines

**1** Disconnect the battery negative lead (see *Disconnecting the battery*).
**2** Remove the inlet manifold as described in Chapter 4A.
**3** Unclip the plastic guard, to expose the wiring terminals at the rear of the starter motor.
**4** Undo the nut and disconnect the wiring from the rear of the starter solenoid **(see illustrations)**.
**5** Unscrew the securing bolts and manoeuvre the starter motor from the transmission bellhousing **(see illustration)**. Note the position of the locating dowel, and ensure it is in place when refitting.

### GDI engine

**6** Remove the engine top cover, and disconnect the battery negative lead (see *Disconnecting the battery*). The starter motor is located at the rear of the engine, at the base of the support bracket for the inlet manifold **(see illustration)**.
**7** Remove the air cleaner and air inlet duct as described in Chapter 4B.
**8** Working in the engine compartment, unscrew the starter motor upper mounting bolt.
**9** Raise the front of the car, and support it on axle stands.

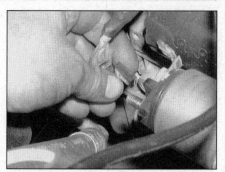

**8.4b . . . and disconnect the wiring from the rear of the starter solenoid**

**10** Remove the nut securing the main starter cable from the solenoid – the cable itself is also secured by two bolted brackets at the base of the inlet manifold support bracket. Unclip the smaller wire above the starter solenoid.
**11** Remove the starter motor lower mounting bolt, then take the starter motor out of its location **(see illustration)**.

## *Refitting*

**12** Refitting is a reversal of removal.

### 9 Starter motor – testing and overhaull

If the starter motor is thought to be suspect, it should be removed from the car and taken to an auto-electrician for testing. Most auto-electricians will be able to supply and fit brushes at a reasonable cost. However, check on the cost of repairs before proceeding as it may prove more economical to obtain a new or exchange motor.

### 10 Ignition switch – removal and refitting

Refer to the information given in Chapter 10.

**8.5 Unscrew the securing bolts and manoeuvre the starter motor from the transmission bellhousing**

**8.6 GDI engine starter motor – seen with the inlet manifold removed**

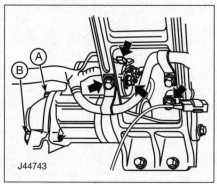

J44743

**8.11 GDI engine starter motor mounting bolts (A and B) and wiring details (arrowed)**

# Chapter 5 Part B:
# Ignition system

## Contents

## Degrees of difficulty

| Easy, suitable for novice with little experience |  | Fairly easy, suitable for beginner with some experience | | Fairly difficult, suitable for competent DIY mechanic |  | Difficult, suitable for experienced DIY mechanic | | Very difficult, suitable for expert DIY or professional | |

## Specifications

### General

System type:
  Up to 2000 model year:
    Non-turbo models . . . . . . . . . . . . . . . . . . . . . . . . . . . . . . . . . . . . Fenix 5.1 engine management system
    Turbo models . . . . . . . . . . . . . . . . . . . . . . . . . . . . . . . . . . . . . . . EMS 2000 engine management system
  2000 model year onwards:
    Non-GDI engine models . . . . . . . . . . . . . . . . . . . . . . . . . . . . . . EMS 2000 engine management system
    GDI engine models . . . . . . . . . . . . . . . . . . . . . . . . . . . . . . . . . Melco engine management system
Firing order . . . . . . . . . . . . . . . . . . . . . . . . . . . . . . . . . . . . . . . . . . 1-3-4-2 (No 1 cylinder at timing belt end of engine)

### Spark plugs

Type . . . . . . . . . . . . . . . . . . . . . . . . . . . . . . . . . . . . . . . . . . . . . . . See Chapter 1 Specifications

### Ignition timing*

1.6 litre engines . . . . . . . . . . . . . . . . . . . . . . . . . . . . . . . . . . . . . 10° ± 3° BTDC @ 750 rpm
1.8 litre non-GDI engines . . . . . . . . . . . . . . . . . . . . . . . . . . . . . . 5° ± 3° BTDC @ 750 rpm
1.8 litre GDI engine . . . . . . . . . . . . . . . . . . . . . . . . . . . . . . . . . . 16° ± 3° BTDC @ 750 rpm
2.0 litre non-turbo engines . . . . . . . . . . . . . . . . . . . . . . . . . . . . . 8° ± 3° BTDC @ 750 rpm
Turbo engines . . . . . . . . . . . . . . . . . . . . . . . . . . . . . . . . . . . . . . . 0° to 15° BTDC @ 750 ± 50 rpm
*Values given are for reference only; no adjustment is possible

### Ignition coil

Primary resistance . . . . . . . . . . . . . . . . . . . . . . . . . . . . . . . . . . . . n/a
Secondary resistance:
  Except GDI engine . . . . . . . . . . . . . . . . . . . . . . . . . . . . . . . . . . 260 to 340 ohms
  GDI engine . . . . . . . . . . . . . . . . . . . . . . . . . . . . . . . . . . . . . . . . 1700 to 2500 ohms

### Torque wrench settings

| | Nm | lbf ft |
|---|---|---|
| Ignition coil | 10 | 7 |
| Knock sensor: | | |
| Except GDI engine | 20 | 15 |
| GDI engine | 30 | 22 |
| Spark plugs | 25 | 18 |

## 1 General information

The Fenix 5.1, EMS 2000 and Melco systems covered in this Chapter are all full engine management systems, controlling both the fuel injection and ignition functions; refer to the Specifications for system application data. As the layout and overall operation of each of the systems is very similar, a general description is given in the following paragraphs. Refer to Chapter 4A or 4B for information relating to the fuel system.

The ignition system is responsible for igniting the compressed fuel/air charge in each cylinder in turn at precisely the right moment for the prevailing engine speed and load. On all models, the ignition system is of the static (distributorless) type, consisting only of two twin-output ignition coils (models with the GDI engine have four separate single-output coils).

### Except GDI engines

Two ignition coils are fitted, each one serving two cylinders. Under the control of the ECU, the ignition coils operate on the wasted-spark principle, ie, each spark plug sparks twice for every cycle of the engine, once during the compression stroke and once during the exhaust stroke. The spark voltage is greatest in the cylinder which is under compression; in the cylinder on its exhaust stroke, the compression is low and this produces a very weak spark which has no effect on the exhaust gases. This arrangement means there's no distributor, and that direct ignition can be employed without the need for a separate ignition coil for each cylinder.

The main components of the ignition side of the system are the ECU and the ignition power stage, the ignition coils, the spark plugs and HT leads, and the various sensors that supply information to the ECU on engine operating conditions. The operation of the system is as follows.

The engine flywheel has a series of teeth machined into its outer edge. A crankshaft sensor is mounted in close proximity to the edge of the flywheel, so that as the flywheel

**1.6 Ignition system failure sensor**

rotates, the teeth pass underneath the tip of the crankshaft sensor. The crankshaft sensor is inductive and so is triggered by the transition between metal (ie, a tooth) and air (ie, space between the teeth). The net result is that the sensor transmits an electrical pulse to the ECU every time the edge of a tooth passes it; the ECU uses this signal to compute engine speed and crankshaft position. The teeth are spaced at equal intervals around the edge of the flywheel, apart from one missing tooth. The ECU recognises the absence of a pulse from the RPM sensor at this point, and uses it to establish the TDC position for No 1 piston. The time interval between pulses, and the location of the missing tooth, allow the ECU to accurately determine the position of the crankshaft and its speed. The camshaft position sensor enhances this information by detecting the rotational position of one of the camshafts, enabling the ECU to detect whether a particular piston is on an inlet or exhaust stroke.

### GDI engine

GDI engines have an ignition coil fitted over each spark plug, fired in sequence by the ECU. The GDI engine is also fitted with an ignition system failure sensor, mounted on the throttle body mounting bracket at the rear of the engine **(see illustration)** – the exact function of this sensor is unclear at the time of writing.

The main components of the ignition side of the system are the ECU and the ignition power stage, the ignition coils, the spark plugs, and the various sensors that supply information to the ECU on engine operating conditions. The operation of the system is as follows.

On the GDI engine, the crankshaft toothed sprocket (at the timing belt end of the engine) is used as a trigger for the crankshaft sensor, with a trigger plate fitted behind the sprocket used to create the pulse required for the ECU to establish TDC position and engine speed. The camshaft position sensor enhances this information by detecting the rotational position of the exhaust camshaft, enabling the ECU to detect whether a particular piston is on an inlet or exhaust stroke.

### All engines

Information on engine load is supplied to the ECU via the manifold absolute pressure sensor, or via the airflow sensor and ambient pressure sensor. Further information is sent to the ECU from the knock sensor. These sensors are sensitive to high frequency vibration which occurs when the engine starts to pink or knock (pre-ignite). Sensors monitoring coolant temperature, throttle position, road speed, automatic transmission gear position (where applicable) and air conditioning system operation provide additional input signals to the ECU on vehicle operating conditions.

From this constantly-changing data, the ECU selects, and if necessary modifies, a particular ignition advance setting from a map of ignition characteristics stored in its memory.

With the firing point established, the ECU sends a signal to the ignition power stage, which is an electronic switch controlling the current to the ignition coil primary windings. On receipt of the signal from the ECU, the power stage interrupts the primary current to the ignition coil, which induces a high-tension voltage in the coil secondary windings. This HT voltage is conducted to the spark plugs, via the HT leads. The cycle is then repeated many times a second for each cylinder in turn.

In the event of a fault in the system due to loss of a signal from one of the sensors, the ECU reverts to an emergency (limp-home) program. This will allow the car to be driven, although engine operation and performance will be limited. A warning light on the instrument panel will illuminate if the fault is likely to cause an increase in harmful exhaust emissions.

## 2 Ignition system – testing

**Warning: Voltages produced by an electronic ignition system are considerably higher than those produced by conventional ignition systems. Extreme care must be taken when working on the system if the ignition is switched on. Persons with surgically-implanted cardiac pacemaker devices should keep well clear of the ignition circuits, components and test equipment.**

### General

**1** The components of the ignition system are normally very reliable; most faults are far more likely to be due to loose or dirty connections, or to tracking of HT voltage due to dirt, dampness or damaged insulation, than to the failure of any of the system's components. **Always** check all wiring thoroughly before condemning an electrical component, and work methodically to eliminate all other possibilities before deciding that a particular component is faulty.

**2** The old practice of checking for a spark by holding the live end of an HT lead a short distance away from the engine is **not** recommended; not only is there a high risk of a powerful electric shock, but the ECU or HT coil may be damaged. Similarly, **never** try to diagnose misfires by pulling off one HT lead at a time. This can introduce unburnt fuel into the catalytic converter causing it to overheat.

**3** The following tests should be carried out when an obvious fault such as non-starting or a clearly detectable misfire exists. Some faults, however, are more obscure and are often disguised by the fact that the ECU will adopt an emergency program (limp-home) mode to maintain as much driveability as possible. Faults of this nature usually appear in the form of excessive fuel consumption, poor idling characteristics, lack of performance, knocking or pinking noises from the engine under certain conditions, or a combination of these conditions.

### Engine will not start

**4** If the engine either will not turn over at all, or only turns very slowly, check the battery and starter motor. Connect a voltmeter across the battery terminals (meter positive probe to battery positive terminal) then note the voltage reading obtained while turning the engine over on the starter for (no more than) ten seconds. If the reading obtained is less than approximately 9.5 volts, first check the battery, starter motor and charging system as described in Part A of this Chapter.

**5** If the engine turns over at normal speed but will not start, check the HT circuit by connecting a timing light (following its manufacturer's instructions) and turning the engine over on the starter motor; if the light flashes, voltage is reaching the spark plugs, so these should be checked first. If the light does not flash, check the condition of the HT leads themselves.

**6** If there is a spark, continue with the checks described in Section 3 of this Chapter.

**7** If there is still no spark, check the condition of the coil, if possible by substitution with a known good unit, or by checking the primary and secondary resistances (the coil primary resistance is not quoted by Volvo, but a fault can be assumed if no sensible reading can be obtained). If the fault persists, the problem lies elsewhere; if the fault is now cleared, a new coil is the obvious cure. However, check carefully the condition of the LT connections themselves before doing so, to ensure that the fault is not due to dirty or poorly-fastened connectors.

**8** If the coil is in good condition, the fault probably lies with one of the system sensors, or related components. Start with the crankshaft position sensor, which can often suffer vibration damage. In this case, a fault code should be logged in the diagnostic unit which may help to isolate the component concerned (see Section 3).

### Engine misfires

**9** An irregular misfire suggests either a loose connection or intermittent fault on the primary circuit, or an HT fault on the ignition coil side of the circuit.

**10** With the ignition switched off, check carefully through the system, ensuring that all connections are clean and securely fastened. If the equipment is available, check the LT circuit as described above.

**11** Check that the ignition coils and the HT leads are clean and dry. Check the leads themselves and the spark plugs (by substitution if necessary) with reference to Chapter 1.

**12** Regular misfiring is most likely to be due to a fault in the HT leads (where fitted), coils (GDI engine) or spark plugs. Use a timing light (paragraph 5) to check whether HT voltage is present at all leads.

**13** If HT voltage is not present on any particular lead, the fault may be in that lead. If HT is present on all leads, the fault will be in the spark plugs; check and renew them if there is any doubt about their condition.

**14** If no HT is present, check the ignition coil; its secondary windings may be breaking down under load.

**15** Any further checking of the system components should be carried out by a Volvo dealer.

### 3 Fault diagnosis – general information

### General information

**1** The fuel and ignition systems on all engines covered by this manual incorporate an on-board diagnostic system to facilitate fault finding and system testing. The diagnostic system works in conjunction with the fuel, and where applicable, the ignition system ECUs to continually monitor the system components. Should a fault occur, the ECU stores a series of signals (or fault codes) for subsequent read-out using dedicated Volvo diagnostic unit equipment.

**2** If driveability problems have been experienced and engine performance is suspect, Volvo diagnostic equipment can be used to pinpoint any problem areas, by extracting any fault codes stored in the engine management systems ECU. Once this has been done, however, further tests may often be necessary to determine the exact nature of the fault; ie, whether a component itself has failed, or whether it is a wiring or other inter-related problem.

### Preliminary checks

**Note:** *When carrying out these checks to trace a fault, remember that if the fault has appeared only a short time after any part of the vehicle has been serviced or overhauled, the first place to check is where that work was carried out, however unrelated it may appear, to ensure that no carelessly-refitted components are causing the problem.*

*If you are tracing the cause of a partial engine fault, such as lack of performance, in addition to the checks outlined below, check the compression pressures. Check also that the fuel filter and air cleaner element have been renewed at the recommended intervals. Refer to Chapter 1, and the relevant part of Chapter 2, for details of these procedures.*

**3** Open the bonnet and check the condition of the battery connections – remake the connections or renew the leads if a fault is found. Use the same techniques to ensure that all earth points in the engine compartment provide good electrical contact through clean, metal-to-metal joints, and that all are securely fastened.

**4** Next work methodically around the engine compartment, checking all visible wiring, and the connections between sections of the wiring loom. What you are looking for at this stage is wiring that is obviously damaged by chafing against sharp edges, or against moving suspension/transmission components and/or the auxiliary drivebelt, by being trapped or crushed between carelessly-refitted components, or melted by being forced into contact with hot engine castings, coolant pipes, etc. In almost all cases, damage of this sort is caused in the first instance by incorrect routing on reassembly after previous work has been carried out (see the note at the beginning of this sub-Section).

**5** Obviously, wires can break or short together inside the insulation so that no visible evidence betrays the fault, but this usually only occurs where the wiring loom has been incorrectly routed so that it is stretched taut or kinked sharply; either of these conditions should be obvious on even a casual inspection. If this is thought to have happened and the fault proves elusive, the suspect section of wiring should be checked very carefully during the more detailed checks which follow.

**6** Depending on the extent of the problem, damaged wiring may be repaired by rejoining the break or splicing-in a new length of wire, using solder to ensure a good connection, and remaking the insulation with adhesive insulating tape or heat-shrink tubing, as desired. If the damage is extensive, given the implications for the vehicle's future reliability, the best long-term answer may well be to renew that entire section of the loom, however expensive this may appear.

**7** When the actual damage has been repaired, ensure that the wiring loom is rerouted correctly, so that it is clear of other components, is not stretched or kinked, and is secured out of harm's way using the plastic clips, guides and ties provided.

**8** Check all electrical connectors, ensuring that they are clean, securely fastened, and that each is locked by its plastic tabs or wire clip, as appropriate. If any connector shows external signs of corrosion (accumulations of white or green deposits, or streaks of rust), or if any is thought to be dirty, it must be unplugged and cleaned using electrical contact cleaner. If the connector pins are severely corroded, the connector must be renewed; note that this may mean the renewal of that entire section of the loom.

**9** If the cleaner completely removes the corrosion to leave the connector in a satisfactory condition, it would be wise to pack the connector with a suitable material which will exclude dirt and moisture, and prevent the corrosion from occurring again; a Volvo dealer or automotive electrical specialist may be able to recommend a suitable product.

**4.3 Disconnect the twin HT leads from the ignition coil terminals**

**4.4 Unplug the LT wiring from the ignition coil at the connector**

**10** Working methodically around the engine compartment, check carefully that all vacuum hoses and pipes are securely fastened and correctly routed, with no signs of cracks, splits or deterioration to cause air leaks, or of hoses that are trapped, kinked, or bent sharply enough to restrict air flow. Check with particular care at all connections and sharp bends, and renew any damaged or deformed lengths of hose.

**11** Working from the fuel tank, via the filter, to the fuel rail (and including the feed and return), check the fuel lines, and renew any that are found to be leaking, trapped or kinked.

**12** Check that the accelerator cable is correctly secured and adjusted; renew the cable if there is any doubt about its condition, or if it appears to be stiff or jerky in operation (later GDI engines do not have an accelerator cable). Refer to Chapter 4A or 4B for further information, if required.

**13** Unclip the air cleaner cover, and check that the air filter is not clogged or soaked. (A clogged air filter will obstruct the inlet air flow, causing a noticeable effect on engine performance.) Renew the filter if necessary; refer to the relevant Section of Chapter 1 for further information, if required.

**14** Start the engine and allow it to idle.

*Caution: Working in the engine compartment while the engine is running requires great care if the risk of personal injury is to be avoided; among the dangers are burns from contact with hot components, or contact with moving components such as the radiator cooling fan or the auxiliary drivebelt. Refer to*

*'Safety first!' at the front of this manual before starting, and ensure that your hands, and long hair or loose clothing, are kept well clear of hot or moving components at all times.*

**15** Working from the air inlet, via the air cleaner assembly and the mass airflow sensor (or inlet air temperature sensor) to the throttle housing and inlet manifold (and including the various vacuum hoses and pipes connected to these), check for air leaks. Usually, these will be revealed by sucking or hissing noises, but minor leaks may be traced by spraying a solution of soapy water on to the suspect joint; if a leak exists, it will be shown by the change in engine note and the accompanying air bubbles (or sucking-in of the liquid, depending on the pressure difference at that point). If a leak is found at any point, tighten the fastening clamp and/or renew the faulty components, as applicable.

**16** Similarly, work from the cylinder head, via the manifold to the tailpipe, to check that the exhaust system is free from leaks. The simplest way of doing this, if the vehicle can be raised and supported safely and with complete security while the check is made, is to temporarily block the tailpipe while listening for the sound of escaping exhaust gases; any leak should be evident. If a leak is found at any point, tighten the fastening clamp bolts and/or nuts, renew the gasket, and/or renew the faulty section of the system, as necessary, to seal the leak.

**17** It is possible to make a further check of the electrical connections by wiggling each electrical connector of the system in turn as

the engine is idling; a faulty connector will be immediately evident from the engine's response as contact is broken and remade. A faulty connector should be renewed to ensure that the future reliability of the system; note that this may mean the renewal of that entire section of the loom.

**18** Switch off the engine. If the fault is not yet identified, the next step is to check the fault code read out at the diagnostic unit as described below.

### *Fault code read-out*

**19** As noted in the general comments at the beginning of this Section, the preliminary checks outlined above should eliminate the majority of faults from the ignition (or fuel) system. If the fault has not yet been identified, the next step is to check whether a fault code has been logged and if so, to interpret the meaning of the code. To do this, the vehicle should be taken to a suitably-equipped fuel injection specialist or Volvo dealer for testing. A wiring block connector is incorporated in the engine management circuit, into which a special electronic diagnostic tester can be plugged; the connector is located inside the vehicle behind the facia, to the side of the centre console. The tester will locate the fault quickly and simply, alleviating the need to test all the system components individually, which is a time-consuming operation that carries a high risk of damaging the ECU.

---

## 4  Ignition HT coil – removal and refitting

### *Non-turbo models*

#### Up to 2000 model year

**1** Disconnect the battery negative lead (see *Disconnecting the battery*).

**2** Remove the screws and detach the plastic cover panel from the top of the engine.

**3** Release the plastic lugs and disconnect the twin HT leads from the ignition coil terminals **(see illustration)**.

**4** Unplug the LT wiring from the ignition coil at the connector **(see illustration)**.

**5** Slacken and withdraw the securing screws and lift the coil from its mounting bracket **(see illustrations)**.

**6** Refit by reversing the removal operations.

#### 2000 model year onwards

**7** The removal and refitting of the later coil-over-plug ignition coils is as described for the turbo models later in this section. For information on removing the GDI engine ignition coils, refer to the spark plug renewal section in Chapter 1.

### *Turbo models*

**8** Disconnect the battery negative lead (see *Disconnecting the battery*).

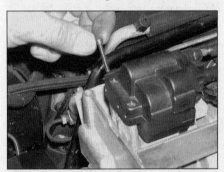

**4.5a Slacken and withdraw the securing screws . . .**

**4.5b . . . and lift the coil from its mounting bracket**

**9** Remove the screws and detach the plastic cover panel from the top of the engine.
**10** Unplug the LT wiring from the side of the coil unit, and the HT lead from the terminal at the side of the coil unit.
**11** Slacken and withdraw the securing screw, then grasp the tabs at the side of the coil unit at withdraw it from the cylinder head cover **(see illustration)**.
**12** Refitting is a reversal of removal.

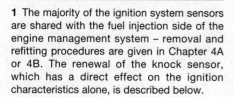

## 5  Ignition system sensors – removal and refitting

**1** The majority of the ignition system sensors are shared with the fuel injection side of the engine management system – removal and refitting procedures are given in Chapter 4A or 4B. The renewal of the knock sensor, which has a direct effect on the ignition characteristics alone, is described below.

### *Knock sensor*

#### Except GDI engine

**2** The knock sensor is located on the front right-hand side of the cylinder block, under the inlet manifold.
**3** Remove the inlet manifold (see Chapter 4A).
**4** Unplug the wiring connector from the knock sensor.
**5** Undo the sensor securing bolt and remove the sensor.
**6** Locate the sensor on the cylinder block and refit and tighten the retaining bolt to the specified torque. Tightening the securing bolt to a torque other than specified will affect the operation of the sensor.
**7** Refit the inlet manifold as described in Chapter 4A.

**4.11  Ignition coil location – turbo models**

#### GDI engine

**8** The GDI engine knock sensor is located at the rear of the engine block, below the inlet manifold, at the timing belt end of the engine. Having located the sensor, trace the wiring along the rear of the engine, freeing it from the twisted-wire cable clips used – note how the wiring is routed for refitting. Finally, disconnect the knock sensor wiring connector which is at the transmission end of the engine, close to No 4 cylinder ignition coil.
**9** As the sensor wiring cannot be detached from the sensor body, either an open-ended spanner or crow's foot spanner will be needed to unscrew it from the engine. Do not drop or strike the sensor during removal, or it will be damaged – similarly, take care not to twist the wiring too much, or it may break.
**10** Clean the mating faces of the sensor and engine, then screw the sensor in by hand. As with removal, take care not to subject the sensor to any kind of impact when it is being fitted, and ensure that the wiring does not become twisted or strained.
**11** The sensor must be tightened to the specified torque for it to function correctly.

Given that a normal socket cannot be used, due to the sensor's attached wiring, accurate torquing is made more difficult. Special slotted sockets are available for fitting exhaust oxygen sensors, which usually suffer the same problem of attached wiring. If not, a crow's foot adaptor could be used with a torque wrench, but using the adaptor will effectively increase the torque applied, so refer to the tool manufacturer for guidance.
**12** Route the knock sensor wiring along the back of the engine, refitting it into all the clips provided, then reconnect its wiring plug.

## 6  Electronic control unit (ECU) – removal and refitting

The ignition and fuel injection systems are controlled by the same engine management system ECU – refer to the information given in Chapter 4A or 4B.

## 7  Ignition timing – checking

The engines covered in this manual are not equipped with timing marks that can be used for ignition timing checking. The markings on the camshaft and crankshaft do not relate directly to piston top dead centre, and are used for repair and assembly only. Consequently, the only way to check the ignition timing accurately is to take the vehicle to a Volvo dealer or auto-electrical specialist equipped with the necessary diagnostic equipment. The ignition timing is under the control of the engine management system ECU, and cannot be adjusted.

# Chapter 6
# Clutch

## Contents

## Degrees of difficulty

| Easy, suitable for novice with little experience  | Fairly easy, suitable for beginner with some experience  | Fairly difficult, suitable for competent DIY mechanic 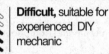 | Difficult, suitable for experienced DIY mechanic | Very difficult, suitable for expert DIY or professional  |
|---|---|---|---|---|

## Specifications

### General
Clutch type . . . . . . . . . . . . . . . . . . . . . . . . . . . . . . . . . . . . . . . . . . . Single dry plate, diaphragm spring, hydraulic actuation (self-adjusting on turbo models)

### Pressure plate
Warp limit . . . . . . . . . . . . . . . . . . . . . . . . . . . . . . . . . . . . . . . . . . . . 0.2 mm

### Driven plate (friction disc)
Diameter:
  Non-turbo models:
    Up to 1998 . . . . . . . . . . . . . . . . . . . . . . . . . . . . . . . . . . . . . 220 mm
    1998 onwards . . . . . . . . . . . . . . . . . . . . . . . . . . . . . . . . . . . 215 mm
  Turbo models . . . . . . . . . . . . . . . . . . . . . . . . . . . . . . . . . . . . . . 240 mm

### Clutch pedal
Height* . . . . . . . . . . . . . . . . . . . . . . . . . . . . . . . . . . . . . . . . . . . . . . 162.5 mm
Free play . . . . . . . . . . . . . . . . . . . . . . . . . . . . . . . . . . . . . . . . . . . . . 1 to 3 mm
Travel (at rest – fully depressed) . . . . . . . . . . . . . . . . . . . . . . . . . . 136 mm
*With a clearance of 1 to 3 mm between the pedal and the stop-bolt*

### Torque wrench settings

| | Nm | lbf ft |
|---|---|---|
| Master cylinder retaining nuts . . . . . . . . . . . . . . . . . . . . . . . . . . . . . | 13 | 10 |
| Pressure plate retaining bolts: | | |
|   Non-turbo models . . . . . . . . . . . . . . . . . . . . . . . . . . . . . . . . . . . . | 21 | 15 |
|   Turbo models . . . . . . . . . . . . . . . . . . . . . . . . . . . . . . . . . . . . . . . | 25 | 18 |
| Slave cylinder retaining bolts: | | |
|   Non-turbo models, except GDI engine . . . . . . . . . . . . . . . . . . . . . | 30 | 22 |
|   GDI engine models . . . . . . . . . . . . . . . . . . . . . . . . . . . . . . . . . . . | 18 | 13 |
|   Turbo models . . . . . . . . . . . . . . . . . . . . . . . . . . . . . . . . . . . . . . . | 10 | 7 |

## 1 General information

A single dry plate diaphragm spring clutch is fitted to all manual transmission models. The clutch is hydraulically operated via a master and slave cylinder.

The main components of the clutch are the pressure plate, the driven plate (sometimes called the friction plate or disc) and the release bearing. The pressure plate is bolted to the flywheel, with the driven plate sandwiched between them. The centre of the driven plate has a splined hub, which engages with the splines on the transmission input shaft. The release bearing slides along a sleeve fitted over the transmission input shaft and acts on the diaphragm spring fingers of the pressure plate.

When the engine is running and the clutch pedal is released, the diaphragm spring clamps the pressure plate, driven plate and flywheel firmly together. Drive is transmitted through the friction surfaces of the flywheel and pressure plate to the linings of the driven plate and thus to the transmission input shaft.

When the clutch pedal is depressed, the pedal movement is transmitted hydraulically to the release bearing, which is pressed against the diaphragm spring fingers. Spring pressure on the pressure plate is relieved, and the flywheel and pressure plate spin without moving the driven plate. As the pedal is released, spring pressure is restored and the drive is gradually taken up.

The clutch hydraulic system consists of a master cylinder, a slave cylinder and the

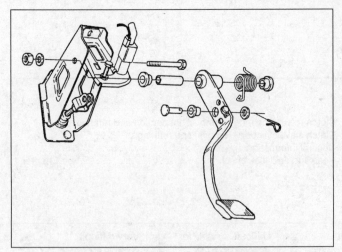

**2.5 Exploded view of the clutch pedal components**

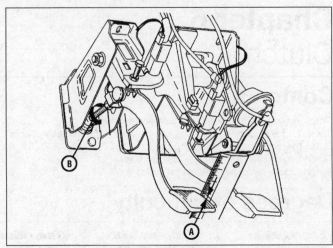

**2.10 To adjust the clutch pedal free play (A), slacken the locknut and turn the pushrod (B)**

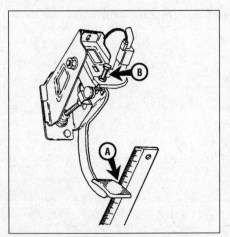

**2.12 To adjust the clutch pedal height (A), slacken the locknut and turn the stop-bolt (B)**

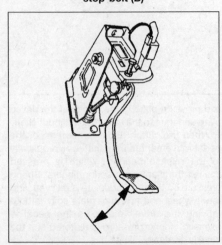

**2.13 Measure and record the distance the clutch pedal travels through**

associated pipes and hoses. The fluid reservoir is shared with the brake master cylinder. On non-turbo models, the slave cylinder is mounted outside the transmission bellhousing, and effort is transmitted to the release bearing via a pivoted release fork. On turbocharged models, the slave cylinder is mounted inside the transmission bellhousing, and fits concentrically over the transmission input shaft, directly behind the release bearing.

Wear in the driven plate linings is compensated for automatically by the hydraulic system components, and no adjustment is necessary. Additionally on turbocharged models, a spring-loaded adjustment ring fitted inside the pressure plate compensates for wear in the driven plate to ensure that the clutch pedal travel remains constant.

### 2 Clutch pedal – removal, refitting and adjustment

#### Removal

1 Disconnect the battery negative lead (see *Disconnecting the battery*).
2 Remove the trim panel under the facia on the driver's side. Where applicable, undo the securing nuts, unplug the wiring and remove the electronic control unit. Move the relay holder to one side.
3 Unscrew the nut from the end of the pedal pivot bolt and remove the washer, then unhook the return spring from the pedal.
4 Fold back the carpet, then withdraw the clip and release the master cylinder pushrod from the clutch pedal.
5 Slide the pivot bolt out as far as possible, then twist the clutch pedal to disengage it from the bolt and remove it from the mounting bracket **(see illustration)**.
6 With the pedal removed, check the condition of the pivot bushes and renew as necessary.

#### Refitting

7 Refit by reversing the removal operations. Apply grease to the pedal bushes, and use a new circlip to secure the pedal if the old one is in any way damaged or distorted.
8 On non-turbo models, measure and if necessary adjust the clutch pedal free travel and height, as described in the following sub-sections.

#### Adjustment

⚠ *Warning: Make no attempt to adjust the clutch pedal height on turbo models – the dimension is factory-set, and should not be altered.*

#### Clutch pedal free play

9 With the clutch pedal in the rest position, measure and record the amount of free play at the clutch pedal rubber. Compare the measurement with the figure given in the Specifications.
10 If adjustment is required, slacken the master cylinder pushrod locknut, then turn the pushrod until the correct free play is achieved **(see illustration)**. Ensure that the pushrod is not pushed into the master cylinder as you do this, as incorrect adjustment will result. Tighten the pushrod locknut on completion.

#### Clutch pedal height

11 With the clutch pedal in the rest position, measure and record the distance between the top surface of the clutch pedal rubber and the floor. Compare the measurement with the figure given in the Specifications.
12 If adjustment is required, slacken the stop-bolt locknut, then turn the stop-bolt until the correct pedal height is achieved. Tighten the stop-bolt locknut on completion **(see illustration)**.

#### Clutch pedal travel

13 Measure and record the distance that the top surface of the clutch pedal rubber travels through, between the rest and fully-depressed positions **(see illustration)**. After carrying out

the previously-described pedal height and free play adjustments, the pedal travel should be as given in the Specifications.

14 Incorrect pedal travel may be caused by air trapped in the clutch hydraulic system (in which case it will be necessary to bleed the system as described in Section 5), a defective master cylinder (see Section 3) or slave cylinder (see Section 4).

## 3 Clutch master cylinder – removal and refitting

**⚠ Warning: Hydraulic fluid is poisonous; wash off immediately and thoroughly in the case of skin contact, and seek immediate medical advice if any fluid is swallowed or gets into the eyes. Certain types of hydraulic fluid are flammable, and may ignite when allowed into contact with hot components; when servicing any hydraulic system, it is safest to assume that the fluid IS flammable, and to take precautions against the risk of fire as though it is petrol that is being handled. Hydraulic fluid is also an effective paint stripper, and will attack plastics; if any is spilt, it should be washed off immediately, using copious quantities of clean water. Finally, it is hygroscopic (it absorbs moisture from the air) – old fluid may be contaminated and unfit for further use. When topping-up or renewing the fluid, always use the recommended type, and ensure that it comes from a newly-opened container.**

**Note:** Master cylinder internal components are not available separately, and no repair or overhaul of the cylinder is possible. In the event of a hydraulic system fault, or any sign of visible fluid leakage on or around the master cylinder or clutch pedal, the unit should be renewed.

### Removal

1 Disconnect the battery negative lead (see *Disconnecting the battery*).
2 On left-hand drive models, refer to Chapter 4A or 4B and remove the air cleaner assembly.
3 Connect a length of hose to the bleed nipple on the clutch slave cylinder. Place the other end of the hose into an empty collecting receptacle. Slacken the bleed nipple and have an assistant depress the clutch pedal slowly several times, to pump the hydraulic fluid into the collecting container. Have ready a container and rags to catch any fluid which may spill. Tighten the bleed nipple again, when no more fluid can be ejected.
4 On left-hand-drive models, remove the engine compartment fusebox lid, then undo the securing screws and move the fusebox to the side of the engine compartment. On models with cruise control, remove the securing screws and position the cruise

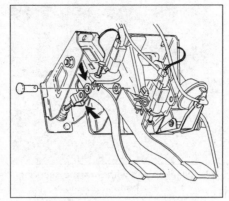

**3.7 Disconnect the master cylinder pushrod from the clutch pedal**

control vacuum pump and regulator to one side.
5 Unscrew the hydraulic pipe union from the end of the clutch master cylinder. Be prepared for further fluid spillage. Cover the open pipe union with a piece of polythene and a rubber band to keep dirt out. Where a snap-on coupling is used on the pipe union, extract the spring clip and pull out the pipe.
6 Remove the trim panel under the facia on the driver's side.
7 Disconnect the master cylinder pushrod from the clutch pedal as described in Section 2 **(see illustration)**.
8 Remove the nuts which secure the master cylinder to the bulkhead **(see illustration)**.
9 Remove the master cylinder from the engine compartment, being careful not to drip fluid onto the paintwork. Recover the gasket.

### Refitting

10 Refit by reversing the removal operations, noting the following points:
   a) If a new master cylinder is being fitted, transfer the fluid supply hose from the old cylinder to the new one prior to installation.
   b) If the hydraulic pipe union is of the snap-on type, fit a new O-ring to the connector.
   c) Tighten the master cylinder retaining nuts to the specified torque.
   d) Refill and bleed the clutch hydraulic system on completion, as described in Section 5.

**4.2 Slave cylinder bleed nipple (arrowed)**

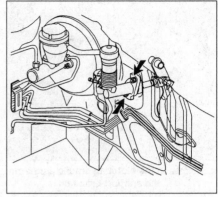

**3.8 Remove the nuts (arrowed) which secure the master cylinder to the bulkhead**

   e) On completion check, and if necessary adjust, the height, free play and travel of the clutch pedal, as described at the end of Section 2.

## 4 Clutch slave cylinder – removal and refitting

**Note:** Slave cylinder internal components are not available separately, and no repair or overhaul of the cylinder is possible. In the event of a hydraulic system fault, or any sign of visible fluid leakage on or around the slave cylinder pushrod or rubber gaiter (where applicable), the unit should be renewed.

### Non-turbo models

#### Removal

**Note:** Refer to the warning at the beginning of Section 3 before proceeding.
1 Remove the air cleaner assembly and associated ducting, as described in Chapter 4A or 4B.
2 Remove the dust cap and connect a length of hose to the bleed nipple on the clutch slave cylinder **(see illustration)**. Place the other end of the hose into an empty collecting receptacle. Slacken the bleed nipple and have an assistant depress the clutch pedal slowly several times, to pump the hydraulic fluid into the collecting container. Have ready a container and rags to catch any fluid which may spill. Tighten the bleed nipple again, when no more fluid can be ejected.
3 Where applicable, withdraw the spring-loaded clip to release the clutch hydraulic pipe from it support bracket **(see illustration)**.
4 Unscrew the hydraulic pipe union at the support bracket, where the rigid pipework joins the flexible rubber hose, and carefully withdraw the pipe. Have ready a container and rags to catch the fluid which will spill. Cover the open pipe union with a piece of polythene and a rubber band to keep dirt out.
5 Slacken and withdraw the securing bolts, then disengage the piston from the clutch release fork and withdraw the slave cylinder

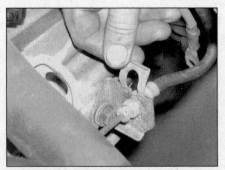

**4.3 Release the clutch hydraulic pipe from the support bracket**

**4.5a Slacken and withdraw the securing bolts . . .**

**4.5b . . . then disengage the piston from the clutch release fork and withdraw the slave cylinder**

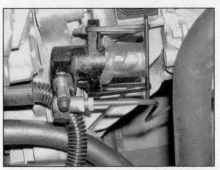

**4.5c Secure the piston in position using a piece of scrap metal and cable-ties**

from the transmission casing. Secure the piston in position using a piece of scrap metal and cable-ties or wire, to prevent it from being pushed out of the slave cylinder **(see illustrations)**. If required, the hydraulic pipe can be disconnected from the slave cylinder at the union.

### Refitting

**6** Refit by reversing the removal operations, noting the following points:
a) *Use new union sealing washers.*
b) *Tighten all fixings and unions to the correct torque, where specified.*
c) *Apply a small amount of grease to the point of contact between the end of the slave cylinder piston and clutch release fork.*
d) *Refill and bleed the clutch hydraulic system on completion (see Section 5).*

## Turbo models

### Removal

**7** Remove the transmission as described in Chapter 7A.
**8** Detach the rubber gaiter from the transmission casing, and slide it along the hydraulic pipe towards the slave cylinder.
**9** Remove the adapter from quick-release coupling on the slave cylinder hydraulic pipe by pulling out the locking bracket. Place the adapter in a plastic bag to prevent contamination.
**10** Undo the securing bolts and remove the slave cylinder, together with the release bearing, from the transmission casing.

### Refitting

**11** Refitting is a reversal of removal, noting the following points:
a) *Fit a new rubber seal to the hydraulic pipe adapter, lubricated with a small amount of brake fluid.*
b) *Ensure that the adapter-to-quick-release coupling locking bracket is securely refitted.*
c) *Tighten the slave cylinder securing bolts to the specified torque.*
d) *On completion, refill and bleed the clutch hydraulic system.*

| 5 | Clutch hydraulic system – bleeding |
|---|---|

**Note:** *Refer to the warning at the beginning of Section 3 before proceeding.*

### General information

**1** Whenever the clutch hydraulic lines are disconnected for service or repair, a certain amount of air will enter the system. The presence of air in any hydraulic system will introduce a degree of elasticity and in the clutch system, this will translate into poor pedal feel and reduced travel, leading to inefficient gearchanges and even clutch system failure. For this reason, the clutch hydraulic system must be topped-up and bled to remove any air bubbles, after carrying out any work.

**2** The clutch hydraulic system can be bled in one of two ways – manually, by pumping the clutch pedal and catching the ejected fluid in a receptacle connected to the bleed pipe, or by using a pressurised brake bleeding kit. These kits are readily available in motor accessory shops, and are extremely effective. The following sub-sections describe both methods.

### Manual bleeding

**3** Top-up the hydraulic fluid reservoir on the brake master cylinder with fresh clean fluid of the specified type (see *Weekly checks*).
**4** Remove the dust cover and fit a length of clear hose over the bleed screw on the slave cylinder **(see illustration 4.2)**. Note that on turbo models where the slave cylinder is mounted inside the clutch bellhousing, the bleed screw is located on the hydraulic fluid pipe that leads into the bellhousing **(see illustration)**. Place the other end of the hose in a jar containing a small amount of hydraulic fluid.
**5** Slacken the bleed screw, and at the same time, have an assistant fully depress the clutch pedal. Tighten the bleed screw when the pedal reaches the lowest point of its travel. Have the assistant release the pedal, then slacken the bleed screw again. The aim is to have the bleed screw open only when the pedal on its downstroke, so that air is not drawn into the system.
**6** Repeat the process until clean fluid, free of air bubbles, emerges from the bleed screw. Tighten the screw at the end of a pedal downstroke, and remove the hose and jar. Refit the dust cover.
**7** Top-up the hydraulic fluid reservoir to the MAX level.

### Pressure bleeding

**8** Locate the bleed screw on the hydraulic pipe leading into the clutch bellhousing, and remove the dust cap.
**9** Fit a ring spanner over the bleed nipple head, but do not slacken it at this point. Connect a length of clear plastic hose over the nipple, and insert the other end into a clean container. Pour hydraulic fluid into the container, such that the end of the hose is covered.

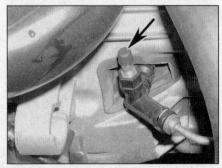

**5.4 Hydraulic system bleed screw location (turbo models)**

**10** Following the kit manufacturer's instructions, pour hydraulic fluid into the bleeding kit vessel.

**11** Unscrew the car's fluid reservoir cap, then connect the bleeding kit fluid supply hose to the reservoir.

**12** Connect the pressure hose to a supply of compressed air – a spare tyre is convenient source.

*Caution: Check that the pressure in the tyre does not exceed the maximum quoted by the kit manufacturer, let some air escape to reduce the pressure, if necessary. Gently open the air valve and allow the air and fluid pressures to equalise. Check that there are no leaks before proceeding.*

**13** Using the spanner, slacken the bleed pipe nipple until fluid and air bubbles can be seen to flow through the tube, into the container. Maintain a steady flow until the emerging fluid is free of air bubbles; keep an eye on the level of fluid in the bleeding kit vessel and the car's fluid reservoir – if it is allowed to drop too low, air may be forced into the system, defeating the object of the exercise. To refill the vessel, turn off the compressed air supply, remove the lid and pour in an appropriate quantity of clean fluid from a new container – **do not** re-use the fluid collected in the receiving container. Repeat as necessary until the ejected fluid is bubble-free.

**14** On completion, pump the clutch pedal several times to assess its feel and travel. If firm, constant pedal resistance is not felt throughout the pedal stroke, it is probable that air is still present in the system; repeat the bleeding procedure, this time with an assistant holding the clutch pedal depressed, until the pedal feel is restored.

**15** Depressurise the bleeding kit and remove it from the car. At this point, the fluid reservoir may be over-full; the excess should be removed using a *clean* pipette to reduce the level to the MAX mark.

**16** Tighten the bleed pipe nipple using the spanner and remove the receiving container. Refit the dust cap.

**17** Finally, road test the car and check the operation of the clutch system whilst changing up and down through the gears, whilst pulling away from a standstill, and from a hill start.

---

**6   Clutch assembly –**
   removal, inspection
   and refitting

⚠ *Warning: Dust created by clutch wear and deposited on the clutch components may contain asbestos, which is a health hazard. DO NOT blow it out with compressed air or inhale any of it. DO NOT use petrol or petroleum-based solvents to clean off the dust. Brake system cleaner or methylated spirit should be used to flush the dust into a suitable receptacle. After the clutch*

*components are wiped clean with rags, dispose of the contaminated rags and cleaner in a sealed, marked container.*
**Note**: *On turbo models, Volvo special tools 9995677 and 9995662 will be required to counterhold the clutch pressure plate automatic adjustment mechanism during removal and refitting.*

### Removal

**1** Remove the transmission as described in Chapter 7A. If the existing clutch is to be refitted, mark the relationship between the pressure plate and the flywheel using a dab of paint **(see illustration)**.

#### Turbo models

**2** Fit Volvo special tool 9995677 to the outer surface of the clutch pressure plate. The three pegs must locate behind the automatic adjuster tension springs on the inner rim of the pressure plate. The spring-loaded hooks should be fitted into the holes drilled into the outer edge of the pressure plate, such that the tool applies tension in an anti-clockwise direction to the pressure plate adjustment mechanism **(see illustration)**.

**3** Fit Volvo special tool 9995662 to the clutch pressure plate. If the clutch is worn, first turn the adjustment mechanism by hand, so that the stamped arrow markings line up. Turn the special tool's handle so that it compresses the pressure plate diaphragm spring, releasing the pressure on the driven plate and the automatic adjustment mechanism **(see**

**6.1  Mark the pressure plate and flywheel using a dab of paint**

**illustration)**. A distinct click can be heard as the diaphragm spring pivots and releases.

#### All models

**4** Undo and remove the clutch pressure plate bolts, working in a diagonal sequence and slackening the bolts only a few turns at a time **(see illustration)**. To prevent the flywheel rotating as the bolts are undone, lock the flywheel using a screwdriver engaged with the ring gear teeth, bracing it against an engine/transmission locating dowel. Alternatively, a locking tool can be fabricated from scrap metal.

**5** Ease the clutch pressure plate off its locating dowels and be prepared to catch the driven plate which will drop out as the pressure plate is removed **(see illustration)**. Note which way round the plate is fitted.

**6.2  Volvo special tool 9995677 in position on the clutch pressure plate**

**6.3  Fit Volvo tool 9995662 and turn the handle to compress the pressure plate diaphragm spring**

**6.4  Undo and remove the clutch pressure plate bolts progressively, in a diagonal sequence**

**6.5  Ease the clutch pressure plate off its locating dowels and catch the driven plate**

6.15 Fit the clutch driven plate so the side of the hub marked 'engine side' faces the flywheel

6.16 Place the clutch pressure plate over the dowels, refit the bolts and tighten them finger-tight

**6** It is important that no oil or grease is allowed to come into contact with the friction material or the pressure plate and flywheel faces during inspection and refitting.

**7** On turbo models, if the original clutch is to be refitted, slacken off special tool 9995662 so that the tension is removed from the clutch pressure plate. There is no need to remove the tool from the clutch completely at this stage. Conversely if the clutch is to be renewed, remove both special tools to allow them to be fitted to the new pressure plate.

⚠ *Warning: Keep your fingers away from the clutch pressure plate assembly rivets as the compression tool is slackened, to avoid pinching.*

## Inspection

**8** With the clutch assembly removed, clean off all traces of asbestos dust using a dry cloth. This is best done outside or in a well-ventilated area; asbestos dust is harmful, and must not be inhaled

**9** Examine the linings of the driven plate for wear and loose rivets, and the rim for distortion, cracks, broken torsion springs and worn splines. The surface of the friction linings may be highly glazed, but, as long as the friction material pattern can be clearly seen, this is satisfactory. If there is any sign of oil contamination, indicated by a continuous or patchy, shiny black discolouration, the plate must be renewed, and the source of the contamination traced and rectified. This will be either a leaking crankshaft oil seal or transmission input shaft oil seal – or both. The driven plate must also be renewed if the lining thickness has worn down to, or just above, the level of the rivet heads.

**10** Check the machined faces of the flywheel and pressure plate. If either is grooved, or heavily scored, renewal is necessary. The pressure plate must also be renewed if any cracks are apparent, if the diaphragm spring is damaged or its pressure suspect, or if there is excessive warpage of the pressure plate face.

**11** With the transmission removed, check the condition of the release bearing, as described in Section 7.

## Refitting

**12** Wipe down the pressure plate and flywheel faces with a clean dry rag before assembly begins, to remove any traces of oil or grease.

### Turbo models

**13** If fitting a new clutch, fit Volvo special tools 9995677 and 9995662 to the clutch pressure plate as described in *Removal*.

**14** Tighten tool 9995662 so that the clutch pressure plate diaphragm is compressed; this should take between 4 and 5 turns of the handle from the centre screw coming into contact with the spring fingers, until a distinct click is heard as the diaphragm spring pivots.

### All models

**15** Place the driven plate in position on the flywheel, orientating it such that the section of the side of the hub marked 'engine side' (which also has the greatest protrusion) faces the flywheel **(see illustration)**.

**16** Place the clutch pressure plate over the dowels, refit the bolts and tighten them finger-tight so that the driven plate is gripped, but can still be moved **(see illustration)**.

6.21 Using a clutch alignment tool (shown with engine removed for clarity)

**17** The plate must now be centralised so that, when the engine and transmission are mated, the splines of the transmission input shaft will pass through the splines in the centre of the driven plate hub.

**18** Centralisation can be carried out quite easily by inserting a makeshift centring tool, such as a round bar or long screwdriver, through the hole in the centre of the driven plate, so that the end of the tool rests in the hole in the end of the crankshaft. Note that on turbo models, the centre screw shaft of special tool 9995662 is drilled to accept a clutch centring tool.

**19** Pivot the centring tool sideways, or up-and-down, to move the clutch driven plate in whichever direction is necessary to achieve centralisation.

**20** Centralisation is easily judged by removing the centring tool and viewing the driven plate hub in relation to the hole in the centre of the crankshaft. When the hole appears exactly in the centre of the driven plate hub, all is correct.

**21** An alternative and more accurate method of centralisation is to use a commercially-available clutch aligning tool obtainable from most accessory shops **(see illustration)**.

**22** Once the clutch is centralised, progressively tighten the pressure plate bolts in a diagonal sequence, until the clutch has been fully advanced along its locating dowels and is resting squarely against the flywheel. The bolts can then be tightened (again in a diagonal sequence) to the torque setting given in the Specifications.

**23** On turbo models, remove the Volvo special tools.

⚠ *Warning: Keep your fingers away from the clutch pressure plate assembly rivets as the compression tool is slackened, to avoid pinching.*

**24** The transmission can now be refitted by referring to the Chapter 7A of this manual.

### 7 Clutch release bearing – removal, inspection and refitting

## *Removal*

### Non-turbo models

**1** Remove the transmission from the engine as described in Chapter 7A.

**2** Having separated the transmission from the engine, detach the bearing from the release fork and slide it off the input shaft guide sleeve **(see illustration)**. Note that on some models, the release bearing is held in position on the release fork by a spring clip.

**3** Free the release fork dust boot from the bellhousing, and withdraw the release fork from the pivot ball-stud **(see illustration)**.

### Turbo models

**4** Remove the clutch slave cylinder as described in Section 4, then separate the release bearing from the slave cylinder.

## *Inspection*

**5** Check the bearing for smoothness of

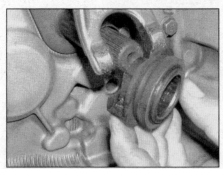

**7.2 Detach the release bearing from the release fork and slide it off the input shaft guide sleeve**

operation, and renew it if there is any roughness or harshness as the bearing is spun. It is a good idea to renew the bearing as a matter of course during clutch overhaul, regardless of its apparent condition. Also check the condition of the dust gaiter, and renew it if any signs of deterioration are apparent.

## *Refitting*

**6** Refitting the release bearing is a reversal of removal. On non-turbo models, lubricate the

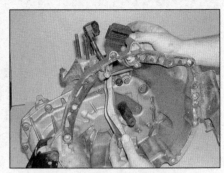

**7.3 Free the release fork dust boot from the bellhousing and withdraw the release fork from the pivot ball-stud**

release fork pivot ball-stud sparingly with molybdenum disulphide grease. Do not apply any grease to the transmission input shaft, the guide sleeve, or the release bearing itself, as these components have a friction-reducing coating which does not require lubrication. With the bearing and release bearing in position, secure the release fork to the slave cylinder lug on the bellhousing with a cable-tie or similar, to hold it in place as the transmission is refitted.

# Chapter 7 Part A:
# Manual transmission

## Contents

## Degrees of difficulty

| Easy, suitable for novice with little experience |  | Fairly easy, suitable for beginner with some experience |  | Fairly difficult, suitable for competent DIY mechanic | | Difficult, suitable for experienced DIY mechanic | | Very difficult, suitable for expert DIY or professional |  |

## Specifications

### General

| | |
|---|---|
| Transmission type . . . . . . . . . . . . . . . . . . . . . . . . . . . . . . . . . . . . | 5 forward gears and one reverse. Synchromesh on all gears |
| Designation: | |
|   1.6 litre and early 1.8 litre (except GDI) . . . . . . . . . . . . . . . . . . . . | M3P |
|   2.0 litre non-turbo and later 1.8 litre (except GDI) . . . . . . . . . . . . | M5P |
|   1.8 litre GDI . . . . . . . . . . . . . . . . . . . . . . . . . . . . . . . . . . . . . . . | M5M42 or F5M45 |
|   1.9 litre turbo T4 . . . . . . . . . . . . . . . . . . . . . . . . . . . . . . . . . . . . | M56L2 |
|   2.0 litre low-pressure turbo . . . . . . . . . . . . . . . . . . . . . . . . . . . . | M56H |

### Lubrication

| | |
|---|---|
| Lubricant type . . . . . . . . . . . . . . . . . . . . . . . . . . . . . . . . . . . . . . . | See *Lubricants and fluids* |
| Capacity: | |
|   M3P, M5P . . . . . . . . . . . . . . . . . . . . . . . . . . . . . . . . . . . . . . . . | 3.4 litres |
|   M5M42 and F5M45 . . . . . . . . . . . . . . . . . . . . . . . . . . . . . . . . . | 2.2 litres |
|   M56 . . . . . . . . . . . . . . . . . . . . . . . . . . . . . . . . . . . . . . . . . . . . | 2.1 litres |

### Torque wrench settings

| | Nm | lbf ft |
|---|---|---|
| Engine support beam to bodywork . . . . . . . . . . . . . . . . . . . . . . . . | 69 | 51 |
| Engine support beam to engine mountings . . . . . . . . . . . . . . . . . . | 52 | 38 |
| Flywheel sensor . . . . . . . . . . . . . . . . . . . . . . . . . . . . . . . . . . . . . | 20 | 15 |
| Gear lever housing bolts . . . . . . . . . . . . . . . . . . . . . . . . . . . . . . . | 25 | 18 |
| Input shaft guide sleeve . . . . . . . . . . . . . . . . . . . . . . . . . . . . . . . | 25 | 18 |
| Release bearing guide sleeve bolts . . . . . . . . . . . . . . . . . . . . . . . | 10 | 7 |
| Reversing light switch . . . . . . . . . . . . . . . . . . . . . . . . . . . . . . . . | 22 | 16 |
| Selector rod adjustment collar nut . . . . . . . . . . . . . . . . . . . . . . . . | 24 | 18 |
| Selector rod to gear lever . . . . . . . . . . . . . . . . . . . . . . . . . . . . . . | 16 | 12 |
| Selector rod to transmission . . . . . . . . . . . . . . . . . . . . . . . . . . . . | 16 | 12 |
| Transmission bellhousing-to-engine bolts . . . . . . . . . . . . . . . . . . | 48 | 35 |
| Transmission drain plug . . . . . . . . . . . . . . . . . . . . . . . . . . . . . . . | 38 | 28 |
| Transmission earth cable . . . . . . . . . . . . . . . . . . . . . . . . . . . . . . | 40 | 30 |
| Transmission filler/level plug . . . . . . . . . . . . . . . . . . . . . . . . . . . | 22 | 16 |

## 1 General information

The manual transmission and final drive are housed in an aluminium casing, bolted directly to the left-hand side of the engine. Gear selection is by a floor-mounted lever assembly operating the transmission selector mechanism via twin cables on turbocharged and GDI models, or a single rod on other non-turbo models.

The transmission internal components comprise the input shaft, the upper and lower layshafts, the final drive differential and the selector mechanism. The input shaft contains the fixed 1st, 2nd and 5th gears, the freewheeling 3rd and 4th gearwheels and the 3rd/4th synchro unit. The upper layshaft contains the freewheeling 5th and reverse gearwheels, the 5th/reverse synchro unit and a final drive pinion. The lower layshaft contains the fixed 3rd and 4th gears, the freewheeling 1st, 2nd and reverse intermediate gearwheels, the 1st/2nd synchro unit and a final drive pinion.

Drive from the engine is transmitted to the input shaft by the clutch. The gears on the input shaft are permanently meshed with the gears on the two layshafts, but when drive is transmitted, only one gear at a time is actually locked to its shaft – the others are

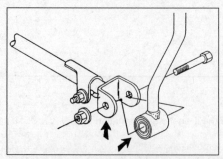

**2.9 Unscrew the flange nut and withdraw the pivot bolt from the selector rod joint at the base of the gear lever**

freewheeling. The selection of gears is by sliding synchro units; movement of the gear lever is transmitted to selector forks, which slide the appropriate synchro unit towards the gear to be engaged and lock it to the relevant shaft. In neutral, none of the gears are locked, all are freewheeling.

Reverse gear is obtained by locking the reverse gearwheel to the upper layshaft. Drive is transmitted through the input shaft to the reverse intermediate gearwheel on the lower layshaft, then to the reverse gearwheel and final drive pinion on the upper layshaft. Reverse is therefore obtained by transmitting power through all three shafts, instead of only two as in the case of the forward gears. By eliminating the need for a separate reverse idler gear, synchromesh can also be provided on reverse gear.

## 2 Gear lever housing – removal and refitting

### GDI and turbo models

#### Removal

**1** Remove the centre console as described in Chapter 11.
**2** Undo the four bolts securing the gear lever housing to the floorpan.
**3** With reference to Section 3, lift up the gear lever housing and prise off the selector inner cable socket joints from the base of the gear lever.

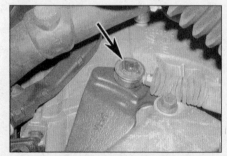

**3.6 Extract the circlip (arrowed) securing the inner cable ends to the transmission selector levers**

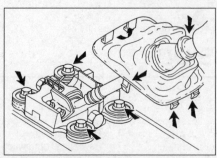

**2.11 Unclip the gaiter, then undo the four bolts securing the housing assembly to the floor**

**4** Extract the retaining clips securing the selector outer cables to the front of the gear lever housing, and remove the housing from the car.

#### Refitting

**5** Refit by reversing the removal operations.
**6** Tighten the four securing bolts to the specified torque. Refit the centre console as described in Chapter 11.

### Other models

#### Removal

**7** Chock the rear wheels, apply the hand-brake, then jack up the front of the car and support it on axle stands.
**8** Where applicable, undo the nuts and remove the cover plate from the floorpan, to expose the base of the gear lever.
**9** Unscrew the flange nut and withdraw the pivot bolt from the selector rod joint at the base of the gear lever. Collect the washers and bushes, making a careful note of their order of fitment **(see illustration)**.
**10** Lower the car to the ground, then remove the centre console as described in Chapter 11.
**11** Undo the four bolts securing the housing assembly to the floor. Recover the washers and then remove the assembly from the car **(see illustration)**.

#### Refitting

**12** Refit by reversing the removal operations. Tighten the four lever housing bolts and the selector rod-to-gear lever bolt to the specified torque. Refit the centre console as described in Chapter 11.

**3.14 The cable with yellow markings (arrowed) connects to the vertical selector lever on the left of the transmission**

## 3 Selector cables/rod – removal and refitting

### GDI and turbo models (cables)

#### Removal

**1** Remove the battery as described in Chapter 5A.
**2** Remove the screws and lift the plastic cover panel from the top of the engine.
**3** Refer to Chapter 4A or 4B and remove the air cleaner assembly.
**4** On turbo models, unbolt the heat shield from above the exhaust manifold (where fitted) and remove it from the engine compartment.
**5** Position a trolley jack underneath the transmission bellhousing and raise it until it is just taking the combined weight of the engine and transmission. Unbolt and remove the engine left-hand mounting from the transmission.
**6** Extract the circlip securing the inner cable ends to the transmission selector levers. Withdraw the washers, and slide the cable ends off the levers **(see illustration)**.
**7** Extract the retaining clips and release the outer cables from the transmission brackets.
**8** Remove the centre console as described in Chapter 11.
**9** Remove the gear lever housing as described in Section 2, then prise the selector inner cable socket joints from the base of the gear lever.
**10** Undo the screws and remove the trim/soundproofing panel from under the facia on the left-hand side.
**11** Where applicable, undo the bolts securing the engine control module (ECM) mounting bracket to the floorpan, noting that one of the bolts secures an earth cable. Move the bracket and control module to one side.
**12** Undo the nuts securing the cable entry cover plate to the bulkhead.
**13** Note the routing of the cables under the facia and in the engine compartment, as an aid to refitting. Release any adjacent components as necessary then pull the cables into the passenger compartment and remove them from the car.

#### Refitting

**14** Refitting is a reversal of removal, noting the following **(see illustration)**:
a) The cable marked at both ends with yellow paint connects to the gear lever housing left-hand link plate, and the vertical selector lever on the left-hand end of the transmission.
b) When routing the selector cables through the passenger and engine compartments, ensure that the cables are not kinked or forced through any sharp bends, as this will impede their operation.
c) Lightly grease the cable ball-end fittings before reconnecting.

**3.20a Remove the nut, withdraw the pivot bolt and detach the selector rod from the transmission**

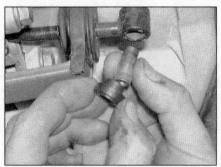

**3.20b Collect the washers and bushes, making a careful note of their order of fitment**

**3.25 Slacken the selector rod adjustment collar locknut to alter the length of the selector rod**

### Other models (rod)

#### Removal

**15** Chock the rear wheels, apply the handbrake, then jack up the front of the car and support it on axle stands.

**16** Where applicable, undo the nuts and remove the cover plate from the floorpan, to expose the base of the gear lever.

**17** Unscrew the flange nut and withdraw the pivot bolt from the selector rod joint at the base of the gear lever.

**18** Collect the washers and bushes, making a careful note of their order of fitment.

**19** Lower the car to the ground, then remove the air cleaner as described in Chapter 4A, and the battery as described in Chapter 5A, to gain access to the top of the transmission.

**20** Slacken and withdraw the pivot bolt and detach the selector rod from the transmission. Collect the washers and bushes, making a careful note of their order of fitment **(see illustrations)**.

**21** Withdraw the selector rod from the underside of the car.

#### Refitting

**22** Refitting is a reversal of removal, noting the following points:
a) *Lubricate the pivot points at either end the end of the selector rod using a suitable multi-purpose grease.*
b) *Insert the selector rod-to-transmission pivot bolt from above and tighten to the specified torque.*
c) *On completion, check and if necessary adjust the length of the selector rod, as described in the next sub-Section.*

#### Adjustment

**23** Move the gear lever into first gear.

**24** Check that the gearchange lever is resting against the end stop at the top right-hand side of the gear lever housing. In this position, check that the distance between the end of the selector rod adjustment collar and the boss at the end of the selector rod is approximately 8 mm.

**25** If adjustment is required, slacken the selector rod adjustment collar locknut and adjust the selector rod until the measurement

described in the previous paragraph is achieved **(see illustration)**.

**26** On completion, tighten the adjustment collar locknut to the specified torque.

---

### 4 Oil seals – renewal

---

### Driveshaft oil seals

**1** Chock the rear wheels, apply the handbrake, then jack up the front of the car and support it on axle stands. Remove the appropriate front roadwheel.

**2** Drain the transmission oil as described in Section 6, or be prepared for oil loss as the driveshaft is removed.

**3** Remove the appropriate driveshaft as described in Chapter 8.

**4** Note the correct fitted depth of the driveshaft oil seal in its housing, then carefully prise it out of position using a large flat-bladed screwdriver. Take great care to avoid scoring the seal housing.

**5** Remove all traces of dirt from the area around the oil seal aperture, then apply a smear of grease to the outer lip of the new oil seal. Ensure the seal is correctly positioned, with its sealing lip facing inwards, and tap it squarely into position, using a suitable tubular drift (such as a socket) which bears only on the hard outer edge of the seal. Ensure the seal is fitted at the same depth in its housing that the original was.

**6** Refit the driveshaft as described in Chapter 8.

**7** Refill/top-up the transmission with the specified type and amount of oil, as described in Section 6.

### Input shaft oil seal

**Note:** *This operation does not apply to 1.6 and 1.8 litre models with the M3P transmission. On these models, the input shaft guide sleeve is pressed into the transmission, and can only be removed using special tools.*

**8** Remove the transmission as described in Section 7.

**9** With reference to Chapter 6, remove the clutch release bearing from the release fork and slide it off the input shaft guide sleeve. On turbo models, remove the clutch slave cylinder from the input shaft guide sleeve.

**10** Where applicable, free the release fork dust gaiter from the bellhousing and withdraw the release fork from the pivot ball-stud.

**11** Undo the bolts and remove the guide sleeve from the bellhousing.

**12** On non-turbo models, carefully lever the old oil seal from the guide sleeve.

**13** On turbo models, carefully lever the old oil seal out of the bellhousing. The seal may also be removed by carefully drilling two holes in the front face of the seal and threading a self-tapping screw into each hole. The seal can then be eased from its seat by pulling on the heads of the self-tapping screws with a pair of pliers. If this method is used, take great care to avoid drilling into the surface of the seal housing or the input shaft.

**14** Thoroughly clean the oil seal housing in the guide sleeve/transmission casing (as applicable)

**15** Lubricate the new seal and fit it to the bellhousing/input shaft sleeve, with the lip facing towards the transmission casing. Use a socket or suitable tubing to drive the seal squarely into its housing.

**16** Refit the input shaft sleeve to the transmission casing, and tighten the securing bolts to the specified torque.

**17** Refitting the remainder of the release bearing components is a reversal of removal. Do not apply any grease to the transmission input shaft, the guide sleeve, or the release bearing itself, as these components have a friction-reducing coating which does not require lubrication.

**18** On non-turbo models, lubricate the release fork pivot ball-stud sparingly with molybdenum disulphide grease. With the bearing and release fork in position, secure the release fork to the slave cylinder lug on the bellhousing with a cable-tie or similar, to hold it in place as the transmission is refitted.

**19** Refit the transmission (see Section 7).

**5.1 Reversing light switch (arrowed) –
GDI engine model**

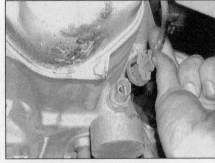

**5.2 Unplug the wiring from the reversing
light switch – M5P transmission**

plug and drain plug. GDI engine models have
the transmission drain plug at the base of the
casing **(see illustration)**, and the filler plug
(marked OIL) on the front of the unit. On all
other models, the drain plug is located on the
underside of the transmission casing.

**3** Unscrew and remove the drain plug and
allow the oil to drain into the container **(see
illustration)**.

**4** When all the oil has drained, refit the drain
plug and tighten it securely.

### Refilling

**5** Wipe clean the area around the filler/level
plug and unscrew the plug from the casing
(refer to Chapter 1, Section 10, for more
details).

**6** Fill the transmission through the filler/level
plug hole with the correct type of oil. The oil
level is correct when the oil begins to run out
of the plug hole.

**7** Wait until the oil level settles (until the oil
flowing from the hole stops), then refit the
filler/level plug, and tighten it securely. Lower
the car to the ground, drive it for a short
distance, then check for leaks.

**8** Dispose of the old oil safely in accordance
with environmental regulations.

---

## 5  Reversing light switch – removal and refitting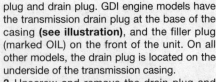

### Removal

**1** The reversing light switch is located on the
upper face of the transmission on turbo and
GDI models **(see illustration)**, or at the rear
of the transmission casing on the left-hand
side of the differential housing on all other
models.

**2** Clean around the switch, disconnect the
wiring connector and unscrew the switch **(see
illustration)**.

### Refitting

**3** Refit by reversing the removal operations.

## 6  Manual transmission oil – draining and refilling

**Note:** *Ideally, the transmission oil should be
drained immediately after the car has been
driven. This will ensure that any contaminants
are drained out along with the oil, rather than
remaining at the bottom of the transmission
casing.*

### Draining

**1** Jack up the front of the car and support it
securely on axle stands (see *Jacking and
vehicle support*). Remove the engine
undershield, and position a suitable container
beneath the transmission.

**2** On the left-hand of the transmission casing
on turbo models, you will see the filler/level

## 7  Manual transmission – removal and refitting

### Removal

**1** Park the car on a level surface and apply
the handbrake.

**2** Put the gear lever in neutral.

**3** Undo the securing screws and lift off the
engine cover panel.

**4** Refer to Chapter 5A and remove the
battery.

**5** Refer to Chapter 4A or 4B, and remove the
air cleaner assembly and all relevant inlet
ducting around the left-hand side of the
engine (left as seen from the driver's seat).

**6** On turbo models, slacken the hose clips
and disconnect the intake air ducting from the
turbocharger and intercooler. Release the
ducting from its support bracket and then
remove it from the engine compartment.

**7** Disconnect the selector cables/rod (as
applicable) from the transmission as
described in Section 3. On models with
selector cables, unbolt the selector mounting
bracket from the top of the transmission
casing, and position it to one side.

**8** Unbolt the earth cable from side of the
transmission casing **(see illustration)**.

**9** Disconnect the wiring connector from the
reversing light switch (see Section 5). On GDI
engine models, also disconnect the
transmission oil temperature sensor on the
front of the casing **(see illustration)**.

**10** Remove the securing screws and detach
the wiring harness clip(s) from the top of the
transmission casing.

**6.2 Transmission oil drain plug –
GDI engine models**

**6.3 Unscrew and remove the drain plug –
M5P transmission**

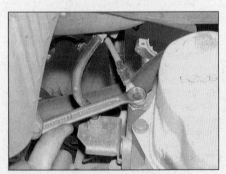

**7.8 Unbolt the earth cable from side of the
transmission casing**

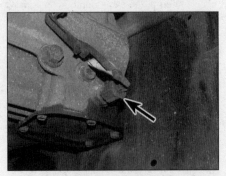

**7.9 Oil temperature sensor wiring plug
(arrowed) – GDI engine model**

**11** Where applicable, disconnect the wiring from the temperature sensor at the left-hand side of the cylinder head **(see illustration)**.

**12** On all except turbo models, remove the clutch slave cylinder from the top of the transmission casing with reference to Chapter 6. Wrap a cable-tie around the slave cylinder to prevent the piston from being pushed out. On turbo models, undo the union and disconnect the slave cylinder hydraulic pipe from at the coupling at the top of the transmission casing; be prepared for some hydraulic fluid spillage.

**13** Remove the spring clip and release the slave cylinder hydraulic pipe from the front of the transmission casing.

**14** On all except GDI engine models, remove the two securing screws and withdraw the crankshaft position (flywheel) sensor from the top of the transmission bellhousing. Move the sensor to one side with the wiring still attached (see Chapter 4A for details).

**15** Remove the starter motor with reference to Chapter 5A.

**16** Undo all the transmission-to-engine retaining bolts that are accessible from above. Note that the bolts are not all of equal length, so make a careful note of where each one is fitted **(see illustration)**.

**17** Position a engine lifting beam across the engine compartment, and attach the jib to the lifting eyelets at both ends of the cylinder head. Adjust the height of the jib so that the load is just taken off the engine mountings.

**18** Unbolt and remove the engine/transmission left-hand mounting together with its bracket, with reference to Chapter 2A or 2B.

**19** Check that the handbrake is applied, then chock the rear wheels, jack up the front of the car and rest it securely on axle stands. Remove both front roadwheels.

**20** Remove the splash guard from the underside of the engine compartment, then remove the splash guard from the left-hand side of the engine compartment via the left-hand wheel arch.

**21** Drain the oil from the transmission as described in Section 6.

**22** On turbo models, slacken the hose clips and disconnect the intake air ducting from the intercooler and throttle body. Release the

**7.11 Disconnecting the cylinder head-mounted temperature sensor – GDI engine**

ducting from its support bracket and remove it from the engine compartment.

**23** Except on GDI engines, unbolt and remove the exhaust downpipe heat shield, to allow access the right-hand driveshaft.

**24** Ensure that the engine lifting beam is supporting the combined weight of the engine and transmission, then unbolt the engine/transmission front and rear mountings from the engine/transmission crossmember, with reference to Chapter 2A or 2B.

**25** Slacken and withdraw the securing bolts and remove the engine/transmission crossmember from the underside of the engine compartment **(see illustrations)**. Collect the bushes, washers, grommets and support plates, making a careful note of their order of fitment to ensure correct reassembly later. Note also that the securing bolts are of unequal lengths.

**26** Where applicable on early models, withdraw the locking pin and disconnect the speedometer drive cable from the transmission.

**27** Referring to Chapter 8, remove the left-hand driveshaft completely, but only remove the right-hand driveshaft from the transmission and the intermediate bearing bracket, leaving it connected at the steering knuckle end. Support the driveshaft using a length of wire, to avoid straining the CV joints.

**28** Support the transmission from below on a trolley jack.

**29** Undo the remaining bolts securing the transmission bellhousing to the engine. Withdraw the transmission squarely off the

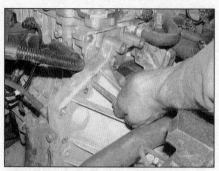

**7.16 Undo all the transmission-to-engine retaining bolts that are accessible from above**

engine dowels, taking care not to allow the weight of the transmission to hang on the clutch driven plate **(see illustration)**. It will be necessary to lower the engine slightly, by adjusting the height of the engine lifting beam jib, to allow the transmission to be withdrawn. Ensure that the exhaust system is not put under undue strain as the engine is lowered – if necessary, release some of the exhaust mountings from under the car.

**30** Lower the jack and remove the transmission from under the car.

### Refitting

**31** The transmission is refitted by a reversal of the removal procedure, bearing in mind the following points.

a) Ensure the bellhousing locating dowels are correctly positioned prior to installation.

b) On non-turbo models, secure the clutch release fork to the slave cylinder lug on the bellhousing with a cable-tie or similar, to hold it in place as the transmission is refitted.

c) Do not apply any grease to the transmission input shaft, the guide sleeve, or the release bearing itself, as these components have a friction-reducing coating which does not require lubrication.

d) Reconnect the selector cables/rod to the transmission as described in Section 3. Where applicable, check the adjustment of the selector rod mechanism as described at the end of Section 3.

**7.25a Unscrew the bolts . . .**

**7.25b . . . and remove the engine/transmission crossmember from below the engine compartment**

**7.29 Withdraw the transmission squarely off the engine dowels**

e) *Refit any exhaust system components which were disturbed, as described in Chapter 4C.*
f) *Tighten all nuts and bolts to the correct torque (where specified).*
g) *Bleed the clutch hydraulic system as described in Chapter 6.*
h) *Refill the transmission with the specified grade and quantity of oil, as described in Section 6.*

## 8  Manual transmission overhaul – general information

Overhauling a manual transmission is a difficult job for the do-it-yourselfer. It involves the dismantling and reassembly of many small parts. Numerous clearances must be precisely measured and, if necessary, changed with selected spacers and circlips. As a result, if transmission problems arise, while the unit can be removed and refitted by a competent do-it-yourselfer, overhaul should be left to a transmission specialist. Rebuilt transmissions may be available – check with your dealer parts department, motor factors, or transmission specialists. At any rate, the time and money involved in an overhaul is almost sure to exceed the cost of a rebuilt unit.

Nevertheless, it's not impossible for an inexperienced mechanic to rebuild a transmission, providing the special tools are available, and the job is done in a deliberate step-by-step manner so nothing is overlooked.

The tools necessary for an overhaul include: internal and external circlip pliers, a bearing puller, a slide hammer, a set of pin punches, a dial test indicator, and possibly a hydraulic press. In addition, a large, sturdy workbench and a vice or transmission stand will be required.

During dismantling of the transmission, make careful notes of how each part comes off, where it fits in relation to other parts, and what holds it in place.

Before taking the transmission apart for repair, it will help if you have some idea what area of the transmission is malfunctioning. Certain problems can be closely tied to specific areas in the transmission, which can make component examination and replacement easier. Refer to the *Fault finding* section at the rear of this manual for information regarding possible sources of trouble.

# Chapter 7 Part B:
# Automatic transmission

## Contents

## Degrees of difficulty

| Easy, suitable for novice with little experience  | Fairly easy, suitable for beginner with some experience  | Fairly difficult, suitable for competent DIY mechanic | Difficult, suitable for experienced DIY mechanic | Very difficult, suitable for expert DIY or professional |
| --- | --- | --- | --- | --- |

## Specifications

### General

| | |
| --- | --- |
| Type . . . . . . . . . . . . . . . . . . . . . . . . . . . . . . . . . . . . . . . . . . . . . . . . . . | Computer-controlled four- or five-speed with torque converter lock-up on three highest gears |
| Designation . . . . . . . . . . . . . . . . . . . . . . . . . . . . . . . . . . . . . . . . . . . . | AW 50-42 (4-speed) or AW55-50 (5-speed) |

### Ratios

| | |
| --- | --- |
| Four-speed transmission: | |
| 1st . . . . . . . . . . . . . . . . . . . . . . . . . . . . . . . . . . . . . . . . . . . . . . . . . . | 3.74 : 1 |
| 2nd . . . . . . . . . . . . . . . . . . . . . . . . . . . . . . . . . . . . . . . . . . . . . . . . . | 2.14 : 1 |
| 3rd . . . . . . . . . . . . . . . . . . . . . . . . . . . . . . . . . . . . . . . . . . . . . . . . . . | 1.42 : 1 |
| 4th . . . . . . . . . . . . . . . . . . . . . . . . . . . . . . . . . . . . . . . . . . . . . . . . . . | 1.02 : 1 |
| Reverse . . . . . . . . . . . . . . . . . . . . . . . . . . . . . . . . . . . . . . . . . . . . . . | 4.09 : 1 |
| Final drive: | |
| Non-turbo models . . . . . . . . . . . . . . . . . . . . . . . . . . . . . . . . . . . | 3.10 : 1 |
| Turbo models . . . . . . . . . . . . . . . . . . . . . . . . . . . . . . . . . . . . . . | 2.76 : 1 |
| Five-speed transmission: | |
| 1st . . . . . . . . . . . . . . . . . . . . . . . . . . . . . . . . . . . . . . . . . . . . . . . . . . | 4.77 : 1 |
| 2nd . . . . . . . . . . . . . . . . . . . . . . . . . . . . . . . . . . . . . . . . . . . . . . . . . | 2.99 : 1 |
| 3rd . . . . . . . . . . . . . . . . . . . . . . . . . . . . . . . . . . . . . . . . . . . . . . . . . . | 1.96 : 1 |
| 4th . . . . . . . . . . . . . . . . . . . . . . . . . . . . . . . . . . . . . . . . . . . . . . . . . . | 1.32 : 1 |
| 5th . . . . . . . . . . . . . . . . . . . . . . . . . . . . . . . . . . . . . . . . . . . . . . . . . . | 1.02 : 1 |
| Final drive: | |
| Non-turbo models . . . . . . . . . . . . . . . . . . . . . . . . . . . . . . . . . . . | 2.86 : 1 |
| Turbo models . . . . . . . . . . . . . . . . . . . . . . . . . . . . . . . . . . . . . . | 2.44 : 1 |

### Lubrication

| | |
| --- | --- |
| Lubricant type . . . . . . . . . . . . . . . . . . . . . . . . . . . . . . . . . . . . . . . . . | See *Lubricants and fluids* |
| Capacity: | |
| Four-speed transmission: | |
| Drain and refill . . . . . . . . . . . . . . . . . . . . . . . . . . . . . . . . . . . . . | 7.7 litres |
| Volume in torque converter . . . . . . . . . . . . . . . . . . . . . . . . . . . | 2.5 litres |
| Difference between MAX and MIN on dipstick . . . . . . . . . . . . . | 0.5 litres |
| Five-speed transmission: | |
| Drain and refill . . . . . . . . . . . . . . . . . . . . . . . . . . . . . . . . . . . . . | 7.5 litres |
| Volume in torque converter . . . . . . . . . . . . . . . . . . . . . . . . . . . | 3.0 litres approx |
| Difference between MAX and MIN on dipstick . . . . . . . . . . . . . | 0.2 litres |

## Torque wrench settings

| | Nm | lbf ft |
|---|---|---|
| Fluid temperature sensor | 25 | 18 |
| Selector cable bracket to transmission | 25 | 18 |
| Selector cable entry cover plate | 10 | 7 |
| Selector housing bolts | 25 | 18 |
| Torque converter-to-driveplate bolts* | 35 | 26 |
| Transmission drain plug | 40 | 30 |
| Transmission speed sensor | 6 | 4 |
| Transmission-to-engine bolts | 48 | 35 |
| Vehicle speed sensor | 6 | 4 |

*New bolts must be used*

---

## 1  General information

The automatic transmission is a computer-controlled four- or five-speed transmission with torque converter lock-up on the highest three gears. The five-speed unit replaced the four-speed for 2001 model year, but apart from the extra ratio and revised software, the new unit is very similar to the old one.

The unit is controlled by an electronic control unit (ECU) which receives signal inputs from various sensors relating to transmission operating conditions. Information on engine parameters are also sent to the ECU from the engine management system. From this data, the ECU can establish the optimum gear shifting speeds and lock-up engagement points according to the driving mode selected.

Drive is taken from the engine to the transmission by a torque converter. This is a type of fluid coupling which under certain conditions has a torque multiplying effect. The torque converter is mechanically locked to the engine, under the control of the ECU, when the transmission is operating in the three highest gears. This eliminates losses due to slip, and improves fuel economy.

On four-speed models, the gear selector has six positions: P, R, N, D, 3 and L. Five-speed versions have an extra selector position, with P, R, N, D, 4, 3, and L. In position P, the transmission is mechanically locked: this position must only be engaged when the vehicle is stationary. In position R, reverse is engaged, in N neutral. In position D, gearchanging is automatic throughout the range. In positions 3 or 4, the next gear up is blocked and automatic gearchanging occurs in the lower gears, making it a suitable selection for driving in mountainous regions. In position L, only first and second gears are available.

On four-speed models, the mode switch has three selectable functions; ECON, SPORT and WINTER. In ECON mode the transmission changes up to a higher gear and engages lock-up as early as possible for maximum economy, whilst in SPORT mode, the gear changing points are selected for maximum performance. In WINTER mode, the transmission will allow starting from rest in a higher than normal gear to avoid wheelspin in poor road conditions. This mode can also be used to restrict gear changing in D, 3 and L when road conditions dictate the need for more direct control of gear selection.

On the later five-speed transmission, the only selectable function is W, for winter mode, which operates in a similar fashion to the earlier unit. The previous sport and economy modes have now been incorporated into the transmission's normal function – the decision as to which operating mode to use is determined by the ECU, based on throttle position and its rate of change (this information is derived from the throttle position sensor signal). In this way, gearchanges can be economy-orientated, but full acceleration is always available on demand.

A kickdown facility causes the transmission to shift down a gear (subject to engine speed) when the throttle is fully depressed. This is useful when extra acceleration is required. Kickdown, like the other transmission functions, is controlled by the ECU.

Generally, the engine can only be started in positions P and N. On certain models, the engine can only be started in position P, thanks to a safety/security feature called Shiftlock. With this system, the ignition key can only be removed from the ignition/steering lock if the selector lever is placed in position P. On restarting the car, the selector lever can only be moved from the P position once the ignition switch is turned to position II and the brake pedal is pressed. If necessary, the Shiftlock system can be overridden by turning the ignition switch to position II and depressing the Shiftlock override button to the right of the selector lever.

In addition to control of the transmission, the ECU incorporates a built-in fault diagnosis facility. A fault is signalled to the driver by the flashing of the warning light on the instrument panel. The ECU then reverts to an emergency (limp-home) program which ensures that two forward gears and reverse will always be available, but gearchanging must be performed manually. If a fault of this nature does occur, the ECU stores a series of signals (or fault codes) for subsequent read-out via the diagnostic unit located in the engine compartment.

The automatic transmission is a complex unit, but if it is not abused it will be reliable and long-lasting. Repair or overhaul operations are beyond the scope of many dealers, let alone the home mechanic; specialist advice should be sought if problems arise which cannot be solved by the procedures given in this Chapter.

## 2  Automatic transmission fluid – draining and refilling

1 Renewal of the automatic transmission fluid is not a service requirement, and will normally only be necessary in the following circumstances:

a) *If the on-board diagnostic system has logged a fault code indicating fluid temperature too high (see Section 11).*

b) *If the fluid is discoloured or has a burnt smell resulting from hard and continuous operation of the transmission.*

c) *Water is present in the fluid, indicated by a grey colour and possible presence of water droplets. If such contamination is found, the source must be traced and rectified, and the transmission and fluid cooler pipes must be thoroughly cleaned and flushed. In severe cases, a new transmission unit may be needed.*

d) *If the car is continuously used for taxi work or extended periods of trailer towing, the fluid should be changed at the 40 000 mile (60 000 km) service interval.*

2 Raise and securely support the front of the car (see *Jacking and vehicle support*).

3 Remove the splash guards from underside of the engine compartment.

4 Remove the drain plug located on the right-hand side of the casing, below and just forward of the driveshaft. Allow the contents of the transmission to drain into a suitable draining container. Refit the drain plug, using a new seal if necessary, and tighten it to the specified torque.

***Caution: If the vehicle has just been run, the transmission fluid may be very hot – protect your hands to avoid scalding.***

5 Refit the splash guard(s) and lower the car to the ground.

6 Refer to Chapter 5A and remove the battery, then unbolt and remove the battery tray; this allows improved access to the top of the transmission.

**7** Clean the fluid cooler return hose union on the transmission, then disconnect the hose at the transmission union. Suitably plug the open union on the transmission.

**8** Attach a clear plastic hose to the end of the fluid cooler return hose. Lead the hose into the draining container.

**9** Temporarily refit the battery tray and battery.

**10** Apply the handbrake and move the gear selector lever to the P (Park) position.

**11** Add 2.0 litres of fresh automatic transmission fluid of the specified type via the dipstick tube.

**12** Start the engine and allow it to idle. Fluid will flow into the draining container. When bubbles appear in the fluid running through the clear hose, stop the engine.

**13** Add a further 2.0 litres of fresh automatic transmission fluid of the specified type via the dipstick tube.

**14** Repeat paragraph 12, then remove the battery and battery tray. Remove the plastic hose and reconnect the fluid cooler return hose to the transmission.

**15** Refit the battery tray and battery securely.

**16** Add a further 2.0 litres of fresh automatic transmission fluid.

**17** Start the engine and allow it to idle. Move the gear selector lever through all the gear positions, stopping for four to five seconds in each position. Return the selector lever to the P position, wait for two minutes then check the fluid level as described in Chapter 1, using the COLD markings on the dipstick. Top-up as necessary.

**18** Dispose of the old fluid safely (see *General repair procedures*).

**19** Any fault codes stored in the transmission control module's memory should now be erased electronically; this operation can only be carried out by a Volvo dealer using dedicated diagnostic equipment.

---

**3** Selector cable –
removal, refitting
and adjustment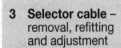

---

### Removal

**1** Park the car on a level surface then refer to Chapter 4A, and remove the air cleaner assembly.

**2** Refer to Chapter 5A and remove the battery and battery tray.

**3** Working in the engine compartment, extract the locking clip and washer securing the selector inner cable to the gear shift position sensor lever.

**4** Undo the two nuts and remove the washers (where fitted) securing the selector outer cable bracket to the transmission. Lift the bracket off the mounting studs and release the inner cable end from the shift position sensor lever.

**5** Release the selector cable from the clip on the wiring connector bracket, at the engine compartment bulkhead.

**3.12 Undo the two nuts (arrowed) securing the cable entry grommet to the bulkhead**

**6** Undo the securing nuts and remove the heat shield from the engine compartment bulkhead.

**7** Remove the centre console as described in Chapter 11.

**8** Extract the retaining clip securing the selector outer cable to the gear selector housing.

**9** Undo the securing bolts and remove the selector lever housing from the floorpan (see Section 4). Extract the retaining clip securing the selector inner cable to the base of the gear selector lever – this is in the form of a roll-pin, pulled out (or tapped out) to the side.

**10** Undo the screws and remove the trim/soundproofing panel from under the facia on the left-hand side.

**11** Where applicable, undo the screws and remove the carpet support plate under the centre of the facia on the left-hand side. Bend back the carpet to allow the support plate to be withdrawn.

**12** Undo the two nuts securing the cable entry grommet to the bulkhead **(see illustration)**. Where applicable, release the shift lock cable from the selector cable.

**13** Note the routing of the cable under the facia, and in the engine compartment, as an aid to refitting. Release any adjacent components as necessary then pull the cable

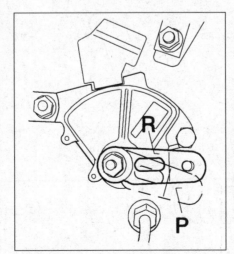

**3.20 Move the gear shift position sensor lever rearward one position to R (Reverse)**

into the passenger compartment and remove it from the car – the help of an assistant will be required to help guide the cable through the bulkhead.

### Refitting and adjustment

**14** From inside the car, carefully feed the cable through into the engine compartment, ensuring correct routing.

**15** Reconnect the cable to the selector lever and housing, and secure with the retaining pin and clips. Refit the selector lever housing to the floorpan, and tighten the securing bolts to the specified torque.

**16** Refit the cable entry grommet, carpet support plate and the trim/soundproofing panel.

**17** Refit the centre console as described in Chapter 11.

**18** Move the gear selector lever to position R (Reverse). Ensure that the gear lever and cable position do not move during subsequent operations.

**19** Working in the engine compartment, move the gear position sensor lever as far forward as it will go to the P (Park) position. Ensure that the correct gear is selected by releasing the handbrake and trying to roll the car; the transmission should be locked. Re-apply the handbrake.

**20** Move the gear shift position sensor lever rearward one position to R (Reverse) **(see illustration)**.

**21** Without moving the selector cable or gear shift position sensor lever, locate the inner cable on the gear shift position sensor lever and position the outer cable bracket on the transmission studs. Secure the bracket with the nuts (and where applicable the washers) and tighten the nuts to the specified torque. Secure the cable inner with the spring clip **(see illustration)**.

**22** Refit the locking clip and washer securing the cable to the transmission.

**23** Check the adjustment of the selector cable, by moving the gear selector lever (inside the car) to the N (neutral) position. Without touching the locking button, move the lever forward slightly then backwards slightly. Play should be felt in both directions.

**24** On completion, refit the heat shield, air cleaner assembly, battery tray and battery.

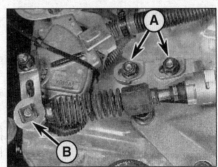

**3.21 Cable bracket nuts (A) and inner cable spring clip (B)**

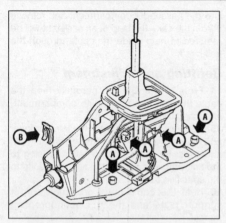

**4.9 Selector lever housing securing bolts (A) and selector cable securing clip (B)**

## 4 Selector lever housing – removal and refitting

### Removal

**1** Disconnect the battery negative lead (see *Disconnecting the battery*).

**2** Grasp the gear lever gaiter around the internal retaining clip, turn the gaiter and clip clockwise through 90° and pull the gaiter down. Ensure that the retaining clip returns to its original position after releasing the gaiter.

**3** Jerk the gear lever knob sharply upwards to remove it from the selector lever. Note that considerable force will be required to release it. Volvo state that the knob cannot be re-used once it has been removed, but there should be no harm in trying to do so.

**4** Refer to Chapter 11 and remove the centre console.

**5** Remove the selector illumination bulbholder from the base of the indicator panel.

**6** Where applicable, remove the shift lock solenoid and microswitch as described in Section 7.

**7** Extract the retaining clip securing the selector outer cable to the gear selector housing **(see illustration 4.9)**.

**8** Release the wiring harness from the clips at the side of the lever housing and unplug the wiring at the connectors.

**9** Slacken and withdraw the bolts which secure the lever housing to the floorpan **(see illustration)**.

**10** Extract the retaining pin securing the selector inner cable to the gear selector lever, as described in Section 3.

**11** Lift the housing from the floorpan and remove it from the car.

### Refitting

**12** Refitting is a reversal of removal, but tighten the lever housing securing bolts to the specified torque. When refitting the gear lever knob, push it firmly into position ensuring that it is securely seated in the snap catches. Also ensure that the lock button locates on the catches in the gear lever pushrod.

## 5 Transmission control system sensors – removal and refitting

### Transmission speed sensor

#### Removal

**1** The transmission speed sensor is located on the upper surface of the transmission casing, underneath the left-hand engine mounting bracket **(see illustration)**.

**2** Remove the plastic cover panel from the top of the engine then refer to Chapter 5A and remove the battery.

**3** Refer to Chapter 4A and remove the air cleaner assembly and inlet ducting.

**4** Unbolt and remove the battery tray and detach the air cleaner bracket.

**5** Unplug the transmission main wiring connector(s) on the top of the transmission housing. Release the harness securing clips then undo the screws and remove the wiring harness bracket.

**6** Remove the engine/transmission left-hand mounting bracket from the transmission, as described in Chapter 2A. Note that this will involve supporting the left-hand side of the engine and transmission using a lifting beam or an engine crane.

**7** Unplug the sensor wiring connector.

**8** Wipe clean the area around the sensor, then undo the retaining bolt and remove the RPM sensor from the top of the transmission housing.

#### Refitting

**9** Smear some clean automatic transmission fluid on the sensor O-ring seal, then locate the sensor in position on the transmission. Secure with the retaining bolt and tighten to the specified torque.

**10** The remainder of the refitting procedure is a reversal of removal. On completion, adjust the selector cable as described in Section 3.

### Vehicle speed sensor

#### Removal

**11** The vehicle speed sensor is mounted on the upper surface of the transmission, towards the rear of the unit, above the differential housing **(see illustration 5.1)**.

**12** Remove the plastic cover panel from the top of the engine, then refer to Chapter 4A and remove the air cleaner assembly and inlet ducting.

**13** Release the wiring harness from the cable-ties at the top of the transmission casing.

**14** Undo the securing screws and detach the wiring harness connector bracket from the transmission.

**15** Wipe clean the area around the sensor, remove the securing screw and then withdraw the sensor from the transmission casing. Unplug the wiring connector.

#### Refitting

**16** Smear some clean automatic transmission fluid on the sensor O-ring seal, then locate the sensor in position on the transmission.

**17** Fit the sensor securing screw and tighten to the specified torque.

**18** Reconnect the wiring plug to the sensor.

**19** Refit the wiring harness connector support bracket and fit the connector to the bracket.

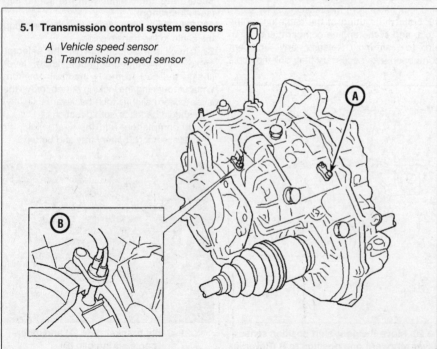

**5.1 Transmission control system sensors**

*A  Vehicle speed sensor*
*B  Transmission speed sensor*

**20** Secure the harness in position with new cable-ties.

**21** Refit the air cleaner assembly with reference to Chapter 4A.

### *Fluid temperature sensor*

#### Removal

**22** The transmission fluid temperature sensor is located on the underside of the transmission **(see illustration).**

**23** Remove the plastic cover panel from the top of the engine then refer to Chapter 5A and remove the battery.

**24** Refer to Chapter 4A and remove the air cleaner assembly and inlet ducting.

**25** Unbolt and remove the battery tray and detach the air cleaner bracket.

**26** Unplug the transmission main wiring connector(s) on the top of the transmission housing. Release the harness securing clips, then undo the screws and remove the wiring harness bracket.

**27** Disconnect the selector cable from the gear shift position sensor, as described in Section 3.

**28** Remove the gearshift position sensor as described later in this section.

**29** Raise the front of the car and support it securely on axle stands.

**30** Drain the transmission fluid as described in Section 2.

**31** Wipe clean the area around the sensor, then unscrew it from the front of the transmission housing. Place a container beneath the sensor as it is unscrewed, as there will be fluid spillage.

**32** Unplug the sensor wiring at the connector. Note the routing of the sensor wiring and carefully pull it clear. Remove the sensor from the car.

#### Refitting

**33** Smear some clean automatic transmission fluid on the sensor O-ring seal, locate the sensor in position and tighten to the specified torque.

**34** The remainder of the refitting procedure is a reversal of removal, but refill the transmission with fresh fluid as described in Section 2.

### *Gear shift position sensor*

#### Removal

**35** Remove the plastic cover panel from the top of the engine, then refer to Chapter 5A and remove the battery.

**36** Refer to Chapter 4A and remove the air cleaner assembly and inlet ducting.

**37** Unbolt and remove the battery tray and detach the air cleaner bracket.

**38** Unplug the transmission main wiring connector(s) on the top of the transmission housing. Release the harness securing clips, then undo the screws and remove the wiring harness bracket.

**39** Disconnect the selector cable from the gear shift position sensor, as described in Section 3.

**40** Remove the securing clip, undo the nut and remove the lever from the gear shift position sensor shaft **(see illustration).**

**41** Lift the dipstick tube upwards from the transmission casing and rotate it to allow the sensor to be removed.

**42** Slacken and withdraw the securing screws and lift the sensor from the top of the transmission casing **(see illustration 5.40).**

#### Refitting

**43** Refitting is a reversal of removal, noting the following points **(see illustration):**

a) *When fitting the sensor to the transmission casing, ensure that, with the sensor shaft in the Neutral position, the flats on either side of the lever are lined up with the marking cast into the top of the sensor body*

b) *Tighten all nuts and bolt to the correct torque, where specified.*

c) *On completion, adjust the selector cable as described in Section 3.*

**5.22  Transmission oil temperature sensor (arrowed)**

### 6  Kickdown switch – removal and refitting

**Note:** *On models built after 1998, the kickdown switch is incorporated into the accelerator cable assembly – refer to Chapter 4A, Section 4, for details.*

#### *Removal*

**1** The kickdown switch is located directly underneath the accelerator pedal.

**2** Before starting work, disconnect the battery negative lead (see *Disconnecting the battery*).

**3** To gain access to the switch, release the carpet from its securing clips and the surrounding trim panels.

**4** Fold up the rubber cap, then depress the retaining lugs and withdraw the kickdown switch from its holder. Unplug the wiring connector.

#### *Refitting*

**5** Refitting is a reversal of removal. If a new switch has been fitted, it is recommended that any fault codes stored in the transmission control system are erased; this operation can only be carried by a Volvo dealer using dedicated diagnostic equipment.

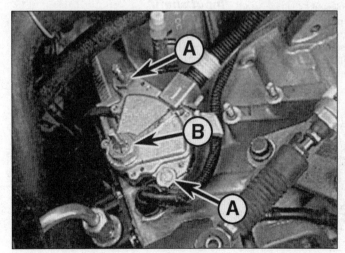

**5.40  Gear position sensor securing screws (A) and shaft lever locknut (B)**

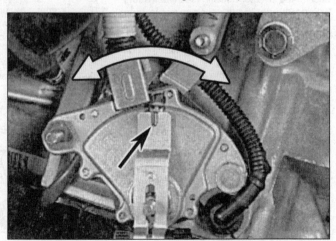

**5.43  With the sensor shaft in the Neutral position, the flats on either side of the lever must line up with the marking (arrowed) cast into the top of the sensor body**

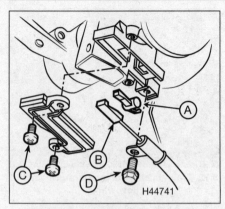

**7.3 Shiftlock cable details at ignition switch end**

A  Cable retaining clip
B  Cable end fitting
C  Cable cover screws
D  Cable securing bolt

## 7  Shiftlock system components – removal and refitting

### Cable

#### Removal

**1** If not already done, select P.
**2** Remove the driver's-side lower facia panel and the steering column lower shroud, as described in Chapters 10 and 11.
**3** Remove the cable securing bolt beneath the ignition switch, then the two cross-head screws securing the cable cover. Remove the cable from the ignition switch, recovering the cable retaining clip for refitting **(see illustration)**.
**4** Remove the centre console as described in Chapter 11.
**5** Pull the inner cable to the rear slightly, and unhook the end fitting from the lever at the base of the selector housing **(see illustration)**.
**6** Slide the cable adjuster and cable outer sideways out of the retaining bracket at the base of the selector housing.
**7** Work back along the cable, releasing it from the securing clips, and noting its routing for use when refitting. Remove the cable from the car.

#### Refitting and adjustment

**8** Refitting is a reversal of removal. Ensure that the selector lever is still in position P, and that the cable is routed as noted during removal. On completion, adjust the cable as follows.
**9** Check the operation of the shiftlock system. When engaged, it should not be possible to select any position other than P, until the ignition switch is turned to position II and the brake pedal (or the shiftlock override button) is pressed. Once the car has been driven, it should not be possible to remove the ignition key until the selector lever is placed in position P.
**10** If adjustment is necessary, turn the cable adjuster sleeve at the base of the selector housing in the required direction until correct operation is achieved **(see illustration)**.

### Solenoid/microswitch

#### Removal

**11** Remove the centre console as described in Chapter 11.
**12** Move the selector lever to position L, using the shiftlock override button if necessary to release the shiftlock system.
**13** Pull the solenoid wiring connector sideways to unclip it from the selector housing, then disconnect the two halves of the plug.
**14** Release the clip securing the solenoid to the selector housing, and remove the solenoid by squeezing together the two retaining lugs **(see illustration)**.

#### Refitting

**15** Refitting is a reversal of removal.

## 8  Electronic control unit (ECU) – removal and refitting

### Removal

**1** The automatic transmission ECU is located in the passenger compartment, behind the facia/centre console. Ensure that the ignition is switched off before starting work (take out the key). The ECU will be damaged if the wiring plug is disconnected with the ignition on. Wait a further two minutes, to ensure that the transmission main relay is fully de-energised. If the engine cooling fan is running when the engine is switched off, wait for it to stop, then wait a further two minutes.
**2** Remove the radio/cassette and/or storage bin from the centre console, as described in Chapter 12 and/or Chapter 11.
**3** Remove the ashtray from the centre console as described in Chapter 11.
**4** Unclip the trim panel from the right-hand side of the centre console.
**5** The ECU is mounted on a bracket, secured by a total of four bolts – remove the bolts, and withdraw the ECU and bracket from under the facia.
**6** Disconnect the ECU wiring connector, and remove the ECU from the car. Take care not to touch the ECU connector pins, as damage from static electricity could result.

### Refitting

**7** Refitting is a reversal of removal. If a new ECU has been fitted, it will be necessary to adapt it to the throttle position sensor signal, as follows.
**8** Switch on the ignition, but do not start the engine. Depress the accelerator pedal fully, so that the kickdown switch operates, and hold it down for five seconds.
**9** Release the accelerator pedal – the new throttle position sensor signal will now be stored in the ECU memory.
**10** Switch off the ignition.

## 9  Oil seals – renewal

### Driveshaft seals

**1** The procedure is the same as that described for the manual transmission in Chapter 7A, Section 4.

### Input shaft/ torque converter seal

**2** Remove the transmission as described in Section 10.
**3** Pull the torque converter squarely out of the transmission. Be careful, it is full of fluid.

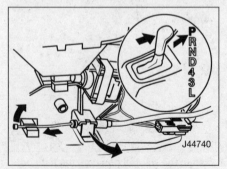

**7.5 Removing the shiftlock cable at the selector lever end**

**7.10 Shiftlock override button (A) and cable adjuster sleeve (B)**

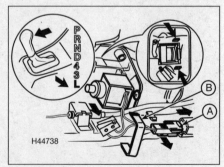

**7.14 Shiftlock solenoid/microswitch removal – wiring connector (A) and retaining clip (B)**

4  Pull or lever out the old seal. Clean the seat and inspect the seal rubbing surface on the torque converter.

5  Lubricate the new seal with clean automatic transmission fluid and fit it, lips inwards. Seat it with a piece of tube.

6  Lubricate the torque converter sleeve with clean automatic transmission fluid, and slide the converter into place, pushing it in as far as it will go.

7  Check that the torque converter is fully seated by measuring the distance from the edge of the transmission housing face to the retaining bolt tabs on the converter. The dimension should be approximately 14 mm.

8  Refit the transmission as described in Section 10.

9  Check the transmission fluid level as described in Chapter 1 on completion.

### Selector shaft seal

10  Remove the gear shift position sensor as described in Section 5.

11  Note the fitted depth of the existing seal, then prise it from the transmission using a flat-bladed screwdriver. Take great care to avoid scoring the seal housing **(see illustration)**.

12  Coat the new seal in clean automatic transmission fluid, then press it into position using a suitable long-reach socket as a drift **(see illustration)**.

13  Refit the gearshift position sensor as described in Section 5.

### 10  Automatic transmission – removal and refitting

**Note:** *Arrangements must be made to support the engine from above to allow the subframe to be detached on the left-hand side. The best way to support the engine is with a lifting beam resting in the bonnet channels with an adjustable jib appropriately placed. Trolley jacks and the help of an assistant will also be required throughout the procedure.*

### Removal

1  Park the car on a level surface and apply the handbrake.

2  Move the gear selector lever to N (neutral).

3  Refer to Chapter 5A and remove the battery, then undo the bolts and remove the battery tray.

4  Refer to Chapter 4A and remove the air cleaner assembly and all relevant inlet ducting around the left-hand side of the engine.

5  Disconnect the selector cable at the transmission end as described in Section 3.

6  Unplug the transmission wiring harness connectors on top of the transmission casing.

7  Remove the cable clamps securing the wiring harness and earth lead.

8  Remove the fluid dipstick tube and seal the opening.

9  Refer to Chapter 5A and remove the starter motor.

**9.11  Prising out the selector shaft oil seal**

**9.12  Press the new seal into position using a suitable long-reach socket as a drift**

10  Undo all the transmission-to-engine retaining bolts that are accessible from above.

11  Position a lifting beam above the engine and attach to the lifting eyelets at the left and right-hand side of the engine. Adjust the height of the jib so that the beam just takes the combined weight of the engine and transmission from the front, rear and left-hand mountings.

12  Remove the splash guard under the radiator and, where applicable, the large splash guard under the engine.

13  Referring to Chapter 8, disconnect both driveshafts from the transmission, leaving them connected at the steering knuckle end. Tie the driveshafts back away from the transmission.

14  Ensure that the engine is securely supported by the lifting beam, then with reference to Chapter 2A, unbolt the left hand engine/transmission mounting from the bodywork and transmission casing. Stabilise the engine and transmission, adjusting the height of the lifting beam jib if necessary, then unbolt the front and rear engine mountings from the engine/transmission crossmember.

15  Unbolt and remove the engine/transmission crossmember from the underside of the engine compartment.

16  Unbolt the earth strap from the transmission.

17  Slacken the unions and disconnect the transmission fluid cooler pipes from the front and underside of the transmission. Cover or seal the disconnected pipes and unions.

18  Rotate the crankshaft, using a socket on the pulley nut, until one of the torque converter-to-driveplate retaining bolts becomes accessible through the opening on the rear facing side of the engine. The bolts are Torx type, size TX50. Working through the opening, undo the bolt. Rotate the crankshaft as necessary and remove the remaining five bolts in the same way. Note that new bolts will be required for refitting.

19  Lower the engine and transmission by adjusting the height of the lifting beam jib, until sufficient clearance exists to enable the transmission to be withdrawn.

20  Position a sturdy trolley jack beneath the transmission. Take care to position the jack head so that the transmission sump cannot be

damaged during removal; the sump is fragile and should not be allowed to bear any load.

21  Make a final check to ensure that all electrical wiring has been disconnected from the transmission and ensure that all fluid pipes are secured away from the transmission.

22  Ensure that the engine is securely supported from above, then undo the remaining bolts securing the transmission to the engine. Withdraw the transmission squarely off the engine dowels making sure that the torque converter remains in position on the transmission. Use the access hole in the transmission housing to hold the converter in place. Move the jack with transmission so that it supports the weight of the unit as it is withdrawn from the engine.

23  Lower the jack and remove the transmission unit from under the car.

### Refitting

24  Before refitting the transmission, flush out the fluid cooler with fresh transmission fluid. To do this, attach a hose to the upper union, pour ATF through the hose and collect it in a container positioned beneath the return hose.

25  Clean the contact surfaces on the torque converter and driveplate, and the transmission and engine mating faces. Lightly lubricate the torque converter guide projection and the engine/transmission locating dowels with grease.

26  Check that the torque converter is fully seated by measuring the distance from the edge of the transmission housing face to the retaining bolt tabs on the converter. The dimension should be approximately 14 mm.

27  Using a trolley jack as a support (as described for the removal procedure), manoeuvre the transmission squarely into position and engage it with the engine guide bushes. Ensure that the guide bushes have engaged correctly with the corresponding holes on the transmission bellhousing, before refitting the transmission-to-engine securing bolts. Refit the lower bolts securing the transmission to the engine and tighten them lightly, to hold the transmission in place.

28  Insert the remainder of the transmission-to-engine securing bolts. Tighten all the bolts progressively and in a diagonal sequence to

the specified torque, to ensure that the transmission is drawn squarely onto the engine.

**29** Attach the torque converter to the driveplate using new securing bolts. Rotate the crankshaft for access to the bolts as was done for removal, then rotate the torque converter by means of the access hole in the transmission housing. Fit and tighten all the bolts hand-tight first of all, but then tighten again to the specified torque.

**30** The remainder of the transmission refitting procedure is a reversal of removal. Tighten all nuts and bolts to the correct torque, where specified, and on completion adjust the selector cable with reference to Section 3. Finally, check and if necessary refill or top-up the automatic transmission fluid level.

## 11 Automatic transmission – fault diagnosis

**1** The automatic transmission electronic control system incorporates an on-board diagnostic facility as an aid to fault-finding and system testing. The diagnostic system is a feature of the electronic control unit (ECU) which continually monitors the system components and their operation. Should a fault occur, the ECU stores in memory a series of signals (or fault codes) for subsequent read-out. It also illuminates the warning light located in the instrument panel.

**2** Fault code retrieval involves the use of dedicated diagnostic equipment, and so can only be carried out by a Volvo dealer or other specialist.

# Chapter 8
# Driveshafts

## Contents

## Degrees of difficulty

| | | | | |
|---|---|---|---|---|
| **Easy,** suitable for novice with little experience  | **Fairly easy,** suitable for beginner with some experience  | **Fairly difficult,** suitable for competent DIY mechanic | **Difficult,** suitable for experienced DIY mechanic | **Very difficult,** suitable for expert DIY or professional |

## Specifications

### Lubrication (overhaul only – see text)

Specified type of grease:
| | |
|---|---|
| Turbo engines . . . . . . . . . . . . . . . . . . . . . . . . . . . . . . . . . . . . . . . . . . | Volvo number 1161429-4* |
| All other engines: | |
|   Manual transmission models: | |
|     Outer joint and right-hand inner joint . . . . . . . . . . . . . . . . . . . | Volvo number 1161029-2* |
|     Left-hand inner joint . . . . . . . . . . . . . . . . . . . . . . . . . . . . . . . . . | Lubricated by transmission oil – no grease required |
|   Automatic transmission models: | |
|     Outer joint . . . . . . . . . . . . . . . . . . . . . . . . . . . . . . . . . . . . . . . | Volvo number 1161429-4* |
|     Inner joint . . . . . . . . . . . . . . . . . . . . . . . . . . . . . . . . . . . . . . . . | Volvo number 1161029-2* |
| Amount per joint: | |
|   Turbo engines . . . . . . . . . . . . . . . . . . . . . . . . . . . . . . . . . . . . . . | 120 gm |
|   All other engines . . . . . . . . . . . . . . . . . . . . . . . . . . . . . . . . . . . . | 80 gm |

*\* See your Volvo dealer for details*

### Torque wrench settings

| | Nm | lbf ft |
|---|---|---|
| Hub nut: | | |
|   Pre-1998 model year . . . . . . . . . . . . . . . . . . . . . . . . . . . . . . . . . | 240 | 177 |
|   1998 model year onwards: | | |
|     Stage 1 . . . . . . . . . . . . . . . . . . . . . . . . . . . . . . . . . . . . . . . . . | 120 | 89 |
|     Stage 2 . . . . . . . . . . . . . . . . . . . . . . . . . . . . . . . . . . . . . . . . . | Angle-tighten a further 60° | |
| Left-hand driveshaft inner gaiter retaining plate bolts . . . . . . . . . . . . | 25 | 18 |
| Roadwheel nuts . . . . . . . . . . . . . . . . . . . . . . . . . . . . . . . . . . . . . . . | 110 | 81 |
| Support bearing bracket bolts – turbo engine . . . . . . . . . . . . . . . . . . | 25 | 18 |

## 1  General information

Drive is transmitted from the differential to the front wheels by means of two solid-steel driveshafts of unequal length. Both driveshafts are splined at their outer ends, to accept the wheel hubs, and are secured to the hub by a large nut. Constant velocity (CV) joints are fitted to each end of the driveshafts, to ensure the smooth and efficient transmission of drive at all the angles possible as the roadwheels move up-and-down with the suspension, and as they turn from side-to-side under steering.

On non-turbo engines with manual transmission, a different inner constant velocity joint arrangement is fitted to each driveshaft. On the right-hand side, the driveshaft is splined to engage with a tripod joint, containing needle roller bearings and cups. The tripod joint is free to slide within the yoke of the joint outer member, which is splined and retained by a roll-pin to the differential sun wheel stub shaft. As on the outer joints, a flexible gaiter secured to the driveshaft and outer member protects the complete assembly. On the left-hand side, the driveshaft also engages with a tripod joint, but the yoke in which the tripod joint is free to slide is an integral part of the differential sun wheel. On this side, the gaiter is secured to the transmission casing with a retaining plate, and to a ball-bearing on the driveshaft with a

retaining clip. The bearing allows the driveshaft to turn within the gaiter, which does not revolve. The outer constant velocity joints on both driveshafts are of the ball-and-cage type.

On non-turbo engines with automatic transmission, the inner end of each driveshaft is splined to the differential side gears, and both inner and outer constant velocity joints are of the ball-and-cage type.

On all turbo engines, the inner end of each driveshaft is splined to the differential side gears, and both inner and outer constant velocity joints are of the ball-and-cage type. On the right-hand driveshaft, the inner constant velocity joint is located approximately halfway along the shaft's length, and the joint outer member is attached to the rear of the cylinder block via a support bearing and bracket.

**2.1 With the car on its wheels, remove the wheel trim/hub cap and slacken the hub nut**

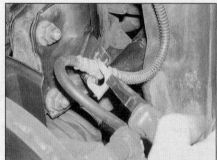

**2.5 Slide out the retaining clip and free the brake hose from its strut bracket**

**2.7 Unscrew the nuts and withdraw the upper bolt which secures the strut to the swivel hub**

## 2 Driveshafts (non-turbo engines) – removal and refitting

**Note:** *A new hub nut will be required on refitting. On some manual transmission models, the driveshaft outer joint splines are coated with sealing agent prior to refitting. Where this is the case, it is likely that a puller/extractor will be required to draw the hub assembly off of the driveshaft end on removal.*

### Removal

**1** Remove the wheel trim/hub cap (as applicable) then slacken the hub nut with the car resting on its wheels **(see illustration)**. Also slacken the wheel nuts.

**2** Chock the rear wheels of the car, firmly apply the handbrake, then jack up the front of the car and support it on axle stands. Remove the appropriate front roadwheel then undo the retaining screws/fasteners (as applicable) and remove the undershield from beneath the engine/transmission. Where necessary, also remove the wheel arch liner.

**3** Slacken and remove the hub nut and (where fitted) washer. If the nut was not slackened with the wheels on the ground (see paragraph 1), have an assistant firmly depress the brake pedal to prevent the front hub from rotating, whilst you slacken and remove the hub nut. Alternatively, a tool can be fabricated

from two lengths of steel strip (one long, one short) and a nut and bolt; the nut and bolt forming the pivot of a forked tool.

**4** Remove the anti-lock braking system (ABS) sensor from the hub as described in Chapter 9.

**5** Slide out the retaining clip(s) and free the front brake caliper hose from its bracket(s) **(see illustration)**.

**6** Extract the split pin, then slacken and remove the nut securing the steering gear track rod end balljoint to the swivel hub. Release the balljoint tapered shank using a universal balljoint separator.

**7** Slacken and remove the two nuts from the bolts securing the swivel hub to the suspension strut. Withdraw the upper bolt, but leave the lower bolt in position at this stage **(see illustration)**. Now proceed as described under the relevant sub-heading.

### Left-hand shaft – manual transmission

**8** Drain the transmission oil as described in Chapter 7A.

**9** Slacken and remove the three bolts securing the flexible gaiter retaining plate to the side of the transmission **(see illustration)**.

**10** Pull the top of the swivel hub outwards until the driveshaft tripod joint is released from its yoke; be prepared for some oil spillage as the joint is withdrawn. Be careful that the rollers on the end of the tripod do not fall off.

**11** Remove the lower bolt securing the swivel hub to the suspension strut. Taking care not to damage the driveshaft gaiters or strain the

brake hose, release the outer constant velocity joint from the hub and remove the driveshaft. Note that it is likely the joint will be a tight fit in the hub splines (see Note at the start of this Section). Try tapping the joint out of position using a hammer and a soft metal drift, whilst an assistant supports the hub assembly. If this fails to move the joint, a suitable puller/extractor will be required to draw the hub assembly off of the driveshaft end. Whilst the driveshaft is removed, support the hub assembly by refitting the bolts to the base of the strut.

### Right-hand shaft – manual transmission

**12** Undo the retaining bolts and remove the exhaust front pipe heat shield **(see illustration)**.

**13** Rotate the driveshaft until the double roll-pin, securing the inner constant velocity joint to the sun wheel shaft, is visible. Using a hammer and a 5 mm diameter pin punch, drive out the double roll-pin **(see illustration)**. Access to the pin is awkward, but can only be improved by supporting the engine and removing the engine/transmission cross-member (see paragraphs 19 and 20).

**14** Pull the top of the swivel hub outwards until the inner constant velocity joint splines are released from the sun wheel shaft. Recover the sealing ring from the sun wheel shaft and take care not to damage the dust shield fitted to the end of the driveshaft joint **(see illustration)**.

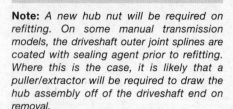

**2.9 On non-turbo models, remove the left-hand driveshaft gaiter retaining plate bolts**

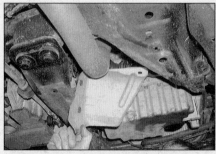

**2.12 Remove the exhaust front pipe heat shield to improve access to the right-hand driveshaft inner joint**

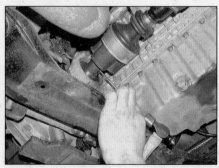

**2.13 Tap out the inner joint roll-pins using a hammer and punch**

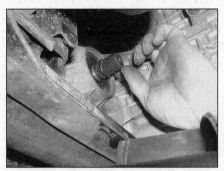

**2.14 Free the driveshaft joint from sun wheel shaft and remove the sealing ring**

**2.15 Free the outer joint from the hub assembly and remove the right-hand driveshaft from the car**

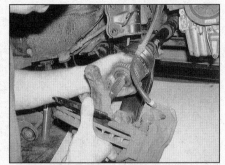

**2.25 Engage the driveshaft joint with the swivel hub then insert the strut to hub bolts**

**15** Remove the driveshaft as described in paragraph 11 **(see illustration)**.

### Left-hand shaft – automatic transmission

**16** Taking care not to damage the housing, insert a flat bar or large screwdriver in between the inner joint and the transmission, and carefully lever the joint out of position. Free the inner joint from the transmission, taking care not to damage the differential oil seal.
**17** Remove the lower bolt securing the swivel hub to the suspension strut. Taking care not to damage the driveshaft gaiters or strain the brake hose, release the outer constant velocity joint from the hub and remove the driveshaft. If necessary, tap the joint out of position using a hammer and a soft metal drift, whilst an assistant supports the hub assembly. Whilst the driveshaft is removed, support the hub assembly by refitting the bolts to the base of the strut.

### Right-hand shaft – automatic transmission

**18** Undo the retaining bolts and remove the exhaust front pipe heat shield. To improve access to the inner joint, remove the engine/transmission crossmember as follows.
**19** Attach a support bar or engine hoist to the lifting hook on the cylinder head and use it to support the weight of the engine transmission. Alternatively support the engine/transmission unit with a jack and block of wood.
**20** Slacken and remove the through-bolts

from the front and rear mountings, then undo the mounting bolts and remove the crossmember from beneath the engine/transmission. Recover the upper and lower mounting rubbers and spacers from the crossmember mountings, noting their correct fitted locations. Renew the mounting rubbers if they show signs of damage or deterioration.
**21** Remove the driveshaft as described in paragraphs 16 and 17.

### Refitting

### Left-hand shaft – manual transmission

**22** Wipe clean the side of the transmission and the outer constant velocity joint splines.
**23** Insert the tripod joint into the sun wheel yoke, keeping the driveshaft horizontal as far as possible. Align the gaiter retaining plate with its bolt holes. Refit the retaining bolts, and tighten them to the specified torque. Ensure that the gaiter is not twisted.
**24** Ensure that the driveshaft outer constant velocity joint and hub splines are clean and dry. If locking compound was present on removal, apply a coat of locking fluid (Volvo recommend sealing agent 1161075-5 – available from your Volvo dealer) to the splines of the driveshaft. On all other models, apply a thin film of grease to the driveshaft splines.
**25** Move the top of the swivel hub inwards, at the same time engaging the driveshaft with the hub **(see illustration)**.
**26** Slide the hub fully onto the driveshaft splines, then insert the suspension strut mounting bolts and fit the nuts. Tighten both nuts by hand, then tighten them to the specified torque (see Chapter 10 Specifications).
**27** Fit the washer (where fitted) and new hub nut, tightening it by hand only at this stage **(see illustration)**.
**28** Reconnect the steering track rod balljoint to the swivel hub, then tighten its retaining nut to the specified torque (see Chapter 10 Specifications) and secure it in position with a new split pin.
**29** Refit the ABS sensor to the hub as described in Chapter 9, then locate the brake

hose in its bracket(s) and secure it in position with the retaining clip(s).
**30** On pre-1998 model year cars, using the method employed during removal to prevent the hub from rotating, tighten the hub nut to the specified torque. Alternatively, lightly tighten the nut at this stage and tighten it to the specified torque once the car is resting on its wheels again.
**31** On cars from 1998 model year onwards, using the method employed during removal to prevent the hub from rotating, tighten the hub nut to the specified Stage 1 torque setting, then angle-tighten it further through the specified Stage 2 angle. It is recommended that an angle-measuring gauge is used during the final stages of the tightening, to ensure accuracy. If a gauge is not available, use white paint to make alignment marks between the nut and hub prior to tightening; the marks can then be used to check that the nut has been rotated through the correct angle. Alternatively, lightly tighten the nut at this stage and tighten once the car is resting on its wheels again.
**32** On all models, check that the hub rotates freely, then refit the engine undershield and wheel arch liner.
**33** Refit the roadwheel, then lower the car to the ground and tighten the roadwheel nuts to the specified torque. If not already having done so, also tighten the hub nut to the specified torque or torque/angle (as applicable) **(see illustrations)**.
**34** Refill the transmission with the specified

**2.27 Fit the new hub nut and lightly tighten**

**2.33a Tighten the hub nut to the specified torque . . .**

**2.33b . . . then, where applicable, tighten further through the Stage 2 angle**

type and amount of oil, and check the level using the information given in Chapter 1.

### Right-hand shaft – manual transmission

35 Before installing the driveshaft, examine the differential oil seal for signs of damage or deterioration and, if necessary, renew it, as described in Chapter 7A, Section 4. It is highly recommended that the seal is renewed, regardless of its apparent condition.

36 Ensure that the inner constant velocity joint and sun wheel shaft splines are clean and dry then fit the sealing ring to the shaft. Ensure the dust shield is correctly fitted to the driveshaft inner joint then engage the driveshaft splines with those of the sun wheel shaft. Make sure that the roll-pin holes are correctly aligned then slide on the driveshaft **(see illustration)**.

37 Drive in the roll-pins with their slots 180° apart, then seal the ends of the pins with sealing compound (Volvo recommend the use of sealing agent 1161058-1 – available from your Volvo dealer) **(see illustrations)**.

38 If the crossmember was removed, ensure the upper and lower mounting rubbers and the spacers are correctly fitted to the engine/transmission crossmember holes, then manoeuvre the crossmember into position (refer to Chapter 2A or 2B if in doubt). Refit the mounting bolts, tightening them to the specified torque, then refit the through-bolts to the engine/transmission mountings. Remove the support bar/hoist/jack (as applicable) and rock the engine to settle it in position. Tighten the engine/transmission rear

**2.37a Tap the roll-pins fully into position . . .**

**2.36 Engage the inner joint with the sun wheel, making sure the roll-pin holes are correctly aligned**

mounting through-bolt to the specified torque setting, then tighten the front mounting through-bolt to the specified torque.

39 Refit the exhaust heat shield to the cylinder block, and tighten its retaining bolts to the specified torque (Chapter 4C).

40 Carry out the procedures described in paragraphs 24 to 33. On completion check and, if necessary, top-up the transmission oil level as described in Chapter 1.

### Left-hand shaft – automatic transmission

41 Before installing the driveshaft, examine the differential oil seal for signs of damage or deterioration and, if necessary, renew it, as described in Chapter 7A, Section 4. It is highly recommended that the seal is renewed, regardless of its apparent condition. Also inspect the inner joint circlip for signs of damage and renew if necessary.

42 Thoroughly clean the driveshaft splines, and the apertures in the transmission and hub assembly. Apply a thin film of grease to the oil seal lips, and to the driveshaft splines and shoulders. Check that all gaiter clips are securely fastened.

43 Offer up the driveshaft, and locate the inner joint splines with those of the differential sun wheel, taking great care not to damage the oil seal. Push the joint fully into position and check that it is securely retained by the circlip.

44 Carry out the procedures described in paragraphs 25 to 33. On completion check and, if necessary, top-up the transmission fluid level as described in Chapter 1.

**2.37b . . . then seal each end of the pin with a smear of sealing compound**

### Right-hand shaft – automatic transmission

45 Refit the driveshaft to the transmission as described in paragraphs 41 to 43.

46 Refit the engine/transmission crossmember as described in paragraphs 38 and 39.

47 Carry out the procedures described in paragraphs 25 to 33. On completion check and, if necessary, top-up the transmission fluid level as described in Chapter 1.

### 3 Driveshafts (turbo engines) – removal and refitting

**Note:** *A new hub nut will be required on refitting.*

### *Removal*

#### Right-hand shaft

1 Remove the wheel trim/hub cap (as applicable) then slacken the hub nut with the car resting on its wheels **(see illustration 2.1)**. Also slacken the wheel nuts.

2 Chock the rear wheels of the car, firmly apply the handbrake, then jack up the front of the car and support it on axle stands. Remove the appropriate front roadwheel then undo the retaining screws/fasteners (as applicable) and remove the undershield from beneath the engine/transmission. Where necessary, also remove the wheel arch liner.

3 Slacken and remove the hub nut and (where fitted) washer. If the nut was not slackened with the wheels on the ground (see paragraph 1), have an assistant firmly depress the brake pedal to prevent the front hub from rotating, whilst you slacken and remove the hub nut. Alternatively, a tool can be fabricated from two lengths of steel strip (one long, one short) and a nut and bolt; the nut and bolt forming the pivot of a forked tool.

4 Remove the anti-lock braking system (ABS) sensor from the hub as described in Chapter 9.

5 Slide out the retaining clip(s) and free the front brake caliper hose from its bracket(s) **(see illustration 2.5)**.

6 Extract the split pin, then slacken and remove the nut securing the steering gear track rod end balljoint to the swivel hub. Release the balljoint tapered shank using a universal balljoint separator.

7 Slacken and remove the two nuts from the bolts securing the swivel hub to the suspension strut. Withdraw the upper bolt, but leave the lower bolt in position at this stage **(see illustration 2.7)**.

8 Support the driveshaft assembly, then slacken and remove the retaining bolts and remove the support bearing bracket clamp.

9 Carefully free the inner end of the driveshaft from the transmission, taking care not to damage the oil seal, and position it clear.

10 Remove the lower bolt securing the swivel hub to the suspension strut. Taking care not to damage the driveshaft gaiters or strain the brake hose, release the outer constant

velocity joint from the hub and remove the driveshaft. If necessary, tap the joint out of position using a hammer and a soft metal drift, whilst an assistant supports the hub assembly. Whilst the driveshaft is removed, support the hub assembly by refitting the bolts to the base of the strut.

### Left-hand shaft

**11** Remove the wheel trim/hub cap (as applicable) then slacken the hub nut with the car resting on its wheels **(see illustration 2.1)**. Also slacken the wheel nuts.

**12** Chock the rear wheels of the car, firmly apply the handbrake, then jack up the front of the car and support it on axle stands. Remove the appropriate front roadwheel then undo the retaining screws/fasteners (as applicable) and remove the undershield from beneath the engine/transmission. Where necessary, also remove the wheel arch liner.

**13** Slacken and remove the hub nut and (where fitted) washer. If the nut was not slackened with the wheels on the ground (see paragraph 1), have an assistant firmly depress the brake pedal to prevent the front hub from rotating, whilst you slacken and remove the hub nut. Alternatively, a tool can be fabricated from two lengths of steel strip (one long, one short) and a nut and bolt; the nut and bolt forming the pivot of a forked tool.

**14** Remove the anti-lock braking system (ABS) sensor from the hub as described in Chapter 9.

**15** Slide out the retaining clip(s) and free the front brake caliper hose from its bracket(s) **(see illustration 2.5)**.

**16** Extract the split pin, then slacken and remove the nut securing the steering gear track rod end balljoint to the swivel hub. Release the balljoint tapered shank using a universal balljoint separator.

**17** Slacken and remove the two nuts from the bolts securing the swivel hub to the suspension strut. Withdraw the upper bolt, but leave the lower bolt in position at this stage **(see illustration 2.7)**.

**18** Taking care not to damage the housing, insert a flat bar or large screwdriver in between the inner joint and the transmission, and carefully lever the joint out of position. Free the inner joint from the transmission taking care not to damage the differential oil seal.

**19** Remove the lower bolt securing the swivel hub to the suspension strut. Taking care not to damage the driveshaft gaiters or strain the brake hose, release the outer constant velocity joint from the hub and remove the driveshaft. If necessary, tap the joint out of position using a hammer and a soft metal drift, whilst an assistant supports the hub assembly. Whilst the driveshaft is removed, support the hub assembly by refitting the bolts to the base of the strut.

### Refitting

### Right-hand shaft

**20** Before installing the driveshaft, examine the differential oil seal for signs of damage or

deterioration and, if necessary, renew it, as described in Chapter 7A, Section 4. It is highly recommended that the seal is renewed, regardless of its apparent condition.

**21** Thoroughly clean the driveshaft splines, and the apertures in the transmission and hub assembly. Apply a thin film of grease to the oil seal lips, and to the driveshaft splines and shoulders. Check that all gaiter clips are securely fastened.

**22** Offer up the driveshaft, and locate the inner joint splines with those of the differential sun wheel, taking great care not to damage the oil seal. Seat the support bearing in its bracket then refit the retaining clamp and tighten its bolts to the specified torque.

**23** The remainder of refitting is as described in paragraphs 27 to 34.

### Left-hand shaft

**24** Before installing the driveshaft, examine the differential oil seal for signs of damage or deterioration and, if necessary, renew it, as described in Chapter 7A, Section 4. It is highly recommended that the seal is renewed, regardless of its apparent condition. Also inspect the inner joint circlip for signs of damage and renew if necessary.

**25** Thoroughly clean the driveshaft splines, and the apertures in the transmission and hub assembly. Apply a thin film of grease to the oil seal lips, and to the driveshaft splines and shoulders. Check that all gaiter clips are securely fastened.

**26** Offer up the driveshaft, and locate the inner joint splines with those of the differential sun wheel, taking great care not to damage the oil seal. Push the joint fully into position and check that it is securely retained by the circlip.

**27** Slide the hub fully onto the driveshaft splines, then insert the suspension strut mounting bolts and fit the nuts. Tighten both nuts by hand, then tighten them to the specified torque (see Chapter 10 Specifications).

**28** Fit the washer (where fitted) and new hub nut, tightening it by hand only at this stage.

**29** Reconnect the steering track rod balljoint to the swivel hub, then tighten its retaining nut to the specified torque (see Chapter 10 Specifications) and secure it in position with a new split pin.

**30** Refit the ABS sensor to the hub as described in Chapter 9, then locate the brake

hose in its bracket(s) and secure it in position with the retaining clip(s).

**31** Using the method employed during removal to prevent the hub from rotating, tighten the hub nut to the specified Stage 1 torque setting, then angle-tighten it through the specified Stage 2 angle. It is recommended that an angle-measuring gauge is used during the final stages of the tightening, to ensure accuracy. If a gauge is not available, use white paint to make alignment marks between the nut and hub prior to tightening; the marks can then be used to check that the nut has been rotated through the correct angle. Alternatively, lightly tighten the nut at this stage and tighten once the car is resting on its wheels again.

**32** Check that the hub rotates freely then refit the undercover and inner wing cover (as applicable).

**33** Refit the roadwheel then lower the car to the ground and tighten the roadwheel nuts to the specified torque. If not already having done so, also tighten the hub nut to the specified stage 1 torque and then through the specified stage 2 angle (see paragraph 31).

**34** On completion check and, if necessary, top-up the transmission oil level as described in Chapter 1.

## 4 Driveshaft outer constant velocity joint gaiter – renewal

**1** Remove the driveshaft from the car as described in Section 2 or 3.

**2** Secure the driveshaft in a vice equipped with soft jaws, and release the gaiter retaining clips. If necessary, the retaining clips can be cut to release them.

**3** Fold back the rubber gaiter to expose the outer constant velocity joint, and scoop out the excess grease. If necessary, cut the gaiter and remove it from the shaft **(see illustration)**.

**4** Using a pair of circlip pliers, spread the joint inner member circlip, then slide the outer constant velocity joint off from the driveshaft **(see illustration)**. If necessary, tap the joint off using a hammer and suitable soft metal drift, making sure the drift contacts only the joint inner member.

**4.3 To improve access, cut the gaiter with a knife and remove it from the shaft**

**4.4 Expand the joint inner member circlip, then remove the constant velocity joint assembly from the shaft**

**4.7 Inspect the joint balls and ball tracks for signs of wear**

**5** Remove the rubber gaiter and retaining clips from the driveshaft and discard them.

**6** With the constant velocity joint removed from the driveshaft, thoroughly clean the joint using paraffin, or a suitable solvent, and dry it thoroughly. Carry out a visual inspection of the joint.

**7** Move the inner splined driving member from side-to-side, to expose each ball in turn at the top of its track **(see illustration)**. Examine the balls for cracks, flat spots, or signs of surface pitting.

**8** Inspect the ball tracks on the inner and outer members. If the tracks have widened, the balls will no longer be a tight fit. At the same time, check the ball cage windows for wear or cracking between the windows.

**9** If the constant velocity joint is found to be worn or damaged, it will be necessary to renew it. If the joint is in satisfactory condition,

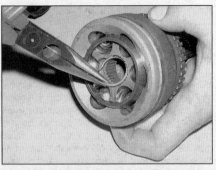

**4.12 Remove the original circlip from the constant velocity joint inner member and install the new one**

**4.13b ... and fill the gaiter with any excess**

**4.11 Tape over the splines then slide on the new gaiter complete with the inner retaining clip**

obtain a new gaiter, retaining clips, a new circlip and the correct type and quantity of grease (see Specifications); a driveshaft gaiter kit containing all the necessary components is available from Volvo.

**10** Tape over the splines on the end of the driveshaft to prevent the new gaiter being damaged.

**11** Fit the inner retaining clip onto the gaiter, then slide the new gaiter onto the shaft **(see illustration)**. Remove the tape and fit the outer retaining clip to the gaiter.

**12** Remove the circlip from the joint inner member and install the new one, making sure it is correctly located **(see illustration)**.

**13** Work the grease well into the ball tracks of the joint, then fill the gaiter with any excess **(see illustrations)**.

**14** Spread the circlip, then locate the outer joint on the driveshaft splines and slide it onto

**4.13a Work the grease well into the joint assembly ...**

**4.16 Secure the retaining clips in position by compressing their raised sections**

the shaft. Remove the circlip pliers, and tap the joint fully onto the shaft until the circlip clicks into position in the shaft groove. Pull on the joint assembly to make sure it is securely retained by the circlip.

**15** Locate the gaiter lips correctly on the driveshaft and joint outer member, and carefully lift the outer lip of the gaiter to equalise the air pressure inside.

**16** Ensure the gaiter is correctly located, then secure it in position with the retaining clips. Each clip is secured in position by compressing its raised section **(see illustration)**. In the absence of the special tool, carefully compress the clip using a pair of side-cutters, taking great care not to cut through the clip.

**17** Check that the constant velocity joint moves freely in all directions before refitting the driveshaft as described in Section 2 or 3.

## 5 Driveshaft inner constant velocity joint gaiter – renewal

**1** Remove the driveshaft as described in Section 2 or 3 and proceed as described under the relevant sub-heading.

### Non-turbo engines

#### Right-hand shaft – manual transmission

**2** Using a pair of grips, push out the gaiter metal cover stakings from the outer member recesses. Great care must be taken as the stakings are being pushed out, to avoid deforming the outer member plate.

**3** Using a pair of snips, cut the gaiter inner retaining clip, then make alignment marks between the joint outer member and the driveshaft.

**4** Using a soft metal drift, tap the gaiter metal cover off the outer member, then slide the outer member off the end of the tripod joint. As the outer member is removed, be prepared to hold the rollers in place, otherwise they may fall off the tripod ends. If necessary, secure the rollers in place using tape after removal of the outer member. **Note:** *The rollers are matched to the tripod joint stems, and it is important that they are not interchanged.*

**5** Using circlip pliers, extract the circlip securing the tripod joint to the driveshaft.

**6** Mark the position of the tripod in relation to the driveshaft, using a dab of paint or a punch, then remove the tripod joint from the shaft. If it is tight, draw the joint off the driveshaft end using a puller – make sure the legs of the puller are located behind the joint inner member, and do not contact the joint rollers **(see illustration)**. Alternatively, support the inner member of the tripod joint, and press the shaft out using a hydraulic press, again ensuring that no load is applied to the joint rollers.

**7** With the tripod joint removed, slide the gaiter off the end of the driveshaft.

**5.6 Using a puller to draw the tripod joint off from the driveshaft**

**8** Wipe clean the joint components, taking care not to remove the alignment marks made on dismantling. **Do not** use paraffin or other solvents to clean this type of joint.

**9** Examine the tripod joint, rollers and outer member for any signs of scoring or wear. Check that the rollers move smoothly on the tripod stems. If wear is evident, renew the affected components. If the joint is in satisfactory condition, obtain a new gaiter, a retaining clip and the correct type and quantity of grease (see Specifications); a driveshaft gaiter kit containing all the necessary components is available from Volvo.

**10** Tape over the driveshaft splines, then slide the inner retaining clip and gaiter onto the driveshaft **(see illustration)**.

**11** Remove the tape then, aligning the marks made on dismantling, engage the tripod joint with the driveshaft splines **(see illustration)**.

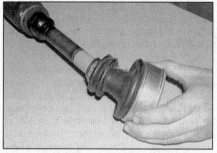

**5.10 Tape over the driveshaft splines then slide on the new gaiter complete with the inner retaining clip**

Use a hammer and soft metal drift to tap the joint onto the shaft, taking great care not to damage the driveshaft splines or joint rollers. Alternatively, support the driveshaft, and press the joint into position using a hydraulic press and suitable tubular spacer which bears only on the joint inner member.

**12** Secure the tripod joint in position with the circlip, ensuring that it is correctly located in the driveshaft groove **(see illustration)**.

**13** Evenly distribute the special grease contained in the repair kit around the tripod joint and inside the outer member **(see illustration)**. Pack the gaiter with the remainder of the grease.

**14** Slide the outer member into position over the tripod joint, aligning the marks made on removal **(see illustration)**.

**15** Slide the gaiter metal cover onto the outer member until it is flush with the plate edge.

**5.11 Align the marks made prior to removal and engage the tripod joint with the driveshaft splines**

Secure the gaiter in position by staking its metal cover into the ring plate cut-outs using a hammer and screwdriver. To prevent the outer member plate being deformed whilst doing this, support it with a suitable diameter socket inserted in between the plate and outer member **(see illustration)**.

**16** Carefully lift the inner lip of the gaiter to equalise the air pressure within, then seat the gaiter inner lip correctly in the driveshaft groove. Ensure the inner lip is correctly seated, then secure it in position with the retaining clip. The retaining clip is secured in position by compressing its raised section – in the absence of the special tool, a pair of side-cutters may be used, taking great care not to cut the clip **(see illustrations)**.

**17** Check that the constant velocity joint moves freely in all directions, then refit the driveshaft as described in Section 2 or 3.

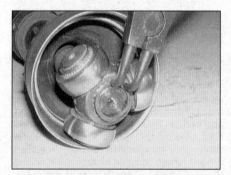

**5.12 Secure the tripod joint with the new circlip, making sure it is located in the driveshaft groove**

**5.13 Fill the joint outer member with fresh grease and coat the joint rollers**

**5.14 Engage the outer member with the tripod joint, aligning the marks made prior to removal**

**5.15 With the gaiter cover correctly positioned, stake it securely into the plate cut-outs**

**5.16a Lift the gaiter inner lip to equalise the air pressure inside . . .**

**5.16b . . . then secure the inner retaining clip in position by compressing its raised section**

## Left-hand shaft – manual transmission

**Note:** *This text assumes the gaiter and bearing are to be renewed as an assembly (this is how Volvo supply new gaiters) which requires the use of a hydraulic press. If the bearing is serviceable, it is possible leave the bearing on the driveshaft and renew the gaiter separately; the gaiter is secured to the bearing by a retaining clip (see paragraph 16).*

18 Remove the tripod joint as described in paragraphs 5 and 6.

19 Unclip the dust cover from the gaiter/bearing and slide it along the driveshaft.

20 Mark the correct fitted position of the gaiter bearing on the driveshaft, then pull/press the gaiter and bearing assembly off, using the same method as employed for tripod joint removal.

21 With the gaiter removed, slide off the dust cover and remove the gaiter retaining plate, noting which way around each one is fitted.

22 Examine the tripod joint, rollers and outer member for any signs of scoring or wear. Check that the rollers move smoothly on the tripod stems. If the joint assembly is worn, renew it.

23 Obtain a new gaiter, which is supplied complete with the small bearing. Owing to the lip-type seal used in the bearing, the bearing and gaiter must be pressed into position. If a hammer and tubular drift are used to drive the assembly onto the driveshaft, there is a risk of distorting the seal.

24 Slide the gaiter retaining plate and the new dust seal onto the driveshaft, ensuring that both components are fitted the correct way around.

25 Support the driveshaft, and press the gaiter bearing onto the shaft, using a tubular spacer which bears only on the bearing inner race. Press the bearing onto the shaft until its is correctly aligned with the mark made prior to removal (this should be approximately 150 mm from the driveshaft end).

26 Once the gaiter bearing is correctly positioned, clip the dust cover securely onto the gaiter/bearing. Check the gaiter spins freely on the shaft before proceeding.

27 Align the marks made on dismantling, and engage the tripod joint with the driveshaft splines. Use a hammer and soft metal drift to tap the joint onto the shaft, taking care not to damage the driveshaft splines or joint rollers. Alternatively, support the driveshaft, and press the joint into position using a tubular spacer which bears only on the joint inner member.

28 Secure the tripod joint in position with the circlip, ensuring that it is correctly located in the driveshaft groove.

29 Refit the driveshaft to the car as described in Section 2 or 3.

## Both shafts – automatic transmission

30 Secure the driveshaft in a vice equipped with soft jaws, and release the gaiter retaining clips. If necessary, the retaining clips can be cut to release them.

31 Fold back the rubber gaiter, then scoop out the excess grease from the joint. Make alignment marks between the joint outer member and the driveshaft using a dab of paint or a punch.

32 Carefully bend back the tabs on the outer member retaining plate, then slide the outer member off the end of the tripod joint **(see illustration)**. As the outer member is removed be prepared to hold the rollers in place, otherwise they will fall off the tripod ends. If necessary, secure the rollers in place using tape after removal of the outer member. **Note:** *The rollers are matched to the tripod joint stems, and it is important that they are not interchanged.*

33 Carry out the operations described in paragraphs 5 to 13.

34 Fit the outer retaining clip over the gaiter, then slide the outer member into position over the tripod joint, aligning the marks made on removal. Secure the outer member in position by bending down the retaining plate tabs back to their original shape.

35 Ensure that there are no sharp edges on the retaining plate and that its outer surface is free from grease then locate the gaiter lips correctly on the driveshaft and joint outer member. With the gaiter correctly seated, carefully lift its inner lip to equalise the air pressure inside.

36 Ensure the gaiter is correctly positioned then secure it in position with the retaining clips. Each clip is secured in position by compressing its raised section. In the absence of the special tool, carefully compress the clip using a pair of side-cutters taking great care not to cut through the clip.

37 Check that the constant velocity joint moves freely in all directions before refitting the driveshaft as described in Section 2 or 3.

## Turbo engines

38 Remove the inner joint from the driveshaft and renew the gaiter as described in Section 4.

## 6 Right-hand driveshaft support bearing (turbo engines) – renewal

1 Remove the driveshaft as described in Section 3.

2 Carry out the operations described in paragraphs 2 to 6 of Section 4 and remove the **inner** constant velocity joint assembly and gaiter from the driveshaft. If the gaiter appears serviceable it can be re-used, although it is recommended that a new one is fitted on reassembly. Whilst the joint is removed, it is recommended that it should be cleaned and checked for wear (see Section 4).

3 Remove all traces of dirt and corrosion from the driveshaft, then extract the circlip securing the support bearing in position.

4 Draw the bearing off from the inner end of the driveshaft using a suitable bearing puller. Alternatively, securely support the bearing

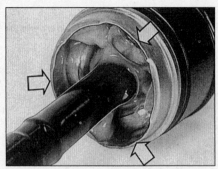

**5.32 Bend up the retaining plate tabs (arrowed) using pliers**

and press/tap the driveshaft out from the bearing.

5 Ensure the inner end of the driveshaft is clean and free from corrosion, and lubricate it with a smear of oil.

6 Securely support the inner race of the new bearing, then locate the driveshaft end squarely in the bearing inner race. Insert a soft metal drift in through the centre of the constant velocity joint inner member, so that it bears against the driveshaft and not the joint inner member, then press/tap the driveshaft into position until the bearing is in contact with the constant velocity joint.

7 Ensure the bearing is correctly fitted then secure it position with the circlip, making sure it is correctly located in the driveshaft groove.

8 Reassembly the driveshaft as described in paragraphs 11 to 17 of Section 4, then refit the driveshaft as described in Section 3.

## 7 Driveshaft overhaul – general information

1 If any of the checks described in Chapter 1 reveal wear in any driveshaft joint, first remove the roadwheel trim or centre cap (as appropriate) and check that the hub nut is tight. If the nut is loose, obtain a new one and tighten it to the specified torque or specified Stage 1 torque and then through the specified Stage 2 angle (as applicable). If the nut is tight, refit the centre cap/trim and repeat the check on the other hub nut.

2 Road test the car, and listen for a metallic clicking from the front as the car is driven slowly in a circle on full-lock. If a clicking noise is heard, this indicates wear in the outer constant velocity joint. This means that the joint must be renewed; reconditioning is not possible.

3 If vibration, consistent with road speed, is felt through the car when accelerating, there is a possibility of wear in the inner constant velocity joints. On turbo engines, also check that the support bearing on the right-hand driveshaft is in good condition.

4 To check the joints for wear, remove the driveshafts, then dismantle them as described in Section 4 or 5; if any wear or free play is found, the affected joint must be renewed.

# Chapter 9
# Braking system

## Contents

## Degrees of difficulty

| **Easy,** suitable for novice with little experience  | **Fairly easy,** suitable for beginner with some experience  | **Fairly difficult,** suitable for competent DIY mechanic | **Difficult,** suitable for experienced DIY mechanic | **Very difficult,** suitable for expert DIY or professional |
|---|---|---|---|---|

## Specifications

### Front brakes

| | |
|---|---|
| Type . . . . . . . . . . . . . . . . . . . . . . . . . . . . . . . . . . . . . . . . . . . . . . . . . . . . . | Disc, with single-piston sliding caliper |
| Disc diameter: | |
|   Up to 1997 . . . . . . . . . . . . . . . . . . . . . . . . . . . . . . . . . . . . . . . . . . | 256 mm |
|   1998 onwards . . . . . . . . . . . . . . . . . . . . . . . . . . . . . . . . . . . . . . . . | 281 mm |
| Disc thickness: | |
|   New . . . . . . . . . . . . . . . . . . . . . . . . . . . . . . . . . . . . . . . . . . . . . . . | 24.0 mm |
|   Minimum . . . . . . . . . . . . . . . . . . . . . . . . . . . . . . . . . . . . . . . . . . . . | 21.5 mm* |
| Maximum disc run-out . . . . . . . . . . . . . . . . . . . . . . . . . . . . . . . . . . . . . | 0.04 mm |
| Brake pad friction material thickness: | |
|   New . . . . . . . . . . . . . . . . . . . . . . . . . . . . . . . . . . . . . . . . . . . . . . . | 9.4 mm |
|   Minimum . . . . . . . . . . . . . . . . . . . . . . . . . . . . . . . . . . . . . . . . . . . . | 2.0 mm |

* If new pads are to be fitted and the disc thickness is 22.1 mm or less then Volvo state that the discs should also renewed.

### Rear disc brakes

| | |
|---|---|
| Type . . . . . . . . . . . . . . . . . . . . . . . . . . . . . . . . . . . . . . . . . . . . . . . . . . . | Disc, with single-piston sliding caliper |
| Disc diameter . . . . . . . . . . . . . . . . . . . . . . . . . . . . . . . . . . . . . . . . . . . . | 260 mm |
| Disc thickness: | |
|   New . . . . . . . . . . . . . . . . . . . . . . . . . . . . . . . . . . . . . . . . . . . . . . . | 10.0 mm |
|   Minimum thickness . . . . . . . . . . . . . . . . . . . . . . . . . . . . . . . . . . . . | 8.4 mm* |
| Maximum disc run-out . . . . . . . . . . . . . . . . . . . . . . . . . . . . . . . . . . . . . | 0.04 mm |
| Brake pad friction material thickness: | |
|   New . . . . . . . . . . . . . . . . . . . . . . . . . . . . . . . . . . . . . . . . . . . . . . . | 9.4 mm |
|   Minimum . . . . . . . . . . . . . . . . . . . . . . . . . . . . . . . . . . . . . . . . . . . . | 2.0 mm |

* If new pads are to be fitted and the disc thickness is 8.9 mm or less then Volvo state that the discs should also renewed.

## Torque wrench settings

| | Nm | lbf ft |
|---|---|---|
| ABS components: | | |
|    Front wheel sensor bolts | 25 | 18 |
|    Rear wheel sensor bolts | 55 | 41 |
| Brake pedal: | | |
|    Mounting bracket nuts/bolts | 25 | 18 |
|    Pivot bolt nut | 45 | 33 |
| Brake pipe unions: | | |
|    Bolts: | | |
|       Front brake caliper | 15 | 11 |
|       Rear brake caliper | 29 | 21 |
|    Nuts | 14 | 10 |
| Front brake caliper: | | |
|    Guide pin bolts | 35 | 26 |
|    Mounting bracket bolts | 100 | 74 |
| Handbrake cable guide bolts | 25 | 18 |
| Handbrake lever bolts | 25 | 18 |
| Master cylinder mounting nuts | 25 | 18 |
| Pressure-regulating valve bolt | 25 | 18 |
| Rear brake caliper: | | |
|    Guide pin bolts | 33 | 24 |
|    Mounting bolt | 55 | 41 |
| Roadwheel nuts | 110 | 81 |
| Vacuum servo unit nuts | 25 | 18 |

## 1 General information

The braking system is of the servo-assisted, dual-circuit hydraulic type. The arrangement of the hydraulic system is such that each circuit operates one front and one rear brake from a tandem master cylinder. Under normal circumstances, both circuits operate in unison. However, in the event of hydraulic failure in one circuit, full braking force will still be available at two wheels.

All models are equipped with disc brakes all round as standard, with anti-lock brakes (ABS) being fitted as standard on all models (refer to Section 18 for further information on ABS operation).

The disc brakes are actuated by single-piston sliding type calipers, which ensure that equal pressure is applied to each disc pad. The rear brake calipers incorporate the handbrake mechanisms which provides an independent mechanical means of rear brake application.

A pressure-regulating valve is situated in the hydraulic circuit to each rear brake. The valves limit the hydraulic pressure applied to the rear brakes to help to prevent rear wheel lock-up during emergency braking.

*Caution: When servicing any part of the system, work carefully and methodically; also observe scrupulous cleanliness when overhauling any part of the hydraulic system. Always renew components (in axle sets, where applicable) if in doubt about their condition, and use only genuine Volvo replacement parts, or at least those of known good quality. Note the warnings given in 'Safety first!' and at relevant points in this Chapter concerning the dangers of asbestos dust and hydraulic fluid.*

## 2 Hydraulic system – bleeding

*Warning: Hydraulic fluid is poisonous; wash off immediately and thoroughly in the case of skin contact, and seek immediate medical advice if any fluid is swallowed or gets into the eyes. Certain types of hydraulic fluid are inflammable, and may ignite when allowed into contact with hot components; when servicing any hydraulic system, it is safest to assume that the fluid IS inflammable, and to take precautions against the risk of fire as though it is petrol that is being handled. Hydraulic fluid is also an effective paint stripper, and will attack plastics; if any is spilt, it should be washed off immediately, using copious quantities of fresh water. Finally, it is hygroscopic (it absorbs moisture from the air) – old fluid may be contaminated and unfit for further use. When topping-up or renewing the fluid, always use the recommended type, and ensure that it comes from a freshly-opened sealed container.*

### General

1 The correct operation of any hydraulic system is only possible after removing all air from the components and circuit; this is achieved by bleeding the system.

2 During the bleeding procedure, add only clean, unused hydraulic fluid of the recommended type; never re-use fluid that has already been bled from the system. Ensure that sufficient fluid is available before starting work.

3 If there is any possibility of incorrect fluid being already in the system, the brake components and circuit must be flushed completely with uncontaminated, correct fluid. It may also be necessary to renew the seals fitted to the various components.

4 If hydraulic fluid has been lost from the system, or air has entered because of a leak, ensure that the fault is cured before proceeding further.

5 Park the car on level ground, securely chock the wheels, then release the hand-brake.

6 Check that all pipes and hoses are secure, unions tight and bleed screws closed. Clean any dirt from around the bleed screws.

7 Unscrew the master cylinder reservoir cap, and top the master cylinder reservoir up to the MAX level line; refit the cap loosely, and remember to maintain the fluid level at least above the MIN level line throughout the procedure, or there is a risk of further air entering the system.

8 One-man, do-it-yourself brake bleeding kits are available from motor accessory shops. It is recommended that one of these kits is used whenever possible, as they greatly simplify the bleeding operation, and also reduce the risk of expelled air and fluid being drawn back into the system. If such a kit is not available, the basic (two-man) method must be used, which is described in detail below.

9 If a kit is to be used, prepare the car as described previously, and follow the kit manufacturer's instructions, as the procedure may vary slightly according to the type being used; generally, they are as outlined below in the relevant sub-section.

10 Whichever method is used, the same sequence must be followed (see paragraphs 11 and 12) to ensure that the removal of all air from the system.

## *Bleeding*

### Sequence

**11** If the system has been only partially disconnected, and suitable precautions were taken to minimise fluid loss, it should be necessary only to bleed that part of the system (ie, the primary or secondary circuit).

**12** If the complete system is to be bled, then it should be done working in the following sequence (ignition off):
a) *Right-hand rear brake.*
b) *Left-hand rear brake.*
c) *Right-hand front brake.*
d) *Left-hand front brake.*

### Basic (two-man) method

**13** Collect a clean glass jar, a suitable length of plastic or rubber tubing which is a tight fit over the bleed screw, and a ring spanner to fit the screw. The help of an assistant will also be required. Make sure the spanner is a good fit on the bleed screw – the screw may be tight, and it's too easy to round-off.

**14** Remove the dust cap from the first screw in the sequence. Fit the spanner and tube to the screw, place the other end of the tube in the jar, and pour in sufficient fluid to cover the end of the tube.

**15** Ensure that the master cylinder reservoir fluid level is maintained at least above the MIN level line throughout the procedure.

**16** Have the assistant fully depress the brake pedal several times to build-up pressure, then maintain it on the final downstroke.

**17** While pedal pressure is maintained, unscrew the bleed screw (approximately one turn) and allow the compressed fluid and air to flow into the jar. The assistant should maintain pedal pressure, following it down to the floor if necessary, and should not release it until instructed to do so. When the flow stops, tighten the bleed screw again, have the assistant release the pedal slowly, and recheck the reservoir fluid level.

**18** Repeat the steps given in paragraphs 16 and 17 until the fluid emerging from the bleed screw is free from air bubbles. If the master cylinder has been drained and refilled, and air is being bled from the first screw in the sequence, allow approximately five seconds between cycles for the master cylinder passages to refill.

**19** When no more air bubbles appear, tighten the bleed screw to the specified torque, remove the tube and spanner, and refit the dust cap. Do not overtighten the bleed screw.

**20** Repeat the procedure on the remaining screws in the sequence, until all air is removed from the system and the brake pedal feels firm again. On completion, lower the car to the ground.

### Using a one-way valve kit

**21** As their name implies, these kits consist of a length of tubing with a one-way valve fitted, to prevent expelled air and fluid being drawn back into the system; some kits include a translucent container, which can be positioned so that the air bubbles can be more easily seen flowing from the end of the tube.

**22** The kit is connected to the bleed screw, which is then opened **(see illustration)**. The user returns to the driver's seat, depresses the brake pedal with a smooth, steady stroke, and slowly releases it; this is repeated until the expelled fluid is clear of air bubbles.

**23** Note that these kits simplify work so much that it is easy to forget the master cylinder reservoir fluid level; ensure that this is maintained at least above the MIN level line at all times.

### Using a pressure-bleeding kit

**24** These kits are usually operated by the reservoir of pressurised air contained in the spare tyre. However, note that it will probably be necessary to reduce the pressure to a lower level than normal; refer to the instructions supplied with the kit.

**25** By connecting a pressurised, fluid-filled container to the master cylinder reservoir, bleeding can be carried out simply by opening each screw in turn (in the specified sequence), and allowing the fluid to flow out until no more air bubbles can be seen in the expelled fluid.

**26** This method has the advantage that the large reservoir of fluid provides an additional safeguard against air being drawn into the system during bleeding.

**27** Pressure-bleeding is particularly effective when bleeding difficult systems, or when bleeding the complete system at the time of routine fluid renewal.

### All methods

**28** When bleeding is complete, and firm pedal feel is restored, wash off any spilt fluid, tighten the bleed screws, and refit their dust caps.

**29** Check the hydraulic fluid level in the master cylinder reservoir, and top-up if necessary (see *Weekly checks*).

**30** Discard any hydraulic fluid that has been bled from the system; it will not be fit for re-use.

**31** Check the feel of the brake pedal. If it feels at all spongy, air must still be present in the system, and further bleeding is required. Failure to bleed satisfactorily after a reasonable repetition of the bleeding procedure may be due to worn master cylinder seals.

**2.22 Bleeding a front brake caliper using a one-way valve kit**

---

### 3 Hydraulic pipes and hoses – renewal

**Note:** *Before starting work, refer to the note at the beginning of Section 2 concerning the dangers of hydraulic fluid.*

**1** If any pipe or hose is to be renewed, minimise fluid loss by first removing the master cylinder reservoir cap, then tightening it down onto a piece of polythene to obtain an airtight seal. Alternatively, flexible hoses can be sealed, if required, using a proprietary brake hose clamp; metal brake pipe unions can be plugged (if care is taken not to allow dirt into the system) or capped immediately they are disconnected. Place a wad of rag under any union that is to be disconnected, to catch any spilt fluid.

**2** If a flexible hose is to be disconnected, unscrew the brake pipe union nut before removing the spring clip which secures the hose to its mounting bracket.

**3** To unscrew the union nuts, it is preferable to obtain a brake pipe spanner of the correct size; these are available from most large motor accessory shops **(see illustration)**. Failing this, a close-fitting open-ended spanner will be required, though if the nuts are tight or corroded, their flats may be rounded-off if the spanner slips. In such a case, a self-locking wrench is often the only way to unscrew a stubborn union, but it follows that the pipe and the damaged nuts must be renewed on reassembly. Always clean a union and surrounding area before disconnecting it. If disconnecting a component with more than one union, make a careful note of the connections before disturbing any of them.

**4** If a brake pipe is to be renewed, it can be obtained, cut to length and with the union nuts and end flares in place, from Volvo dealers. All that is then necessary is to bend it to shape, following the line of the original, before fitting it to the car. Alternatively, most motor accessory shops can make up brake pipes from kits, but this requires very careful measurement of the original, to ensure that the new one is of the correct length. The

**3.3 Using a brake pipe spanner to unscrew a union nut**

**4.2a Slacken and remove the lower guide pin bolt . . .**

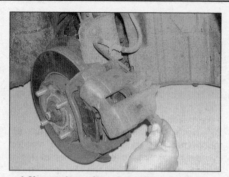

**4.2b . . . then pivot the caliper upwards and away from the mounting bracket**

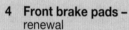
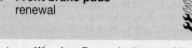

**4.3a Remove the brake pads from the mounting bracket . . .**

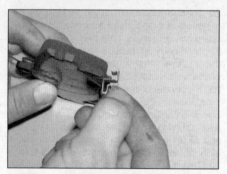

**4.3b . . . and unclip the wear indicator from the inner pad**

safest answer is usually to take the original to the shop as a pattern.

5 On refitting, do not overtighten the union nuts. It is not necessary to exercise brute force to obtain a sound joint.

6 Ensure that the pipes and hoses are correctly routed, with no kinks, and that they are secured in the clips or brackets provided. After fitting, remove the polythene from the reservoir, and bleed the hydraulic system as described in Section 2. Wash off any spilt fluid, and check carefully for fluid leaks.

## 4  Front brake pads – renewal

⚠ *Warning: Renew both sets of front brake pads at the same time – never renew the pads on only one*

**4.4 Measuring brake pad friction material thickness**

*wheel, as uneven braking may result. Note that the dust created by wear of the pads may contain asbestos, which is a health hazard. Never blow it out with compressed air, and don't inhale any of it. An approved filtering mask should be worn when working on the brakes. DO NOT use petrol or petroleum-based solvents to clean brake parts; use brake cleaner or methylated spirit only.*

1 Apply the handbrake, loosen the front wheel nuts, then jack up the front of the car and support it on axle stands. Remove the front roadwheels.

2 Slacken and remove the caliper lower guide pin bolt, then pivot the caliper away from the brake pads and mounting bracket, and tie it to the coil spring using a suitable piece of wire (see illustrations).

3 Withdraw the pads from the mounting bracket and unclip the wear indicator from the

**4.6 Check the guide pin gaiters for signs of damage and renew if split**

inner pad, noting its correct fitted location (see illustrations).

4 First measure the thickness of each brake pad's friction material (see illustration). If either pad is worn at any point to the specified minimum thickness or less, all four pads must be renewed. Also, the pads should be renewed if any are fouled with oil or grease; there is no satisfactory way of degreasing friction material, once contaminated. If any of the brake pads are worn unevenly, or are fouled with oil or grease, trace and rectify the cause before reassembly.

5 If the brake pads are still serviceable, carefully clean them using a clean, fine wire brush or similar, paying particular attention to the sides and back of the metal backing. Clean out the grooves in the friction material, and pick out any large embedded particles of dirt or debris. Carefully clean the pad locations in the caliper mounting bracket.

6 Prior to fitting the pads, check that the guide pins are free to slide easily in the caliper body bushes, and their gaiters are undamaged (see illustration). Brush the dust and dirt from the caliper and piston, but do not inhale it, as it is a health hazard. Inspect the dust seal around the piston for damage, and the piston for evidence of fluid leaks, corrosion or damage. If attention to any of these components is necessary, refer to Section 7.

7 If new brake pads are to be fitted, the caliper piston must be pushed back into the cylinder to make room for them. Either use a G-clamp or similar tool, or use suitable pieces of wood as levers. Provided that the master cylinder reservoir has not been overfilled with hydraulic fluid, there should be no spillage, but keep a careful watch on the fluid level while retracting the piston. If the fluid level rises above the MAX level line at any time, the surplus should be syphoned off or ejected via a plastic tube connected to the bleed screw (see Section 2).

⚠ *Warning: When the caliper pistons are pushed back into the calipers, the reversed fluid flow can (in rare cases) cause the master cylinder seals to turn, resulting in loss of braking. To avoid this possibility, connect a pipe to the caliper bleed screw, then open the screw as the piston is pushed back, allowing the fluid to flow into a container. The brakes will, of course, require bleeding on completion.*

8 Clip the wear indicator onto the inner pad then fit both brake pads to the caliper mounting bracket, ensuring that the friction material of each pad is against the brake disc.

9 Pivot the caliper down into position over the pads, making sure the pad anti-rattle springs are correctly positioned against the caliper body (see illustration).

10 Press down on the caliper and screw in the guide pin bolt, tightening it to the specified torque setting (see illustration).

11 Depress the brake pedal repeatedly, until

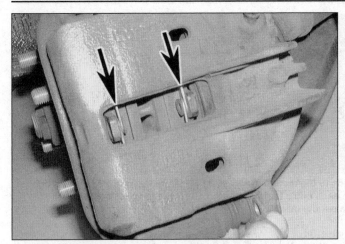

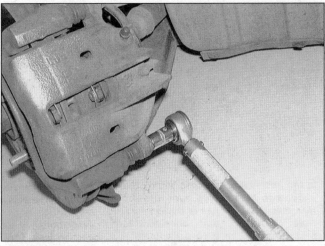

4.9 Pivot the caliper back down into position making sure the pad anti-rattle springs (arrowed) are correctly located against the caliper body

4.10 Refit the guide pin bolt and tighten it to the specified torque

the pads are pressed into firm contact with the brake disc, and normal (non-assisted) pedal pressure is restored.

**12** Repeat the above procedure on the remaining front brake caliper.

**13** Refit the roadwheels, then lower the car to the ground and tighten the roadwheel nuts to the specified torque setting.

**14** Check the hydraulic fluid level as described in *Weekly checks*.

> **HAYNES HiNT** *New pads will not give full braking efficiency until they have bedded-in. Be prepared for this, and avoid hard braking as far as possible for the first hundred miles or so after pad renewal.*

## 5 Rear brake pads – renewal

⚠️ *Warning: Renew both sets of rear brake pads at the same time – never renew the pads on only one wheel, as uneven braking may result. Note that the dust created by wear of the pads may contain asbestos, which is a health hazard. Never*

*blow it out with compressed air, and don't inhale any of it. An approved filtering mask should be worn when working on the brakes. DO NOT use petrol or petroleum-based solvents to clean brake parts; use brake cleaner or methylated spirit only.*

**Note:** *The caliper guide pin bolts must be renewed whenever they are unscrewed.*

**1** Chock the front wheels, loosen the rear wheel nuts, then jack up the rear of the car and support it on axle stands. Remove the rear wheels then fully release the handbrake.

**2** Slide out the retaining clip and free the brake hose from its bracket **(see illustration)**.

**3** Slacken and remove the caliper upper guide pin bolt, using an open-ended spanner to prevent the guide pin from rotating **(see illustration)**. Discard the guide pin bolt – a new bolt must be used on refitting.

**4** Pivot the caliper backwards until its is possible to withdraw the two brake pads from the caliper mounting bracket. Unclip the wear indicator from the inner pad noting its correct fitted location **(see illustrations)**.

**5** First measure the thickness of each brake pad's friction material **(see illustration)**. If either pad is worn at any point to the specified minimum thickness or less, **all four** pads must

5.2 Slide out the retaining clip securing the rear brake caliper hose in position . . .

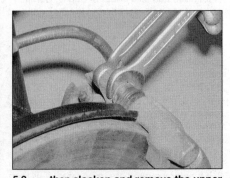

5.3 . . . then slacken and remove the upper guide pin bolt

5.4a Pivot the caliper backwards and manoeuvre the brake pads out of position

5.4b Unclip the wear indicator from the inner pad, noting its correct fitted location

5.5 Measuring rear brake pad friction material thickness

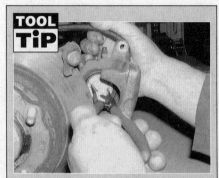

**In the absence of the special tool, the piston can be screwed back into the rear caliper using a pair of circlip pliers. Note, however, that considerable pressure may have to be applied – proper piston-retracting tools are available from motor accessory shops.**

**5.9 Fit the brake pads to the mounting bracket making sure each pad's friction material is against the disc**

**5.11 Fit the new guide pin bolt and tighten to the specified torque**

be renewed. Also, the pads should be renewed if any are fouled with oil or grease; there is no satisfactory way of degreasing friction material, once contaminated. If any of the brake pads are worn unevenly, or fouled with oil or grease, trace and rectify the cause before reassembly. New brake pads are available from Volvo dealers.

**6** If the brake pads are still serviceable, carefully clean them using a clean, fine wire brush or similar, paying particular attention to the sides and back of the metal backing. Clean out the grooves in the friction material (where applicable), and pick out any large embedded particles of dirt or debris. Carefully clean the pad locations in the caliper body/mounting bracket.

**7** Prior to fitting the pads, check that the guide pins are free to slide easily in the caliper bracket, and check that the rubber guide pin gaiters are undamaged. Brush the dust and dirt from the caliper and piston, but **do not** inhale it, as it maybe injurious to health. Inspect the dust seal around the piston for damage, and the piston for evidence of fluid leaks, corrosion or damage. If attention to any of these components is necessary, refer to Section 8.

**8** If new brake pads are to be fitted, it will be necessary to retract the piston fully into the

**6.3 Measuring brake disc thickness with a micrometer**

caliper bore, by rotating it in a clockwise direction **(see Tool Tip)**. While turning the piston, apply pressure so it is forced back into the bore. Provided that the master cylinder reservoir has not been overfilled with hydraulic fluid, there should be no spillage, but keep a careful watch on the fluid level while retracting the piston. If the fluid level rises above the MAX level line at any time, the surplus should be syphoned off, or ejected through a plastic tube connected to the bleed screw (see Section 2).

⚠️ **Warning: When the caliper pistons are pushed back into the calipers, the reversed fluid flow can (in rare cases) cause the master cylinder seals to turn, resulting in loss of braking. To avoid this possibility, connect a pipe to the caliper bleed screw, then open the screw as the piston is pushed back, allowing the fluid to flow into a container. The brakes will, of course, require bleeding on completion.**

**9** Clip the wear indicator correctly onto the inner pad then locate the pads in the mounting bracket, ensuring that each pad's friction material is against the brake disc **(see illustration)**.

**10** Slide the caliper back into position over the pads, ensuring the pad anti-rattle springs are correctly positioned against the caliper body.

**11** Press the caliper into position then install the new guide pin bolt, tightening it to the specified torque setting whilst retaining the guide pin with an open-ended spanner **(see illustration)**.

**12** Locate the brake hose in the bracket and secure it in position with the retaining clip.

**13** Depress the brake pedal repeatedly, until the pads are pressed into firm contact with the brake disc, and normal (non-assisted) pedal pressure is restored.

**14** Repeat the above procedure on the remaining rear brake caliper.

**15** Refit the roadwheels, then lower the car to the ground and tighten the wheel nuts to the specified torque setting.

**16** Check the hydraulic fluid level as described in *Weekly checks*.

**17** On completion check and, if necessary,

adjust the handbrake as described in Section 13.

> **HAYNES HiNT** *New pads will not give full braking efficiency until they have bedded-in. Be prepared for this, and avoid hard braking as far as possible for the first hundred miles or so after pad renewal.*

## 6 Brake disc – inspection, removal and refitting

**Note:** *Before starting work, refer to the note at the beginning of Section 4 concerning the dangers of asbestos dust.*

### Inspection

**Note:** *If either disc requires renewal, BOTH should be renewed at the same time, to ensure even and consistent braking. New brake pads should also be fitted.*

**1** If the front discs are to be checked, apply the handbrake, loosen the front wheel nuts, then jack up the front of the car and support it on axle stands. If the rear discs are to be checked, chock the front wheels, loosen the rear wheel nuts, then jack up the rear of the car and support it on axle stands. Remove the appropriate roadwheel and continue as follows.

**2** Slowly rotate the brake disc so that the full area of both sides can be checked; remove the brake pads if better access is required to the inboard surface. Light scoring is normal in the area swept by the brake pads, but if heavy scoring or cracks are found, the disc must be renewed.

**3** It is normal to find a lip of rust and brake dust around the disc's perimeter; this can be scraped off if required. If, however, a lip has formed due to excessive wear of the brake pad swept area, then the disc's thickness must be measured using a micrometer **(see illustration)**. Take measurements at several places around the disc, at the inside and outside of the pad swept area; if the disc has worn at any point to the specified minimum thickness or less, the disc must be renewed.

4 If the disc is thought to be warped, it can be checked for run-out. First secure the disc firmly to the hub by refitting at least two roadwheel nuts (if necessary fit spacers to the studs). Either use a dial gauge mounted on any convenient fixed point, while the disc is slowly rotated, or use feeler blades to measure (at several points all around the disc) the clearance between the disc and a fixed point, such as the caliper mounting bracket **(see illustration)**. If the measurements obtained are at the specified maximum or beyond, the disc is excessively warped, and must be renewed; however, it is worth checking first that the hub bearing is in good condition (Chapters 1 and/or 10).

5 Check the disc for cracks, especially around the wheel nut stud holes, and any other wear or damage, and renew if necessary.

### Removal

**Note:** *New caliper mounting bolts will be required on refitting.*

6 With the roadwheel removed, slide out the retaining clip and free the caliper brake hose from its bracket.

7 Slacken and remove the two bolts securing the brake caliper mounting bracket to the swivel hub/trailing arm (as applicable). Slide the caliper assembly off of the disc, and tie the assembly to the coil spring, using a piece of wire or string, to avoid placing any strain on the hydraulic brake hose **(see illustration)**. Discard the bolts; new ones should be used on refitting.

8 Use chalk or paint to mark the relationship of the disc to the hub (if the disc is to be refitted), then slacken and remove the retaining screw (where fitted) and remove the disc **(see illustrations)**. If it is tight, lightly tap its rear face with a hide or plastic mallet to free it from the hub.

### Refitting

9 Refitting is the reverse of the removal procedure, noting the following points:
 a) *Ensure that the mating surfaces of the disc and hub are clean and flat (remove all traces of corrosion).*
 b) *On refitting, align (if applicable) the marks made on removal.*
 c) *If a new disc has been fitted, use a suitable solvent to wipe any preservative coating from the disc, before refitting the caliper.*
 d) *Slide the caliper into position, making sure the pads pass either side of the disc, then fit the new mounting bolts and tighten them to the specified torque setting.*
 e) *Refit the roadwheel, then lower the car to the ground and tighten the wheel nuts to the specified torque. Apply the footbrake several times to force the pads back into contact with the disc before driving the car.*

**6.4  Checking disc run-out with a dial gauge**

---

### 7  Front brake caliper –
removal, overhaul and refitting

**Note:** *Before starting work, refer to the note at the beginning of Section 2 concerning the dangers of hydraulic fluid, and to the warning at the beginning of Section 4 concerning the dangers of asbestos dust.*

### Removal

1 Apply the handbrake, loosen the front wheel nuts, then jack up the front of the car and support it on axle stands. Remove the relevant front roadwheel.

2 Minimise fluid loss by first removing the master cylinder reservoir cap, and then tightening it down onto a piece of polythene, to obtain an airtight seal. Alternatively, use a brake hose clamp, a G-clamp or a similar tool to clamp the flexible hose.

3 Clean the area around the brake hose union on the caliper. Slacken and remove the bolt, and recover the sealing washers which are fitted on each side of the hose union. Plug the hose end to minimise fluid loss and prevent dirt entry. Discard the sealing washers; new ones must be used on refitting. Wash off any spilt fluid immediately with cold water.

4 Slacken and remove the upper and lower caliper guide pin bolts, then lift the caliper away from the brake disc and remove it from the car; the brake pads can be left in position in the caliper mounting bracket.

**6.8a  On the rear disc, with the caliper removed, slacken and remove the retaining screw . . .**

---

**6.7  On the front brake, unbolt the caliper, then mark the disc position on the hub before removing it**

### Overhaul

5 With the caliper on the bench, wipe away all traces of dust and dirt, but *avoid inhaling the dust, as it is a health hazard.*

6 Withdraw the partially-ejected piston from the caliper body, and remove the dust seal.

> **HAYNES HiNT**
> *If the piston cannot be withdrawn by hand, it can be pushed out by applying compressed air to the brake hose union hole. Only low pressure should be required, such as is generated by a foot pump. As the piston is expelled, take great care not to trap your fingers between the piston and caliper.*

7 Using a small screwdriver, extract the piston hydraulic seal, taking care not to damage the caliper bore.

8 Thoroughly clean all components, using only methylated spirit, isopropyl alcohol or clean hydraulic fluid as a cleaning medium. Never use mineral-based solvents such as petrol or paraffin, as they will attack the hydraulic system's rubber components. Dry the components immediately, using compressed air or a clean, lint-free cloth. Use compressed air to blow clear the fluid passages.

9 Check all components, and renew any that are worn or damaged. Check particularly the cylinder bore and piston; these should be renewed (note that this means the renewal of the complete body assembly) if they are

**6.8b  . . . then remove the disc from the hub**

scratched, worn or corroded in any way. Similarly check the condition of the guide pins and their gaiters; both pins should be undamaged and (when cleaned) a reasonably-tight sliding fit in the caliper bracket. If there is any doubt about the condition of any component, renew it.

**10** If the assembly is fit for further use, obtain the appropriate repair kit; the components are available from Volvo dealers in various combinations. All rubber seals should be renewed as a matter of course; these should never be re-used.

**11** On reassembly, ensure that all components are clean and dry.

**12** Soak the piston and the new piston (fluid) seal in clean hydraulic fluid. Smear clean fluid on the cylinder bore surface.

**13** Fit the new piston (fluid) seal, using only your fingers (no tools) to manipulate it into the cylinder bore groove.

**14** Fit the new dust seal to the rear of the piston, and seat the outer lip of the seal in the caliper body groove. Carefully ease the piston squarely into the cylinder bore using a twisting motion. Press the piston fully into position and seat the inner lip of the dust seal in the piston groove.

**15** If the guide pins are being renewed, lubricate the pin shafts with silicone grease, or a copper-based brake grease or anti-seize compound (Volvo recommend the use of silicone grease 1161325-4 – available from your Volvo dealer) and fit the gaiters to the pin grooves. Insert the pins into the caliper bracket and seat the gaiters correctly in the bracket grooves.

**16** Prior to refitting, fill the caliper with fresh hydraulic fluid by slackening the bleed screw and pumping the fluid through the caliper until bubble-free fluid is expelled from the union hole.

### Refitting

**17** Ensure that the brake pads are still correctly fitted in the caliper mounting bracket.

**18** Manoeuvre the caliper into position over the pads, making sure the pad anti-rattle springs are correctly positioned against the caliper body.

**19** Press down on the caliper and screw in the guide pin bolts, tightening them to the specified torque setting.

**20** Position a new sealing washer on each side of the brake hose union, and screw in the union bolt. Ensure the hose end fitting is correctly positioned, then tighten the union bolt to the specified torque.

**21** Remove the brake hose clamp or polythene (where fitted) and bleed the hydraulic system as described in Section 2. Note that, providing the precautions described were taken to minimise brake fluid loss, it should only be necessary to bleed the relevant front brake.

**22** Refit the roadwheel, then lower the car to the ground and tighten the roadwheel nuts to the specified torque.

## 8 Rear brake caliper – removal, overhaul and refitting

**Note:** *Before starting work, refer to the note at the beginning of Section 2 concerning the dangers of hydraulic fluid, and to the warning at the beginning of Section 5 concerning the dangers of asbestos dust.*

### Removal

**Note:** *New guide pin bolts must be used on refitting.*

**1** Chock the front wheels, loosen the rear wheel nuts, then jack up the rear of the car and support it on axle stands. Remove the relevant rear wheel.

**2** Referring to Section 13, release the handbrake lever, then back off the handbrake cable adjuster to obtain maximum freeplay in the cables.

**3** Free the handbrake cable from the caliper lever, then unclip the outer cable from the caliper body.

**4** Minimise fluid loss by first removing the master cylinder reservoir cap, and then tightening it down onto a piece of polythene, to obtain an airtight seal. Alternatively, use a brake hose clamp, a G-clamp or a similar tool to clamp the flexible hose.

**5** Clean the area around the brake hose union on the caliper. Slacken and remove the bolt and recover the sealing washers which are fitted on each side of the hose union **(see illustration)**. Plug the hose end, to minimise fluid loss and prevent dirt entry. Discard the sealing washers; new ones must be used on refitting. Wash off any spilt fluid immediately with cold water.

**6** Slacken and remove the upper and lower caliper guide pin bolts, using a slim open-ended spanner to prevent the guide pin itself from rotating. Lift the caliper away from the brake disc and remove it from the car; the brake pads can be left in position in the caliper mounting bracket. Discard the bolts; new ones should be used on refitting.

### Overhaul

**Note:** *It is not possible to overhaul the brake caliper handbrake mechanism. If the*

**8.5 Unscrew the union bolt and detach the brake hose from the rear brake caliper**

*mechanism is faulty, or fluid is leaking from the handbrake lever seal, the caliper assembly must be renewed.*

**7** With the caliper on the bench, wipe away all traces of dust and dirt, but avoid inhaling the dust, as it is a health hazard.

**8** Remove the piston from the caliper bore by rotating it in an anti-clockwise direction. This can be achieved using a suitable pair of circlip pliers engaged in the caliper piston slots. Once the piston turns freely but does not come out any further, the piston can be withdrawn by hand.

> **HAYNES HINT**
> *If the piston cannot be withdrawn by hand, it can be pushed out by applying compressed air to the brake hose union hole. Only low pressure should be required, such as is generated by a foot pump. As the piston is expelled, take care not to trap your fingers between the piston and caliper.*

**9** Remove the dust seal from the piston then, using a small screwdriver, carefully extract the piston hydraulic seal from the caliper bore. Take care not to mark the caliper bore.

**10** Withdraw the guide pins from the caliper mounting bracket, and remove the guide sleeve gaiters.

**11** Inspect all the caliper components as described in Section 7, paragraphs 8 to 10, and renew as necessary, noting that the handbrake mechanism **must not** be dismantled.

**12** On reassembly, ensure all components are clean and dry.

**13** Soak the piston and the new piston (fluid) seal in clean hydraulic fluid. Smear clean fluid on the cylinder bore surface. Fit the new piston (fluid) seal, using only the fingers (no tools) to manipulate into the cylinder bore groove.

**14** Fit the new dust seal to the rear of the piston, and seat the outer lip of the seal in the caliper body groove. Carefully ease the piston squarely into the cylinder bore using a twisting motion. Turn the piston in a clockwise direction, using the method employed on dismantling, until it is fully retracted into the caliper bore, then seat the inner lip of the dust seal in the piston groove.

**15** Apply silicone grease, or a copper-based brake grease or anti-seize compound (Volvo recommend the use of silicone grease 1161325-4 – available from your Volvo dealer) to the guide pins. Fit the new gaiters to the guide pins and fit the pins to the caliper mounting bracket, ensuring that the gaiters are correctly located in the grooves on both the pins and bracket.

**16** Prior to refitting, fill the caliper with fresh hydraulic fluid by slackening the bleed screw and pumping the fluid through the caliper until bubble-free fluid is expelled from the union hole.

**9.2 Release the clip and detach the clutch master cylinder hose (arrowed) from the reservoir**

**9.3 Disconnect the wiring connector from the brake fluid level sender unit (arrowed)**

**9.4 Unscrew the union nuts and disconnect the brake pipes from the master cylinder**

## Refitting

**17** Ensure that the brake pads are still correctly fitted in the caliper mounting bracket.

**18** Manoeuvre the caliper into position over the pads, making sure the pad anti-rattle springs are correctly positioned against the caliper body.

**19** Press down on the caliper and screw in the new guide pin bolts, tightening them to the specified torque setting whilst retaining the guide pin with an open-ended spanner.

**20** Position a new sealing washer on each side of the brake hose union and screw in the union bolt. Ensure the hose end fitting is correctly positioned then tighten the union bolt to the specified torque.

**21** Remove the brake hose clamp or polythene (where fitted) and bleed the hydraulic system as described in Section 2. Note that, providing the precautions described were taken to minimise brake fluid loss, it should only be necessary to bleed the relevant rear brake.

**22** Reconnect the handbrake cable securely to the caliper, and adjust as described in Section 13.

**23** Refit the roadwheel, then lower the car to the ground and tighten the roadwheel nuts to the specified torque.

---

**9   Master cylinder –**
removal, overhaul and refitting

---

**Note:** *Before starting work, refer to the warning at the beginning of Section 2 concerning the dangers of hydraulic fluid.*

## Removal

### Right-hand-drive models

**1** Ensure the ignition is switched off (take out the key), then wipe clean the master cylinder fluid reservoir and remove the reservoir cap. Syphon the hydraulic fluid from the reservoir or, alternatively, open any convenient bleed screw in the system, and gently pump the brake pedal to expel the fluid through a plastic tube connected to the screw (see Section 2).

*Caution: Do not syphon the fluid by mouth, as it is poisonous; use a syringe or an old poultry baster.*

**2** On manual transmission models, disconnect the clutch master cylinder hose from the reservoir **(see illustration)**. Plug the hose end, to minimise fluid loss and prevent the entry of dirt into the system.

**3** Disconnect the wiring connector from the brake fluid level sender unit **(see illustration)**.

**4** Wipe clean the area around the brake pipe unions on the side of the master cylinder, and place absorbent rags beneath the pipe unions to catch any surplus fluid. Make a note of the correct fitted positions of the unions, then unscrew the union nuts and carefully withdraw the pipes **(see illustration)**. Plug or tape over the pipe ends and master cylinder orifices, to minimise the loss of brake fluid, and to prevent the entry of dirt into the system. Wash off any spilt fluid immediately with cold water.

**5** Slacken and remove the two nuts securing the master cylinder to the vacuum servo unit, then withdraw the unit from the engine compartment. Recover the sealing ring fitted to the rear of the master cylinder and discard it; a new one must be used on refitting.

### Left-hand-drive models

**6** Disconnect the battery negative lead (see *Disconnecting the battery*).

**7** To improve access, undo the retaining bolts securing the fuse/relay box to the suspension mounting turret, and position it clear. Where necessary, remove the cruise control pump mounting bolts, and position the pump clear of the master cylinder.

**8** Carefully ease the vacuum hose check valve out from the servo unit, taking care not to damage the sealing grommet.

**9** Slacken and remove the bolt securing the rear brake pressure-regulating valve to its bracket.

**10** Remove the master cylinder as described in paragraphs 1 to 5, noting that it will be necessary to free the servo support bracket from the studs to enable removal.

## Overhaul

**11** If the master cylinder is faulty, it must be renewed. Repair kits are not available from

Volvo dealers, so the cylinder must be treated as a sealed unit.

**12** The only item which can be renewed is the mounting seal for the fluid reservoir; if these show signs of deterioration, remove the retaining pin then ease off the reservoir and remove the old seal. Lubricate the new seal with clean brake fluid, and ease into the master cylinder ports. Refit the fluid reservoir, and secure it in position with the roll pin.

## Refitting

### Right-hand-drive models

**13** Remove all traces of dirt from the master cylinder and servo unit mating surfaces, and fit a new sealing ring to the rear of the master cylinder body.

**14** Fit the master cylinder to the servo unit, ensuring that the servo unit pushrod enters the master cylinder bore centrally. Refit the master cylinder mounting nuts and tighten them to the specified torque.

**15** Wipe clean the brake pipe unions, then refit them to the master cylinder ports and tighten them to the specified torque.

**16** Where necessary, securely reconnect the clutch master cylinder fluid hose to the reservoir.

**17** Reconnect the fluid level sender unit wiring connector.

**18** Refill the master cylinder reservoir with new fluid, and bleed the complete hydraulic system as described in Section 2.

### Left-hand-drive models

**19** Refit the master cylinder as described in paragraphs 13 to 17, remembering to locate the support bracket on the studs before refitting the master cylinder retaining nuts.

**20** Refit the pressure-regulating valve bolt, tightening it to the specified torque.

**21** Taking care not to displace the rubber grommet, carefully reconnect the vacuum hose valve to the servo unit.

**22** Refit the cruise control air pump (where fitted) and relay box tightening their retaining bolts securely.

**23** Refill the master cylinder reservoir with new fluid, and bleed the complete hydraulic system as described in Section 2.

## 10 Brake pedal –
removal and refitting

### Removal

#### Right-hand-drive models

**1** Disconnect the battery negative lead (see *Disconnecting the battery*).

**2** Undo the retaining screws (the lower screw is hidden behind a trim cap) and remove the driver's side lower panel from the facia, disconnecting the wiring connector from the footwell light **(see illustrations)**.

**3** On models with cruise control, remove the vacuum reservoir from the brake pedal bracket (see Chapter 4A, Section 12).

**4** Unclip the control module, then undo the retaining nuts and remove the control module holder **(see illustrations)**. Position the relay box clear of the pedal mounting bracket.

**5** Slide off the retaining clip and washer, and withdraw the clevis pin securing the pushrod to the pedal **(see illustration)**.

**6** Slacken and remove the nut and washer from the pedal pivot bolt. Slide the bolt out, tilting the pedal as necessary, and manoeuvre the pedal assembly out of its bracket.

**7** Examine all components for signs of wear or damage, paying particular attention to the pivot bushes and spacer, renewing them as necessary.

#### Left-hand-drive models

**8** Carry out the operations described in paragraphs 1 to 3.

**9** Unhook the accelerator cable end fitting from the top of the pedal.

**10** Disconnect the wiring connector from the stop-light switch.

**11** Slide off the retaining clip and washer, and withdraw the clevis pin securing the pushrod to the pedal.

**12** Carefully unhook the end of the return spring, then slacken and remove the nut and washer from the pedal pivot bolt.

**13** Slacken and remove the steering column bolts and support the column.

**14** Slacken and remove the servo unit mounting nuts, and the nuts on the side of the

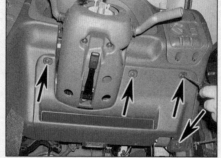
**10.2a Remove the screws (arrowed) securing the driver's side lower panel . . .**

bracket, then free the pedal mounting bracket from the bulkhead.

**15** Slide out the pedal pivot bolt and manoeuvre the pedal assembly out of position, noting the correct fitted position of the return spring.

**16** Examine all components for signs of wear or damage, paying particular attention to the pivot bushes and spacer, renewing them as necessary.

### Refitting

#### Right-hand-drive models

**17** Refitting is the reverse of removal, noting the following points:

a) *Prior to refitting, apply a smear of multi-purpose grease to the pedal pivot bushes and spacer and the pushrod clevis pin.*

b) *Tighten the pedal pivot bolt nut to the specified torque.*

c) *Ensure the return spring is correctly engaged with the pedal.*

d) *On completion, reconnect the battery then check and, if necessary, adjust the stop-light switch as described in Section 17.*

#### Left-hand-drive models

**18** Refitting is the reverse of removal, noting the following points:

a) *Prior to refitting, apply a smear of multi-purpose grease to the pedal pivot bushes and spacer and the pushrod clevis pin.*

b) *Tighten the pedal pivot bolt nut and the servo and pedal bracket nuts to their specified torque settings.*

**10.2b . . . and disconnect the wiring connector from the footwell illumination light**

c) *Ensure the return spring is correctly engaged with the pedal.*

d) *Reconnect the accelerator cable and check the cable adjustment (see Chapter 4A or 4B).*

e) *On completion reconnect the battery then check and, if necessary, adjust the stop-light switch as described in Section 17.*

## 11 Vacuum servo unit –
testing, removal and refitting

### Testing

**1** To test the operation of the servo unit, depress the footbrake several times to exhaust the vacuum, then start the engine whilst keeping the pedal firmly pressed. As the engine starts, there should be a noticeable give in the brake pedal as the vacuum builds up. Allow the engine to run for at least two minutes, then switch it off. If the brake pedal is now pressed, it should feel normal, but further applications should result in the pedal feeling firmer, with the pedal stroke decreasing with each application.

**2** If the servo does not operate as described, first inspect the servo unit check valve as described in Section 12.

**3** If the servo unit still fails to operate satisfactorily, the fault lies within the unit itself. Repairs to the unit are not possible – if faulty, the servo unit must be renewed.

**10.4a Unclip the control module then undo the retaining nuts (arrowed) . . .**

**10.4b . . . and remove the holder from the facia**

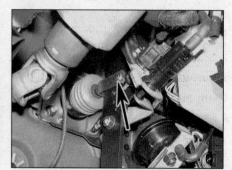
**10.5 Slide off the clip, then withdraw the clevis pin (arrowed) securing the servo pushrod to the pedal**

## Removal

### Right-hand-drive models

**4** Disconnect the battery negative lead (see *Disconnecting the battery*).

**5** To improve access, undo the retaining screws and lift off the cover from the top of the engine. Unclip the coolant expansion tank from its mountings, and position it clear of the servo.

**6** Wipe clean the area around the master cylinder and servo unit, then slacken and remove the bolt securing the brake pipe retaining clip to the body.

**7** Remove the master cylinder as described in Section 9.

**8** On manual transmission models, remove the clutch master cylinder as described in Chapter 6.

**9** On all models, carefully ease the vacuum hose valve out from the servo unit, taking care not to damage the rubber grommet.

**10** Undo the retaining screws (the lower screw is hidden behind a trim cap) and remove the driver's side lower panel from the facia, disconnecting the wiring connector from the footwell light.

**11** Unclip the control module, then undo the retaining nuts and remove the control module holder. Position the relay box clear of the pedal mounting bracket.

**12** Slide off the retaining clip and washer, and withdraw the clevis pin securing the pushrod to the pedal.

**13** Slacken and remove the servo unit retaining nuts, then return to the engine compartment.

**14** Carefully manoeuvre the servo unit out of position, and recover the gasket which is fitted between the servo and bulkhead. If necessary, free the power steering/air conditioning system pipes (as applicable) from their fixings to gain the necessary clearance required for removal. Examine the gasket for signs of wear or damage, and renew if necessary.

### Left-hand-drive models

**15** Remove the master cylinder as described in Section 9.

**16** Undo the retaining screws (the lower screw is hidden behind a trim cap) and remove the driver's side lower panel from the facia, disconnecting the wiring connector from the footwell light.

**17** Slide off the retaining clip and washer, and withdraw the clevis pin securing the pushrod to the pedal.

**18** Slacken and remove the servo unit retaining nuts, then return to the engine compartment.

**19** Carefully manoeuvre the servo unit out of position, and recover the gasket which is fitted between the servo and bulkhead. Examine the gasket for signs of wear or damage, and renew if necessary.

## Refitting

### Right-hand-drive models

**20** Ensure the servo unit and bulkhead mating surfaces are clean, fit the gasket to the rear of the servo unit and manoeuvre the unit into position.

**21** From inside the car, make sure the pushrod is correctly engaged with the pedal, then refit the servo unit nuts and tighten them to the specified torque.

**22** Apply a smear of multi-purpose grease to the clevis pin, then align the pedal with the pushrod and insert the pin. Refit the washer and secure it in position with the retaining clip.

**23** Secure the control module and relay box in position then refit the facia panel.

**24** Reconnect the vacuum hose to the servo, then clip the coolant expansion tank back into position.

**25** On manual transmission models, refit the clutch master cylinder as described in Chapter 6.

**26** Refit the braking system master cylinder as described in Section 9.

**27** Bleed the complete hydraulic braking system as described in Section 2, then bleed the clutch system as described in Chapter 6.

### Left-hand drive models

**28** Carry out the operations described in paragraphs 20 to 22.

**29** Refit the master cylinder as described in Section 9, and bleed the complete hydraulic system as described in Section 2.

---

## 12 Vacuum servo unit check valve – removal, testing and refitting

**Note:** *On some models, the valve is an integral part of the servo unit vacuum hose and is not available separately.*

## Removal

**1** To improve access to the valve, undo the retaining screws and remove the cover from the top of the engine.

**2** Carefully ease the check valve out from the servo unit, taking care not to damage the grommet **(see illustration)**.

**3** On models where the valve is available separately, carefully ease the valve out of the end of the hose and remove it from the car.

**4** On models where the valve is an integral part of the hose, work back along the hose, freeing it from all the relevant retaining clips whilst noting its correct routing. Release the retaining clip and remove the hose assembly from the car; the hose is secured to the manifold with a quick-release fitting, depress the collar to release it.

## Testing

**5** Examine the vacuum hose for signs of damage, and renew if necessary. The valve may be tested by blowing through it in both directions. Air should flow through the valve in one direction only – when blown through from the servo unit end of the valve. Renew the valve if this is not the case.

**12.2 Check valve (arrowed) is a push-fit in the servo unit sealing grommet (valve shown is integral with hose)**

**6** Examine the servo unit rubber sealing grommet for signs of damage or deterioration, and renew as necessary.

## Refitting

**7** Refitting is the reverse of removal, noting the following:

a) *Take great care not to displace or damage the sealing grommet when refitting the valve.*

b) *On models where the valve is part of the hose, ensure the hose is correctly routed and retained by all the relevant clips then securely connect it to the manifold. Make sure the hose is securely retained by the quick-release fitting.*

c) *On completion, start the engine and check the check valve-to-servo unit connection for signs of air leaks.*

---

## 13 Handbrake – adjustment

**1** The handbrake will normally be kept in adjustment by the action of the rear brake caliper handbrake mechanisms. Occasionally, the handbrake mechanism may require adjustment to compensate for cable stretch, but adjustment should only be needed if the brake calipers, cables or handbrake lever are disturbed.

**2** Prior to checking the handbrake adjustment, firmly apply the footbrake several times to ensure that the rear brake caliper self-adjusting mechanism is correctly set.

**3** Handbrake adjustment is checked by counting the number of clicks emitted from the lever ratchet mechanism whilst apply the handbrake. Fully release the handbrake lever and apply as normal; the handbrake should be fully applied between the 5th and 7th notch of the ratchet mechanism.

**4** If adjustment is necessary, remove the rear section of the centre console to gain access to the handbrake lever (see Chapter 11).

**5** First check that the handbrake cable balancer plate, located at the rear of the handbrake lever, is at a right-angle to the lever cable **(see illustration)**. If not, then either the handbrake cables or the brake caliper

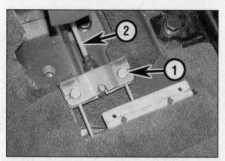

13.5 Prior to adjustment, ensure the balancer plate (1) is at a right-angle to the lever cable (2)

13.7a Release the handbrake lever and back off the adjuster nut . . .

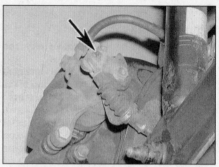

13.7b . . . until both rear brake caliper handbrake levers are against their stops

handbrake mechanisms are faulty, resulting in the force not being applied equally to each rear brake. The most likely cause is that one or both of the handbrake cables are binding. If necessary, trace and rectify the problem before continuing.

**6** If the balancer plate is correctly positioned, chock the front wheels, then jack up the rear of the car and support it on axle stands.

**7** With the handbrake lever fully released, back off the cable adjuster nut until both rear brake caliper handbrake levers are in contact with their stops **(see illustrations)**. Slowly tighten the adjuster nut until the point is reached where all freeplay is removed from the adjuster cable, but both levers remain in contact with their stops.

**8** Check both rear wheels rotate freely, then check the adjustment as described in paragraph 3 and, if necessary, repeat the adjustment procedure.

**9** Once the handbrake is correctly adjusted, lower the car to the ground then refit the centre console rear section.

## 14 Handbrake lever – removal and refitting

### Removal

**1** Remove the rear section of the centre console as described in Chapter 11.
**2** Chock the wheels, then fully release the handbrake lever.

14.3 Detach the adjuster cable from the balancer plate (2) then undo the handbrake lever retaining bolts (1)

**3** Back off the cable adjuster nut until it is possible to unhook the adjuster cable from the balancer plate **(see illustration)**.
**4** Disconnect the wiring connector from the handbrake lever warning light switch.
**5** Slacken and remove the mounting bolts and remove the handbrake lever from the car.

### Refitting

**6** Refitting is a reversal of removal, tightening the handbrake lever bolts to the specified torque. Prior to refitting the centre console section, adjust the handbrake as described in Section 13.

## 15 Handbrake cables – removal and refitting

### Removal

**1** The handbrake cable consists of three sections, a right- and a left-hand section, which connects each rear brake to the balancer plate, and a short adjuster cable which links the balancer plate to the handbrake lever. Each section can be removed individually as follows.

### Adjuster cable

**2** Chock the wheels, then fully release the handbrake lever.
**3** Remove the rear section of the centre console as described in Chapter 11.
**4** Unscrew the adjuster nut from the cable, and remove the spring clip.
**5** Bend back the retaining tang, then free the cable from the handbrake lever cam and balancer plate, and remove it from the car.

### Left- and right-hand cables

**6** Each cable can be removed as follows.
**7** Chock the front wheels, then jack up the rear of the car and support it on axle stands. If the left-hand cable is being removed, remove the retaining screws/fastener and remove the fuel filter protective cover to gain access to the cable.
**8** Remove the rear section of the centre console as described in Chapter 11, then remove the rear seat cushion.
**9** Back off the cable adjuster nut to obtain

maximum freeplay in the cables, then unhook the front end of the cable from the balancer plate.
**10** Release the retaining clips and lift up the carpet to reveal the cable guide. Undo the retaining bolts securing the guide to the floor, then free the cable from its guide and release the cable sealing grommet from the floor.
**11** From underneath the car, unhook the inner cable from the brake caliper lever then unclip the outer cable from its bracket.
**12** Slacken and remove the bolts securing the cable clips to the trailing arm/underbody and remove the cable from the car **(see illustration)**.

### Refitting

### Adjuster cable

**13** Engage the cable with the balancer plate, and seat it in the handbrake lever cam. Position the cable so that its nipple is positioned vertically in the balancer plate, then secure it in position with the retaining tang.
**14** Refit the spring clip and adjuster nut to the cable then adjust the cable as described in Section 13. Operate the handbrake lever several times to settle the cable is position and recheck the adjustment before refitting the centre console rear section.

### Left- and right-hand cables

**15** Feed the front end of the cable up through the floor, and seat its sealing grommet correctly in position.
**16** Ensure the cable is correctly routed then

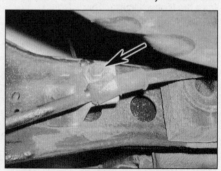

15.12 Undo the retaining bolts securing the handbrake cable clips to the trailing arm and underbody

refit its retaining clip bolts, tightening them securely. Where necessary, refit the protective cover.

**17** Hook the inner cable back onto the brake caliper lever and clip the outer cable securely into its bracket.

**18** Working inside the car, engage the front end of the cable with the balancer plate, then refit the cable guide. Ensure the cable is correctly located, then refit the guide retaining bolts, tightening them to the specified torque.

**19** Seat the carpet correctly in position then refit the rear seat cushion as described in Chapter 11.

**20** Refit the spring clip and adjuster nut to the cable then adjust the cable as described in Section 13. Operate the handbrake lever several times to settle the cable is position and recheck the adjustment before refitting the centre console rear section.

## 16 Rear brake pressure-regulating valve – testing, removal and refitting

### Testing

**1** The hydraulic circuit to each rear brake is equipped with a pressure-regulating valve arrangement, to help prevent the rear wheels locking up under hard braking. The valve assembly is of the pressure-sensitive type, located on the left-hand side of the engine compartment bulkhead; on left-hand drive models, it is mounted onto the front of the servo unit **(see illustration)**. The regulating valve acts as a restrictor and limits the hydraulic pressure being applied to the rear brakes, ensuring that the front brakes are always applied with a greater force.

**2** Specialist equipment is required to check the performance of the valve. Therefore, if there is thought to be a fault, the car should be taken to a suitably-equipped Volvo dealer for testing. If faulty, the valve assembly must be renewed.

### Removal

**Note:** *Before starting work, refer to the warning at the beginning of Section 2 concerning the dangers of hydraulic fluid.*

**3** Minimise fluid loss by first removing the master cylinder reservoir cap, and then tightening it down onto a piece of polythene, to obtain an airtight seal.

**4** Wipe clean the area around the brake pipe unions on the valve, and place absorbent rags beneath the pipe unions to catch any surplus fluid. To avoid confusion on refitting, make alignment marks between the pipes and valve assembly.

**5** Slacken the union nuts and disconnect the brake pipes from the valve. Plug or tape over the pipe ends and valve orifices, to minimise the loss of brake fluid, and to prevent the entry of dirt into the system. Wash off any spilt fluid immediately with cold water.

**6** Slacken and remove the retaining bolt, and remove the valve assembly from the car.

### Refitting

**7** Manoeuvre the valve assembly into position, and locate all the brake pipes in their specific unions. Tighten the union nuts lightly only at this stage.

**8** Refit the valve retaining bolt and tighten it to the specified torque, then tighten all the brake pipe union nuts to their specified torque setting.

**9** Remove the polythene from the master cylinder reservoir, and bleed the complete hydraulic system as described in Section 2.

## 17 Stop-light switch – removal, refitting and adjustment

### Removal

**1** The stop-light switch is located on the pedal bracket behind the facia. On models with cruise control, there are two switches on the brake pedal; the stop-light switch is the upper of the two switches, and has no vacuum pipe connected to it.

**2** Undo the retaining screws (the lower screw is hidden behind a trim cap) and remove the driver's side lower panel from the facia, disconnecting the wiring connector from the footwell light **(see illustrations)**.

**3** Disconnect the wiring connector, then unscrew the switch and remove it from the bracket **(see illustration)**.

**16.1 Rear brake pressure-regulating valve assembly (arrowed) on the engine compartment bulkhead**

### Refitting and adjustment

**4** Push the switch gently into position in the pedal mounting bracket.

**5** Connect a continuity tester (ohmmeter or self-powered test light) across the switch terminals. Screw the switch in until an open-circuit is present between the switch terminals (infinite resistance, or light goes out). Gently depress the pedal, and check that continuity exists between the switch terminals (zero resistance, or light comes on) after the pedal has travelled approximately 5 mm. Screw the switch in or out (as necessary) until it operates as specified. **Note:** *It is essential that the stop-light switch is correctly adjusted, otherwise the anti-lock braking system performance maybe affected (see Section 18).*

**6** In the absence of a continuity tester, the same adjustment can be made by reconnecting the switch and having an assistant observe the stop-lights (ignition on).

**7** Once the stop-light switch is correctly adjusted, reconnect the wiring connector and refit the panel to the facia. Recheck the operation of the stop-lights before using the car on the road.

## 18 Anti-lock braking system (ABS) – general information

**1** ABS was fitted as standard to all models in the range. The system is comprised of the ABS unit (which contains both the system hydraulics

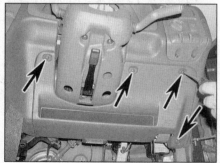

**17.2a Remove the driver's side lower panel (retaining screws arrowed) from facia . . .**

**17.2b . . . disconnecting the wiring connector from the footwell illumination light**

**17.3 Disconnect the wiring connector (arrowed – model with cruise control shown) then unscrew the switch from the bracket**

**19.3 Release the retaining clip and disconnect the wiring connector (arrowed) from the ABS unit**

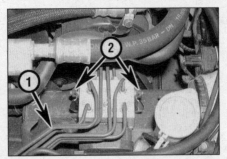

**19.4 Disconnect the brake pipes (1), then slacken the nuts (2) and remove the ABS unit from its bracket**

and electronics), the four roadwheel sensors, and the stop-light switch. The purpose of the system is to prevent the wheel(s) locking during heavy braking. This is achieved by automatic release of the brake on the relevant wheel, followed by re-application of the brake.

**2** The electric pump and eight hydraulic solenoid valves (two for each brake – one inlet and one outlet) in the ABS unit are controlled by the electronic control unit (ECU), which itself receives signals from the four wheel sensors (which are fitted to the hubs) and the stop-light switch. The wheel sensors monitor the speed of rotation of each wheel and the stop-light switch informs the ECU when the brake is being applied.

**3** When the brakes are being applied (stop-light switch operated), the ECU compares the signal from each wheel sensor. The ECU can then determine when a wheel is decelerating at an abnormal rate, compared to the speed of the car, and therefore predicts when a wheel is about to lock.

**4** During normal braking, the hydraulic system functions in the same way as a non-ABS braking system with the ABS unit having no effect. The ABS unit inlet solenoid valves are all open and the outlet valves are all closed and the electrically-operated pump is switched off.

**5** If the ECU senses that a wheel is about to lock, it closes the relevant inlet solenoid valve in the hydraulic unit, which then isolates the relevant brake on the wheel which is about to lock from the master cylinder, effectively sealing-in the hydraulic pressure. The ABS unit pump is now turned on.

**19.10 Removing the wheel arch liner**

**6** If the speed of rotation of the wheel continues to decrease at an abnormal rate, the ECU opens the outlet solenoid valve(s) on the relevant brake(s) and the pump draws the hydraulic fluid back into the ABS unit accumulator chambers, releasing the brake. Once the speed of rotation of the wheel returns to an acceptable rate, the pump stops; the solenoid valves switch again, allowing the hydraulic master cylinder pressure to return to the caliper, which then re-applies the brake. This cycle can be carried out many times a second.

**7** The action of the solenoid valves and pump creates pulses in the hydraulic circuit. When the ABS system is functioning, these pulses may be felt through the brake pedal.

**8** The ABS system performs a self-check every time the car is driven. When the ignition is switched on, the warning light will be illuminated for approximately 4 seconds and then go out if no faults are found. The first time the car exceeds a speed of around 20 mph, a functional check of the hydraulic system will be carried out. If any faults are diagnosed, the ECU will automatically shut down the ABS unit and illuminate the warning light on the instrument panel to inform the driver that the ABS system is not operational. Normal braking will still be available, however.

**9** If a fault does develop in the ABS system, the car must be taken to a Volvo dealer for fault diagnosis and repair.

## 19 Anti-lock braking system (ABS) components – removal and refitting

### ABS unit

**Note:** *Volvo state that the operation of the hydraulic unit should be checked using special test equipment after refitting. Bearing this in mind, it is recommended that removal and refitting of the unit is entrusted to a Volvo dealer. If you decide to remove/refit the unit yourself, ensure that the operation of the braking system is checked at the earliest opportunity by a Volvo dealer.*

### Removal

**1** Disconnect the battery negative lead (see *Disconnecting the battery*).

**2** Minimise fluid loss by first removing the master cylinder reservoir cap, and then tightening it down onto a piece of polythene, to obtain an airtight seal.

**3** Release the retaining clip and disconnect the wiring connector from the ABS unit ECU **(see illustration)**.

**4** Wipe clean the area around all the pipes unions and mark the locations of the hydraulic fluid pipes to ensure correct refitting **(see illustration)**. Unscrew the union nuts and disconnect the pipes from the ABS unit. Be prepared for fluid spillage, and plug the open ends of the pipes and the hydraulic unit unions, to prevent dirt ingress and further fluid loss.

**5** Slacken the mounting nuts and remove the ABS unit from the engine compartment. If necessary, the mounting bracket can then be unbolted and removed from the car. Renew the regulator mountings if they show signs of wear or damage. **Note:** *Keep the hydraulic unit upright to minimise the risk of fluid loss, resulting in airlocks inside the unit.*

**6** If necessary, the ECU and ABS unit hydraulic modulator can be separated. Evenly and progressively slacken and remove the retaining bolts, then **carefully** ease the ECU squarely away from the modulator, taking care not to damage the wiring pins.

### Refitting

**7** Refitting is the reverse of removal, noting the following points:

a) *Where necessary, align the ECU wiring pins with the modulator, and ease the unit squarely into position. Fit the four Torx screws and tighten them, then refit and tighten the central bolt. Never tighten the Torx screws to more than 8 Nm (6 lbf ft).*

b) *Reconnect the hydraulic pipes to the correct unions and tighten the union nuts to the specified torque.*

c) *Ensure the wiring connector is securely reconnected.*

d) *On completion, fill the fluid reservoir with fresh fluid and bleed the complete hydraulic system as described in Section 2. Thoroughly check the operation of the braking system before using the car on the road. If there is any doubt about the function of the ABS system, have it checked by a Volvo dealer at the earliest possible opportunity.*

### Front wheel sensor

#### Removal

**8** Disconnect the battery negative lead (see *Disconnecting the battery*).

**9** Apply the handbrake, loosen the front wheel nuts, then jack up the front of the car and support securely on axle stands. Remove the roadwheel.

**10** Remove the retaining screws/fasteners and remove the wheel arch liner to gain access to the sensor wiring connector **(see illustration)**.

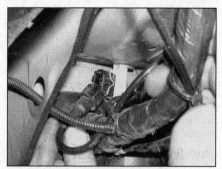

**19.11a Disconnect the wiring connector . . .**

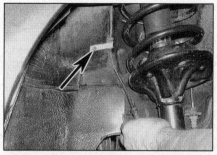

**19.11b . . . then undo the wiring clip screw (arrowed) and free the wiring grommets from their retaining clips**

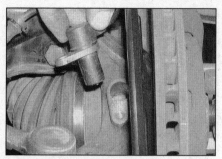

**19.12 Slacken and remove the retaining bolt and remove the wheel sensor from the swivel hub**

**19.14 Ensure the sensor is correctly located in the hub then tighten its retaining bolt to the specified torque**

**19.19 Remove the fuel filter protective cover . . .**

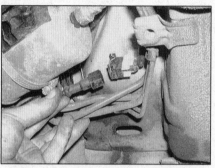

**19.20 . . . to gain access to the left-hand sensor wiring connector**

**11** Disconnect the wiring connector, then undo the retaining screws and remove the clips securing the sensor wiring to the inner wing **(see illustrations)**.

**12** Unclip the sensor wiring grommets from the lower retaining clips, then undo the retaining bolt and remove the sensor from the swivel hub assembly **(see illustration)**.

### Refitting

**13** Ensure that the mating faces of the sensor and the swivel hub are clean, and remove all traces of dirt from the sensor toothed ring on the driveshaft.

**14** Ensure the sensor tip is clean, then apply a little multi-purpose grease to the swivel hub bore. Ease the sensor into position, then refit the retaining bolt and tighten it to the specified torque **(see illustration)**.

**15** Ensure the sensor wiring is correctly routed, and clip its lower grommets into their brackets. Refit the wiring retaining clips, tightening their retaining screws securely, and reconnect the wiring connector.

**16** Refit the wheel arch liner and roadwheel, then lower the car to the ground. Tighten the wheel nuts to the specified torque, then reconnect the battery.

### Rear wheel sensor

#### Removal

**17** Disconnect the battery negative lead (see *Disconnecting the battery*).

**18** Remove the rear hub assembly as described in Chapter 10.

**19** If the work is being carried out on the left-

hand side, remove the retaining screws/ fastener and remove the fuel filter protective cover to gain access to the sensor wiring **(see illustration)**.

**20** Work back along the sensor wiring and unscrew the nut/bolts securing the wiring clamps to the trailing arm. Disconnect the connector so the wiring is free to be removed with the sensor **(see illustration)**.

**21** Slacken and remove the retaining bolts, and remove the sensor from the car **(see illustration)**.

### Refitting

**22** Ensure that the mating surfaces of the sensor and backplate are clean and dry, and remove all traces of dirt from the toothed ring on the rear of the hub.

**23** Lubricate the sensor surface with a little grease, then feed the wiring in through the backplate and seat the sensor in position.

**19.21 Undo the retaining bolts and remove the rear wheel sensor**

Ensure the sensor is correctly located, then refit the retaining bolts and tighten to the specified torque **(see illustration)**.

**24** Work along the wiring, ensuring it is correctly routed, and secure the retaining clamps to the trailing arm. Securely tighten the clamp retaining nut/bolts, then reconnect the wiring connector. Where necessary, refit the fuel filter protective cover to the car.

**25** Refit the hub assembly as described in Chapter 10 and reconnect the battery.

### Front wheel sensor toothed ring

#### Removal

**26** Remove the driveshaft as described in Chapter 8.

**27** Remove the toothed ring from the outer constant velocity (CV) joint by carefully tapping between the inner edge of the ring and the joint with a small chisel.

**19.23 Ensure the rear wheel sensor is correctly located then tighten its retaining bolts to the specified torque**

**19.32 Undo the two bolts and remove the rear wheel sensor toothed ring from the rear of the hub assembly**

### Refitting

**28** Ensure the CV joint and toothed ring mating surfaces are clean and dry.

**29** Apply a smear of multi-purpose grease to the inner edge of the ring, then tap the ring squarely onto the CV joint. Ensure the toothed ring is tapped fully onto the joint, then wipe away any excess grease.

**30** Refit the driveshaft as described in Chapter 8.

### *Rear wheel sensor toothed ring*

### Removal

**31** Remove the rear hub assembly as described in Chapter 10.

**32** Undo the retaining bolts and remove the toothed ring from the rear of the hub **(see illustration)**.

### Refitting

**33** Ensure the toothed ring and hub mating surfaces are clean and dry, then seat the ring in position. Refit the retaining bolts and tighten them securely.

**34** Refit the hub assembly as described in Chapter 10.

### *Stop-light switch*

**35** See Section 17.

# Chapter 10
# Suspension and steering

## Contents

## Degrees of difficulty

| | | | | |
|---|---|---|---|---|
| **Easy,** suitable for novice with little experience  | **Fairly easy,** suitable for beginner with some experience | **Fairly difficult,** suitable for competent DIY mechanic | **Difficult,** suitable for experienced DIY mechanic | **Very difficult,** suitable for expert DIY or professional |

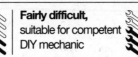

## Specifications

### Front wheel alignment and steering angles

| | |
|---|---|
| Toe setting | 0.15° ± 0.05° toe-in per wheel |
| Camber: | |
|   Standard setting: | |
|     Up to May 2000 | 0° ± 1° |
|     May 2000 onwards: | |
|       Standard | -0.16° ± 0.5° |
|       Sport | -0.33° ± 0.5° |
|       Comfort | -0.07° ± 0.5° |
|   Maximum difference between sides | 0.68° |
| Castor: | |
|   Standard setting: | |
|     Pre-1998 model year | 2.2° ± 1° |
|     1998 model year to May 2000 | 3.2° ± 1° |
|     May 2000 onwards: | |
|       Standard | 4° ± 1° |
|       Sport | 4.15° ± 1° |
|       Comfort | 3.86° ± 1° |
|   Maximum difference between sides | 0.68° |
| Kingpin inclination angle: | |
|   Up to May 2000 | 12.68° ± 1° |
|   May 2000 onwards: | |
|     Standard | 13.68° ± 1° |
|     Sport | 14.07° ± 1° |
|     Comfort | 13.26° ± 1° |
|   Maximum difference between sides | 0.68° |

## Rear wheel alignment

| | |
|---|---|
| Toe setting | 0.15° ± 0.05° toe-in per wheel |
| Camber: | |
| Standard | -0.67° ± 0.25° |
| Sport | -0.90° ± 0.25° |
| Sport/Dynamic with nivomat | -1.16° ± 0.25° |
| Maximum difference between sides | 0.68° |

## Roadwheels

| | |
|---|---|
| Type | Pressed-steel or aluminium alloy (depending on model) |
| Size | 5.5J x 14, 6J x 15 or 6.5J x 16 (depending on model) |
| Tyre pressures | See *Weekly checks* |

## Torque wrench settings

| | Nm | lbf ft |
|---|---|---|
| **Front suspension** | | |
| Anti-roll bar: | | |
| Connecting link nuts | 45 | 33 |
| Mounting clamp bolts | 25 | 18 |
| Hub nut: | | |
| Pre-1998 model year | 240 | 177 |
| 1998 model year onwards: | | |
| Stage 1 | 120 | 89 |
| Stage 2 | Angle-tighten a further 60° | |
| Lower arm: | | |
| Balljoint nut | 67 | 49 |
| Front pivot bolt | 90 | 66 |
| Rear mounting clamp bolts | 90 | 66 |
| Subframe front mounting bolts | 108 | 80 |
| Suspension strut: | | |
| Piston nut | 65 | 48 |
| Strut-to-swivel hub bolts | 90 | 66 |
| Upper mounting nuts | 45 | 33 |
| **Rear suspension** | | |
| Anti-roll bar: | | |
| Connecting link balljoint nut | 45 | 33 |
| Mounting clamp bolts | 25 | 18 |
| Backplate/caliper mounting bracket bolts | 55 | 41 |
| Control link: | | |
| Link-to-body pivot bolt | 80 | 59 |
| Link-to-trailing arm bolts | 35 | 26 |
| Hub nut: | | |
| Pre-1998 model year | 175 | 129 |
| 1998 model year onwards: | | |
| Stage 1 | 120 | 89 |
| Stage 2 | Angle-tighten a further 30° | |
| Lower arm: | | |
| Arm-to-body pivot bolt | 80 | 59 |
| Arm-to-trailing arm pivot bolt | 90 | 66 |
| Trailing arm front pivot bolt | 90 | 66 |
| Suspension strut: | | |
| Upper mounting nuts | 50 | 37 |
| Lower mounting bolt | 90 | 66 |
| Piston nut: | | |
| Standard shock absorber | 30 | 22 |
| Nivomat shock absorber | 25 | 18 |
| Upper link: | | |
| Link-to-body bolts | 35 | 26 |
| Link-to-trailing arm pivot bolt | 90 | 66 |
| **Steering** | | |
| Power steering pump: | | |
| Mounting bolts: | | |
| Except GDI engine | 25 | 18 |
| GDI engine | 45 | 33 |
| Outlet pipe union nut | 19 | 14 |
| Steering column: | | |
| Mounting nuts and bolts | 25 | 18 |
| Universal joint clamp bolt | 17 | 13 |

## Torque wrench settings (continued)

| | Nm | lbf ft |
|---|---|---|
| **Steering (continued)** | | |
| Steering gear: | | |
| Mounting bolts .......................................... | 69 | 51 |
| Hydraulic pipe union nuts ................................. | 15 | 11 |
| Steering wheel retaining nut ................................. | 43 | 32 |
| Track rod: | | |
| Balljoint locknut .......................................... | 42 | 31 |
| Balljoint-to-swivel hub nut* ................................. | 24 | 18 |
| Inner balljoint-to-steering rack ............................. | 88 | 65 |
| *If the split pin holes are not correctly aligned at the specified torque, tighten the nut slightly more to bring the holes into alignment.* | | |
| **Roadwheels** | | |
| Wheel nuts ................................................. | 110 | 81 |

---

## 1  General information

The independent front suspension is of the MacPherson strut type, incorporating coil springs and integral telescopic shock absorbers. The MacPherson struts are located by transverse lower suspension arms, which utilise rubber inner mounting bushes, and incorporate a balljoint at the outer ends. The front swivel hubs, which carry the wheel/hub bearings, brake calipers and the hub/disc assemblies, are bolted to the MacPherson struts, and connected to the lower arms via the balljoints. A front anti-roll bar is fitted to all models. The anti-roll bar is rubber-mounted onto the subframe, and is connected to each suspension strut via a connecting link.

In May 2000 (the time of the Phase 2 facelift), the front suspension was modified, with new lower arms, hubs, struts and changes to the front geometry, intended principally to improve ride comfort. After 2001, various Sport models were added to the range, featuring further tweaks to the suspension. In neither case was the fundamental suspension layout changed, however, and repair procedures are hardly affected.

The independent rear suspension incorporates trailing arms and suspension struts. The trailing arms are connected to the body by transverse lower suspension arms and by upper links and control links. The suspension struts incorporate coil springs and integral telescopic shock absorbers and link the lower arm to the body. A rear anti-roll bar is fitted to reduce body roll. The anti-roll bar is rubber mounted onto the underbody and is connected to each lower arm via a connecting link.

The steering column is secured to the steering gear pinion by means of a clamp bolt. The lower end of the column incorporates two universal joints in between which a collapsible section is fitted. In the event of impact, this section of steering column is designed to deform and, if necessary, break in an effort to prevent the steering column being forced towards the driver.

The steering gear is mounted onto the subframe and is connected by two track rods, with balljoints at their outer ends, to the steering arms projecting rearwards from the swivel hubs. The track rod ends are threaded, to facilitate adjustment. The hydraulic steering system is powered by a pump which is belt-driven off the crankshaft pulley.

**Note:** *Self-locking (Nyloc) nuts are used to secure many components in position, and it is recommended that these are renewed whenever they are disturbed. This is particularly important if resistance cannot be felt when the locking portion passes over the bolt or stud thread.*

## 2  Front suspension swivel hub – removal and refitting

**Note:** *A new hub nut and new brake caliper mounting bolts will be required on refitting.*
**Note:** *On non-turbo manual transmission models, the driveshaft outer joint splines may be coated with sealing agent prior to refitting. Where this is the case, it is likely that a puller/extractor will be required to draw the hub assembly off the driveshaft end on removal.*

**2.1 Remove the wheel trim/hub cap and slacken the hub nut with the car standing on its wheels**

### Removal

1 Remove the wheel trim/hub cap (as applicable) then slacken the hub nut with the car resting on its wheels **(see illustration)**. Also slacken the wheel nuts.
2 Chock the rear wheels of the car, firmly apply the handbrake, then jack up the front of the car and support it on axle stands. Remove the appropriate front roadwheel.
3 Slacken and remove the hub nut and (where fitted) washer; discard the nut, a new one should be used on refitting. If the nut was not slackened with the wheels on the ground (see paragraph 1), have an assistant firmly depress the brake pedal to prevent the front hub from rotating, whilst you slacken and remove the hub nut. Alternatively, a tool can be fabricated from two lengths of steel strip (one long, one short) and a nut and bolt; the nut and bolt forming the pivot of a forked tool.
4 Remove the anti-lock braking system (ABS) sensor from the hub as described in Chapter 9.
5 Slide out the retaining clip(s) and free the front brake caliper hose from its bracket(s).
6 Remove the brake disc as described in Chapter 9. Discard the brake caliper mounting bolts – they must be renewed whenever they are disturbed.
7 Extract the split pin, then slacken and remove the nut securing the steering gear track rod end balljoint to the swivel hub **(see illustration)**. Release the balljoint tapered shank using a universal balljoint separator.

**2.7 Extract the split pin, then slacken and remove the track rod balljoint nut**

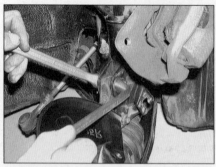

**2.8 Unscrew the nuts and withdraw the bolts securing the swivel hub to the strut**

**2.9 Free the swivel hub from the strut, then release the driveshaft joint from the hub splines**

**2.10a Unscrew the lower arm balljoint nut . . .**

**2.10b . . . then free the swivel hub assembly from the balljoint and remove it**

**2.12 Engage the swivel hub with the lower arm balljoint and tighten the balljoint nut to the specified torque**

**8** Loosen the lower arm balljoint nut slightly then slacken and remove the nuts and withdraw the bolts securing the swivel hub to the suspension strut **(see illustration)**. Discard the nuts and bolts, new ones should be used on refitting.

**9** Taking care not to damage the driveshaft gaiter, release the outer constant velocity joint splines from the hub **(see illustration)**. If the joint is a tight fit, try tapping it out of position using a hammer and a soft metal drift, whilst an assistant supports the hub assembly. If this fails to move the joint, a suitable puller/extractor will be required to draw the hub assembly off the driveshaft end. **Note:** *Support the driveshaft by suspending it with wire or string – do not allow it to hang under its weight, or the joints/gaiters may be damaged.*

**10** Unscrew the nut from the lower arm

balljoint, then free the swivel hub assembly from the balljoint shank and remove it from the car **(see illustrations)**. If necessary, use a balljoint separator to free the hub.

## Refitting

**11** Ensure that the driveshaft outer constant velocity joint and hub splines are clean and dry. If locking compound was present on removal, apply a coat of locking fluid (Volvo recommend sealing agent 1161075-5 – available from your Volvo dealer) to the splines of the driveshaft. On all other models apply a thin film of grease to the driveshaft splines.

**12** Manoeuvre the hub assembly into position, and engaging it with the lower arm balljoint, and screw on the balljoint nut and tighten to the specified torque **(see illustration)**.

**13** Move the top of the swivel hub inwards, at the same time engaging the driveshaft with the hub.

**14** Slide the hub fully onto the driveshaft splines, then insert the two new suspension strut mounting bolts and refit the retaining nuts. Tighten both nuts by hand, then tighten them to the specified torque **(see illustrations)**.

**15** Fit the washer (where fitted) and new hub nut, tightening it by hand only at this stage.

**16** Reconnect the steering track rod balljoint to the swivel hub, then tighten its retaining nut to the specified torque and secure it in position with a new split pin **(see illustration)**.

**17** Refit the brake disc to the hub, referring to Chapter 9 for further information. Slide the caliper into position, making sure the pads pass either side of the disc, then fit the new mounting bolts and tighten them to the specified torque setting (see Chapter 9).

**18** Refit the ABS sensor to the hub as described in Chapter 9 then locate the brake hose in its bracket(s) and secure it in position with the retaining clip(s).

**19** On pre-1998 model year cars, using the method employed during removal to prevent the hub from rotating, tighten the hub nut to the specified torque. Alternatively, lightly tighten the nut at this stage and tighten it to the specified torque once the car is resting on its wheels again.

**20** On cars from 1998 model year onwards, using the method employed during removal to prevent the hub from rotating, tighten the hub

**2.14a Engage the driveshaft joint with the hub then align the swivel hub with the strut . . .**

**2.14b . . . and refit the strut-to-swivel hub bolts, tightening their nuts to the specified torque**

**2.16 Tighten the track rod balljoint to the specified torque, then secure it with a new split pin**

nut to the specified Stage 1 torque setting, then angle-tighten it through the specified Stage 2 angle. It is recommended that an angle-measuring gauge is used during the final stages of the tightening, to ensure accuracy. If a gauge is not available, use white paint to make alignment marks between the nut and hub prior to tightening; the marks can then be used to check that the nut has been rotated through the correct angle. Alternatively, lightly tighten the nut at this stage, and tighten once the car is resting on its wheels again.

**21** Check that the hub rotates freely, then refit the roadwheel and lower the car to the ground. Tighten the wheel nuts to the specified torque then, if not already done, tighten the hub nut **(see illustrations)**.

### 3  Front hub bearings – renewal

**Note:** *The bearing is a pre-adjusted, double-row roller type, and is intended to last the car's entire service life without maintenance or attention. Never overtighten the hub nut in an attempt to adjust the bearing.*

**Note:** *A press will be required to dismantle and rebuild the assembly; if such a tool is not available, a large bench vice and spacers (such as large sockets) may serve as an adequate substitute. The bearing's inner races are an interference fit on the hub; if the inner race remains on the hub when it is pressed out of the hub carrier, a knife-edged bearing puller will be required to remove it.*

**1** Remove the swivel hub assembly as described in Section 2.

**2** Support the swivel hub securely on blocks or in a vice. Using a tubular spacer which bears only on the inner end of the hub flange, press the hub flange out of the bearing. If the bearing's outboard inner race remains on the hub, remove it using a bearing puller (see note above).

**3** Lever out the oil seals, then extract the bearing retaining circlip from the inner end of the swivel hub assembly.

**2.21a  Tighten the hub nut to the specified torque (pre-1998 model year) . . .**

**2.21b  . . . or to the specified torque and angle (1998 model year onwards)**

**4** Where necessary, refit the inner race back in position over the ball cage, and securely support the inner face of the swivel hub. Using a tubular spacer which bears only on the inner race, press the complete bearing assembly out of the swivel hub.

**5** Thoroughly clean the hub and swivel hub, removing all traces of dirt and grease, and polish away any burrs or raised edges which might hinder reassembly. Check both for cracks or any other signs of wear or damage, and renew them if necessary. Renew the circlip, regardless of its apparent condition.

**6** On reassembly, apply a light film of oil to the bearing outer race and hub flange shaft, to aid installation of the bearing.

**7** Securely support the swivel hub, and locate the bearing in the hub. Press the bearing fully into position, ensuring that it enters the hub squarely, using a tubular spacer which bears only on the bearing outer race.

**8** Once the bearing is correctly seated, secure it in position with the new circlip, ensuring that it is correctly located in the groove in the swivel hub.

**9** Turn the swivel hub assembly over and press the new outer oil seal squarely into position. Ensure the seal is pressed fully into position and lubricate its sealing lip with a smear of grease.

**10** Securely support the outer face of the hub flange and, taking care not to damage the oil seal, locate the swivel hub bearing inner race over the end of the hub flange. Press the bearing onto the hub, using a tubular spacer

which bears only on the inner race of the hub bearing, until it seats against the hub shoulder. Check that the hub flange rotates freely, and wipe off any excess oil or grease.

**11** Pack the bearing with grease (Volvo recommend the use of grease 1161001-1 – available from your Volvo dealer) then press the new inner oil seal squarely into position.

**12** Refit the swivel hub assembly as described in Section 2.

### 4  Front suspension strut – removal and refitting

**Note:** *New anti-roll bar connecting link nuts will be required on refitting.*

#### Removal

**1** Chock the rear wheels, apply the handbrake, then jack up the front of the car and support on axle stands. Remove the appropriate roadwheel.

**2** Slide out the retaining clip(s) and free the front brake caliper hose from its bracket(s) on the strut. Also unclip the ABS wiring from its brackets on the strut **(see illustrations)**.

**3** Unscrew the nut securing the anti-roll bar connecting link to the strut, and position the link clear of the strut **(see illustration)**.

**4** Slacken and remove the nuts and withdraw the bolts securing the swivel hub to the suspension strut **(see illustration)**. Note which way round they are fitted, for refitting.

**4.2a  Remove the retaining clip and free the brake hose from its strut bracket . . .**

**4.2b  . . . then unclip the ABS wheel sensor wiring from the strut**

**4.3  Unscrew the retaining nut and free the anti-roll bar connecting link from the strut**

**4.4  Unscrew the nuts and withdraw the strut-to-swivel hub bolts**

**4.5a  Slacken and remove the strut upper mounting nuts . . .**

**4.5b  . . . then manoeuvre the strut assembly out from underneath the wing**

**5** Working in the engine compartment, slacken and remove the three suspension strut upper mounting nuts, then free the strut from the swivel hub and manoeuvre it out from under the wheel arch **(see illustrations)**.

### Refitting

**6** Manoeuvre the strut into position and refit the upper mounting nuts, tightening them by hand only at this stage.
**7** Engage the lower end of the strut with the swivel hub, then insert the strut-to-hub bolts, and tighten to the specified torque setting.
**8** Reconnect the anti-roll bar connecting link to the strut using a new nut, and tighten it to the specified torque.
**9** Clip the ABS sensor and brake hose wiring onto the strut brackets.
**10** Refit the roadwheel, then lower the car to the ground and tighten the wheel nuts to the specified torque.

**11** With the car standing on its wheels, tighten the strut upper mounting nuts to the specified torque.

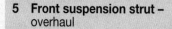

### 5  Front suspension strut – overhaul

⚠️ *Warning: Before attempting to dismantle the front suspension strut, a suitable tool to hold the coil spring in compression must be obtained. Adjustable coil spring compressors are readily-available, and are recommended for this operation. Any attempt to dismantle the strut without such a tool is likely to result in damage or personal injury.*

**1** With the strut removed from the car, clean away all external dirt, then mount it upright in a

vice. Fit the spring compressor and compress the coil spring until tension is relieved from the spring seats **(see illustration)**.
**2** Remove the dust cap from the centre of upper mounting then unscrew the shock absorber piston nut **(see illustrations)**. If necessary, prevent piston rotation by retaining the upper spring seat with a peg spanner located in the spring seat alignment holes.
**3** Remove the nut then lift off the upper mounting followed by the upper spring seat and spring rubber **(see illustrations)**.
**4** Lift off the coil spring, noting which way around it is fitted, and remove the bump stop and dust sleeve and from the shock absorber piston **(see illustration)**.
**5** Examine the shock absorber for signs of fluid leakage. Check the piston for signs of pitting along its entire length, and check the shock body for signs of damage. While

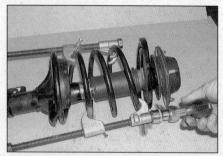

**5.1  Fit the spring compressors and compress the strut spring to relieve tension from the spring seats**

**5.2a  Remove the dust cap . . .**

**5.2b  . . . and unscrew the shock absorber piston nut**

**5.3a  Remove the upper mounting assembly . . .**

**5.3b  . . . then lift off the upper spring seat and the spring rubber**

**5.4  Slide off the bump stop and dust sleeve from the shock absorber piston**

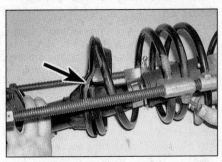

**5.8  Refit the coil spring, making sure its lower end is against the spring seat stop (arrowed)**

**5.10a  Refit the upper spring seat, making sure its holes (arrowed) . . .**

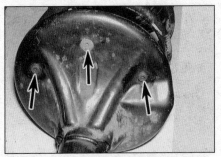

**5.10b  . . . are correctly aligned with the three bolts (arrowed) on the lower spring seat**

holding it in an upright position, test the operation of the shock absorber by moving the piston through a full stroke, and then through short strokes of 50 to 100 mm. In both cases, the resistance felt should be smooth and continuous. If the resistance is jerky, or uneven, or if there is any visible sign of wear or damage to the shock absorber, renewal is necessary. **Note:** *Shock absorbers must be renewed in pairs.*

6 Inspect all other components for signs of damage or deterioration, and renew any that are suspect. If the upper mounting bearing is worn the complete mounting assembly must be renewed.
7 Clip the dust sleeve onto the bump stop, lubricate the bump stop with petroleum jelly, and fit the assembly to the piston.
8 Refit the coil spring to the strut base, making sure its flatter surface is at the top,

and position its end against the spring seat stop **(see illustration)**.
9 Fit the spring rubber and upper spring seat to the to the top of the coil spring.
10 On all models except later (2000-on) Sport or Dynamic models, make sure the spring seat holes are correctly aligned with the three bolts on the strut lower spring seat **(see illustrations)**.
11 On 2000-on Sport or Dynamic models, the reference hole in the upper spring seat should be turned clockwise so it sits at 20° to the corresponding bolt in the lower spring seat **(see illustration)**. Both left- and right-hand strut upper seats are rotated clockwise.
12 Ensure the spring seat is correctly engaged with the strut piston, then refit the upper mounting assembly and screw on the piston nut. Retain the spring seat, and tighten the piston nut to the specified torque.
13 Ensure the coil spring lower end is in contact with the spring seat stop, and the upper and lower seats are still correctly aligned, then carefully release the spring compressor and remove it from the strut.
14 Refit the strut to the car as described in Section 4.

## 6  Front suspension lower arm – removal, overhaul and refitting

**Note:** *New front pivot bolt nuts will be required on refitting.*

### Removal

1 Chock the rear wheels, firmly apply the handbrake, then loosen the appropriate front wheel nuts. Jack up the front of the car and support on axle stands, then remove the front wheel.
2 Slacken and remove the lower arm rear mounting bracket bolts, and the front pivot bolt and nut, then free the lower arm from the subframe.
3 Unscrew the lower arm balljoint nut a few turns, then free the balljoint shank from the swivel hub using a universal balljoint separator. Remove the nut completely, and manoeuvre the arm away from the car.

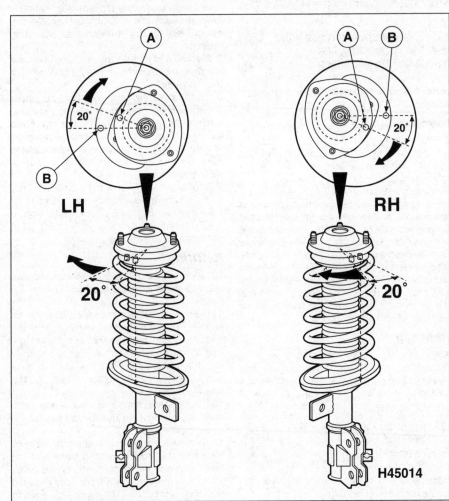

**5.11  On 2000-on Sport and Dynamic models, spring upper seat is rotated 20° clockwise**

*A  Hole in upper spring seat*          *B  Bolt in lower spring seat*

**7.2a Slacken and remove the balljoint nuts . . .**

**7.2b . . . and remove the anti-roll bar connecting link**

## Overhaul

**4** Thoroughly clean the lower arm and the area around the arm mountings, removing all traces of dirt and underseal if necessary, then check carefully for cracks, distortion or any other signs of wear or damage, paying particular attention to the pivot bushes and balljoint. The balljoint is an integral part of the lower arm, and cannot be renewed separately. If the arm or balljoint are damaged, then the complete arm must be renewed.

**5** If the balljoint is serviceable but the gaiter shows signs of damage or deterioration, the gaiter should be renewed. Release the retaining springs and slide the gaiter off the balljoint. Grease the balljoint, then slide the new gaiter into position. Ensure the gaiter is correctly located on the lower arm, then secure it in position with the retaining springs, making sure they are correctly seated in the gaiter grooves.

**6** Renewal of either pivot bush will require the use of a hydraulic press and several spacers, and is therefore best entrusted to a Volvo dealer or garage with access to the necessary equipment. If the equipment is available, the front bush can be pressed out and the new one installed, making sure the bush is positioned so it projects from the arm by the same amount on either side. The positioning of the rear bush in relation to the lower arm is even more critical. Prior to removal, note the **exact** position of the bush locating pin in relation to the lower arm. Press on the new bush, making sure its locating pin is positioned in exactly the same position; failure to do this will result in excess load being placed on the bush rubber material, leading to its failure.

## Refitting

**7** Manoeuvre the lower arm into position, and locate the balljoint shank in the base of the swivel hub. Refit the retaining nut to the balljoint, tightening it by hand only.

**8** Locate the lower arm front bush in the subframe, then insert the pivot bolt and fit the new nut, tightening by hand only at this stage.

**9** Refit the lower arm rear mounting bracket, making sure it is correctly engaged with the pivot bush, and tighten its retaining bolts to the specified torque.

**10** Tighten the balljoint nut to the specified torque.

**11** Refit the roadwheel, then lower the car to the ground and tighten the wheel nuts to the specified torque.

**12** Rock the car to settle the lower arm in position then, with the car resting on wheels, tighten the front pivot bolt to the specified torque.

**13** Check and, if necessary, adjust the front wheel alignment as described in Section 29.

---

### 7 Front suspension anti-roll bar connecting link – removal and refitting

**Note:** New retaining nuts will be required on refitting.

## Removal

**1** Firmly apply the handbrake, then jack up the front of the car and support it on axle stands. To improve access, remove the roadwheel.

**2** Slacken and remove the nuts securing the connecting link to the suspension strut and anti-roll bar, and remove the link from the car. To prevent rotation, retain the balljoint shank with an Allen key as the nuts are slackened **(see illustrations)**.

**3** Examine the connecting link for signs of damage, paying particular attention to the balljoints, and renew if necessary. Note that the connecting link retaining nuts must be renewed as a matter of course.

## Refitting

**4** Refitting is a reversal of the removal procedure, using new retaining nuts and tightening them to the specified torque setting.

---

### 8 Front suspension anti-roll bar – removal and refitting

**Note:** New anti-roll bar connecting link nuts will be required on refitting.
**Note:** An engine support bar or hoist will be required to support the engine/transmission whilst the subframe is unbolted.

## Removal

**1** Peel back the carpet from around the base of the steering column to gain access to the column lower joint. Position the steering wheel so that the joint clamp bolt is accessible, then engage the steering lock.

**2** Unscrew the clamp bolt from the steering column lower universal joint. Using paint or a suitable marker pen, make alignment marks between the joint and steering gear pinion, then disengage the steering column from the pinion.

**3** Fold back the carpet, then unscrew the retaining bolts securing the steering gear sealing plate to the bulkhead. Cut the cable-tie (early models), then free the plate from the steering gear and remove it from the car.

**4** Carry out the operations described in paragraphs 1 to 8 of Section 9.

**5** Slacken and remove the retaining bolts and remove the rear mounting clamps from the left- and right-hand lower suspension arms.

**6** Place a jack and a suitable block of wood under the subframe, then slacken and remove the two subframe front mounting bolts. Taking care not to strain any pipes/hoses, carefully lower the subframe assembly until access can be gained to the anti-roll bar mounting clamps.

**7** Slacken and remove the retaining bolts and washers, then remove mounting clamps from the subframe.

**8** Manoeuvre the anti-roll bar out from underneath the car and remove its mounting bushes, noting each one's correct fitted location. If the anti-roll bar is to be removed for any length of time, raise the subframe back up into position and loosely refit its mounting bolts.

**9** Carefully examine the anti-roll bar components for signs of wear, damage or deterioration, paying particular attention to the mounting bushes. Renew worn components as necessary.

## Refitting

**10** Slide the mounting bushes into position, aligning them with the tape on the anti-roll bar.

**11** Refit the anti-roll bar, making sure the flat surface of each mounting bush is against the subframe, and refit the mounting brackets. Ensure the brackets are correctly engaged with the rubbers, then refit the retaining bolts and washers, and tighten them to the specified torque.

**12** Raise the subframe assembly into position, taking care not to trap any of the wiring/pipes/hoses.

**13** Ensure the subframe is correctly located, then refit the front mounting bolts and the lower arm rear mounting brackets and bolts. Make sure the brackets are correctly engaged with the pivot bushes, then tighten all bolts to their specified torque settings.

**14** Working inside the car, refit the steering gear sealing plate to the bulkhead and securely tighten its retaining bolts. Ensure the gaiter is correctly located on the steering gear housing, and (on early models) secure it in position with a new cable-tie.

**15** Align the marks made prior to removal, and engage the steering column joint with the steering gear pinion. Refit the clamp bolt, tighten it to the specified torque, then seat the carpet back in position.

**16** Carry out the operations described in paragraphs 20 to 27 of Section 9.

## 9  Front suspension subframe – removal and refitting

**Note:** *New lower arm front pivot bolt nuts and anti-roll bar connecting link nuts will be required on refitting.*

**Note:** *An engine support bar or hoist will be required to support the engine/transmission whilst the subframe is removed.*

### Removal

**1** Chock the rear wheels, firmly apply the handbrake, then loosen the front wheel nuts. Jack up the front of the car and support on axle stands. Remove both front roadwheels.

**2** Remove the retaining screws/fasteners, and remove the undershield from beneath the engine/transmission.

**3** Remove the exhaust system front pipe as described in Chapter 4C.

**4** Undo the retaining bolts and remove the exhaust front pipe heat shield (where fitted).

**5** Attach a support bar or engine hoist to the lifting hook on the cylinder head, and use it to support the weight of the engine and transmission. Alternatively, support the engine/transmission with a jack and block of wood.

**6** Slacken and remove the through-bolts from the front and rear mountings, then undo the mounting bolts and remove the crossmember from beneath the engine/transmission. Recover the upper and lower mounting rubbers and spacers from the crossmember mountings, noting their correct fitted locations. Renew the mounting rubbers if they show signs of damage or deterioration.

**7** Referring to Chapter 7A, disconnect the gearchange selector cables/rod (as applicable) from the transmission.

**8** Slacken and remove the nuts securing the left- and right-hand connecting links to the anti-roll bar. To prevent rotation, retain the balljoint shanks with an Allen key as the nuts are unscrewed. Discard the nuts – new ones should be used on refitting.

**9** Slacken and remove the retaining bolts then remove the steering gear mounting clamps from the subframe. Free the steering gear, then slacken and remove the bolts securing the hydraulic pipe/hose brackets to the subframe. Free the pipes/hoses, and position them clear so they do not hinder subframe removal.

**10** Slacken and remove the retaining bolts and remove the rear mounting clamps from the left- and right-hand lower suspension arms.

**11** Slacken and remove the nuts and withdraw the front pivot bolts securing the lower suspension arms to the subframe. Free both lower arms from the subframe, and position them clear.

**12** Make a final check that all control cables/hoses attached to the subframe have been released and positioned clear so that they will not hinder the removal procedure.

**13** Place a jack and a suitable block of wood under the subframe to support the subframe as it is lowered.

**14** Slacken and remove the two subframe front mounting bolts, then carefully lower the subframe assembly out of position and remove it from underneath the car.

### Refitting

**15** Raise the subframe assembly into position, taking care not to trap any of the wiring/pipes/hoses. Ensure the subframe is correctly located, then refit the front mounting bolts, tightening them by hand only at this stage.

**16** Ensure the steering gear is correctly seated on the subframe and all pipes and hoses are correctly routed before continuing.

**17** Engage the lower arms with the subframe and insert the front pivot bolts. Fit the new nuts to the pivot bolts, tightening them lightly only at this stage.

**18** Refit the rear mounting brackets to the lower arms, making sure they are correctly engaged with the pivot bushes, and tighten the retaining bolts to the specified torque.

**19** Tighten the subframe front mounting bolts to the specified torque setting.

**20** Seat the steering gear assembly on the subframe and fit the mounting clamps. Refit the mounting bolts, tightening them all by hand first, then go around and tighten them to the specified torque. Ensure the pipes and hoses are correctly routed, then refit the bracket bolts and tighten securely

**21** Reconnect the connecting links to the anti-roll bar and fit the new nuts to the balljoints, tightening them to the specified torque.

**22** Reconnect the gearchange selector cables/rod (as applicable) to the transmission as described in Chapter 7A.

**23** Ensure the upper and lower mounting rubbers and the spacers are correctly fitted to the engine/transmission crossmember holes, then manoeuvre the crossmember into position. Refit the mounting bolts, tightening them to the specified torque, then refit the through-bolts to the engine/transmission mountings. Lower the engine, and rock it to settle it in position. Tighten the engine/transmission rear mounting through-bolt to the specified torque setting, then tighten the front mounting through-bolt to the specified torque.

**24** Refit the exhaust heat shield (where fitted) to the cylinder block, and tighten its retaining bolts to the specified torque (see Chapter 4C).

**25** Refit the exhaust front pipe as described in Chapter 4C.

**26** Securely refit the undershield, then refit the roadwheels and lower the car to the ground. Tighten the wheel nuts to the specified torque.

**27** Rock the car to settle the suspension in position then, with the car resting on wheels, tighten the lower arm front pivot bolts to the specified torque.

**28** Check and, if necessary, adjust the front wheel alignment as described in Section 29.

## 10  Rear hub assembly – removal and refitting

**Note:** *A new hub nut and new brake caliper mounting bolts will be needed on refitting.*

### Removal

**1** Remove the brake disc as described in Chapter 9.

**2** Remove the hub cap, then slacken and remove the hub nut **(see illustrations)**. Discard the nut; a new one should be used on refitting.

**3** Remove the hub assembly from the stub axle **(see illustration)**. Inspect the hub assembly for signs of wear or damage, and renew if necessary.

**10.2a  Carefully tap off the hub cap . . .**  **10.2b  . . . then slacken and remove the hub nut . . .**

**10.3** . . . and pull the rear hub assembly off the stub axle

**10.6 Tighten the rear hub nut to the specified torque (pre-1998 model year)**

**10.7 Tighten the rear hub nut to the specified torque and angle (1998 model year onwards)**

### *Refitting*

**4** Prior to refitting, remove all traces of dirt from the ABS sensor and the toothed ring which is fitted to the rear of the hub.

**5** Slide the hub assembly onto the stub axle, and screw on the new hub nut.

**6** On pre-1998 model year cars, tighten the hub nut to the specified torque, then securely refit the hub cap **(see illustration)**.

**7** On later models, tighten the hub nut to the specified stage 1 torque setting, then angle-tighten it through the specified stage 2 angle. It is recommended that an angle-measuring gauge is used during the final stages of the tightening, to ensure accuracy **(see illustration)**. If a gauge is not available, use white paint to make alignment marks between the nut and hub prior to tightening; the marks can then be used to check that the nut has been rotated through the correct angle. Once the hub nut is correctly tightened securely refit the hub cap.

**8** On all models, refit the brake disc as described in Chapter 9.

### 11 Rear hub bearings – renewal

**Note:** *The bearing is a pre-adjusted, double-row roller type, and is intended to last the car's entire service life without maintenance or attention. Never overtighten the hub nut in an attempt to adjust the bearing.*

**1** The rear hub bearings are an integral part of the hub assembly, and are not available separately. If the bearings are worn, renew the hub assembly as described in Section 10.

### 12 Rear suspension strut – removal and refitting

**Note:** *A new strut lower mounting bolt nut and upper mounting nuts will be required on refitting, as will a new lower suspension arm-to-trailing arm bolt nut.*

### *Removal*

#### Saloon models

**1** Open the boot lid, then undo the retaining screws and remove the luggage compartment floor panel. Peel the boot lid sealing strip away from the relevant side and base of the boot lid aperture, then carefully unclip the luggage compartment rear trim panel in an upwards direction and remove it from the car.

**2** Remove the relevant luggage compartment side trim panel rear fasteners (loosen the centre screws a few turns, then pull out the complete fastener) and fold the rear of trim panel inwards to gain access to the strut upper mounting. To improve access, remove the front fasteners (located behind the rear seat back) and remove the panel completely.

**3** With the car resting on its wheels, slacken and remove the retaining bolts from the rear anti-roll bar mounting clamps.

**4** Chock the front wheels, then loosen the rear roadwheel nuts. Jack up the rear of the car and support it securely on axle stands. Remove the rear wheels.

**5** Unscrew the nut from the lower suspension arm-to-trailing arm bolt, and from the strut lower mounting bolt, then withdraw both bolts. Have an assistant support the strut then remove the sealing cap from the strut upper mounting. Slacken and remove the upper mounting nuts (do not loosen the strut's larger central nut) and manoeuvre the strut out of position.

#### Estate models

**6** Undo the retaining screws and remove the luggage compartment floor panel.

**7** Peel off the tailgate sealing strip from around the base of the tailgate aperture, then unclip and remove the sill trim panel from the rear of the luggage compartment **(see illustration)**.

**8** Carefully prise out the luggage compartment courtesy light from the relevant rear pillar trim panel, and disconnect its wiring.

**9** Prise out the speaker grille, then undo the retaining screws and carefully unclip the trim panel and remove it from the pillar **(see illustrations)**.

**10** Fold the rear seat cushion and back forwards to gain access to the seat back side cushion retaining bolt. Undo the bolt, then slide the side cushion upwards and out of position **(see illustrations)**.

**12.7 On Estate models, peel off the sealing strip then unclip the sill trim panel from the tailgate aperture**

**12.9a Undo the retaining screws (arrowed) . . .**

**12.9b . . . and unclip the rear pillar upper trim panel**

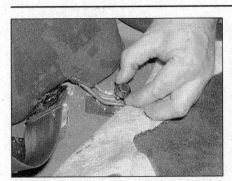

**12.10a Slacken and remove the retaining bolt . . .**

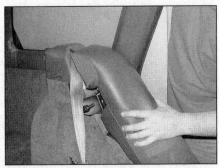

**12.10b . . . then lift the seat back side cushion out of position**

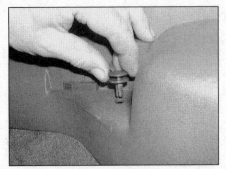

**12.11a Remove the retaining fasteners (rear fastener shown) . . .**

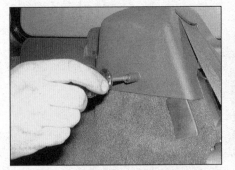

**12.11b . . . then undo the retaining screw . . .**

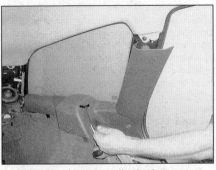

**12.11c . . . and unclip the luggage compartment upper trim panel, freeing it from the seat belt**

**12.12a Release the fasteners/screws and fold back the luggage compartment side trim panel**

**11** Remove the two retaining fasteners and the retaining screw, then carefully unclip the luggage compartment upper trim panel and remove it from the car, freeing it from the side seat belt **(see illustrations)**.

**12** Remove the rear retaining fastener(s) and screw(s), and fold the luggage side trim panel inwards. Remove the insulation panel and foam to gain access to the strut upper mounting **(see illustrations)**.

**13** Remove the strut as described in paragraphs 3 to 5 **(see illustration)**.

### Refitting

**14** Manoeuvre the strut assembly into position, making sure the lower end of the coil spring is facing towards the rear of the car, and have an assistant screw on the new upper mounting nuts. Tighten the mounting nuts to the specified torque, then refit the sealing cap.

**15** Engage the lower end of the strut with the lower arm, then insert the lower arm bolt and the strut lower mounting bolt. Fit the new nuts to the bolts, tightening them lightly only at this stage.

**16** Refit the roadwheel, then lower the car to the ground and tighten the wheel nuts to the specified torque.

**17** Align the anti-roll bar mounting clamps with its mountings and refit the retaining bolts, tightening them lightly only.

**18** Rock the car to settle the rear suspension components in position, then tighten the anti-

roll bar mounting clamp bolts to the specified torque. Rock the car again, then tighten the strut lower mounting bolt and the lower arm-

**12.12b Remove the insulation panel . . .**

**12.13 Remove the two rear strut upper mounting nuts – do not loosen the larger centre nut**

to-trailing arm bolt to their specified torque settings **(see illustration)**. Securely refit all the luggage compartment trim panels.

**12.12c . . . and the foam block to gain access to the strut upper mounting**

**12.18 Tighten the strut lower mounting bolt and the other specified fixings with the car resting on its wheels**

**14.3 Unscrew the nut and withdraw the upper link-to-trailing arm pivot bolt . . .**

### 13 Rear suspension strut – overhaul

⚠️ *Warning: Before attempting to dismantle the suspension strut, a suitable tool to hold the coil spring in compression must be obtained. Adjustable coil spring compressors are readily available, and are recommended for this operation. Any attempt to dismantle the strut without such a tool is likely to result in damage or personal injury.*

**Note:** *A new shock absorber piston nut will be required on reassembly.*

1 With the strut removed from the car, clean away all external dirt, then mount it upright in a vice.

2 Fit the spring compressor and compress the coil spring until tension is relieved from the spring seats.

3 Slacken the shock absorber piston nut whilst retaining the piston with a suitable Allen key or spanner (as applicable).

4 Remove the nut, then lift off the washer, mounting plate assembly and spring rubber.

5 Lift off the coil spring, then slide off the dust cover from the piston.

6 Examine the shock absorber for signs of fluid leakage. Check the piston for signs of pitting along its entire length, and check the shock body for signs of damage. While holding it in an upright position, test the operation of the shock absorber by moving the piston through a full stroke, and then

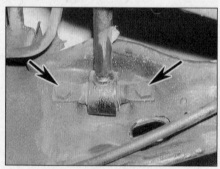

**15.4 Control link-to-trailing arm bolts (arrowed)**

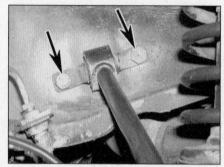

**14.4 . . . then undo the two bolts (arrowed) and remove the upper link**

through short strokes of 50 to 100 mm. In both cases, the resistance felt should be smooth and continuous. If the resistance is jerky, or uneven, or if there is any visible sign of wear or damage to the shock absorber, renewal is necessary. **Note:** *Shock absorbers must be renewed in pairs.*

7 Inspect all other components for signs of damage or deterioration, and renew any that are suspect.

8 Fully extend the piston rod, and slide on the dust cover.

9 Refit the coil spring, making sure the spring end abuts the spring seat stop.

10 Fit the spring rubber to the top of the spring, then refit the upper mounting and washer.

11 Screw on the new piston nut, and tighten it to the specified torque.

12 Ensure all components are correctly positioned, then carefully release the spring compressor and remove it from the strut.

13 Ensure the lower end of the spring is tight against the stop and the spring rubber is parallel to the upper mounting, then refit the strut as described in Section 12.

### 14 Rear suspension upper link – removal and refitting

**Note:** *A new pivot bolt nut will be required on refitting.*

#### Removal

1 Chock the front wheels, then loosen the relevant rear wheel nuts. Jack up the rear of the car and support it securely on axle stands. Remove the relevant roadwheel.

2 Position a jack beneath the lower suspension arm, and raise it until it is just supporting the weight of the arm.

3 Unscrew the nut and withdraw the bolt securing the upper link to the trailing arm **(see illustration)**.

4 Undo the bolts securing the upper link to the body, and remove it from the car **(see illustration)**.

5 Inspect the link bushes for signs of damage or deterioration. If the bushes are damaged, the complete link assembly must be renewed.

#### Refitting

6 Manoeuvre the link into position, and insert its mounting bolts and the trailing arm bolt. Tighten the link-to-body bolts to the specified torque, then fit the new nut to the trailing arm bolt, tightening it lightly only at this stage.

7 Refit the roadwheel, then lower the car to the ground and tighten the wheel nuts to the specified torque.

8 Rock the car to settle the rear suspension components in position, then tighten the link-to-trailing arm bolt to the specified torque.

9 If a new upper link has been installed, check the rear wheel alignment as described in Section 29.

### 15 Rear suspension control link – removal and refitting

**Note:** *A new pivot bolt nut will be required on refitting.*

#### Removal

1 Chock the front wheels, then loosen the relevant rear wheel nuts. Jack up the rear of the car and support it securely on axle stands. Remove the relevant roadwheel.

2 Position a jack beneath the lower suspension arm, and raise it until it is just supporting the weight of the arm.

3 Clean the area around the control link-to-body pivot bolt. Make alignment marks between the bolt eccentric washer and the body bracket; these marks can be used on refitting to preserve the rear wheel alignment.

4 Slacken and remove the two bolts securing the control link to the trailing arm **(see illustration)**.

5 Unscrew the nut from the pivot bolt, and remove the washer. Withdraw the pivot bolt and manoeuvre the control link out of position; the eccentric washer is an integral part of the bolt.

6 Inspect the link bushes for signs of damage or deterioration. If the bushes are damaged, the complete link assembly must be renewed.

#### Refitting

7 Manoeuvre the link into position and insert its trailing arm mounting bolts.

8 Slide the link pivot bolt into position, making sure it is correctly located. Fit the washer and new nut to the bolt, tightening it lightly only at this stage.

9 Tighten the control link trailing arm bolts to the specified torque.

10 Refit the roadwheel, then lower the car to the ground and tighten the wheel nuts to the specified torque.

11 Rock the car to settle the rear suspension components in position. Ensure the marks made prior to removal are correctly aligned, then tighten the control link-to-body bolt to the specified torque.

12 On completion, check the rear wheel alignment as described in Section 29.

**16.1 Unscrew the nut and detach the anti-roll bar connecting link from the lower arm**

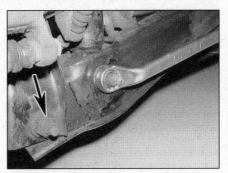

**16.4 Remove the nut and withdraw the strut lower mounting bolt (lower arm-to-trailing arm pivot bolt arrowed)**

**16.6 Unscrew the nut, then remove the inner pivot bolt and remove the lower arm from the car**

## 16 Rear suspension lower arm – removal, overhaul and refitting

**Note:** *New pivot bolt nuts will be required on refitting, as will a new suspension strut lower mounting bolt nut and an anti-roll bar connecting link nut.*

### Removal

**1** With the car resting on its wheels, slacken and remove the nut securing the anti-roll bar connecting link to the relevant lower arm, and free the link balljoint **(see illustration)**.

**2** Chock the front wheels then jack up the rear of the car and support it securely on axle stands. Remove the relevant roadwheel.

**3** Clean the area around the lower arm to body pivot bolt. Make alignment marks between the bolt eccentric washer and the body bracket; these marks can be used on refitting to preserve the rear wheel alignment.

**4** Slacken and remove the nut and withdraw the suspension strut lower mounting bolt from the lower arm **(see illustration)**.

**5** Unscrew the nut and withdraw the outer pivot bolt which secures the lower arm to the trailing arm.

**6** Unscrew the nut from the lower arm inner pivot bolt and remove the washer **(see illustration)**. Withdraw the pivot bolt and manoeuvre the lower arm out of position; the eccentric washer is an integral part of the bolt.

### Overhaul

**7** Thoroughly clean the lower arm and the area around the arm mountings, removing all traces of dirt and underseal if necessary, then check carefully for cracks, distortion or any other signs of wear or damage, paying particular attention to the pivot bushes. Renewal of either pivot bush will require the use of a hydraulic press and several spacers, and is therefore best entrusted to a Volvo dealer or garage with access to the necessary equipment. If the equipment is available, each bush can be pressed out and the new one installed, making sure that it is positioned centrally.

### Refitting

**8** Manoeuvre the lower arm into position, and slide the inner pivot bolt into position, making sure the eccentric washer is correctly located. Fit the washer and new nut to the bolt, tightening it lightly only at this stage.

**9** Pass the strut through the lower arm, then align the lower arm with the trailing arm and insert the outer pivot bolt. Fit the new nut to the pivot bolt, tightening it lightly only at this stage.

**10** Align the strut lower mounting with the lower arm, and insert the mounting bolt. Fit the new nut to the bolt, tightening it lightly only.

**11** Refit the roadwheel, then lower the car to the ground and tighten the wheel nuts to the specified torque.

**12** Rock the car to settle the rear suspension components in position, then tighten the lower arm outer pivot bolt and the suspension strut lower mounting bolt to their specified torque settings. Ensure the marks made prior to removal are correctly aligned, then tighten the lower arm inner pivot bolt to the specified torque.

**13** Engage the anti-roll bar connecting link balljoint with the lower arm, then fit the new retaining nut, tightening it to the specified torque.

**14** On completion, check the rear wheel alignment as described in Section 29.

## 17 Rear suspension trailing arm – removal, overhaul and refitting

**Note:** *New upper link and lower arm pivot bolt nuts will be required on refitting.*

### Removal

**1** Remove the control link as described in Section 15.

**2** Undo the retaining screws/fastener and remove the protective cover from the front of the trailing arm **(see illustrations)**.

**3** Referring to Chapter 9, carry out the following procedures:

*a) Detach the handbrake cable from the brake caliper, then undo the retaining nut/bolts and free the cable from the trailing arm.*

*b) Remove the brake disc.*

*c) Disconnect the ABS wheel sensor wiring connector. Unclip the wiring so the sensor is free to be removed with the trailing arm. If the trailing arm is being renewed, remove the sensor completely.*

**4** If the trailing arm is being renewed, remove the hub assembly as described in Section 10. Slacken and remove the retaining bolts, and remove the brake backplate and caliper mounting bracket from the arm.

**5** With the lower arm supported, slacken and remove the nuts and pivot bolts securing the upper link and lower arm to the trailing arm.

**17.2a Remove the retaining screws/fastener . . .**

**17.2b . . . and remove the cover to access the trailing arm front mounting (left-hand side shown)**

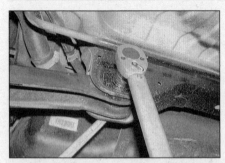

**17.13 All lower arm fixings must be tightened to the specified torque only with the car resting on its wheels**

**6** Slacken and remove the trailing arm-to-body front mounting bolt, and remove the arm from the car.

## Overhaul

**7** Thoroughly clean the trailing arm and the area around the arm mountings, removing all traces of dirt and underseal if necessary, then check carefully for cracks, distortion or any other signs of wear or damage, paying particular attention to the front pivot bush. Renewal of the pivot bush will require the use of a hydraulic press and several spacers, and is therefore best entrusted to a Volvo dealer or garage with access to the necessary equipment. If the equipment is available, the bush can be pressed out and the new one installed, making sure that it is positioned centrally in the arm.

## Refitting

**8** Manoeuvre the arm into position and refit its front mounting bolt, tightening it lightly only at this stage.
**9** Insert the pivot bolts securing the upper link and lower arm to the trailing arm and fit the new nuts, tighten both only lightly at this stage.
**10** Where necessary, refit the brake caliper mounting bracket and backplate to the trailing arm, tightening the retaining bolts to the specified torque, then refit the hub assembly as described in Section 10.
**11** Referring to Chapter 9, carry out the following:
  *a) Refit the rear wheel ABS sensor (where removed) and reconnect the wiring connector.*

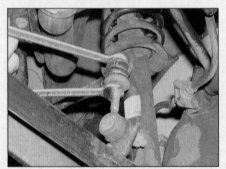

**18.1 Unscrew the anti-roll bar connecting link nut**

*b) Refit the brake disc and caliper.*
*c) Reconnect the handbrake cable to the trailing arm and caliper, and adjust the cable.*
**12** Refit the control link as described in Section 15.
**13** With the car resting on its wheels, rock it to settle the trailing arm in position, then tighten the lower arm outer pivot bolt, the upper link outer pivot bolt, and the trailing arm front mounting bolt to their specified torque settings **(see illustration)**. Once all bolts are correctly tightened, refit the protective cover to the car underbody.
**14** On completion, check the rear wheel alignment as described in Section 29.

## 18 Rear suspension anti-roll bar connecting link – removal and refitting

**Note:** *New connecting link nuts will be required on refitting.*

### Removal

**1** With the car resting on its wheels, slacken and remove the nut securing the connecting link to the anti-roll bar, and remove the upper washer and rubber spacer **(see illustration)**.
**2** Slacken and remove the nut securing the connecting link balljoint to the lower arm, then remove the connecting link complete with the anti-roll bar lower rubber spacer and washer. If necessary, prevent the balljoint shank rotating by retaining it with an Allen or Torx key whilst the nut is slackened.
**3** Inspect the connecting link balljoint and the anti-roll bar rubber spacers for signs of damage or deterioration, and renew if necessary. The nuts should be renewed as a matter of course.

### Refitting

**4** Fit the lower washer and rubber spacer to the connecting link, then manoeuvre the link into position. Engage the link with the anti-roll bar, then fit the upper rubber spacer and washer and screw on the new nut.
**5** Locate the balljoint shank in the lower arm bracket, then fit the new retaining nut and tighten to the specified torque.

**18.6 Measuring the thread visible above the top of the nut**

**6** Tighten the nut securing the link to the anti-roll bar until 3 to 5 mm of the connecting link thread is visible **(see illustration)**.

## 19 Rear suspension anti-roll bar – removal and refitting

**Note:** *New connecting link nuts will be required on refitting.*

### Removal

**1** With the car resting on its wheels, slacken and remove the anti-roll bar mounting clamp bolts, and remove both clamps.
**2** Unscrew the nuts securing the connecting links to the ends of the anti-roll bar, and remove the upper washer and rubber spacer from each link.
**3** Manoeuvre the anti-roll bar out from underneath the car, and remove its mounting bushes, noting each one's correct fitted location. Also remove the lower rubber spacers and washers from the connecting links, and store them with the bar.
**4** Carefully examine the anti-roll bar components for signs of wear, damage or deterioration, paying particular attention to the mounting bushes and spacers. Renew worn components as necessary.

### Refitting

**5** Slide the mounting bushes into position on the anti-roll bar, then refit the lower washers and rubber spacers to the connecting links.
**6** Manoeuvre the anti-roll bar into position, making sure that the flat surface of each mounting bush is against the bracket, and refit the mounting clamps. Ensure the clamps are correctly engaged with the rubbers, then refit the retaining bolts, tightening them by hand only.
**7** Engage the anti-roll bar ends with the connecting links, and install the upper rubber spacers and washers. Fit the new nuts to the connecting links, and tighten each one until 3 to 5 mm of the connecting link thread is visible.
**8** Rock the car to settle the anti-roll bar in position, then tighten the mounting clamp bolts to the specified torque.

## 20 Steering wheel – removal and refitting

⚠️ **Warning: Refer to the precautions given in Chapter 12 before proceeding.**

### Removal

**1** Remove the airbag as described in Chapter 12, Section 25.
**2** Position the front wheels in the straight-ahead position, and engage the steering lock.
**3** Slacken and remove the steering wheel

retaining nut **(see illustration)**. Hold the wheel rim as the nut is undone – do not rely on the steering lock alone, or the lock may be damaged. Mark the steering wheel and steering column shaft in relation to each other.

**4** Remove the locking screw from the plastic strip. Securely fit it to the airbag contact unit lug, and tighten it lightly to lock the unit in position **(see illustrations)**. **Do not** attempt to rotate the contact unit once the locking screw is in position.

**5** Lift the steering wheel off the column splines, taking care not to damage the contact unit wiring **(see illustration)**.

**HAYNES HiNT** *If the wheel is tight, tap it up near the centre, using the palm of your hand, or twist it from side-to-side, whilst pulling upwards to release it from the shaft splines.*

## Refitting

**6** Prior to refitting, ensure that the indicator column switch is in its central (off) position. Failure to do this could lead to the steering wheel lug breaking the switch tab as the steering wheel is refitted.

**7** Pass the contact unit wiring through the steering wheel centre, and seat the wheel on the column splines, aligning the marks made on removal.

**8** Refit the steering wheel retaining nut, and tighten it to the specified torque.

**9** Remove the locking screw from the contact unit lug, then refit it to the plastic strip and screw it back into the wheel.

**10** Refit the airbag as described in Chapter 12, Section 25.

**21 Steering column –**
removal, inspection
and refitting

## Removal

**1** Disconnect the battery negative lead (see *Disconnecting the battery*).

**2** Remove the steering wheel as described in Section 20.

**3** Slacken and remove the retaining screws (the lower screw is hidden behind a trim cap) and remove the lower panel from the driver's side of the facia, disconnecting the wiring from the footwell light **(see illustrations)**.

**4** Release the height adjustment lever, then undo the retaining screws and unclip the upper and lower shrouds from the steering column **(see illustrations)**.

**5** Remove the combination switch holder assembly from the steering column as described in Chapter 12, Section 4.

**6** Disconnect the wiring connector from the ignition switch, and free the wiring from the steering column.

**20.3 Remove the steering wheel retaining nut**

**20.4b . . . and screw it lightly into the airbag contact unit lug to lock it**

**7** Using paint or a suitable marker pen, make alignment marks between the column universal joint and the steering gear pinion, then slacken and remove the clamp bolt **(see illustration)**.

**21.3a Undo the screws (arrowed) and remove the driver's side lower panel . . .**

**21.4a Undo the screws (arrowed) . . .**

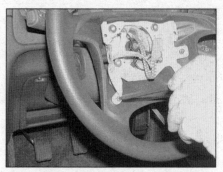
**20.4a Remove the locking screw from the plastic strip . . .**

**20.5 Remove the steering wheel, feeding the wiring through as it is removed**

**8** Slacken and remove the column mounting nuts and bolts, then free the column from the steering gear pinion and manoeuvre it out of position **(see illustration)**.

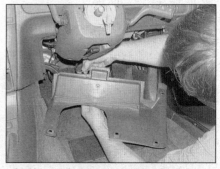
**21.3b . . . disconnecting the wiring from the footwell illumination light**

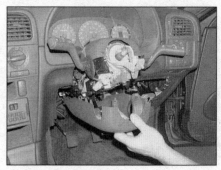
**21.4b . . . and unclip the column shrouds**

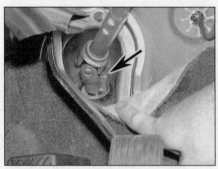

**21.7 Fold back the carpet to access the steering column lower clamp bolt (arrowed)**

**21.8 Steering column mounting nuts and bolts (arrowed)**

### Inspection

**9** Before refitting the steering column, examine the column and mountings for signs of damage and deformation, and renew as necessary. Check the steering shaft for signs of free play in the column bushes, check the universal joints for signs of damage or roughness in the joint bearings, and the lower coupling for signs of wear. If any damage or wear is found on the steering column universal joint or shaft bushes, the column must be renewed as an assembly.

### Refitting

**10** Manoeuvre the column assembly into position, and engage the column universal joint with the steering gear pinion, aligning the marks made prior to removal.

**11** Locate the column on its mountings, then refit the mounting nuts and bolts and tighten then to the specified torque.

**12** Insert the column universal joint clamp bolt, and tighten it to the specified torque setting.

**13** Reconnect the wiring connector to the ignition switch, then refit the switch assembly to the top of the column. Ensure all the wiring is correctly routed, and retained by all the necessary clips and ties.

**14** Clip the steering column upper shroud firmly into position, then refit the lower shroud and securely tighten its retaining screws. Refit the lower panel to the facia.

**15** Refit the steering wheel as described in Section 20.

| 22 | Ignition switch/ steering column lock – removal and refitting |

### Lock cylinder

#### Removal

**1** Disconnect the battery negative lead (see *Disconnecting the battery*).

**2** Release the height adjustment lever, then undo the retaining screws and remove/unclip the upper and lower shrouds from the steering column.

**3** Insert the ignition key and turn the switch to position I.

**4** Depress the lock cylinder detent by inserting a 2 mm punch into the lock housing hole, then withdraw the cylinder from the housing (see illustration).

#### Refitting

**5** Insert the key into the new lock cylinder, and turn it to position I.

**6** Depress the detent with the punch, and slide the lock cylinder fully into position.

**7** Check the operation of the lock assembly, then clip the steering column upper shroud firmly into position. Refit the lower shroud and securely tighten its retaining screws.

**8** Reconnect the battery negative lead.

### Lock housing assembly

**Note:** *New shear-bolts will be required on refitting.*

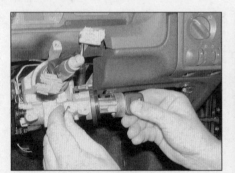

**22.4 Removing the steering/ignition lock cylinder**

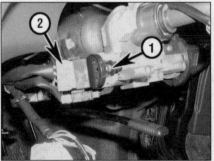

**22.18 Ignition switch retaining screw (1) and wiring connector (2)**

#### Removal

**9** Remove the steering column as described in Section 21.

**10** Clamp the column securely in a vice, taking great care not to distort the column tube.

**11** Using a hammer and suitable punch, tap the lock housing retaining clamp bolts around until they can be unscrewed by hand. Alternatively, carefully drill the heads off the shear-bolts.

**12** Remove the bolts and the mounting clamp, and lift the lock assembly away from the steering column.

#### Refitting

**13** Engage the lock assembly with the column, then refit the mounting clamp and screw in the new shear-bolts.

**14** Evenly and progressively tighten the shear-bolts until both are lightly tightened. Check the operation of the lock assembly to ensure it is correctly positioned, then tighten each bolt until its head shears off.

**15** Refit the steering column as described in Section 21.

### Ignition switch

#### Removal

**16** Disconnect the battery negative lead (see *Disconnecting the battery*).

**17** Release the height adjustment lever, then undo the retaining screws and remove the lower shroud from the steering column.

**18** Undo the retaining screw and remove the switch assembly from the end of the lock housing. Disconnect the wiring connector and remove the switch from the car (see illustration).

#### Refitting

**19** Refitting is the reverse of removal, ensuring the switch insert is correctly engaged with the lock cylinder pin.

| 23 | Steering gear assembly – removal, overhaul and refitting |  |

**Note:** *An engine support bar or hoist will be required to support the engine/transmission whilst the crossmember is removed.*

### Removal

**1** Peel back the carpet from around the base of the steering column to gain access to the column lower joint. Position the steering wheel so that the joint clamp bolt is accessible, then engage the steering lock.

**2** Unscrew the clamp bolt from the steering column lower universal joint. Using paint or a suitable marker pen, make alignment marks between the joint and steering gear pinion, then disengage the steering column from the pinion.

**3** Unscrew the retaining bolts securing the steering gear sealing plate to the bulkhead, then cut the cable-tie (early models only) and free the plate from the steering gear.

**4** Chock the rear wheels, firmly apply the handbrake, then loosen the front wheel nuts. Jack up the front of the car and support on axle stands. Remove both front roadwheels.

**5** Remove the retaining screws and fasteners, and remove the undershield beneath the engine/transmission.

**6** Remove the exhaust system front pipe as described in Chapter 4C.

**7** Undo the retaining bolts and remove the exhaust front pipe heat shield (where fitted).

**8** Attach a support bar or engine hoist to the lifting hook on the cylinder head and use it to support the weight of the engine transmission. Alternatively support the engine/transmission with a jack and block of wood.

**9** Slacken and remove the through-bolts from the front and rear mountings then undo the mounting bolts and remove the crossmember from beneath the engine/transmission. Recover the upper and lower mounting rubbers and spacers from the crossmember mountings, noting their correct fitted locations. Renew the mounting rubbers if they show signs of damage or deterioration.

**10** Unbolt the engine/transmission rear mounting and remove it from the transmission housing.

**11** To improve access to the steering gear, move the engine/transmission slightly forwards and secure it in position by inserting a block of wood in between the transmission and subframe. To ensure no excess strain is placed on the wiring/pipes/hoses as the engine/transmission is moved, release all the necessary clips and ties.

**12** Undo the retaining bolts and clips and remove the heat shield from the steering gear housing.

**13** Using brake hose clamps, clamp both the supply and return hoses near the power steering fluid reservoir. This will minimise fluid loss during subsequent operations.

**14** Mark the unions to ensure they are correctly positioned on reassembly, then unscrew the feed and return pipe union nuts from the steering gear assembly – be prepared for fluid spillage, and position a suitable container beneath the pipes whilst unscrewing the union nuts.

**15** Free the power steering pipes from any retaining clips, and position them clear of the steering gear. Recover the sealing rings from the pipe unions, then plug the pipe ends and steering gear orifices to prevent fluid leakage and to keep dirt out of the hydraulic system. Discard the sealing rings, new ones must be used on refitting.

**16** Extract the split pins, then unscrew the retaining nut from each track rod balljoint, and free both balljoints from the hubs. If the balljoints are tight, use a universal balljoint separator to free them.

**17** Slacken and remove the retaining bolts, then remove the steering gear mounting clamps from the subframe. Manoeuvre the steering gear assembly out from underneath the car, complete with its mounting rubbers.

### Overhaul

**18** Examine the steering gear assembly for signs of wear or damage, and check that the rack moves freely throughout the full length of its travel, with no signs of roughness or excessive free play between the steering gear pinion and rack. Inspect all the fluid unions for signs of leakage, and check that all union nuts are securely tightened. Renew the mounting rubbers if they show signs of damage or deterioration.

**19** If the steering gear assembly is in need of overhaul, seek the advice of a Volvo dealer or a local steering gear overhaul specialist. They will be able to inform you whether it is possible to overhaul the original steering gear or whether a new unit will be required. The only components which can be renewed easily by the home mechanic are the steering gear gaiters, the track rod balljoints and the track rods. Track rod balljoint/balljoint gaiters, steering gear gaiter and track rod renewal procedures are covered elsewhere in this Chapter.

### Refitting

**20** Ensure the steering gear and subframe mating surfaces are clean and dry, then manoeuvre the steering gear into position.

**21** Ensure both steering gear mounting rubbers are positioned with their flat surfaces against the subframe, then refit the mounting clamps and tighten the mounting bolts evenly and progressively to the specified torque.

**22** Working inside the car, refit the steering gear sealing plate to the bulkhead and securely tighten its retaining bolts. Ensure the gaiter is correctly located on the steering gear housing – on early models, secure it in position with a new cable-tie.

**23** Align the marks made prior to removal, and engage the steering column joint with the steering gear pinion. Refit the clamp bolt, tighten it to the specified torque, then seat the carpet back in position.

**24** Fit new sealing rings to the power steering pipes and reconnect them to the steering gear, tightening the union nuts lightly only. Ensure the pipes are correctly routed and retained by all the necessary clips, then tighten both union nuts to the specified torque. Remove the brake hose clamp from the fluid reservoir hoses.

**25** Locate the track rod balljoints in the swivel hubs, and tighten the retaining nuts to the specified torque. Secure each nut in position with a new split pin; if the split pin holes are not correctly aligned at the specified torque, it is permissible to overtighten the nut slightly to bring the holes into alignment.

**26** Wipe away all spilt fluid, then securely refit the heat shield to the steering gear.

**27** Move the engine back to its normal position and refit the rear mounting to the transmission, tightening its retaining bolts to the specified torque.

**28** Ensure the upper and lower mounting rubbers and the spacers are correctly fitted to the engine/transmission crossmember holes, then manoeuvre the crossmember into position. Refit the mounting bolts, tightening them to the specified torque, then refit the through-bolts to the engine/transmission mountings. Remove the support bar/hoist/jack (as applicable) and rock the engine to settle it in position. Tighten the engine/transmission rear mounting through-bolt to the specified torque setting, then tighten the front mounting through-bolt to the specified torque.

**29** Refit the exhaust heat shield (where fitted) and tighten its retaining bolts to the specified torque (Chapter 4C).

**30** Refit the exhaust front pipe as described in Chapter 4C.

**31** Top-up the fluid reservoir and bleed the hydraulic system as described in Section 25.

**32** Securely refit the engine undershield, then refit the roadwheels and lower the car to the ground. Tighten the wheel nuts to the specified torque.

**33** On completion check and, if necessary, adjust the front wheel alignment as described in Section 29.

### 24 Steering gear rubber gaiter – renewal

**1** Remove the track rod balljoint and locknut as described in Section 27.

**2** Mark the correct fitted position of the gaiter on the track rod, then release the retaining clips and slide the gaiter off the steering gear housing and track rod end.

**3** Thoroughly clean the track rod and the steering gear housing, using fine abrasive paper to polish off any corrosion, burrs or sharp edges, which might damage the new gaiter's sealing lips on installation. Scrape off all the grease from the old gaiter, and apply it to the track rod inner balljoint. (This assumes that grease has not been lost or contaminated as a result of damage to the old gaiter. Use fresh grease if in doubt – Volvo recommend the use of grease 1161001-1.)

**4** Carefully slide the new gaiter onto the track rod end, and locate it on the steering gear housing. Align the outer edge of the gaiter with the mark made on the track rod prior to removal, then secure it in position with new retaining clips.

**5** Refit the track rod balljoint as described in Section 27.

### 25 Power steering system – bleeding

**1** This procedure will only be necessary when any part of the hydraulic system has been disconnected.

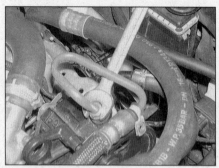

**26.6 Unscrew the union nut and disconnect the outlet pipe from the power steering pump**

**2** Referring to *Weekly checks*, remove the fluid reservoir filler cap, and top-up with the specified fluid to the upper level mark on the dipstick.

**3** Jack up the front of the car and support it on axle stands to remove the weight from the front wheels.

**4** With the engine stopped, move the steering from lock-to-lock several times to purge out the trapped air, then top-up the level in the fluid reservoir. Repeat this procedure until the fluid level in the reservoir does not drop any further.

**5** Lower the car to the ground again and top-up the fluid level to the dipstick level mark.

**6** Have an assistant start the engine and allow it to idle with the front wheels in the straight-ahead position. Whilst the engine is running, keep an eye on the fluid level in the reservoir, topping-up as necessary. Have your assistant slowly move the steering from lock-to-lock several times to purge out any remaining air in the system. Repeat this procedure until bubbles cease to appear in the fluid reservoir. Once air bubbles stop appearing in the fluid reservoir, switch off the engine.

**7** Check that fluid level is up to the relevant dipstick level mark, topping-up if necessary then securely refit the reservoir cap. **Note:** *If an abnormal noise is heard from the fluid lines when the steering wheel is turned, it indicates that there is still air in the system and further bleeding is necessary.*

**27.4 Extract the split pin, then unscrew the track rod balljoint nut**

## 26 Power steering pump – removal and refitting

### Removal

**1** Firmly apply the handbrake, then jack up the front of the car and support it on axle stands.

**2** Remove the retaining screws and fasteners, and remove the undershield beneath the engine/transmission.

**3** Remove the auxiliary drivebelt as described in Chapter 1.

**4** Using brake hose clamps, clamp both the supply and return hoses near the power steering fluid reservoir. This will minimise fluid loss during subsequent operations.

**5** Wipe clean the area around the power steering pump fluid pipe unions.

### Except GDI engine

**6** Slacken the retaining clip and disconnect the fluid supply hose from the pump. Unscrew the union nut and the retaining clip bolt, and disconnect the outlet pipe **(see illustration)**. Be prepared for some fluid spillage as the pipe and hose are disconnected, and plug the hose/pipe ends and pump unions, to minimise fluid loss and prevent the entry of dirt into the system. Discard the outlet pipe sealing ring; a new one must be used on refitting.

**7** Working through the cut-outs in the pump pulley, slacken and remove the bolts securing the front mounting bracket to the pump. Unscrew the bolts securing the mounting bracket to the cylinder block, and remove the bracket from the engine.

**8** Undo the bolts securing the pump to the rear bracket, and manoeuvre the pump out of position.

### GDI engine

**9** Unbolt the steering fluid reservoir, and place it to one side.

**10** Work along the fluid outlet (pressure) pipe, and unbolt the pipe clamps from the car body.

**11** Disconnect the wiring plug from the pressure switch at the front of the pump, and release the wiring from the retaining clips.

**12** Release (or cut off) the clip securing the low-pressure hose to the top of the pump, and remove the hose.

**13** Unscrew the fluid outlet pipe union bolt, recover the washer and O-ring, and remove the pipe from the pump. Be prepared for fluid loss as this is done. Plug the pump openings and pipe ends, to prevent further fluid loss and the entry of dirt into the system.

**14** Slacken and remove the three pump mounting bolts, and remove the steering pump from the engine mounting bracket.

### All engines

**15** If the power steering pump is faulty, it must be renewed. The pump is a sealed unit, and cannot be overhauled.

### Refitting

**16** Refitting is a reversal of removal, noting the following points:

a) *Fit new O-ring seals and washers where necessary, ensure all union fittings are clean, and that all hoses are securely reconnected (use new pipe clips if required).*

b) *Tighten the pump mounting bolts securely.*

c) *Refit the auxiliary drivebelt and tension it as described in Chapter 1.*

d) *Refit the undershield, ensuring it is securely held by all its retaining screws and fasteners.*

e) *On completion, bleed the hydraulic system as described in Section 25.*

## 27 Track rod balljoint – removal and refitting

### Removal

**1** Apply the handbrake, then loosen the relevant front wheel nuts. Jack up the front of the car and support it on axle stands. Remove the appropriate front roadwheel.

**2** If the balljoint is to be re-used, use a straight-edge and a scriber, or similar, to mark its relationship to the track rod and locknut.

**3** Hold the track rod, and unscrew the balljoint locknut by a quarter of a turn. Do not move the locknut from this position, as it will serve as a handy reference mark on refitting.

**4** Extract the split pin, then unscrew the retaining nut from the track rod balljoint, and free the balljoint from the hub **(see illustration)**. If the balljoint is tight, use a universal balljoint separator to free it.

**5** Counting the **exact** number of turns necessary to do so, unscrew the balljoint from the track rod end.

**6** If necessary, count the number of exposed threads between the end of the track rod and the locknut, and record this figure. Unscrew the locknut and remove it from the track rod.

**7** Carefully clean the balljoint and the threads. Renew the balljoint if its movement is sloppy or too stiff, if excessively worn, or if damaged in any way; carefully check the stud taper and threads. If the balljoint gaiter is damaged, the complete balljoint assembly must be renewed.

### Refitting

**8** Where necessary, screw the locknut onto the track rod, and position it so that the same number of exposed threads are visible, as was noted prior to removal.

**9** Screw the balljoint into the track rod by the number of turns noted on removal. This should bring the balljoint to within a quarter of a turn from the locknut, with the alignment marks that were made on removal (if applicable) lined up.

**10** Locate the track rod balljoint in the hub, and tighten its nut to the specified torque. Secure the nut with a new split pin; if the split pin holes are not correctly aligned at the specified torque, it is permissible to overtighten the nut slightly to align the holes **(see illustration)**.
**11** Refit the roadwheel, then lower the car to the ground and tighten the roadwheel nuts to the specified torque.
**12** Check and, if necessary, adjust the front wheel alignment as described in Section 29, then tighten the balljoint locknut to the specified torque.

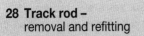
## 28 Track rod –
removal and refitting

**Note:** *A new locking plate will be required on refitting.*

### Removal
**1** Remove the track rod balljoint and locknut as described in Section 27.
**2** Remove all traces of dirt from around the steering gear and gaiter, then mark the correct fitted position of the gaiter on the housing and track rod. Release the retaining clips, and slide the gaiter off the steering gear housing and track rod end.
**3** Wrap a layer of insulating tape around the end of steering gear rack, to prevent possible damage, then grip the rack with an adjustable spanner.
**4** Bend back the locking plate then, using a pair of grips, unscrew the track rod inner balljoint from the steering rack end. As the balljoint is being slackened, retain the rack with the spanner to prevent excess strain being placed on the steering gear assembly.
**5** Remove the track rod assembly, and discard the locking plate. Examine the track rod inner balljoint for signs of slackness or tight spots, and check that the track rod itself is straight and free from damage. If necessary, renew the track rod; it is also recommended that the steering gear gaiter is renewed.

### Refitting
**6** Fit a new locking plate to the track rod balljoint, then screw the balljoint into the steering rack.
**7** Tighten the track rod balljoint to the specified torque, retaining the steering rack with an open-ended spanner to prevent any excess strain being placed on the steering gear assembly. Once the balljoint is correctly tightened, remove the tape from the steering rack, and secure the balljoint in position by bending down the locking plate.
**8** Ensure the track rod balljoint is adequately lubricated (Volvo recommend the use of grease 1161001-1 – available from your Volvo dealer) then carefully slide the gaiter onto the track rod end and locate it on the steering gear housing.

**27.10 Tighten the track rod balljoint nut to the specified torque, then secure it with a new split pin**

**9** Ensure the gaiter is not twisted, then align its outer edges with the marks made prior to removal, and secure it in position with the retaining clips.
**10** Refit the track rod balljoint as described in Section 27.

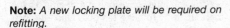
## 29 Wheel alignment and steering angles –
general information

### Definitions
**1** A car's steering and suspension geometry is defined in four basic settings – all angles are expressed in degrees; the steering axis is defined as an imaginary line drawn through the axis of the suspension strut, extended where necessary to contact the ground.
**2 Camber** is the angle between each roadwheel and a vertical line drawn through its centre and tyre contact patch, when viewed from the front or rear of the car. Positive camber is when the roadwheels are tilted outwards from the vertical at the top; negative camber is when they are tilted inwards. The front wheel camber angle can be altered slightly by repositioning the swivel hub in relation to the strut and the rear wheel camber angle can be adjusted by rotating the suspension lower arm inner pivot bolt.
**3 Castor** is the angle between the steering axis and a vertical line drawn through each roadwheel's centre and tyre contact patch, when viewed from the side of the car. Positive castor is when the steering axis is tilted so that it contacts the ground ahead of the vertical; negative castor is when it contacts the ground behind the vertical. The castor angle is not adjustable.
**4 Toe** is the difference, viewed from above, between lines drawn through the roadwheel centres and the car's centre-line. Toe-in is when the roadwheels point inwards, towards each other at the front, while toe-out is when they splay outwards from each other at the front. The front wheel toe setting is adjusted by screwing the track rod into/out of the outer balljoint, to alter the effective length of the track rod assembly, and the rear wheel toe

setting can be adjusted by rotating the control link pivot bolt.
**5 Kingpin inclination (sometimes referred to as steering axis inclination)** – is the angle between the steering axis and a vertical line drawn through each roadwheel's centre and tyre contact patch, when viewed from the front or rear of the car. The kingpin inclination angle is not adjustable.

### Checking and adjustment
**6** Due to the special measuring equipment necessary to check the wheel alignment and steering angles, and the skill required to use it properly, the checking and adjustment of these settings is best left to a Volvo dealer or similar expert. Note that most tyre-fitting shops now possess sophisticated checking equipment. The following is provided as a guide, should the owner decide to carry out a DIY check.
**7** For the measurements to be accurate it is important that the car is unladen, except for the spare wheel and tool kit, and that the tyres are correctly inflated (see *Weekly checks*). Rock the car several times to settle all suspension components in position and ensure the front wheels are positioned in the straight-ahead position before taking any measurements.

#### Front wheel toe setting
**8** To check the toe setting, a tracking gauge must first be obtained. Two types of gauge are available, and can be obtained from motor accessory shops. The first type measures the distance between the front and rear inside edges of the roadwheels with the car stationary. The second type, known as a scuff plate, measures the actual position of the contact surface of the tyre, in relation to the road surface, with the car in motion. This is achieved by pushing or driving the front tyre over a plate, which then moves slightly according to the scuff of the tyre, and shows this movement on a scale. Both types have their advantages and disadvantages, but either can give satisfactory results if used correctly and carefully.
**9** If adjustment is necessary, apply the handbrake, then jack up the front of the car and support it securely on axle stands. Turn the steering wheel onto full-left lock, and measure the amount of exposed thread on the right-hand track rod end. Now turn the steering onto full-right lock, and measure the amount of thread on the left-hand side. If there is the same amount of thread visible on both sides, then subsequent adjustment should be made equally on both sides. If there is more thread visible on one side than the other, it will be necessary to compensate for this during adjustment. **Note:** *It is most important that after adjustment, the same amount of thread is visible on each track rod end (Volvo state that up to 2 mm difference is allowable).*
**10** First clean the track rod threads; if they

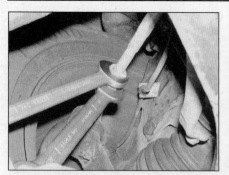

**29.11 Hold the track rod balljoint and slacken the locknut**

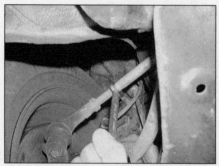

**29.12 Screw the track rod into/out of the balljoint to adjust the front wheel toe setting**

are corroded, apply penetrating fluid before starting adjustment. Release the steering gear rubber gaiter outboard clips and peel back the gaiters; apply a smear of grease to the inside of the gaiters, so that both are free, and will not be twisted or strained as their respective track rods are rotated.

**11** Use a straight-edge and a scriber or similar to mark the relationship of each track rod to its balljoint then, holding each track rod balljoint in turn, unscrew the locknut fully **(see illustration)**.

**12** Alter the length of the track rods, bearing in mind the note made in paragraph 9. Screw them into or out of the balljoints, rotating the track rod using an open-ended spanner fitted to the flats provided on the track rod **(see illustration)**. Shortening the track rods (screwing them into their balljoints) will reduce toe-in/increase toe-out.

**13** When the setting is correct, hold the track rods and tighten the balljoint locknuts to the specified torque setting. Check that the balljoints are seated correctly in their sockets, and count the exposed threads to check the

length of both track rods. If they are not the same, then the adjustment has not been made equally, and problems will be encountered with tyre scrubbing in turns; also, the steering wheel spokes will no longer be horizontal when the wheels are in the straight-ahead position.

**14** If the track rod lengths are the same (see paragraph 9), lower the car to the ground and recheck the toe setting; re-adjust if necessary. When the setting is correct, tighten the track rod balljoint locknuts to the specified torque. Ensure that the rubber gaiters are seated correctly, and are not twisted or strained, and secure them in position with the retaining clips.

**15** If after adjustment, the steering wheel spokes are no longer horizontal when the wheels are in the straight-ahead position, remove the steering wheel and reposition it (see Section 20).

## Front wheel camber setting

**16** If access to camber angle measuring equipment can be gained, the camber angle

can be altered as follows. **Note:** *Only a very small amount of camber adjustment is possible.*

**17** Attach the gauges to the car and check the camber angle is within the specified limits.

**18** If adjustment is necessary, apply the handbrake, then jack up the front of the car and support it securely on axle stands.

**19** Slacken the bolts securing the suspension strut to the swivel hub, and alter the camber by moving the swivel hub assembly in relation to the strut. Once the hub is correctly positioned, tighten both bolts to the specified torque, then lower the car to the ground.

**20** Recheck the camber angle again and, if necessary, repeat the adjustment procedure.

## Rear wheel toe setting

**21** Check the toe setting as described in paragraph 8.

**22** If adjustment is necessary, slacken the control link inner pivot bolt nut, then alter the toe setting by rotating the bolt. Once the bolt is correctly positioned, hold it stationary and tighten its nut to the specified torque.

**23** Recheck the toe setting again and, if necessary, repeat the adjustment procedure.

## Rear wheel camber setting

**24** If access to camber angle measuring equipment can be gained, the camber angle can be adjusted as follows.

**25** Attach the gauges to the car, and check the camber angle is within the specified limits.

**26** If adjustment is necessary, slacken the suspension lower arm inner pivot bolt nut, then alter the camber setting by rotating the bolt. Once the bolt is correctly positioned, hold it stationary and tighten its nut to the specified torque.

**27** Recheck the camber angle again and, if necessary, repeat the adjustment procedure.

# Chapter 11
# Bodywork and fittings

## Contents

## Degrees of difficulty

| Easy, suitable for novice with little experience  | Fairly easy, suitable for beginner with some experience | Fairly difficult, suitable for competent DIY mechanic | Difficult, suitable for experienced DIY mechanic | Very difficult, suitable for expert DIY or professional 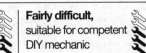 |
|---|---|---|---|---|

## Specifications

| Torque wrench settings | Nm | lbf ft |
|---|---|---|
| Bonnet hinge bolts | 24 | 18 |
| Bonnet lock bolts | 8 | 6 |
| Boot lid hinge bolts | 21 | 15 |
| Boot lid lock bolts | 10 | 7 |
| Door hinge bolts | 21 | 15 |
| Door lock: | | |
|   Exterior handle bolts | 10 | 7 |
|   Lock retaining screws | 6 | 4 |
|   Striker plate screws | 21 | 15 |
| Door window: | | |
|   Guide bolts | 10 | 7 |
|   Regulator bolts | 8 | 6 |
|   Window-to-regulator bolts | 8 | 6 |
| Exterior mirror bolts | 10 | 7 |
| Facia panel bolts | 12 | 9 |
| Front bumper mounting bolts | 40 | 30 |
| Front seat belt: | | |
|   Buckle bolt | 45 | 33 |
|   Inertia reel bolts | 48 | 35 |
|   Lower mounting bolt | 45 | 33 |
| Front seat mounting nuts and bolts | 40 | 30 |
| Rear bumper: | | |
|   Mounting bolts | 50 | 37 |
|   Mounting nuts | 5 | 4 |
| Rear seat belt: | | |
|   Buckle bolts | 48 | 35 |
|   Guide bolts – Saloon model | 18 | 13 |
|   Inertia reel bolt | 48 | 35 |
|   Lower mounting bolt | 30 | 22 |
| Rear seat cushion bolts | 23 | 17 |
| Roadwheel nuts | 110 | 81 |
| Tailgate hinge bolts | 24 | 18 |
| Tailgate lock bolts | 10 | 7 |

## 1 General information

The bodyshell is made of pressed-steel sections. Most components are welded together, but some use is made of structural adhesives.

The bonnet, door and some other vulnerable panels are made of zinc-coated metal, and are further protected by being coated with an anti-chip primer before being sprayed.

Extensive use is made of plastic materials, mainly in the interior, but also in exterior components. The front and rear bumpers, and front grille are injection-moulded from a synthetic material that is very strong and yet light. Plastic components such as wheel arch liners are fitted to the underside of the car, to improve the body's resistance to corrosion.

## 2 Maintenance – bodywork and underframe

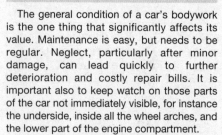

The general condition of a car's bodywork is the one thing that significantly affects its value. Maintenance is easy, but needs to be regular. Neglect, particularly after minor damage, can lead quickly to further deterioration and costly repair bills. It is important also to keep watch on those parts of the car not immediately visible, for instance the underside, inside all the wheel arches, and the lower part of the engine compartment.

The basic maintenance routine for the bodywork is washing – preferably with a lot of water, from a hose. This will remove all the loose solids which may have stuck to the car. It is important to flush these off in such a way as to prevent grit from scratching the finish. The wheel arches and underframe need washing in the same way, to remove any accumulated mud which will retain moisture and tend to encourage rust. The best time to clean the underframe and wheel arches is in wet weather, when the mud is thoroughly wet and soft. In very wet weather, the underframe is usually cleaned of large accumulations automatically, and this is a good time for inspection.

Periodically, except on cars with a wax-based underbody protective coating, it is a good idea to have the whole of the underframe of the car steam-cleaned, engine compartment included, so that a thorough inspection can be carried out to see what minor repairs and renovations are necessary. Steam-cleaning is available at many garages, and is necessary for the removal of the accumulation of oily grime, which sometimes is allowed to become thick in certain areas. If steam-cleaning facilities are not available, there are some excellent grease solvents available which can be brush-applied; the dirt can then be simply hosed off. Note that these methods should not be used on cars with wax-based underbody protective coating, or the coating will be removed. Such cars should

be inspected annually, preferably just before Winter, when the underbody should be washed down, and repair any damage to the wax coating. Ideally, a completely fresh coat should be applied. It would also be worth considering the use of such wax-based protection for injection into door panels, sills, box sections, etc, as an additional safeguard against rust damage, where such protection is not provided by the manufacturer.

After washing paintwork, wipe off with a chamois leather to give an unspotted clear finish. A coat of clear protective wax polish will give added protection against chemical pollutants in the air. If the paintwork sheen has dulled or oxidised, use a cleaner/polisher combination to restore the brilliance of the shine. This requires a little effort, but such dulling is usually caused because regular washing has been neglected. Care needs to be taken with metallic paintwork, as special non-abrasive cleaner/polisher is required to avoid damage to the finish. Always check that the door and ventilator opening drain holes and pipes are completely clear, so that water can be drained out. Brightwork should be treated in the same way as paintwork. Windscreens and windows can be kept clear of the smeary film which often appears, by proprietary glass cleaner. Never use any form of wax or other body or chromium polish on glass.

## 3 Maintenance – upholstery and carpets

Mats and carpets should be brushed or vacuum-cleaned regularly, to keep them free of grit. If they are badly stained, remove them from the car for scrubbing or sponging, and make quite sure they are dry before refitting. Seats and interior trim panels can be kept clean by wiping with a damp cloth. If they do become stained (which can be more apparent on light-coloured upholstery), use a little liquid detergent and a soft nail brush to scour the grime out of the material. Do not forget to keep the headlining clean in the same way as the upholstery. When using liquid cleaners inside the car, do not over-wet the surfaces being cleaned. Excessive damp could get into the seams and padded interior, causing stains, offensive odours or even rot. If the inside of the car gets wet accidentally, it is worthwhile taking some trouble to dry it out properly, particularly where carpets are involved. Do not leave oil or electric heaters inside the car for this purpose.

## 4 Minor body damage – repair

### Scratches

If the scratch is very superficial, and does not penetrate to the metal of the bodywork,

repair is very simple. Lightly rub the area of the scratch with a paintwork renovator or a very fine cutting paste to remove loose paint from the scratch, and to clear the surrounding bodywork of wax polish. Rinse the area with clean water.

In the case of metallic paint, the most commonly-found scratches are not in the paint, but in the lacquer top coat, and appear white. If care is taken , these can sometimes be rendered less obvious by very careful use of paintwork renovator (which would otherwise not be used on metallic paintwork); otherwise, repair of these scratches can be achieved by applying lacquer with a fine brush.

Apply touch-up paint to the scratch using a fine paint brush; continue to apply fine layers of paint until the surface of the paint in the scratch is level with the surrounding paintwork. Allow the new paint at least two weeks to harden, then blend it into the surrounding paintwork by rubbing the scratch area with a paintwork renovator or a very fine cutting paste. Finally, apply wax polish.

Where the scratch has penetrated right through to the metal of the bodywork, causing the metal to rust, a different repair technique is required. Remove any loose rust from the bottom of the scratch with a penknife, then apply rust-inhibiting paint to prevent the formation of rust in the future. Using a rubber or nylon applicator, fill the scratch with body-stopper paste. If required, this paste can be mixed with cellulose thinners to provide a very thin paste which is ideal for filling narrow scratches. Before the stopper-paste in the scratch hardens, wrap a piece of smooth cotton rag around the top of a finger. Dip the finger in cellulose thinners, and quickly sweep it across the surface of the stopper-paste in the scratch; this will ensure that the surface of the stopper-paste is slightly hollowed. The scratch can now be painted over as described earlier in this Section.

### Dents

When deep denting of the car's bodywork has taken place, the first task is to pull the dent out, until the affected bodywork almost attains its original shape. There is little point in trying to restore the original shape completely, as the metal in the damaged area will have stretched on impact, and cannot be reshaped fully to its original contour. It is better to bring the level of the dent up to a point which is about 3 mm below the level of the surrounding bodywork. In cases where the dent is very shallow anyway, it is not worth trying to pull it out at all. If the underside of the dent is accessible, it can be hammered out gently from behind, using a mallet with a wooden or plastic head. Whilst doing this, hold a suitable block of wood firmly against the outside of the panel, to absorb the impact from the hammer blows and thus prevent a large area of the bodywork from being 'belled-out'.

Should the dent be in a section of the

bodywork which has a double skin, or some other factor making it inaccessible from behind, a different technique is called for. Drill several small holes through the metal inside the area – particularly in the deeper section. Then screw long self-tapping screws into the holes, just sufficiently for them to gain a good purchase in the metal. Now the dent can be pulled out by pulling on the protruding heads of the screws with a pair of pliers.

The next stage of the repair is the removal of the paint from the damaged area, and from an inch or so of the surrounding 'sound' bodywork. This is accomplished most easily by using a wire brush or abrasive pad on a power drill, although it can be done just as effectively by hand, using sheets of abrasive paper. To complete the preparation for filling, score the surface of the bare metal with a screwdriver or the tang of a file, or alternatively, drill small holes in the affected area. This will provide a good 'key' for the filler paste.

To complete the repair, see the Section on filling and respraying.

### Rust holes or gashes

Remove all paint from the affected area, and from an inch or so of the surrounding 'sound' bodywork, using an abrasive pad or a wire brush on a power drill. If these are not available, a few sheets of abrasive paper will do the job most effectively. With the paint removed, you will be able to judge the severity of the corrosion, and therefore decide whether to renew the whole panel (if this is possible) or to repair the affected area. New body panels are not as expensive as most people think, and it is often quicker and more satisfactory to fit a new panel than to attempt to repair large areas of corrosion.

Remove all fittings from the affected area, except those which will act as a guide to the original shape of the damaged bodywork. Then, using tin snips or a hacksaw blade, remove all loose metal and any other metal badly affected by corrosion. Hammer the edges of the hole inwards, to create a slight depression for the filler paste.

Wire-brush the affected area to remove the powdery rust from the surface of the remaining metal. Paint the affected area with rust-inhibiting paint; if the back of the rusted area is accessible, treat this also.

Before filling can take place, it will be necessary to block the hole in some way. This can be achieved with aluminium or plastic mesh, or aluminium tape.

Aluminium or plastic mesh, or glass-fibre matting, is probably the best material to use for a large hole. Cut a piece to the approximate size and shape of the hole to be filled, then position it in the hole so that its edges are below the level of the surrounding bodywork. It can be retained in position by several blobs of filler paste around its periphery.

Aluminium tape should be used for small or very narrow holes. Pull a piece off the roll, trim it to the approximate size and shape required,

then pull off the backing paper (if used) and stick the tape over the hole; it can be overlapped if the thickness of one piece is insufficient. Burnish down the edges of the tape with the handle of a screwdriver or similar, to ensure that the tape is securely attached to the metal underneath.

### Filling and respraying

Before using this Section, see the Sections on dent, deep scratch, rust holes and gash repairs.

Many types of bodyfiller are available, but generally speaking, those proprietary kits which contain a tin of filler paste and a tube of resin hardener are best for this type of repair which can be used directly from the tube. A wide, flexible plastic or nylon applicator will be found invaluable for imparting a smooth and well-contoured finish to the surface of the filler.

Mix up a little filler on a clean piece of card or board – measure the hardener carefully (follow the maker's instructions on the pack), otherwise the filler will set too rapidly or too slowly. Using the applicator, apply the filler paste to the prepared area; draw the applicator across the surface of the filler to achieve the correct contour and to level the surface. When a contour that approximates to the correct one is achieved, stop working the paste – if you carry on too long, the paste will become sticky and begin to 'pick-up' on the applicator. Continue to add thin layers of filler paste at 20-minute intervals, until the level of the filler is just proud of the surrounding bodywork.

Once the filler has hardened, the excess can be removed using a metal plane or file. From then on, progressively-finer grades of abrasive paper should be used, starting with a 40-grade production paper, and finishing with a 400-grade wet-and-dry paper. Always wrap the abrasive paper around a flat rubber, cork, or wooden block – otherwise the surface of the filler will not be completely flat. During the smoothing of the filler surface, the wet-and-dry paper should be periodically rinsed in water. This will ensure that a very smooth finish is imparted to the filler at the final stage.

At this stage, the 'dent' should be surrounded by a ring of bare metal, which in turn should be encircled by the finely 'feathered' edge of the good paintwork. Rinse the repair area with clean water, until all the dust produced by the rubbing-down operation has gone.

Spray the whole area with a light coat of primer – this will show up any imperfections in the surface of the filler. Repair these imperfections with fresh filler paste or bodystopper, and again smooth the surface with abrasive paper. If bodystopper is used, it can be mixed with cellulose thinners, to form a thin paste which is ideal for filling small holes. Repeat this spray-and-repair procedure until you are satisfied that the surface of the filler, and the feathered edge of the paintwork, are perfect. Clean the repair area with clean water, and allow to dry fully.

The repair area is now ready for final spraying. Paint spraying must be carried out in a warm, dry, windless and dust-free atmosphere. This condition can be created artificially if you have access to a large indoor working area, but if you are forced to work in the open, you will have to pick your day very carefully. If you are working indoors, dousing the floor in the work area with water will help to settle the dust which would otherwise be in the atmosphere. If the repair area is confined to one body panel, mask off the surrounding panels; this will help to minimise the effects of a slight mis-match in paint colours. Bodywork fittings (eg chrome strips, door handles etc) will also need to be masked off. Use genuine masking tape, and several thickness of newspaper, for the masking operations.

Before starting to spray, agitate the aerosol can thoroughly, then spray a test area (an old tin, or similar) until the technique is mastered. Cover the repair area with a thick coat of primer; the thickness should be built up using several thin layers of paint, rather than one thick one. Using 400 grade wet-and-dry paper, rub down the surface of the primer until it is smooth. While doing this, the work area should be thoroughly doused with water, and the wet-and-dry paper periodically rinsed in water. Allow to dry before spraying on more paint.

Spray on the top coat, again building up the thickness by using several thin layers of paint. Start spraying at the top of the repair area, and then, using a side-to-side motion, work downwards until the whole repair area and about 2 inches of the surrounding original paintwork is covered. Remove all masking material 10 to 15 minutes after spraying on the final coat of paint.

Allow the new paint at least two weeks to harden, then, using a paintwork renovator or a very fine cutting paste, blend the edges of the paint into the existing paintwork. Finally, apply wax polish.

### Plastic components

With the use of more and more plastic body components by the manufacturers (eg bumpers. spoilers, and in some cases major body panels), rectification of more serious damage to such items has become a matter of either entrusting repair work to a specialist in this field, or renewing complete components. Repair of such damage by the DIY owner is not feasible, owing to the cost of the equipment and materials required for effecting such repairs. The basic technique involves making a groove along the line of the crack in the plastic, using a rotary burr in a power drill. The damaged part is then welded back together, using a hot air gun to heat up and fuse a plastic filler rod into the groove. Any excess plastic is then removed, and the area rubbed down to a smooth finish. It is important that a filler rod of the correct plastic is used, as body components can be made of a variety of different types (eg polycarbonate, ABS, polypropylene).

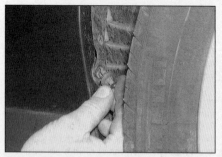

**6.4 Remove the fasteners/screws securing the wheel arch liners to the bumper**

Damage of a less-serious nature (abrasions, minor cracks etc) can be repaired by the DIY owner using a two-part epoxy filler repair material which can be used directly from the tube. Once mixed in equal proportions, this is used in similar fashion to the bodywork filler used on metal panels. The filler is usually cured in twenty to thirty minutes, ready for sanding and painting.

If the owner is renewing a complete component himself, or if he has repaired it with epoxy filler, he will be left with the problem of finding a suitable paint for finishing which is compatible with the type of plastic used. At one time, the use of a universal paint was not possible, owing to the complex range of plastics met with in body component applications. Standard paints, generally speaking, will not bond to plastic or rubber satisfactorily, but professional matched paints, to match any plastic or rubber finish, can be

**6.5 Disconnect the headlight washer hose from the T-piece**

obtained from some dealers. However, it is now possible to obtain a plastic body parts finishing kit which consists of a preprimer treatment, a primer and coloured top coat. Full instructions are normally supplied with a kit, but basically the method of use is to first apply the preprimer to the component concerned, and allow it to dry for up to 30 minutes. Then the primer is applied, and left to dry for about an hour before finally applying the special-coloured top coat. The result is a correctly coloured component, where the paint will flex with the plastic or rubber, a property that standard paint does not normally possess.

## 5 Major body damage – repair

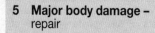

Where serious damage has occurred, or

large areas need renewal due to neglect, it means that complete new panels will need welding-in, and this is best left to professionals. If the damage is due to impact, it will also be necessary to check completely the alignment of the bodyshell, and this can only be carried out accurately by a Volvo dealer using special jigs. If the body is left misaligned, it is primarily dangerous, as the car will not handle properly, and secondly, uneven stresses will be imposed on the steering, suspension and possibly transmission, causing abnormal wear, or complete failure, particularly to such items as the tyres.

## 6 Front bumper – removal and refitting

### Removal

**1** To improve access, firmly apply the handbrake, then jack up the front of the car and support it on axle stands.

**2** Remove the front indicator light units as described in Chapter 12 – this is not essential, but it removes the risk of damaging the painted bumper surface during removal (and refitting). As an alternative, apply several strips of masking tape to the bumper, in the area below the headlights and front indicators.

**3** Undo the retaining screws/fasteners and remove the front section of the engine/transmission undershield from beneath the bumper.

**4** Remove the fasteners and screws securing the left- and right-hand wheel arch liners to the bumper ends **(see illustration)**.

**5** Position the headlight wiper arms clear of the headlights, then trace the headlight washer hoses back to the T-piece connector. Disconnect the washer reservoir hose from the T-piece and plug its end to minimise fluid loss **(see illustration)**.

**6** Disconnect the wiring connectors from the headlight wiper motors, the foglights and the bumper sidelights. Unclip the temperature sensor (where fitted) from the front of the bumper, then release the wiring from its bumper retaining clips **(see illustrations)**. On models for cold-climate markets, remove the fuse by the air cleaner, and disconnect the earth lead for the engine block heater.

**7** Undo the screw securing each end of the bumper to the front wings **(see illustration)**.

**8** From underneath the car, remove the clips securing the lower edge of the bumper to the body, then remove the two bumper mounting bolts which are located directly behind each headlight **(see illustrations)**.

**9** With the aid of an assistant, manoeuvre the bumper assembly forwards and away from the car **(see illustration)**. As the bumper is removed, make sure that the wiring has been released from all the relevant clips.

**10** Inspect the bumper mounting brackets and the reinforcement panel for signs of damage, and renew if necessary.

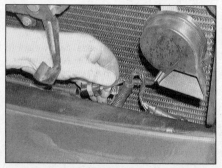

**6.6a Disconnect the wiring from the headlight wiper motors and foglights . . .**

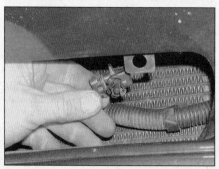

**6.6b . . . and unclip the temperature sensor from the front bumper**

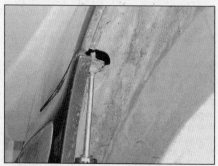

**6.7 Remove the screw securing each end of the bumper to the wings**

**6.8a Remove the clips from the lower edge of the bumper . . .**

## Refitting

**11** Refitting is a reverse of the removal procedure, ensuring that the bumper mounting bolts are tightened to the specified torque.

## 7 Rear bumper –
removal and refitting

## Removal

**1** Remove the retaining screws/fasteners and remove the wheel arch liners from the left- and right-hand sides of the bumper. Remove the screw securing each end of the bumper to the body **(see illustrations)**.
**2** Unclip the bumper sidelight wiring connectors from the body, then disconnect the wiring connectors so the lights are free to be removed with the bumper **(see illustration)**.
**3** Remove the fastener securing the base of the bumper in position **(see illustration)**.
**4** Undo the retaining screws and remove the luggage compartment floor panel.
**5** Peel off the sealing strip from around the base of the boot lid/tailgate aperture, then unclip and remove the sill trim panel from the rear of the luggage compartment **(see illustration)**.
**6** On Saloon models, remove the luggage compartment left- and right-hand side trim panel rear fasteners (loosen the centre screws a few turns, then pull out the complete fastener) and fold the rear of each trim panel inwards to gain access to bumper retaining nuts and bolts **(see illustration)**. To further improve access, remove the front fasteners (located behind the rear seat backs) and remove the panels completely.
**7** On Estate models, remove the retaining fastener/screw(s) (as applicable) securing the rear of each luggage compartment side trim panel in position. Free the rear of each panel and fold it inwards slightly to enable access to be gained to the bumper retaining nuts and bolts. If necessary, to improve access even further, remove the rear pillar and luggage compartment upper trim panels, and fold the side trim panels fully in (see Chapter 10, Section 12).
**8** As there is a risk of damaging the painted

**6.8b** . . . then remove the mounting bolts (arrowed – seen from below) behind each headlight

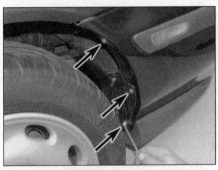

**7.1a** Remove the screws (arrowed) and take out the wheel arch liners. . .

bumper surface during removal (and refitting), it is advisable to apply several strips of masking tape to the bumper, in the area below the tail lights and in front of the towbar (if fitted).

**6.9** Removing the front bumper assembly

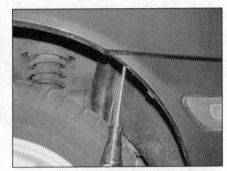

**7.1b** . . . then remove the screw securing each end of the bumper to the body

**9** Remove the bumper retaining bolts (x2) and nuts (x4) then, with the aid of an assistant, free the bumper ends from their mountings and remove the bumper from the car **(see illustration)**.

**7.2** Unclip the bumper sidelight wiring connectors from the body, and disconnect them

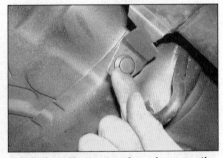

**7.3** Pull out the centre pin and remove the fastener securing the base of the bumper to the body

**7.5** On Estate models, peel off the sealing strip then unclip the tailgate sill trim panel

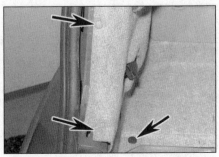

**7.6** On Saloon models, remove the rear fasteners (three arrowed) and fold back the side trim

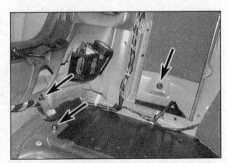

**7.9** Bumper left-hand side fixings (arrowed) – luggage compartment side trim panel removed

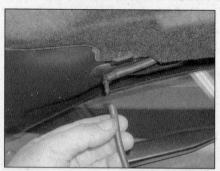

8.3 Disconnect the washer hose from the bonnet

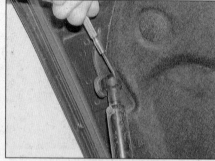

8.4 Support the bonnet then unclip the support strut from its balljoint

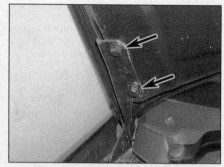

8.5 Slacken and remove the hinge bolts (arrowed) and remove the bonnet

### Refitting

10 Refitting is a reverse of the removal procedure, tightening the retaining nuts and bolts to their specified torques.

## 8 Bonnet –
removal, refitting and adjustment

### Removal

1 Open the bonnet and place a wad of rag underneath each corner of the bonnet, to protect against possible damage should the bonnet slip.
2 Using a pencil or felt tip pen, mark the outline of each hinge relative to the bonnet, to use as a guide on refitting.
3 Disconnect the washer hose from the bonnet (see illustration).
4 Have an assistant support the bonnet then, using a small flat-bladed screwdriver, carefully lift the retaining clips and unhook the support strut from bonnet balljoint (see illustration).
5 Remove the left- and right-hand hinge-to-bonnet bolts, and carefully remove the bonnet from the car (see illustration).
6 Inspect the bonnet hinges for signs of wear and free play at the pivots, and if necessary renew. The hinges are bolted to the body; remove the windscreen wiper motor cover panel (see Chapter 12) to gain access to the hinge fixings.

### Refitting and adjustment

7 With the aid of an assistant, align the bonnet with the hinges and refit the retaining bolts, tightening them by hand only. Align the hinges with the marks made on removal, then tighten the retaining bolts to the specified torque.
8 Clip the support strut back onto the balljoint and check it is securely retained by the spring clip.
9 Securely reconnect the washer hose.
10 Close the bonnet, and check for alignment with the adjacent panels. If necessary, slacken the hinge bolts and re-align the bonnet to suit; the height of the bonnet can be altered by screwing the rubber stoppers into/out of the bonnet lock crossmember. Once the bonnet is correctly aligned, tighten the bonnet bolts to the specified torque.

## 9 Bonnet release cable –
removal and refitting

### Removal

1 Unbolt the bonnet lock from the crossmember, and detach the cable from the lock.
2 Firmly apply the handbrake, then loosen the driver's side front wheel nuts. Jack up the front of the car and remove the wheel.
3 Remove the retaining screws and fasteners,

and manoeuvre out the wheel arch liner from under the driver's side wing (see illustration).
4 Free the bonnet release cable from its clips and ties, and pull it through under the wheel arch, noting its correct routing.
5 Working inside the car, undo the retaining screws (the lower screw is hidden behind a trim cap) and remove the driver's side lower facia panel, disconnecting the wiring connector from the footwell light (see illustrations).
6 Remove the retaining screws, then free the bonnet release lever from the body and unhook it from the end of the cable.
7 Return to the outside of the car, and withdraw the cable from underneath the wheel arch.

### Refitting

8 Feed the cable back in through the bulkhead grommet and into the passenger compartment.
9 Reconnect the release lever to the cable then refit the lever to the body, tightening its retaining screws securely. Refit the lower panel to the facia.
10 Route the cable correctly underneath the wing and through to the front of the car, securing it in position with all the necessary clips and ties.
11 Refit the bonnet lock as described in Section 10.
12 Check the operation of the lock, then refit the wheel arch liner and roadwheel. Lower the car to the ground, and tighten the wheel nuts to the specified torque.

9.3 Remove the screws/fasteners and take out the driver's side wheel arch liner

9.5a Remove the screws (arrowed) and take off the driver's side lower panel from the facia . . .

9.5b . . . disconnecting the wiring from the footwell illumination light

## 10 Bonnet lock –
### removal, refitting and adjustment

### Removal

**1** Open up the bonnet then remove the protective cover (where fitted) from the bonnet lock.

**2** If the lock is fitted with a microswitch (for the alarm system), trace the wiring back from the switch, and free it from its retaining clips. Unclip the wiring connector from the body, and disconnect it from the main wiring harness so the switch is free to be removed with the lock assembly **(see illustration)**.

**3** Remove the retaining bolts, then free the lock assembly from the crossmember. Unclip the release cable and remove the lock from the car **(see illustrations)**.

### Refitting and adjustment

**4** Reconnect the release cable correctly to the lock, then seat the lock in position on the crossmember. Refit the lock retaining bolts and tighten to the specified torque.

**5** Where necessary, ensure the microswitch wiring is correctly routed and retained by all the necessary clips, then reconnect the connector and clip it back into position.

**6** Check the operation of the release lever and cable, then close the bonnet and check the operation of the lock. If necessary, adjust the lock operation by slackening the retaining bolts and repositioning the lock on the crossmember. Once the lock is correctly positioned, tighten the retaining bolts to the specified torque. Lubricate the lock with multi-purpose grease, then (where necessary) refit the protective cover.

## 11 Door –
### removal, refitting and adjustment

### Removal

**1** Disconnect the battery negative lead (see *Disconnecting the battery*).

**2** Using a hammer and punch, carefully tap out the roll pin securing the door check link to the pillar **(see illustration)**.

**3** If work is being carried out on the front door, unclip the wiring harness gaiter and retaining plate from the pillar, then depress the retaining clip and disconnect the door wiring connector **(see illustration)**. In practice, it's easier to disconnect the connector once the door has been freed from its hinges.

**4** If work is being carried out on the rear door, free the door wiring harness gaiter and retaining plate from the pillar, and withdraw the wiring until the connector appears. Release the retaining clip and disconnect the door wiring from the main harness, ensuring

**10.2 Disconnect the bonnet lock microswitch wiring connector (arrowed) and free the wiring from its clips**

**10.3b . . . then free the lock assembly from the body . . .**

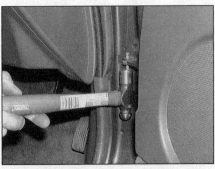

**11.2 Tap out the roll pin and detach the door check link from the pillar**

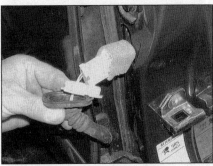

**11.4 Withdraw the wiring from the rear door pillar and disconnect it**

**10.3a Slacken and remove the retaining bolts . . .**

**10.3c . . . and detach it from the release cable (arrowed)**

the wiring connector does not disappear into the pillar **(see illustration)**.

**5** On all doors, using a pencil or felt tip pen, mark the outline of each hinge relative to the door, to use as a guide on refitting.

**6** Have an assistant support the door, then remove the hinge retaining bolts and remove the door from the car **(see illustration)**.

**7** Examine the hinges for signs of wear or damage and, if necessary, renew. If the front

**11.3 On the front door, unclip the wiring harness gaiter from the pillar and disconnect the connector**

**11.6 Remove the hinge bolts (arrowed) and remove the door**

**11.8 Ensure the gaiter is correctly located on the retaining plate, then clip the plate into the pillar**

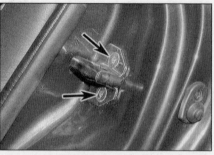

**11.14 Adjust the lock striker by slackening the screws (arrowed) and repositioning it as necessary**

damaged, paint the affected area with a suitable touch-in brush to prevent corrosion.
**14** Once the door is correctly aligned, check that the lock striker enters the door lock centrally and holds the door firmly shut when locked. If necessary, slacken the retaining screws and adjust the lock striker position as necessary **(see illustration)**. Once the striker plate is correctly positioned, tighten its retaining screws to the specified torque.

door hinges are to be renewed, it will be necessary to remove the wheel arch liner, and withdraw the foam insulation from behind the wing to gain access to the hinge bolts. Mark the position of the hinge on the body, then undo the retaining bolts and remove the hinge from the car. Fit the new hinge, aligning the marks made prior to removal, and tighten its retaining bolts to the specified torque.

### Refitting

**8** With the aid of an assistant, offer up the door to the car and securely reconnect the wiring connector. Ensure the connector is securely connected, then seat the wiring gaiter on its retaining plate and clip the plate back into the pillar **(see illustration)**.
**9** Refit the hinge bolts, then align the hinges with the marks made before removal and tighten the retaining bolts to the specified torque.

**10** Align the check link with its bracket and refit the roll pin, tapping it securely into the position.
**11** Check the door alignment and, if necessary, adjust then reconnect the battery negative lead. If the paintwork around the hinges has been damaged, paint the area with a suitable touch-in brush to prevent corrosion.

### Adjustment

**12** Close the door and check the door alignment with surrounding body panels. If necessary, slight adjustment of the door position can be made by slackening the hinge retaining bolts and repositioning the hinge/door as necessary. Note that it will be necessary to remove the wheel arch liner and foam insulation from behind the wing to access the front door hinge-to-body bolts.
**13** Once the door is correctly positioned, tighten the hinge bolts to the specified torque. If the paintwork around the hinges has been

## 12 Door inner trim panel – removal and refitting

**Note:** *Door trim panel design varies according to the equipment level. Some trim panel fastener locations on your car might be different to those shown in the accompanying illustrations.*

### Removal

**1** Disconnect the battery lead (see *Disconnecting the battery*) and proceed as described under the relevant sub-heading.

#### Front door

**2** Pull off the control knob (manual mirror only), then unclip the exterior mirror inner trim panel and remove it from the door **(see illustration)**.
**3** Undo the door lock inner handle surround retaining screw, then lift the handle and remove the surround from around the handle **(see illustrations)**.
**4** On models with manually-operated windows, push/lever out the regulator handle spring clip, then remove the handle and spacer from the regulator spindle. In the absence of the clip removal tool **(see illustration 12.10a)**, the clip can be released by feeding a strip of cloth between the handle and spacer; pull the ends of cloth upwards, and use a 'sawing' action to catch the spring ends.
**5** On all models, unclip and remove the speaker grille from the base of the trim panel **(see illustration)**.
**6** Remove the trim caps (where fitted) then remove the trim panel retaining screws from the front and rear of the panel. Further screws are located in the armrest pocket and door bin **(see illustrations)**.
**7** Unclip and remove the armrest pocket and

**12.2 Unclip the mirror inner trim panel from the door**

**12.3a Undo the retaining screw . . .**

**12.3b . . . and remove the door lock inner handle surround**

**12.5 Unclip the speaker grille from the door trim panel**

**12.6a Prise off the trim caps (arrowed) then remove the screws from the rear of the panel . . .**

12.6b . . . the front of the panel
(arrowed) . . .

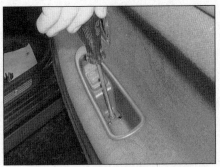

12.6c . . . and the armrest pocket

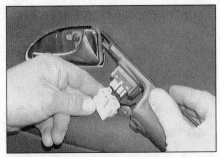

12.7  Remove the armrest pocket from the
trim panel, disconnecting the switch wiring
connector

remove it from the trim panel. Where necessary, disconnect the wiring connector from the window switch as the pocket is removed **(see illustration)**.

**8** Carefully unclip the base of the trim panel

from the door, then lift the panel upwards and away from the door **(see illustration)**. Where necessary, free the wiring harness from the panel and disconnect any relevant wiring connectors as soon as they become accessible.

### Rear door

**9** Carefully unclip the small trim panel from the rear of the window frame **(see illustration)**.

**10** On models with manual windows, push/lever out the regulator handle retaining clip, then remove the handle and spacer from the regulator spindle **(see illustrations)**. In the absence of the clip removal tool, the clip can be released by feeding a strip of cloth between the handle and spacer; pull the ends of cloth upwards, and use a 'sawing' action to catch the spring ends.

**11** On all models, undo the door lock inner handle surround retaining screw, then lift the handle and remove the surround from around the handle **(see illustrations)**.

**12** Remove the trim caps (where fitted), then remove the trim panel retaining screws from the rear of the panel and the armrest pocket **(see illustrations)**.

12.8  Unclip the base of the trim panel then
lift it away from the door

12.9  Unclip the inner trim panel from the
rear of the rear door

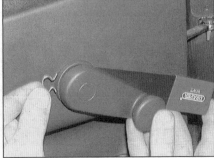

12.10a  On models with manually-operated
windows, slide out the retaining clip . . .

12.10b . . . then remove the regulator
handle and spacer from the spindle

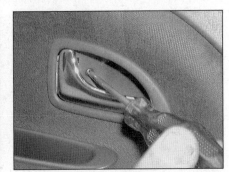

12.11a  Undo the retaining screw . . .

12.11b . . . and remove the door lock inner
handle surround

12.12a  Remove the trim caps, then undo
the screws located in the armrest
pocket . . .

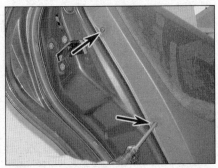

12.12b . . . and on the trim panel rear edge
(arrowed)

**12.13 Remove the armrest pocket from the trim panel**

**13** Unclip and remove the armrest pocket and remove it from the trim panel **(see illustration)**. Where necessary, disconnect the wiring connector from the window switch as the pocket is removed.

**14** Carefully unclip the base of the trim panel from the door, then lift the panel upwards and away from the door **(see illustration)**. Where necessary, free the wiring harness from the panel, and disconnect any relevant wiring connectors as soon as they become accessible.

### *Refitting*

**15** Refitting of the trim panel is the reverse of removal. Prior to clipping the panel in position, ensuring all the wiring (where necessary) is correctly routed and passed through the relevant apertures.

**12.14 Unclip the base of the trim panel then lift the panel away from the rear door**

## 13 Door handle and lock components – removal and refitting

### *Removal*

**1** Remove the inner trim panel as described in Section 12, and proceed as described under the relevant sub-heading.

### Door lock inner handle

**2** Prise out the inner section of the handle link rod clip, and free the rod from the handle **(see illustration)**.

**3** Remove the retaining screws and remove the handle from the door **(see illustration)**.

### Front door lock assembly

**4** Remove the inner handle as described above.

**5** Carefully peel the insulation panel away from the rear of the door sufficiently to give access to the lock components. If the insulation panel is to be completely removed, it will first be necessary to undo the screws and remove the loudspeaker and the trim panel support bracket. On some models, the support bracket may be riveted in position; carefully drill out the rivets and obtain new rivets for use on refitting **(see illustrations)**. **Note:** *The insulation panel must be renewed if it is damaged.*

**6** Undo the retaining screws and remove the side impact protection system (SIPS) striker and insert from the door **(see illustrations)**.

**7** Fully close the window (on models with electric windows, temporarily reconnect the battery and switch to do this) then free the window sealing strip from its rear guide. Remove the screw from the base of the guide, then manoeuvre the guide out through the door aperture, freeing it from the wiring clip **(see illustrations)**.

**8** Unclip the inner handle link rod guide from the door, and slide it off the rod **(see illustration)**.

**9** Unclip the lock button link rod from its guide on the door **(see illustration)**.

**10** Remove the lock retaining screws, then free the lock from the door and disconnect the wiring connector from the central locking actuator. Release the retaining clips and detach the exterior handle and lock button link rods, then manoeuvre the lock assembly out through the door aperture **(see illustrations)**.

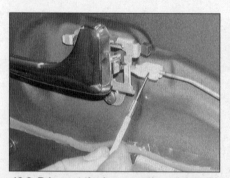

**13.2 Prise out the inner section of the clip to free the link rod . . .**

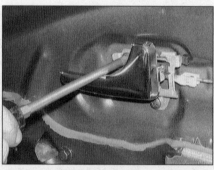

**13.3 . . . then undo the screws and remove the lock inner handle from the door**

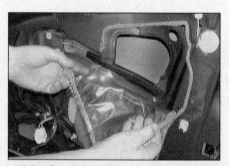

**13.5a Carefully peel back the insulation panel to gain access to the lock components**

**13.5b If the trim panel support bracket is riveted in position, carefully drill off the rivet heads**

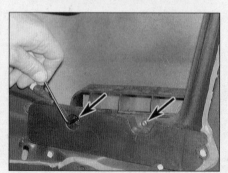

**13.6a Undo the retaining screws (arrowed) and remove the SIPS striker . . .**

**13.6b . . . and insert from the door**

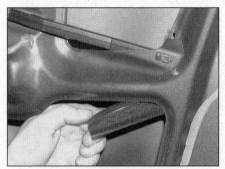

**13.7a Free the sealing strip from the rear guide . . .**

**13.7b . . . then undo the retaining bolt . . .**

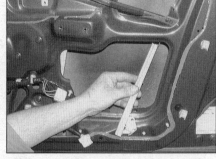

**13.7c . . . and remove the guide from the door**

### Front door exterior handle

**11** Carry out the operations in paragraphs 4 to 8.

**12** Carefully unclip the handle link rods from the door lock assembly. Trace the wiring back from the lock microswitch(es) and disconnect the wiring connector **(see illustration)**.

**13** Remove the retaining bolts, then unclip the inner and outer sections of the handle assembly and manoeuvre them out from the door. Where necessary, the microswitch(es) can then be unclipped and removed the handle **(see illustrations)**.

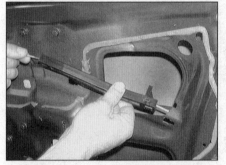

**13.8 Unclip the guide from the door and slide it off the link rod**

**13.9 Unclip the lock button link rod from its guide**

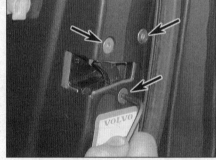

**13.10a Slacken and remove the retaining screws (arrowed) . . .**

**13.10b . . . then detach exterior handle and lock button link rods . . .**

**13.10c . . . and manoeuvre the lock assembly out of position**

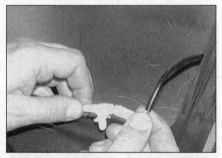

**13.12 Unclip the wiring connector and disconnect the lock microswitch wiring connector**

**13.13a Undo the retaining bolts . . .**

**13.13b . . . and remove the inner . . .**

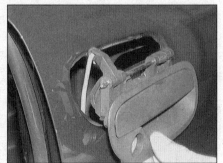

**13.13c . . . and outer sections of the exterior handle assembly**

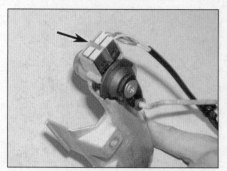

**13.13d  The microswitches can be unclipped from the handle**

**13.15a  Unhook the link rod . . .**

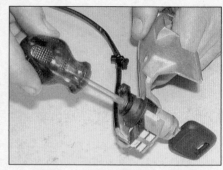

**13.15b  . . . then undo the retaining screw . . .**

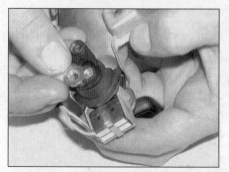

**13.15c  . . . and remove the spacer . . .**

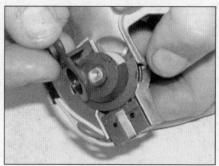

**13.15d  . . . and operating crank, noting each component's correct fitted location**

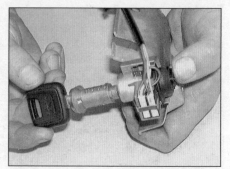

**13.16  Withdraw the lock cylinder from the handle**

## Front door lock cylinder

**14**  Remove the exterior handle from the door as described earlier in this Section.

**15**  Insert the key into the cylinder. Unhook the link rod, remove the retaining screw then,

**13.18a  Peel back the insulation panel to gain access to the lock components**

**13.18b  If the trim panel support bracket is riveted in position, carefully drill off the rivet heads**

noting each component's correct fitted location, remove the spacer and operating crank whilst holding the return spring assembly firmly in position on the handle **(see illustrations)**.

**16**  Withdraw the lock cylinder and key assembly from the handle **(see illustration)**.

## Rear door lock assembly

**17**  Remove the inner handle as described in paragraphs 2 and 3.

**18**  Carefully peel the insulation panel away from the rear of the door sufficiently to give access to the lock components. If the insulation panel is to be completely removed, it will first be necessary to undo the screws and remove the trim panel support bracket from the door. On some models, the support bracket may be riveted in position; carefully drill out the rivets and obtain new rivets for use on refitting **(see illustrations)**. **Note:** *The*

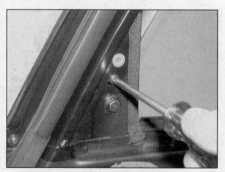

**13.19a  Undo the retaining screw . . .**

*insulation panel must be renewed if it is damaged on removal.*

**19**  Open the window (on models with electric windows, temporarily reconnect the battery and switch to do this) then undo the retaining screw and remove the small outer trim panel from the rear of the door window frame **(see illustrations)**.

**20**  Remove the retaining bolts securing the window glass rear guide to the door. Free the sealing strip from the guide, then manoeuvre the guide out of position **(see illustrations)**. With the guide removed, fully raise the window again.

**21**  Release the retaining clip and detach the lock link rod from the inner button pivot. Where the link rod is hooked in position, press out the centre pin, then unclip the inner button pivot from the door and detach it from the end of the rod **(see illustrations)**.

**13.19b  . . . and remove the outer trim panel from the rear door**

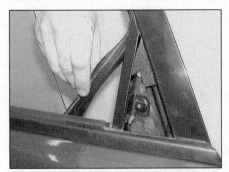

13.20a  Free the sealing strip from the guide . . .

13.20b  . . . then undo the retaining bolts (arrowed) . . .

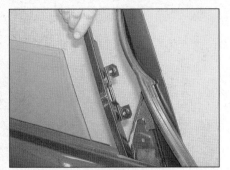

13.20c  . . . and remove the window glass guide from the door

13.21a  Push out the centre pin . . .

13.21b  . . . then unclip the inner button pivot from the door and detach it from the link rod

13.23a  Undo the retaining screws (arrowed) . . .

22  Release the exterior handle link rod from its clip on the lock assembly.
23  Remove the lock retaining screws, then unclip the link rods from their guides. Remove the lock assembly from the door, disconnecting the wiring connector from

the central locking actuator **(see illustrations)**.

### Rear door exterior handle

24  Carry out the operations in paragraphs 17 to 20.

25  Unclip the exterior handle link rod from the lock assembly.
26  Remove the access plug from the door, then remove the handle retaining bolts. Unclip the handle assembly from the door and manoeuvre out the retaining plate **(see illustrations)**.

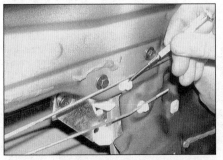

13.23b  . . . then unclip the link rods from the guides

13.23c  Manoeuvre the lock assembly out from the door . . .

13.23d  . . . and disconnect the wiring connector from the central locking actuator

13.26a  Remove the access plug . . .

13.26b  . . . then slacken and remove the retaining bolts . . .

13.26c  . . . and remove the exterior handle from the door

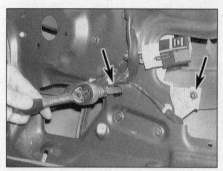

14.5a Slacken the glass retaining bolts . . .

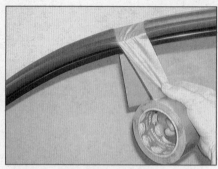

14.5b . . . then lift the glass fully up and tape it to the door frame

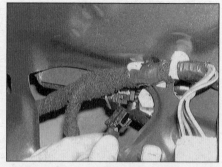

14.6 Unbolt the regulator assembly from the door and disconnect the motor wiring connector

## Refitting

**27** Refitting is the reverse of removal, noting the following points:

a) *Tighten all fasteners to the specified torque settings (where given).*

b) *Ensure that all link rods are securely clipped in position and (where possible) are correctly adjusted. On some link rods, adjustments can be made by repositioning the link rod in its retaining clip.*

c) *Check the operation of the lock/handles before sticking the insulation panel back onto the door and refitting the trim panel as described in Section 12.*

d) *On completion, check the operation of the lock. Also check that the rear edge of the door is flush to the body once shut. If necessary, adjustments can be made by slackening the retaining screws and repositioning the lock striker slightly. Once the striker is correctly positioned, tighten the retaining screws to the specified torque.*

## 14 Door window glass and regulator – removal and refitting

## Removal

**1** Remove the inner trim panel as described in Section 12, then proceed as described under the relevant sub-heading.

### Front door window regulator

**2** Carefully peel the insulation panel away from the rear of the door sufficiently to give access to the window regulator assembly. If the insulation panel is to be completely removed, it will first be necessary to undo the retaining screws and remove the loudspeaker and the trim panel support bracket. On some models, the support bracket may be riveted in position; carefully drill out the rivets and obtain new rivets for use on refitting. **Note:** *The insulation panel must be renewed if it is damaged.*

**3** On models up to May 2000, undo the screws and remove the side impact protection system (SIPS) striker and insert from the door.

**4** Fully close the window (on models with electric windows, temporarily reconnect the battery and switch to do this) then carefully free the window sealing strip from its rear guide. Remove the retaining screw from the base of the guide, then manoeuvre the guide out through the door aperture, freeing it from the wiring clip.

**5** Position the window so that the bolts securing the window glass to the regulator are accessible through the door aperture. Remove both bolts, then lift the glass fully up and tape it to the top of the door frame to hold it in position **(see illustrations)**.

**6** Remove the retaining bolts securing the regulator assembly to the door, then (where

necessary) disconnect the wiring connector from the regulator motor **(see illustration)**.

**7** Manoeuvre the regulator assembly out through the door aperture **(see illustration)**. Note that the regulator assembly is only available as a complete unit, and must not be dismantled (though there's no harm in doing so, if a new one's the only other option).

### Rear door window regulator

**8** Remove the door lock inner handle as described in Section 13.

**9** Undo the retaining screws and remove the trim panel support bracket from the door. On some models the support bracket maybe secured in position with pop rivets; carefully drill out the rivets and obtain new rivets for use on refitting.

**10** Carefully peel off the insulation panel and remove it from the door. **Note:** *The insulation panel must be renewed if it is damaged on removal.*

**11** Position the window so that the bolts securing the window glass to the regulator are accessible through the door aperture (on models with electric windows temporarily reconnect the battery and switch to do this). Remove both bolts then lift the glass fully up and tape it to the top of the door frame to hold it in position **(see illustrations)**.

**12** Remove the retaining bolts securing the regulator assembly to the door then (where necessary) disconnect the wiring connector from the regulator motor **(see illustration)**.

14.7 Removing the regulator assembly from the front door

14.11a Slacken the glass retaining bolts . . .

14.11b . . . then lift the glass fully up and tape it to the door frame

**14.12 Slacken and remove the retaining bolts (arrowed) . . .**

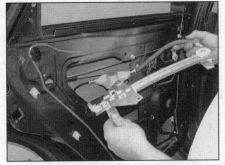

**14.13 . . . then manoeuvre the regulator assembly out of the rear door**

**14.15 Unclip the window inner sealing strip and remove it from the front door**

**13** Manoeuvre the regulator assembly out through the door aperture **(see illustration)**. Note that the regulator assembly is only available as a complete unit, and must not be dismantled (though there's no harm in doing so, if a new one's the only other option).

### Front door window

**14** Carry out the operations described in paragraphs 2 to 5.

**15** Unclip the window inner sealing strip and remove it from the top of the door **(see illustration)**.

**16** Free the window from its guides and manoeuvre it out from the top of the door **(see illustration)**.

### Rear door window

**17** Carry out the operations described in paragraphs 8 to 10.

**18** Open the window (on models with electric windows temporarily reconnect the battery and switch to do this) then undo the retaining screw and remove the small outer trim panel from the rear of the door window frame **(see illustrations 13.19a and 13.19b)**.

**19** Remove the retaining bolts securing the window glass rear guide to the door. Free the sealing strip from the guide, then manoeuvre the guide out of position **(see illustrations 13.20a to 13.20c)**.

**20** Unclip the window inner sealing strip and remove it from the top of the door **(see illustration)**.

**21** Remove the retaining screw from each end of the window outer sealing strip, and remove the strip from the door **(see illustrations)**.

**22** Position the window so that the bolts

securing the window glass to the regulator are accessible through the door aperture. Remove both bolts, then lift the glass upwards and out of the door **(see illustration)**.

### Refitting

**23** Refitting is the reverse of the relevant removal procedure, noting the following:

a) Ensure all sealing strips are correctly located.

b) On refitting the window glass, take care to ensure it engages correctly with its guides.

c) When refitting the regulator, install all the bolts hand-tight, then tighten the three bolts securing the winder/motor mounting to the specified torque. Engage the glass with the regulator, and loosely refit its bolts. Move the regulator mechanism up and down a few times to settle it in position, then tighten the remaining regulator bolts and the window glass bolts to the specified torque. Close the window and check it seats correctly in the door frame; if necessary, slight adjustments can be made by slackening the bolts and moving the glass slightly on the regulator.

d) Once the window is correctly positioned, refit the insulation panel securely to the door and install the inner trim panel (see Section 12).

**14.16 Manoeuvre the window glass out of the top of the door**

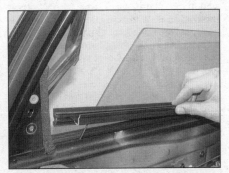

**14.20 Unclip the window inner sealing strip and remove it from the rear door**

**14.21a Remove the retaining screw from each end . . .**

**14.21b . . . then lift off the window outer sealing strip**

**14.22 Manoeuvre the window glass out of the top of the door**

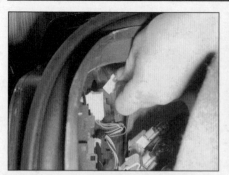

15.3a Disconnect the boot lid wiring connector . . .

15.3b . . . then unclip the gaiter and mounting plate, and withdraw the harness

15.4 Lift the retaining clip and detach the support struts from the boot lid

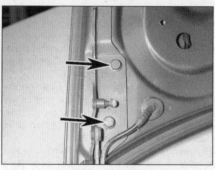

15.6 Unscrew the bolts (arrowed) and lift the boot lid away

## 15 Boot lid – removal and refitting

### Removal

#### Boot lid

1 Open the boot lid, then disconnect the battery negative lead (see *Disconnecting the battery*).

2 Release the retaining clip and open up the left-hand rear light unit trim panel cover to gain access to the boot lid wiring harness connector, which is situated above the rear light unit. To improve access, peel off the boot lid sealing strip, unclip the luggage compartment sill trim panel, then remove the fasteners securing the rear of the side trim panel in position and fold it inwards slightly.

3 Disconnect the boot lid wiring connector, then unclip the wiring harness gaiter and mounting plate from the body **(see illustrations)**. Withdraw the wiring from the body until the connector appears.

4 Using a small, flat-bladed screwdriver, carefully lift the retaining clips and detach the support struts from their upper balljoints **(see illustration)**.

5 Using a pencil or felt tip pen, mark the outline of the hinges relative to the boot lid, to use as a guide on refitting.

6 Remove the retaining bolts and remove the boot lid from the car **(see illustration)**.

7 Inspect the hinges for signs of wear and free play at the pivots, and if necessary renew; the hinges are bolted to the body.

#### Support strut

8 Open up the boot lid then, using a small, flat-bladed screwdriver, carefully lift the retaining clips and detach the support strut from the hinge balljoints.

### Refitting

#### Boot lid

9 Refitting is the reverse of removal, aligning the hinges with the marks made before removal, and tightening the retaining bolts to the specified torque.

10 On completion, close the boot lid and check its alignment with the surrounding panels. If necessary, slacken the hinge bolts and re-align the boot lid to suit; the height of the boot lid can be altered by screwing the rubber stoppers into/out of the boot lid. Once the boot lid is correctly aligned, tighten the hinge bolts to the specified torque. If the paintwork around the hinges has been damaged, paint the affected area with a suitable touch-in brush to prevent corrosion.

#### Support strut

11 Refitting is the reverse of removal, ensuring the strut is securely clipped in position.

## 16 Boot lid lock components – removal and refitting

### Removal

#### Lock assembly

1 Open up the boot lid then remove the fasteners (unscrew each centre screw slightly then pull out the complete fastener) and remove the boot lid inner trim panel **(see illustrations)**.

2 Prise out the inner section of the link rod clip and free the link rod from the lock button **(see illustration)**.

3 Remove the retaining bolts and manoeuvre the lock out of position, disconnecting the wiring connector(s) as they become accessible **(see illustrations)**.

16.1a Unscrew the centre screws slightly, then pull out all the fasteners . . .

16.1b . . . and remove the inner trim panel from the boot lid

16.2 Prise out the inner section of the retaining clip and detach the link rod from the lock button

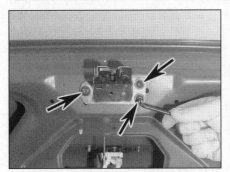

**16.3a  Undo the retaining screws (arrowed) . . .**

**16.3b  . . . then remove the lock assembly from the boot lid and disconnect the wiring connectors**

**16.5  Undo the retaining screw and pivot the support bracket away from the lock button**

## Lock button assembly

**4** Carry out the operations in paragraphs 1 and 2.

**5** Unclip the central locking actuator link rod from the lock button, then slacken the retaining screw and pivot the support bracket away from the button **(see illustration)**.

**6** Remove the retaining nuts and remove the lock button surround panel from the outside of the boot lid **(see illustration)**.

**7** Manoeuvre the lock button assembly out of position **(see illustration)**.

## *Refitting*

**8** Refitting is the reverse of removal, noting the following points:

a) *Ensure that all link rods are securely clipped in position and (where possible) are correctly adjusted. On some link rods, adjustments can be made by repositioning the link rod in its retaining clip.*

b) *Check the operation of the lock/button before refitting the trim panel.*

c) *On completion, check the operation of the lock and check that boot lid is held firmly shut. If necessary, adjustments can be made by slacken the screws and repositioning the lock striker slightly. Once the striker is correctly positioned, securely tighten the screws.*

## 17 Tailgate – removal and refitting

## *Removal*

## Tailgate

**1** Open the tailgate, then disconnect the battery negative lead (see *Disconnecting the battery*).

**2** Undo the two screws located in the handle aperture, then unclip the inner trim panel and remove it from the tailgate **(see illustrations)**.

**3** Remove the high-level stop-light unit as described in Chapter 12, Section 7.

**4** Disconnect the hose from the tailgate washer jet, and free the grommet and hose from the tailgate **(see illustration)**.

**5** Disconnect the wiring connectors from the tailgate electrical components, and tie a piece

**16.6  Remove the lock button surround panel . . .**

**17.2a  Slacken and remove the two retaining screws . . .**

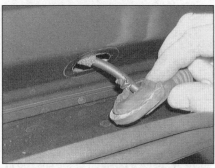

**17.4  Disconnect the washer hose from the jet and free it from the tailgate**

of string to the end of the wiring. Free the wiring from its retaining clips then withdraw it from the tailgate **(see illustration)**. When the end of the wiring appears, untie the string and

**16.7  . . . then withdraw the lock button assembly from the boot lid**

leave it in position; it can then be used to draw the wiring back into position on refitting.

**6** Draw around the outline of each hinge on the tailgate using a suitable marker pen.

**17.2b  . . . then unclip the inner trim panel from the tailgate**

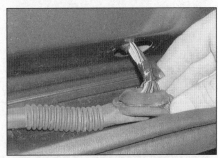

**17.5  Free the wiring grommet from the tailgate and withdraw the tailgate wiring harness**

**17.7 Lift the retaining clips and detach the support struts from the tailgate**

7 Have an assistant support the tailgate, then carefully lift the retaining clips and detach both support struts from their balljoints **(see illustration)**.

8 Remove the bolts securing the hinges to the tailgate, and remove the tailgate from the car **(see illustration)**.

9 Examine the hinges for signs of wear or damage. If renewal is necessary, remove the rear pillar upper trim panels (remove the courtesy lights and speaker grilles, then undo the screws and unclip the panels) then unclip and lower the rear of the headlining, taking care not to crease it. Mark the position of the hinge on the body, then undo the nuts and remove the hinge assembly, along with any relevant shims positioned between the hinge and body. Fit the new hinge and (where necessary) shims, and securely tighten the retaining nuts.

**18.3 Remove the tailgate lock and disconnect its wiring connectors**

**18.9 Removing the tailgate lock button assembly**

**17.8 Undo the hinge bolts (arrowed) and remove the tailgate from the car**

### Support strut

10 Have an assistant support the tailgate then, using a small flat-bladed screwdriver, carefully lift the retaining clips and unhook the strut from its balljoints.

## *Refitting*

### Tailgate

11 Refitting is the reverse of removal, noting the following:

a) *Align the hinges with the marks made before removal, and tighten the hinge bolts to the specified torque.*

b) *Prior to refitting the trim panel, connect the battery and check the operation of all the tailgate electrical components.*

c) *Ensure the tailgate is correctly aligned*

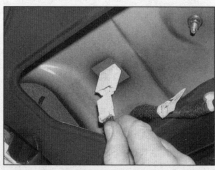

**18.6 Disconnect the wiring connector from the tailgate light unit**

**18.10 Adjust the position of the link rod in the clip, then secure it with the inner part of the clip**

with all its surrounding body components; adjustments can be made by slackening the hinge bolts and repositioning the tailgate on its hinges. If height adjustment of the tailgate is necessary, it will be necessary to fit/remove shims between the hinge and body (see paragraph 9).

d) *If the paintwork around the hinges has been damaged, paint the affected area with a suitable touch-in brush to prevent corrosion.*

### Support strut

12 Refitting is the reverse of removal, making sure the strut is clipped securely in position.

---

## 18 Tailgate lock components – removal, refitting and adjustment

## *Removal*

### Lock assembly

1 Open up the tailgate, then undo the two screws located in the handle aperture, and unclip the inner trim panel from the tailgate.

2 Reach in behind the lock then release the retaining clip and detach the link rod from the lock.

3 Remove the retaining bolts then manoeuvre the lock out of position, disconnecting the wiring connectors as they become accessible **(see illustration)**.

### Lock button assembly

4 Remove the tailgate trim panel as described in paragraph 1.

5 Undo the screws and remove the number plate from the tailgate.

6 Disconnect the main wiring connector from the tailgate light unit assembly **(see illustration)**.

7 Undo the nuts, then remove the complete light unit assembly from the tailgate, complete with its rubber seal. The seal must be renewed if damaged.

8 Prise out the inner section of the button link rod clip, and detach the central locking actuator rod from the button.

9 Manoeuvre the lock button assembly out of position, complete with its rubber seal **(see illustration)**.

## *Refitting*

10 Refitting is the reverse of removal, noting the following points:

a) *When refitting the lock button, ensure the button is correctly engaged with the lock link rod before refitting the rear light unit.*

b) *Ensure that all link rods are securely clipped in position and (where possible) are correctly adjusted. The lock link rod can be adjusted by repositioning the link rod in the two-piece retaining clip (see illustration).*

**19.2  Door lock central locking actuator retaining screws (arrowed)**

**19.4  Unclip the link rod from the lock button**

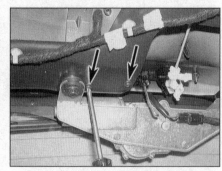

**19.5a  Undo the retaining screws . . .**

c) *Check the operation of the lock/button before refitting the trim panel and light unit.*
d) *On completion, check the operation of the lock, and ensure that the tailgate is held firmly shut. If necessary, adjustments can be made by slackening the screws and repositioning the lock striker slightly. Once the striker is correctly positioned, securely tighten its screws.*

## 19  Central locking components – removal and refitting

## Removal

### Door lock actuator

**1** Remove the relevant door lock assembly as described in Section 13.
**2** Undo the retaining screws then free the actuator from the lock assembly **(see illustration)**.

### Tailgate lock actuator

**3** Open up the tailgate, undo the two screws located in the handle aperture, and unclip the inner trim panel from the tailgate.
**4** Detach the actuator link rod from the lock button **(see illustration)**.
**5** Undo the two retaining screws and remove the actuator from the tailgate, disconnecting the wiring connector as it becomes accessible **(see illustrations)**.

### Boot lid lock actuator

**6** Open up the boot lid, then remove the fasteners (unscrew each centre screw slightly, then pull out the complete fastener) and remove the boot lid inner trim panel **(see illustrations 16.1a and 16.1b)**.
**7** Detach the actuator link rod from the lock button **(see illustration)**.
**8** Undo the two screws and remove the actuator from the boot lid, disconnecting the wiring connector as it becomes accessible **(see illustrations)**.

## Refitting

**9** Refitting is the reverse of removal, checking the operation of the central locking system before refitting the insulation/trim panel.

## 20  Electric window components – removal and refitting

## Window switch

**1** Refer to Chapter 12, Section 4.

## Window winder motors

**2** At the time of writing, it was unclear whether the window winder motors were available separately, or whether the complete regulator assembly would have to be renewed. Refer to your Volvo dealer for the latest information. Regulator removal and refitting is given in Section 14.

**19.5b  . . . and remove the tailgate central locking actuator, then disconnect the wiring**

## 21  Exterior mirrors and associated components – removal and refitting

## Manual mirror

**1** Pull off the control knob from the mirror adjustment handle, then unclip and remove the mirror inner trim panel from the door.
**2** Undo the retaining bolts and remove the mirror from the door. Recover the insulation which is fitted between the door and mirror; if it is damaged it must be renewed.
**3** Refitting is the reverse of removal, tightening the retaining bolts to the specified torque.

**19.7  Detach the link rod from the lock button . . .**

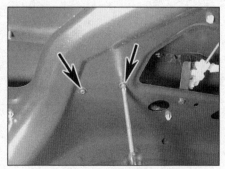

**19.8a  . . . then undo the two retaining screws (arrowed) . . .**

**19.8b  . . . and remove the boot lid lock actuator, disconnecting its wiring**

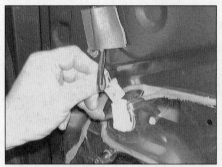

**21.5a Disconnect the wiring connector . . .**

**21.5b . . . then undo the retaining screws
(arrowed) . . .**

**21.5c . . . and remove the exterior mirror
from the door**

### Electric mirror

**4** Remove the door inner trim panel as described in Section 12.
**5** Disconnect the mirror wiring connector, then undo the retaining bolts and remove the mirror from the door **(see illustrations)**. Recover the insulation which is fitted between the door and mirror; if it is damaged it must be renewed.
**6** Refitting is the reverse of removal, tightening the retaining bolts to the specified torque.

### Mirror glass

**Note:** *The mirror glass is clipped into position. Removal of the glass is likely to result in breakage if carried out carelessly. If the glass is already broken (or even if it's not), wear gloves to avoid injury.*
**7** Tilt the mirror glass fully inwards. Using a screwdriver behind the outer edge of the glass, release the retaining clips, then carefully prise the glass from the motor/adjuster **(see illustration)**. Take great care when removing the glass; do not use excessive force as the glass is easily broken.
**8** Remove the glass from the mirror. Where necessary, disconnect the wiring connectors from the mirror heating element.
**9** On refitting, reconnect the wiring (where fitted) to the glass and clip the glass onto the motor/adjuster, taking great care not to break it. Apply force only to the centre of the glass, to minimise the risk of breakage. Ensure the glass is clipped securely into position, and adjust as necessary.

### Mirror switch

**10** Refer to Chapter 12, Section 4.

### Electric mirror motor

**11** Remove the mirror glass as described in paragraphs 7 and 8.
**12** Undo the retaining screws and remove the motor assembly, disconnecting its wiring as it becomes accessible **(see illustration)**.
**13** On refitting, securely reconnect the wiring, then seat the motor in position. Securely tighten the motor retaining screws, then refit the glass as described in paragraph 9.

## 22 Windscreen, tailgate and rear window glass – general information

These areas of glass are secured by the tight fit of the weatherstrip in the body aperture, and are bonded in position with a special adhesive. Renewal of such fixed glass is a difficult, messy and time-consuming task, which is beyond the scope of the home mechanic. It is difficult, unless one has plenty of practice, to obtain a secure, waterproof fit. Furthermore, the task carries a high risk of breakage; this applies especially to the laminated glass windscreen. In view of this, owners are strongly advised to have this sort of work carried out by one of the many specialist windscreen fitters or a Volvo dealer.

## 23 Sunroof – general information

**1** Due to the complexity of the sunroof mechanism, considerable expertise is needed to repair, replace or adjust the sunroof components successfully. Removal of the roof first requires the headlining to be removed, which is a complex and tedious operation, and not a task to be undertaken lightly. Therefore, any problems with the sunroof should be referred to a Volvo dealer.
**2** If the sunroof motor fails to operate, first check the relevant fuse. If the fault cannot be traced and rectified, the sunroof can be opened and closed manually as follows.

**3** Carefully prise out the courtesy light lenses from the overhead console, then undo the retaining screws and lower the console assembly away from the headlining.
**4** Prise out the cap and remove the screw from the centre of the sunroof motor, noting the correct fitted location of its washer, shim(s) and spacer. Do not lose any of these components, as the motor will not function without them.
**5** Using an Allen key (there is one supplied with the vehicle toolkit), rotate the motor spindle and close the sunroof. Ensure the spacer, shim(s) and washer are correctly positioned, then refit the centre bolt to the motor and tighten securely. Refit the overhead console, tightening its retaining screws securely, and clip the lenses back into position. Investigate the cause of the problem at the earliest possible opportunity.

## 24 Body exterior fittings – removal and refitting

### Underpanels and wheel arch liners

**1** The various plastic covers fitted to the underside of the car are secured in position by a mixture of screws, nuts and retaining clips and removal will be fairly obvious on inspection. Work methodically around the panel, removing its retaining screws and releasing its retaining clips until the panel is free and can be removed from the underside

**21.7 Tilt the mirror glass inwards and carefully unclip it from the motor/adjuster**

**21.12 Mirror motor retaining screws (arrowed)**

25.5a Unclip the access cover from the side of the seat . . .

25.5b . . . then slide the protective tool over the SIPS sensor unit . . .

25.5c . . . making sure it is clipped securely in position

of the car. Most clips used on the car are simply prised out. Other clips can be released by unscrewing/prising out the centre screw/pin, and then removing the clip.
2 On refitting, renew any retaining clips that may have been broken on removal, and ensure that the panel is securely retained by all the relevant clips and screws.

### Body trim strips and badges

3 The various body trim strips and badges are held in position with a special adhesive tape. Removal requires the trim/badge to be heated, to soften the adhesive, and then cut away from the surface. Due to the high risk of damage to the car's paintwork during this operation, it is recommended that this task be entrusted to a Volvo dealer.

## 25 Side impact protection system (SIPS) airbags – general information

⚠ *Warning: Before carrying out any work whatsoever on the SIPS/airbag system, switch off the ignition, disconnect the battery negative lead (see 'Disconnecting the battery'), and wait for at least 2 minutes before proceeding.*

⚠ *Warning: On models before May 2000, do not subject the area of the seat around the sensor to any form of shock which could accidentally trigger the SIPS airbag.*

⚠ *Warning: Do not subject the seat assembly to temperatures in excess of 100ºC.*

⚠ *Warning: Never attempt to dismantle or repair the front seat assembly or SIPS airbag components. Any repairs should be entrusted to a Volvo dealer.*

⚠ *Warning: If the SIPS sensor shows signs of damage, the complete SIPS assembly must be renewed by a Volvo dealer.*

⚠ *Warning: Volvo state that the SIPS airbag units should be renewed every 10 years. The expiry date of the units are given on a sticker attached to driver's side door pillar.*

**Note:** *Refer to Chapter 12 for information on the supplementary restraint system (SRS) which operates the driver's and passenger's front airbags.*

### Front seat airbags

#### Up to May 2000

1 Both front seats are equipped with a side impact protection system (SIPS) airbag. In the event of a side impact, the relevant airbag inflates and forms a cushion between the driver/passenger (as applicable) and the door, significantly reducing the possibility of serious injury. The SIPS airbag system components are all contained within each seat assembly – there are no external components, and the seats are not linked in any way.
2 Each front seat assembly houses a sensor unit and an airbag unit; the sensor is fitted to the outside of the seat cushion frame and the airbag is fitted to the outside of the seat back frame. The sensor and airbag are linked by two tubes which are filled with a combustible gas.
3 The sensor unit is calibrated to set off the airbag only when the impact is significant enough that the deformed door contacts the seat at a speed of 2 m/s or faster. Lesser impacts will not set the airbag off.
4 If the impact is severe enough, the sensor cover is deformed by the door, which forces the sensor firing pin to set off the ignition charge. The ignition charge ignites the combustible gas in the tubes linking the sensor to the airbag, which transmits the force of the charge to the gas generators in the airbag unit. The gas generators then inflate the airbag within milliseconds, forcing it rip open the seat upholstery and form a protective cushion between the seat occupant's torso and door. After impact, the airbag deflates almost immediately.
5 If work is being carried out on the front seats, it is important to fit the protective tool over the SIPS sensor unit to prevent the system being accidentally triggered. To do this, carefully unclip the access cover from the rear of the seat cushion side trim panel, and remove the protective tool from its holder. Carefully slide the tool into position over the sensor, making sure it is correctly located **(see illustrations)**. Once the work is complete,

slide off the tool, clip it back into its holder and securely refit the access cover to the seat.
6 Note the warnings at the start of this Section before contemplating any work on the front seats.

#### May 2000 onwards

7 The airbags in the front seats of later models are not self-contained, but are integrated instead into a SIPS which includes side curtain airbags. The front seats still contain airbags, which when triggered, operate in a similar fashion to those on earlier models – the difference lies in the triggering process.
8 Side impact sensors, mounted in the B- and C-pillars of the car body, constantly monitor for a severe side impact. Minor side impacts will not trigger the system – only when there is a serious risk of the bodyshell being deformed will any action be taken. As with the previous system, the side airbags will only deploy on the side of the car which has suffered impact.
9 Since the later-type front seats do not contain the side impact sensors, handling the seats once they have been removed carries less risk of triggering the seat airbags. The only precaution required is when disconnecting the front seat wiring, which should **only** be done at least two minutes after the battery has been disconnected. An additional precaution would be to tape up the seat wiring plug once it has been disconnected, to avoid any chance of a static charge firing the seat airbag. When reconnecting the seat wiring afterwards, ensure that the ignition is switched off.

### Side curtain airbags

10 The side curtain airbags fitted from May 2000 onwards deploy from the roof panels fitted between the tops of the side doors and the headlining. Their principle of operation is similar to any other airbag – they are triggered by the side impact sensors mounted in the B- and C-pillars, in the event of a severe side impact. Their purpose is to protect the passengers from head or upper body injury.
11 The presence of the curtain airbags will not normally have any impact on DIY procedures, but their location should be borne in mind if fitting any aftermarket equipment which might involve drilling in the area.

**26.3 Unscrew the mounting bolt and detach the seat belt from the front seat**

**26.4 Unclip the trim covers to gain access to the front seat rear outer bolt ...**

off the protective tool from the SIPS sensor, and clip it back into its holder before refitting the access cover securely to the seat trim panel.

### Rear seat

#### Seat cushion

**8** Fold the seat cushions fully forwards. Remove the hinge bolts and remove the seat cushion assembly from the car **(see illustration)**.
**9** Refitting is the reverse of removal, tightening the retaining bolts to the specified torque.

#### Seat back

**10** Fold the seat cushions fully forwards.
**11** Remove the bolts securing the right-hand seat back mountings to the floor, then remove the seat back from the car **(see illustration)**.
**12** To remove the left-hand seat back, undo the two screws and remove the luggage compartment floor panel to gain access to the inner bracket nut. Remove the nut and the outer bracket bolt, then undo the seat belt lower mounting bolt and remove the seat back assembly from the car **(see illustrations)**.
**13** Refitting is the reverse of removal, ensuring the left-hand seat back is fitted first.

## 26 Seats –
### removal and refitting

### Front seat

**Note:** *Side impact protection system airbags are fitted to the front seats. Refer to the warnings given in the Section 25 before proceeding.*

#### Removal

**1** Disconnect the battery negative lead (see *Disconnecting the battery*), and wait at least two minutes before proceeding. On models up to May 2000, refer to Section 25 and fit the protective tool supplied to the SIPS airbag sensor, to prevent the system being accidentally triggered.
**2** Remove the rear section of the centre console as described in Section 30.

**3** Remove the mounting bolt and detach the seat belt lower mounting from the seat frame **(see illustration)**. Recover the spacer which is fitted between the seat belt and seat.
**4** Unclip the trim cover from the seat rear outer mounting bolt **(see illustration)**.
**5** Slide off the trim cover from the front of the seat rail to reveal the outer mounting nut **(see illustration)**.
**6** Remove the front and rear mounting nuts and bolts then carefully manoeuvre the seat out of position, disconnecting the wiring connector(s) as they become accessible.

### Refitting

**7** Refitting is the reverse of removal, tightening the mounting nuts and bolts and the seat belt bolt to their specified torque settings **(see illustration)**. Ensure that the ignition is switched off before reconnecting the seat wiring plug. Where applicable, slide

## 27 Seat belt tensioners –
### general information

**Note:** *The front seat belt tensioners are part of the supplementary restraint system (SRS). Refer to Chapter 12 for further information.*

**26.5 ... and the front outer nut**

**26.7 Tighten the front seat mounting nuts and bolts to the specified torque**

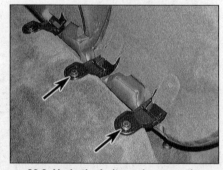

**26.8 Undo the bolts and remove the relevant section of the rear seat cushion**

**26.11 Right-hand seat back inner mounting bracket bolts**

**26.12a Unscrew the inner mounting bracket retaining nut ...**

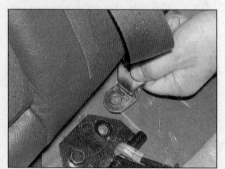

**26.12b ... and the seat belt lower mounting bolt, then remove the seat back**

**28.3 Unscrew the lower mounting bolt and detach the seat belt**

**28.4a Unclip the rear door sill trim panel . . .**

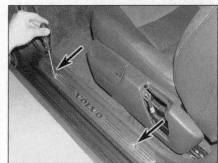

**28.4b . . . then undo the retaining screws . . .**

**1** All models covered in this manual are fitted with front seat belt tensioners. The tensioners are designed to instantaneously take up any slack in the seat belt in the case of a sudden frontal impact, therefore reducing the possibility of injury to the front seat occupants. Each front seat is fitted with the system, the tensioner being attached directly to the seat belt inertia reel.

**2** The seat belt tensioners are operated by the supplementary restraint system (SRS) control unit (see Chapter 12). The tensioner is electrically triggered by a frontal impact above a predetermined force. Lesser impacts, including impacts from behind or from the side, will not trigger the system.

**3** When the system is triggered, the fuel inside the tensioner cylinder ignites. This forces the tensioner piston downwards, which then removes all slack from the seat belt by retracting and locking the inertia reel. The strength of the explosion in the tensioner cylinder is calibrated to retract the seat belt sufficiently to securely retain the occupant of the seat without forcing them into the seat. Once the tensioner has been triggered, the seat belt will be permanently locked and the assembly must be renewed.

**4** To prevent the risk of injury if the system is triggered inadvertently when working on the car, if any work is to be carried out on the front seat belts, switch off the ignition then disconnect the battery (see *Disconnecting the battery*) and wait a few minutes before proceeding.

**5** Note the following warnings before contemplating any work on the front seat belts:

 *Warning: If the tensioner mechanism is dropped, it must be renewed, even it has suffered no apparent damage.*

 *Warning: Do not allow any solvents to come into contact with the tensioner mechanism.*

 *Warning: Do not subject the tensioner assembly to temperatures in excess of 100ºC.*

*Warning: Volvo state the seat belt tensioners should be renewed every 10 years, regardless of their apparent condition. The expiry*

**28.4c . . . and remove the front door sill trim panel**

*date of the units are given on a sticker attached to driver's side door pillar.*

### 28 Seat belt components – removal and refitting

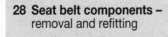

### *Removal*

#### Front seat belt

 *Warning: Refer to the warnings given in Section 27 before proceeding.*

**1** Disconnect the battery negative lead (see *Disconnecting the battery*) and wait a few minutes.

**2** Unclip the access cover from the rear of the seat cushion outer side trim panel. On models before May 2000, as a precaution, unclip the

**28.6a . . . then unclip the upper trim panel . . .**

**28.5 Unclip the lower trim panel from the door pillar . . .**

protective tool from its holder, and carefully slide it into position over the SIPS sensor to prevent the airbag being accidentally triggered (see Section 25).

**3** Remove the mounting bolt and detach the seat belt lower mounting from the seat frame. Recover the spacer which is fitted between the seat belt and seat **(see illustration)**.

**4** Unclip the trim panel from the rear door sill, then undo the retaining screws and remove the front door sill trim panel **(see illustrations)**.

**5** Carefully unclip the door pillar lower trim panel and remove it from the car **(see illustration)**.

**6** Peel back the door sealing strips, then unclip the base of the upper trim panel from the pillar then free the panel upper retaining clip. Feed the seat belt through the panel and remove the trim panel from the car **(see illustrations)**.

**28.6b . . . and free it from the seat belt**

**28.7 Disconnect the wiring connector from the seat belt tensioner mechanism**

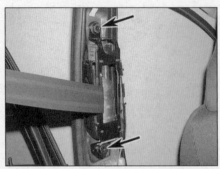

**28.8 Undo the inertia reel retaining bolts and remove the front seat belt**

**28.14a On Saloon models, open up the seat belt guide trim cover, then remove the bolt . . .**

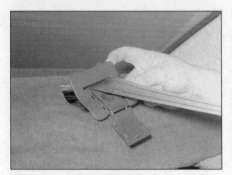

**28.14b . . . and slide each guide off from the belt**

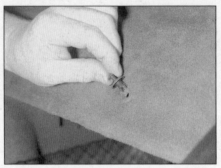

**28.15a Unscrew the centre screw a few turns, and pull out the complete fastener . . .**

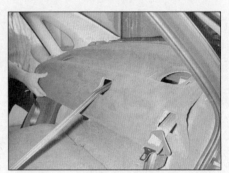

**28.15b . . . then slide the parcel shelf forwards and remove it**

7 Disconnect the wiring connector from the seat belt tensioner mechanism **(see illustration)**.

8 Remove the mounting bolts securing the inertia reel assembly to the door pillar, then remove the assembly from the car **(see illustration)**.

*Caution: Do not attempt to dismantle the inertia reel/tensioner assembly – the belt assembly is only available as a complete unit.*

### Front seat belt buckle

9 Remove the rear section of the centre console as described in Section 30.

10 Slide the seat fully backwards, then remove the mounting bolt.

11 Remove the buckle, disconnecting its wiring connector as it becomes accessible.

### Rear seat belt – Saloon models

12 Remove the rear loudspeakers as described in Chapter 12.

13 Fold the seat cushions forwards then remove all the seat belt lower mounting bolts.

14 Open up the trim covers on each parcel shelf seat belt guide, to gain access to the guide retaining screw. Undo the retaining screws and remove all the belt guides from the parcel shelf and slide them off the seat belts **(see illustrations)**.

15 Remove the parcel shelf retaining clip (loosen the centre screw a few turns, then pull out the complete fastener) then slide the shelf forwards and out of position, freeing it from the seat belts **(see illustrations)**.

16 Remove the inertia reel mounting bolt and remove the relevant seat belt assembly from the car **(see illustration)**.

### Rear seat side belt – Estate models

17 Fold the seat cushion forwards then remove the seat belt lower mounting bolt.

18 Remove the seat back side cushion retaining bolt, then slide the side cushion upwards and remove it **(see illustrations)**.

19 Carefully prise out the luggage compartment courtesy light from the relevant rear pillar trim panel and disconnect it from its wiring. Prise out the speaker grille then undo the retaining screws and carefully unclip the trim panel and remove it from the pillar **(see illustrations)**.

20 Remove the two fasteners and the retaining screw, then carefully unclip the luggage compartment upper trim panel and remove it from the car, freeing it from the side seat belt **(see illustrations)**.

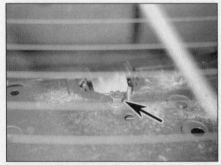

**28.16 Undo the bolt (arrowed) and remove the rear seat belt assembly**

**28.18a Slacken and remove the retaining bolt . . .**

**28.18b . . . then lift the rear seat side cushion out**

**28.19a** Undo the retaining screws (arrowed) . . .

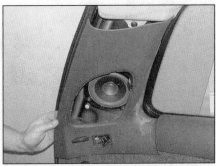

**28.19b** . . . and unclip the trim panel from the rear pillar

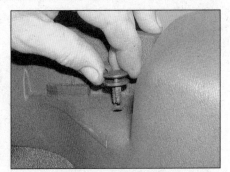

**28.20a** Remove the fasteners (rear one shown) . . .

**28.20b** . . . and retaining screw . . .

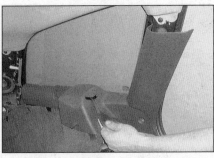

**28.20c** . . . then unclip the luggage compartment upper trim panel and free it from the seat belt

**28.21** Unscrew the inertia reel bolt and remove the seat side belt assembly

**21** Remove the inertia reel mounting bolt and remove the seat belt assembly from the car **(see illustration)**.

### Rear seat centre belt – Estate models

**Note:** *New headrest guides will be required on refitting.*

**22** Remove the seat back as described in Section 26.

**23** Depress the locking buttons, and slide out the headrests from the seat assembly.

**24** Remove the all headrest guides from the seat. To do this, grip each headrest guide firmly, rotate it to break its retaining tabs then pull it out from the seat assembly. If this fails to remove the guides, saw off the guide head, taking great care not to damage the seat upholstery (make up a protective template to protect the upholstery) **(see illustrations)**.

**25** Undo the screws securing the lock assembly cover to the seat back. Unclip the

knob from the lock lever, then remove the cover from the seat. With the cover removed, unclip the indicator button from the lock link rod **(see illustrations)**.

**28.24a** Remove the headrest guides by twisting and pulling/levering them out of the seat . . .

**26** Unclip the armrest from the seat back, then carefully unclip and remove the armrest trim panel **(see illustrations)**.

**27** Undo the retaining screws and remove

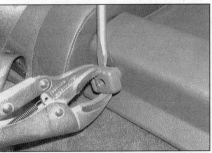

**28.24b** . . . or alternatively saw the head off from the guide (note template protecting upholstery)

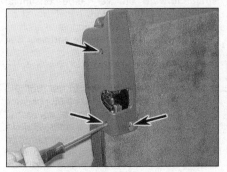

**28.25a** Undo the retaining screws . . .

**28.25b** . . . then pull off the lock lever knob . . .

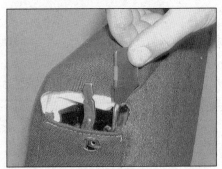

**28.25c** . . . and remove the lock cover and indicator button

28.26a Remove the armrest . . .

28.26b . . . and unclip the armrest trim panel from the seat

28.27 Undo the retaining screws and remove the seat belt guide . . .

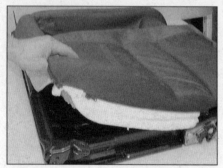

28.28 . . . then unzip the upholstery and free it from the seat back

28.29a Remove the seat belt guide screw . . .

28.29b . . . and inertia reel nut, and remove the seat centre belt assembly from the seat back

the seat belt guide from the seat back **(see illustration)**.

**28** Free the upholstery from its retaining clips in the armrest aperture, then undo the zips and free the upholstery and foam assembly from the seat back **(see illustration)**.

**29** Remove the seat belt guide screws and the inertia reel nut, and separate the belt and seat back **(see illustrations)**.

### Rear lap belt and belt buckles

**30** Tilt the rear seat cushion forwards, then remove the buckle retaining bolts **(see illustration)**. Remove the buckle assembly, and recover the spacers which are fitted between the buckle and floor.

### Refitting

**31** Refitting is the reverse of removal, noting the following points:

a) Remove all traces of locking compound

28.30 Slacken and remove the bolts and remove the seat belt buckle assembly from the floor

from the threads of the rear seat belt mounting bolts. Prior to refitting the bolts, apply a few drops of fresh locking compound to the threads of each bolt.

b) Make sure the inertia reel is correctly located, and the washers and/or spacers (as applicable) are correctly positioned on all the belt mounting points.

c) Tighten all fasteners to the specified torque (where given).

d) Check the condition of all trim panel retaining clips, and renew any that are damaged. Ensure all panels are securely retained by their clips, and are correctly joined with all adjoining panels/sealing strips.

### 29 Interior trim – removal and refitting

### Interior trim panels

**1** The interior trim panels are secured using either screws or various types of trim fasteners, usually studs or clips.

**2** Check that there are no other panels overlapping the one to be removed; usually there is a sequence that has to be followed that will become obvious on close inspection.

**3** Remove all obvious fasteners, such as screws. If the panel will not come free, it is held by hidden clips or fasteners. These are usually situated around the edge of the panel and can be prised up to release them; note, however, that they can break quite easily so replacements should be available. The best way

of releasing such clips without the correct type of tool, is to use a large flat-bladed screwdriver. Note in many cases that the adjacent sealing strip must be prised back to release a panel.

**4** When removing a panel, **never** use excessive force or the panel may be damaged; always check carefully that all fasteners have been removed or released before attempting to withdraw a panel.

**5** Refitting is the reverse of the removal procedure; renew any clips/fasteners damaged on removal and ensure that all disturbed components are correctly secured to prevent rattles.

### Carpets

**6** The passenger compartment floor carpet is in one piece and is secured at its edges by screws or clips, usually the same fasteners used to secure the various adjoining trim panels.

**7** Carpet removal and refitting is reasonably straightforward but very time-consuming because all adjoining trim panels must be removed first, as must components such as the seats, the centre console and seat belt lower anchorages.

### Headlining

**8** The headlining is clipped to the roof and can be withdrawn only once all fittings such as the grab handles, sun visors, sunroof (if fitted), windscreen and rear quarter windows and related trim panels have been removed and the door, tailgate and sunroof aperture sealing strips have been prised clear. On models with side curtain airbags, remember that the curtain airbag units are housed

30.2a  Remove the ashtray from the rear of the centre console . . .

30.2b  . . . and lift out the drinks holder insert

30.3a  Undo the retaining screws (arrowed) . . .

30.3b  . . . and remove the centre console rear section

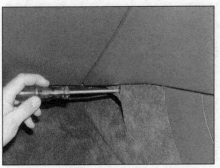

30.4a  Undo the retaining screw . . .

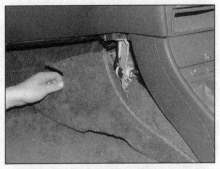

30.4b  . . . and remove both side panels from the front of the centre console

behind the trim panels between the tops of the doors and the headlining.

**9** Note that headlining removal requires considerable skill and experience if it is to be carried out without damage and is therefore best entrusted to an expert.

## 30 Centre console – removal and refitting

### *Removal*

#### Models up to May 2000

**1** Disconnect the battery negative lead (see *Disconnecting the battery*).

**2** Remove the ashtray from the rear of the console then lift out the drinks holder insert to gain access to the console rear section retaining screws **(see illustrations)**.

**3** Remove the retaining screws and remove the console rear section from the car **(see illustrations)**.

**4** Undo the retaining screws securing the left- and right-hand side panels, then carefully unclip the panels and remove them from the front of the centre console **(see illustrations)**.

**5** On manual transmission models, unclip the gearchange lever gaiter from the centre console and fold it back over the lever **(see illustration)**.

**6** On automatic transmission models, carefully prise the selector lever position indicator panel out from the console. Free the bulbholders from the rear of the panel and remove the panel from the car.

**7** On all models, ease the window switch panel assembly out of position and disconnect its wiring connectors **(see illustration)**.

**8** Remove the audio unit as described in Chapter 12.

**9** Where necessary, unclip and remove the storage compartment from the centre of the facia **(see illustration)**.

**10** Undo the retaining screws and remove the ashtray/cigarette lighter assembly, disconnecting the wiring as it becomes accessible **(see illustrations)**.

**11** Remove the screws securing the rear of the centre console front section to the floor **(see illustration)**.

**12** Fully apply the handbrake, then lift the rear of the console front section over the handbrake lever and manoeuvre it out of position, disconnecting the switch wiring connectors as they become accessible **(see illustration)**.

30.5  On manual transmission models, unclip the gaiter and fold it back over the lever

30.7  Push the window switch panel assembly out and disconnect its wiring

30.9  Unclip the storage compartment from the facia

**30.10a Undo the retaining screws (arrowed) . . .**

**30.11 Undo the retaining screws (arrowed) . . .**

### Models from May 2000 onwards

**13** Remove the rubber tray in front of the gear lever.

**14** On manual transmission models, unclip the gaiter from the gear lever trim panel.

**31.5a On models with electronic climate control, release the clips (arrowed) . . .**

**31.6a On manual heating/ventilation controls, pull off the three control knobs . . .**

**30.10b . . . and remove the ashtray/cigarette lighter, disconnecting its wiring**

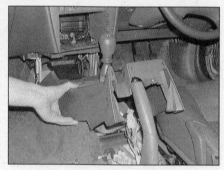

**30.12 . . . and manoeuvre out the front section of the centre console**

**15** Carefully release the lugs around the edges of the gear lever trim panel, then ease the panel out and disconnect the wiring plug from it.

**16** Inside the oddments tray at the rear of the console, prise up the screw cover, and remove the two screws underneath it.

**31.5b . . . then carefully unclip the faceplate from the control panel**

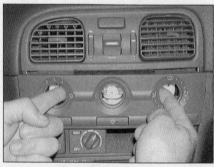

**31.6b . . . then pull the faceplate assembly off from the control panel**

**17** Remove the two console retaining screws behind the gear lever.

**18** Fully apply the handbrake, then lift the rear of the console front section over the handbrake lever and manoeuvre it out of position, disconnecting the switch wiring connectors as they become accessible.

**19** To remove the front section of the console, remove the audio unit (see Chapter 12).

**20** Remove the two screws at the base of the radio aperture, then the console can be twisted out of its location – for refitting, note that it slots into a guide under the centre section of the facia panel, and into the console side panels.

**21** To remove the console side panels (if required), take out the panel's single retaining screw at the base of the facia, then move the panel down and towards the footwell. The panel is secured to the heater unit by several clips, and a cable-tie (which will have to be cut – obtain a new one for reassembly).

### Refitting

**22** Refitting is the reverse of removal, making sure all fasteners are securely tightened. On completion, reconnect the battery and check the operation of all switches.

### 31 Facia panel assembly – removal and refitting

> **HAYNES HiNT**
>
> *Attach an identification label to each wiring connector as it is disconnected. The labels can then be used on refitting to help ensure that all wiring is correctly routed through the relevant facia apertures.*

### Removal

**1** Disconnect the battery negative lead (see *Disconnecting the battery*).

**2** Remove the centre console (see Section 30).

**3** Remove the steering wheel as described in Chapter 10.

**4** Remove the combination switch assembly from the top of the steering column as described in Chapter 12, Section 4.

**5** On models with an electronic climate control (ECC) air conditioning system, remove the faceplate from the heater control panel. To do this, release the faceplate retaining clips by inserting a small, flat-bladed screwdriver in through the top vent on either side, then carefully ease the faceplate out of position **(see illustrations)**.

**6** On models with a manually-controlled heating/ventilation system (with or without air conditioning), pull off all the control knobs from the heating/ventilation control panel. Reach in through the control knob apertures and carefully ease the faceplate squarely off from the front of the control panel **(see illustrations)**.

31.8a Undo the retaining screw . . .

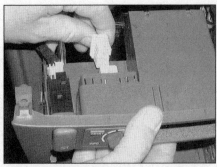

31.8b . . . then ease the centre panel out and disconnect the switch wiring

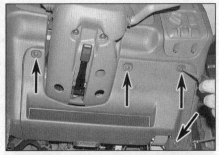

31.10a Undo the screws (arrowed) and remove the driver's side lower facia panel . . .

31.10b . . . disconnecting the wiring from the footwell illumination light

31.11 Undo the retaining screws and remove the glovebox insert

31.12 Unclip the instrument panel wiring connectors and free them from the facia

**7** On all models, remove the heater control panel retaining screws, and free the panel from the facia.

**8** Remove the retaining screw from the base of the facia centre panel, then carefully ease the panel out. Disconnect the switch wiring connectors, and remove the centre panel from the facia **(see illustrations)**.

**9** Remove the retaining screws and fastener, and remove the lower panel from the passenger side of the facia.

**10** Undo the retaining screws (the lower screw is hidden behind a trim cap) and remove the driver's side lower facia panel, disconnecting the wiring connector from the footwell light **(see illustrations)**.

**11** Open the glovebox, then undo the retaining screws and remove the glovebox insert **(see illustration)**.

**12** Remove the instrument panel as described in Chapter 12. With the panel removed, release the speedometer cable (where fitted) and panel wiring connectors from their facia mountings **(see illustration)**.

**13** Remove the facia loudspeakers as described in Chapter 12.

**14** On models with an electronic climate control (ECC) air conditioning system, remove the sun sensor from the passenger side loudspeaker and disconnect it from the wiring connector.

**15** Remove the bonnet release lever mounting bracket bolts, and free the lever bracket from the facia **(see illustration)**.

**16** Unscrew the fusebox retaining nut, then

unbolt the fusebox lower bracket from the body. Lower the fusebox slightly to enable the four facia wiring connectors to be disconnected from it **(see illustrations)**.

**17** Release the retaining clip and detach the

31.15 Unbolt the bonnet release lever bracket and position it clear of the facia

31.16b . . . and lower the fusebox to disconnect the four facia wiring connectors

facia centre vent air temperature control cable from the driver's side of the heater/ventilation housing.

**18** Remove the facia retaining bolts located in the instrument panel aperture, loudspeaker

31.16a Unscrew the fusebox nut, then unbolt the bracket . . .

31.18a Unscrew the facia retaining bolts in the instrument panel aperture . . .

31.18b . . . the loudspeaker apertures . . .

31.18c . . . and the glovebox aperture

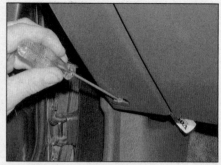

31.19a Prise out the trim cap and remove the passenger-side facia bolt . . .

31.19b . . . and the two centre retaining bolts (arrowed)

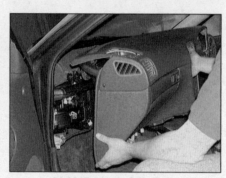

31.20 Removing the facia

apertures and the glovebox insert aperture **(see illustrations)**.

**19** Work along the bottom edge of the facia, and remove the lower retaining bolts located on each end of the facia (the passenger side bolt is hidden behind a trim cap) and the two bolts located in the centre of the facia **(see illustrations)**.

**20** With the aid of an assistant, manoeuvre the facia away from the bulkhead and remove it from the car, freeing its wiring from any relevant retaining clips **(see illustration)**.

### Refitting

**21** Refitting is a reversal of the removal procedure. Prior to refitting the facia retaining bolts, ensure the centre vent cable and all the necessary wiring is correctly routed. Refit the bolts and tighten them all by hand at first before going around and tightening them to the specified torque. On completion, reconnect the battery and check that all the electrical components and switches function correctly.

# Chapter 12
# Body electrical system

## Contents

## Degrees of difficulty

| | | | | |
|---|---|---|---|---|
| **Easy,** suitable for novice with little experience  | **Fairly easy,** suitable for beginner with some experience  | **Fairly difficult,** suitable for competent DIY mechanic | **Difficult,** suitable for experienced DIY mechanic | **Very difficult,** suitable for expert DIY or professional |

## Specifications

**System type** . . . . . . . . . . . . . . . . . . . . . . . . . . . . . . . . . . . . . . . . . 12 volt, negative-earth

| Bulbs | Wattage |
|---|---|
| **Exterior lights** | |
| Headlight: | |
|    Combined main/dipped beam bulb . . . . . . . . . . . . . . . . . . . . . . . | 60/55 (H4 type) |
|    Separate main and dipped beam bulbs: | |
|       Conventional headlight . . . . . . . . . . . . . . . . . . . . . . . . . . . . . | 55 (H7 type) |
|       Xenon headlight: | |
|          Dipped beam . . . . . . . . . . . . . . . . . . . . . . . . . . . . . . . . . . | 55 (H7 type) |
|          Main beam . . . . . . . . . . . . . . . . . . . . . . . . . . . . . . . . . . . . | 35 (D2R Xenon type) |
| Front foglight: | |
|    Up to May 2000 . . . . . . . . . . . . . . . . . . . . . . . . . . . . . . . . . . . . . | 55 (H3 type) |
|    May 2000 onwards . . . . . . . . . . . . . . . . . . . . . . . . . . . . . . . . . . | 55 (H1 type) |
| Front sidelight . . . . . . . . . . . . . . . . . . . . . . . . . . . . . . . . . . . . . . . . . | 4 |
| Bumper sidelights . . . . . . . . . . . . . . . . . . . . . . . . . . . . . . . . . . . . . . | 4 |
| Direction indicator . . . . . . . . . . . . . . . . . . . . . . . . . . . . . . . . . . . . . . | 21 |
| Direction indicator side repeater . . . . . . . . . . . . . . . . . . . . . . . . . . . | 5 |
| Number plate light . . . . . . . . . . . . . . . . . . . . . . . . . . . . . . . . . . . . . . | 5 |
| Rear foglight . . . . . . . . . . . . . . . . . . . . . . . . . . . . . . . . . . . . . . . . . . | 21 |
| Reversing light . . . . . . . . . . . . . . . . . . . . . . . . . . . . . . . . . . . . . . . . . | 21 |
| Stop-light . . . . . . . . . . . . . . . . . . . . . . . . . . . . . . . . . . . . . . . . . . . . . | 21 |
| Tail light . . . . . . . . . . . . . . . . . . . . . . . . . . . . . . . . . . . . . . . . . . . . . . | 5 |
| **Interior lights** | |
| Courtesy light: | |
|    Front . . . . . . . . . . . . . . . . . . . . . . . . . . . . . . . . . . . . . . . . . . . . . | 5 |
|    Rear . . . . . . . . . . . . . . . . . . . . . . . . . . . . . . . . . . . . . . . . . . . . . . | 10 |
| Door trim panel light . . . . . . . . . . . . . . . . . . . . . . . . . . . . . . . . . . . . | 10 |
| Reading light . . . . . . . . . . . . . . . . . . . . . . . . . . . . . . . . . . . . . . . . . . | 5 |
| Luggage compartment light . . . . . . . . . . . . . . . . . . . . . . . . . . . . . . | 5 |
| Instrument panel bulbs: | |
|    Warning lights . . . . . . . . . . . . . . . . . . . . . . . . . . . . . . . . . . . . . . | 3 |
|    Illumination lights . . . . . . . . . . . . . . . . . . . . . . . . . . . . . . . . . . . | 1.2 |
| Heater control panel light . . . . . . . . . . . . . . . . . . . . . . . . . . . . . . . . | 1.2 |

## Torque wrench settings

| | Nm | lbf ft |
|---|---|---|
| Headlight retaining nuts | 7 | 5 |
| Headlight wiper arm nut | 4 | 3 |
| Rear light unit retaining nuts | 7 | 5 |
| SRS system fixings: | | |
|   Control unit bolts | 10 | 7 |
|   Driver's airbag contact unit screws | 3 | 2 |
|   Driver's airbag unit screws | 10 | 7 |
|   Passenger airbag unit bolts | 10 | 7 |
| Windscreen wiper motor/linkage: | | |
|   Linkage retaining nuts | 10 | 7 |
|   Motor crank spindle nut | 20 | 15 |
| Windscreen/tailgate wiper arm nut | 16 | 12 |

## 1 General information and precautions

⚠️ **Warning: Before carrying out any work on the electrical system, read through the precautions given in 'Safety first!' at the beginning of this manual and Chapter 5A.**

**1** The electrical system is of the 12 volt negative-earth type. Power for the lights and all electrical accessories is supplied by a lead-acid type battery which is charged by the alternator.

**2** This Chapter covers repair and service procedures for the various electrical components not associated with engine. Information on the battery, alternator and starter motor can be found in Chapter 5A.

**3** It should be noted that, prior to working on any component in the electrical system, the battery negative lead should first be disconnected to prevent the possibility of electrical short-circuits and/or fires (see *Disconnecting the battery*).

## 2 Electrical fault finding – general information

**Note:** *Refer to the precautions given in 'Safety first!' and in Section 1 of this Chapter before starting work. The following tests relate to testing of the main electrical circuits, and should not be used to test delicate electronic circuits (such as anti-lock braking systems), particularly where an electronic control module (ECU) is used.*

**1** A typical electrical circuit consists of an electrical component, any switches, relays, motors, fuses, fusible links or circuit breakers related to that component, and the wiring and connectors which link the component to both the battery and the chassis. To help to pinpoint a problem in an electrical circuit, wiring diagrams are included at the end of this Chapter.

**2** Before attempting to diagnose an electrical fault, first study the appropriate wiring diagram to obtain a complete understanding of the components included in the particular circuit concerned. The possible sources of a fault can be narrowed down by noting if other components related to the circuit are operating properly. If several components or circuits fail at one time, the problem is likely to be related to a shared fuse or earth connection.

**3** Electrical problems usually stem from simple causes, such as loose or corroded connections, a faulty earth connection, a blown fuse, a melted fusible link, or a faulty relay (refer to Section 3 for details of testing relays). Visually inspect the condition of all fuses, wires and connections in a problem circuit before testing the components. Use the wiring diagrams to determine which terminal connections will need to be checked in order to pinpoint the trouble spot.

**4** The basic tools required for electrical fault-finding include a circuit tester or voltmeter (a 12 volt bulb with a set of test leads can also be used for certain tests); a self-powered test light (sometimes known as a continuity tester); an ohmmeter (to measure resistance); a battery and set of test leads; and a jumper wire, preferably with a circuit breaker or fuse incorporated, which can be used to bypass suspect wires or electrical components. Before attempting to locate a problem with test instruments, use the wiring diagram to determine where to make the connections.

**5** To find the source of an intermittent wiring fault (usually due to a poor or dirty connection, or damaged wiring insulation), a wiggle test can be performed on the wiring. This involves wiggling the wiring by hand to see if the fault occurs as the wiring is moved. It should be possible to narrow down the source of the fault to a particular section of wiring. This method of testing can be used in conjunction with any of the tests described in the following sub-Sections.

**6** Apart from problems due to poor connections, two basic types of fault can occur in an electrical circuit – open-circuit, or short-circuit.

**7** Open-circuit faults are caused by a break somewhere in the circuit, which prevents current from flowing. An open-circuit fault will prevent a component from working, but will not cause the relevant circuit fuse to blow.

**8** Short-circuit faults are caused by a short somewhere in the circuit, which allows the current flowing in the circuit to escape along an alternative route, usually to earth. Short-circuit faults are normally caused by a breakdown in wiring insulation, which allows a feed wire to touch either another wire, or an earthed component such as the bodyshell. A short-circuit fault will normally cause the relevant circuit fuse to blow.

### Finding an open-circuit

**9** To check for an open-circuit, connect one lead of a circuit tester or voltmeter to either the negative battery terminal or a known good earth.

**10** Connect the other lead to a connector in the circuit being tested, preferably nearest to the battery or fuse.

**11** Switch on the circuit, bearing in mind that some circuits are live only when the ignition switch is moved to a particular position.

**12** If voltage is present (indicated either by the tester bulb lighting or a voltmeter reading, as applicable), this means that the section of the circuit between the relevant connector and the battery is problem-free.

**13** Continue to check the remainder of the circuit in the same fashion.

**14** When a point is reached at which no voltage is present, the problem must lie between that point and the previous test point with voltage. Most problems can be traced to a broken, corroded or loose connection.

### Finding a short-circuit

**15** To check for a short-circuit, first disconnect the load(s) from the circuit (loads are the components which draw current from a circuit, such as bulbs, motors, heating elements, etc).

**16** Remove the relevant fuse from the circuit, and connect a circuit tester or voltmeter to the fuse connections.

**17** Switch on the circuit, bearing in mind that some circuits are live only when the ignition switch is moved to a particular position.

**18** If voltage is present (indicated either by the tester bulb lighting or a voltmeter reading, as applicable), this means that there is a short-circuit.

**19** If no voltage is present, but the fuse still blows with the load(s) connected, this indicates an internal fault in the load(s).

### Finding an earth fault

**20** The battery negative terminal is connected to 'earth' – the metal of the engine/transmission and the car body – and most systems are wired so that they only receive a positive feed, the current returning via the metal of the car body.

**3.2a The fuses are in the fusebox behind the driver's side lower facia panel (shown with panel removed) . . .**

**3.2b . . . and in the fuse/relay box in the engine compartment**

This means that the component mounting and the body form part of that circuit.

**21** Loose or corroded mountings can therefore cause a range of electrical faults, ranging from total failure of a circuit, to a puzzling partial fault. In particular, lights may shine dimly (especially when another circuit sharing the same earth point is in operation), motors (eg, wiper motors or the radiator cooling fan motor) may run slowly, and the operation of one circuit may have an apparently-unrelated effect on another.

**22** Note that on many vehicles, earth straps are used between certain components, such as the engine/transmission and the body, usually where there is no metal-to-metal contact between components due to flexible rubber mountings, etc.

**23** To check whether a component is properly earthed, disconnect the battery and connect one lead of an ohmmeter to a known good earth point. Connect the other lead to the wire or earth connection being tested. The resistance reading should be zero; if not, check the connection as follows.

**24** If an earth connection is thought to be faulty, dismantle the connection and clean back to bare metal both the bodyshell and the wire terminal or the component earth connection mating surface. Be careful to remove all traces of dirt and corrosion, then use a knife to trim away any paint, so that a clean metal-to-metal joint is made.

**25** On reassembly, tighten the joint fasteners securely; if a wire terminal is being refitted, use serrated washers between the terminal and the bodyshell to ensure a clean and

secure connection. When the connection is remade, prevent the onset of corrosion in the future by applying a coat of petroleum jelly or silicone-based grease. Alternatively, spray on (at regular intervals) a proprietary ignition sealer, or a water-dispersant lubricant.

## 3  Fuses and relays – general information

### Fuses

**1** The fuses are located in the fusebox situated behind the lower cover on the driver's side of the facia panel, with additional fuses being located in the fuse/relay box located in the left-hand rear corner of the engine compartment.

**2** To gain access to the fusebox, reach up behind the driver's side lower facia panel and unclip the cover from the fusebox. To gain access to the fuses in the engine compartment, simply release the retaining clip and remove the cover from the fuse/relay box **(see illustrations)**.

**3** A list of the circuits each fuse protects is given on the cover.

**4** To remove a fuse, first switch off the circuit concerned (or the ignition), then pull the fuse out of its terminals using the fuse removal tool which is clipped onto the cover **(see illustrations)**. The wire within the fuse should be visible; if the fuse is blown it will be broken or melted.

**5** Always renew a fuse with one of an identical rating; never use a fuse with a

different rating from the original or substitute anything else. Never renew a fuse more than once without tracing the source of the trouble. The fuse rating is stamped on top of the fuse; note that the fuses are also colour-coded for easy recognition.

**6** If a new fuse blows immediately, find the cause before renewing it again; a short to earth as a result of faulty insulation is most likely. Where a fuse protects more than one circuit, try to isolate the defect by switching on each circuit in turn (if possible) until the fuse blows again. Always carry a supply of spare fuses of each relevant rating on the car, a spare of each rating should be clipped into the base of the fusebox.

### Relays

**7** The majority of relays are either located behind the driver's side facia lower panel, both in the upper half of the fusebox and in separate holder next to the fusebox, and in the fuse/relay box in the engine compartment. Exceptions to this are the driver's-side window automatic relay which is fitted to the driver's door, and the window wiper relay which is an integral part of the switch assembly.

**8** To gain access to those behind the facia, undo the retaining screws (the lower screw is located behind a trim cap) and remove the driver's side lower facia panel, disconnecting the wiring connector from the footwell light.

**9** To gain access to those in the engine compartment, release the clip and remove the cover from the fuse/relay box.

**10** If a circuit or system controlled by a relay develops a fault and the relay is suspect, operate the system; if the relay is functioning, it should be possible to hear it click as it is energised. If this is the case, the fault lies with the components or wiring of the system. If the relay is not being energised, then either the relay is not receiving a main supply or a switching voltage, or the relay itself is faulty. Testing is by the substitution of a known good unit but be careful; while some relays are identical in appearance and in operation, others look similar but perform different functions.

**11** To renew a relay, first ensure that the ignition switch is off. The relay can then simply be pulled out from the socket and the new relay pressed in **(see illustration)**.

**3.4a Unclip the removal tool from the cover . . .**

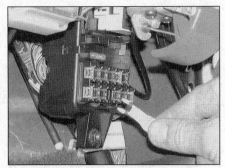

**3.4b . . . then use the tool to pull the relevant fuse out of position**

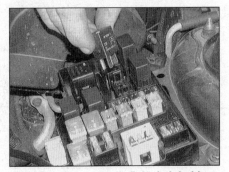

**3.11 Relays are a push-fit in their holders**

### 4 Switches – removal and refitting

**Note:** *Disconnect the battery negative lead before removing any switch (see 'Disconnecting the battery').*

#### Ignition switch

**1** Refer to Chapter 10.

#### Steering column switches

**2** Remove the steering wheel (see Chapter 10).
**3** Release the height adjustment lever, then undo the three screws underneath, and unclip the upper and lower shrouds from the steering column **(see illustrations)**.
**4** Remove the airbag contact unit assembly as described in Section 25.
**5** Undo the two screws securing the switch

**4.3a Slacken and remove the retaining screws (arrowed) . . .**

**4.3b . . . and remove the upper and lower shrouds from the steering column**

holder assembly to the top of the steering column. Lift the assembly out, disconnecting the wiring connectors as they become accessible **(see illustrations)**.
**6** Undo the retaining screws and carefully

remove the relevant switch assembly from the holder, noting that it will be necessary to disconnect the horn wiring connector from the right-hand switch assembly **(see illustrations)**.
**7** Refitting is the reverse of removal, ensuring the wiring is correctly routed and all connectors are securely reconnected.

#### Centre console switches

**8** On manual transmission models, unclip the gear lever gaiter from the centre console, and fold it back over the lever **(see illustration)**.
**9** On automatic transmission models, carefully prise the selector lever position indicator panel out from the console. Free the bulbholders from the rear of the panel, and remove the panel from the car.
**10** On all models, reach in behind and unclip the switch panel assembly from the console. Disconnect the wiring connectors and remove switch panel from the car **(see illustrations)**.

**4.5a Slacken and remove the retaining screws (arrowed) . . .**

**4.5b . . . and remove the combination switch holder assembly from the column**

**4.6a To remove the right-hand switch assembly, undo the retaining screws . . .**

**4.6b . . . then free the switch and disconnect the horn wiring (arrowed)**

**4.6c The left-hand switch assembly is retained by three screws (arrowed)**

**4.8 Unclip the gaiter from the console and fold it back over the lever**

**4.10a Push the switch panel out from the console . . .**

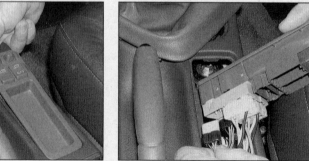

**4.10b . . . and disconnect the wiring connectors**

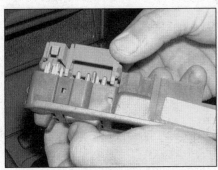

**4.11a Unclip the holder from the base of the switch panel . . .**

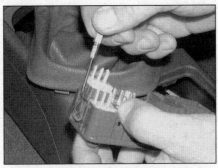

**4.11b . . . then unclip the relevant switch**

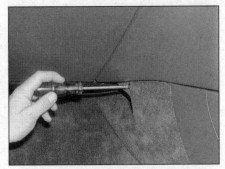

**4.12a Undo the retaining screw . . .**

**4.12b . . . and unclip the side panel from the front of the centre console**

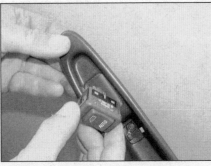

**4.13a Push the switch out from the centre console . . .**

**4.13b . . . and disconnect it from the wiring connector**

**11** Unclip the holder from the base of the panel, then release the retaining clips and ease the relevant switch out **(see illustrations)**.
**12** To remove the switches located at the front of the console on early models, first

undo the screw then carefully unclip the relevant side panel from the front of the centre console **(see illustrations)**.
**13** Reach in behind the console and ease the relevant switch out from the centre console,

disconnecting the wiring connector as it becomes accessible **(see illustrations)**.
**14** Refitting is the reverse of removal.

### Door switches

**15** Remove the trim cap, then undo the screw securing the armrest pocket **(see illustration)**.
**16** Unclip the armrest pocket from the trim panel, and disconnect the wiring connector from the switch. Unclip the switch and remove it from the pocket **(see illustration)**.
**17** Refitting is the reverse of removal.

### Lighting switch

**18** Undo the screws securing the switch panel to the facia. Unclip and remove the panel assembly, disconnecting the wiring connectors as they become accessible **(see illustrations)**.
**19** Unclip the switch assembly and remove it from the vent panel **(see illustration)**.
**20** Refitting is the reverse of removal.

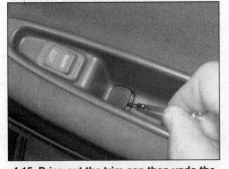

**4.15 Prise out the trim cap then undo the screw and lift out the armrest pocket**

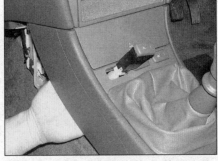

**4.16 Disconnect the wiring connector then separate the switch from the pocket**

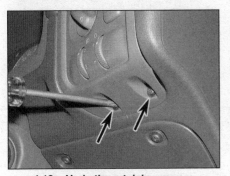

**4.18a Undo the retaining screws (arrowed) . . .**

**4.18b . . . then withdraw the panel from the facia and disconnect the wiring**

**4.19 Unclip the lighting switch assembly and separate it from the vent panel**

4.22 Unclip the storage compartment and remove it from the facia

4.26a Undo the retaining screw . . .

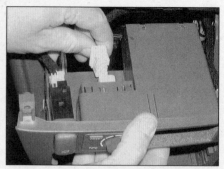

4.26b . . . and remove the facia centre panel, disconnecting the switch wiring

## Facia centre panel switches

**Note:** *These are the switches mounted either side of the trip computer, between the audio unit and heating/ventilation control panel. On models from May 2000, the child lock and alarm reduction switches can be removed by carefully prising them from the panel – with these removed, it may also be possible to remove other nearby switches, by pressing them out from behind.*

21 Remove the audio unit as described in Section 18.

22 Where necessary, unclip and remove the storage compartment from the centre of the facia **(see illustration)**.

23 On models with an electronic climate control (ECC) air conditioning system, remove the faceplate from the heater control panel. To do this, release the faceplate retaining clips by inserting a small, flat-bladed screwdriver in through the top vent on either side then carefully ease the faceplate out of position.

24 On models with a manually-controlled heating/ventilation system (with or without air conditioning), pull off all the control knobs from the heating/ventilation controls. Reach in through the control knob apertures and carefully ease the faceplate squarely off from the front of the control panel.

25 On all models, slacken and remove the heating/ventilation control panel lower retaining screws.

26 Slacken and remove the screw securing the base of the facia centre panel, then ease the panel out and remove it from the facia, disconnect its wiring connectors as they become accessible **(see illustrations)**.

27 Remove the relevant switch by depressing its retaining clips and sliding it out **(see illustration)**.

28 Refitting is the reverse of removal.

## Hazard warning light switch

29 On models with an electronic climate control (ECC) air conditioning system, remove the faceplate from the heater control panel. To do this, release the faceplate retaining clips by inserting a small, flat-bladed screwdriver in through the top vent on either side, then carefully ease the faceplate out.

30 On models with a manually-controlled heating/ventilation system (with or without air conditioning), pull off all the control knobs from the heating/ventilation controls. Reach in through the control knob apertures and carefully ease the faceplate squarely off from the front of the control panel.

31 On all models, slacken and remove the heating/ventilation control panel upper retaining screws **(see illustration)**.

32 Carefully prise the facia centre vent outlets out with a small, flat-bladed screwdriver inserted in between the inner edge of the vent and panel **(see illustration)**. As the outlets are removed take care not to lose the rubber washer and spring clips from their pivot pins.

33 Release the centre vent upper retaining clips (carefully lever the clips down using a flat-bladed screwdriver) and ease the vent panel out until access can be gained to the hazard warning light switch wiring connector **(see illustration)**.

34 Disconnect the wiring connector and unclip the hazard warning light switch from the rear of the vent assembly **(see illustrations)**.

35 Refitting is the reverse of removal,

4.27 Release the retaining clips and slide the switch out from the facia panel

4.31 Slacken and remove the heating/ventilation panel upper screws (arrowed)

4.32 Carefully prise out the vents from the centre outlet

4.33 Release the retaining clips (arrowed) then ease the vent panel out from the facia

4.34a Disconnect the wiring connector . . .

**4.34b . . . then unclip the hazard warning light switch from the vent assembly**

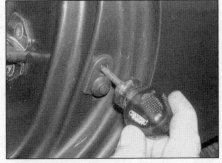

**4.36a  Slacken and remove the retaining screw . . .**

**4.36b . . . then remove the courtesy light switch, disconnecting the wiring connector**

ensuring the switch is clipped securely in position. Clip the outlets back into the vent housing, making sure the rubber washers and spring clips are correctly positioned, before clipping the housing into the facia.

### Courtesy light switches

**36** Undo the retaining screw and ease the switch out from the pillar. Disconnect the wiring connector and tape it to the body to prevent it disappearing into the pillar **(see illustrations)**.

**37** On refitting, reconnect the wiring connector, then refit the switch to the pillar and securely tighten its retaining screw.

### Stop-light switch

**38** Refer to Chapter 9.

### Handbrake lever switch

**39** Remove the rear section of the centre console as described in Chapter 11.

**40** Disconnect the wiring connector, then undo the retaining screw and remove the switch from the handbrake lever **(see illustration)**.

**41** Refitting is the reverse of removal. Check the operation of the switch before refitting the centre console.

### Overhead console switches

**42** Carefully prise the courtesy light lenses out from the overhead console **(see illustration)**.

**43** Undo the retaining screws, then lower the console assembly away from the headlining

**4.40  Disconnect the wiring then remove the handbrake switch screw (arrowed)**

and disconnect its wiring connectors **(see illustrations)**. The switches are not available separately – if any switch is faulty, the complete console assembly must be renewed.

**44** Refitting is the reverse of removal.

### Automatic transmission mode switches

#### Models up to May 2000

**45** Refer to paragraphs 8 to 11.

#### Models from May 2000 onwards

**46** Remove the centre console front section as described in Chapter 11, then remove the switch by carefully bending the switch locating tabs with a small screwdriver.

### Luggage area light switch

**47** The luggage compartment light switch is

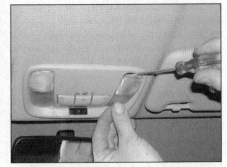

**4.42  Prise out both lenses from the overhead console . . .**

an integral part of the lock assembly, and is not available separately. If the switch is faulty, renew the lock as described in Chapter 11.

### Heating/ventilation control switches

#### Manual heating/ventilation system

**48** Pull off the control knobs from the heating/ventilation controls **(see illustration)**.

**49** Reach in through the control knob apertures and carefully ease the faceplate squarely off from the front of the control panel **(see illustration)**.

**50** Carefully unclip the switch circuit board and remove it from the rear of the faceplate, the switches are an integral part of the board **(see illustration)**.

**51** Refitting is the reverse of removal ensuring the faceplate wiring terminals are correctly aligned with the control panel.

**4.43a . . . undo the retaining screws (arrowed) . . .**

**4.43b . . . then lower the console and disconnect the wiring connectors**

**4.48  On manually-controlled heating/ventilation, remove all the control knobs . . .**

4.49 . . . and pull off the faceplate

4.50 Unclip the switch circuit board and separate it from the rear of the faceplate

4.55 Unclip the surround from around the blower motor switch . . .

### Electronic climate control air conditioning system

**52** The switches are an integral part of the control unit. If any switch is faulty, renew the control panel assembly as described in Chapter 3.

### *Blower motor switch*

#### Manual heating/ventilation system

**53** Carry out the operations described in paragraphs 21 to 26 and remove the centre panel from the facia.

**54** Slacken and remove the heater/ventilation control panel upper retaining screws, then unclip the panel assembly and manoeuvre it out from the facia.

**55** Disconnect the blower motor switch wiring connector, then unclip the switch surround from the front of the control panel **(see illustration)**.

**56** Release the retaining clips and remove the switch assembly from the rear of the panel **(see illustration)**.

**57** Refitting is the reverse of removal.

### Electronic climate control air conditioning system

**58** The switch is an integral part of the control unit. If the switch is faulty, renew the control panel assembly as described in Chapter 3.

---

### 5 Bulbs (exterior lights) – renewal

---

### *General*

**1** Whenever a bulb is renewed, note the following points:

4.56 . . . then unclip the switch and remove it from the rear of the panel (shown with facia removed)

a) *Ensure the ignition switch is switched off.*
b) *Remember that if the light has just been in use the bulb may be extremely hot.*
c) *Always check the bulb contacts and holder, ensuring that there is clean metal-to-metal contact between the bulb and its live(s) and earth. Clean off any corrosion or dirt before fitting a new bulb.*
d) *Wherever bayonet-type bulbs are fitted, ensure that the live contact(s) bear firmly against the bulb contact.*
e) *Always ensure that the new bulb is of the correct rating and that it is completely clean before fitting it; this applies particularly to headlight/foglight bulbs (see below).*

### *Conventional headlight*

**2** On turbo models, lift the securing clip and remove the plastic cover to gain access to the rear of the headlight unit **(see illustration)**.

**3** On headlights which incorporate a combined main/dipped beam bulb, rotate the access cover anti-clockwise and remove it from the rear of the headlight unit **(see illustration)**. On headlight units with separate main and dipped beam bulbs, remove the relevant rubber cover from the rear of the headlight.

**4** Disconnect the wiring connector from the bulb, then unhook and release the ends of the bulb retaining clip and release it from the rear of the light unit. Withdraw the bulb **(see illustrations)**.

**5** When handling the new bulb, use a tissue or clean cloth to avoid touching the glass with the fingers; moisture and grease from the skin

5.2 On turbo models, lift the clip and remove the plastic cover to access the rear of the headlight

5.3 Remove the access cover from the rear of the headlight . . .

5.4a . . . and pull the wiring from the headlight bulb (normal headlight shown, battery removed for clarity)

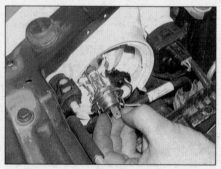

5.4b Release the retaining clip and remove the headlight bulb

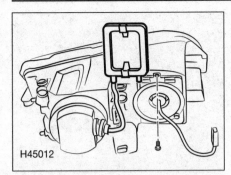

**5.8 On Xenon headlights, remove the high-voltage unit to access the rear cover, held on by a single screw**

can cause blackening and rapid failure of this type of bulb. If the glass is accidentally touched, wipe it clean using methylated spirit.
**6** Install the new bulb, ensuring that its locating tabs are correctly located in the light cut-outs, and secure it in position with the retaining clip. Reconnect the wiring connector and securely refit the cover(s).

### Xenon headlight

**7** Due to the high-voltage nature of Xenon headlights, it is essential that the system is only worked on when the ignition is switched off, and the battery disconnected (see *Disconnecting the battery*).

#### Main beam

**8** The bulb renewal procedure is very similar to that for conventional units. The only additional work to be carried out is removing the high-voltage unit fitted to the rear of the headlight – this is secured by one screw on the base, and the unit then unclips. Disconnect the wiring from the unit only as necessary. Access to the bulb is then gained by removing the single screw from the small cover fitted to the rear of the headlight **(see illustration)**.

#### Dipped beam

**9** Unclip the cover from the rear of the headlight, then disconnect the high-voltage connector from the bulb.
**10** The bulb is retained in position by a locking ring – note the position of this ring before removing it. Twist the locking ring to

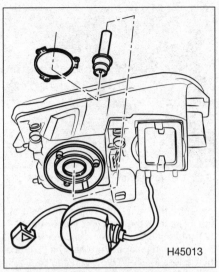

**5.10 Renewing the Xenon-type dipped-beam bulb**

remove it from the headlight, and free the bulb **(see illustration)**.
**11** As with conventional headlight bulbs, the Xenon bulbs must be handled with care, and should not be touched by bare fingers. Refitting is a reversal of removal, ensuring that the bulb is located securely, and all wiring connections are correctly remade.

### Front sidelight

**12** On turbo models, lift the securing clip and remove the plastic cover to gain access to the rear of the headlight unit.
**13** On headlights which incorporate a combined main/dipped beam bulb, rotate the access cover anti-clockwise and remove it from the rear of the headlight unit. On headlight units with separate main and dipped beam bulbs, unclip the access cover then remove the relevant rubber cover from the rear of the headlight.
**14** On models with Xenon headlights, refer to paragraph 8 and gain access to the main beam bulb.
**15** Rotate the sidelight bulbholder anti-clockwise and release it from the headlight unit. The bulb is of the bayonet type, and is removed by pushing it inwards slightly and rotating anti-clockwise **(see illustrations)**.

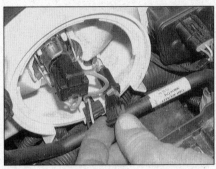

**5.15a Rotate the sidelight bulbholder anti-clockwise and free it from the rear of the headlight . . .**

**16** Refitting is the reverse of the removal procedure.

### Front direction indicator

**17** Locate the indicator light unit retaining screw, which is situated in between the indicator and headlight unit. Back the retaining screw off by approximately two turns, then (where applicable) release the clip at the side of the unit, and slide the light out **(see illustration)**.
**18** Rotate the bulbholder anti-clockwise and remove it from the rear of the light unit. The bulb is a bayonet fit in the holder, and can be removed by pressing it and twisting in an anti-clockwise direction **(see illustration)**.
**19** Refitting is a reverse of the removal procedure, ensuring the light unit peg is correctly located in its hole (or that the side clip is engaged), and the unit is securely retained by the screw.

### Front foglight

**20** Firmly apply the handbrake, then jack up the front of the car and support it on axle stands.
**21** Remove the screws/fasteners securing the relevant end of the engine undershield front section, and lower it to access the back of the foglight.
**22** Release the retaining clip and remove the access cover from the rear of the foglight **(see illustration)**.
**23** Disconnect the foglight bulb wiring connector **(see illustration)**.

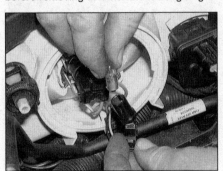

**5.15b . . . then remove the bulb**

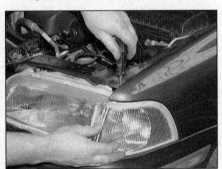

**5.17 Slacken the retaining screw and slide the indicator out**

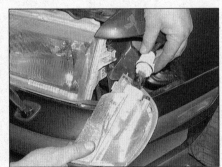

**5.18 Free the bulbholder from the rear of the light, and remove the bulb**

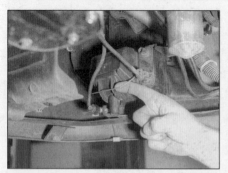

5.22 **Release the retaining clip and remove the access cover from the foglight**

5.23 **Disconnect the wiring connector . . .**

5.24 **. . . then release the retaining clip and withdraw the foglight bulb**

24 Release the retaining clip and withdraw the bulb from the light unit **(see illustration)**.
25 When handling the new bulb, use a tissue or clean cloth to avoid touching the glass with the fingers; moisture and grease from the skin can cause blackening and rapid failure of this type of bulb. If the glass is accidentally touched, wipe it clean using methylated spirit.
26 Install the new bulb, ensuring that its locating tabs are correctly located in the reflector cut-outs, and secure it in position with the retaining clip.
27 Reconnect the bulb wiring connector.
28 Refit the access cover to the foglight, and secure it in position with the retaining clip.
29 Secure the undershield in position with all the screws/fasteners.
30 Lower the car to the ground.

### Direction indicator side repeater

31 Carefully move the light unit slightly

forwards, then ease the rear of the light out and free it from the wing **(see illustration)**.
32 Rotate the bulbholder anti-clockwise and free it from the rear of the lens. The bulb is of the capless (push-fit) type, and can be simply pulled out of its holder **(see illustrations)**.
33 Refitting is the reverse of removal, ensuring the lens unit is clipped securely in position.

### Rear light unit

34 Undo the retaining clip and open up the trim panel cover to gain access to the rear of the light unit **(see illustration)**.
35 Disconnect the wiring connector then release the retaining clips and free the bulbholder assembly from the light unit **(see illustration)**.
36 All bulbs have bayonet fittings. The relevant bulb can be removed by pressing in and rotating anti-clockwise **(see illustration)**.

37 Refitting is the reverse of the removal sequence, ensuring the bulbholder is securely retained by the catches.

### High-level stop-light

38 The bulbs are an integral part of the light unit assembly, and cannot be renewed separately. If faulty, the complete light assembly must be renewed (see Section 7).

### Number plate light

#### Saloon models

39 Open up the boot lid then remove the fasteners (unscrew each centre screw slightly, then pull out the complete fastener) and remove the boot lid inner trim panel.
40 Remove the bulbholder from the rear of the light unit. The bulb is of the capless (push-fit) type, and can be simply pulled out of the holder **(see illustrations)**.

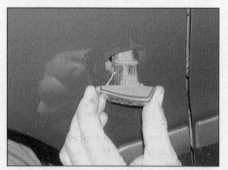

5.31 **Unclip the side repeater light unit from the wing**

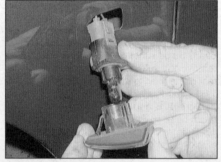

5.32a **Free the bulbholder from the rear of the lens . . .**

5.32b **. . . and pull out the bulb**

5.34 **Open up the rear light access cover . . .**

5.35 **. . . then disconnect the wiring and unclip the bulbholder assembly**

5.36 **Remove the relevant bulb by pushing it in and rotating anti-clockwise**

5.40a  On Saloon models, pull the bulbholder from behind the number plate light . . .

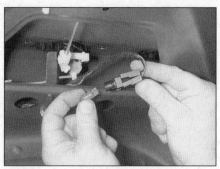

5.40b  . . . then remove the bulb from the holder

5.42  On Estate models, undo the screws and free the number plate light . . .

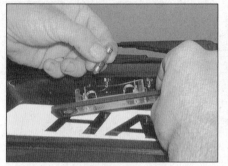

5.43  . . . then ease the bulb out from its contacts

5.46  Reach through the indicator aperture and unclip the sidelight from the bumper

5.51  Remove the wheel arch liner from the rear bumper to access the sidelight

**41** Refitting is the reverse of removal.

### Estate models

**42** Undo the retaining screws and lower the light unit out from the tailgate **(see illustration)**.
**43** Free the bulb from its contacts and remove it from the light unit **(see illustration)**.
**44** Refitting is the reverse of removal, ensuring the bulb is securely held by the contacts. Do not overtighten the light unit retaining screws, as the plastic is easily cracked.

### *Front bumper sidelight*

#### Up to May 2000

**45** Remove the direction indicator light as described in paragraphs 17 and 18.
**46** Reach in behind the bumper and release the light unit retaining clip **(see illustration)**. Disconnect the wiring connector and remove the light unit from the car. Note that the light must be treated as a sealed unit; if the bulb

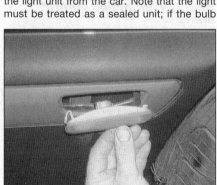

5.53  Removing the sidelight from the rear bumper

has blown, renew the complete light unit. If necessary, remove the engine undershield screws/fasteners to improve access.
**47** Refitting is the reverse of removal, ensuring the indicator light unit is correctly refitted (see paragraph 19).

#### May 2000 onwards

**48** Carefully push the light unit rearwards (taking care not to damage the paint if tools have to be used), and unhook the front end of the light from the bumper.
**49** With the light removed, twist the bulbholder anti-clockwise for access to the bulb.
**50** Refitting is a reversal of removal. Ensure that the light unit is properly clipped back into the bumper on completion.

### *Rear bumper sidelight*

#### Up to May 2000

**51** Remove the screws/fasteners (as applicable) and remove the relevant wheel arch liner from the rear bumper **(see illustration)**.
**52** Slacken and remove the screw securing the bumper to the car body.
**53** Unclip and disconnect the wiring connector, then reach in behind the bumper and release the light unit retaining clip **(see illustration)**. Remove the light unit from the car, noting that it must be treated as a sealed unit; if the bulb has blown, the light unit must be renewed.
**54** Refitting is the reverse of removal.

#### May 2000 onwards

**55** Proceed as described for the front bumper sidelight (paragraphs 48 to 50).

### 6  Bulbs (interior lights) – renewal

### *General*

**1** Refer to Section 5, paragraph 1.

### *Front courtesy light*

**2** Carefully prise the lens out from the overhead console **(see illustration)**.
**3** Free the bulb from its contacts and remove it from the light unit **(see illustration)**.
**4** Refitting is the reverse of removal, ensuring the bulb is securely held by the contacts.

### *Rear courtesy light*

**5** Carefully prise the lens out from the roof **(see illustration)**.

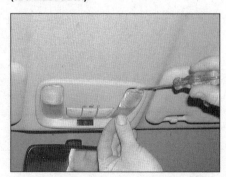

6.2  Prise out the lens from the overhead console . . .

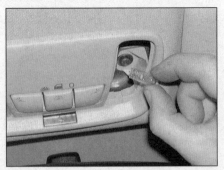

6.3 . . . and remove the front courtesy light bulb from its contacts

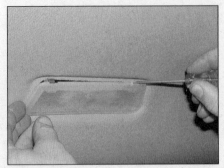

6.5 Prise the rear courtesy light out from the headlining . . .

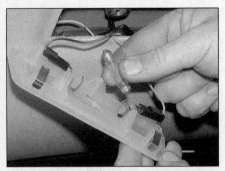

6.6 . . . then unclip the bulb from the light unit

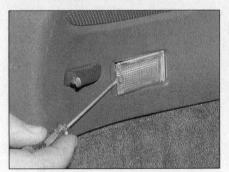

6.11 Prise out the luggage compartment light. . .

6.12 . . . and free the bulb from its contacts (Estate)

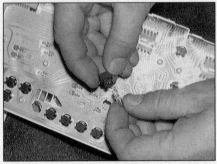

6.18 Free the bulbholder from the rear of the instrument panel and pull out the bulb

6 Free the bulb from its contacts and remove it from the light unit (see illustration).
7 Refitting is the reverse of removal, ensuring the bulb is securely held by the contacts.

### Vanity mirror light

8 Fold down the sun visor and open up the mirror flap.
9 Carefully ease off the lens, then free the bulb from its contacts and remove it from the light unit.
10 Refitting is the reverse of removal, ensuring the bulb is securely held by the contacts.

### Luggage area light

11 Using a small, flat-bladed screwdriver, carefully prise light unit assembly out to gain access to the bulb (see illustration).
12 Free the bulb from its contacts and remove it from the light unit (see illustration).

13 Refitting is the reverse of removal, ensuring the bulb is securely held by the contacts.

### Front footwell light

14 Using a small, flat-bladed screwdriver, carefully prise light unit assembly out to gain access to the bulb.
15 Unclip the cover, then free the bulb from its contacts and remove it from the light unit.
16 Refitting is the reverse of removal, ensuring the bulb is securely held by the contacts.

### Instrument illumination/warning lights

17 Remove the instrument panel as described in Section 9.
18 Twist the relevant bulbholder anti-clockwise and withdraw it from the rear of the panel. Most bulbs are of the capless-type and

are a push-fit in their holders, but some maybe integral with their holders (see illustration). Be very careful to ensure the new bulbs are of the correct rating, the same as those removed.
19 Refit the bulbholder to the rear of the instrument panel, then refit the instrument panel as described in Section 9.

### Lighting switch illumination

20 Undo the retaining screws securing the switch panel to the facia. Unclip and remove the panel assembly, disconnecting the wiring connectors as they become accessible.
21 Twist the bulbholder anti-clockwise and withdraw it from the rear of the faceplate; the bulb is integral with the holder.
22 Refitting is the reverse of removal.

### Heating/ventilation control lights

#### Manual heating/ventilation system

23 Pull off all the control knobs from the heating/ventilation controls.
24 Reach in through the control knob apertures and carefully ease the faceplate squarely off from the front of the control panel (see illustration).
25 Twist the relevant bulbholder anti-clockwise and withdraw it from the rear of the faceplate; the bulbs are integral with their holders (see illustration).
26 Refitting is the reverse of removal, ensuring the faceplate wiring terminals are correctly aligned with the control panel.

6.24 Removing the faceplate from the heating/ventilation control panel

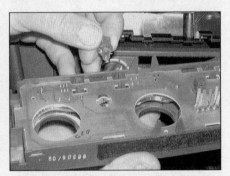

6.25 Twist the bulbholder anti-clockwise and remove it from behind the faceplate

**6.28a  Using a flat-bladed screwdriver, rotate the bulbholder anti-clockwise . . .**

**6.28b  . . . then remove it from the rear of the control panel**

**6.30  Carefully prise out the glovebox illumination light**

### Electronic climate control air conditioning system

27 Remove the heating/ventilation control panel as described in Chapter 3.
28 Using a long, flat-bladed screwdriver, rotate the relevant bulbholder slightly anti-clockwise then withdraw the bulbholder assembly from the rear of the panel (see illustrations).
29 Fit the new bulbholder assembly securely to the panel then refit the control panel as described in Chapter 3.

### Glovebox light

30 Open up the glovebox then carefully prise the light unit assembly out of position, taking care not to displace the bulb rear cover from the facia (see illustration).
*Caution: If the bulb cover is displaced, it will fall down behind the facia. Remove the passenger side lower cover and centre console side panel to enable it to be retrieved.*
31 Free the bulb from its contacts and remove it from the light unit.
32 Refitting is the reverse of removal, ensuring the bulb is securely held by the contacts. Prior to refitting the light unit, make sure the bulb cover is securely located on the facia.

### Automatic transmission selector light

33 Remove either the front section of the centre console, or just the console side panel, as described in Chapter 11.
34 Unplug the bulbholder from the base of the light unit, and remove the bulb.

35 Refitting is a reversal of removal.

### Automatic transmission mode switch light

#### May 2000 onwards

36 To renew the mode switch illumination bulb, remove the switch as described in Section 4. The bulbholder is removed by turning it a quarter-turn with a screwdriver.
37 Refitting is a reversal of removal.

### Hazard warning light switch bulb

38 Remove the switch as described in Section 4. The bulbholder is removed by turning it a quarter-turn with a screwdriver.
39 Refitting is a reversal of removal.

### Cigar lighter illumination

40 First, the cigar lighter itself must be removed as described in Section 12.
41 Using a small screwdriver, carefully release the plastic tabs securing the cigar lighter socket, and remove it. The bulbholder can now be slid off the side of the cigar lighter socket, and the bulb renewed.
42 Refitting is a reversal of removal.

### 7  Exterior light units – removal and refitting

**Note:** *Disconnect the battery negative lead before removing any light unit (see 'Disconnecting the battery').*

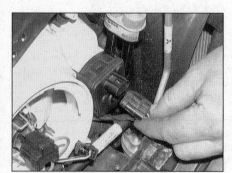

**7.4  Disconnect the wiring connectors from the headlight bulbs and the levelling motor**

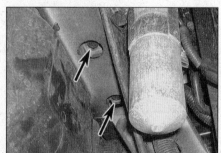

**7.5  Slacken and remove the bumper mounting bolts (arrowed – viewed from underneath)**

### Headlight

1 Firmly apply the handbrake, then jack up the front of the car and support it on axle stands. On turbo models, lift the securing clip and remove the plastic cover to gain access to the rear of the headlight unit.
2 Remove the front direction indicator light as described in paragraph 10.
3 On headlights which incorporate a combined main/dipped beam bulb, rotate the access cover anti-clockwise and remove it from the rear of the headlight unit. On headlight units with separate main and dipped beam bulbs, unclip the access cover then remove the rubber covers from the rear of the headlight. On Xenon headlights, proceed to paragraph 4.
4 Disconnect the wiring connectors from the headlight bulb(s) and sidelight bulb, then free the wiring from the rear of the light unit. Also disconnect the wiring connector from the headlight levelling motor (see illustration).
5 Working underneath the car, slacken and remove the two bumper mounting bolts (located directly behind the headlight unit) on the side which the headlight is to be removed (see illustration). If necessary, to improve access to the bolts, remove the engine undershield.
6 Undo the screw securing the relevant end of the front bumper to the wing, then free the bumper end and move it forwards slightly to gain the necessary clearance required for headlight removal. Fold the headlight wiper arm forwards.
7 Slacken and remove the four retaining nuts then carefully manoeuvre the headlight unit out of position. The headlight levelling motor can be removed by rotating it slightly, to free the motor body from the light unit, and unclipping its balljoint from the rear of the reflector (see illustrations).
8 If necessary, carefully prise off the retaining clips then remove the lens and seal from the light (see illustration). If the seal is damaged it must be renewed. On refitting ensure the lens and reflector unit are perfectly clean and dry. Seat the seal in the headlight groove then refit the lens and secure it in position with all the retaining clips.

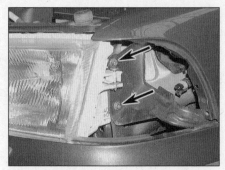

**7.7a Slacken and remove the outer . . .**

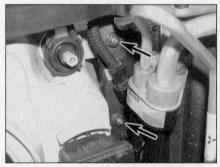

**7.7b . . . and inner retaining nuts . . .**

**7.7c . . . and remove the headlight unit**

**7.7d Rotate the levelling motor to free it from the headlight unit . . .**

**7.7e . . . then unclip it from the rear of the reflector**

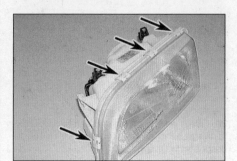

**7.8 The headlight lens can be removed once the retaining clips have been prised off**

9 Refitting is a direct reversal of the removal procedure, tightening the headlight nuts to the specified torque. On completion, the headlight beam alignment should be checked using the information given in Section 8.

## Front direction indicator light

10 Locate the indicator light unit retaining screw, which is situated in between the indicator and headlight unit. Back the retaining screw off by approximately two turns, then

(where applicable) release the clip at the side of the unit, and slide the light out. Disconnect the wiring plug from the back of the unit as soon as it is accessible **(see illustrations)**.

11 Refitting is a reverse of the removal procedure, ensuring the light unit peg is correctly located in its hole (or that the side clip is engaged), and the unit is securely retained by the screw.

## Front foglight

12 Firmly apply the handbrake, then jack up the front of the car and support it on axle stands.

13 Remove the screws/fasteners securing the relevant end of the undershield front section in position, and lower the shield to gain access to the foglight. To improve access, remove the cover completely.

14 If the right-hand foglight unit is to be removed, it will be necessary to remove the carbon canister (see Chapter 4C, Section 8) to access the light unit.

15 Disconnect the wiring connector from the foglight, then unclip the wiring harness from the light **(see illustration)**.

16 Remove the lower fastener (push out the centre pin, then remove the fastener body) and the two upper bolts, and manoeuvre the foglight out **(see illustrations)**.

17 Refitting is the reverse of removal. If necessary, adjust the foglight aim using the adjuster located on the rear of the light **(see illustration)**.

## Direction indicator side repeater

18 Carefully move the light slightly forwards, then ease the rear of the light out and free it

**7.10a Slacken the retaining screw . . .**

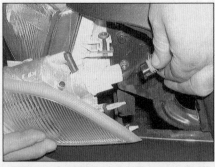
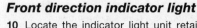

**7.10b . . . then slide the indicator unit out and disconnect the wiring connector**

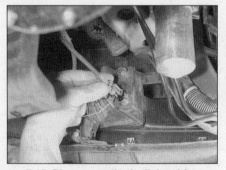

**7.15 Disconnect the foglight wiring connector**

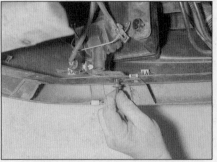

**7.16a Remove the lower fastener and the upper bolts . . .**

7.16b . . . then manoeuvre the foglight out from underneath the bumper

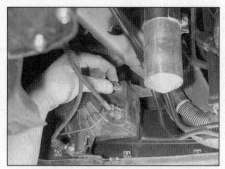

7.17 The foglight aim can be adjusted by rotating the adjuster on the rear

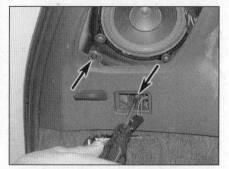

7.26a Undo the retaining screws (arrowed) . . .

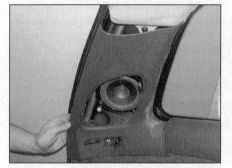

7.26b . . . then unclip the rear trim panel

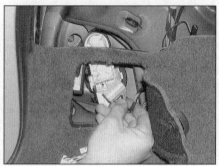

7.27 Disconnect the wiring connector . . .

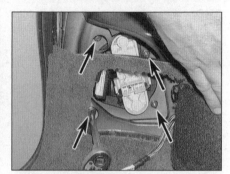

7.28 . . . then undo the retaining nuts and remove the light

from the wing. Free the bulbholder and remove the lens unit from the car.

19 Refitting is the reverse of removal, ensuring the lens unit is clipped securely in position.

### Rear light unit – Saloon models

20 Undo the retaining clip and open up the trim panel cover to gain access to the rear of the light unit. To improve access, peel off the boot lid sealing strip, unclip the luggage compartment sill trim panel, then remove the fasteners securing the rear of the side trim panel in position and fold it inwards slightly.

21 Disconnect the wiring connectors from the bulbholders.

22 Unscrew the retaining nuts and remove the light unit from the car, along with its seal. Inspect the seal for signs of damage or deterioration, and renew if necessary.

23 Refitting is the reverse of the removal sequence, ensuring the seal is correctly fitted.

### Rear light unit – Estate models

#### Body-mounted

24 Carefully prise the speaker grille out from the relevant luggage compartment rear pillar upper trim panel.

25 Unclip the luggage compartment light unit from the trim panel and disconnect it from the wiring connector.

26 Undo the trim panel retaining screws (located in the light and speaker grille apertures), then unclip the panel from the body and remove it from the car (see illustrations).

27 Disconnect the wiring connector from the light unit (see illustration).

28 Unscrew the retaining nuts and remove the light unit from the car, along with its seal (see illustration). Inspect the seal for signs of damage, and renew if necessary.

29 Refitting is the reverse of the removal sequence, ensuring the light unit seal is

correctly fitted. Renew any trim panel retaining clips which show signs of damage, and ensure all clips are correctly fitted to the panel before refitting the panel to the car.

#### Tailgate-mounted

30 Open up the tailgate, then undo the two screws in the handle aperture, and unclip the inner trim panel from the tailgate.

31 Disconnect the wiring connector from the light unit (see illustration).

32 Slacken and remove the retaining nuts, then remove the light unit assembly from the tailgate, complete with its rubber seal (see illustration). The seal must be renewed if damaged.

33 Refitting is the reverse of removal, tightening the retaining nuts securely.

### High-level stop-light

34 Release the retaining clips and remove the cover from the rear of the light unit (see illustration).

7.31 Disconnect the light unit wiring connector . . .

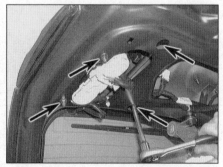

7.32 . . . then undo the nuts (four arrowed) and remove the tailgate light unit

7.34 Unclip the high-level stop-light rear cover and disconnect the wiring connector . . .

7.35 . . . then undo the screws and remove the light unit (Estate)

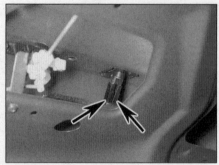

7.38 On Saloon models, disconnect the wiring connectors (arrowed) . . .

7.40 . . . then unclip the light unit from the boot lid

**35** Disconnect the wiring connector, then undo the screws and remove the light unit **(see illustration)**.
**36** Refitting is the reverse of removal.

### Number plate light

#### Saloon models

**37** Open up the boot lid then remove the fasteners (unscrew each centre screw slightly then pull out the complete fastener) and remove the boot lid inner trim panel.
**38** Disconnect the wiring connectors from the relevant number plate light **(see illustration)**.
**39** Unscrew the retaining nuts, then lift off the lock button surround panel from the boot lid.
**40** Carefully unclip the light unit and remove it from the boot lid **(see illustration)**.
**41** Refitting is the reverse of removal.

#### Estate models

**42** Undo the retaining screws and lower the light unit out from the tailgate, disconnecting the wiring connectors as they become accessible.

**43** Refitting is the reverse of removal. Do not overtighten the light unit retaining screws, as the plastic is easily cracked.

### Bumper sidelights

**44** See Section 5.

---

## 8 Headlight beam alignment – general information

**1** Accurate adjustment of the headlight beam is only possible using optical beam-setting equipment, and this work should therefore be carried out by a Volvo dealer or suitably-equipped workshop.
**2** For reference, the headlights can be adjusted by rotating the adjusters on the rear of the unit; the inner adjuster can be accessed through the hole in the bonnet lock cross-member **(see illustration)**. **Note:** *Ensure that the headlight beam adjuster switch is set to position 0 before the headlights are adjusted.*

---

## 9 Instrument panel – removal and refitting

### Removal

**1** Disconnect the battery negative terminal (see *Disconnecting the battery*).
**2** Remove the two column upper mounting bolts (accessible through the holes in the steering column lower shroud) then fully lower the column down **(see illustrations)**.
**3** Undo the retaining screws and remove the instrument panel shroud from the facia **(see illustration)**.
**4** Slacken and remove the instrument panel retaining screws **(see illustration)**.
**5** Release the upper retaining clip and withdraw the instrument panel squarely from the facia; the wiring connectors and (where fitted) speedometer cable are clipped to the facia, and will automatically be disconnected as the panel is withdrawn **(see illustration)**.

### Refitting

**6** Prior to refitting ensure the wiring connectors and (where fitted) speedometer

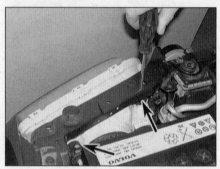

8.2 Headlight beam alignment adjusters (arrowed) on the rear of the unit

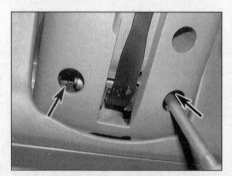

9.2a Working through the holes in the column lower shroud . . .

9.2b . . . remove the steering column upper mounting bolts

9.3 Undo the screws (arrowed) and remove the instrument panel shroud

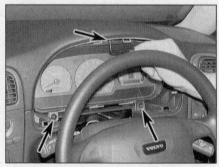

9.4 Undo the retaining screws (arrowed) . . .

cable are securely clipped into their facia brackets.

**7** Manoeuvre the instrument panel squarely back into position. Ensure the panel is correctly aligned with the connectors/cable, then clip it securely into the facia aperture.

**8** Refit the instrument panel shroud and securely tighten its retaining screws.

**9** Align the steering column with its mountings and refit the mounting bolts, tightening them to the specified torque (see Chapter 10).

**10** On completion, reconnect the battery and check the operation of the panel warning lights.

## 10  Instrument panel components – removal and refitting

At the time of writing, it was unclear if any of the instrument panel components were available separately. Refer to your Volvo dealer for the latest parts information; they will be able to advise you on the best course of action should the instrument(s) develop a fault.

## 11  Speedometer cable – removal and refitting

**Note:** *A speedometer cable is only fitted to models with an analogue (mechanical) mileometer. On models with an electronic (LCD) mileometer (2000 model year onwards), the speedometer is electronically-operated.*

### Removal

**1** Remove the instrument panel as described in Section 9.

**2** Release cable end fitting clip from the facia bracket then remove the clip from the cable.

**3** Working in the engine compartment, trace the speedometer cable down to the fitting on the transmission. Remove the retaining clip and disconnect the cable from the speedometer drive.

**4** Work back along the cable, freeing it from any relevant retaining clips, whilst noting its correct routing. Free the cable grommet from the bulkhead, then pull the upper end of the

**9.5 . . . and unclip the instrument panel from the facia**

cable through into the engine compartment and remove the cable from the car.

### Refitting

**5** Feed the cable through the bulkhead from the engine compartment. Ensure the cable end fitting is correctly routed through the facia bracket, then securely seat the grommet in the bulkhead.

**6** Ensure the cable is correctly routed and retained by all the relevant clips, then reconnect it to the transmission. Secure the cable in position with the retaining clip.

**7** Refit the instrument panel as described in Section 9.

## 12  Cigar lighter – removal and refitting

### Removal

#### Models up to May 2000

**1** Remove the audio unit as described in Section 18.

**2** Where necessary, unclip and remove the storage compartment from directly above the ashtray.

**3** Undo the retaining screws and remove the ashtray/cigar lighter assembly, disconnecting the wiring as it becomes accessible **(see illustrations)**.

#### Models from May 2000 onwards

**4** Remove the relevant section of the centre console as described in Chapter 11.

### All models

**5** If necessary, unclip the bulbholder from the lighter, then release the retaining clips and slide the lighter element out.

### Refitting

**6** Refitting is a reversal of the removal procedure, ensuring all the wiring connectors are securely reconnected.

## 13  Horn – removal and refitting

### Removal

**1** With the bonnet open, unscrew the retaining bolt and free the horn from the bonnet lock crossmember; disconnect it from the wiring connector.

### Refitting

**2** Securely reconnect the wiring connector, then refit the horn to the crossmember and securely tighten its retaining bolt.

## 14  Windscreen/ tailgate wiper arm – removal and refitting

### Removal

**1** Operate the wiper motor, then switch it off so that the wiper arm returns to the at-rest position.

**2** If a windscreen wiper arm is being removed, open up the bonnet then prise off the trim cap from the wiper arm retaining nut **(see illustration)**. If the tailgate wiper arm is being removed, lift up the trim cover to gain access to the retaining nut.

> **HAYNES HINT**
> *To make lining-up the wiper arm easier when refitting, mark the position of the wiper blade on the glass using a strip of masking tape.*

**3** Slacken and remove the wiper arm retaining nut, then lift the blade off of the glass

**12.3a  Undo the retaining screws (arrowed) . . .**

**12.3b . . . and remove the ashtray/cigarette lighter assembly**

**14.2  Remove the trim cap from the wiper arm to access the retaining nut**

15.2a Prise out the fasteners . . .

15.2b . . . and remove the cover panel (shown with bonnet removed)

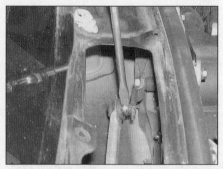

15.3 Carefully lever the wiper linkage off the wiper arm balljoint

15.4 On RHD models, undo the bolts and move the fuse/relay box clear

15.5a Remove the wiper motor cover . . .

15.5b . . . and disconnect the motor wiring connector

and pull the wiper arm off its spindle. If necessary, carefully ease the arm off of the spindle using a pair of grips.

### Refitting

**4** Ensure the wiper and spindle are clean and dry, then refit the arm. Ensure the arm is correctly positioned, then refit the retaining nut, tightening it to the specified torque. Refit the retaining nut trim cap/cover.

### 15 Windscreen wiper motor and linkage – removal and refitting

### Wiper motor

#### Removal

**1** Remove the wiper arms as described in Section 14.

**2** Prise out all the fasteners, then carefully unclip and remove the wiper linkage cover panel from the base of the windscreen **(see illustrations)**.

**3** Using a large, flat-bladed screwdriver, carefully lever the wiper linkage off from the motor crank balljoint **(see illustration)**.

**4** On right-hand-drive models, to improve access to the motor, remove the cover from the fuse/relay box, then undo the retaining bolts and free the box from the body **(see illustration)**.

**5** On all models, remove the motor cover then disconnect the wiper motor wiring connector **(see illustrations)**.

**6** Slacken and remove the four bolts securing the motor mounting plate to the bulkhead, then manoeuvre the assembly out and remove it from the car **(see illustrations)**. Inspect the mounting rubbers for signs of damage or deterioration, and renew if necessary.

**7** To separate the motor from the mounting

plate, first make alignment marks between the motor crank and the mounting plate. Slacken and remove the motor spindle nut; if necessary, prevent rotation by retaining the crank with an open-ended spanner whilst the nut is slackened **(see illustration)**. Remove the crank, then undo the three mounting bolts and separate the motor and mounting plate.

### Refitting

**8** Where necessary, refit the motor to the mounting plate, and securely tighten its mounting bolts. Refit the crank to the motor, aligning the marks made prior to removal, and tighten the spindle nut to the specified torque. To ensure the motor crank is correctly positioned, reconnect the wiring connector then operate the motor a few times prior to refitting.

**9** Manoeuvre the motor assembly into position, and securely tighten the mounting plate bolts.

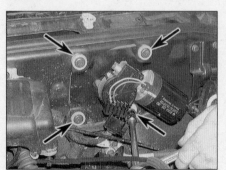

15.6a Slacken and remove the mounting bolts (arrowed) . . .

15.6b . . . then manoeuvre the motor assembly out of position

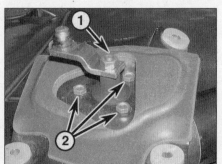

15.7 Wiper motor spindle nut (1) and mounting bolts (2)

**15.10 Securely clip the linkage back onto the motor crank balljoint**

**15.13a Slacken and remove the wiper spindle nuts (arrowed) . . .**

**15.13b . . . then manoeuvre the linkage assembly out of position**

**10** Reconnect the wiring connector to the motor, then securely clip the linkage back onto the motor crank balljoint **(see illustration)**.
**11** Refit the wiper motor cover panel, then refit the wiper arms as described in Section 14. On right-hand drive models, refit the fuse/relay box bolts, tightening them securely, and refit the cover.

### Wiper linkage

#### Removal

**12** Carry out the operations described in paragraphs 1 to 3.
**13** Slacken and remove the nuts securing the wiper spindle mountings to the body, then manoeuvre the linkage assembly out **(see illustrations)**.
**14** Inspect the linkage assembly for signs of wear, and renew if necessary.

#### Refitting

**15** Manoeuvre the linkage assembly into position, and refit the retaining nuts. Ensure the spindle mountings are both correctly positioned, then tighten the nuts to the specified torque setting.
**16** Securely clip the linkage back onto the motor crank balljoint, then refit the wiper motor cover panel.
**17** Refit the wiper arms as described in Section 14.

**16 Tailgate wiper motor (Estate models) –** removal and refitting

### Removal

**1** Remove the wiper arm as described in Section 14.

**2** Remove the cap from the wiper spindle, then slacken and remove the spindle nut and mounting bush **(see illustrations)**.
**3** Open the tailgate and undo the two screws located in the handle aperture. Unclip the inner trim panel and remove it from the tailgate.
**4** Disconnect the wiring connector from the motor **(see illustration)**.
**5** Undo the bolts securing the motor mounting bracket to the tailgate, then manoeuvre the wiper motor assembly out and recover the motor sealing grommet from the tailgate **(see illustrations)**. If necessary, unscrew the mounting bolts and separate the motor and mounting bracket. Inspect the motor mounting rubbers for signs of damage or deterioration, and renew if necessary.

### Refitting

**6** Ensure the grommet is correctly located in the tailgate, then manoeuvre the motor into position and loosely fit the retaining bolts.
**7** Slide on the mounting bush (aligning its mounting lug correctly) onto the motor spindle, then refit the spindle nut. Ensure the bush is correctly located, then securely tighten the spindle nut and refit the trim cap.
**8** Securely tighten the motor mounting bracket bolts, then reconnect the wiring.
**9** Clip the inner trim panel into position on the tailgate, and securely tighten its retaining screws.
**10** Refit the wiper arm as described in Section 14.

**16.2a Remove the wiper motor spindle cap, then unscrew the nut (arrowed) . . .**

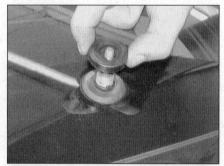

**16.2b . . . and lift off the mounting bush**

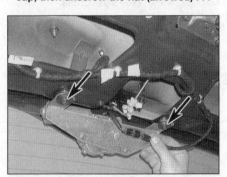

**16.4 Disconnect the wiring, then undo the mounting bolts (arrowed) . . .**

**16.5a . . . and remove the wiper motor from the tailgate**

**16.5b Check the sealing grommet condition**

**17.6 Disconnect the washer hose(s) at the connections near the reservoir neck**

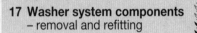

### 17 Washer system components – removal and refitting

**1** The washer reservoir is located in the front right-hand corner of the engine compartment; on models equipped with headlight washers, the reservoir also supplies the headlight washer jets via an additional pump. On Estate models, an additional pump is fitted to the reservoir to supply the tailgate washer jet.

#### Washer system reservoir

**2** Firmly apply the handbrake, then loosen the right-hand front wheel nuts. Jack up the front of the car and support it on axle stands. Remove the right-hand front roadwheel.
**3** Remove the screws/fasteners, and take out the right-hand wheel arch liner from underneath the right-hand wing. Similarly,

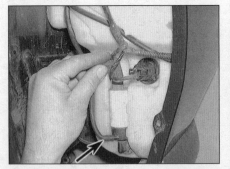

**17.11 Disconnect the wiring connector and washer hose (arrowed) . . .**

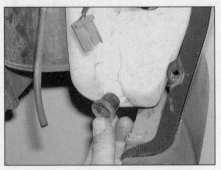

**17.12b . . . and remove its sealing grommet**

**17.8 Removing the washer reservoir**

lower or completely remove the engine undershield, to gain access to the reservoir.
**4** Remove the right-hand front indicator light (see Section 7). On models fitted with front foglights, remove the right-hand foglight unit.
**5** Disconnect the wiring connectors from the washer reservoir fluid level sensor and the washer pump(s).
**6** Working in the engine compartment, disconnect the washer hose(s) at the valve connection(s) on the washer reservoir neck **(see illustration)**.
**7** Remove the bolts securing the charcoal canister to the washer reservoir, and position the canister clear.
**8** Remove the reservoir retaining bolts, then lower the reservoir out **(see illustration)**. If necessary, slacken and remove the screw securing the bumper end to the wing, to obtain extra clearance to enable the reservoir to be removed.

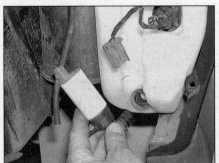

**17.12a . . . then ease the washer pump out of position . . .**

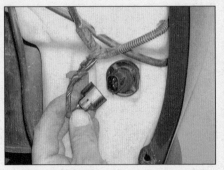

**17.20 Disconnect the wiring connector . . .**

**9** Refitting is the reverse of removal, ensuring that the hose(s) and wiring are securely reconnected. Refill the reservoir and check for leakage.

#### Washer pump

##### Windscreen/headlight

**10** Carry out the operations described in paragraphs 2 and 3. The windscreen washer pump is fitted to the rear of the reservoir.
**11** Position a container beneath the reservoir to catch the fluid, then disconnect the wiring connector and washer hose(s) from the pump **(see illustration)**.
**12** Carefully ease the pump out from the reservoir, and recover its sealing grommet **(see illustrations)**.
**13** Refitting is the reverse of removal, using a new sealing grommet if the original one shows signs of damage or deterioration. Refill the reservoir and check the pump grommet for leaks.

##### Tailgate

**14** Firmly apply the handbrake, then jack up the front of the car and support it on axle stands. The tailgate washer pump is fitted to the front of the reservoir.
**15** Remove the retaining screws/fasteners and remove the front section of the engine/transmission undercover.
**16** Position a container beneath the reservoir to catch the fluid then disconnect the wiring connector and washer hose(s) from the pump.
**17** Carefully ease the pump out from the reservoir and recover its sealing grommet.
**18** Refitting is the reverse of removal, using a new sealing grommet if the original one shows signs of damage or deterioration. Refill the reservoir and check the pump grommet for leaks.

#### Washer fluid level sensor

**19** Carry out the operations described in paragraphs 2 and 3. The fluid level sensor is fitted to the rear of the reservoir.
**20** Disconnect the wiring connector from the sensor **(see illustration)**.
**21** Position a container beneath the reservoir to catch the fluid, then carefully ease the sensor out from the reservoir and recover its sealing grommet **(see illustration)**.

**17.21 . . . then ease out the fluid level sensor and sealing grommet (arrowed)**

**22** Refitting is the reverse of removal, using a new sealing grommet if necessary. Refill the reservoir and check the sensor grommet for leaks.

### Washer jets

#### Windscreen

**23** Open the bonnet, then prise out the retaining clips and fold back the insulation panel to gain access to the rear of the washer jets.
**24** Disconnect the washer hose, then release the retaining clips and ease the jet out from the bonnet.
**25** On refitting, securely clip the jet into position in the bonnet, then reconnect the washer hose. Secure the insulation panel in position, then close the bonnet and check the operation of the jet.
**26** If necessary adjust the nozzles using a pin, aiming one nozzle to a point slightly above the centre of the swept area and the other to slightly below the centre point to ensure complete coverage. Note that only vertical adjustment is possible.

#### Tailgate

**27** Remove the high-level stop-light unit as described in Section 7.
**28** Depress the retaining clips then ease the jet out and disconnect it from the washer hose.
**29** Refitting is the reverse of removal.

### Headlight wiper motor

**30** Lift up the trim cover, then slacken and remove the wiper arm retaining nut. Lift the blade off of the headlight, then pull the wiper arm off its spindle and disconnect the washer hose **(see illustrations)**. If necessary, carefully ease the arm off the spindle using a pair of grips.
**31** Remove the headlight unit as described in Section 7.
**32** Disconnect the wiring connector from the wiper motor, then undo the retaining bolts and remove the motor from the bumper **(see illustrations)**.
**33** Refitting is the reverse of removal. Prior to refitting the wiper arm, operate the motor to ensure it is correctly set to the at-rest position.

**17.30a  Unscrew the retaining nut . . .**

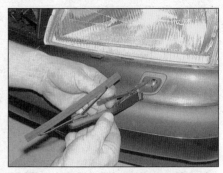
**17.30b  . . . then pull the wiper arm from its spindle and disconnect the washer hose**

**17.32a  Disconnect the wiring connector . . .**

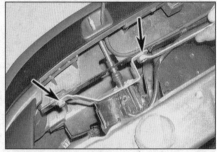
**17.32b  . . . then undo the bolts (arrowed) and remove the wiper motor from the bumper**

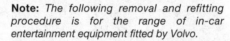
## 18  Radio/cassette/CD player – removal and refitting

**Note:** *The following removal and refitting procedure is for the range of in-car entertainment equipment fitted by Volvo.*

### Removal

**1** Disconnect the battery negative lead (see *Disconnecting the battery*).
**2** Using a small, flat-bladed screwdriver, carefully depress the audio unit removal handles to free them from the unit **(see illustration)**.
**3** Fully extend the left- and right-hand handles and pull the unit out from the facia **(see illustration)**.
**4** Disconnect the aerial lead and wiring connectors and remove the audio unit **(see illustration)**.

### Refitting

**5** Refitting is the reverse of the removal procedure. On completion, connect the battery negative terminal and enter the security code.

## 19  Speakers – removal and refitting

### Removal

#### Facia-mounted speaker

**1** Carefully prise out the speaker grille and remove it from the facia **(see illustration)**.
**2** Unclip the speaker and remove from the facia, disconnecting the wiring as it becomes accessible **(see illustrations)**.

**18.2  Depress and extend the removal handles . . .**

**18.3  . . . then use the handles to pull the audio unit out**

**18.4  Disconnect the wiring plugs and aerial lead as they become accessible**

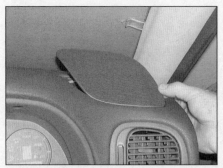

19.1 Unclip the speaker grille . . .

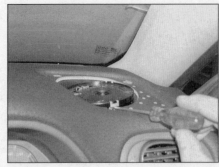

19.2a . . . then prise the speaker out from the facia . . .

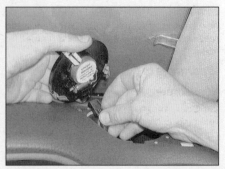

19.2b . . . and disconnect it from the wiring

19.3 Unclip the speaker grille from the door trim panel . . .

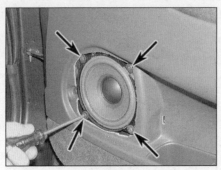

19.4a . . . then undo the retaining screws (arrowed) . . .

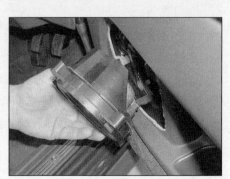

19.4b . . . and withdraw the speaker from the door

### Front door-mounted speaker

3 Unclip and remove the speaker grille from the door inner trim panel **(see illustration)**.
4 Undo the retaining screws and remove the speaker from the panel, disconnecting the wiring as it becomes accessible **(see illustrations)**.

### Rear speakers – Saloon models

5 Unclip and remove the speaker grille from the rear parcel shelf **(see illustration)**.

6 Undo the retaining screws and remove the speaker from the panel, disconnecting the wiring as it becomes accessible **(see illustration)**.

### Rear speakers – Estate models

7 Unclip and remove the speaker grille from the rear pillar trim panel **(see illustration)**.
8 Undo the retaining screws and remove the speaker, disconnecting the wiring as it becomes accessible **(see illustrations)**.

### *Refitting*

9 Refitting is the reverse of removal.

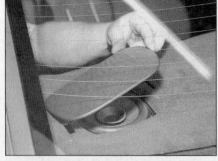

19.5 On Saloon models, unclip the speaker grille from the rear parcel shelf . . .

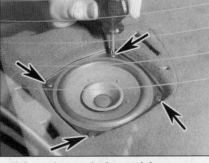

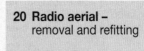

19.6 . . . then undo the retaining screws (arrowed) and lift out the rear speaker

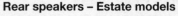

## 20 Radio aerial – removal and refitting

### *Saloon models*

1 Open the boot lid, then undo the retaining

19.7 On Estate models, unclip the speaker grille from the rear pillar trim panel . . .

19.8a . . . then undo the retaining screws (arrowed) . . .

19.8b . . . and remove the speaker, disconnecting its wiring connectors

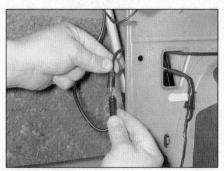

**20.4a On Saloon models, disconnect the aerial lead . . .**

**20.4b . . . and unbolt the earth lead from the body**

**20.5 Free the drain tube grommet from the body so it can be removed with the aerial**

screws and remove the luggage compartment floor panel.

**2** Peel the boot lid sealing strip away from the left-hand side and base of the boot lid aperture, then carefully unclip the luggage compartment rear trim panel upwards and remove it.

**3** Remove the luggage compartment left-hand side trim panel rear fasteners (loosen the centre screws a few turns, then pull out the complete fastener) and fold the rear of trim panel inwards to gain access to the aerial. To improve access, remove the front fasteners (located behind the rear seat back) and remove the panel completely.

**4** Disconnect the aerial lead, then undo the retaining bolt securing the aerial earth lead to the body **(see illustrations)**.

**5** Trace the drain tube back from the base of the aerial and free its sealing grommet from body **(see illustration)**.

**6** Slacken and remove the mounting bolt, then disconnect the wiring connector from the aerial **(see illustrations)**.

**7** Free the upper end of the aerial from the sealing grommet and remove it from the car. Remove the sealing grommet from the body and store it with the aerial **(see illustrations)**.

**8** Refitting is the reverse of removal. Prior to refitting the mounting bolt, ensure the sealing grommet is correctly fitted and the aerial mounting lug is correctly located in its slot in the body.

### Estate models

**9** Using a small, flat-bladed screwdriver, carefully prise the rear courtesy light unit out from the headlining to gain access to the base of the aerial.

**10** Unclip the connectors from the roof, then disconnect both the aerial lead and wiring connector. Take care not to allow the vehicle

end of the lead/wiring to disappear behind the roof lining.

**11** Unscrew the retaining nut and lift the aerial off from the roof, noting its rubber seal.

**12** Refitting is the reverse of removal, ensuring the rubber seal is in good condition.

---

### 21 Cruise control system – general information and component renewal

Refer to Chapter 4A.

---

### 22 Alarm/engine immobiliser system – general information

**Note:** *This information is applicable only to the anti-theft alarm and immobiliser systems fitted by Volvo as standard equipment.*

### Alarm system

**1** Most models fitted with remote central locking are also equipped with an anti-theft alarm system. The alarm is automatically armed and disarmed when the car is locked/unlocked with the remote central locking transmitter. When the car is locked, the indicator lights will stay on for 1 second and the alarm system LED on the facia will flash slowly; the alarm system will become active approximately 25 seconds (50 seconds, on early models) after locking the doors. If the LED stays on continuously when the doors are locked this indicates that either a door, the bonnet or the tailgate/boot lid are not correctly shut, or the ultrasonic sensors have detected movement within the car.

**2** The alarm system has switches on the bonnet, tailgate/boot lid and each of the doors, and ultrasonic sensors on the door pillar to detect movement inside the car. Should a door, the tailgate/boot lid or the bonnet be opened without first using the remote central locking transmitter to unlock the doors, or movement be detected within the car, the alarm system will be triggered. When the system is triggered, the horn will sound and the indicator lights will flash for approximately 30 seconds. After this time the

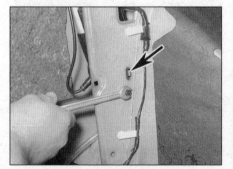

**20.6a Unscrew the mounting bolt (note locating lug – arrowed) . . .**

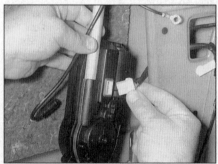

**20.6b . . . then disconnect the aerial wiring connector**

**20.7a Remove the aerial assembly from the boot . . .**

**20.7b . . . and recover the sealing grommet from the body**

system automatically resets, although the LED will continue to flash for approximately 5 minutes. If the alarm has been activated, when the car is unlocked the LED will flash continuously until the ignition switch is turned on.

3 If the horn wiring is tampered with while the system is active (and even if the wires are cut), the horn will sound for 5 minutes.

4 Should the alarm system become faulty, the car should be taken to a Volvo dealer for examination. If a fault is present in the system, the LED will flash rapidly whenever the ignition is switched on.

### Immobiliser system

5 An engine immobiliser system is fitted as standard to all models and the system is operated automatically every time the ignition key is inserted/removed.

6 The immobiliser system ensures that the car can only be started using the original Volvo ignition key. The key contains an electronic chip (transponder) which is programmed with a code. When the key is inserted into the ignition switch, it uses the current present in the sensor coil (which is fitted to the switch housing) to send a signal to the immobiliser electronic control unit (ECU). The ECU checks this code every time the ignition is switched on. If the key code does not match the ECU code, the ECU will disable the starter, fuel and ignition circuits to prevent the engine being started.

7 An engine immobiliser warning light is fitted to the instrument panel to confirm that the immobiliser system is functioning correctly. If all is well, the light should illuminate for approximately 3 seconds every time the ignition is switched on and then go out. If the warning light fails to come on (check the bulb first before assuming the system is faulty), remains illuminated after the initial period or comes on at any time when the engine is running then a fault is present in the system and the car should be taken to a Volvo dealer for testing. **Note:** *If the warning light flashes continuously when the ignition is switched on, the key code is not being recognised by the ECU.*

8 If the ignition key is lost, a new one can be obtained from a Volvo dealer. They have access to the correct key code for the immobiliser system of your car and will be able to supply a new coded key. If necessary, your Volvo dealer can reprogram the system ECU and supply new keys to suit, rendering the original key useless.

## 23 Heated front seat components – removal and refitting

Renewal of the front seat heater pads should be entrusted to a Volvo dealer. Renewal involves dismantling of the complex seat assembly. Heater pad renewal is especially difficult to achieve successfully. In practice, it will be very difficult for the home mechanic to carry out the job without ruining the upholstery. The only item which is easily removed/refitted are the relays or operating switches (see Section 3 or 4).

## 24 Airbag system – general information and precautions

**Note:** *Refer to Chapter 11 for information on the side impact protection system (SIPS) airbags.*

1 All models are equipped with a supplementary restraint system (SRS) which incorporates a driver's airbag and front seat belt tensioners. On some models, a front passenger airbag is also incorporated in the system; these models can be identified by the SRS AIRBAG marking on the top of the passenger side of the facia.

2 The system comprises of the airbag unit(s) (complete with gas generators), the control unit (with an integral impact sensor), the seat belt tensioners, and a warning light in the instrument panel.

3 The system is triggered in the event of a heavy frontal impact above a predetermined force; triggering is also dependent on the point of impact. The airbags are inflated within milliseconds, and form a safety cushion between the driver and steering wheel and (where fitted) the passenger and facia. This prevents contact between the upper body and wheel/facia, and therefore greatly reduces the risk of injury. The airbag then deflates almost immediately. At the same time, the control unit also operates the front seat belt tensioner mechanisms (see Chapter 11 for details).

4 Every time the ignition is switched on, the SRS control unit performs a self-test. During this time, the SRS warning light in the instrument panel is illuminated. After the self-test has been completed (this takes approximately 10 seconds) the warning light should go out; if the engine is started before this time, the light will go out straightaway. If the warning light fails to come on (check the bulb first before assuming the system is faulty), remains illuminated after the initial period, or comes on at any time when the engine is running, there is a fault in the system. The car be taken to a Volvo dealer for examination at the earliest possible opportunity.

> ⚠ **Warning:** *Before carrying out any operations on the system, disconnect the battery negative terminal and wait at least two minutes. Refer to 'Disconnecting the battery' in the Reference section of this manual. When operations are complete, make sure no one is inside the car when the battery is reconnected then, with the driver's door open, switch the ignition on from outside the car.*

> ⚠ **Warning:** *Note that the airbag(s) must not be subjected to temperatures in excess of 100ºC.*

When the airbag is removed, ensure that it is stored the correct way up to prevent possible inflation.

> ⚠ **Warning:** *Do not allow any solvents or cleaning agents to contact the airbag assemblies. They must be cleaned using only a damp cloth.*

> ⚠ **Warning:** *The airbags and control unit(s) are both sensitive to impact. If either is dropped onto a hard surface or are damaged, they should be renewed.*

> ⚠ **Warning:** *Disconnect the SRS control unit wiring plug prior to using arc-welding equipment on the car.*

> ⚠ **Warning:** *Volvo state that the airbag units should be renewed every 10 years. The expiry date of the units are given on a sticker attached to driver's side door pillar. On some vehicles, when the expiry date is reached, the airbag warning light will be permanently illuminated.*

> ⚠ **Warning:** *Never fit a child seat to the front passenger seat if a passenger airbag is fitted to the car. Only fit child seats in the rear of the car.*

## 25 Airbag system components – removal and refitting
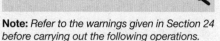

**Note:** *Refer to the warnings given in Section 24 before carrying out the following operations.*

1 Disconnect the battery negative terminal, wait at least two minutes before proceeding (see *Disconnecting the battery*).

### Driver's airbag

#### Removal

2 Though not essential, to improve access, release the steering column height adjustment lever, then undo the retaining screws and unclip the upper and lower shrouds. Slacken and remove the two airbag retaining screws located behind the steering wheel, rotating the wheel as necessary to gain access to the screws **(see illustration)**. The screws are Torx T30 type, and are fitted at an angle.

**25.2  Slacken and remove the airbag unit retaining screws . . .**

**25.3 . . . then lift the unit away from the steering wheel and disconnect its wiring**

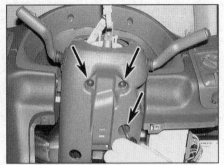

**25.7a  Undo the retaining screws (arrowed) . . .**

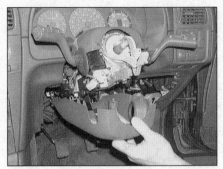

**25.7b . . . then unclip the upper and lower column shrouds**

**3** Return the steering wheel to the straight-ahead position, then carefully lift the airbag assembly away from the steering wheel, disconnecting the wiring connector from the rear of the unit **(see illustration)**. Note that the airbag must not be knocked or dropped, and should be stored with its padded surface uppermost.

### Refitting

**4** Reconnect the wiring connector, then seat the airbag unit centrally in the steering wheel, making sure the wire does not become trapped. Fit the retaining screws and tighten them to the specified torque setting. Refit the column shrouds, if removed.
**5** Ensure no one is inside the car, and reconnect the battery. With the driver's door open, turn on the ignition switch from outside the car, and check the operation of the airbag warning light.

## Driver's airbag contact unit

### Removal

**6** Remove the airbag as described in paragraphs 2 and 3, then refer to Chapter 10 and remove the steering wheel.
**7** If not already done, release the steering column height adjustment lever, then undo the retaining screws and unclip the upper and lower shrouds **(see illustrations)**.
**8** Disconnect the wiring connector from the contact unit **(see illustration)**.
**9** Remove the screws, then unclip and remove the contact unit from the switch

holder, disconnecting the horn contact wiring connector as it becomes accessible **(see illustrations)**.

### Refitting

**10** Prior to refitting, it is necessary to ensure that the contact unit is centralised. If the locking screw was correctly used on removal, this will not be a problem. New contact units are supplied correctly positioned. If there is any doubt, centralise the unit as follows. Undo the locking screw, then retain the outside of the contact unit and rotate the centre fully anti-clockwise until resistance is felt. From this point, rotate the centre approximately three turns in a clockwise direction to bring the centre locking lug into alignment with the screw locating point, then lightly tighten the screw to lock the contact unit in position.
**11** Reconnect the horn wiring connector, then clip the contact unit securely onto the switch holder. Refit the retaining screws and tighten them to the specified torque.
**12** Ensure the wiring is correctly routed, then reconnect the wiring connector to the contact unit.
**13** Refit the steering column shrouds correctly to the column and securely tighten their retaining screws.
**14** Refit the steering wheel as described in Chapter 10. When the battery is reconnected, ensure no one is inside the car. With the driver's door open, turn on the ignition switch from outside the car and check the operation of the airbag warning light.

## Passenger airbag

### Removal

**15** Remove the facia (see Chapter 11).
**16** Undo the retaining screws and remove the heating/ventilation duct assembly from the rear of the facia.
**17** Disconnect the wiring connector, then remove the retaining bolts and airbag unit from the facia. Note that the airbag must not be knocked or dropped, and should be stored with its bag surface uppermost.

### Refitting

**18** Manoeuvre the airbag into position and refit the retaining bolts, tightening them to the specified torque setting.
**19** Ensure the wiring is correctly routed, then securely reconnect the wiring connector.
**20** Refit the heating/ventilation duct assembly, making sure it is correctly engaged with the facia vents, and securely tighten its retaining screws.
**21** Refit the facia as described in Chapter 11. When the battery is reconnected, ensure no one is inside the car. With the driver's door open, turn on the ignition switch from outside the car and check the operation of the airbag warning light.

## SRS control unit

### Removal

**22** Remove the centre console as described in Chapter 11.

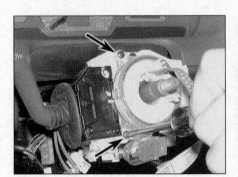

**25.9a . . . then undo the retaining screws (arrowed) . . .**

**25.9b . . . and lift the unit away, disconnecting the horn wiring**

**25.8  Disconnect the wiring connector from the contact unit . . .**

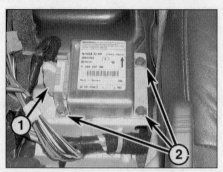

**25.23 SRS control unit wiring connector (1) and retaining bolts (2)**

**23** Release the retaining clip and disconnect the wiring connector from the control unit **(see illustration)**.

**24** Unscrew the retaining bolts and remove the control unit from the car.

### Refitting

**25** Ensure the mating surfaces of the control unit and body are clean and dry, then manoeuvre the SRS control unit into position. Refit the mounting bolts and tighten to the specified torque.

**26** Reconnect the wiring connector to the control unit, and secure it in position with the retaining clip.

**27** Refit the centre console as described in Chapter 11. When the battery is reconnected, ensure no one is inside the car. With the driver's door open, turn on the ignition switch from outside the car and check the operation of the airbag warning light.

### Seat belt tensioners

**28** Refer to Chapter 11.

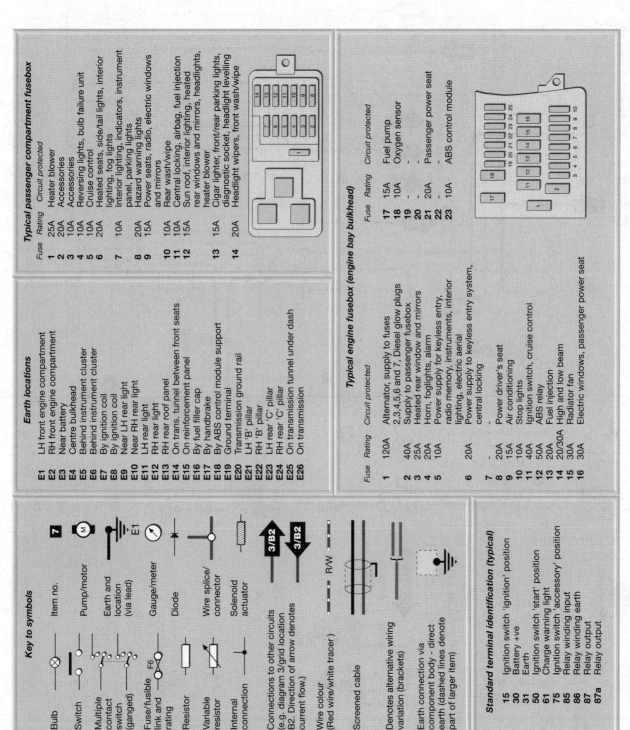

## Key to symbols

- Bulb
- Switch
- Multiple contact switch (ganged)
- Fuse/fusible link and rating  F6
- Resistor
- Variable resistor
- Internal connection
- Connections to other circuits (e.g. diagram 3/grid location. B2. Direction of arrow denotes current flow.)
- Wire colour (Red wire/white tracer)  R/W
- Screened cable
- Denotes alternative wiring variation (brackets)
- Earth connection via component body - direct earth (dashed lines denote part of larger item)

- Item no.  7
- Pump/motor  M
- Earth and location (via lead)  E1
- Gauge/meter
- Diode
- Wire splice/ connector
- Solenoid actuator
- 3/B2
- 3/B2

## Standard terminal identification (typical)

| | |
|---|---|
| 15 | Ignition switch 'ignition' position |
| 30 | Battery +ve |
| 31 | Earth |
| 50 | Ignition switch 'start' position |
| 61 | Charge warning light |
| 75 | Ignition switch 'accessory' position |
| 85 | Relay winding input |
| 86 | Relay winding earth |
| 87 | Relay output |
| 87a | Relay output |

## Earth locations

| | |
|---|---|
| E1 | LH front engine compartment |
| E2 | RH front engine compartment |
| E3 | Near battery |
| E4 | Centre bulkhead |
| E5 | Behind instrument cluster |
| E6 | Behind instrument cluster |
| E7 | By ignition coil |
| E8 | By ignition coil |
| E9 | Near LH rear light |
| E10 | Near RH rear light |
| E11 | LH rear light |
| E12 | RH rear light |
| E13 | RH rear roof panel |
| E14 | On trans. tunnel between front seats |
| E15 | On reinforcement panel |
| E16 | By fuel filler cap |
| E17 | By handbrake |
| E18 | By ABS control module support |
| E19 | Ground terminal |
| E20 | Transmission ground rail |
| E21 | LH 'B' pillar |
| E22 | RH 'B' pillar |
| E23 | LH rear 'C' pillar |
| E24 | RH rear 'C' pillar |
| E25 | On transmission tunnel under dash |
| E26 | On transmission |

## Typical passenger compartment fusebox

| Fuse | Rating | Circuit protected |
|---|---|---|
| 1 | 25A | Heater blower |
| 2 | 20A | Accessories |
| 3 | 20A | Accessories |
| 4 | 10A | Reversing lights, bulb failure unit |
| 5 | 10A | Cruise control |
| 6 | 20A | Heated seats, side/tail lights, interior lighting, fog lights |
| 7 | 10A | Interior lighting, indicators, instrument panel, parking lights |
| 8 | 20A | Hazard warning lights |
| 9 | 15A | Power seats, radio, electric windows and mirrors |
| 10 | 10A | Rear wash/wipe |
| 11 | 10A | Central locking, airbag, fuel injection |
| 12 | 15A | Sun roof, interior lighting, heated rear windows and mirrors, headlights, heater blower |
| 13 | 15A | Cigar lighter, front/rear parking lights, diagnostic socket, headlight levelling |
| 14 | 20A | Headlight wipers, front wash/wipe |

## Typical engine fusebox (engine bay bulkhead)

| Fuse | Rating | Circuit protected |
|---|---|---|
| 1 | 120A | Alternator, supply to fuses 2,3,4,5,6 and 7, Diesel glow plugs |
| 2 | 40A | Supply to passenger fusebox |
| 3 | 25A | Heated rear window and mirrors |
| 4 | 20A | Horn, foglights, alarm |
| 5 | 10A | Power supply for keyless entry, radio memory, instruments, interior lighting, electric aerial |
| 6 | 20A | Power supply to keyless entry system, central locking |
| 7 | - | - |
| 8 | 20A | Power driver's seat |
| 9 | 15A | Air conditioning |
| 10 | 10A | Stop lights |
| 11 | 40A | Ignition switch, cruise control |
| 12 | 50A | ABS relay |
| 13 | 30A | Fuel injection |
| 14 | 20/30A | High and low beam |
| 15 | 30A | Radiator fan |
| 16 | 30A | Electric windows, passenger power seat |
| 17 | 15A | Fuel pump |
| 18 | 10A | Oxygen sensor |
| 19 | - | - |
| 20 | - | - |
| 21 | 20A | Passenger power seat |
| 22 | - | - |
| 23 | 10A | ABS control module |

**Diagram 1 : Information for wiring diagrams - typical**

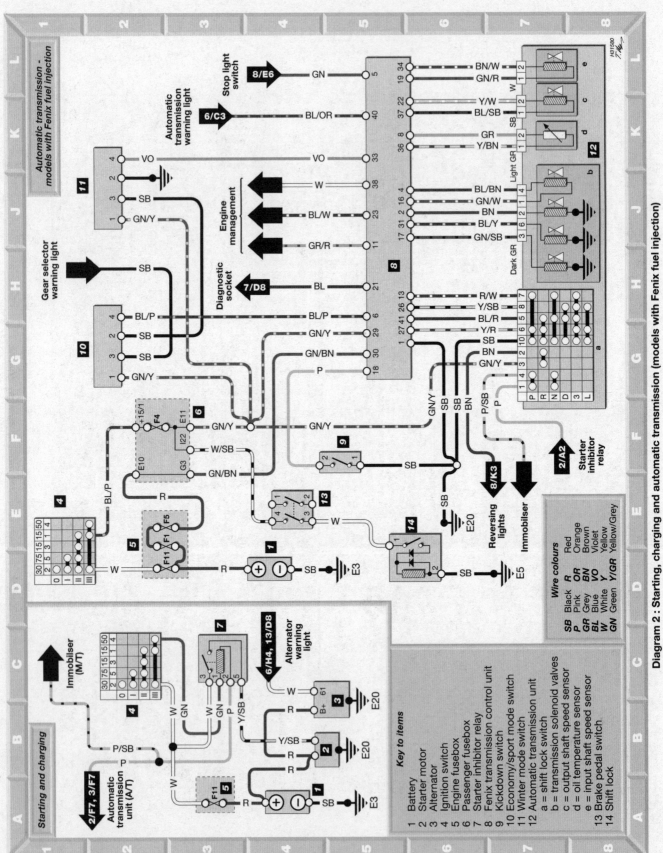

Diagram 2 : Starting, charging and automatic transmission (models with Fenix fuel injection)

**Automatic transmission - models with Fenix fuel injection**

Stop light switch **8/E6**

Automatic transmission warning light **6/C3**

Engine management

Gear selector warning light

Diagnostic socket **7/D8**

Starter inhibitor relay **2/A2**

Reversing lights **8/K3**

Immobiliser

**Starting and charging**

Immobiliser (M/T)

Automatic transmission unit (A/T) **2/F7, 3/F7**

Alternator warning light **6/H4, 13/D8**

**Wire colours**

| | | | |
|---|---|---|---|
| **SB** | Black | **R** | Red |
| **P** | Pink | **OR** | Orange |
| **GR** | Grey | **BN** | Brown |
| **BL** | Blue | **VO** | Violet |
| **W** | White | **Y** | Yellow |
| **GN** | Green | **Y/GR** | Yellow/Grey |

**Key to items**

1 Battery
2 Starter motor
3 Alternator
4 Ignition switch
5 Engine fusebox
6 Passenger fusebox
7 Starter inhibitor relay
8 Fenix transmission control unit
9 Kickdown switch
10 Economy/sport mode switch
11 Winter mode switch
12 Automatic transmission unit
    a = shift lock switch
    b = transmission solenoid valves
    c = output shaft speed sensor
    d = oil temperature sensor
    e = input shaft speed sensor
13 Brake pedal switch
14 Shift lock

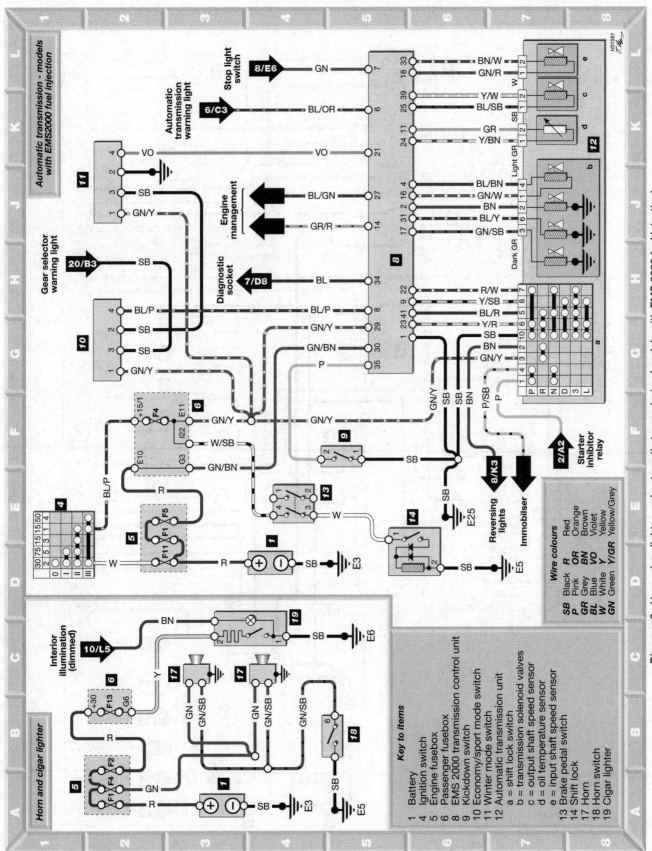

Diagram 3 : Horn, cigar lighter and automatic transmission (models with EMS 2000 fuel injection)

**Wire colours**

| | | | |
|---|---|---|---|
| **SB** | Black | **R** | Red |
| **P** | Pink | **OR** | Orange |
| **GR** | Grey | **BN** | Brown |
| **BL** | Blue | **VO** | Violet |
| **W** | White | **Y** | Yellow |
| **GN** | Green | **Y/GR** | Yellow/Grey |

**Key to items**

1  Battery
4  Ignition switch
5  Engine fusebox
6  Passenger fusebox
8  EMS 2000 transmission control unit
9  Kickdown switch
10  Economy/sport mode switch
11  Winter mode switch
12  Automatic transmission unit
  a = shift lock switch
  b = transmission solenoid valves
  c = output shaft speed sensor
  d = oil temperature sensor
  e = input shaft speed sensor
13  Brake pedal switch
14  Shift lock
17  Horn
18  Horn switch
19  Cigar lighter

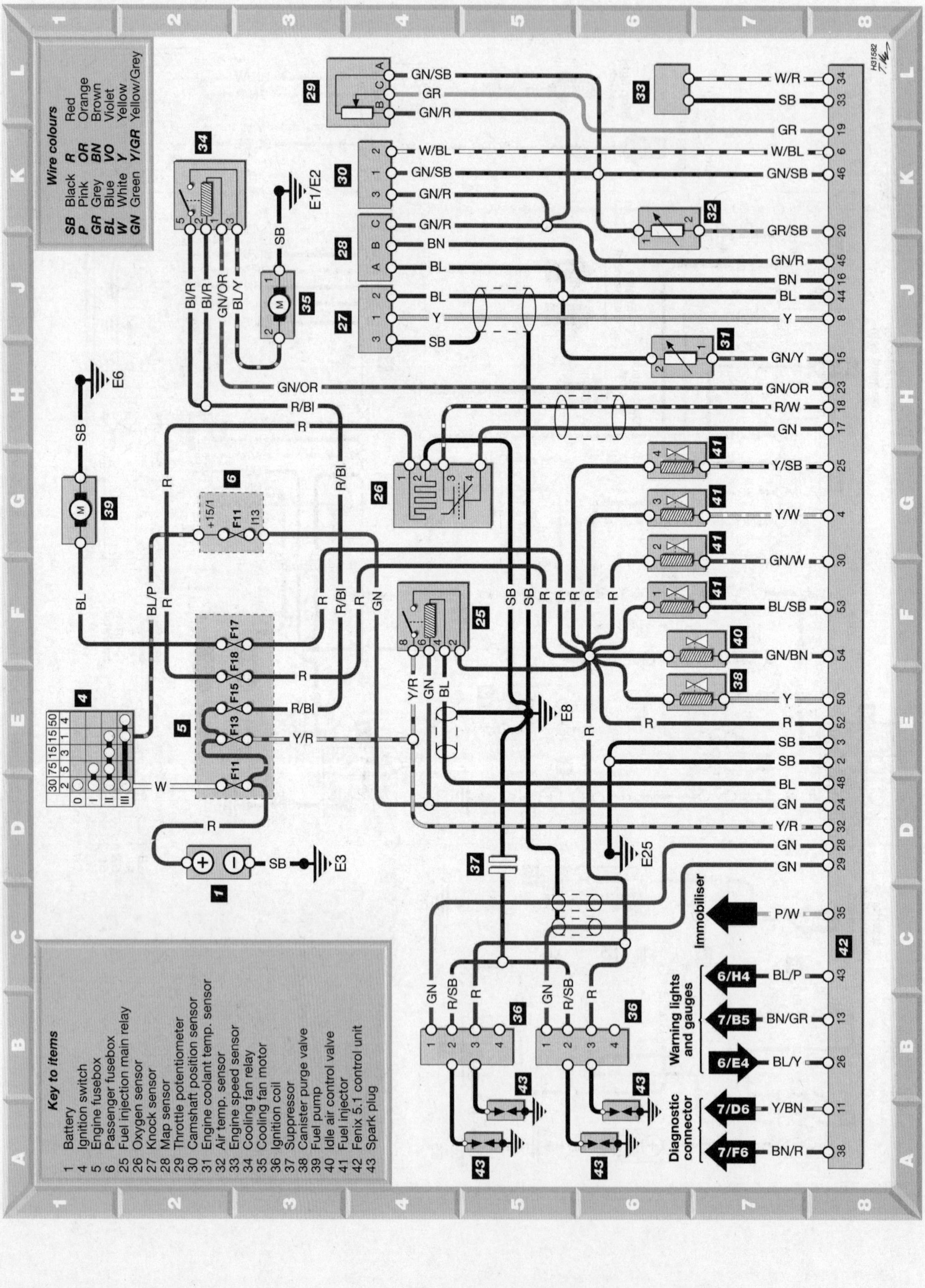

Diagram 4 : Fenix 5.1 fuel injection

**Wire colours**

| | | | |
|---|---|---|---|
| **SB** | Black | **R** | Red |
| **P** | Pink | **OR** | Orange |
| **GR** | Grey | **BN** | Brown |
| **BL** | Blue | **VO** | Violet |
| **W** | White | **Y** | Yellow |
| **GN** | Green | **Y/GR** | Yellow/Grey |

**Key to items**

1 Battery
4 Ignition switch
5 Engine fusebox
6 Passenger fusebox
25 Fuel injection main relay
26 Oxygen sensor
27 Knock sensor
28 Map sensor
29 Throttle potentiometer
30 Camshaft position sensor
31 Engine coolant temp. sensor
32 Air temp. sensor
33 Engine speed sensor
34 Cooling fan relay
35 Cooling fan motor
36 Ignition coil
37 Suppressor
38 Canister purge valve
39 Fuel pump
40 Idle air control valve
41 Fuel injector
42 Fenix 5.1 control unit
43 Spark plug

Immobiliser

Warning lights and gauges

Diagnostic connector

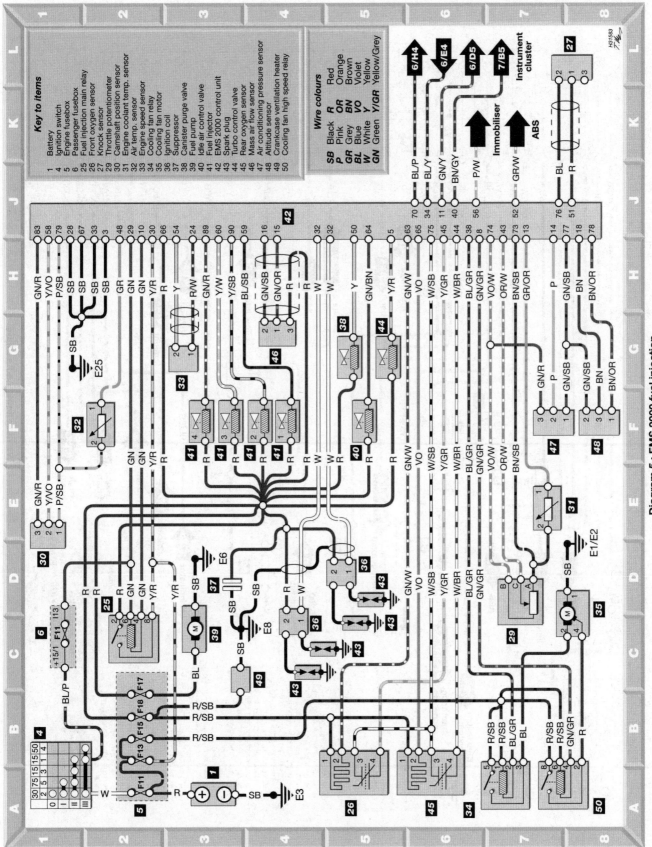

**Key to items**

1 Battery
4 Ignition switch
5 Engine fusebox
6 Passenger fusebox
25 Fuel injection main relay
26 Front oxygen sensor
27 Knock sensor
29 Throttle potentiometer
30 Camshaft position sensor
31 Engine coolant temp. sensor
32 Air temp. sensor
33 Engine speed sensor
34 Cooling fan relay
35 Cooling fan motor
36 Ignition coil
37 Suppressor
38 Canister purge valve
39 Fuel pump
40 Idle air control valve
41 Fuel injector
42 EMS 2000 control unit
43 Spark plug
44 Turbo control valve
45 Rear oxygen sensor
46 Mass air flow sensor
47 Air conditioning pressure sensor
48 Altitude sensor
49 Crankcase ventilation heater
50 Cooling fan high speed relay

**Wire colours**

| SB | Black | R | Red |
|----|-------|-----|--------|
| P | Pink | OR | Orange |
| GR | Grey | BN | Brown |
| BL | Blue | VO | Violet |
| W | White | Y | Yellow |
| GN | Green | Y/GR | Yellow/Grey |

Instrument cluster

Immobiliser

ABS

Diagram 5 : EMS 2000 fuel injection

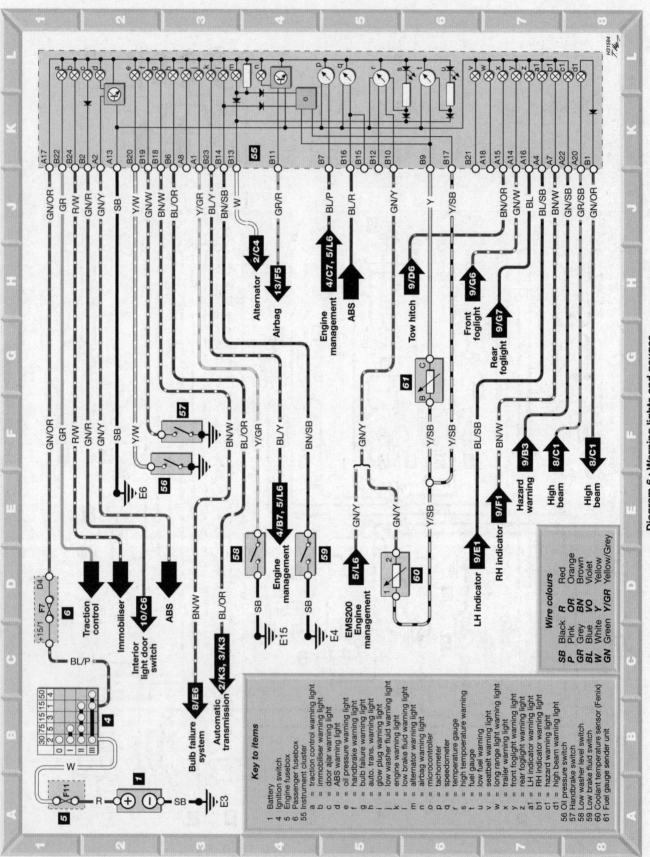

Diagram 6 : Warning lights and gauges

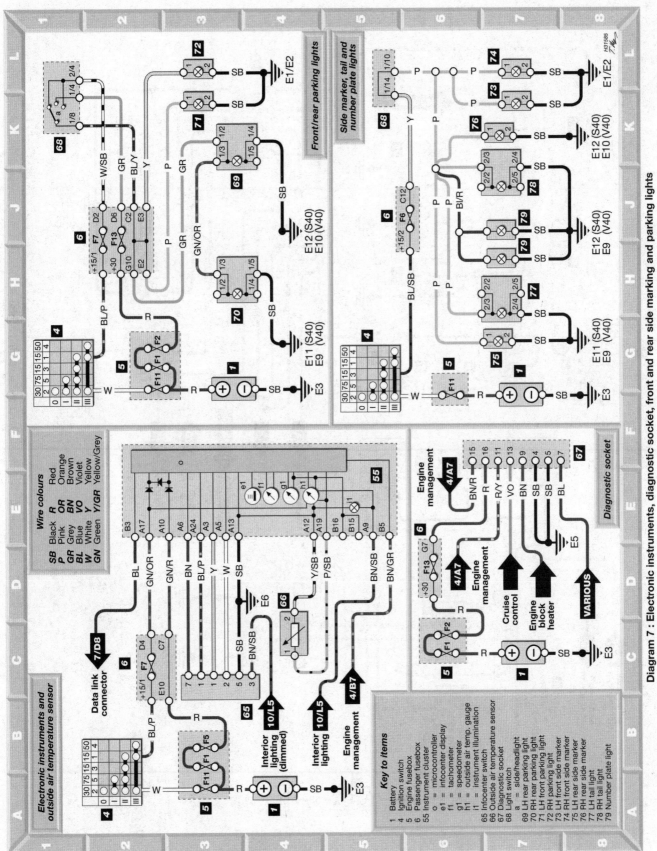

**Front/rear parking lights**

**Side marker, tail and number plate lights**

**Electronic instruments and outside air temperature sensor**

**Wire colours**

| | | | |
|---|---|---|---|
| *SB* | Black | *R* | Red |
| *P* | Pink | *OR* | Orange |
| *GR* | Grey | *BN* | Brown |
| *BL* | Blue | *VO* | Violet |
| *W* | White | *Y* | Yellow |
| *GN* | Green | *Y/GR* | Yellow/Grey |

**Data link connector**

**Interior lighting (dimmed)**

**Interior lighting**

**Engine management**

**Engine management**

**Cruise control**

**Engine block heater**

**VARIOUS**

**Diagnostic socket**

**Key to items**

1 Battery
2 Ignition switch
5 Engine fusebox
6 Passenger fusebox
55 Instrument cluster
  o = microcontroller
  e1 = infocenter display
  f1 = tachometer
  g1 = speedometer
  h1 = outside air temp. gauge
  i1 = instrument illumination
65 Infocenter switch
66 Outside air temperature sensor
67 Diagnostic socket
68 Light switch
  a = side/headlight
69 LH rear parking light
70 RH rear parking light
71 LH front parking light
72 RH front parking light
73 LH front side marker
74 RH front side marker
75 LH rear side marker
76 RH rear side marker
77 LH tail light
78 RH tail light
79 Number plate light

**Diagram 7 : Electronic instruments, diagnostic socket, front and rear side marking and parking lights**

H91585

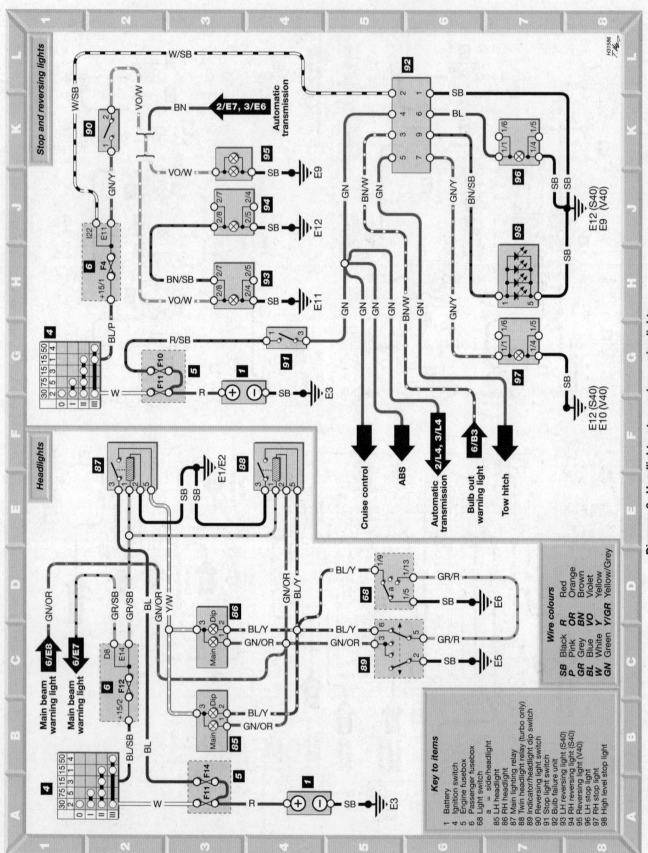

Diagram 8 : Headlights, stop and reversing lights

**Stop and reversing lights**

**Headlights**

**Main beam warning light** 6/E8

**Main beam warning light** 6/E7

**Automatic transmission** 2/E7, 3/E6

**Cruise control**

**ABS**

**Automatic transmission** 2/L4, 3/L4

**Bulb out warning light** 6/B3

**Tow hitch**

E12 (S40)
E9 (V40)

E12 (S40)
E10 (V40)

**Wire colours**

| | | | | |
|---|---|---|---|---|
| **SB** | Black | **R** | Red | |
| **P** | Pink | **OR** | Orange | |
| **GR** | Grey | **BN** | Brown | |
| **BL** | Blue | **VO** | Violet | |
| **W** | White | **Y** | Yellow | |
| **GN** | Green | **Y/GR** | Yellow/Grey | |

**Key to items**

1 Battery
4 Ignition switch
5 Engine fusebox
6 Passenger fusebox
68 Light switch
  a = side/headlight
85 LH headlight
86 RH headlight
87 Main lighting relay
88 Twin headlight relay (turbo only)
89 Indicator/headlight dip switch
90 Stop light switch
91 Stop light switch
92 Bulb failure unit
93 LH reversing light (S40)
94 RH reversing light (S40)
95 Reversing light (V40)
96 LH stop light
97 RH stop light
98 High level stop light

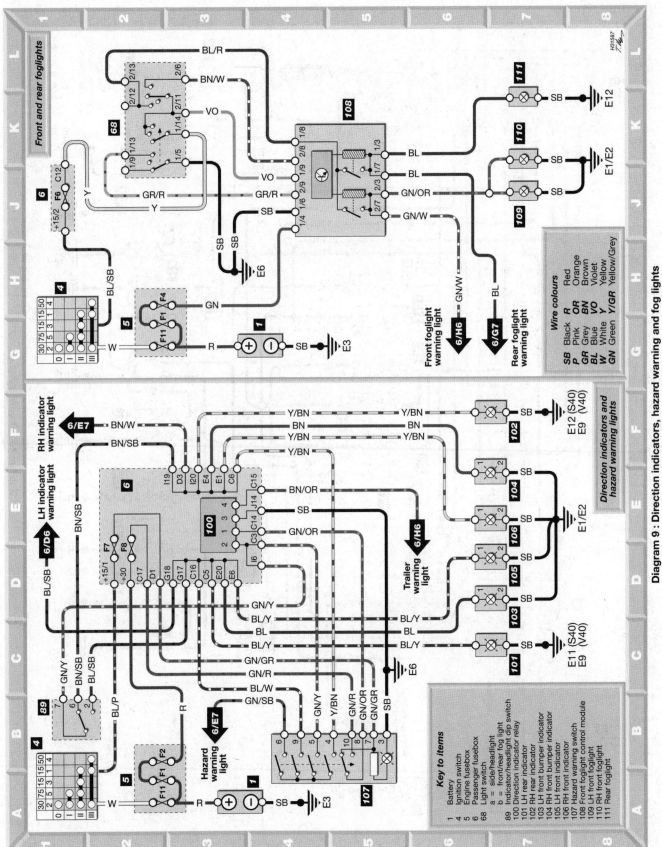

Diagram 9 : Direction indicators, hazard warning and fog lights

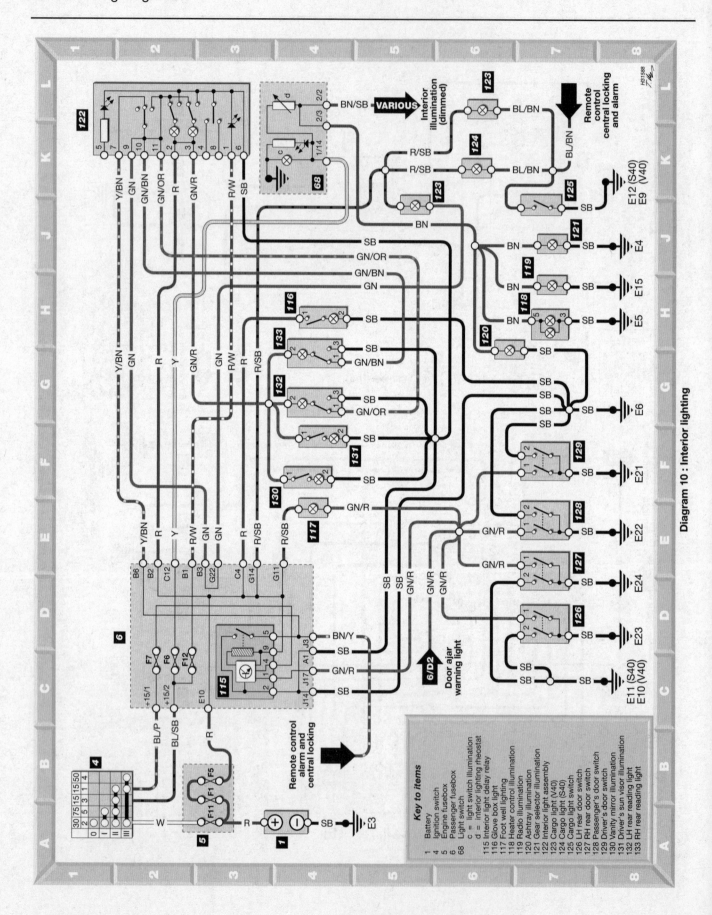

Diagram 10 : Interior lighting

**Key to items**

1   Battery
4   Ignition switch
5   Engine fusebox
6   Passenger fusebox
68  Light switch
    c = light switch illumination
    d = interior lighting rheostat
115 Interior light delay relay
116 Glove box light
117 Foot well lighting
118 Heater control illumination
119 Radio illumination
120 Ashtray illumination
121 Gear selector illumination
122 Interior light assembly
123 Cargo light (V40)
124 Cargo light (S40)
125 Cargo light switch
126 LH rear door switch
127 RH rear door switch
128 Passenger's door switch
129 Driver's door switch
130 Vanity mirror illumination
131 Driver's sun visor illumination
132 LH rear reading light
133 RH rear reading light

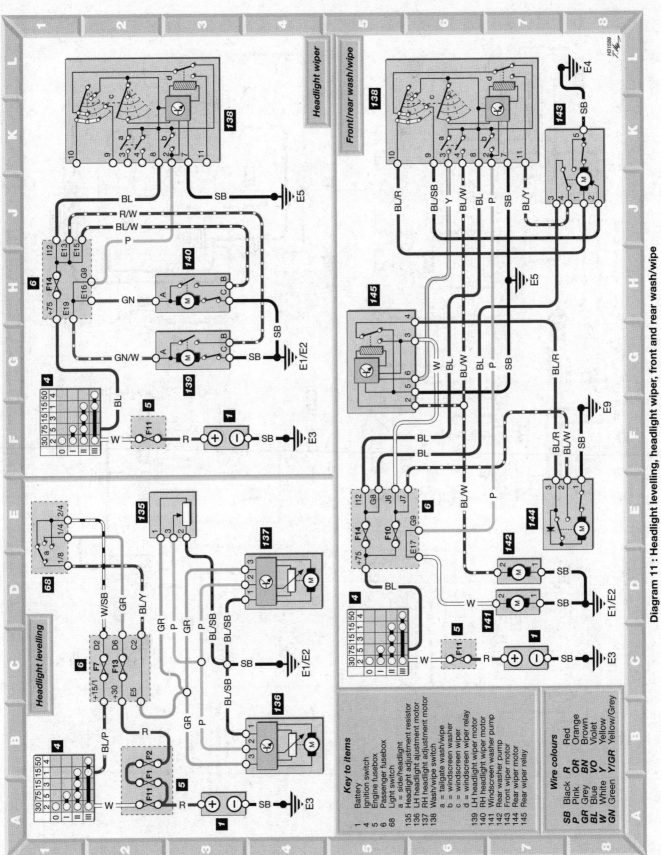

Diagram 11 : Headlight levelling, headlight wiper, front and rear wash/wipe

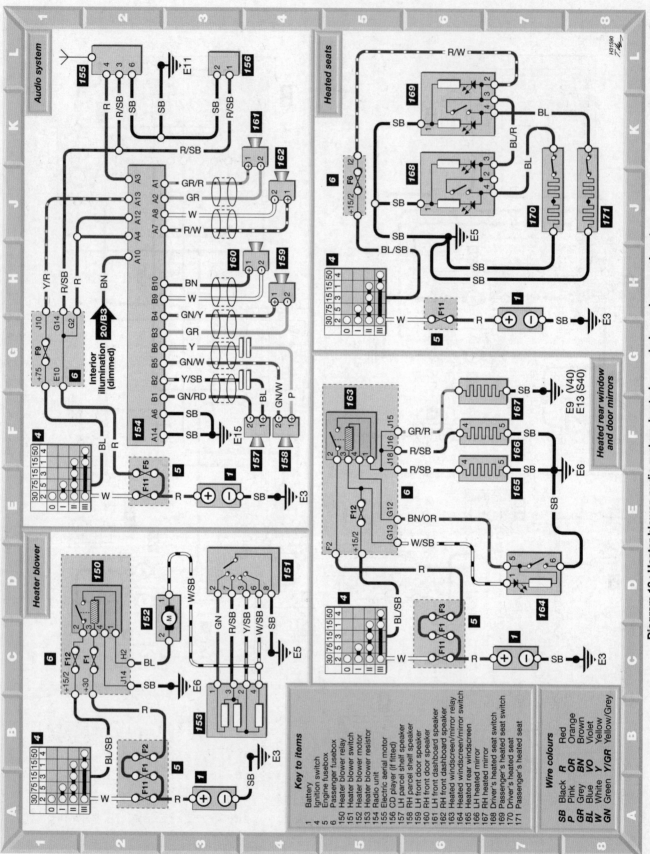

**Diagram 12 : Heater blower, audio system, heated rear window, mirrors and seats**

**Key to items**

1 Battery
4 Ignition switch
5 Engine fusebox
6 Passenger fusebox
150 Heater blower relay
151 Heater blower switch
152 Heater blower motor
153 Heater blower resistor
154 Radio unit
155 Electric aerial motor
156 CD player (if fitted)
157 LH parcel shelf speaker
158 RH parcel shelf speaker
159 LH front door speaker
160 RH front door speaker
161 LH front dashboard speaker
162 RH front dashboard speaker
163 Heated windscreen/mirror relay
164 Heated windscreen/mirror switch
165 Heated rear windscreen
166 LH heated mirror
167 RH heated mirror
168 Driver's heated seat switch
169 Passenger's heated seat switch
170 Driver's heated seat
171 Passenger's heated seat

**Wire colours**

| | | | |
|---|---|---|---|
| **SB** | Black | **R** | Red |
| **P** | Pink | **OR** | Orange |
| **GR** | Grey | **BN** | Brown |
| **BL** | Blue | **VO** | Violet |
| **W** | White | **Y** | Yellow |
| **GN** | Green | **Y/GR** | Yellow/Grey |

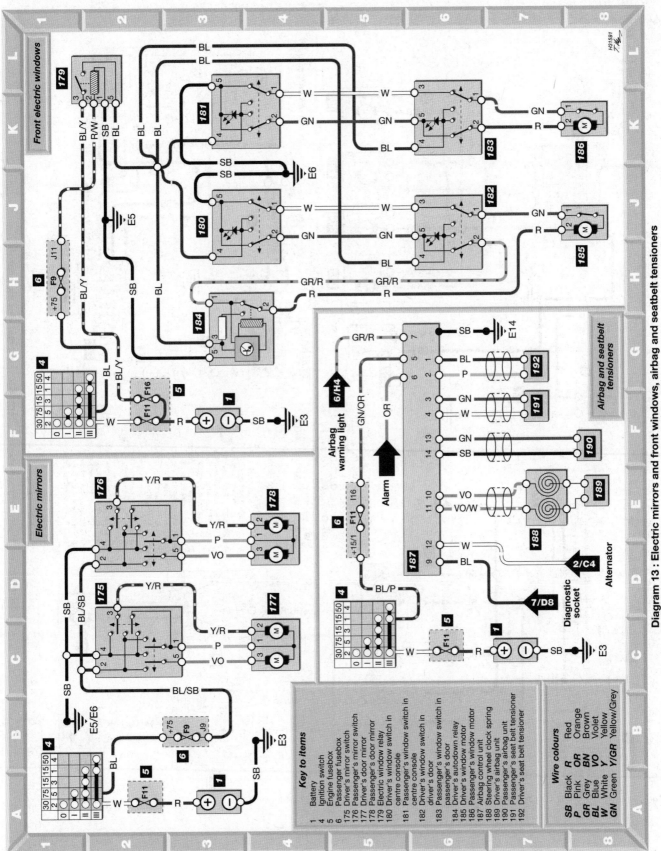

**Front electric windows**

**Electric mirrors**

**Airbag and seatbelt tensioners**

**Alternator**

**Diagnostic socket**

Airbag warning light

Alarm

**Key to items**

| | |
|---|---|
| 1 | Battery |
| 4 | Ignition switch |
| 5 | Engine fusebox |
| 6 | Passenger fusebox |
| 175 | Driver's mirror switch |
| 176 | Passenger's mirror switch |
| 177 | Driver's door mirror |
| 178 | Passenger's door mirror |
| 179 | Electric window relay |
| 180 | Driver's window switch in centre console |
| 181 | Passenger's window switch in centre console |
| 182 | Driver's window switch in driver's door |
| 183 | Passenger's window switch in passenger's door |
| 184 | Driver's autodown relay |
| 185 | Passenger's window motor |
| 186 | Driver's window motor |
| 187 | Airbag control unit |
| 188 | Steering wheel clock spring |
| 189 | Driver's airbag unit |
| 190 | Passenger's airbag unit |
| 191 | Passenger's seat belt tensioner |
| 192 | Driver's seat belt tensioner |

**Wire colours**

| | | | |
|---|---|---|---|
| SB | Black | R | Red |
| P | Pink | OR | Orange |
| GR | Grey | BN | Brown |
| BL | Blue | VO | Violet |
| W | White | Y | Yellow |
| GN | Green | Y/GR | Yellow/Grey |

**Diagram 13 : Electric mirrors and front windows, airbag and seatbelt tensioners**

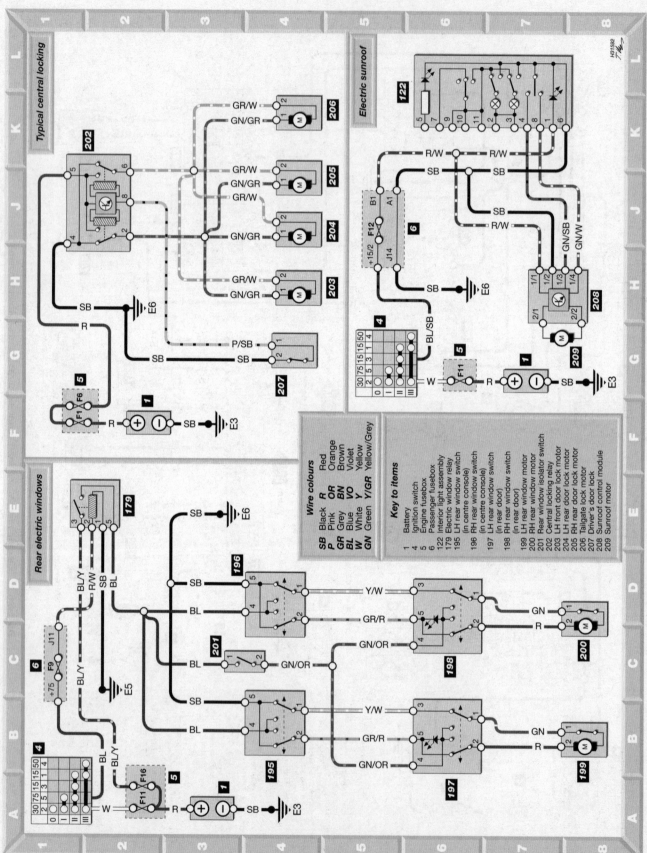

Diagram 14 : Rear electric windows, central locking and electric sunroof

**Wire colours**

| | |
|---|---|
| **SB** | Black |
| **P** | Pink |
| **GR** | Grey |
| **BL** | Blue |
| **W** | White |
| **GN** | Green |
| **R** | Red |
| **OR** | Orange |
| **BN** | Brown |
| **VO** | Violet |
| **Y** | Yellow |
| **Y/GR** | Yellow/Grey |

**Key to items**

1 Battery
4 Ignition switch
5 Engine fusebox
6 Passenger fusebox
122 Electric window relay
179 Interior light assembly
195 LH rear window switch (in centre console)
196 RH rear window switch (in centre console)
197 LH rear window switch (in rear door)
198 RH rear window switch (in rear door)
199 LH rear window motor
200 RH rear window motor
201 Rear window isolator switch
202 Central locking relay
203 LH front door lock motor
204 LH rear door lock motor
205 RH rear door lock motor
206 Tailgate lock motor
207 Driver's door lock
208 Sunroof control module
209 Sunroof motor

# Dimensions and weights

**Note:** *All figures are approximate, and may vary according to model. Refer to manufacturer's data for exact figures.*

## Dimensions

Overall length:
   Up to May 2000 . . . . . . . . . . . . . . . . . . . . . . . . . . . . . 4483 mm
   May 2000 onwards . . . . . . . . . . . . . . . . . . . . . . . . . . . 4516 mm
Overall width (including mirrors) . . . . . . . . . . . . . . . . . . . . . 1717 mm (1897 mm)
Overall height:
   Up to May 2000 . . . . . . . . . . . . . . . . . . . . . . . . . . . . . 1411 mm
   May 2000 onwards:
      S40 . . . . . . . . . . . . . . . . . . . . . . . . . . . . . . . . . . . . 1422 mm
      V40 . . . . . . . . . . . . . . . . . . . . . . . . . . . . . . . . . . . . 1425 mm
Wheelbase:
   Up to May 2000 . . . . . . . . . . . . . . . . . . . . . . . . . . . . . 2550 mm
   May 2000 onwards . . . . . . . . . . . . . . . . . . . . . . . . . . . 2562 mm

## Weights

Kerb weight (typical) . . . . . . . . . . . . . . . . . . . . . . . . . . . . . . 1250 kg
Maximum gross vehicle weight (typical) . . . . . . . . . . . . . . . . 1720 kg
Maximum roof rack load . . . . . . . . . . . . . . . . . . . . . . . . . . . 100 kg
Maximum trailer weight:
   Unbraked . . . . . . . . . . . . . . . . . . . . . . . . . . . . . . . . . . 645 kg
   Braked:
      1.6 litre models . . . . . . . . . . . . . . . . . . . . . . . . . . . . 1000 kg
      1.8 litre models . . . . . . . . . . . . . . . . . . . . . . . . . . . . 1200 kg
      1.9 and 2.0 litre models . . . . . . . . . . . . . . . . . . . . . . 1400 kg

# Conversion factors

## Length (distance)

| | | | | | |
|---|---|---|---|---|---|
| Inches (in) | x 25.4 | = Millimetres (mm) | x 0.0394 | = | Inches (in) |
| Feet (ft) | x 0.305 | = Metres (m) | x 3.281 | = | Feet (ft) |
| Miles | x 1.609 | = Kilometres (km) | x 0.621 | = | Miles |

## Volume (capacity)

| | | | | | |
|---|---|---|---|---|---|
| Cubic inches (cu in; in³) | x 16.387 | = Cubic centimetres (cc; cm³) | x 0.061 | = | Cubic inches (cu in; in³) |
| Imperial pints (Imp pt) | x 0.568 | = Litres (l) | x 1.76 | = | Imperial pints (Imp pt) |
| Imperial quarts (Imp qt) | x 1.137 | = Litres (l) | x 0.88 | = | Imperial quarts (Imp qt) |
| Imperial quarts (Imp qt) | x 1.201 | = US quarts (US qt) | x 0.833 | = | Imperial quarts (Imp qt) |
| US quarts (US qt) | x 0.946 | = Litres (l) | x 1.057 | = | US quarts (US qt) |
| Imperial gallons (Imp gal) | x 4.546 | = Litres (l) | x 0.22 | = | Imperial gallons (Imp gal) |
| Imperial gallons (Imp gal) | x 1.201 | = US gallons (US gal) | x 0.833 | = | Imperial gallons (Imp gal) |
| US gallons (US gal) | x 3.785 | = Litres (l) | x 0.264 | = | US gallons (US gal) |

## Mass (weight)

| | | | | | |
|---|---|---|---|---|---|
| Ounces (oz) | x 28.35 | = Grams (g) | x 0.035 | = | Ounces (oz) |
| Pounds (lb) | x 0.454 | = Kilograms (kg) | x 2.205 | = | Pounds (lb) |

## Force

| | | | | | |
|---|---|---|---|---|---|
| Ounces-force (ozf; oz) | x 0.278 | = Newtons (N) | x 3.6 | = | Ounces-force (ozf; oz) |
| Pounds-force (lbf; lb) | x 4.448 | = Newtons (N) | x 0.225 | = | Pounds-force (lbf; lb) |
| Newtons (N) | x 0.1 | = Kilograms-force (kgf; kg) | x 9.81 | = | Newtons (N) |

## Pressure

| | | | | | |
|---|---|---|---|---|---|
| Pounds-force per square inch (psi; lbf/in²; lb/in²) | x 0.070 | = Kilograms-force per square centimetre (kgf/cm²; kg/cm²) | x 14.223 | = | Pounds-force per square inch (psi; lbf/in²; lb/in²) |
| Pounds-force per square inch (psi; lbf/in²; lb/in²) | x 0.068 | = Atmospheres (atm) | x 14.696 | = | Pounds-force per square inch (psi; lbf/in²; lb/in²) |
| Pounds-force per square inch (psi; lbf/in²; lb/in²) | x 0.069 | = Bars | x 14.5 | = | Pounds-force per square inch (psi; lbf/in²; lb/in²) |
| Pounds-force per square inch (psi; lbf/in²; lb/in²) | x 6.895 | = Kilopascals (kPa) | x 0.145 | = | Pounds-force per square inch (psi; lbf/in²; lb/in²) |
| Kilopascals (kPa) | x 0.01 | = Kilograms-force per square centimetre (kgf/cm²; kg/cm²) | x 98.1 | = | Kilopascals (kPa) |
| Millibar (mbar) | x 100 | = Pascals (Pa) | x 0.01 | = | Millibar (mbar) |
| Millibar (mbar) | x 0.0145 | = Pounds-force per square inch (psi; lbf/in²; lb/in²) | x 68.947 | = | Millibar (mbar) |
| Millibar (mbar) | x 0.75 | = Millimetres of mercury (mmHg) | x 1.333 | = | Millibar (mbar) |
| Millibar (mbar) | x 0.401 | = Inches of water (inH₂O) | x 2.491 | = | Millibar (mbar) |
| Millimetres of mercury (mmHg) | x 0.535 | = Inches of water (inH₂O) | x 1.868 | = | Millimetres of mercury (mmHg) |
| Inches of water (inH₂O) | x 0.036 | = Pounds-force per square inch (psi; lbf/in²; lb/in²) | x 27.68 | = | Inches of water (inH₂O) |

## Torque (moment of force)

| | | | | | |
|---|---|---|---|---|---|
| Pounds-force inches (lbf in; lb in) | x 1.152 | = Kilograms-force centimetre (kgf cm; kg cm) | x 0.868 | = | Pounds-force inches (lbf in; lb in) |
| Pounds-force inches (lbf in; lb in) | x 0.113 | = Newton metres (Nm) | x 8.85 | = | Pounds-force inches (lbf in; lb in) |
| Pounds-force inches (lbf in; lb in) | x 0.083 | = Pounds-force feet (lbf ft; lb ft) | x 12 | = | Pounds-force inches (lbf in; lb in) |
| Pounds-force feet (lbf ft; lb ft) | x 0.138 | = Kilograms-force metres (kgf m; kg m) | x 7.233 | = | Pounds-force feet (lbf ft; lb ft) |
| Pounds-force feet (lbf ft; lb ft) | x 1.356 | = Newton metres (Nm) | x 0.738 | = | Pounds-force feet (lbf ft; lb ft) |
| Newton metres (Nm) | x 0.102 | = Kilograms-force metres (kgf m; kg m) | x 9.804 | = | Newton metres (Nm) |

## Power

| | | | | | |
|---|---|---|---|---|---|
| Horsepower (hp) | x 745.7 | = Watts (W) | x 0.0013 | = | Horsepower (hp) |

## Velocity (speed)

| | | | | | |
|---|---|---|---|---|---|
| Miles per hour (miles/hr; mph) | x 1.609 | = Kilometres per hour (km/hr; kph) | x 0.621 | = | Miles per hour (miles/hr; mph) |

## Fuel consumption*

| | | | | | |
|---|---|---|---|---|---|
| Miles per gallon, Imperial (mpg) | x 0.354 | = Kilometres per litre (km/l) | x 2.825 | = | Miles per gallon, Imperial (mpg) |
| Miles per gallon, US (mpg) | x 0.425 | = Kilometres per litre (km/l) | x 2.352 | = | Miles per gallon, US (mpg) |

## Temperature

Degrees Fahrenheit = (°C x 1.8) + 32          Degrees Celsius (Degrees Centigrade; °C) = (°F - 32) x 0.56

*It is common practice to convert from miles per gallon (mpg) to litres/100 kilometres (l/100km), where mpg x l/100 km = 282*

Spare parts are available from many sources, including maker's appointed garages, accessory shops, and motor factors. To be sure of obtaining the correct parts, it may sometimes be necessary to quote the vehicle identification number. If possible, it can also be useful to take the old parts along for positive identification. Items such as starter motors and alternators may be available under a service exchange scheme – any parts returned should always be clean.

Our advice regarding spare part sources is as follows:

## Officially-appointed garages

This is the best source of parts which are peculiar to your car, and are not otherwise generally available (eg badges, interior trim, certain body panels, etc). It is also the only place at which you should buy parts if the vehicle is still under warranty.

## Accessory shops

These are very good places to buy materials and components needed for the maintenance of your car (oil, air and fuel filters, spark plugs, light bulbs, drivebelts, oils and greases, brake pads, touch-up paint, etc). Parts like this sold by a reputable shop are of the same standard as those used by the car manufacturer.

## Motor factors

Good factors will stock all the more important components which wear out comparatively quickly, and can sometimes supply individual components needed for the overhaul of a larger assembly. They may also handle work such as cylinder block reboring, crankshaft regrinding and balancing, etc.

## Tyre and exhaust specialists

These outlets may be independent or members of a local or national chain. They frequently offer competitive prices when compared with a main dealer or local garage, but it will pay to obtain several quotes before making a decision. Also ask what 'extras' may be added to the quote – for instance, fitting a new valve and balancing the wheel are both often charged on top of the price of a new tyre.

## Other sources

Beware of parts of materials obtained from market stalls, car boot sales or similar outlets. Such items are not invariably sub-standard, but there is little chance of compensation if they do prove unsatisfactory. In the case of safety-critical components such as brake pads there is the risk not only of financial loss but also of an accident causing injury or death.

Second-hand components or assemblies obtained from a car breaker can be a good buy in some circumstances, but this sort of purchase is best made by the experienced DIY mechanic.

# Vehicle identification numbers

Modifications are a continuing and unpublicised process in vehicle manufacture, quite apart from major model changes. Spare parts manuals and lists are compiled upon a numerical basis, the individual vehicle identification numbers being essential to correct identification of the component concerned.

When ordering spare parts, always give as much information as possible. Quote the vehicle type and year, vehicle identification number (VIN), and engine number, as appropriate.

The *vehicle identification number* (VIN) is riveted to the centre of the engine compartment bulkhead, and is visible with the bonnet open. The vehicle identification (chassis) number is also stamped onto the bulkhead, next to the VIN plate, and on a plate attached to the driver's end of the facia, which is visible through the windscreen **(see illustration)**. Throughout the manual, it is sometimes necessary to identify the model year of the car, which can be done using the tenth digit of the vehicle identification number, as follows:

| VIN 10th letter | Model year |
| --- | --- |
| T | 1996 |
| V | 1997 |
| W | 1998 |
| X | 1999 |
| Y | 2000 |
| Z | 2001 |
| A | 2002 |
| B | 2003 |
| C | 2004 |

The *engine code, engine number* and manufacturing number can be found on the sticker attached to the top of the timing belt cover **(see illustration)**. The engine number is also stamped on the front of the cylinder block, at the transmission end.

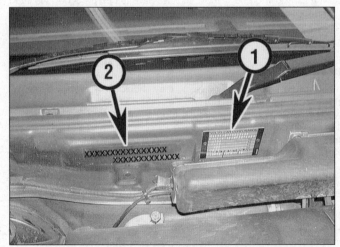

The VIN plate (1) is riveted to the engine compartment bulkhead, and the VIN (chassis) number (2) is also stamped next to it

The sticker attached to the timing belt cover has the engine code, engine number and manufacturing numbers on it

Whenever servicing, repair or overhaul work is carried out on the car or its components, observe the following procedures and instructions. This will assist in carrying out the operation efficiently and to a professional standard of workmanship.

### Joint mating faces and gaskets

When separating components at their mating faces, never insert screwdrivers or similar implements into the joint between the faces in order to prise them apart. This can cause severe damage which results in oil leaks, coolant leaks, etc upon reassembly. Separation is usually achieved by tapping along the joint with a soft-faced hammer in order to break the seal. However, note that this method may not be suitable where dowels are used for component location.

Where a gasket is used between the mating faces of two components, a new one must be fitted on reassembly; fit it dry unless otherwise stated in the repair procedure. Make sure that the mating faces are clean and dry, with all traces of old gasket removed. When cleaning a joint face, use a tool which is unlikely to score or damage the face, and remove any burrs or nicks with an oilstone or fine file.

Make sure that tapped holes are cleaned with a pipe cleaner, and keep them free of jointing compound, if this is being used, unless specifically instructed otherwise.

Ensure that all orifices, channels or pipes are clear, and blow through them, preferably using compressed air.

### Oil seals

Oil seals can be removed by levering them out with a wide flat-bladed screwdriver or similar implement. Alternatively, a number of self-tapping screws may be screwed into the seal, and these used as a purchase for pliers or some similar device in order to pull the seal free.

Whenever an oil seal is removed from its working location, either individually or as part of an assembly, it should be renewed.

The very fine sealing lip of the seal is easily damaged, and will not seal if the surface it contacts is not completely clean and free from scratches, nicks or grooves. If the original sealing surface of the component cannot be restored, and the manufacturer has not made provision for slight relocation of the seal relative to the sealing surface, the component should be renewed.

Protect the lips of the seal from any surface which may damage them in the course of fitting. Use tape or a conical sleeve where possible. Lubricate the seal lips with oil before fitting and, on dual-lipped seals, fill the space between the lips with grease.

Unless otherwise stated, oil seals must be fitted with their sealing lips toward the lubricant to be sealed.

Use a tubular drift or block of wood of the appropriate size to install the seal and, if the seal housing is shouldered, drive the seal down to the shoulder. If the seal housing is unshouldered, the seal should be fitted with its face flush with the housing top face (unless otherwise instructed).

### Screw threads and fastenings

Seized nuts, bolts and screws are quite a common occurrence where corrosion has set in, and the use of penetrating oil or releasing fluid will often overcome this problem if the offending item is soaked for a while before attempting to release it. The use of an impact driver may also provide a means of releasing such stubborn fastening devices, when used in conjunction with the appropriate screwdriver bit or socket. If none of these methods works, it may be necessary to resort to the careful application of heat, or the use of a hacksaw or nut splitter device.

Studs are usually removed by locking two nuts together on the threaded part, and then using a spanner on the lower nut to unscrew the stud. Studs or bolts which have broken off below the surface of the component in which they are mounted can sometimes be removed using a stud extractor. Always ensure that a blind tapped hole is completely free from oil, grease, water or other fluid before installing the bolt or stud. Failure to do this could cause the housing to crack due to the hydraulic action of the bolt or stud as it is screwed in.

When tightening a castellated nut to accept a split pin, tighten the nut to the specified torque, where applicable, and then tighten further to the next split pin hole. Never slacken the nut to align the split pin hole, unless stated in the repair procedure.

When checking or retightening a nut or bolt to a specified torque setting, slacken the nut or bolt by a quarter of a turn, and then retighten to the specified setting. However, this should not be attempted where angular tightening has been used.

For some screw fastenings, notably cylinder head bolts or nuts, torque wrench settings are no longer specified for the latter stages of tightening, "angle-tightening" being called up instead. Typically, a fairly low torque wrench setting will be applied to the bolts/nuts in the correct sequence, followed by one or more stages of tightening through specified angles.

### Locknuts, locktabs and washers

Any fastening which will rotate against a component or housing during tightening should always have a washer between it and the relevant component or housing.

Spring or split washers should always be renewed when they are used to lock a critical component such as a big-end bearing retaining bolt or nut. Locktabs which are folded over to retain a nut or bolt should always be renewed.

Self-locking nuts can be re-used in non-critical areas, providing resistance can be felt when the locking portion passes over the bolt or stud thread. However, it should be noted that self-locking stiffnuts tend to lose their effectiveness after long periods of use, and should then be renewed as a matter of course.

Split pins must always be replaced with new ones of the correct size for the hole.

When thread-locking compound is found on the threads of a fastener which is to be re-used, it should be cleaned off with a wire brush and solvent, and fresh compound applied on reassembly.

### Special tools

Some repair procedures in this manual entail the use of special tools such as a press, two or three-legged pullers, spring compressors, etc. Wherever possible, suitable readily-available alternatives to the manufacturer's special tools are described, and are shown in use. In some instances, where no alternative is possible, it has been necessary to resort to the use of a manufacturer's tool, and this has been done for reasons of safety as well as the efficient completion of the repair operation. Unless you are highly-skilled and have a thorough understanding of the procedures described, never attempt to bypass the use of any special tool when the procedure described specifies its use. Not only is there a very great risk of personal injury, but expensive damage could be caused to the components involved.

### Environmental considerations

When disposing of used engine oil, brake fluid, antifreeze, etc, give due consideration to any detrimental environmental effects. Do not, for instance, pour any of the above liquids down drains into the general sewage system, or onto the ground to soak away. Many local council refuse tips provide a facility for waste oil disposal, as do some garages. If none of these facilities are available, consult your local Environmental Health Department, or the National Rivers Authority, for further advice.

With the universal tightening-up of legislation regarding the emission of environmentally-harmful substances from motor vehicles, most vehicles have tamperproof devices fitted to the main adjustment points of the fuel system. These devices are primarily designed to prevent unqualified persons from adjusting the fuel/air mixture, with the chance of a consequent increase in toxic emissions. If such devices are found during servicing or overhaul, they should, wherever possible, be renewed or refitted in accordance with the manufacturer's requirements or current legislation.

**Note: It is antisocial and illegal to dump oil down the drain. To find the location of your local oil recycling bank, call this number free.**

The jack supplied with the vehicle tool kit should **only** be used for changing the roadwheels in an emergency – see *Wheel changing* at the front of this book. When carrying out any other kind of work, raise the vehicle using a heavy-duty hydraulic (or 'trolley') jack, and always supplement the jack with axle stands positioned under the vehicle jacking points. If the roadwheels do not have to be removed, consider using wheel ramps – if wished, these can be placed under the wheels once the vehicle has been raised using a hydraulic jack, and the vehicle lowered onto the ramps so that it is resting on its wheels.

Only ever jack the vehicle up on a solid, level surface. If there is even a slight slope, take great care that the vehicle cannot move as the wheels are lifted off the ground. Jacking up on an uneven or gravelled surface is not recommended, as the weight of the vehicle will not be evenly distributed, and the jack may slip as the vehicle is raised.

As far as possible, do not leave the vehicle unattended once it has been raised, particularly if children are playing nearby.

Before jacking up the front of the car, ensure that the handbrake is firmly applied. When jacking up the rear of the car, place wooden chocks in front of the front wheels, and engage first gear (or P).

To raise the front of the car, place the jack head underneath the braced underbody section behind the lower arm rear mounting. To raise the rear of the car, the jack head should be positioned under the outer end of the lower suspension arm, directly beneath the strut lower mounting. Always use a flat piece of wood on the jack head, to prevent damage.

When the car's been raised to the required height, support it on an axle stand placed under one of the vehicle jack location points on the sill. To protect the sill edge, use a block of wood with a slot cut in it, on the head of the axle stand.

The jack supplied with the car should be located under the lifting points provided at the front and rear of the sills. The lifting points are marked by two notches on the sill edge – models with plastic sill covers will have an arrow marking to indicate the jacking points. Ensure the jack head is correctly located on the sill edge before trying to raise the car.

**Never** work under, around, or near a raised vehicle, unless it is adequately supported on stands. Do not rely on a jack alone, as even a hydraulic jack could fail under load. Makeshift methods should not be used to lift and support the car during servicing work.

# Disconnecting the battery

Several systems fitted to the car require battery power to be available at all times (permanent live), either to ensure their continued operation (such as the clock) or to maintain control unit memories (such as that in the engine management system's ECU) which would be wiped if the battery were to be disconnected. Whenever the battery is to be disconnected therefore, first note the following, to ensure that there are no unforeseen consequences of this action:

a) *First, on any car with central locking, it is a wise precaution to remove the key from the ignition, and to keep it with you, so that it does not get locked in if the central locking should engage accidentally when the battery is reconnected!*

b) *The engine management system's ECU will lose the information stored in its memory when the battery is disconnected. This includes idling and operating values, and any fault codes detected – in the case of the fault codes, if it is thought likely that the system has developed a fault for which the corresponding code has been logged, the car must be taken to a Volvo dealer for the codes to be read, using the special diagnostic equipment necessary for this (see Chapter 4A or 4B). Whenever the battery is disconnected, the information relating to idle speed control and other operating values will have to be re-programmed into the unit's memory. The ECU does this by itself, but until then, there may be surging, hesitation, erratic idle and a generally inferior level of performance. To allow the ECU to relearn these values, start the engine and run it as close to idle speed as possible until it reaches its normal operating temperature, then run it for approximately two minutes at 1200 rpm. Next, drive the car as far as necessary – approximately 5 miles of varied driving conditions is usually sufficient – to complete the relearning process.*

c) *If the battery is disconnected while the alarm system is armed or activated, the alarm will remain in the same state when the battery is reconnected. The same applies to the engine immobiliser system (where fitted).*

d) *If a trip computer is in use, any information stored in memory will be lost.*

e) *If a Volvo audio unit is fitted, and the unit and/or the battery is disconnected, the unit will not function again on reconnection until the correct security code is entered. Details of this procedure, which varies according to the unit and model year, are given in the car's handbook. Ensure you have the correct code before you disconnect the battery. For obvious security reasons, the procedure is not given in this manual. If you do not have the code or details of the correct procedure, but can supply proof of ownership and a legitimate reason for wanting this information, the car's selling dealer may be able to help.*

Devices known as 'memory-savers' (or 'code-savers') can be used to avoid some of the above problems. Precise details vary according to the device used. Typically, it is plugged into the cigarette lighter, and is connected by its own wires to a spare battery; the car's own battery is then disconnected from the electrical system, leaving the 'memory-saver' to pass sufficient current to maintain audio unit security codes and ECU memory values, and also to run permanently-live circuits such as the clock, all the while isolating the battery in the event of a short-circuit occurring while work is carried out.

⚠ ***Warning: Some of these devices allow a considerable amount of current to pass, which can mean that many of the car's systems are still operational when the main battery is disconnected. If a 'memory-saver' is used, ensure that the circuit concerned is actually 'dead' before carrying out any work on it!***

## Introduction

A selection of good tools is a fundamental requirement for anyone contemplating the maintenance and repair of a motor vehicle. For the owner who does not possess any, their purchase will prove a considerable expense, offsetting some of the savings made by doing-it-yourself. However, provided that the tools purchased meet the relevant national safety standards and are of good quality, they will last for many years and prove an extremely worthwhile investment.

To help the average owner to decide which tools are needed to carry out the various tasks detailed in this manual, we have compiled three lists of tools under the following headings: *Maintenance and minor repair, Repair and overhaul*, and *Special*. Newcomers to practical mechanics should start off with the *Maintenance and minor repair* tool kit, and confine themselves to the simpler jobs around the vehicle. Then, as confidence and experience grow, more difficult tasks can be undertaken, with extra tools being purchased as, and when, they are needed. In this way, a *Maintenance and minor repair* tool kit can be built up into a *Repair and overhaul* tool kit over a considerable period of time, without any major cash outlays. The experienced do-it-yourselfer will have a tool kit good enough for most repair and overhaul procedures, and will add tools from the *Special* category when it is felt that the expense is justified by the amount of use to which these tools will be put.

## Maintenance and minor repair tool kit

The tools given in this list should be considered as a minimum requirement if routine maintenance, servicing and minor repair operations are to be undertaken. We recommend the purchase of combination spanners (ring one end, open-ended the other); although more expensive than open-ended ones, they do give the advantages of both types of spanner.

☐ *Combination spanners:*
  *Metric - 8 to 19 mm inclusive*
☐ *Adjustable spanner - 35 mm jaw (approx.)*
☐ *Spark plug spanner (with rubber insert) - petrol models*
☐ *Spark plug gap adjustment tool - petrol models*
☐ *Set of feeler gauges*
☐ *Brake bleed nipple spanner*
☐ *Screwdrivers:*
  *Flat blade - 100 mm long x 6 mm dia*
  *Cross blade - 100 mm long x 6 mm dia*
  *Torx - various sizes (not all vehicles)*
☐ *Combination pliers*
☐ *Hacksaw (junior)*
☐ *Tyre pump*
☐ *Tyre pressure gauge*
☐ *Oil can*
☐ *Oil filter removal tool*
☐ *Fine emery cloth*
☐ *Wire brush (small)*
☐ *Funnel (medium size)*
☐ *Sump drain plug key (not all vehicles)*

## Repair and overhaul tool kit

These tools are virtually essential for anyone undertaking any major repairs to a motor vehicle, and are additional to those given in the *Maintenance and minor repair* list. Included in this list is a comprehensive set of sockets. Although these are expensive, they will be found invaluable as they are so versatile - particularly if various drives are included in the set. We recommend the half-inch square-drive type, as this can be used with most proprietary torque wrenches.

The tools in this list will sometimes need to be supplemented by tools from the *Special* list:

☐ *Sockets (or box spanners) to cover range in previous list (including Torx sockets)*
☐ *Reversible ratchet drive (for use with sockets)*
☐ *Extension piece, 250 mm (for use with sockets)*
☐ *Universal joint (for use with sockets)*
☐ *Flexible handle or sliding T "breaker bar" (for use with sockets)*
☐ *Torque wrench (for use with sockets)*
☐ *Self-locking grips*
☐ *Ball pein hammer*
☐ *Soft-faced mallet (plastic or rubber)*
☐ *Screwdrivers:*
  *Flat blade - long & sturdy, short (chubby), and narrow (electrician's) types*
  *Cross blade – long & sturdy, and short (chubby) types*
☐ *Pliers:*
  *Long-nosed*
  *Side cutters (electrician's)*
  *Circlip (internal and external)*
☐ *Cold chisel - 25 mm*
☐ *Scriber*
☐ *Scraper*
☐ *Centre-punch*
☐ *Pin punch*
☐ *Hacksaw*
☐ *Brake hose clamp*
☐ *Brake/clutch bleeding kit*
☐ *Selection of twist drills*
☐ *Steel rule/straight-edge*
☐ *Allen keys (inc. splined/Torx type)*
☐ *Selection of files*
☐ *Wire brush*
☐ *Axle stands*
☐ *Jack (strong trolley or hydraulic type)*
☐ *Light with extension lead*
☐ *Universal electrical multi-meter*

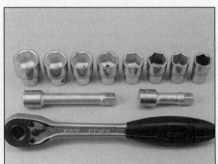

**Sockets and reversible ratchet drive**

**Brake bleeding kit**

**Torx key, socket and bit**

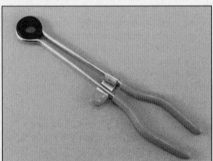

**Hose clamp**

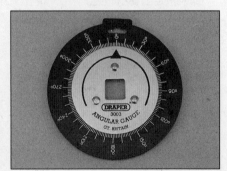

**Angular-tightening gauge**

## Special tools

The tools in this list are those which are not used regularly, are expensive to buy, or which need to be used in accordance with their manufacturers' instructions. Unless relatively difficult mechanical jobs are undertaken frequently, it will not be economic to buy many of these tools. Where this is the case, you could consider clubbing together with friends (or joining a motorists' club) to make a joint purchase, or borrowing the tools against a deposit from a local garage or tool hire specialist. It is worth noting that many of the larger DIY superstores now carry a large range of special tools for hire at modest rates.

The following list contains only those tools and instruments freely available to the public, and not those special tools produced by the vehicle manufacturer specifically for its dealer network. You will find occasional references to these manufacturers' special tools in the text of this manual. Generally, an alternative method of doing the job without the vehicle manufacturers' special tool is given. However, sometimes there is no alternative to using them. Where this is the case and the relevant tool cannot be bought or borrowed, you will have to entrust the work to a dealer.

☐ Angular-tightening gauge
☐ Valve spring compressor
☐ Valve grinding tool
☐ Piston ring compressor
☐ Piston ring removal/installation tool
☐ Cylinder bore hone
☐ Balljoint separator
☐ Coil spring compressors (where applicable)
☐ Two/three-legged hub and bearing puller
☐ Impact screwdriver
☐ Micrometer and/or vernier calipers
☐ Dial gauge
☐ Stroboscopic timing light
☐ Dwell angle meter/tachometer
☐ Fault code reader
☐ Cylinder compression gauge
☐ Hand-operated vacuum pump and gauge
☐ Clutch plate alignment set
☐ Brake shoe steady spring cup removal tool
☐ Bush and bearing removal/installation set
☐ Stud extractors
☐ Tap and die set
☐ Lifting tackle
☐ Trolley jack

## Buying tools

Reputable motor accessory shops and superstores often offer excellent quality tools at discount prices, so it pays to shop around.

Remember, you don't have to buy the most expensive items on the shelf, but it is always advisable to steer clear of the very cheap tools. Beware of 'bargains' offered on market stalls or at car boot sales. There are plenty of good tools around at reasonable prices, but always aim to purchase items which meet the relevant national safety standards. If in doubt, ask the proprietor or manager of the shop for advice before making a purchase.

## Care and maintenance of tools

Having purchased a reasonable tool kit, it is necessary to keep the tools in a clean and serviceable condition. After use, always wipe off any dirt, grease and metal particles using a clean, dry cloth, before putting the tools away. Never leave them lying around after they have been used. A simple tool rack on the garage or workshop wall for items such as screwdrivers and pliers is a good idea. Store all normal spanners and sockets in a metal box. Any measuring instruments, gauges, meters, etc, must be carefully stored where they cannot be damaged or become rusty.

Take a little care when tools are used. Hammer heads inevitably become marked, and screwdrivers lose the keen edge on their blades from time to time. A little timely attention with emery cloth or a file will soon restore items like this to a good finish.

## Working facilities

Not to be forgotten when discussing tools is the workshop itself. If anything more than routine maintenance is to be carried out, a suitable working area becomes essential.

It is appreciated that many an owner-mechanic is forced by circumstances to remove an engine or similar item without the benefit of a garage or workshop. Having done this, any repairs should always be done under the cover of a roof.

Wherever possible, any dismantling should be done on a clean, flat workbench or table at a suitable working height.

Any workbench needs a vice; one with a jaw opening of 100 mm is suitable for most jobs. As mentioned previously, some clean dry storage space is also required for tools, as well as for any lubricants, cleaning fluids, touch-up paints etc, which become necessary.

Another item which may be required, and which has a much more general usage, is an electric drill with a chuck capacity of at least 8 mm. This, together with a good range of twist drills, is virtually essential for fitting accessories.

Last, but not least, always keep a supply of old newspapers and clean, lint-free rags available, and try to keep any working area as clean as possible.

**Micrometers**

**Dial test indicator ("dial gauge")**

**Strap wrench**

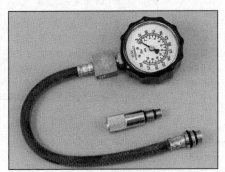

**Compression tester**

**Fault code reader**

This is a guide to getting your vehicle through the MOT test. Obviously it will not be possible to examine the vehicle to the same standard as the professional MOT tester. However, working through the following checks will enable you to identify any problem areas before submitting the vehicle for the test.

Where a testable component is in borderline condition, the tester has discretion in deciding whether to pass or fail it. The basis of such discretion is whether the tester would be happy for a close relative or friend to use the vehicle with the component in that condition. If the vehicle presented is clean and evidently well cared for, the tester may be more inclined to pass a borderline component than if the vehicle is scruffy and apparently neglected.

It has only been possible to summarise the test requirements here, based on the regulations in force at the time of printing. Test standards are becoming increasingly stringent, although there are some exemptions for older vehicles.

An assistant will be needed to help carry out some of these checks.

The checks have been sub-divided into four categories, as follows:

**1** Checks carried out **FROM THE DRIVER'S SEAT**

**2** Checks carried out **WITH THE VEHICLE ON THE GROUND**

**3** Checks carried out **WITH THE VEHICLE RAISED AND THE WHEELS FREE TO TURN**

**4** Checks carried out on **YOUR VEHICLE'S EXHAUST EMISSION SYSTEM**

---

**1** Checks carried out **FROM THE DRIVER'S SEAT**

### Handbrake

☐ Test the operation of the handbrake. Excessive travel (too many clicks) indicates incorrect brake or cable adjustment.
☐ Check that the handbrake cannot be released by tapping the lever sideways. Check the security of the lever mountings.

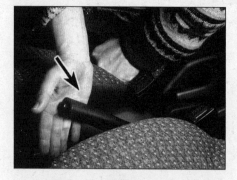

☐ Check that the brake pedal is secure and in good condition. Check also for signs of fluid leaks on the pedal, floor or carpets, which would indicate failed seals in the brake master cylinder.
☐ Check the servo unit (when applicable) by operating the brake pedal several times, then keeping the pedal depressed and starting the engine. As the engine starts, the pedal will move down slightly. If not, the vacuum hose or the servo itself may be faulty.

### Footbrake

☐ Depress the brake pedal and check that it does not creep down to the floor, indicating a master cylinder fault. Release the pedal, wait a few seconds, then depress it again. If the pedal travels nearly to the floor before firm resistance is felt, brake adjustment or repair is necessary. If the pedal feels spongy, there is air in the hydraulic system which must be removed by bleeding.

### Steering wheel and column

☐ Examine the steering wheel for fractures or looseness of the hub, spokes or rim.
☐ Move the steering wheel from side to side and then up and down. Check that the steering wheel is not loose on the column, indicating wear or a loose retaining nut. Continue moving the steering wheel as before, but also turn it slightly from left to right.
☐ Check that the steering wheel is not loose on the column, and that there is no abnormal movement of the steering wheel, indicating wear in the column support bearings or couplings.

### Windscreen, mirrors and sunvisor

☐ The windscreen must be free of cracks or other significant damage within the driver's field of view. (Small stone chips are acceptable.) Rear view mirrors must be secure, intact, and capable of being adjusted.

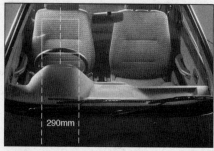

☐ The driver's sunvisor must be capable of being stored in the "up" position.

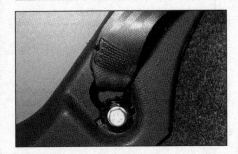

## Seat belts and seats

**Note:** *The following checks are applicable to all seat belts, front and rear.*

☐ Examine the webbing of all the belts (including rear belts if fitted) for cuts, serious fraying or deterioration. Fasten and unfasten each belt to check the buckles. If applicable, check the retracting mechanism. Check the security of all seat belt mountings accessible from inside the vehicle.

☐ Seat belts with pre-tensioners, once activated, have a "flag" or similar showing on the seat belt stalk. This, in itself, is not a reason for test failure.

☐ The front seats themselves must be securely attached and the backrests must lock in the upright position.

## Doors

☐ Both front doors must be able to be opened and closed from outside and inside, and must latch securely when closed.

## 2 Checks carried out WITH THE VEHICLE ON THE GROUND

## Vehicle identification

☐ Number plates must be in good condition, secure and legible, with letters and numbers correctly spaced – spacing at (A) should be at least twice that at (B).

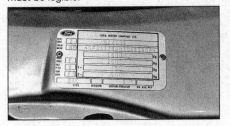

☐ The VIN plate and/or homologation plate must be legible.

## Electrical equipment

☐ Switch on the ignition and check the operation of the horn.

☐ Check the windscreen washers and wipers, examining the wiper blades; renew damaged or perished blades. Also check the operation of the stop-lights.

☐ Check the operation of the sidelights and number plate lights. The lenses and reflectors must be secure, clean and undamaged.

☐ Check the operation and alignment of the headlights. The headlight reflectors must not be tarnished and the lenses must be undamaged.

☐ Switch on the ignition and check the operation of the direction indicators (including the instrument panel tell-tale) and the hazard warning lights. Operation of the sidelights and stop-lights must not affect the indicators - if it does, the cause is usually a bad earth at the rear light cluster.

☐ Check the operation of the rear foglight(s), including the warning light on the instrument panel or in the switch.

☐ The ABS warning light must illuminate in accordance with the manufacturers' design. For most vehicles, the ABS warning light should illuminate when the ignition is switched on, and (if the system is operating properly) extinguish after a few seconds. Refer to the owner's handbook.

## Footbrake

☐ Examine the master cylinder, brake pipes and servo unit for leaks, loose mountings, corrosion or other damage.

☐ The fluid reservoir must be secure and the fluid level must be between the upper (**A**) and lower (**B**) markings.

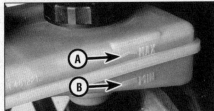

☐ Inspect both front brake flexible hoses for cracks or deterioration of the rubber. Turn the steering from lock to lock, and ensure that the hoses do not contact the wheel, tyre, or any part of the steering or suspension mechanism. With the brake pedal firmly depressed, check the hoses for bulges or leaks under pressure.

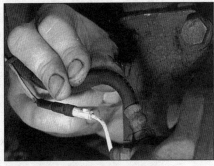

## Steering and suspension

☐ Have your assistant turn the steering wheel from side to side slightly, up to the point where the steering gear just begins to transmit this movement to the roadwheels. Check for excessive free play between the steering wheel and the steering gear, indicating wear or insecurity of the steering column joints, the column-to-steering gear coupling, or the steering gear itself.

☐ Have your assistant turn the steering wheel more vigorously in each direction, so that the roadwheels just begin to turn. As this is done, examine all the steering joints, linkages, fittings and attachments. Renew any component that shows signs of wear or damage. On vehicles with power steering, check the security and condition of the steering pump, drivebelt and hoses.

☐ Check that the vehicle is standing level, and at approximately the correct ride height.

## Shock absorbers

☐ Depress each corner of the vehicle in turn, then release it. The vehicle should rise and then settle in its normal position. If the vehicle continues to rise and fall, the shock absorber is defective. A shock absorber which has seized will also cause the vehicle to fail.

## Exhaust system

☐ Start the engine. With your assistant holding a rag over the tailpipe, check the entire system for leaks. Repair or renew leaking sections.

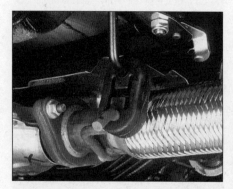

**3** Checks carried out **WITH THE VEHICLE RAISED AND THE WHEELS FREE TO TURN**

*Jack up the front and rear of the vehicle, and securely support it on axle stands. Position the stands clear of the suspension assemblies. Ensure that the wheels are clear of the ground and that the steering can be turned from lock to lock.*

## Steering mechanism

☐ Have your assistant turn the steering from lock to lock. Check that the steering turns smoothly, and that no part of the steering mechanism, including a wheel or tyre, fouls any brake hose or pipe or any part of the body structure.

☐ Examine the steering rack rubber gaiters for damage or insecurity of the retaining clips. If power steering is fitted, check for signs of damage or leakage of the fluid hoses, pipes or connections. Also check for excessive stiffness or binding of the steering, a missing split pin or locking device, or severe corrosion of the body structure within 30 cm of any steering component attachment point.

## Front and rear suspension and wheel bearings

☐ Starting at the front right-hand side, grasp the roadwheel at the 3 o'clock and 9 o'clock positions and rock gently but firmly. Check for free play or insecurity at the wheel bearings, suspension balljoints, or suspension mountings, pivots and attachments.

☐ Now grasp the wheel at the 12 o'clock and 6 o'clock positions and repeat the previous inspection. Spin the wheel, and check for roughness or tightness of the front wheel bearing.

☐ If excess free play is suspected at a component pivot point, this can be confirmed by using a large screwdriver or similar tool and levering between the mounting and the component attachment. This will confirm whether the wear is in the pivot bush, its retaining bolt, or in the mounting itself (the bolt holes can often become elongated).

☐ Carry out all the above checks at the other front wheel, and then at both rear wheels.

## Springs and shock absorbers

☐ Examine the suspension struts (when applicable) for serious fluid leakage, corrosion, or damage to the casing. Also check the security of the mounting points.

☐ If coil springs are fitted, check that the spring ends locate in their seats, and that the spring is not corroded, cracked or broken.

☐ If leaf springs are fitted, check that all leaves are intact, that the axle is securely attached to each spring, and that there is no deterioration of the spring eye mountings, bushes, and shackles.

☐ The same general checks apply to vehicles fitted with other suspension types, such as torsion bars, hydraulic displacer units, etc. Ensure that all mountings and attachments are secure, that there are no signs of excessive wear, corrosion or damage, and (on hydraulic types) that there are no fluid leaks or damaged pipes.

☐ Inspect the shock absorbers for signs of serious fluid leakage. Check for wear of the mounting bushes or attachments, or damage to the body of the unit.

## Driveshafts
## (fwd vehicles only)

☐ Rotate each front wheel in turn and inspect the constant velocity joint gaiters for splits or damage. Also check that each driveshaft is straight and undamaged.

## Braking system

☐ If possible without dismantling, check brake pad wear and disc condition. Ensure that the friction lining material has not worn excessively, (A) and that the discs are not fractured, pitted, scored or badly worn (B).

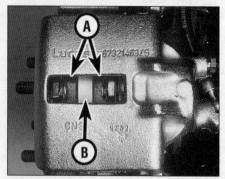

☐ Examine all the rigid brake pipes underneath the vehicle, and the flexible hose(s) at the rear. Look for corrosion, chafing or insecurity of the pipes, and for signs of bulging under pressure, chafing, splits or deterioration of the flexible hoses.

☐ Look for signs of fluid leaks at the brake calipers or on the brake backplates. Repair or renew leaking components.

☐ Slowly spin each wheel, while your assistant depresses and releases the footbrake. Ensure that each brake is operating and does not bind when the pedal is released.

□ Examine the handbrake mechanism, checking for frayed or broken cables, excessive corrosion, or wear or insecurity of the linkage. Check that the mechanism works on each relevant wheel, and releases fully, without binding.

□ It is not possible to test brake efficiency without special equipment, but a road test can be carried out later to check that the vehicle pulls up in a straight line.

## Fuel and exhaust systems

□ Inspect the fuel tank (including the filler cap), fuel pipes, hoses and unions. All components must be secure and free from leaks.

□ Examine the exhaust system over its entire length, checking for any damaged, broken or missing mountings, security of the retaining clamps and rust or corrosion.

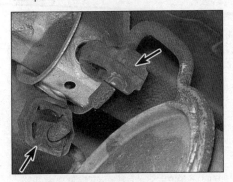

## Wheels and tyres

□ Examine the sidewalls and tread area of each tyre in turn. Check for cuts, tears, lumps, bulges, separation of the tread, and exposure of the ply or cord due to wear or damage. Check that the tyre bead is correctly seated on the wheel rim, that the valve is sound and properly seated, and that the wheel is not distorted or damaged.

□ Check that the tyres are of the correct size for the vehicle, that they are of the same size and type on each axle, and that the pressures are correct.

□ Check the tyre tread depth. The legal minimum at the time of writing is 1.6 mm over at least three-quarters of the tread width. Abnormal tread wear may indicate incorrect front wheel alignment.

### Body corrosion

□ Check the condition of the entire vehicle structure for signs of corrosion in load-bearing areas. (These include chassis box sections, side sills, cross-members, pillars, and all suspension, steering, braking system and seat belt mountings and anchorages.) Any corrosion which has seriously reduced the thickness of a load-bearing area is likely to cause the vehicle to fail. In this case professional repairs are likely to be needed.

□ Damage or corrosion which causes sharp or otherwise dangerous edges to be exposed will also cause the vehicle to fail.

## 4 Checks carried out on YOUR VEHICLE'S EXHAUST EMISSION SYSTEM

### Petrol models

□ Have the engine at normal operating temperature, and make sure that it is in good tune (ignition system in good order, air filter element clean, etc).

□ Before any measurements are carried out, raise the engine speed to around 2500 rpm, and hold it at this speed for 20 seconds. Allow the engine speed to return to idle, and watch for smoke emissions from the exhaust tailpipe. If the idle speed is obviously much too high, or if dense blue or clearly-visible black smoke comes from the tailpipe for more than 5 seconds, the vehicle will fail. As a rule of thumb, blue smoke signifies oil being burnt (engine wear) while black smoke signifies unburnt fuel (dirty air cleaner element, or other carburettor or fuel system fault).

□ An exhaust gas analyser capable of measuring carbon monoxide (CO) and hydrocarbons (HC) is now needed. If such an instrument cannot be hired or borrowed, a local garage may agree to perform the check for a small fee.

### CO emissions (mixture)

□ At the time of writing, for vehicles first used between 1st August 1975 and 31st July 1986 (P to C registration), the CO level must not exceed 4.5% by volume. For vehicles first used between 1st August 1986 and 31st July 1992 (D to J registration), the CO level must not exceed 3.5% by volume. Vehicles first

used after 1st August 1992 (K registration) must conform to the manufacturer's specification. The MOT tester has access to a DOT database or emissions handbook, which lists the CO and HC limits for each make and model of vehicle. The CO level is measured with the engine at idle speed, and at "fast idle". The following limits are given as a general guide:

*At idle speed -*
CO level no more than 0.5%
*At "fast idle" (2500 to 3000 rpm) -*
CO level no more than 0.3%
*(Minimum oil temperature 60ºC)*

□ If the CO level cannot be reduced far enough to pass the test (and the fuel and ignition systems are otherwise in good condition) then the carburettor is badly worn, or there is some problem in the fuel injection system or catalytic converter (as applicable).

### HC emissions

□ With the CO within limits, HC emissions for vehicles first used between 1st August 1975 and 31st July 1992 (P to J registration) must not exceed 1200 ppm. Vehicles first used after 1st August 1992 (K registration) must conform to the manufacturer's specification. The MOT tester has access to a DOT database or emissions handbook, which lists the CO and HC limits for each make and model of vehicle. The HC level is measured with the engine at "fast idle". The following is given as a general guide:

*At "fast idle" (2500 to 3000 rpm) -*
HC level no more than 200 ppm
*(Minimum oil temperature 60ºC)*

□ Excessive HC emissions are caused by incomplete combustion, the causes of which can include oil being burnt, mechanical wear and ignition/fuel system malfunction.

### Diesel models

□ The only emission test applicable to Diesel engines is the measuring of exhaust smoke density. The test involves accelerating the engine several times to its maximum unloaded speed.

**Note:** *It is of the utmost importance that the engine timing belt is in good condition before the test is carried out.*

□ The limits for Diesel engine exhaust smoke, introduced in September 1995 are:
*Vehicles first used before 1st August 1979:*
Exempt from metered smoke testing, but must not emit "dense blue or clearly visible black smoke for a period of more than 5 seconds at idle" or "dense blue or clearly visible black smoke during acceleration which would obscure the view of other road users".
*Non-turbocharged vehicles first used after*
*1st August 1979:* 2.5m$^{-1}$
*Turbocharged vehicles first used after*
*1st August 1979:* 3.0m$^{-1}$

□ Excessive smoke can be caused by a dirty air cleaner element. Otherwise, professional advice may be needed to find the cause.

## Engine

- [ ] Engine fails to rotate when attempting to start
- [ ] Engine rotates, but will not start
- [ ] Engine difficult to start when cold
- [ ] Engine difficult to start when hot
- [ ] Starter motor noisy or excessively-rough in engagement
- [ ] Engine starts, but stops immediately
- [ ] Engine idles erratically
- [ ] Engine misfires at idle speed
- [ ] Engine misfires throughout the driving speed range
- [ ] Engine hesitates on acceleration
- [ ] Engine stalls
- [ ] Engine lacks power
- [ ] Engine backfires
- [ ] Oil pressure warning light illuminated with engine running
- [ ] Engine runs-on after switching off
- [ ] Engine noises

## Cooling system

- [ ] Overheating
- [ ] Overcooling
- [ ] External coolant leakage
- [ ] Internal coolant leakage
- [ ] Corrosion

## Fuel and exhaust systems

- [ ] Excessive fuel consumption
- [ ] Fuel leakage and/or fuel odour
- [ ] Excessive noise or fumes from exhaust system

## Clutch

- [ ] Pedal travels to floor – no pressure or very little resistance
- [ ] Clutch fails to disengage (unable to select gears)
- [ ] Clutch slips (engine speed increases, with no increase in vehicle speed)
- [ ] Judder as clutch is engaged
- [ ] Noise when depressing or releasing clutch pedal

## Manual transmission

- [ ] Noisy in neutral with engine running
- [ ] Noisy in one particular gear
- [ ] Difficulty engaging gears
- [ ] Jumps out of gear
- [ ] Vibration
- [ ] Lubricant leaks

## Automatic transmission

- [ ] Fluid leakage
- [ ] Transmission fluid brown, or has burned smell
- [ ] General gear selection problems
- [ ] Transmission will not downshift (kickdown) with accelerator pedal fully depressed
- [ ] Engine will not start in any gear, or starts in gears other than Park or Neutral
- [ ] Transmission slips, shifts roughly, is noisy, or has no drive in forward or reverse gears

## Driveshafts

- [ ] Vibration when accelerating or decelerating
- [ ] Clicking or knocking noise on turns (at slow speed on full-lock)

## Braking system

- [ ] Vehicle pulls to one side under braking
- [ ] Noise (grinding or high-pitched squeal) when brakes applied
- [ ] Excessive brake pedal travel
- [ ] Brake pedal feels spongy when depressed
- [ ] Excessive brake pedal effort required to stop vehicle
- [ ] Judder felt through brake pedal or steering wheel when braking
- [ ] Brakes binding
- [ ] Rear wheels locking under normal braking

## Suspension and steering

- [ ] Vehicle pulls to one side
- [ ] Wheel wobble and vibration
- [ ] Excessive pitching and/or rolling around corners, or during braking
- [ ] Wandering or general instability
- [ ] Excessively-stiff steering
- [ ] Excessive play in steering
- [ ] Lack of power assistance
- [ ] Tyre wear excessive

## Electrical system

- [ ] Battery will not hold a charge for more than a few days
- [ ] Ignition/no-charge warning light remains illuminated with engine running
- [ ] Ignition/no-charge warning light fails to come on
- [ ] Lights inoperative
- [ ] Instrument readings inaccurate or erratic
- [ ] Horn inoperative, or unsatisfactory in operation
- [ ] Windscreen wipers inoperative, or unsatisfactory in operation
- [ ] Windscreen washers inoperative, or unsatisfactory in operation
- [ ] Electric windows inoperative, or unsatisfactory in operation
- [ ] Central locking system inoperative, or unsatisfactory in operation

# Introduction

The vehicle owner who does his or her own maintenance according to the recommended service schedules should not have to use this section of the manual very often. Modern component reliability is such that, provided those items subject to wear or deterioration are inspected or renewed at the specified intervals, sudden failure is comparatively rare. Faults do not usually just happen as a result of sudden failure, but develop over a period of time. Major mechanical failures in particular are usually preceded by characteristic symptoms over hundreds or even thousands of miles. Those components which do occasionally fail without warning are often small and easily carried in the vehicle.

With any fault-finding, the first step is to decide where to begin investigations. Sometimes this is obvious, but on other occasions, a little detective work will be necessary. The owner who makes half a dozen haphazard adjustments or replacements may be successful in curing a fault (or its symptoms), but will be none the wiser if the fault recurs, and ultimately may have spent more time and money than was necessary. A calm and logical approach will be found to be more satisfactory in the long run. Always take into account any warning signs or abnormalities that may have been noticed in the period preceding the fault – power loss, high or low gauge readings, unusual smells, etc – and remember that failure of components such as fuses or spark plugs may only be pointers to some underlying fault.

The pages which follow provide an easy-reference guide to the more common problems which may occur during the operation of the vehicle. These problems and their possible causes are grouped under headings denoting various components or systems, such as Engine, Cooling system, etc. The general Chapter which deals with the problem is also shown in brackets; refer to the relevant part of that Chapter for system-specific information. Whatever the fault, certain basic principles apply. These are as follows:

*Verify the fault.* This is simply a matter of being sure that you know what the symptoms are before starting work. This is particularly important if you are investigating a fault for someone else, who may not have described it very accurately.

*Don't overlook the obvious.* For example, if the vehicle won't start, is there fuel in the tank? (Don't take anyone else's word on this particular point, and don't trust the fuel gauge either!) If an electrical fault is indicated, look for loose or broken wires before digging out the test gear.

*Cure the disease, not the symptom.* Substituting a flat battery with a fully-charged one will get you off the hard shoulder, but if the underlying cause is not attended to, the new battery will go the same way. Similarly, changing oil-fouled spark plugs for a new set will get you moving again, but remember that the reason for the fouling (if it wasn't simply an incorrect grade of plug) will have to be established and corrected.

*Don't take anything for granted.* Particularly, don't forget that a 'new' component may itself be defective (especially if it's been rattling around in the boot for months), and don't leave components out of a fault diagnosis sequence just because they are new or recently-fitted. When you do finally diagnose a difficult fault, you'll probably realise that all the evidence was there from the start.

*Consider what work, if any, has recently been carried out.* Many faults arise through careless or hurried work. For instance, if any work has been performed under the bonnet, could some of the wiring have been dislodged or incorrectly routed, or a hose trapped? Have all the fasteners been properly tightened? Were new, genuine parts and new gaskets used? There is often a certain amount of detective work to be done in this case, as an apparently-unrelated task can have far-reaching consequences.

# Engine

## Engine fails to rotate when attempting to start

- ☐ Battery terminal connections loose or corroded (see *Weekly checks*)
- ☐ Battery discharged or faulty (Chapter 5A)
- ☐ Broken, loose or disconnected wiring in the starting circuit (Chapter 5A)
- ☐ Defective starter solenoid or ignition switch (Chapter 5A or 12)
- ☐ Defective starter motor (Chapter 5A)
- ☐ Starter pinion or flywheel ring gear teeth loose or broken (Chapter 2 or 5A)
- ☐ Engine earth strap broken or disconnected (Chapter 5A)
- ☐ Engine suffering 'hydraulic lock' (eg from water ingested after traversing flooded roads, or from a serious internal coolant leak) – consult a Volvo dealer for advice
- ☐ Automatic transmission not in position P or N (Chapter 7B)

## Engine rotates, but will not start

- ☐ Fuel tank empty
- ☐ Battery discharged (engine rotates slowly) (Chapter 5A)
- ☐ Battery terminal connections loose or corroded (see *Weekly checks*)
- ☐ Ignition components damp or damaged (Chapter 1 or 5B)
- ☐ Immobiliser fault, or 'uncoded' ignition key being used (Chapter 12 or 'Roadside repairs')
- ☐ Crankshaft sensor fault (Chapter 4A or 4B)
- ☐ Broken, loose or disconnected wiring in the ignition circuit (Chapter 1 or 5B)
- ☐ Worn, faulty or incorrectly-gapped spark plugs (Chapter 1)
- ☐ Fuel injection system fault (Chapter 4A or 4B)
- ☐ Major mechanical failure (eg timing belt snapped) (Chapter 2A or 2B)

## Engine difficult to start when cold

- ☐ Battery discharged (Chapter 5A)
- ☐ Battery terminal connections loose or corroded (see *Weekly checks*)
- ☐ Worn, faulty or incorrectly-gapped spark plugs (Chapter 1)
- ☐ Other ignition system fault (Chapter 1 or 5B)
- ☐ Fuel injection system fault (Chapter 4A or 4B)
- ☐ Wrong grade of engine oil used (*Weekly checks* or Chapter 1)
- ☐ Low cylinder compressions (Chapter 2A or 2B)

## Engine difficult to start when hot

- ☐ Air filter element dirty or clogged (Chapter 1)
- ☐ Fuel injection system fault (Chapter 4A or 4B)
- ☐ Low cylinder compressions (Chapter 2A or 2B)

## Starter motor noisy or excessively-rough

- ☐ Starter pinion or flywheel ring gear teeth loose or broken (Chapter 2 or 5A)
- ☐ Starter motor mounting bolts loose or missing (Chapter 5A)
- ☐ Starter motor internal components worn or damaged (Chapter 5A)

## Engine starts, but stops immediately

- ☐ Loose or faulty electrical connections in the ignition circuit (Chapter 1 or 5B)
- ☐ Vacuum leak at the throttle body or inlet manifold (Chapter 4A or 4B)
- ☐ Blocked injectors/fuel injection system fault (Chapter 4A or 4B)

## Engine idles erratically

- ☐ Air filter element clogged (Chapter 1)
- ☐ Vacuum leak at the throttle body, inlet manifold or associated hoses (Chapter 4A or 4B)
- ☐ Worn, faulty or incorrectly-gapped spark plugs (Chapter 1)
- ☐ Uneven or low cylinder compressions (Chapter 2A or 2B)
- ☐ Camshaft lobes worn (Chapter 2A or 2B)
- ☐ Timing belt incorrectly fitted (Chapter 2A or 2B)
- ☐ Blocked injectors/fuel injection system fault (Chapter 4A or 4B)

## Engine misfires at idle speed

- ☐ Worn, faulty or incorrectly-gapped spark plugs (Chapter 1)
- ☐ Faulty spark plug HT leads – non-GDI engines (Chapter 1)
- ☐ Vacuum leak at the throttle body, inlet manifold or associated hoses (Chapter 4A or 4B)
- ☐ Blocked injectors/fuel injection system fault (Chapter 4A or 4B)
- ☐ Uneven or low cylinder compressions (Chapter 2A or 2B)
- ☐ Disconnected, leaking, or perished crankcase ventilation hoses (Chapter 4C)

# Engine (continued)

### Engine misfires throughout the driving speed range

- ☐ Fuel filter choked (Chapter 1)
- ☐ Fuel pump faulty, or delivery pressure low (Chapter 4A or 4B)
- ☐ Fuel tank vent blocked, or fuel pipes restricted (Chapter 4A or 4B)
- ☐ Vacuum leak at the throttle body, inlet manifold or associated hoses (Chapter 4A or 4B)
- ☐ Worn, faulty or incorrectly-gapped spark plugs (Chapter 1)
- ☐ Faulty spark plug HT leads – non-GDI engines (Chapter 1)
- ☐ Faulty ignition coil(s) (Chapter 5B)
- ☐ Uneven or low cylinder compressions (Chapter 2A or 2B)
- ☐ Blocked injector/fuel injection system fault (Chapter 4A or 4B)
- ☐ Blocked catalytic converter (Chapter 4A or 4B)
- ☐ Engine overheating (Chapter 3)

### Engine hesitates on acceleration

- ☐ Worn, faulty or incorrectly-gapped spark plugs (Chapter 1)
- ☐ Vacuum leak at the throttle body, inlet manifold or associated hoses (Chapter 4A or 4B)
- ☐ Blocked injectors/fuel injection system fault (Chapter 4A or 4B)

### Engine stalls

- ☐ Vacuum leak at the throttle body, inlet manifold or associated hoses (Chapter 4A or 4B)
- ☐ Fuel filter choked (Chapter 1)
- ☐ Fuel pump faulty, or delivery pressure low (Chapter 4A or 4B)
- ☐ Fuel tank vent blocked, or fuel pipes restricted (Chapter 4A or 4B)
- ☐ Blocked injectors/fuel injection system fault (Chapter 4A or 4B)

### Engine lacks power

- ☐ Air filter element blocked (Chapter 1)
- ☐ Fuel filter choked (Chapter 1)
- ☐ Fuel pipes blocked or restricted (Chapter 4A or 4B)
- ☐ Worn, faulty or incorrectly-gapped spark plugs (Chapter 1)
- ☐ Accelerator cable problem (Chapter 4A or 4B)
- ☐ Vacuum leak at the throttle body, inlet manifold or associated hoses (Chapter 4A or 4B)
- ☐ Blocked injectors/fuel injection system fault (Chapter 4A or 4B)
- ☐ Timing belt incorrectly fitted (Chapter 2A or 2B)
- ☐ Fuel pump faulty, or delivery pressure low (Chapter 4A or 4B)
- ☐ Uneven or low cylinder compressions (Chapter 2A or 2B)
- ☐ Blocked catalytic converter (Chapter 4A or 4B)
- ☐ Brakes binding (Chapter 1 or 9)
- ☐ Clutch slipping (Chapter 6)

### Engine backfires

- ☐ Timing belt incorrectly fitted (Chapter 2A or 2B)
- ☐ Vacuum leak at the throttle body, inlet manifold or associated hoses (Chapter 4A or 4B)
- ☐ Blocked injectors/fuel injection system fault (Chapter 4A or 4B)
- ☐ Blocked catalytic converter (Chapter 4A or 4B)
- ☐ Spark plug HT leads incorrectly fitted – non-GDI engines (Chapter 1 or 5B)
- ☐ Ignition coil unit faulty (Chapter 5B)

### Oil pressure warning light illuminated with engine running

- ☐ Low oil level, or incorrect oil grade (see *Weekly checks*)
- ☐ Faulty oil pressure sensor, or wiring damaged (Chapter 5A)
- ☐ Worn engine bearings and/or oil pump (Chapter 2A or 2B)
- ☐ High engine operating temperature (Chapter 3)
- ☐ Oil pump pressure relief valve defective (Chapter 2A or 2B)
- ☐ Oil pump pick-up strainer clogged (Chapter 2A or 2B)

### Engine runs-on after switching off

- ☐ Excessive carbon build-up in engine (Chapter 2)
- ☐ High engine operating temperature (Chapter 3)
- ☐ Fuel injection system fault (Chapter 4A or 4B)

### Engine noises

#### Pre-ignition (pinking) or knocking during acceleration or under load

- ☐ Ignition timing incorrect/ignition system fault (Chapter 1 or 5B)
- ☐ Incorrect grade of spark plug (Chapter 1)
- ☐ Incorrect grade of fuel (Chapter 4)
- ☐ Knock sensor faulty – GDI engine models (Chapter 4B)
- ☐ Vacuum leak at the throttle body, inlet manifold or associated hoses (Chapter 4A or 4B)
- ☐ Excessive carbon build-up in engine (Chapter 2)
- ☐ Blocked injector/fuel injection system fault (Chapter 4A or 4B)

#### Whistling or wheezing noises

- ☐ Leaking inlet manifold or throttle body gasket (Chapter 4A or 4B)
- ☐ Leaking exhaust manifold gasket or pipe-to-manifold joint (Chapter 4C)
- ☐ Leaking vacuum hose (Chapter 4, 5 or 9)
- ☐ Blowing cylinder head gasket (Chapter 2A or 2B)
- ☐ Partially blocked or leaking crankcase ventilation system (Chapter 4C)

#### Tapping or rattling noises

- ☐ Worn valve gear or camshaft (Chapter 2A or 2B)
- ☐ Ancillary component fault (coolant pump, alternator, etc) (Chapter 3, 5A, etc)

#### Knocking or thumping noises

- ☐ Worn big-end bearings (regular heavy knocking, perhaps less under load) (Chapter 2C)
- ☐ Worn main bearings (rumbling and knocking, perhaps worsening under load) (Chapter 2C)
- ☐ Piston slap – most noticeable when cold, caused by piston/bore wear (Chapter 2C)
- ☐ Ancillary component fault (coolant pump, alternator, etc) (Chapter 3, 5A, etc)
- ☐ Engine mountings worn or defective (Chapter 2A or 2B)
- ☐ Front suspension or steering components worn (Chapter 10)

# Cooling system

### Overheating

- [ ] Insufficient coolant in system (see *Weekly checks*)
- [ ] Thermostat faulty (Chapter 3)
- [ ] Radiator core blocked, or grille restricted (Chapter 3)
- [ ] Cooling fan faulty (Chapter 3)
- [ ] Inaccurate cylinder head temperature sender (Chapter 3, 4A or 4B)
- [ ] Airlock in cooling system (Chapter 3)
- [ ] Expansion tank pressure cap faulty (Chapter 3)
- [ ] Engine management system fault (Chapter 4A or 4B)

### Overcooling

- [ ] Thermostat faulty (Chapter 3)
- [ ] Inaccurate coolant temperature sender (Chapter 3, 4A or 4B)
- [ ] Cooling fan faulty (Chapter 3)
- [ ] Engine management system fault (Chapter 4A or 4B)

### External coolant leakage

- [ ] Deteriorated or damaged hoses or hose clips (Chapter 1)
- [ ] Radiator core or heater matrix leaking (Chapter 3)
- [ ] Expansion tank pressure cap faulty (Chapter 1)
- [ ] Coolant pump internal seal leaking (Chapter 3)
- [ ] Coolant pump gasket leaking (Chapter 3)
- [ ] Boiling due to overheating (Chapter 3)
- [ ] Cylinder block core plug leaking (Chapter 2C)

### Internal coolant leakage

- [ ] Leaking cylinder head gasket (Chapter 2A or 2B)
- [ ] Cracked cylinder head or cylinder block (Chapter 2)

### Corrosion

- [ ] Infrequent draining and flushing (Chapter 1)
- [ ] Incorrect coolant mixture or inappropriate coolant type (see *Weekly checks*)

# Fuel and exhaust systems

### Excessive fuel consumption

- [ ] Air filter element dirty or clogged (Chapter 1)
- [ ] Fuel injection system fault (Chapter 4A or 4B)
- [ ] Crankcase ventilation system blocked (Chapter 4C)
- [ ] Tyres under-inflated (see *Weekly checks*)
- [ ] Brakes binding (Chapter 1 or 9)
- [ ] Fuel leak, causing apparent high consumption (Chapter 1, 4A or 4B)

### Fuel leakage and/or fuel odour

- [ ] Damaged or corroded fuel tank, pipes or connections (Chapter 4A or 4B)
- [ ] Evaporative emissions system fault (Chapter 4C)

### Excessive noise or fumes from exhaust system

- [ ] Leaking exhaust system or manifold joints (Chapter 1 or 4C)
- [ ] Broken mountings causing body or suspension contact (Chapter 1)

# Clutch

### Pedal travels to floor – no pressure or very little resistance

- ☐ Air in hydraulic system/faulty master or slave cylinder (Chapter 6)
- ☐ Faulty hydraulic release system (Chapter 6)
- ☐ Clutch pedal return spring detached or broken (Chapter 6)
- ☐ Broken clutch release bearing or fork (Chapter 6)
- ☐ Broken diaphragm spring in clutch pressure plate (Chapter 6)

### Clutch fails to disengage (unable to select gears)

- ☐ Air in hydraulic system/faulty master or slave cylinder (Chapter 6)
- ☐ Faulty hydraulic release system (Chapter 6)
- ☐ Clutch disc sticking on transmission input shaft splines (Chapter 6)
- ☐ Clutch disc sticking to flywheel or pressure plate (Chapter 6)
- ☐ Faulty pressure plate assembly (Chapter 6)
- ☐ Clutch release mechanism worn or incorrectly assembled (Chapter 6)

### Clutch slips (engine speed increases, with no increase in vehicle speed)

- ☐ Faulty hydraulic release system (Chapter 6)
- ☐ Clutch disc linings excessively worn (Chapter 6)
- ☐ Clutch disc linings contaminated with oil or grease (Chapter 6)
- ☐ Faulty pressure plate or weak diaphragm spring (Chapter 6)

### Judder as clutch is engaged

- ☐ Clutch disc linings contaminated with oil or grease (Chapter 6)
- ☐ Clutch disc linings excessively worn (Chapter 6)
- ☐ Faulty or distorted pressure plate or diaphragm spring (Chapter 6).
- ☐ Worn or loose engine or transmission mountings (Chapter 2A or 2B)
- ☐ Clutch disc hub or transmission input shaft splines worn (Chapter 6)

### Noise when depressing or releasing clutch pedal

- ☐ Worn clutch release bearing (Chapter 6)
- ☐ Worn or dry clutch pedal bushes (Chapter 6)
- ☐ Worn or dry clutch master cylinder piston (Chapter 6)
- ☐ Faulty pressure plate assembly (Chapter 6)
- ☐ Pressure plate diaphragm spring broken (Chapter 6)
- ☐ Broken clutch disc cushioning springs (Chapter 6)

# Manual transmission

### Noisy in neutral with engine running

- ☐ Lack of oil (Chapter 1)
- ☐ Input shaft bearings worn (noise apparent with clutch pedal released, but not when depressed) (Chapter 7A)*
- ☐ Clutch release bearing worn (noise apparent with clutch pedal depressed, possibly less when released) (Chapter 6)

### Noisy in one particular gear

- ☐ Worn, damaged or chipped gear teeth (Chapter 7A)*

### Difficulty engaging gears

- ☐ Clutch fault (Chapter 6)
- ☐ Worn, damaged, or poorly-adjusted gearchange linkage (Chapter 7A)
- ☐ Lack of oil (Chapter 1)
- ☐ Worn synchroniser units (Chapter 7A)*

### Jumps out of gear

- ☐ Worn, damaged, or poorly-adjusted gearchange linkage (Chapter 7A)
- ☐ Worn synchroniser units (Chapter 7A)*
- ☐ Worn selector forks (Chapter 7A)*

### Vibration

- ☐ Lack of oil (Chapter 1)
- ☐ Worn bearings (Chapter 7A)*

### Lubricant leaks

- ☐ Leaking driveshaft or selector shaft oil seal (Chapter 7A)
- ☐ Leaking housing joint (Chapter 7A)*
- ☐ Leaking input shaft oil seal (Chapter 7A)*

*Although the corrective action necessary to remedy the symptoms described is beyond the scope of the home mechanic, the above information should be helpful in isolating the cause of the condition, so that the owner can communicate clearly with a professional mechanic.*

# Automatic transmission

**Note:** *Due to the complexity of the automatic transmission, it is difficult for the home mechanic to properly diagnose and service this unit. For problems other than the following, the vehicle should be taken to a dealer service department or automatic transmission specialist. Do not be too hasty in removing the transmission if a fault is suspected, as most of the testing is carried out with the unit still fitted. Remember that, besides the sensors specific to the transmission, many of the engine management system sensors described in Chapter 4A are essential to the correct operation of the transmission.*

## Fluid leakage

☐ Automatic transmission fluid is usually dark red in colour. Fluid leaks should not be confused with engine oil, which can easily be blown onto the transmission by airflow.

☐ To determine the source of a leak, first remove all built-up dirt and grime from the transmission housing and surrounding areas using a degreasing agent, or by steam-cleaning. Drive the vehicle at low speed, so airflow will not blow the leak far from its source. Raise and support the vehicle, and determine where the leak is coming from. The following are common areas of leakage:

a) *Fluid pan*
b) *Dipstick tube (Chapter 1)*
c) *Transmission-to-fluid cooler unions (Chapter 7B)*

## Transmission fluid brown, or has burned smell

☐ Transmission fluid level low (Chapter 1)

## General gear selection problems

☐ Chapter 7B deals with checking the selector cable on automatic transmissions. The following are common problems which may be caused by a faulty cable or sensor:

a) *Engine starting in gears other than Park or Neutral.*
b) *Indicator panel indicating a gear other than the one actually being used.*
c) *Vehicle moves when in Park or Neutral.*
d) *Poor gear shift quality or erratic gear changes.*

## Transmission will not downshift (kickdown) with accelerator pedal fully depressed

☐ Low transmission fluid level (Chapter 1)
☐ Engine management system fault (Chapter 4A)
☐ Faulty transmission sensor or wiring (Chapter 7B)
☐ Incorrect selector cable adjustment (Chapter 7B)

## Engine will not start in any gear, or starts in gears other than Park or Neutral

☐ Faulty transmission sensor or wiring (Chapter 7B)
☐ Engine management system fault (Chapter 4A or 4B)
☐ Incorrect selector cable adjustment (Chapter 7B)

## Transmission slips, shifts roughly, is noisy, or has no drive in forward or reverse gears

☐ Transmission fluid level low (Chapter 1)
☐ Faulty transmission sensor or wiring (Chapter 7B)
☐ Engine management system fault (Chapter 4A)

**Note:** *There are many probable causes for the above problems, but diagnosing and correcting them is considered beyond the scope of this manual. Having checked the fluid level and all the wiring as far as possible, a dealer or transmission specialist should be consulted if the problem persists.*

# Driveshafts

## Vibration when accelerating or decelerating

☐ Worn inner constant velocity joint (Chapter 8)
☐ Bent or distorted driveshaft (Chapter 8)
☐ Worn intermediate bearing (Chapter 8)

## Clicking or knocking noise on turns (at slow speed on full-lock)

☐ Worn outer constant velocity joint (Chapter 8)
☐ Lack of constant velocity joint lubricant, possibly due to damaged gaiter (Chapter 8)
☐ Worn intermediate bearing (Chapter 8)

# Braking system

**Note:** *Before assuming that a brake problem exists, make sure that the tyres are in good condition and correctly inflated, that the front wheel alignment is correct, and that the vehicle is not loaded with weight in an unequal manner. Apart from checking the condition of all pipe and hose connections, any faults occurring on the anti-lock braking system should be referred to a Volvo dealer for diagnosis.*

### Vehicle pulls to one side under braking

☐ Worn, defective, damaged or contaminated brake pads/shoes on one side (Chapter 1 or 9)
☐ Seized or partially-seized brake caliper piston/wheel cylinder (Chapter 1 or 9)
☐ A mixture of brake pad/shoe lining materials fitted between sides (Chapter 1 or 9)
☐ Brake caliper/backplate mounting bolts loose (Chapter 9)
☐ Worn or damaged steering or suspension components (Chapter 1 or 10)

### Noise (grinding or high-pitched squeal) when brakes applied

☐ Brake pad/shoe friction lining material worn down to metal backing (Chapter 1 or 9)
☐ Excessive corrosion of brake disc/drum – may be apparent if car has been standing for some time (Chapter 1 or 9)
☐ Foreign object (stone chipping, etc) trapped between brake disc and shield (Chapter 1 or 9)

### Excessive brake pedal travel

☐ Faulty master cylinder (Chapter 9)
☐ Air in hydraulic system (Chapter 1, 6 or 9)
☐ Faulty vacuum servo unit (Chapter 9)

### Brake pedal feels spongy when depressed

☐ Air in hydraulic system (Chapter 1, 6 or 9)
☐ Deteriorated flexible rubber brake hoses (Chapter 1 or 9)
☐ Master cylinder mounting nuts loose (Chapter 9)
☐ Faulty master cylinder (Chapter 9)

### Excessive brake pedal effort required to stop vehicle

☐ Faulty vacuum servo unit (Chapter 9)
☐ Faulty vacuum pump (Chapter 9)
☐ Disconnected, damaged or insecure brake servo vacuum hose (Chapter 9)
☐ Primary or secondary hydraulic circuit failure (Chapter 9)
☐ Seized brake caliper/wheel cylinder piston (Chapter 9)
☐ Brake pads/shoes incorrectly fitted (Chapter 9)
☐ Incorrect grade of brake pads/shoes fitted (Chapter 9)
☐ Brake pad/shoe linings contaminated (Chapter 1 or 9)

### Judder felt through brake pedal or steering wheel when braking

**Note:** *Under heavy braking on models equipped with ABS, vibration may be felt through the brake pedal. This is a normal feature of ABS operation, and does not constitute a fault*

☐ Excessive run-out or distortion of discs/drums (Chapter 1 or 9)
☐ Brake pad/shoe linings worn (Chapter 1 or 9)
☐ Brake caliper/backplate mounting bolts loose (Chapter 9)
☐ Wear in suspension or steering components or mountings (Chapter 1 or 10)
☐ Front wheels out of balance (see *Weekly checks*)

### Brakes binding

☐ Seized brake caliper/wheel cylinder piston (Chapter 9)
☐ Incorrectly-adjusted handbrake mechanism (Chapter 9)
☐ Faulty master cylinder (Chapter 9)

### Rear wheels locking under normal braking

☐ Rear brake pad/shoe linings contaminated or damaged (Chapter 1 or 9)
☐ Rear brake discs/drums warped (Chapter 1 or 9)
☐ Rear brake load sensing proportioning valve faulty – Estate models (Chapter 9)

# Suspension and steering

**Note:** *Before diagnosing suspension or steering faults, be sure that the trouble is not due to incorrect tyre pressures, mixtures of tyre types, or binding brakes.*

## Vehicle pulls to one side

- ☐ Defective tyre (see *Weekly checks*)
- ☐ Excessive wear in suspension or steering components (Chapter 1 or 10)
- ☐ Incorrect front wheel alignment (Chapter 10)
- ☐ Accident damage to steering or suspension components (Chapter 1)

## Wheel wobble and vibration

- ☐ Front wheels out of balance (vibration felt mainly through the steering wheel) (see *Weekly checks*)
- ☐ Rear wheels out of balance (vibration felt throughout the vehicle) (see *Weekly checks*)
- ☐ Roadwheels damaged or distorted (see *Weekly checks*)
- ☐ Faulty or damaged tyre (see *Weekly checks*)
- ☐ Worn steering or suspension joints, bushes or components (Chapter 1 or 10)
- ☐ Wheel nuts loose (Chapter 1)

## Excessive pitching and/or rolling around corners, or during braking

- ☐ Defective shock absorbers (Chapter 1 or 10)
- ☐ Broken or weak spring and/or suspension component (Chapter 1 or 10)
- ☐ Worn or damaged anti-roll bar or mountings (Chapter 1 or 10)

## Wandering or general instability

- ☐ Incorrect front wheel alignment (Chapter 10)
- ☐ Worn steering or suspension joints, bushes or components (Chapter 1 or 10)
- ☐ Roadwheels out of balance (see *Weekly checks*)
- ☐ Faulty or damaged tyre (see *Weekly checks*)
- ☐ Wheel nuts loose (Chapter 1)
- ☐ Defective shock absorbers (Chapter 1 or 10)

## Excessively-stiff steering

- ☐ Seized steering linkage balljoint or suspension balljoint (Chapter 1 or 10)
- ☐ Broken or incorrectly-adjusted auxiliary drivebelt (Chapter 1)
- ☐ Incorrect front wheel alignment (Chapter 10)
- ☐ Steering rack damaged (Chapter 10)

## Excessive play in steering

- ☐ Worn steering column/intermediate shaft joints (Chapter 10)
- ☐ Worn track rod balljoints (Chapter 1 or 10)
- ☐ Worn steering rack (Chapter 10)
- ☐ Worn steering or suspension joints, bushes or components (Chapter 1 or 10)

## Lack of power assistance

- ☐ Broken or incorrectly-adjusted auxiliary drivebelt (Chapter 1)
- ☐ Incorrect power steering fluid level (see *Weekly checks*)
- ☐ Restriction in power steering fluid hoses (Chapter 1)
- ☐ Faulty power steering pump (Chapter 10)
- ☐ Faulty steering rack (Chapter 10)

## Tyre wear excessive

### Tyres worn on inside or outside edges

- ☐ Tyres under-inflated (wear on both edges) (see *Weekly checks*)
- ☐ Incorrect camber or castor angles (wear on one edge only) (Chapter 10)
- ☐ Worn steering or suspension joints, bushes or components (Chapter 1 or 10)
- ☐ Excessively-hard cornering or braking
- ☐ Accident damage

### Tyre treads exhibit feathered edges

- ☐ Incorrect toe setting (Chapter 10)

### Tyres worn in centre of tread

- ☐ Tyres over-inflated (see *Weekly checks*)

### Tyres worn on inside and outside edges

- ☐ Tyres under-inflated (see *Weekly checks*)

### Tyres worn unevenly

- ☐ Tyres/wheels out of balance (see *Weekly checks*)
- ☐ Excessive wheel or tyre run-out
- ☐ Worn shock absorbers (Chapter 1 or 10)
- ☐ Faulty tyre (see *Weekly checks*)

# Electrical system

**Note:** *For problems associated with the starting system, refer to the faults listed under 'Engine' earlier in this Section.*

## Battery will not hold a charge for more than a few days

- [ ] Battery defective internally (Chapter 5A)
- [ ] Battery terminal connections loose or corroded (see *Weekly checks*)
- [ ] Auxiliary drivebelt worn or incorrectly adjusted (Chapter 1)
- [ ] Alternator not charging at correct output (Chapter 5A)
- [ ] Alternator or voltage regulator faulty (Chapter 5A)
- [ ] Short-circuit causing continual battery drain (Chapter 5A or 12)

## Ignition/no-charge warning light remains illuminated with engine running

- [ ] Auxiliary drivebelt broken, worn, or incorrectly adjusted (Chapter 1)
- [ ] Internal fault in alternator or voltage regulator (Chapter 5A)
- [ ] Broken, disconnected, or loose wiring in charging circuit (Chapter 5A or 12)

## Ignition/no-charge warning light fails to come on

- [ ] Warning light bulb blown (Chapter 12)
- [ ] Broken, disconnected, or loose wiring in warning light circuit (Chapter 5A or 12)
- [ ] Alternator faulty (Chapter 5A)

## Lights inoperative

- [ ] Bulb blown (Chapter 12)
- [ ] Corrosion of bulb or bulbholder contacts (Chapter 12)
- [ ] Blown fuse (Chapter 12)
- [ ] Faulty relay (Chapter 12)
- [ ] Broken, loose, or disconnected wiring (Chapter 12)
- [ ] Faulty switch (Chapter 12)

## Instrument readings inaccurate or erratic

### Instrument readings increase with engine speed

- [ ] Faulty instrument panel voltage regulator (Chapter 12)

### Fuel or temperature gauges give no reading

- [ ] Faulty gauge sender unit (Chapter 3, 4A or 4B)
- [ ] Wiring open-circuit (Chapter 12)
- [ ] Faulty gauge (Chapter 12)

### Fuel or temperature gauges give continuous maximum reading

- [ ] Faulty gauge sender unit (Chapter 3, 4A or 4B)
- [ ] Wiring short-circuit (Chapter 12)
- [ ] Faulty gauge (Chapter 12)

## Horn inoperative, or unsatisfactory in operation

### Horn operates all the time

- [ ] Horn push either earthed or stuck down (Chapter 12)
- [ ] Horn cable-to-horn push earthed (Chapter 12)

### Horn fails to operate

- [ ] Blown fuse (Chapter 12)
- [ ] Cable or connections loose, broken or disconnected (Chapter 12)
- [ ] Faulty horn (Chapter 12)

### Horn emits intermittent or unsatisfactory sound

- [ ] Cable connections loose (Chapter 12)
- [ ] Horn mountings loose (Chapter 12)
- [ ] Faulty horn (Chapter 12)

## Windscreen wipers inoperative, or unsatisfactory in operation

### Wipers fail to operate, or operate very slowly

- [ ] Wiper blades stuck to screen, or linkage seized or binding (Chapter 12)
- [ ] Blown fuse (Chapter 12)
- [ ] Battery discharged (Chapter 5A)
- [ ] Cable or connections loose, broken or disconnected (Chapter 12)
- [ ] Faulty relay (Chapter 12)
- [ ] Faulty wiper motor (Chapter 12)

### Wiper blades sweep over too large or too small an area of the glass

- [ ] Wiper blades incorrectly fitted, or wrong size used (see *Weekly checks*)
- [ ] Wiper arms incorrectly positioned on spindles (Chapter 12)
- [ ] Excessive wear of wiper linkage (Chapter 12)
- [ ] Wiper motor or linkage mountings loose or insecure (Chapter 12)

### Wiper blades fail to clean the glass effectively

- [ ] Wiper blade rubbers dirty, worn or perished (see *Weekly checks*)
- [ ] Wiper blades incorrectly fitted, or wrong size used (see *Weekly checks*)
- [ ] Wiper arm tension springs broken, or arm pivots seized (Chapter 12)
- [ ] Insufficient windscreen washer additive to adequately remove road film (see *Weekly checks*)

## Windscreen washers inoperative, or unsatisfactory in operation

### One or more washer jets inoperative

- [ ] Blocked washer jet
- [ ] Disconnected, kinked or restricted fluid hose (Chapter 12)
- [ ] Insufficient fluid in washer reservoir (see *Weekly checks*)

### Washer pump fails to operate

- [ ] Broken or disconnected wiring or connections (Chapter 12)
- [ ] Blown fuse (Chapter 12)
- [ ] Faulty washer switch (Chapter 12)
- [ ] Faulty washer pump (Chapter 12)

### Washer pump runs for some time before fluid is emitted from jets

- [ ] Faulty one-way valve in fluid supply hose (Chapter 12)

## Electric windows inoperative, or unsatisfactory in operation

### Window glass will only move in one direction

- [ ] Faulty switch (Chapter 12)

### Window glass slow to move

- [ ] Battery discharged (Chapter 5A)
- [ ] Regulator seized or damaged, or in need of lubrication (Chapter 11)
- [ ] Door internal components or trim fouling regulator (Chapter 11)
- [ ] Faulty motor (Chapter 11)

## Window glass fails to move

- [ ] Blown fuse (Chapter 12)
- [ ] Faulty relay (Chapter 12)
- [ ] Broken or disconnected wiring or connections (Chapter 12)
- [ ] Faulty motor (Chapter 11)

# Electrical system (continued)

*Central locking system inoperative, or unsatisfactory in operation*

### Complete system failure

☐ Remote handset battery discharged, where applicable
☐ Blown fuse (Chapter 12)
☐ Faulty relay (Chapter 12)
☐ Broken or disconnected wiring or connections (Chapter 12)
☐ Faulty motor (Chapter 11)

### Latch locks but will not unlock, or unlocks but will not lock

☐ Remote handset battery discharged, where applicable
☐ Faulty master switch (Chapter 12)
☐ Broken or disconnected latch operating rods or levers (Chapter 11)
☐ Faulty relay (Chapter 12)
☐ Faulty motor (Chapter 11)

### One solenoid/motor fails to operate

☐ Broken or disconnected wiring or connections (Chapter 12)
☐ Faulty operating assembly (Chapter 11)
☐ Broken, binding or disconnected latch operating rods or levers (Chapter 11)
☐ Fault in door latch (Chapter 11)

## A

**ABS (Anti-lock brake system)** A system, usually electronically controlled, that senses incipient wheel lockup during braking and relieves hydraulic pressure at wheels that are about to skid.

**Air bag** An inflatable bag hidden in the steering wheel (driver's side) or the dash or glovebox (passenger side). In a head-on collision, the bags inflate, preventing the driver and front passenger from being thrown forward into the steering wheel or windscreen.

**Air cleaner** A metal or plastic housing, containing a filter element, which removes dust and dirt from the air being drawn into the engine.

**Air filter element** The actual filter in an air cleaner system, usually manufactured from pleated paper and requiring renewal at regular intervals.

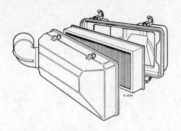

*Air filter*

**Allen key** A hexagonal wrench which fits into a recessed hexagonal hole.

**Alligator clip** A long-nosed spring-loaded metal clip with meshing teeth. Used to make temporary electrical connections.

**Alternator** A component in the electrical system which converts mechanical energy from a drivebelt into electrical energy to charge the battery and to operate the starting system, ignition system and electrical accessories.

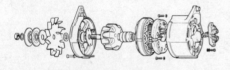

*Alternator (exploded view)*

**Ampere (amp)** A unit of measurement for the flow of electric current. One amp is the amount of current produced by one volt acting through a resistance of one ohm.

**Anaerobic sealer** A substance used to prevent bolts and screws from loosening. Anaerobic means that it does not require oxygen for activation. The Loctite brand is widely used.

**Antifreeze** A substance (usually ethylene glycol) mixed with water, and added to a vehicle's cooling system, to prevent freezing of the coolant in winter. Antifreeze also contains chemicals to inhibit corrosion and the formation of rust and other deposits that

would tend to clog the radiator and coolant passages and reduce cooling efficiency.

**Anti-seize compound** A coating that reduces the risk of seizing on fasteners that are subjected to high temperatures, such as exhaust manifold bolts and nuts.

*Anti-seize compound*

**Asbestos** A natural fibrous mineral with great heat resistance, commonly used in the composition of brake friction materials. Asbestos is a health hazard and the dust created by brake systems should never be inhaled or ingested.

**Axle** A shaft on which a wheel revolves, or which revolves with a wheel. Also, a solid beam that connects the two wheels at one end of the vehicle. An axle which also transmits power to the wheels is known as a live axle.

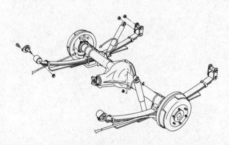

*Axle assembly*

**Axleshaft** A single rotating shaft, on either side of the differential, which delivers power from the final drive assembly to the drive wheels. Also called a driveshaft or a halfshaft.

## B

**Ball bearing** An anti-friction bearing consisting of a hardened inner and outer race with hardened steel balls between two races.

*Bearing*

**Bearing** The curved surface on a shaft or in a bore, or the part assembled into either, that permits relative motion between them with minimum wear and friction.

**Big-end bearing** The bearing in the end of the connecting rod that's attached to the crankshaft.

**Bleed nipple** A valve on a brake wheel cylinder, caliper or other hydraulic component that is opened to purge the hydraulic system of air. Also called a bleed screw.

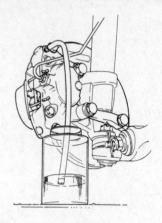

*Brake bleeding*

**Brake bleeding** Procedure for removing air from lines of a hydraulic brake system.

**Brake disc** The component of a disc brake that rotates with the wheels.

**Brake drum** The component of a drum brake that rotates with the wheels.

**Brake linings** The friction material which contacts the brake disc or drum to retard the vehicle's speed. The linings are bonded or riveted to the brake pads or shoes.

**Brake pads** The replaceable friction pads that pinch the brake disc when the brakes are applied. Brake pads consist of a friction material bonded or riveted to a rigid backing plate.

**Brake shoe** The crescent-shaped carrier to which the brake linings are mounted and which forces the lining against the rotating drum during braking.

**Braking systems** For more information on braking systems, consult the *Haynes Automotive Brake Manual*.

**Breaker bar** A long socket wrench handle providing greater leverage.

**Bulkhead** The insulated partition between the engine and the passenger compartment.

## C

**Caliper** The non-rotating part of a disc-brake assembly that straddles the disc and carries the brake pads. The caliper also contains the hydraulic components that cause the pads to pinch the disc when the brakes are applied. A caliper is also a measuring tool that can be set to measure inside or outside dimensions of an object.

**Camshaft** A rotating shaft on which a series of cam lobes operate the valve mechanisms. The camshaft may be driven by gears, by sprockets and chain or by sprockets and a belt.

**Canister** A container in an evaporative emission control system; contains activated charcoal granules to trap vapours from the fuel system.

*Canister*

**Carburettor** A device which mixes fuel with air in the proper proportions to provide a desired power output from a spark ignition internal combustion engine.

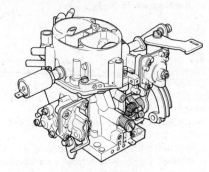

*Carburettor*

**Castellated** Resembling the parapets along the top of a castle wall. For example, a castellated balljoint stud nut.

*Castellated nut*

**Castor** In wheel alignment, the backward or forward tilt of the steering axis. Castor is positive when the steering axis is inclined rearward at the top.

**Catalytic converter** A silencer-like device in the exhaust system which converts certain pollutants in the exhaust gases into less harmful substances.

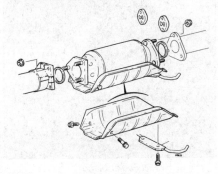

*Catalytic converter*

**Circlip** A ring-shaped clip used to prevent endwise movement of cylindrical parts and shafts. An internal circlip is installed in a groove in a housing; an external circlip fits into a groove on the outside of a cylindrical piece such as a shaft.

**Clearance** The amount of space between two parts. For example, between a piston and a cylinder, between a bearing and a journal, etc.

**Coil spring** A spiral of elastic steel found in various sizes throughout a vehicle, for example as a springing medium in the suspension and in the valve train.

**Compression** Reduction in volume, and increase in pressure and temperature, of a gas, caused by squeezing it into a smaller space.

**Compression ratio** The relationship between cylinder volume when the piston is at top dead centre and cylinder volume when the piston is at bottom dead centre.

**Constant velocity (CV) joint** A type of universal joint that cancels out vibrations caused by driving power being transmitted through an angle.

**Core plug** A disc or cup-shaped metal device inserted in a hole in a casting through which core was removed when the casting was formed. Also known as a freeze plug or expansion plug.

**Crankcase** The lower part of the engine block in which the crankshaft rotates.

**Crankshaft** The main rotating member, or shaft, running the length of the crankcase, with offset "throws" to which the connecting rods are attached.

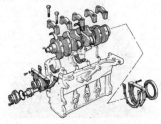

*Crankshaft assembly*

**Crocodile clip** See Alligator clip

# D

**Diagnostic code** Code numbers obtained by accessing the diagnostic mode of an engine management computer. This code can be used to determine the area in the system where a malfunction may be located.

**Disc brake** A brake design incorporating a rotating disc onto which brake pads are squeezed. The resulting friction converts the energy of a moving vehicle into heat.

**Double-overhead cam (DOHC)** An engine that uses two overhead camshafts, usually one for the intake valves and one for the exhaust valves.

**Drivebelt(s)** The belt(s) used to drive accessories such as the alternator, water pump, power steering pump, air conditioning compressor, etc. off the crankshaft pulley.

*Accessory drivebelts*

**Driveshaft** Any shaft used to transmit motion. Commonly used when referring to the axleshafts on a front wheel drive vehicle.

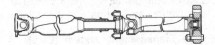

*Driveshaft*

**Drum brake** A type of brake using a drum-shaped metal cylinder attached to the inner surface of the wheel. When the brake pedal is pressed, curved brake shoes with friction linings press against the inside of the drum to slow or stop the vehicle.

*Drum brake assembly*

# E

**EGR valve** A valve used to introduce exhaust gases into the intake air stream.

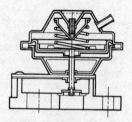

*EGR valve*

**Electronic control unit (ECU)** A computer which controls (for instance) ignition and fuel injection systems, or an anti-lock braking system. For more information refer to the *Haynes Automotive Electrical and Electronic Systems Manual*.

**Electronic Fuel Injection (EFI)** A computer controlled fuel system that distributes fuel through an injector located in each intake port of the engine.

**Emergency brake** A braking system, independent of the main hydraulic system, that can be used to slow or stop the vehicle if the primary brakes fail, or to hold the vehicle stationary even though the brake pedal isn't depressed. It usually consists of a hand lever that actuates either front or rear brakes mechanically through a series of cables and linkages. Also known as a handbrake or parking brake.

**Endfloat** The amount of lengthwise movement between two parts. As applied to a crankshaft, the distance that the crankshaft can move forward and back in the cylinder block.

**Engine management system (EMS)** A computer controlled system which manages the fuel injection and the ignition systems in an integrated fashion.

**Exhaust manifold** A part with several passages through which exhaust gases leave the engine combustion chambers and enter the exhaust pipe.

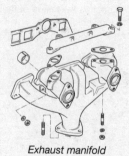

*Exhaust manifold*

# F

**Fan clutch** A viscous (fluid) drive coupling device which permits variable engine fan speeds in relation to engine speeds.

**Feeler blade** A thin strip or blade of hardened steel, ground to an exact thickness, used to check or measure clearances between parts.

*Feeler blade*

**Firing order** The order in which the engine cylinders fire, or deliver their power strokes, beginning with the number one cylinder.

**Flywheel** A heavy spinning wheel in which energy is absorbed and stored by means of momentum. On cars, the flywheel is attached to the crankshaft to smooth out firing impulses.

**Free play** The amount of travel before any action takes place. The "looseness" in a linkage, or an assembly of parts, between the initial application of force and actual movement. For example, the distance the brake pedal moves before the pistons in the master cylinder are actuated.

**Fuse** An electrical device which protects a circuit against accidental overload. The typical fuse contains a soft piece of metal which is calibrated to melt at a predetermined current flow (expressed as amps) and break the circuit.

**Fusible link** A circuit protection device consisting of a conductor surrounded by heat-resistant insulation. The conductor is smaller than the wire it protects, so it acts as the weakest link in the circuit. Unlike a blown fuse, a failed fusible link must frequently be cut from the wire for replacement.

# G

**Gap** The distance the spark must travel in jumping from the centre electrode to the side

*Adjusting spark plug gap*

electrode in a spark plug. Also refers to the spacing between the points in a contact breaker assembly in a conventional points-type ignition, or to the distance between the reluctor or rotor and the pickup coil in an electronic ignition.

**Gasket** Any thin, soft material - usually cork, cardboard, asbestos or soft metal - installed between two metal surfaces to ensure a good seal. For instance, the cylinder head gasket seals the joint between the block and the cylinder head.

*Gasket*

**Gauge** An instrument panel display used to monitor engine conditions. A gauge with a movable pointer on a dial or a fixed scale is an analogue gauge. A gauge with a numerical readout is called a digital gauge.

# H

**Halfshaft** A rotating shaft that transmits power from the final drive unit to a drive wheel, usually when referring to a live rear axle.

**Harmonic balancer** A device designed to reduce torsion or twisting vibration in the crankshaft. May be incorporated in the crankshaft pulley. Also known as a vibration damper.

**Hone** An abrasive tool for correcting small irregularities or differences in diameter in an engine cylinder, brake cylinder, etc.

**Hydraulic tappet** A tappet that utilises hydraulic pressure from the engine's lubrication system to maintain zero clearance (constant contact with both camshaft and valve stem). Automatically adjusts to variation in valve stem length. Hydraulic tappets also reduce valve noise.

# I

**Ignition timing** The moment at which the spark plug fires, usually expressed in the number of crankshaft degrees before the piston reaches the top of its stroke.

**Inlet manifold** A tube or housing with passages through which flows the air-fuel mixture (carburettor vehicles and vehicles with throttle body injection) or air only (port fuel-injected vehicles) to the port openings in the cylinder head.

## J

**Jump start** Starting the engine of a vehicle with a discharged or weak battery by attaching jump leads from the weak battery to a charged or helper battery.

## L

**Load Sensing Proportioning Valve (LSPV)** A brake hydraulic system control valve that works like a proportioning valve, but also takes into consideration the amount of weight carried by the rear axle.

**Locknut** A nut used to lock an adjustment nut, or other threaded component, in place. For example, a locknut is employed to keep the adjusting nut on the rocker arm in position.

**Lockwasher** A form of washer designed to prevent an attaching nut from working loose.

## M

**MacPherson strut** A type of front suspension system devised by Earle MacPherson at Ford of England. In its original form, a simple lateral link with the anti-roll bar creates the lower control arm. A long strut - an integral coil spring and shock absorber - is mounted between the body and the steering knuckle. Many modern so-called MacPherson strut systems use a conventional lower A-arm and don't rely on the anti-roll bar for location.

**Multimeter** An electrical test instrument with the capability to measure voltage, current and resistance.

## N

**NOx** Oxides of Nitrogen. A common toxic pollutant emitted by petrol and diesel engines at higher temperatures.

## O

**Ohm** The unit of electrical resistance. One volt applied to a resistance of one ohm will produce a current of one amp.

**Ohmmeter** An instrument for measuring electrical resistance.

**O-ring** A type of sealing ring made of a special rubber-like material; in use, the O-ring is compressed into a groove to provide the sealing action.

*O-ring*

**Overhead cam (ohc) engine** An engine with the camshaft(s) located on top of the cylinder head(s).

**Overhead valve (ohv) engine** An engine with the valves located in the cylinder head, but with the camshaft located in the engine block.

**Oxygen sensor** A device installed in the engine exhaust manifold, which senses the oxygen content in the exhaust and converts this information into an electric current. Also called a Lambda sensor.

## P

**Phillips screw** A type of screw head having a cross instead of a slot for a corresponding type of screwdriver.

**Plastigage** A thin strip of plastic thread, available in different sizes, used for measuring clearances. For example, a strip of Plastigage is laid across a bearing journal. The parts are assembled and dismantled; the width of the crushed strip indicates the clearance between journal and bearing.

*Plastigage*

**Propeller shaft** The long hollow tube with universal joints at both ends that carries power from the transmission to the differential on front-engined rear wheel drive vehicles.

**Proportioning valve** A hydraulic control valve which limits the amount of pressure to the rear brakes during panic stops to prevent wheel lock-up.

## R

**Rack-and-pinion steering** A steering system with a pinion gear on the end of the steering shaft that mates with a rack (think of a geared wheel opened up and laid flat). When the steering wheel is turned, the pinion turns, moving the rack to the left or right. This movement is transmitted through the track rods to the steering arms at the wheels.

**Radiator** A liquid-to-air heat transfer device designed to reduce the temperature of the coolant in an internal combustion engine cooling system.

**Refrigerant** Any substance used as a heat transfer agent in an air-conditioning system. R-12 has been the principle refrigerant for many years; recently, however, manufacturers have begun using R-134a, a non-CFC substance that is considered less harmful to the ozone in the upper atmosphere.

**Rocker arm** A lever arm that rocks on a shaft or pivots on a stud. In an overhead valve engine, the rocker arm converts the upward movement of the pushrod into a downward movement to open a valve.

**Rotor** In a distributor, the rotating device inside the cap that connects the centre electrode and the outer terminals as it turns, distributing the high voltage from the coil secondary winding to the proper spark plug. Also, that part of an alternator which rotates inside the stator. Also, the rotating assembly of a turbocharger, including the compressor wheel, shaft and turbine wheel.

**Runout** The amount of wobble (in-and-out movement) of a gear or wheel as it's rotated. The amount a shaft rotates "out-of-true." The out-of-round condition of a rotating part.

## S

**Sealant** A liquid or paste used to prevent leakage at a joint. Sometimes used in conjunction with a gasket.

**Sealed beam lamp** An older headlight design which integrates the reflector, lens and filaments into a hermetically-sealed one-piece unit. When a filament burns out or the lens cracks, the entire unit is simply replaced.

**Serpentine drivebelt** A single, long, wide accessory drivebelt that's used on some newer vehicles to drive all the accessories, instead of a series of smaller, shorter belts. Serpentine drivebelts are usually tensioned by an automatic tensioner.

*Serpentine drivebelt*

**Shim** Thin spacer, commonly used to adjust the clearance or relative positions between two parts. For example, shims inserted into or under bucket tappets control valve clearances. Clearance is adjusted by changing the thickness of the shim.

**Slide hammer** A special puller that screws into or hooks onto a component such as a shaft or bearing; a heavy sliding handle on the shaft bottoms against the end of the shaft to knock the component free.

**Sprocket** A tooth or projection on the periphery of a wheel, shaped to engage with a chain or drivebelt. Commonly used to refer to the sprocket wheel itself.

**Starter inhibitor switch** On vehicles with an automatic transmission, a switch that prevents starting if the vehicle is not in Neutral or Park.

**Strut** See MacPherson strut.

# T

**Tappet** A cylindrical component which transmits motion from the cam to the valve stem, either directly or via a pushrod and rocker arm. Also called a cam follower.

**Thermostat** A heat-controlled valve that regulates the flow of coolant between the cylinder block and the radiator, so maintaining optimum engine operating temperature. A thermostat is also used in some air cleaners in which the temperature is regulated.

**Thrust bearing** The bearing in the clutch assembly that is moved in to the release levers by clutch pedal action to disengage the clutch. Also referred to as a release bearing.

**Timing belt** A toothed belt which drives the camshaft. Serious engine damage may result if it breaks in service.

**Timing chain** A chain which drives the camshaft.

**Toe-in** The amount the front wheels are closer together at the front than at the rear. On rear wheel drive vehicles, a slight amount of toe-in is usually specified to keep the front wheels running parallel on the road by offsetting other forces that tend to spread the wheels apart.

**Toe-out** The amount the front wheels are closer together at the rear than at the front. On front wheel drive vehicles, a slight amount of toe-out is usually specified.

**Tools** For full information on choosing and using tools, refer to the *Haynes Automotive Tools Manual.*

**Tracer** A stripe of a second colour applied to a wire insulator to distinguish that wire from another one with the same colour insulator.

**Tune-up** A process of accurate and careful adjustments and parts replacement to obtain the best possible engine performance.

**Turbocharger** A centrifugal device, driven by exhaust gases, that pressurises the intake air. Normally used to increase the power output from a given engine displacement, but can also be used primarily to reduce exhaust emissions (as on VW's "Umwelt" Diesel engine).

# U

**Universal joint or U-joint** A double-pivoted connection for transmitting power from a driving to a driven shaft through an angle. A U-joint consists of two Y-shaped yokes and a cross-shaped member called the spider.

# V

**Valve** A device through which the flow of liquid, gas, vacuum, or loose material in bulk may be started, stopped, or regulated by a movable part that opens, shuts, or partially obstructs one or more ports or passageways. A valve is also the movable part of such a device.

**Valve clearance** The clearance between the valve tip (the end of the valve stem) and the rocker arm or tappet. The valve clearance is measured when the valve is closed.

**Vernier caliper** A precision measuring instrument that measures inside and outside dimensions. Not quite as accurate as a micrometer, but more convenient.

**Viscosity** The thickness of a liquid or its resistance to flow.

**Volt** A unit for expressing electrical "pressure" in a circuit. One volt that will produce a current of one ampere through a resistance of one ohm.

# W

**Welding** Various processes used to join metal items by heating the areas to be joined to a molten state and fusing them together. For more information refer to the *Haynes Automotive Welding Manual.*

**Wiring diagram** A drawing portraying the components and wires in a vehicle's electrical system, using standardised symbols. For more information refer to the *Haynes Automotive Electrical and Electronic Systems Manual.*

**Note:** *References throughout this index are in the form "Chapter number" • "Page number"*